OUT OF THE WHIRLWIND

A Reader of Holocaust Literature

Edited by
ALBERT H. FRIEDLANDER

Illustrated by
Jacob Landau

REVISED AND EXPANDED EDITION

UAHC PRESS   NEW YORK

TO THE 6,000,000

Library of Congress Cataloging-in-Publication Data

Out of the Whirlwind : a reader of Holocaust literature / edited by
   Albert H. Friedlander : illustrated by Jacob Landau.—Rev. and
   expanded ed.
       p.   cm.
     ISBN 0-8074-0703-8 (pbk. : alk. paper)
     1. Holocaust, Jewish (1939–1945)   2. Holocaust, Jewish
   (1939–1945)—Personal narratives.   3. Holocaust (Jewish theology)
   I. Friedlander, Albert H.
   D804.3.087   1999
   940.53'18—dc21   96-49236
                                                                            CIP

This book is printed on acid-free paper.
Copyright © 1968, 1999 by the UAHC Press
Manufactured in the United States of America
10 9 8 7 6 5 4 3 2 1

CONTENTS

> ## INTERLUDE
> Songs in the Night
> The Art and Music of the Shoah 259

EPILOGUE
Second Kings, Chapter 2
A Parable   593

PREFACE

The first edition of *Out of the Whirlwind* in 1968, over three decades ago, responded to the growing interest of a postwar generation in learning about the Shoah (the Hebrew term for Holocaust). The events of the sixties, including the Eichmann trial, the near-destruction of Israel in the Six-Day War, and America's growing involvement in the Vietnam War, all stimulated interest in the most climactic event of the century, namely, the Shoah. Many students were more willing to look closely at this event than their parents' generation who had lived through the war years and often tried to submerge or surmount its harrowing memories.

At that time, Holocaust literature was in its first stages as a special record of a personal and permanent Jewish tragedy; a younger generation saw it as that, but also in broader terms, as an event impacting on every civilized person living in this century. Pioneering works had begun to appear, among them Elie Wiesel's *Night,* and in these students found a new audience of listeners. Survivors became their teachers as the silence surrounding the Shoah was broken. The intention of this anthology was to assemble and present a sampling of the best Holocaust writing in a variety of genres, to serve as an introduction to the involved and receptive student readers.

Today, our knowledge of the history of the Shoah has increased a thousandfold, as Holocaust diaries and journals have been unearthed and translated, and numerous first-person accounts have been written and published. Many new historical works in what has come to be known as Holocaust studies have appeared and its images have been captured in the artistic media of film, art, poetry, and music. The Shoah has entered the popular consciousness on an unprecedented level as the abyss of modern civilization. The silence has indeed been broken, but there is a new anxiety: that we will become inured to these images and cease to feel them. As the generation of survivors departs from us and the baby-boomer generation enters middle age, we see a serious attempt to preserve memory in the construction of new libraries and teaching museums dedicated to the Shoah, as well as commemorative monuments. Yet I fear a sense of closure in these memorials for an event that should never be closed. I am concerned that the intense desire to document every detail of this experience will reduce the Shoah to the point where it can be absorbed, classified, and put to rest.

I still believe that literature of testimony has the most staying power to keep the event alive in the hearts and minds of successive generations. When this book first appeared, I wrote "a whirlwind cannot be taught; it must be experienced." In reissuing this anthology, I believe that the classics presented here remain classics and that their writers' words continue to speak to us across the abyss of time. Many of these selections have gained the status of art, but art in the service of making us feel and understand the darkest experience of modern civilization, the moment when all boundaries were crossed. From them, we learn what it is to be human and what keeps us human. And we mourn for the pain and the loss, repeated six million times.

This expanded edition includes a new last section entitled "Looking Back," which presents excerpts from works of fiction and nonfiction that have appeared since the original publication of this book. In choosing from the vast body of Holocaust literature now available, I decided to focus on themes and questions of particular interest to contemporary readers and works that have stimulated contemporary discussion of these issues.

Looking back, novelist Aharon Appelfeld re-creates a world situated on a precipice, a period in which German Jews were still ignorant of the full extent of the Nazis' murderous intentions. From the distance of time, this snapshot of "the world before" takes on a chilling quality in the mind of the reader. Ida Fink's sketches and Margarete Buber-Neumann's memoir of her friend Milena capture the experiences specifically of women in the ghettos and the camps. Historian Lucy S. Dawidowicz, in a personal memoir, recalls the reactions of American Jews as wave upon wave of disastrous news reached America throughout the war years. Primo Levi, who endured Auschwitz as a young man, reflects on the phenomenon of survivor guilt and shame for impossible choices in the camps.

Experiences that so profoundly affected an entire generation also cast long shadows on the generations born after the Holocaust. The "second-generation" pieces that follow represent serious attempts to understand this epoch-making event and the ways in which it changed our personal and public lives. "All Around Atlantis," an excerpt from a fictional work by Deborah Eisenberg, describes the world of the child of a survivor, growing up in America and trying to make sense of the differences in her home. Political scientist Daniel Jonah Goldhagen takes up the issue of the complicity of ordinary Germans in the mass murder of the Jews. An excerpt from the novel *The Reader* by German jurist Bernhard Schlink portrays the anguish and confusion of a German born after the war confronting the crimes of the previous generation. Artist Art Spiegelman has chosen an illustrated format in *Maus* to explore his relationship with his father and the enduring impact of the Shoah on both the survivor and the child of survivors. Writer and filmmaker Theo Richmond records his fascination with Konin, his parents' former hometown in Poland, researching its history, interviewing survivors, and finally visiting the present-day Konin.

Section Seven in this new edition benefited immeasurably from the vision, enthusiasm, and dedication of my editor, Bonny Fetterman, who saw the need for this project and who helped in all aspects of selecting and editing the new material. I am truly grateful to her.

This book began with a parable about the prophet Elijah and ends with his successor Elisha. That, too, is a generational shift. Elisha remembers what Elijah experienced. We are the generations of Elisha. As George Steiner reminds us, we continue to be "remembrancers" with a special task to perform. The knowledge of the Holocaust is more alive in our time than ever before, despite attempts to push the memory into a dusty archive of the mind where it can be ignored. Nevertheless, the preservation of memory depends on the living. As written in the Epilogue, it is up to us to say the Kaddish for those who had none to recite it for them, and for those whose hopes live on in each one of us.

AHF
January 1999

PROLOGUE

AN EVENING GUEST

ELIE WIESEL

LIKE ALL THE PERSECUTED JEWISH CHILDREN, I PASSIONATELY LOVED
the Prophet Elijah, the only saint who went up to Heaven alive,
in a chariot of fire, to go on through the centuries as the herald
of deliverance.

For no accountable reason I thought of him as a Yemenite Jew:
tall, sombre, unfathomable. A prince ageless and rootless, turning
up wherever he was being waited for. He would move forward, all
wild, never stopping for anything. It was the end that drew him on
in all things, since he was the only one who knew its mystery. On
his way along he would console the graybeard, the orphan, the abandoned widow. He would march on, drawing the world along after
him. In his eyes he would bear a promise that he would like to
free everyone, but he doesn't have either the right to or the power.
Not yet.

In my fancy I assigned him the majestic beauty of Saul, the
strength of Samson. He had only to raise his arm—and our enemies
would fling themselves flat on the ground. He had only to shout
an order, and the universe would tremble: the time was running
out more rapidly so that we might more rapidly attain the celestial
palace where ever since the first day of Creation—and even, accord-

Reprinted with permission of the author. Translated from the French by JOEL
CARMICHAEL.

3

ing to certain mystics, a long time before that—the Messiah was awaiting us.

A Yemenite Jew—I can no longer think why. Perhaps because I had never seen one. For me as a child the Yemen was not located on a map, but somewhere else, in a realm of dreams where all sad children, from every city and from every century, took each other's hand to defy compulsion, time, and death.

Later on I was to see the Prophet, and I had to admit my mistake. To be sure, he was a Jew, but all he came from was Poland. On top of that there was nothing about him like a giant, like a legendary hero. Puny, his back bowed, he pressed his lips together when he looked at you. The way he moved showed how weary he was, but his eyes were ablaze. You felt that the past was, for him, a unique haven.

It was the first night of our Passover. All lit up, the house was preparing to celebrate the Festival of Freedom. My mother and my two older sisters were busy in the kitchen, the little one was setting the table. Father had not yet come back from the synagogue.

I was morose: we were going to sit down to the traditional meal just as a family, and I would have preferred a guest to join us, as in the years before. I was put in a good temper again when the door opened and Father appeared, accompanied by some poorly dressed, shivering, timid stranger. Father had accosted him in the street with the ritual formula: *kol dichfin yethei veyekhul*, let him who is hungry come eat with us. "I'm not hungry," the stranger had answered. "That doesn't matter, come along anyhow, no one should stay out of doors on a festival evening."

My little sister happily set another place. I poured the wine. "Should we begin?" asked my father. "Everything's ready," said my mother. Father blessed the wine, washed his hands, and readied himself to tell us, according to custom, of the feats of our ancestors, of their flight from Egypt in their headlong leap into the grandiose adventure of their encounter with God and with their history.

"I'm not hungry," our guest said, suddenly. "But I'm going to talk to you."

"Later," said my father, a little startled.

"I have no time. Even now it's too late."

I didn't know that this was to be the last Seder, the last Passover feast ever celebrated in my father's house.

It was 1944. The German army had just occupied the whole region. In Budapest the Fascists had taken power. The Eastern front was at Korosmezo, hardly fifteen miles away from us. You could hear the cannon firing, and at night the sky on the other side of the mountains turned red. We thought that the war was coming to an end, that liberation was close at hand; that we were living, like our ancestors, through the final hours of our bondage.

Jews were being abused in the streets, humiliated, covered with insults. A rabbi was forced to sweep the sidewalk. Our dear Hungarian neighbors were yelling: Death to the Jews! But our optimism remained unshakable. It was only a question of holding out for a few days, a few weeks. Then the front would shift and once again the God of Abraham would rescue His people at the last minute, as He always did, just when everything seemed to be lost.

The *Haggadah,* with its account of the Exodus, endorsed our hopefulness. Didn't it say that every Jew had to think of himself, always and everywhere, as having come out of Egypt himself? And that the miracle would come about in each generation once again?

Yet our guest did not look at things in the same way. Troubled, his forehead wrinkled, he was upsetting to us. Morose, angry, he kept trying to anger us in our turn.

"Close these books of yore," he said. "That's all ancient history, finished and done for. Listen to me instead."

Politely, we hid our impatience. In a trembling voice he started describing the sufferings of Israel in the hour of chastisement—the massacre of the Jewish community in Kolomai, then of the community in Kamenetz-Podolsk. Father let him speak, then took up the ancient recitation again as though nothing had happened. My little sister asked the four ritual questions that were supposed to give my father a chance to answer by explaining the meaning and the aim of the feast. Why and in what way is this night different from other nights? Because, under the Pharaohs, we were slaves, but on this night God has made us free men.

Dissatisfied with the question and with the answer to it, our guest took them up again in his own way: Why is this night not different from other nights? Why does the suffering go on this way? And why is it us, always us? And why doesn't God intervene? Where is the miracle? What is He waiting for? When is He going to put Himself in between us and the butchers?

His unexpected interruptions produced a feeling of embarrassment around the table. The moment any one of us opened his mouth he cut him short: "You keep thinking about a past that's more than three thousand years old, and you turn away from the present; Pharaoh is not dead, open your eyes and look—he is destroying our people. Moses is dead, it's true, but not Pharaoh; he is alive, he's coming, soon he'll be at the gates of this city, at the doors of this house; are you sure you'll be spared?"

Then, shrugging his shoulders, he read a few passages from the *Haggadah;* in his mouth the words of praise turned into blasphemies. Father tried to soothe him, to reassure him: "Don't, my friend, you're depressed. Tonight we're at a feast, full of joy and gratitude."

The guest shot him a burning look, and said: "Gratitude, did you say? What for? Have you seen children having their throats cut in front of their mothers? I have, I've seen them."

"Later," said my father. "You'll tell us all that later."

I listened to the guest and kept wondering: Who is he? What does he want? I thought he was sick and unhappy, perhaps mad. It was not until afterwards that I understood: he was the Prophet Elijah. And if he had scarcely any resemblance to the one in the Bible, nor to the one in my dreams, it was because each generation puts forth a prophet in its own image. In the olden days, when there were the kings, he appeared as an angry preacher, setting mountains and hearts on fire; then he repented, and took to begging in the streets of besieged Jerusalem, becoming a student in Babylonia, a messenger in Rome, a beadle in Mainz, Toledo or Kiev. That day he had the face and the fate of a poor Polish Jewish refugee who with his own eyes had seen too often and too close the victory of death over man and his prayers.

I remain convinced that it was he who was our guest. Very often, of course, I can't manage to believe it. Those who've succeeded in seeing him are few and far between. The path leading to him is obscure and dangerous, the slightest trip-up will bring about the loss of the soul. My own rabbi would gladly have given his life to catch a glimpse of him for the space of a single flash of lightning, of a single heartbeat. Why should I have deserved what has been denied so many others? I don't know. But I maintain that it was he who was our guest.

For that matter I had the proof of it immediately.

Tradition requires that after the meal, before prayers are resumed, a goblet of wine be offered the Prophet who on that evening visits all Jewish homes, at the same moment, as though to emphasize the indestructibility of their ties with God. Accordingly Father took the beautiful silver chalice no one ever used and filled it to the brim. Then he signaled to my little sister to go to the door and ask our illustrious visitor to come in and taste our wine. And we meant to tell him: you see, we trust you—in spite of our enemies, in spite of the blood that has been shed, we have not been abandoned by gaiety, we offer you this because we believe in your promise.

Silently, aware of how important the moment was, we rose to our feet to make a solemn salute to the Prophet, with all the honor and the respect that are his due. My little sister left the table and started going toward the door when our guest suddenly cried out:

"No! Little girl—come back! I'll open the door myself!"

There was something in his voice that made us start. We watched him plunge toward the door and open it with a crash:

"Look," he cried out. "There's no one there! No one! D'you hear me?"

And then he leaped outside, leaving the door open.

Standing up, holding our glasses, petrified, we waited for him to come back. My little sister, on the brink of tears, covered her mouth with both hands. Father was the first to get hold of himself. In a gentle voice he called out after our guest: "Where are you, my friend? Come back!" Silence. Father repeated his call in a more urgent tone. Nothing. My cheeks were on fire, I ran outside, sure I would find him on the landing: he wasn't there. I rushed down the steps: he couldn't be too far away. But the only footsteps that rang out in the courtyard were my own. The garden? There were a great many shadows under the trees—except his.

Father, Mother, my sisters, and even our old servant, not knowing what to think, came out to join me. Father said: "I don't understand." Mother murmured: "Where can he be hiding? Why?"

My sisters and I went out into the street and cast about as far as the corner—no one. I started calling out: "H-e-e-y, my friend, where are you?" A number of windows opened up: "What's going on?" "Has any one seen a foreign Jew with a bent back?" "No."

Out of breath, we all came together again in the courtyard. Mother murmured: "The earth might have swallowed him up." And Father repeated: "I don't understand."

It was then that a sudden thought flashed through my mind, and became a certainty: Mother is mistaken, it's the sky and not the earth that's split wide open, in order to take him in. It's pointless chasing after him, he's not here any more. In his fiery chariot he's gone back to his dwelling-place on high, to inform the Lord of what His blessed people is going to undergo in the days to come.

"Friend, come back," my father called out one last time. "Come back, we'll listen to you."

"He can't hear you any more," I said. "He's a long way off by now."

Our hearts heavy, we returned to the table and raised our glasses one more time. We recited the customary blessings, the Psalms, and to finish we sang *Chad Gadya*, that terrifying song in which, in the name of justice, evil catches evil, death calls death, until the Angel of Destruction, in his turn, has his throat cut by the Eternal, blessed-be-He. I loved this naive little song in which everything seemed so simple, so primitive: the cat and the dog, the water and the fire, executioners and victims turn and turn about, all undergoing the same punishment inside the same scheme. But that evening the song upset me, I rebelled against the resignation it implied. Why does God always act too late? Why didn't He get rid of the Angel of Death before he even committed his first murder? If our guest had stayed with us he's the one who would have asked these questions. Since he was gone I asked them myself.

The ceremony was coming to an end, and we didn't dare look at one another. Father raised his glass one last time and we repeated after him. "Next year in Jerusalem." None of us could know that this was the last Passover meal we would have as a family. I saw our guest a few weeks later. The first convoy was leaving the Ghetto; he was in it. He seemed to be more at ease than his companions, as though he had already taken this route a thousand times. Men, women and children, everyone was carrying bags on their backs, blankets, valises. Only he had empty hands.

Today I know what I didn't know then: at the end of a long trip that was to last four days and three nights he got out in a small railway station, near a peaceful little town, somewhere in Silesia, where his fiery chariot was waiting to carry him up to the skies. Isn't that enough proof that he was the Prophet Elijah?

GENERAL INTRODUCTION

A WHIRLWIND CANNOT BE TAUGHT; IT MUST BE EXPERIENCED. AND we cannot know what happened during the *Shoah*—that whirlwind of destruction in which Hitler's Germany killed six million Jews—solely by learning historical facts and figures and scholarly explanations. Facts, figures, and explanations are necessary. But we must also touch and feel and taste the dark days and the burning nights. Our hearts must constrict in terror and grief. Our minds must expand to make room for the incredible. And our love for the goodness of life must grow strong enough to reach into the darkness and to discover the heart of that darkness, the experience itself.

Darkness pervaded every street of every town, city, and country occupied by Nazi Germany. The innermost circle of this geography of hell was the concentration camp. Once inside this circle, humanity moved from the light of day to the valley of the shadow of death. Yet, life did go on. And the testimony of survivors of that life reaches out to us, demanding our concern, our attention, our anguish, and our dedication for tasks left undone, for an expansion of our own existence which must come to encompass those six million lives and bring them back into a world which must not and dares not forget all that took place.

And so we must enter the past. But what passport will gain us entry into hell? Recognizing the fact that the world we are about to enter is utterly alien to the world we know, how can we expand the horizons of our awareness so that hell and the experience of it become real? Two paths are open to us: we can add to our knowledge of the past and strive to understand the outer structure and details of the police state achieved by Hitler Germany. And we can add to our knowledge of ourselves, of man's inner nature—of that range of emotions moving from love to hate and fear of death—only as we experience the daily lives of those who lived within the hell that was Nazi Germany. Facts are of little use in this second quest. But in the literature of that period it is not only facts but emotions which are transmitted. And the knowledge of the evil which can reside in us is too heavy a burden for reason or intellect to carry. Somehow, we must enter the Holocaust and its geography in this twofold way: with a clear mind, and with the humility and openness linked in the Bible with the contrite soul. Only then will we see, and seeing, understand.

The Historical Quest

The persecution and slaughter of Jews is an old and familiar story. But today we live in an ordered world of international law; we think of the state and its institutions as a protection against criminals and evil. And as we look at the record of Nazi Germany, we find it difficult to believe that it is the record of the very same land which gave birth to Bach, Beethoven, Mozart, Goethe, Schiller, Heine—the very same land which has prided itself on its genius and culture.

There are no simple reasons or answers to why and how the Holocaust was allowed to take place. We now know that the vaunted culture of Germany contained much evil and decay beneath its polished surface. We have learned of the weaknesses in its political system —a system which permitted a Hitler to take power. And historians tell us of other factors—political and economic—which produced National Socialism and its venomous ideology. And although the unfolding of evil in Germany does not mean that all Germans were evil, yet, for the first time in modern history, a condition of living was created in which the citizens of a country were encouraged to live as criminals: violence was rewarded and decency punished.

Here, then, is the first clue towards a solution of our question. *A criminal state was created.* We are accustomed to due process of law, to a government which rules for the benefit of those who are being governed. When Hitler and his Brown Shirts came to power, they ignored all rules of law and justice. In order to maintain control, they changed the laws. In order to enforce their laws, they changed the courts and filled them with their hirelings. And in order to maintain themselves and their hirelings in perpetuity, they established a rule of fear: concentration camp and the death penalty threatened all who opposed them.

It is difficult to oppose a police state. To a certain extent, this serves as an answer to the question of why more Germans did not oppose Hitler. But it is not a sufficient answer. The vast majority of Germans supported their leader, ignoring his methods, condoning or closing their eyes to the evils he perpetrated. The rabbis remind us not to judge our fellow man until we stand in his place. But the sin of silence is well known, and this sin of silent acquiescence did as much to destroy the Jews of Europe as the direct actions of the criminals; and law courts find it necessary to punish direct as well as indirect accomplices. We cannot possibly hope to understand the Holocaust if we do not look behind the police state, to *those who were silent and did not protest.*

A police state was established, conducted by criminals in terms of their own twisted values and carved out for their own benefit. From the very beginning, Hitler appealed to the prejudices of the German community. Many Germans, wracked with old prejudices, eagerly participated in the attack upon the Jews; almost no one protested. From the time of the Crusades, bloody pogroms against the German Jewish community are reported in European history. The period of Enlightenment brought with it emancipation for the Jew; but as romantic thinking replaced the rationalism of the Enlightenment, the Jew, once again, became the disliked and feared alien. Germany had a solid foundation of prejudice and Hitler used this in building his case against the Jews. Using twentieth century propaganda techniques, he built on old, deep-rooted feelings. Above all he appealed to man's innate violence and diabolical inclination to break all bounds of conscience—all in the name of patriotism! He succeeded. While the campaign against the Jews was only one plank in Hitler's political platform, it proved one of the most powerful weapons at his command.

The flood of anti-Semitic propaganda included pornographic newspapers, pseudo-scientific "studies" to "substantiate" malignities against the Jewish people, posters, paintings, speeches, and scurrilous mailings. After 1933, when Hitler came to power, much of the state's resources were thrown into attacking the Jewish community. In March of that year, the Nazi Party organized a full scale boycott of Jewish places of business. In 1935, when Hitler felt more secure, he utilized ᵗhe national party meeting in Nuremberg to promulgate the so-called "Nuremberg Laws," which deprived the Jews of their rights as citizens and which gave legal sanction to the fiction that the Jews were an inferior race. The professions were closed to Jews, depriving many of their only means of livelihood, and marriages between Jews and non-Jews were prohibited.

In 1933, the Jewish community organized itself. The Association of Jews in Germany, under the leadership of Rabbi Leo Baeck, became the government of a besieged and imprisoned people. And, while their incomes declined with each new Nazi law, their needs continued to increase. Deprived of their incomes, old, middle-aged, and young Jews needed money to live; as the children were driven out of the German school system, new schools had to be established; special training for emigration was needed—these and countless other costs had to be borne by a community which, though receiving help from abroad, never had enough.

In America, there were Jewish community leaders who went on record saying that interference with Hitler would only worsen the situation; that the answer was definitely not full-scale emigration, but rather a digging in, a waiting out of the storm which would eventually abate. But the Nazis were determined that the storm would take its toll before coming to an end; and even they may not have fully realized the ultimate evil at the end of their road.

In 1938, they discarded all disguise of their criminal actions. In November of that year, on the infamous "Crystal Night"—so-called because of the many windows smashed in this nation-wide pogrom—the Nazis burned most of the 600 synagogues in Germany, destroyed over 800 Jewish business establishments valued at billions of dollars, and arrested more than 30,000 Jews. This was followed by the confiscation of much Jewish capital—as a punishment "for having aroused the anger of the Nazis." New laws followed one after another—excluding Jews from all areas of business, from any social intercourse with their "Aryan" neighbors, requiring all Jews to adopt Jewish names, and making it mandatory that each Jew wear the Star of David so that victims would be more easily marked for persecution. Finally, a law was passed placing Jews outside the realm of the law itself.

There was no escape. A 1938 conference dealing with Jewish refugees, in Evian, had clearly shown that the outside world was unwilling to take decisive measures in helping the Jews; and when war broke out in 1939, there was very little anyone could do. The criminal state had already taken over Austria and its Jews, had made an alliance with Italy which delivered its Jewish community to the Nazis, and then, with the invasion of Poland, the large and venerable Eastern Jewish community fell into Nazi hands. With their military victories to sustain them, the Nazi criminals no longer found it necessary to conceal their actions. They had decided to murder all Jews and proceeded systematically to execute their plan.

From all German controlled territories, Jews were herded towards the Eastern European zone. Ghettos were established, in places like Lodz, Lublin, Cracow, and Warsaw. And nearly three million Jews —those left after the Germans and the large number of Polish anti-Semites had had their sport—were pressed into these sealed off areas until the killing process could be worked out in all its intricate detail. At a top level Nazi conference (the "Wannsee Conference," held January 20, 1942), a "Final Solution" was indeed worked out; and the greatest crime of our time moved towards consummation. The Nazis had already destroyed all aspects of justice and law in the territory they controlled; they were now ready for the wholesale destruction of human beings. The land of Beethoven and Goethe here made a new contribution to European culture: the extermination camps—whether in Auschwitz, Dachau, Bergen-Belsen, or else-where—in which human beings could be burned or gassed to death and could be rendered into soap and lampshades.

The Warsaw Ghetto Uprising

There are no silver linings surrounding the unrelieved blackness of the Holocaust. History cannot be approached by keeping score be-tween the forces of light and the forces of darkness. But when we weary overmuch in our examination of the evil done in those years, we can find at least some measure of relief in looking at the victims and reflecting upon their heroism. In the end, it is of little comfort: they, too, died.

They did not all die as heroes—and we would be playing the Nazis' game if we were to demand heroism from them. They were victims. Had there been any means of escape, they might have taken it. But they had no choice—none except the manner of their death. As we study this period, we will learn that heroism comes in many different shapes and forms. Some heroism goes almost unnoticed, while others stand out starkly against the background of their times.

One such story, in its way as great as any event in Jewish history, is the story of the Warsaw Ghetto. Approximately three hundred and thirty thousand Jews lived in Warsaw when the war started. In October of 1940, the Nazis herded them behind hastily erected ghetto walls and leisurely proceeded with the task of extermination. In the early years of the ghetto, this was done through the simple process of starvation; the Nazis severely limited the amount of food that could be brought into the ghetto. But by the summer of 1942, the extermination camps were in full operation and clamored for victims. The Warsaw Ghetto supplied the victims by the tens of thousands. By October of 1942, the number of ghetto inhabitants had been reduced to fifty thousand. The deportations starting in the summer had been only too successful. And in the spring of 1943, the remainder was to be shipped to the death camps.

But the death camps were cheated of many of their victims: the Jews rebelled. With almost no weapons, they confronted an enemy composed of German army units, SS troupers, Ukrainians, Polish blue police, and Lithuanian uniformed auxiliaries which had entered the ghetto walls on Passover eve. The Jews of the ghetto fought flame throwers, machine guns, and tanks, and they threw back the army. General Stroop, commander of the German forces, petulantly reported to his superiors that "the Jews return to the flames rather than risk falling into our hands . . . not a single Jew gave himself up voluntarily."

For more than a month, the embarrassed Nazi war machine found itself unable to suppress the uprising. In the end, the ghetto was razed building by building, block by block. The majority of the Jews living in the ghetto at the time of the uprising were killed in battle; the survivors almost all perished in the death camps. But the manner in which they lived and died spoke to the world in an unforgettable way. And, as we consider what might have been if the Jewish community would have received significant help from its neighbors, the story of the Warsaw Ghetto becomes less of an isolated episode and more of an indication of the dimensions of Jewish existence in a world of evil.

The Extermination Camps

Details of life in extermination camps are found in the memoirs and novels of survivors; they are clear enough. But dry facts and numbers can have a language all their own. At Auschwitz and the adjacent Birkenau alone, more than 1,750,000 Jews were murdered in less than two years. At Maidanek, nearly 1,500,000 Jews were killed. When we place the horror of camps like Treblinka and Bergen-Belsen alongside these numbers, the geography of hell becomes distinct to us with anguishing clarity.

Raul Hilberg's *The Destruction of the European Jews* gives us a matter-of-fact account of the organization of these camps in their all-too-German thoroughness. One could almost "sympathize" with the problems of German executives trying to get cyklon B gas into full production! And there was always the problem of being under-staffed. But they managed. At Auschwitz the number of "employees" rose from circa 65 (in May, 1940) to circa 3,500 (in December, 1943); in all, more than 7,000 Germans worked there. Between March of 1942 and April of 1945, records indicate that in all con-centration camps more than 45,000 people were employed in the task of exterminating Jews.

Men had to be trained to accept killing as an ordinary task. And some became too involved in their work. Personnel problems did exist for the Germans: the sadism of guards, the corruption of camp officials. We might note, for instance, that on one occasion, when SS men and German political prisoners tossed 90 Jewish women from a third-floor window of one of the Auschwitz buildings into a courtyard below, the SS men were transferred to another post.

The task of killing Jews was by no means easy. The Germans had to work long, hard hours in order to keep track of the great numbers of Jews passing through the camps. It took a great deal of time as-signing numbers to each new inmate, recording it in their files, and then tattooing it on the prisoner's arm. And they had to spend long hours at roll calls checking to see that no prisoners had escaped. Even with all this meticulous care, it was difficult to keep track of the numbers that died daily of starvation, of camp-induced illness, at the hands of sadistic guards and medical researchers and from the guns of the SS men supervising burial details. It was a difficult task indeed, keeping track of all those who "cheated" the gas cham-bers. But more often than not these difficulties were overcome, and careful records were kept. In the last year of the war, fearing retribu-tion, the Germans feverishly destroyed as much of their criminal record as possible.

More than six million had been murdered. The old did not have the young to mourn for them—they died together. But if individuals thus did not leave a memory, European Jewry is remembered and mourned by the rest of world Jewry. And some of the concentra-tion camps have been preserved as museums (for the present, at least) by the German community which has, since the end of the war, striven to atone for its sins. The gas chambers—disguised as shower rooms to deceive the victims—stand in mute accusation. Some of the buildings remain. And the names—Auschwitz, Bergen-Belsen, and the rest—will not be forgotten.

A new textbook is now making its way into the German schools (*The Burden of Guilt*, Oxford University Press, 1964). Hannah Vogt, the German author, discusses the fate of the Jews under Hitler.

The figures she lists give us an approximation of the work done within the extermination camps, and of the success of the "Final Solution." It is probably low in its estimate, but the death of European Jewry should not become a dispute over numbers.

Country:	Jewish Population September 1939	Jews killed	Percentage of Jewish deaths
1. Poland	3,300,000	2,800,000	85%
2. USSR (occupied territory)	2,100,000	1,500,000	71.4%
3. Rumania	850,000	425,000	50%
4. Hungary	404,000	200,000	49.5%
5. Czechoslovakia	315,000	260,000	82.5%
6. France	300,000	90,000	30%
7. Germany	210,000	170,000	81%
8. Lithuania	150,000	135,000	90%
9. Holland	150,000	90,000	60%
10. Latvia	95,000	85,000	89.5%
11. Belgium	90,000	40,000	44.4%
12. Greece	75,000	60,000	80%
13. Yugoslavia	75,000	55,000	73.3%
14. Austria	60,000	40,000	66.6%
15. Italy	57,000	15,000	26.3%
16. Bulgaria	50,000	7,000	14%
17. Others	20,000	6,000	30%
	8,301,000	5,978,000	72%

(Quoted from German edition, p. 192)

These 6,000,000 victims of the Nazi criminal state are the concern of this anthology. The death of these 6,000,000 does not constitute the sum of the German crimes, since any consideration of the Nazi Holocaust would be parochial if it did not consider all of the 29,000,000 victims of World War II. Nor was this crime of genocide, the attempt to destroy a people, limited to the Jews; the Nazis had also set their sights on exterminating the Gypsies. All the occupied countries suffered under German rule.

These are the facts and figures. They give us the actual structure, they tell us that what happened really did happen. Once we have mastered these, we may be able to penetrate deeper into the darkness; we may be able to feel what happened; areas of our own existence may take on new form and meaning—facts, feelings, the outer and inner structure of our existence.

The Inner Quest

In the literature of the Holocaust, there is conveyed that which cannot be transmitted by a thousand facts and figures. We learn to suffer in these pages; and we learn anger. It is that anger which must serve to instruct us. For if we are angry, we care. And if we care, our concern must outstrip the fact, once again. We learn to ask questions. And we also learn that sometimes there are no clear-cut answers which reason can give.

As we move from scholarly reports to literary accounts, our minds and hearts are touched by moral values which are a reality in human existence. If we are pessimists, we can say: "It is not enough!" And it *is* not enough—not nearly sufficient to permit implicit trust in a better future. It is enough, on the other hand, to affirm human existence; it is enough to have the courage to be.

If we are optimists, we can acknowledge the world for what it was; we must not try to explain away the terror and evil of that time. It did happen; and the veil has been torn away from the face of evil which is one aspect of humanity. We cannot sustain the old belief in man, nor the old belief in God and His moral ordering of the world, but we can search for new beliefs. And once we have wept for man, we can also glory in the indomitable spirit of man which yet endures. As we turn to this dark period, we recognize that in confronting the worst, man has produced the best within himself. We look at the Age of Evil and we come to celebrate the vision of man's goodness, the songs of the night that join together with the morning stars and sing of the crowning glory of God's creation—the human soul.

When Dante left the "Inferno," he once more looked up at the stars. The stars have moved further away from the world since then. But, as we enter the inferno of the Holocaust, we know that it is a journey which we cannot avoid. We will look for the stars when we emerge.

The Geography of Hell

How doth the city sit solitary.... LAMENTATIONS 1:1

INTRODUCTION

T HERE WERE MESSENGERS OF DOOM BUT PEOPLE DID NOT LISTEN; there were warnings of imminent danger but few paid any attention. Then came death and it no longer mattered how or whether one knew or suspected the evil intent of the enemy. It was too late. German-dominated Europe had become a geography of hell from which there was no escape.

As we examine the fabric of those days, it crumbles dry and dusty between our fingers. Was there really so little love, so little understanding, so little help from the Gentile neighbors of the Jewish community? We have already noted the corrosive effect of a criminal state upon its citizens and have taken into account the deep-rooted prejudices and hatreds which emerged in that atmosphere of fanatic nationalism. But was the whole landscape one raging inferno? Was there no place where humane feelings created islands of compassion? In search of understanding, we walk into the famous "Achterhuis," the attic where the Frank family, aided by Gentile friends, found temporary refuge from hell. With this account, we enter the actual experience of the Holocaust. We listen. We learn. And we begin to feel.

We digress from the experience for a while and move into its analysis. Some victims, looking back, wonder whether Jews should have hidden at all. They wonder whether the Jews, by their lack of resistance, did not aid rather than hinder the Nazis in their attempt at genocide. It is a subject which has caused much controversy in recent years.

We move on. Reentering the world of darkness—this time, the concentration camp itself—we learn that there is a resistance of the spirit as well as of the body, and this moral resistance, too, must be taken into account.

How did the Jewish community react under stress? What are the sacrifices demanded of victims? What constitutes moral resistance under extreme conditions? Does this type of resistance have any effect on the victims or the persecutors? These are the questions we must keep in mind as we begin to examine the landscape of hell.

1. *THE DIARY OF A YOUNG GIRL*

ANNE FRANK

Natives of Frankfurt, Germany, the Frank family fled to Holland to escape persecution. When the Germans invaded, Mr. Frank prepared a hiding place in the attic of his business establishment. This "secret annex" became their prison, and Anne's diary became one of the great classics of prison literature. It records the triumphs and defeats of the imprisoned human spirit, the beginnings of maturity and love in the life of a young girl, and the anguish of Jewish history. The Franks were betrayed and Anne died in Bergen-Belsen; but the words in her little schoolbook have reached out to teen-agers and adults throughout the world.

THURSDAY, 6 APRIL, 1944

Dear Kitty,

You asked me what my hobbies and interests were, so I want to reply. I warn you, however, that there are heaps of them, so don't get a shock!

First of all: writing, but that hardly counts as a hobby.

Number two: family trees. I've been searching for family trees of the French, German, Spanish, English, Austrian, Russian, Norwegian, and Dutch royal families in all newspapers, books, and pamphlets I can find. I've made great progress with a lot of them, as, for a long time already, I've been taking down notes from all the biographies and history books that I read; I even copy out many passages of history.

My third hobby then is history, on which Daddy has already bought me a lot of books. I can hardly wait for the day that I shall be able to comb through the books in a public library.

Number four is Greek and Roman mythology. I have various books about this too.

Other hobbies are film stars and family photos. Mad on books and reading. Have a great liking for history of art, poets and painters. I may go in for music later on. I have a great loathing for algebra, geometry, and figures.

I enjoy all the other school subjects, but history above all!

> Yours,
> *Anne*

TUESDAY, 11 APRIL, 1944

Dear Kitty,

My head throbs, I honestly don't know where to begin.

On Friday (Good Friday) we played Monopoly, Saturday afternoon too. These days passed quickly and uneventfully. On Sunday afternoon, on my invitation, Peter came to my room at half past four; at a quarter past five we went to the front attic, where we remained until six o'clock. There was a beautiful Mozart concert on the radio from six o'clock until a quarter past seven. I enjoyed it all very much, but especially the "Kleine Nachtmusik." I can hardly listen in the room because I'm always so inwardly stirred when I hear lovely music.

On Sunday evening Peter and I went to the front attic together and, in order to sit comfortably, we took with us a few divan cushions that we were able to lay our hands on. We seated ourselves on one packing case. Both the case and the cushions were very narrow, so we sat absolutely squashed together, leaning against other cases. Boche kept us company too, so we weren't unchaperoned.

Suddenly, at a quarter to nine, Mr. Van Daan whistled and asked if we had one of Dussel's cushions. We both jumped up and went downstairs with cushion, cat, and Van Daan.

A lot of trouble arose out of this cushion, because Dussel was annoyed that we had one of his cushions, one that he used as a pillow. He was afraid that there might be fleas in it and made a great commotion about his beloved cushion! Peter and I put two hard brushes in his bed as a revenge. We had a good laugh over this little interlude!

Our fun didn't last long. At half past nine Peter knocked softly on the door and asked Daddy if he would just help him upstairs over a difficult English sentence. "That's a blind," I said to Margot, "anyone could see through that one!" I was right. They were in the act of breaking into the warehouse. Daddy, Van Daan, Dussel, and Peter were downstairs in a flash. Margot, Mummy, Mrs. Van Daan, and I stayed upstairs and waited.

Four frightened women just have to talk, so talk we did, until we heard a bang downstairs. After that all was quiet, the clock struck a quarter to ten. The color had vanished from our faces, we were still quiet, although we were afraid. Where could the men be? What was that bang? Would they be fighting the burglars? Ten o'clock, footsteps on the stairs: Daddy, white and nervous, entered, followed by Mr. Van Daan. "Lights out, creep upstairs, we expect the police in the house!"

There was no time to be frightened: the lights went out, I quickly grabbed a jacket, and we were upstairs. "What has happened? Tell us quickly!" There was no one to tell us, the men having disappeared downstairs again. Only at ten past ten did they reappear; two kept watch at Peter's open window, the door to the landing was closed, the swinging cupboard shut. We hung a jersey round the night light, and after that they told us:

Peter heard two loud bangs on the landing, ran downstairs, and saw there was a large plank out of the left half of the door. He dashed upstairs, warned the "Home Guard" of the family, and the four of them proceeded downstairs. When they entered the warehouse, the burglars were in the act of enlarging the hole. Without further thought Van Daan shouted: "Police!"

A few hurried steps outside, and the burglars had fled. In order to avoid the hole being noticed by the police, a plank was put against it, but a good hard kick from outside sent it flying to the ground. The men were perplexed at such impudence, and both

Van Daan and Peter felt murder welling up within them; Van Daan beat on the ground with a chopper, and all was quiet again. Once more they wanted to put the plank in front of the hole. Disturbance! A married couple outside shone a torch through the opening, lighting up the whole warehouse. "Hell!" muttered one of the men, and now they switched over from their role of police to that of burglars. The four of them sneaked upstairs, Peter quickly opened the doors and windows of the kitchen and private office, flung the telephone onto the floor, and finally the four of them landed behind the swinging cupboard.

The married couple with the torch would probably have warned the police: it was Sunday evening, Easter Sunday, no one at the office on Easter Monday, so none of us could budge until Tuesday morning. Think of it, waiting in such fear for two nights and a day! No one had anything to suggest, so we simply sat there in pitch-darkness, because Mrs. Van Daan in her fright had unintentionally turned the lamp right out; talked in whispers, and at every creak one heard "Sh! Sh!"

It turned half past ten, eleven, but not a sound; Daddy and Van Daan joined us in turns. Then a quarter past eleven, a bustle and noise downstairs. Everyone's breath was audible, otherwise no one moved. Footsteps in the house, in the private office, kitchen, then . . . on our staircase. No one breathed audibly now, footsteps on our staircase, then a rattling of the swinging cupboard. This moment is indescribable. "Now we are lost!" I said, and could see us all being taken away by the Gestapo that very night. Twice they rattled at the cupboard, then there was nothing, the footsteps withdrew, we were saved so far. A shiver seemed to pass from one to another, I heard someone's teeth chattering, no one said a word.

There was not another sound in the house, but a light was burning on our landing, right in front of the cupboard. Could that be because it was a secret cupboard? Perhaps the police had forgotten the light? Would someone come back to put it out? Tongues loosened, there was no one in the house any longer, perhaps there was someone on guard outside.

Next we did three things: we went over again what we supposed had happened, we trembled with fear, and we had to go to the lavatory. The buckets were in the attic, so all we had was Peter's tin wastepaper basket. Van Daan went first, then Daddy, but Mummy was too shy to face it. Daddy brought the wastepaper basket into the room, where Margot, Mrs. Van Daan, and I gladly made use of it. Finally Mummy decided to do so too. People kept on asking for paper—fortunately I had some in my pocket!

The tin smelled ghastly, everything went on in a whisper, we were tired, it was twelve o'clock. "Lie down on the floor then and sleep." Margot and I were each given a pillow and one blanket; Margot lying just near the store cupboard and I between the table legs. The smell wasn't quite so bad when one was on the floor, but still Mrs. Van Daan quietly brought some chlorine, a tea towel over the pot serving as a second expedient.

Talk, whispers, fear, stink, flatulation, and always someone on the pot; then try to go to sleep! However, by half past two I was so tired that I knew no more until half past three. I awoke when Mrs. Van Daan laid her head on my foot.

"For heaven's sake, give me something to put on!" I asked. I was given something, but don't ask what—a pair of woolen knickers over my pajamas, a red jumper, and a black skirt, white oversocks and a pair of sports stockings full of holes. Then Mrs. Van Daan sat in the chair and her husband came and lay on my feet. I lay thinking till half past three, shivering the whole time, which prevented Van Daan from sleeping. I prepared myself for the return of the police, then we'd have to say that we were in hiding; they would either be good Dutch people, then we'd be saved, or N.S.B.-ers,* then we'd have to bribe them!

"In that case, destroy the radio," sighed Mrs. Van Daan. "Yes, in the stove!" replied her husband. "If they find us, then let them find the radio as well!"

"Then they will find Anne's diary," added Daddy. "Burn it then," suggested the most terrified member of the party. This, and when the police rattled the cupboard door, were my worst moments. "Not my diary; if my diary goes, I go with it!" But luckily Daddy didn't answer.

There is no object in recounting all the conversations that I can still remember; so much was said. I comforted Mrs. Van Daan, who was very scared. We talked about escaping and being questioned by the Gestapo, about ringing up, and being brave.

"We must behave like soldiers, Mrs. Van Daan. If all is up now,

* The Dutch National Socialist Movement.

then let's go for Queen and Country, for freedom, truth, and right, as they always say on the Dutch News from England. The only thing that is really rotten is that we get a lot of other people into trouble too."

Mr. Van Daan changed places again with his wife after an hour, and Daddy came and sat beside me. The men smoked non-stop, now and then there was a deep sigh, then someone went on the pot and everything began all over again.

Four o'clock, five o'clock, half past five. Then I went and sat with Peter by his window and listened, so close together that we could feel each other's bodies quivering; we spoke a word or two now and then, and listened attentively. In the room next door they took down the blackout. They wanted to call up Koophuis at seven o'clock and get him to send someone around. Then they wrote down everything they wanted to tell Koophuis over the phone. The risk that the police on guard at the door, or in the warehouse, might hear the telephone was very great, but the danger of the police returning was even greater.

The points were these:

Burglars had broken in: police have been in the house, as far as the swinging cupboard, but no further.

Burglars apparently disturbed, forced open the door in the warehouse and escaped through the garden.

Main entrance bolted, Kraler must have used the second door when he left. The typewriters and adding machine are safe in the black case in the private office.

Try to warn Henk and fetch the key from Elli, then go and look around the office—on the pretext of feeding the cat.

Everything went according to plan. Koophuis was phoned, the typewriters which we had upstairs were put in the case. Then we sat around the table again and waited for Henk or the police.

Peter had fallen asleep and Van Daan and I were lying on the floor, when we heard loud footsteps downstairs. I got up quietly: "That's Henk."

"No, no, it's the police," some of the others said.

Someone knocked at the door, Miep whistled. This was too much for Mrs. Van Daan, she turned as white as a sheet and sank limply into a chair; had the tension lasted one minute longer she would have fainted.

Our room was a perfect picture when Miep and Henk entered, the table alone would have been worth photographing! A copy of *Cinema and Theater,* covered with jam and a remedy for diarrhea, opened at a page of dancing girls, two jam pots, two started loaves of bread, a mirror, comb, matches, ash, cigarettes, tobacco, ash tray, books, a pair of pants, a torch, toilet paper, etc., etc., lay jumbled together in variegated splendor.

Of course Henk and Miep were greeted with shouts and tears. Henk mended the hole in the door with some planks, and soon went off again to inform the police of the burglary. Miep had also found a letter under the warehouse door from the night watchman Slagter, who had noticed the hole and warned the police, whom he would also visit.

So we had half an hour to tidy ourselves. I've never seen such a change take place in half an hour. Margot and I took the bedclothes downstairs, went to the W.C., washed, and did our teeth and hair. After that I tidied the room a bit and went upstairs again. The table there was already cleared, so we ran off some water and made coffee and tea, boiled the milk, and laid the table for lunch. Daddy and Peter emptied the potties and cleaned them with warm water and chlorine.

At eleven o'clock we sat round the table with Henk, who was back by that time, and slowly things began to be more normal and cozy again. Henk's story was as follows:

Mr. Slagter was asleep, but his wife told Henk that her husband had found the hole in our door when he was doing his tour round the canals, and that he had called a policeman, who had gone through the building with him. He would be coming to see Kraler on Tuesday and would tell him more then. At the police station they knew nothing of the burglary yet, but the policeman had made a note of it at once and would come and look round on Tuesday. On the way back Henk happened to meet our greengrocer at the corner, and told him that the house had been broken into. "I know that," he said quite coolly. "I was passing last evening with my wife and saw the hole in the door. My wife wanted to walk on, but I just had a look in with my torch; then the thieves cleared at once. To be on the safe side, I didn't ring up the police, as with you I didn't think it was the thing to do. I don't know anything, but I guess a lot."

Henk thanked him and went on. The man obviously guesses that we're here, because he always brings the potatoes during the lunch hour. Such a nice man!

It was one by the time Henk had gone and we'd finished doing the dishes. We all went for a sleep. I awoke at a quarter to three and saw that Mr. Dussel had already disappeared. Quite by chance, and with my sleepy eyes, I ran into Peter in the bathroom; he had just come down. We arranged to meet downstairs.

I tidied myself and went down. "Do you still dare to go to the front attic?" he asked. I nodded, fetched my pillow, and we went up to the attic. It was glorious weather, and soon the sirens were wailing; we stayed where we were. Peter put his arms around my shoulder, and I put mine around his and so we remained, our arms around each other, quietly waiting until Margot came to fetch us for coffee at four o'clock.

We finished our bread, drank lemonade and joked (we were able to again), otherwise everything went normally. In the evening I thanked Peter because he was the bravest of us all.

None of us has ever been in such danger as that night. God truly protected us; just think of it—the police at our secret cupboard, the light on right in front of it, and still we remained undiscovered.

If the invasion comes, and bombs with it, then it is each man for himself, but in this case the fear was also for our good, innocent protectors. "We are saved, go on saving us!" That is all we can say.

This affair has brought quite a number of changes with it. Mr. Dussel no longer sits downstairs in Kraler's office in the evenings, but in the bathroom instead. Peter goes round the house for a checkup at half past eight and half past nine. Peter isn't allowed to have his window open at nights any more. No one is allowed to pull the plug after half past nine. This evening there's a carpenter coming to make the warehouse doors even stronger.

Now there are debates going on all the time in the "Secret Annexe." Kraler reproached us for our carelessness. Henk, too, said that in a case like that we must never go downstairs. We have been pointedly reminded that we are in hiding, that we are Jews in chains, chained to one spot, without any rights, but with a thousand duties. We Jews mustn't show our feelings, must be brave and strong, must accept all inconveniences and not grumble, must do what is within our power and trust in God. Sometimes this terrible war will be over. Surely the time will come when we are people again, and not just Jews.

Who has inflicted this upon us? Who has made us Jews different from all other people? Who has allowed us to suffer so terribly up till now? It is God that has made us as we are, but it will be God, too, who will raise us up again. If we bear all this suffering and if there are still Jews left, when it is over, then Jews, instead of being doomed, will be held up as an example. Who knows, it might even be our religion from which the world and all peoples learn good, and for that reason and that reason only do we have to suffer now. We can never become just Netherlanders, or just English, or representatives of any country for that matter, we will always remain Jews, but we want to, too.

Be brave! Let us remain aware of our task and not grumble, a solution will come, God has never deserted our people. Right through the ages there have been Jews, through all the ages they have had to suffer, but it has made them strong too; the weak fall, but the strong will remain and never go under!

During that night I really felt that I had to die, I waited for the police, I was prepared, as the soldier is on the battlefield. I was eager to lay down my life for the country, but now, now I've been saved again, now my first wish after the war is that I may become Dutch! I love the Dutch, I love this country, I love the language and want to work here. And even if I have to write to the Queen myself, I will not give up until I have reached my goal.

I am becoming still more independent of my parents, young as I am, I face life with more courage than Mummy; my feeling for justice is immovable, and truer than hers. I know what I want, I have a goal, an opinion, I have a religion and love. Let me be myself and then I am satisfied. I know that I'm a woman, a woman with inward strength and plenty of courage.

If God lets me live, I shall attain more than Mummy ever has done, I shall not remain insignificant, I shall work in the world and for mankind!

And now I know that first and foremost I shall require courage and cheerfulness!

Yours,
Anne

2. *THE INFORMED HEART*

BRUNO BETTELHEIM

In 1938, Dr. Bruno Bettelheim spent one year as a prisoner in Buchenwald and Dachau. He has written extensively about his experiences and observations, and is considered an authority in the area of behavior under extreme circumstances. His statements about the passivity of camp inmates and the behavior of the Frank family are shocking and challenging. It has been argued that his position, based on observations made before the concentration camps realized their full nature as extermination camps, cannot be equated with the experiences of those later, terrible days; and some reject his position as a slander upon the Jewish victims. But can we ignore the questions he raises?

▬▬

Behavior in extermination camps

The analysis of behavior inside the extermination camps, while more horrid, offers less of psychological interest, since prisoners there had no time or occasion to change much psychologically.

The only psychological phenomenon that seems pertinent in this report is the fact that these prisoners knew they were destined to die and still made almost no effort to revolt. The few exceptions, less than a handful among millions, I shall ignore for the moment, since they represent the behavior of such a tiny minority.

On occasions, only one or two German guards would be escorting up to four hundred prisoners toward the extermination camps over lonesome roads. There was every chance that the four hundred could have overpowered their armed guards.[1] Even if some prisoners had been killed in the process, the majority would have been free to join partisan groups. At the very least they could have enjoyed a temporary revenge without loss to themselves, since they were slated for death anyway.

A nonpsychological analysis of the behavior of these prisoners does not seem adequate for explaining such docility. In order to understand the phenomenon of men not fighting back, although certain death awaited them,[2] it must be realized that the most active individuals had long ago made their efforts to fight National Socialism and were now either dead or exhausted. The Polish and Jewish prisoners who formed a majority in the extermination camps were mostly persons who for some reason had failed to escape and were not fighting back.

Their feeling of defeat does not imply they felt no strong hostility toward their oppressors. Weakness and submission are often charged with greater hostility than open counter-aggression. In counter-aggression, as for instance in the partisan or resistance movements, the opponents of German fascism found outlets for some of their hostilities through offensive action. But within the oppressed person who did not resist lay accumulating hostilities he was unable to discharge in action. Not even the mild relief of verbal aggression was open to him, because even that, he was afraid, would bring destruction by the SS.

The more hostility accumulated, the more terrified the prisoner became that it might break through in an explosive act spelling destruction for him. To prevent this, he felt he must at all times remain convinced of the extremely dangerous character of the aggressor; in that way his own fear would restrain him more effectively. So for his own protection he invested the SS with those features most threatening to himself. These, in turn, increased his anxiety, frustration, and hostility, and to keep them all under control, the SS had to be seen as even more murderous.[3]

---

[1] Even Hoess, in his memoirs, wondered why the prisoners did not revolt, since they could often have done it with ease, given their vast numbers.

[2] This knowledge of certain death made their case different from those other prisoners who could still hope for eventual liberation.

[3] This mechanism differs only in degree from the widespread use of projection as a psychological defense in the "ordinary" concentration camps.

The twin process of repressing all hostility and inflating the terrible image of the SS devoured almost all his emotional energy. If anything was left, it was soon used up by the fight against depression due to loss of status, separation from family, exhaustion due to malnutrition and disease, and the absolute hopelessness of the situation.

In the concentration camps some hostility could be discharged in the fight among prisoner factions. While the battles lasted the hope still lived that one's own party might win, bringing better conditions for oneself. "Moslems" of course no longer fought, did not belong to factions, did not discharge hostility but turned it against the self, like the prisoners in the extermination camps. And like them, they died. In the extermination camps the prisoners were also deprived of anything that might have restored self respect or the will to live, while the pent-up hostility grew uninterruptedly.

All this may explain the docility of prisoners who walked to the gas chambers or who dug their own graves and then lined up before them so that, shot down, they would fall into the graves. It may be assumed that most of these prisoners were by then suicidal. Walking to the gas chamber was committing suicide in a way that asked for none of the energy usually needed for deciding and planning to kill oneself. Psychologically speaking, most prisoners in the extermination camps committed suicide by submitting to death without resistance.

If this speculation is correct, then one may say that in the extermination camps the goals of the SS found their ultimate realization. Through the use of terror the SS succeeded in forcing its opponents to do, out of their own will, what it wished them to do. Millions of people submitted to extermination because SS methods had forced them to see it not as a way out, but as the only way to put an end to conditions in which they could no longer live as human beings.

Since these remarks may seem farfetched, it should be added that the process just described is similar to what can be observed in some psychotic patients. The assumption that these prisoners developed states of mind similar to those observed in psychotic persons seems borne out by the behavior of former prisoners of extermination camps after their liberation. Their symptoms depended, of course, on initial personality assets and what the individual experienced after liberation. In some persons the symptoms appeared more severe, in others less so; some showed that their symptoms were reversible, others not.

Immediately after liberation nearly all prisoners engaged in asocial behavior that could only be explained by far reaching disintegration of their former personality structures. A few former inmates of extermination camps have been studied. Their grip on reality was extremely tenuous. Some were still suffering from delusions of persecution, others suffered from delusions of grandeur. The latter were the counterpart of guilt feelings for having been spared while parents or siblings had all perished. They were trying to justify and explain their own survival by delusionally inflating their importance. It also enabled them to compensate for the extreme damage done to their narcissism by the experience they had undergone.

Business as usual

A few words about the world's reaction to the concentration camps: the terrors committed in them were experienced as uncanny by most civilized persons. It came as a shock to their pride that supposedly civilized nations could stoop to such inhuman acts. The implication that modern man has such inadequate control over his cruelty was felt as a threat. Three different psychological mechanisms were most frequently used for dealing with the phenomenon of the concentration camp: (a) its applicability to man in general was denied by asserting (contrary to available evidence) that the acts of torture were committed by a small group of insane or perverted persons; (b) the truth of the reports was denied by ascribing them to deliberate propaganda. This method was favored by the German government which called all reports on terror in the camps horror propaganda (Greuelpropaganda); (c) the reports were believed, but the knowledge of the terror was repressed as soon as possible.

All three mechanisms could be seen at work after liberation. At first, after the "discovery" of the camps, a wave of extreme outrage swept the Allied nations. It was soon followed by a general repression of the discovery. It may be that this reaction of the general public was due to something more than the shock dealt their narcissism by the fact that cruelty is still rampant among men. It may also be that the memory of the tortures was repressed out of some dim realization that the modern state now has available the means for changing personality. To have to accept that one's personality may be changed against one's will is the greatest threat to one's self respect. It must therefore be dealt with by action, or by repression.

The universal success of the *Diary of Anne Frank* suggests how much the tendency to deny is still with us, while her story itself demonstrates how such denial can hasten our own destruction. It is an onerous task to take apart such a humane and moving story, arousing so much compassion for gentle Anne Frank. But I believe that its world-wide acclaim cannot be explained unless we recognize our wish to forget the gas chambers and to glorify attitudes of extreme privatization, of continuing to hold on to attitudes as usual even in a holocaust. Exactly because their going on with private life as usual brought destruction did it have to be glorified; in that way we could overlook the essential fact of how destructive it can be under extreme social circumstances.

While the Franks were making their preparations for going passively into hiding, thousands of other Jews in Holland and elsewhere in Europe were trying to escape to the free world, the better to survive or to be able to fight their executioners. Others who could not do so went underground—not simply to hide from the SS, waiting passively, without preparation for fight, for the day when they would be caught—but to fight the Germans, and with it for humanity. All the Franks wanted was to go on with life as nearly as possible in the usual fashion.

Little Anne, too, wanted only to go on with life as usual, and nobody can blame her. But hers was certainly not a necessary fate, much less a heroic one; it was a senseless fate. The Franks could have faced the facts and survived, as did many Jews living in Holland. Anne could have had a good chance to survive, as did many Jewish children in Holland. But for that she would have had to be separated from her parents and gone to live with a Dutch family as their own child.

Everybody who recognized the obvious knew that the hardest way to go underground was to do it as a family; that to hide as a family made detection by the SS most likely. The Franks, with their excellent connections among gentile Dutch families should have had an easy time hiding out singly, each with a different family.

But instead of planning for this, the main principle of their planning was to continue as much as possible with the kind of family life they were accustomed to. Any other course would have meant not merely giving up the beloved family life, but also accepting as reality man's inhumanity to man. Most of all it would have forced them to accept that going on with life as usual was not an absolute value, but can sometimes be the most destructive of all attitudes.

There is little doubt that the Franks, who were able to provide themselves with so much, could have provided themselves with a gun or two had they wished. They could have shot down at least one or two of the "green police" who came for them. There was no surplus of such police. The loss of an SS with every Jew arrested would have noticeably hindered the functioning of the police state. The fate of the Franks wouldn't have been any different, because they all died anyway except for Anne's father, though he hardly meant to pay for his survival with the extermination of his whole family. But they could have sold their lives dearly instead of walking to their death.

There is good reason why the so successful play ends with Anne stating her belief in the good in all men. What is denied is the importance of accepting the gas chambers as real so that never again will they exist. If all men are basically good, if going on with intimate family living no matter what else is what is to be most admired, then indeed we can all go on with life as usual and forget about Auschwitz. Except that Anne Frank died because her parents could not get themselves to believe in Auschwitz. And her story found wide acclaim because for us too, it denies implicitly that Auschwitz ever existed. If all men are good, there was never an Auschwitz.

High time

At various places in this book I have mentioned how submitting to the total state leads to a disintegration of what once seemed a well integrated personality, plus a return to many infantile attitudes. At this point perhaps a theoretical speculation may be helpful. Years ago Freud postulated two opposite tendencies: the life instincts, which he called eros or sex, and the destructive tendencies, which he named the death instinct. The more mature the person becomes, the more he should be able to "fuse" these two opposing tendencies, making the resultant "ego" energy available for the task of meeting and shaping reality.

The more immature the person, the more these tendencies are apt to push the total personality, at one moment in one direction, at the next moment in the other. Thus the so-called childlike friendliness of some primitive people, followed in the next moment by extreme "thoughtless" cruelty. But the disintegration, or perhaps one should better say the "defusion" of ego energy under extreme stress—at one moment into pure destructive tendencies ("Let it be over, no matter how"), at the next moment into irrational life tendencies ("Let's get something to eat now, even if it means death in short order")[4]—was only one aspect of man's primitivization in the total state. Another was engaging in infantile thought processes such as wishful thinking in place of a more mature evaluation of reality, and an infantile disregard for the possibility of death. These led many to think that they of all others would be spared and survive, and many more to simply disbelieve in the possibility of their own death. Not believing in its possibility, they did not prepare for it, including no preparation for how to defend their lives even when death became inescapable. Defending their lives before such time might have hastened their death. So up to a point, this "rolling with the punches" that the enemy dealt out was protective of life. But beyond that point it was destructive of both one's own life and that of others whose survival might be more certain too if one risked one's own life. The trouble is that the longer one "rolls" with the punches, the more likely it becomes that one will no longer have the strength to resist when death becomes imminent, particularly if this yielding to the enemy is accompanied not by an inner strengthening of the personality (which it would require) but an inner disintegration.[5]

Those who did not deny validity to death, who neither denied

---

[4] For example, those prisoners who ate the whole day's ration the moment they got it had nothing left for their faltering energies toward the end of the working day. Those who divided the little food they had and saved some for the moment when exhaustion threatened them most, fared much better in the long run.

[5] This, too, could be observed in the story of the Franks who bickered with each other over trifles, instead of supporting each other's desire to resist the demoralizing impact of their living conditions.

nor repressed its possibility, who embraced no childish belief in their indestructibility, were those who prepared for it in time as a real possibility. It meant risking one's life for a self chosen purpose and in doing so, saving one's own life or that of others, or both. When Jews in Germany were restricted to their homes, those who did not allow inertia to take over used the imposing of such restrictions as a warning that it was high time to go underground, join the resistance movement, provide themselves with forged papers, etc., if they had not done so long ago. Most of them survived.

An example out of the lives of some distant relatives of mine may further illustrate. Early in the war, a young man living in a small Hungarian town banded together with a number of other Jews and they prepared themselves for what to do when the Germans invaded. As soon as the Nazis imposed curfews on the Jews, his group left for Budapest since the bigger the city, the better the chances for escaping detection. There, similar groups from other towns converged and joined those of Budapest. From among them they selected typically "Aryan" looking men who, equipped with false papers, immediately joined the Hungarian SS so as to be able to warn of impending actions, to report in advance when a particular district would be searched, etc.

This worked so well that most of the groups survived intact. But they had also equipped themselves with small arms, so that when detected they could put up enough of a fight for the majority to escape while a few would die fighting to gain time for the escape.[6] A few of the Jews who had joined the SS were discovered and immediately shot, probably a death preferable to one in the gas chambers. But even among their special group the majority survived, hiding within the SS up to the last moment.

My young relative was unable to convince some members of his family to go with him when he left. Three times, at tremendous risk to himself he returned, pointing out first the growing persecu-

---

[6] Compare this to the Franks' selection of a hiding place that was basically a trap without an outlet, and that in all their months there no emergency escape route was constructed through which some of their group could at least have tried to escape while one or two of the men blocked and defended one of the small entrances with a homemade barricade. Compare also, Mr. Frank's teaching typically academic high school subjects to the youngsters, rather than how to make a getaway: a token of the same inability to face the possibility of death.

tion of the Jews, later the fact that their transport to the gas chambers had already begun. He could not convince them to move out of their homes, to leave their possessions. On each visit he pleaded more desperately, on each visit he found them less willing or able to listen to him, much less able to take action. It was as if each time they were more on their way to the crematoria where they all in fact died.

On each visit his family clung more desperately to the old living arrangements, the possessions they had accumulated over a lifetime. It was like a parallel process in which their life energies were drained away while their possessions seemed to give them a pseudo-security to replace the real assurance that no longer came from planning for their lives. Again like children, they preferred to cling desperately to some objects in which they had invested all the meaning they could no longer find in their lives. As they withdrew from the fight for survival, their lives began to reside more and more in these dead objects and the persons in them died piece by piece, little object by little object.

In Buchenwald, I talked to hundreds of German Jewish prisoners who were brought there in the fall of 1938. I asked them why they had not left Germany because of the utterly degrading conditions they were subjected to. Their answer was: How could we leave? It would have meant giving up our homes, our places of business. Their earthly possessions had so taken possession of them that they could not move; instead of using them, they were run by them.[7]

How the investing of possessions with one's life energy made people die piece by piece is also evident in the course of the Nazi attitude toward Jews. At the time of the first boycott of Jewish stores the whole external goal of the Nazis was the possessions of the Jews. They even let Jews take some of them out of the country if they would just go, leaving the bulk of their possessions behind. For a long time the intention of the Nazis, and of their first discriminatory laws, was to force undesirable minorities, including Jews, into emigration. Only when this did not work was the extermination policy instituted, though it also followed the inner logic of the Nazi racial ideology. But one wonders if the notion that

---

[7] The Franks, too, postponed going into hiding because they wished first to transfer more of their possessions to their hideout. They postponed it so long that it was nearly too late for Anne's sister, who was called to the SS.

millions of Jews (and later foreign nationals) would submit to extermination did not also result from seeing how much degradation
they would accept without fighting back. The persecution of the
Jews worsened, slow step by slow step, when no violent resistance
occurred. It may have been Jewish acceptance, without fight, of
ever harsher discrimination and degradation that first gave the SS
the idea that they could be gotten to the point where they would
walk to the gas chambers on their own.

Most Jews in Poland who did not believe in business as usual
survived the Second World War. As the Germans approached, they
left everything behind and fled to Russia, much as many of them
distrusted the Soviet system. But there, while perhaps citizens of a
second order, they were at least accepted as human beings. Those
who stayed on to continue business as usual moved toward their
own destruction and perished. Thus in the deepest sense the walk to
the gas chamber was only the last consequence of a philosophy of
business as usual; a last step in no longer defying the death instinct, which might also be called the principle of inertia. Because
the first step was taken long before one entered the death camp.

True, the same suicidal behavior has another meaning. It means
that man can be pushed so far and no further; that beyond a certain
point he chooses death to an inhuman existence. But the initial
step toward this terrible choice was inertia.

Those who give in to it, who have withdrawn all vital energy
from the world, can no longer act with initiative, and are threatened by it in others. They can no longer accept reality for what it
is; having grown infantile, they see it only in the infantile perspective of a wishful denial of what is too unpleasant, of a wishful belief
in their personal immortality. All this is dramatically illustrated in
an experience of Lengyel's.[8] She reports that although she and her
fellow prisoners lived just a few hundred yards from the crematoria
and the gas chambers and knew what they were all about, yet after
months most prisoners denied knowledge of them.[9] Realization of
their true situation might have helped them to save either the life
they were going to lose anyway, or the lives of others. But that

[8] Lengyel, O., *Five Chimneys*, The Story of Auschwitz, Chicago: Ziff Davis, 1947,
pp. 54–55.

[9] German gentile civilians denied the gas chambers, too, but the same denial in
them did not have the same meaning. By that time, civilians who faced facts and
rebelled invited death. Prisoners at Auschwitz were already doomed.

realization they could not afford. When Lengyel and many other prisoners were selected to be sent to the gas chambers, they did not try to break away, as she successfully did. Worse, the first time she tried it, some of the fellow prisoners selected with her for the gas chambers called the supervisors, telling them she was trying to get away. Lengyel desperately asks the question: How was it possible that people denied the existence of the gas chambers when all day long they saw the crematoria burning and smelled the odor of burning flesh? How come they preferred not to believe in the extermination just to prevent themselves from fighting for their very own lives? She offers no explanation except that they begrudged anyone who might save himself from the common fate, because they lacked enough courage to risk action themselves. I believe they did it because they had given up their will to live, had permitted their death tendencies to flood them. As a result they now identified more closely with the SS who were devoting themselves to destruction, than to those fellow prisoners who still had a grip on life and hence managed to escape death.

Human competence for what?

When prisoners began to serve their executioners, to help them speed the death of their own kind, things had gone beyond simple inertia. By then, death instinct running rampant had been added to inertia. Those who tried to serve their executioners in what were once their civilian capacities were merely continuing if not business, then life as usual. Whereby they opened the door to their death.

Lengyel speaks of a Dr. Mengele, SS physician at Auschwitz, in a typical example of the "business as usual" attitude that enabled some prisoners, and certainly the SS, to retain whatever inner balance they could despite what they were doing. She describes how Dr. Mengele took all correct medical precautions during childbirth, rigorously observing all aseptic principles, cutting the umbilical cord with greatest care, etc. But only half an hour later he sent mother and infant to be burned in the crematorium.[10]

---

[10] *Op. cit.*, p. 147.

Still, having made his choice, Dr. Mengele and others like him had, after all, to delude themselves at times to be able to live with themselves and their experience. Only one personal document on the subject has come to my attention, that of Dr. Nyiszli, a prisoner serving as "research physician" at Auschwitz.[11] How Dr. Nyiszli fooled himself can be seen, for example, in his repeatedly referring to himself as a doctor, though he worked as the assistant of a criminal. He speaks of the Institute for Race, Biological, and Anthropological Investigation as "one of the most qualified medical centers of the Third Reich" though it was devoted to proving falsehoods. That Nyiszli was a doctor didn't at all change the fact that he, like any of the prisoner officials who served the SS better than some SS were willing to serve it, was a participant, an accessory to the crimes of the SS. How then could he do it and survive?

The answer was: by taking pride in his professional skills, irrespective of what purpose they were used for. Again and again this pride in his professional skill permeates his story of his own and other prisoners' sufferings. The important issue here is that Dr. Nyiszli, Dr. Mengele, and hundreds of other far more prominent physicians, men trained long before the advent of Hitler to power, were participants in these human experiments and in the pseudoscientific investigations that went with them.[12] It is this pride in professional skill and knowledge, irrespective of moral implications, that is so dangerous. As a feature of modern society oriented toward technological competence it is still with us, though the concentration camps and the crematoria are no longer here. Auschwitz is gone, but as long as this attitude remains with us we shall not be safe from the indifference to life at its core.

It is easy to see that achieving a subtle balance between extremes may be an ideal way of life. It is harder to accept that this holds true even in a holocaust. But even in extreme conditions, to give way only to the heart or only to the mind is neither a good way to live, nor the way to survive. Living only to keep his family intact, even

---

[11] Nyiszli, Dr. Miklos, *Auschwitz: A Doctor's Eyewitness Account*, New York: Frederick Fell, Inc., 1960.

[12] Among the heads of clinics or chairmen of departments who participated knowingly in the experiments were Professors Sauerbruch of the University of Munich and Eppinger of the University of Vienna—teachers of whole generations of physicians before Hitler. Dr. Gebhardt, the president of the German Red Cross, was also among them. (Mitscherlich, A., and Mielke, F., *Doctors of Infamy*, New York: Henry Schuman, Inc., 1949.)

all Mr. Frank's love did not keep them alive, as a better informed heart might have done. Dr. Nyiszli, carried away by his high level training as a pathologist, and against the prompting of the heart, lent himself to such debasement of his deepest pride, his medical science, that one wonders what can have survived except his body.

I have met many Jews, as well as gentile anti-Nazis, who survived in Germany and in the occupied countries, like the group in Hungary described earlier. But they were all people who realized that when a world goes to pieces, when inhumanity reigns supreme, man cannot go on with business as usual. One then has to radically re-evaluate all of what one has done, believed in, stood for. In short, one has to take a stand on the new reality, a firm stand, and not one of retirement into even greater privatization.

If today, Negroes in Africa march against the guns of a police that defends *apartheid*—even if hundreds of them will be shot down and tens of thousands rounded up in concentration camps—their march, their fight, will sooner or later assure them of a chance for liberty and equality. Millions of the Jews of Europe who did not or could not escape in time or go underground as many thousands did, could at least have marched as free men against the SS, rather than to first grovel, then wait to be rounded up for their own extermination, and finally walk themselves to the gas chambers.

Yet the story of the extermination camps shows that even in such an overpowering environment, certain defenses do offer some protection, most important of which is understanding what goes on in oneself, and why. With enough understanding, the individual does not fool himself into believing that with every adjustment he makes he is protecting himself. He is able to recognize that much that on the surface seems protective, is actually self destructive. A most extreme example were those prisoners who volunteered to work in the gas chambers hoping it would somehow save their lives. All of them were killed after a short time. But many of them died sooner, and after weeks of a more horrible life, than might have been true if they had not volunteered.

Fighting back

Did no one of those destined to die fight back? Did none of them wish to die not by giving in but by asserting themselves in attacking the SS? A very few did. One of them was the twelfth *Sonder-kommando,* prisoners working in the gas chambers.[13] Now all these *Kommandos* knew their fate since the first task of every new *Sonder-kommando* was to cremate the corpses of the preceding *Kommando,* exterminated just a few hours before.

In this single revolt of the twelfth *Sonderkommando,* seventy SS were killed, including one commissioned officer and seventeen non-commissioned officers; one of the crematoria was totally destroyed and another severely damaged. True, all eight hundred and fifty-three prisoners of the *Kommando* died. But this proves that a position in the *Sonderkommando* gave prisoners a chance of about ten to one to destroy the SS, a higher ratio than in the ordinary concentration camp.

The one *Sonderkommando* that revolted and took such heavy toll of the enemy did not die much differently than all other *Sonder-kommandos.* Why, then—and this is the question that haunts all who study the extermination camps—why then did millions walk quietly, without resistance, to their death when right before them were examples such as this *Kommando* that managed to destroy and damage part of their own chambers of death and kill almost 10% of their number in SS? Why did so few of the millions of prisoners die like men, as did the men of only one of these *Kom-mandos?* Why did the rest of these *Kommandos* not revolt, but march themselves willingly to their death. Or what did it take for the exception to do so?

Perhaps another rare instance, an example of supreme self assertion, can shed light on the question. Once, a group of naked prisoners about to enter the gas chamber stood lined up in front of it. In some way the commanding SS officer learned that one of the women prisoners had been a dancer. So he ordered her to dance for him. She did, and as she danced, she approached him, seized his gun, and shot him down. She too was immediately shot to death.[14]

But isn't it probable that despite the grotesque setting in which

---

13 Nyiszli, *op. cit.* Scattered revolts in the death camps (Treblinka, etc.) are mentioned elsewhere in the literature, though I have not myself seen witnessed reports. Civilian uprisings began to occur with the turn of the war tide against Germany, but as in the case of the Warsaw uprising, the hour was far too late for the millions already dead.

14 Kogon, *op. cit.,* p. 132.

she danced, dancing made her once again a person? Dancing, she was singled out as an individual, asked to perform in what had once been her chosen vocation. No longer was she a number, a nameless, depersonalized prisoner, but the dancer she used to be. Transformed, however momentarily, she responded like her old self, destroying the enemy bent on her destruction, even if she had to die in the process.

Despite the hundreds of thousands of living dead men who moved quietly to their graves, this one example, and there were several like her, shows that in an instant the old personality can be regained, its destruction undone, once we decide on our own that we wish to cease being units in a system. Exercising the last freedom that not even the concentration camp could take away—to decide how one wishes to think and feel about the conditions of one's life—this dancer threw off her real prison. This she could do because she was willing to risk her life to achieve autonomy once more. If we do that, then if we cannot live, at least we die as men.

3. *JEWISH RESISTANCE*

ALEXANDER DONAT

In this selection, Alexander Donat, a survivor of the Holocaust, deals specifically with the issues of passivity and resistance raised by Dr. Bettelheim. His answers are diametrically opposed to the previous selection. He brands Bettelheim's conclusions false, mustering factual material to document the validity of his position.

▬▬▬

"LIKE SHEEP TO THE SLAUGHTER"

Truth and Interpretation

To Dr. Isaac Schipper, the Polish-Jewish historian who was my closest neighbor in the potato-peeling brigade at the Maidanek concentration camp, I owe an insight which has haunted me ever since my stay there.

"There is no such thing as historical truth," he would say with his sad smile when we dreamed about how after the war the survivors of the camps would tell the world *the whole truth*. "There is just interpretation," he said. "It depends on who writes the history of our time. Should *they* write the story of this war, our destruction will be presented as one of the most glorious exploits in world history. But if *we* write the story we will have the thankless task of

Reprinted with permission of Waldon Press, Inc., from *Jewish Resistance* by ALEXANDER DONAT. Copyright © 1964 by Alexander Donat.

proving to a disbelieving world that we really are Abel, the murdered brother."

Not even twenty years have passed since Schipper spoke these words, and reality has already proved darker than his forebodings. Our tragedy has not yet had time to become history, its witnesses and survivors still live, their memories remain vivid; yet a malicious myth about our experience keeps rising before our eyes. The myth is both open and covert; its sources are at best ignorance and mis-information—at worst, vested interest. After the initial shock, the truth proved too horrible to live with. Then, so much the worse for the truth; it must be doctored, and of doctors there is no lack: the Germans, the Poles, the Vatican, the capitals of the world, and, worst, the Jews themselves.

We are now far from the time when Karl Jaspers could blame every German for "crimes committed in his presence or with his knowledge. If I fail to do whatever I can to prevent them, I too am guilty. If I was present at the murder of others without risking my life to prevent it, I feel guilty."[1] According to Raul Hilberg,[2] about two million Germans were connected with the Nazi genocide organization. Other millions profiteered from the loot. Today, it seems that all the crimes were committed by a handful of Nazi criminals; the German people were not present, they "didn't know." Not only were the Germans "ignorant of the crimes," but the measly flicker of German resistance—late in the day (1944) and actually an ultra-nationalist response to the possibility of Hitler's losing—has now been inflated by some historians into a "soundless rebellion" in which almost the whole German nation ("soundlessly") took part.[3] Everything becomes simple. The small Nazis carried out the orders of the bigger ones, and the bigger ones the orders of the Führer himself. Since Hitler is dead, the guilt and responsibility are heaped on a small group of Nazi villains—most of them now conveniently dead—so that the German conscience is left free and clear.

Konrad Adenauer is perhaps an enlightened representative of the German conscience—or perhaps he is simply smarter. One thing is sure: he made the better deal with his "Reparations" and "Restitutions" to the victims and to Israel. than the claimants. He did

---

[1] Karl Jaspers, *The Question of German Guilt*, New York, 1947.
[2] Raul Hilberg, *The Destruction of the European Jews*, Chicago, 1961.
[3] Gunther Weisenborn, *Der lautlose Aufstand*, Hamburg, 1953.

just enough to disarm the victims morally and to buy Germany's respectability in the eyes of the world. At the same time his countrymen—the murderers, their spouses, their families—are comfortably immersed in the prosperity of the *Wirschaftswunder,* pump-primed by U. S. dollars. Such a spectacle could only come about as the result of the shameful American-Soviet race for the favors of their yesterday's enemy. The political wisdom of this race is, for my purpose, irrelevant; the moral aspects are my concern; the depraved spectacle of the *Faust-Volk* periodically selling its soul to the devil, turning into a nation of barbarians, and then being promoted to the role of defender of civilization.

As for Poland, it now seems there is hardly a man in that country who somehow hadn't "participated" in rescuing Jews from the Nazi murderers. This legend, carefully fomented by the official propaganda, is so well-rooted that the young Polish generation, Jews as well as Gentiles, believe in it entirely.

Each of the political parties participating in the revolt of the Warsaw Ghetto and the Jewish resistance has tried its best to appropriate the biggest slice of posthumous glory: the Zionists, the Bund, the Communists. The Communists tend to grossly overstate their part in the Ghetto resistance and in the aid they rendered to the Ghetto.[4] The Polish non-Communist underground, the Home Army (Armia Krajowa), states through one of its leaders, Andrzej Pomian, that "we Poles are not burdened by the sin of indifference to the Jews' sufferings. In order to alleviate their fate, the leadership of our Underground did everything within the limits of our then very modest means."[5]

But the historical facts are not exactly thus. The late Dr. Isaac Schwarzbart, deputy in the Polish National Council in London during the war, told me more than once, with tears in his eyes, how it really looked—and inside Poland it was even worse. I cite from my yet unpublished memoirs:

> In vain did we implore help from our Polish brothers, with whom we had shared good and bad fortune alike for seven centuries. They were utterly unmoved in our hour of need. They did not even express ordinary human compassion at the spectacle of our ordeal—let alone some manifestation of

---

[4] B. Mark, *Walka i zaglada warszawskiego getta,* Warsaw, 1959.
[5] Zygmunt Nagórski, Sr. et al, *Dialog polsko-zydowski,* New York, 1958.

Christian charity. They did not even let political good sense guide them—after all, objectively, we *were allies* in a struggle against a common enemy. While we bled and died, their attitude was at best indifference, and all too often it was "friendly neutrality" toward the Germans. ("Let the Germans do this dirty job for us.") And there were far too many cases of willing, active, enthusiastic Polish assistance to the Nazi murderers.

There was a handful of noble Poles, of course, but nobody listened to them. Their voices never carried above the continual screams of hatred. Heroically, they managed to save individuals, but they could not bring about the slightest mitigation of Nazi ferocity.

Two forces only were in a position to influence the Polish masses: the London-led underground, and the pulpit. Neither used its influence to change the climate of indifference toward the martyred Jews.

The question of the clergy and its role in our tragedy is a very delicate one, but of extreme importance. "A Christian who witnesses inactively a crime becomes its accomplice." In our crucial moment in two nominally Christian nations there were to be found only a handful of true Christians. Of course, it is common knowledge that some Catholic priests, both at the very top and the bottom of the hierarchy, assumed a courageous attitude in a true Christian spirit.[6] But the over-all picture, it must in candor be said, is most depressing. The Vatican's archives are locked, and the true story of the Church's role in our holocaust has not been revealed to the world. The Vatican and Treblinka, the Vatican and Auschwitz—when will the Vatican archives be opened? When will we obtain the fully documented answer: did the Vatican play the part of Pilate, or did it side with the crucified martyrs?

Only the great capitals of the world might have stopped the eradication of the Jews: by a simple threat of retaliation. What was done? They followed the letter of the gospel: they were silent. From

---

[6] The names of the Archbishop of Toulouse, later elevated to Cardinal Monsignor Jules Gerard Saliège; the Bishop of Montauban, Monsignor Pierre-Marie Theas; the Primate of France and Archbishop of Lyons, Cardinal Gerlier; Father Marie-Benoit (Padre Benedetti, "Father of the Jews"); Metropolitan Andreas Szeptycki, Archbishop of Lvov, the head of the Ukrainian Greek Catholic (Uniate) Church in Galicia; and many superiors of monasteries, convents and Catholic orphanages, will forever remain in the grateful hearts of the persecuted. (Cf. Philip Friedman, *Their Brothers' Keepers*, New York, 1957.)

paper protests, of course, they never shirked. But practically they did nothing to relieve the plight of six million innocent Jews. There is reason to believe that the Nazis would have retreated before a strong worldwide reaction to their atrocities, and that they took world passivity as a green light to go ahead with their genocide. The reasons and excuses for this passivity can all be reduced to two: genuine indifference, and fear lest the Western powers be suspected of waging a "Jewish war." A too-resourceful defense of the Jews just "didn't pay," politically and diplomatically.[7] The sympathies of world Jewry were taken for granted (what alternative did they have?), and there was no need, as in World War I, to win them over with a Balfour declaration.

And the Jews, last and most painful of all. What did the free Jews in America and Europe do when the abyss of biological destruction opened in front of one-third of their people, the crux and the reservoir of their national existence? Did they stone the parliaments, ministries and embassies? Did they besiege the Congress, and the White House? Did they dynamite the diplomatic outposts of the Nazis? Shmul Zygelboim ("Artur"), representative of the Bund in the Polish National Council in London, committed suicide when his efforts to stir world opinion against the Nazi murders proved futile, in the hope that his sacrifice would arouse the world; but how many Shmul Zygelboims were there, and how many *were* aroused by his act among the millions of Jews spared by the conflagration? Certainly they talked a great deal, and even wept and passed resolutions. But, what did they really *do*?

Thus the litmus test "What did you do *then*?" is amazingly efficient. There are too many participants and onlookers who don't care to remember the details of the spectacle, let alone to be reminded of it.

By a sad irony, all the escapist, revisionistic, and distorting versions of the martyrdom, some arising from guilty consciences, others from shame and still others from "the anti-Semitism of guilt," were helped by some voices coming from Israel. These voices, by no means general, were conceived in a desperate negation of the *galuth*, in a determined dissociation from the tragic yesterday of the ghetto.

---

[7] Cf. G. Reitlinger, *The Final Solution of the Jewish Question,* New York, 1953. See also H. G. Adler, *Der Kampf gegen die "Endlösung der Judenfrage,"* Bonn, 1958.

Helpless hatred of the murderers turned into shame and hatred toward the victims—"Why did they let themselves be murdered?" They forget that Israel owes to the *sherit hapleta*, the survivors, at least what they owe her, that Israel is the bone and flesh of the Jewish people all over the world and that it cannot sever the umbilical cord with two thousand years of Jewish history. They seem to forget that the new Jew-as-warrior was cast in the crucible of a profound moral revolution that the People of the Book went through in the flames of the Warsaw Ghetto revolt. In hating the murderers of their people, in painfully reflecting upon the world gone forever, they were the first to coin the self-flagellating indictment-lamentation: "The European Jewry left the historical stage without dignity," declared Itzhak Greenbaum, one of the leaders of Polish Jewry in the twenties and early thirties, who emigrated to Palestine before World War II.[8]

There came also to light a purely pragmatic attitude of "nation-building realism." Out of the blood of the ghettos and gas chambers came the realization of the 2000-year-old dream, the State of Israel —and now practically the sole beneficiary of the billion-dollar reparations, and one of the few friends of West Germany! "Let's be realistic." The murdered millions cannot be restored to life anyway, and sound geopolitical realism suggests that "our social scriptures teach that sons cannot be held responsible for their fathers' sins." So let bygones be bygones! Let's bury the past. . . . And to those of us who cannot so swiftly change our hearts a bitter reproach is thrown: "We *read* memoirs, you still *live* them!"

The Victims on the Defendants' Bench

And then—it was but one more step—the defendants' bench was marked by a new addition: the victims. From all sides obliging pseudoscientists, historians and psychoanalysts started amassing "learned evidence" that the victims were actually co-guilty. These experts said that not only did the Jews not defend themselves but that by their attitude, due to a centuries-long tradition of passivity

---

[8] The very same people from the ghettos and camps were to become the most devoted soldiers of the Israel underground and Liberation War.

and servility, "they went like sheep to the slaughter..." and "collaborated in their own destruction." (Trevor-Roper.)

In this campaign desecrating the memory of our martyrs, the lead belongs to a professor of history at the University of Vermont, Dr. Raul Hilberg. In his 800-page work, *The Destruction of the European Jews,* he concludes with the following verdict: "The reaction pattern of the Jews is characterized by almost complete lack of resistance." "Anticipatory compliance" with the murderers' orders was the only weapon in the Jewish arsenal. Conditioned by 2000 years of submission and passivity they displayed an exceptional capacity for self-delusion. "The Jewish victims, caught in the straitjacket of their history, plunged themselves physically and psychologically into catastrophe." Thus the author condemns the Jews for their "role in their own destruction."

Even more appalling are the pseudo-scientific utterances of the Chicago psychologist Bruno Bettelheim. Because of his work in the Viennese Social Democratic party, he spent a year in 1938 in Dachau and Buchenwald. After his release he went to the USA where he became an "expert" on concentration camps and published several books, the latest of which, *The Informed Heart,*[9] analyzes the behavior of individuals and groups in concentration camps. From the safety of America, Bettelheim chose to start a war against—Anne Frank. "There is little doubt," he writes, "that the Franks could have provided themselves with a gun or two had they wished. They could have sold their lives dearly instead of walking to their deaths." "Millions of the Jews of Europe who did not or could not escape in time or go underground as many thousands did, could at least have marched as free men against the SS, rather than to first grovel, then wait to be rounded up for their own extermination, and finally walk themselves to the gas chambers."[10]

---

[9] Bruno Bettelheim, *The Informed Heart,* New York, 1961.
[10] Amazingly soon Bettelheim found willing disciples and imitators. A particularly coarse example: In their best-selling novel *Fail-Safe,* Eugene Burdick and Harvey Wheeler, without any logical context within the narrative, treat us to the following tirade: "Anne Frank and her family acted like imbeciles. . . . If each Jew in Germany had been prepared to take one SS trooper with him before he was sent to the camps and the gas ovens, precious few Jews would have been arrested. At some point Hitler and the SS would have stopped. . . . If every Jew who was arrested had walked to the door with a pistol in his hand and started shooting at the local heroes, how long would the Nazis have kept it up? But the first Jews who shuffled quietly off to death camps or hid like mice in attics were instruments of destruction of the rest."

In 1962, from the comfort of Chicago, Bettelheim presumes to award patents of heroism and/or cowardice to Hitler's martyrs. In 1962, armed with a knowledge which the Jews *and everyone else* lacked in 1942, Bettelheim lectures them on how they should have behaved. The moral level of this advice is best illustrated by the story he admiringly tells of his Hungarian-Jewish relatives who, looking typically "Aryan," *joined the Hungarian SS* and so enabled themselves and some few other Jews to survive. He does not even realize the moral degradation unavoidably involved in such "heroism." Is Bettelheim naive enough to suppose that by serving the SS these Hungarian Jews didn't become participants in and accessories to the crimes of the SS? Survival at any price—is this Bettelheim's notion of heroism?

Bettelheim freely applies his experiences of the "extreme situations" in Dachau and Buchenwald in 1938 to the "extreme situations" in the Warsaw Ghetto, Maidanek and Auschwitz in 1943. *He forgets that by comparison to the later camps, the camps in 1938 were like summer resorts.* Bettelheim is fully aware that "one could easily arrive at erroneous opinions if findings made in the psychoanalytic setting were applied outside the context of that particular environment." But the temptation to do just that is too strong for him, and so he commits this gross error.

In his masterly and unfortunately too short article, "Jewish Resistance to the Nazis" (*Commentary*, November 1962), Professor Oscar Handlin disposes of these charges: "It is simply not true that the Jews did not resist; there are ample instances of their capacity for fighting back. Nor is it true that greater, or more persistent, or better organized efforts of resistance would have staved off the catastrophe."

In my already mentioned memoirs I find the following paragraphs about the Warsaw Ghetto:

> There was a stubborn, unending, continuous battle to survive. In view of the unequal forces, it was a labor of Sisyphus. Jewish resistance was the resistance of a fish caught in a net, a mouse in a trap, an animal at bay. It is pure myth that the Jews were merely "passive," that they did not resist the Nazis who had decided on their destruction. The Jews fought back against their enemies to a degree no other community anywhere in the world would have been capable of doing were it to find itself similarly beleaguered. They fought against

hunger and starvation, against epidemic disease, against the deadly Nazi economic blockade. They fought against the German murderers and against the traitors within their own ranks, *and they were utterly alone in their fight.* They were forsaken by God and man, surrounded by the hatred or indifference of the Gentile population.

Ours was not a romantic war. Although there was much heroism, there was little beauty; much toil and suffering, but no glamor. We fought back on every front where the enemy attacked—the biological front, the economic front, the propaganda front, the cultural front—with every weapon we possessed.

In the end it was ruse, deception and cunning beyond anything the world has ever seen, which accomplished what hunger and disease could not achieve. What defeated us, ultimately, was Jewry's indestructible optimism, our eternal faith in the goodness of man—or rather, in the limits of his degradation. For generations, the Jews of Eastern Europe had looked to Berlin as to the very symbol of lawfulness, enlightenment and culture. We just could not believe that a German, even disguised as a Nazi, would so far renounce his own humanity as to murder women and children—coldly and systematically. We paid a terrible price for our hope, which turned out to be a delusion: the delusion that the nation of Kant, Goethe, Mozart and Beethoven cannot be a nation of murderers. And when, finally, we saw how we had been deceived, and we resorted to the weapons for which we were least well prepared—historically, philosophically, psychologically—when we finally took up arms, we inscribed in the annals of history the unforgettable epic of the Warsaw Ghetto uprising.

A few basic facts, and I commend them particularly to Trevor-Roper, Hilberg, Bettelheim and all the other retrospective heroes: at the start of the big "Resettlement" action in Warsaw (July 22, 1942) a clandestine meeting of representatives of all organizations active in the Ghetto (except the Revisionists) was urgently summoned. The majority was against an immediate resistance, arguing that it would serve as an excuse for a total massacre. "Painful as it is," they argued, "it is better to sacrifice 70,000 Jews destined for deportation than to endanger the lives of half a million. Since the Nazis apply the principle of collective responsibility, it will bring disaster." The participants in the meeting did not know at that time that deportation meant death. Dr. Emanuel Ringelblum, the archivist of the Ghetto, testifies: "To normally thinking people it was difficult to accept the idea that a Government pretending to the name of European can be found on the globe which would murder millions of innocent people." Today it is easy to sneer at such pathetic delusions and wax morally superior; but what would our combative professors and psychologists have done if they had been confronted, day by day, with the agony of such choices?

The more-militant Left-Zionist youth groups disagreed with the majority and decided to act on their own. *Six* days later (July 28, 1942) the nucleus of what was later to become the Jewish Fighters' Organization was born. *In the second half of August one revolver was smuggled into the Ghetto as a gift from the Polish Workers Party.* Note this well, Messrs. Bettelheim and Hilberg, our resistance began with *one* revolver. This revolver was used by the *Shomer* Israel Kanal in his attempt on the chief of the Ghetto police, Szerynski, on August 25, 1942, the date that is considered the beginning of the armed Ghetto resistance. By the end of December 1942 (when the massacre was practically completed) the Home Army turned over to the Jewish fighters in Warsaw *ten* pistols, and then *fifty* grenades and *fifty* revolvers in February 1943. In Bialystok and Vilna the Jewish fighters received nothing.

Just consider the *quantities* involved: *one, ten, fifty.* This was the help received from the Polish underground. But to Bruno Bettelheim it seems that the Franks (and of course all the remaining million Jewish families in Europe) could "easily" get "one or two" guns—which would have amounted to 1 or 2 million guns! To say things like this is not merely to mock the victims, but to reveal a total failure to imagine what life was like under the Nazis.

Mr. Bettelheim also disapproves of "the Franks' selection [!] of a hiding place that was basically a trap without an outlet." Doesn't the man know that hundreds of thousands of Jews perished because they had *no* place to hide, with or without an outlet? That it wasn't a matter of choice—we could not advertise in the *New York Times* —but of grasping whatever we could? How relevant and realistic Bettelheim's advices are is best illustrated by my own experience: In our shelter in the Warsaw Ghetto there was *one* revolver among the forty persons present. The man with the gun was very anxious to make the Nazis pay dearly for our lives. *He was not even given the chance.* The Germans were careful enough never to approach us within shooting (let alone stabbing) distance. The SS General

Stroop, responsible for the destruction of the Warsaw Ghetto, ordered his troops to set fire to *every* building in the Ghetto. Special engineer brigades poured gasoline on the ground floors and wooden staircases, then threw grenades and gas bombs into cellar bunkers. Thousands of Jews perished in flames and smoke without a physical chance to fight, even if they *had* had the weapons. For Mr. Bettelheim's comfort: Our shelter *did* have an emergency exit. When flames and smoke reached our shelter, the man with the gun ordered its evacuation. About half of the occupants preferred potassium cyanide to surrender. The others momentarily escaped, only to be captured and killed eventually, one way or another. Balance: only *two survived* (my wife and I). Not because we "did not believe in business as usual" and they did. It was just a succession of miracles. Ironically, the man with the gun did not survive.

Bettelheim says: "Anne Frank died because her parents could not get themselves to believe in Auschwitz." But the truth is, Mr. Bettelheim, that nobody could, not you nor I nor anyone else at the time. But what can one expect from a man who could bring himself to write so calloused, so ignorant a sentence as: "Most Jews in Poland who did not believe in business as usual survived the Second World War." Before such a display of bad faith and outrageous stupidity, language is helpless.

Says the Polish journalist Wanda Pelczynska in her review of Hilberg's book:

> Hilberg, educated and living in a free world, doesn't understand how people locked-up in jail, in camp, in the ghetto, people not protected by any law, exposed to enemy violence —save themselves by an illusion of hope. These people are easily told lies and by lies are brought without resistance to the execution trench. Thus the NKVD doublecrossed thousands of Polish officers [presumably not contaminated by the Jewish ethos of passivity]; they transported them to Katyn by telling them that this was a change from a worse camp to a better one. And these people, mind you, were brought up on the principle that "violence will be met with violence" and "when our hour to die will come—it will be in combat."

Says Walter Z. Laqueur (*Survey*, October 1962):

> In more than one sense the Russians were unprepared for the German onslaught in June 1941. Sholokhov, in his *The Science of Hatred*, has described the shock experienced by Soviet

citizens when they realized that the behavior of the Germans in the occupied territories was very far indeed from their traditional image of the civilized and orderly German; they could not believe the news about mass killings, mass robbery and brutal oppression. They had always held the Germans in special esteem. As Stalin told Emil Ludwig in a famous interview, "The Germans were a solid, reliable, sober people who could be trusted."

Witnesses Higher SS and Police Chief Erich von dem Bach Zelewsky:

> The mass of the Jewish people were taken completely by surprise. Never before has a people gone so unsuspectingly to its disaster. After the first anti-Jewish actions of the Germans, they thought now the wave was over and so they walked back to their undoing.

Hilberg himself admits that "one of the most giant hoaxes in world history was perpetrated on five million people noted for their intellect."

There is abundant evidence that Jews took at face value German assurances that it was a bona fide resettlement. Resettlements and relocations of one kind or another had been commonplace since the beginning of the war, and no one for a moment imagined that *this one* would be different. Hundreds of thousands came to Auschwitz, loaded with food and clothes and their life's savings. Thousands of young people in the Warsaw Ghetto with knapsacks and bags volunteered at the *Umschlagplatz* to "join their families previously resettled." Full credit must be given to the Nazi stage-managers that the deceiving appearances, camouflage, psychological warfare and the torture of hope were maintained to the very last moment. Any unbiased person can see the tragedy of the Jews' ignorance. But not Bettelheim and Hilberg: to them the Jews "collaborated in self-destruction."

The tragic truth is, and this is to a great extent our fault as survivors, that twenty years after it occurred, the catastrophe of European Jewry and the epic of the Warsaw Ghetto uprising is little known and even less understood. For three years the Warsaw Ghetto had been systematically bled: by savage Nazi repression and discrimination, by famine and disease, by the Gestapo, by traitors among us, by the misgovernment of the *Judenrat*. The toll of deaths was 100,000 human beings, 25 per cent of its entire population. It was stripped of its political and intellectual leaders who were abroad as a result of the 1939 exodus. The same applies also to the majority of its young men who were either in USSR or in other countries. For some reasons, the male mortality in the Ghetto was twice that of females. Thus, in 1943, the Ghetto was a famished, broken city of women and children.

And still our record stands the toughest scrutiny when compared to the French Huguenots, to the massacred Armenians, not to mention Andersonville, Eupen-Malmedy, or Soviet prisoners-of-war. And what about Czechoslovakia in 1938? And France in 1940?

Let us remember too the anything but heroic performance of the American people, including the intellectuals, in the McCarthy era. Try to imagine McCarthy in war time, endowed with total power, with limitless facilities for terror and destruction, with no legal opposition and with full control of press, radio and television. Imagine McCarthy with his cohorts determined to physically exterminate and plunder a minority segment of the nation, all "for the glory of America." I am by no means sure about the conduct under such circumstances of the majority of Americans nor of the reaction of our vociferous "heroes," had they had the misfortune to belong to that doomed minority.

Lord Moran, who spent three years as army physician in Flanders during World War I, and a year with the RAF in World War II, observes how soldiers' morale cracks under the strain of tension, shock, and monotony in the trenches, and how their resistance to fear is lowered by sickness, fatigue, loss of sleep and other hardships. "Courage is will-power, whereof no man has an unlimited stock; and when in war it is used up, he is finished."[11] Has it ever occurred to our retrospective heroes who now assault the victims of Nazism that after years in the ghetto and camps, after endless "conditioning," after the loss of their dearest ones, a point comes when it no longer matters whether one dies with a piece of hardware in his hand—the so-called "hero's death"—or dies passively in a gas chamber? Bettelheim has written about "extreme situations," but he does not know—and perhaps no one can who did not live through it—what an extreme situation really is.

I purposely leave aside the wide range of problems that border on

---

[11] Lord Moran, *The Anatomy of Courage*, London, 1945.

psychology, philosophy, and ethics: where does the natural self-preservative instinct stop and fear and anxiety begin? Where is the line between controlled fear and cowardice? Is discipline cowardice or courage, collaboration or responsibility? And, on the other side of the spectrum: how long can responsibility (individual and collective) be stretched before it becomes courage, and at what point does an idea greater than fear transform courage into heroism? Heroism carried one step too far can be irresponsibility. Was the Warsaw uprising in 1944 an act of heroism or suicidal folly? Was Czechoslovakia's surrender after Munich an act of cowardice or tragic realism? And, in purely practical terms and not just for the glorious record, did Poland with her romantic adventurism fare better than Czechoslovakia with her pragmatism?

The heroism of the handful of Warsaw youths shook the imagination of our generation, *blasés* as we have become toward acts of daring. But that heroism at the same time concealed the much more profound and shattering sacrifice of 50,000 defenseless men, women and children, who in a magnificent gesture of unarmed resistance defeated the Nazi bestial violence. As never before in mankind's history, heroism and martyrdom flashed in the lightning of doom. It takes a Tolstoy or a Gandhi to appreciate the grandeur of the spectacle. In the climax of our history martyrdom reached its most sublime expression, and in the unprecedented revolutionary tension there appeared a heroism that was the turning point of Jewish history and created a new type of Jew. Martyrdom was the mainstream of Jewish history for millennia. In our catastrophe martyrdom and heroism became inseparable ingredients. No one can tell whether and when the two ingredients will cross again. They are both equally tragic and equally sublime.

We are blessed and burdened with the memory of both; neither can be taken from us; and neither could save us.

Hatred and Soap

There is a widespread belief that the Jewish tragedy is a result of Hitler's psychopathic hatred of the Jews, that it was conceived in the obsession of a maniac. William Shirer defines our catastrophe as "the shattering cost of [Hitler's] aberration." Handlin thinks that

"Hitler . . . was determined, for reasons which were totally irrational, expensive, and contrary to the interests of the state, to liquidate the Jews."

To reduce the origins of genocide to Hitler's psychopathic hatred
is both historically and politically naive. The anti-Jewish policy of
the Nazis was a worked-out calculation. Hermann Rauschning (*Ge-
spräche mit Hitler*, Zurich 1940) quotes Hitler that anti-Semitism is
"die wichtigste Waffe in unserem Propaganda-Arsenal."[12] And Robert Ley, the leader of the Deutsche Arbeitsfront, stated in May
1944: "Anti-Semitism is our second secret weapon."

Irrational hatred sometimes results in murder, but a passionate
murderer does not manufacture soap out of the fat of his victim.
The anti-Jewish war was a coldly premeditated political action carried out with the most monstrous precision. Says Professor Golo
Mann, the son of Thomas Mann: "The German nation in its overwhelming majority was not at all passionately anti-Semitic, no more
so than other peoples are . . . . Maybe this makes it even more appalling. That they have murdered without belief, without hatred,
without conviction, without any sense; only upon order." (*Der Anti-
semitismus,* Frankfort, 1961.) Of course, the war on the Jews eventually became a gathering point for the wicked and the sadistic, a
mobilization of scum and degeneration, a university of cruelty and
crime. Many a murderer became a captive of the ideology, and intoxicated by hatred. Perhaps the calculation did turn out to be
erroneous and, as Handlin wrote, "contrary to the interests of the
[German] state," but nobody can deny that for years it was a powerful weapon. Torture of Jews not only sowed demoralization among
the vanquished nations; anti-Semitism was the link uniting the scum
of the world with the Nazi masterminds.

"Soapmaking," the cold-blooded machinery to exploit all the advantages of the murder—financial, economic, political, propagandistic—was by no means a by-product of the extermination of the
Jews, but a basic ingredient of this action. Plundering Jewish property, exploitation of the Jewish labor force, filling all the Jewish
economic and cultural positions with Germans, bribing the native
mob with shreds of Jewish "wealth," and, finally, the bestial machinery of destruction and exploitation even of human fat and
hair—all these stages of soapmaking were by no means accidental.

---

[12] The most important weapon in our propaganda arsenal.

That anti-Semitism was a powerful weapon in the Nazi aggression is shown by a host of shameful instances. Even Roosevelt and Churchill did not dare to wage an open war on this front. Stalin didn't even try to resist.

Viewed in this light the Jewish resistance against the Nazis must be thoroughly reappraised. To begin with, we have to expose the fallacy which equates the Jewish resistance with the general resistance movements in Europe. The difference consists not only in the two-front situation of the Jews, so penetratingly pointed out by Handlin: Jews fought as members of the general resistance of a given nation, not as Jews but as nationals, but in addition to this they fought as a branded community pushed to a uniquely "extreme situation."[13] It is clear that from the moment the decision for their extermination was taken, their destiny was sealed and the diapason of Jewish resistance could not influence the result. European Jewry was an object and not a subject in this struggle, and as the death sentence came from the outside so too could salvation come only from the outside, through the counter-action of the Great Powers, and the Gentile population. The resistance and partisan movements of other nations had the support of their governments (whether in exile or at home), commanding centers, supplies of arms and funds, not to mention a base among the majority of the populace. The situation of the Jews was different in every respect.

Under these circumstances it would not have been surprising had the Jews really given up all resistance. It is a miracle that in spite of these appalling conditions the Jews often did fight, and heroically.

The Central Issue

Abundant factual material proves beyond a doubt that allegations of the Bettelheim-Hilberg kind are false. True, history did not make us into a trigger-happy nation, but we are by no means exceptions in this respect. We did not believe that the enlightened Germans could be transformed into a nation of soapmakers, but in 1942

---

13 And in this last capacity they were in most cases left to their own fate. "Where a government and a people fought Nazi encroachments," states Philip Friedman (*Their Brothers' Keepers*), "many Jews were saved from extermination. Such were the experiences in Denmark, Finland, Bulgaria, and Italy."

neither Mr. Bettelheim nor Mr. Hilberg knew about it. We dearly paid for this delusion about the nature of Germans, and we should not feel ashamed of it.

With each passing day the tragedy of European Jewry, the greatest crime in the annals of mankind, recedes into the storehouse of history. A new generation arises that "knew not Joseph." Less and less is it a political, financial, demographic problem. But it will never cease to be a moral problem.

And as a moral problem, paradoxical as this may sound, it is less and less a Jewish problem, and more and more a universal one. Auschwitz is modern civilization's declaration of bankruptcy. It is a disaster of humanity. It explodes as the anti-Semitism of guilty conscience: one hates the innocent victim whom one wronged. It makes the East European governments dismally surrender to Hitler's heritage, helpless to cope with the scourge of anti-Semitism. And, finally, the worst loser of all is Christianity itself, whose two thousand years turned out to be an historical mirage.

I do not believe in metaphysical historical justice. But we have daily evidence that crime has in it the seeds of forthcoming punishment, and that unpunished crime boomerangs on the criminals.

Item: When the fighting Warsaw Ghetto begged for arms from the alert and combat-ready "Aryan" Warsaw, icy silence was the answer. What moral right of protest had this very same Warsaw less than a year and a half later when it begged for help from the Red Army across the river, obtaining in answer a similarly "political" silence?

Item: What moral right of protest do the Germans have against the Berlin wall, they who invented this disgrace? Germany from wall to wall—this certainly has its irony.

Item: How can Christianity regain its face? What does it have to offer post-war man, horrified by the specter of atomic war? How can an honest man believe, after Auschwitz?

Item: What moral right of protest do we all have against atomic holocaust? In the name of what principle? If one can with impunity murder six million people, why not six hundred million? Will tomorrow's genocide be stopped by the technicality that the next victim will not be Jewish any more but German, Russian or American? Morals know neither arithmetic nor geography.

There is a sense in which nothing anyone writes or does can

redeem the tragedy of our century. But the one thing that those of us who have survived can do is to keep clean the memory of the victims.

Meanwhile, a few concluding remarks may be useful. Whether the Jews resisted or were able to resist, whether they should or could have behaved other than they did—such questions reveal, as a rule, an incapacity even to imagine the extremity of our situation under Nazi totalitarianism. The shame and horror of our century have to do with the conduct of the European powers, the Gentile world. Even if not one Jew had resisted, there would be no justification either to condemn the victims or to divert attention from the crimes of the murderers. The central issue must not be forgotten; it is a moral issue, the issue of what the world has done and permitted to be done. To insist upon making the world uncomfortable with the memory of its guilt is a necessity for that moral reconstruction which may alone prevent a repetition of our holocaust.

4. *THE TEREZÍN REQUIEM*

JOSEF BOR

The Terezín Requiem is a true story. The events described occurred. The section presented here is the climax of this short classic in which prisoners rehearse Verdi's *Requiem* in a camp which utilized "cultural activities" to deceive the world about the nature of the "Final Solution." New musicians were constantly brought in to replace others killed during rehearsals. Their performance—before Eichmann and his henchmen— was an affirmation of their beliefs. And the question of what constitutes moral resistance is here presented in all its anguish.

━━━

The military order to the SS read: "Evacuate the Jewish hospital."

Armed with clubs and pistols they tramped into the ghetto. Through the streets rang the martial cry: *"Bewegung! Bewegung!"* ("Get moving!")

The Camp Commandant himself, present on the spot and in the foremost rank, directed the operation. He had already hurled his entire motor pool into action. Three tractors with twelve trailers, two trucks, sixteen wagons and drays from the farm, and four manure carts. Forty-eight Jewish funeral cars. . . . And countless two-wheeled carts and carriages for cripples. Only the heavy truck was kept in reserve; they used it for carrying the boxes with the dead bodies to the crematorium, and it was waiting in readiness.

Reprinted with permission of Alfred A. Knopf from *The Terezin Requiem* by JOSEF BOR. Translated from the Czech by EDITH PARGETER. Copyright © 1963 by Edith Pargeter.

But all these vehicles were not enough. Carry the sick, ordered the leader.

The ghetto seethed; crowds of terrified people ran through the streets. Everybody had someone in the hospital: father, wife, child, or at least a friend. The sick were lying everywhere: in the halls, in the rooms, in the corridors, even on the stairs. In their hundreds. And now, come on, get moving with them, throw them out into the street, take them somewhere, anywhere.

All hell had broken out in front of the hospital. Cries, moans, wounds, and shots.

You'll kill him, he has to lie quietly! *"Bewegung! Bewegung!"*

Where are you taking them? What are you going to do with them? *"Bewegung! Bewegung!"*

The houses are locked, the streets closed. Only one way is open. To the attics of the Terezín barracks.

And the attics of the Terezín barracks are enormous. A heavy framework of beams holds the roof aloft and divides the brick floor into a vast maze of dark garrets. Only a beam on the ground is the frontier of the attic, so huge that a sick man would never be able to climb or crawl over it.

And here there is nothing. No water, no light, not even breathable air. And here you are forbidden to place anything, straw mattress, coverlet, pillow, anything inflammable. But you won't easily set fire to a human body.

At long intervals the chinks of narrow windows gleam dully. They neither light the garrets nor freshen the air. But you can get out through them, and make at least a single step. Into emptiness.

No doctor will find the sick here. Nor can the patients call for a doctor. Here you will know the dead by the stench. Old man or child. Truly, no one will look for the sick here.

The military operation is completed. In two hours and twenty minutes the hospital is empty. And the Camp Commandant gives the order:

Transform the building into a theater.

"This day will be inscribed in letters of gold in the annals of the SS garrison of Terezín."

That was how the Camp Commandant put it in his reply to Eichmann's speech, and it expressed what he really felt. This was indeed a happy day for him. Even in the morning it had been a great relief to him when he had seen Eichmann stepping out of the car. And then, the later events! They had proceeded to the celebratory parade, and still no one had had the slightest idea what they had to celebrate. An award of decorations! Today, in this ticklish situation, when for a long time there had been no distribution of decorations to the *Wehrmacht*. And, indeed, Eichmann in his speech had made witty reference to that very fact.

"Distinctions are not handed out lightly nowadays," he had remarked ironically, "but this time they are awarded as by right. To the worth of the SS statistics, bear witness. Here there's no need for reflection: the successes in reaching the prescribed military targets are shown in positive figures, and the language they speak is clear and convincing."

So they had distributed today, for "military merit," decorations, medals, and crosses, KVK, KVK II, even KVK I; and finally Eichmann had pinned on the breasts of Günther and the Camp Commandant, these two alone of all the company, the *Kriegsverdienstkreuz* with sword. It was Himmler's order that they should be awarded here, he said, in Terezín, in the important military sector of the SS, so that everyone would realize the significance of the action that was hastening to its culmination on the territory of the Protectorate of Bohemia and Moravia.

Eichmann was a beautiful speaker, and it was a pleasure to listen to him when he came to hang a KVK II with sword on your tunic. The Camp Commandant congratulated himself. He had not received any distinction for two years now. Eichmann was right: they weren't giving away war-service crosses for nothing these days; they had to be earned laboriously. And it was just at this moment that they had remembered, in such a period of strain, and everyone was delighted about it. Everybody liked it here in Terezín. Just look at Eichmann: amiable, friendly, a changed man; not even among his subordinates was his pleasure dimmed today.

"Every time a company of SS sits down to a meal!" he joked when they took their places at the table, "it breaks some regulation or other." And promptly he went on to invite the Camp Commandant to sit at the head of the table with the highest.

So here sat the Commandant at the head of the table between

Eichmann and Moese, in sheer delight; and he had already given orders for champagne to be brought, for this glorious day must certainly be celebrated.

"And how are we going to finish the day? What are these Jewish artists of yours going to perform for us?" asked Moese with interest.

"Verdi's Requiem," replied the Camp Commandant, as he had been taught.

"I beg your pardon?" Eichmann blurted out in astonishment. "Jews singing the Requiem in Terezín?"

The company of SS had fallen silent, every one of them watching Eichmann with strained attention. The man was twitching, trying to keep his gravity, but it was more than he could manage. He could not get over the surprise, that Jews, sharp and cunning Jews, should be singing a Requiem, never dreaming that. . . . Fools fools, if they had had the slightest suspicion of what awaited them now, they would hardly have found it any singing matter. Eichmann could no longer control himself; the laughter he had been restraining by force convulsed his face in a spasmodic grin and tore his throat in a yell of mirth.

His table companions stared stupidly at one another, without a notion of what was amusing him; but their chief was laughing, and that was an order. The company of SS men burst into loud and lusty laughter.

But Moese did not laugh. He alone remained grave and silent, for he alone understood and knew what Eichmann found so amusing in the idea of the Requiem. The Jews would be singing it for themselves, as though tolling their own death knell; that was what Eichmann found so funny. But Moese did not agree with Eichmann. The Jews surely knew very well for whom the bell was tolling now throughout Europe; even in the camp they received reliable reports of what was happening outside, and they were not fools. Let's wait, rather, until this evening; then we shall know what there is to laugh at here.

Nor was the Camp Commandant amused. Never before had he seen Eichmann laugh aloud, and what the devil was he laughing at now? And at whom? At the Jews or at him? What could there possibly be so ridiculous in this program? Pure art, the Jewish elder had assured him, a unique performance such as you're never likely to hear again, Jews singing the ancient Catholic prayers from the twelfth century. Surely there could be nothing improper in that. And the Jewish elder would never dare to make a fool of the Camp Commandant; besides, he didn't even know why he had asked him to arrange this show, and had no suspicion that he was composing a program for the SS. But trust a sly Jew and he'll jerk your feet from under you when you least expect it.

But Eichmann had already calmed himself, and he clapped the Commandant amiably on the shoulder: a splendid idea, my good friend, excellent, we shall be very glad to hear the Jews sing the Requiem.

"Gentlemen," he said, raising his voice, and everyone at the table rose. "I give you our host! To the Camp Commandant of Terezín!"

A drawn curtain veiled the stage. A fortunate idea of the Commandant's, to have that hung. He wanted to have everything here properly appointed: gleaming footlights, dimmed auditorium, everything as in a real theater. And he had no suspicion that this arrangement suited everyone; the SS always preferred to stare out from darkness, and the singers at least would not have to look at the faces of their audience.

The stage was full of the sound and commotion of musical instruments being tuned. The singers were already in their place. Schächter wiped his forehead and cheeks with a handkerchief; he did not feel well, and breathing was difficult. This would be a strange performance; they had not even been able to rehearse or make any other preparations. Perhaps it was better this way; he would not even have known what to say to them. Somehow they must surpass themselves tonight—hold together as one and maintain the tempo.

He glanced at Jirka, the tympanist; Jirka would have to help him out tonight. An orchestra has always two conductors; the one with the baton may sometimes flag and lose his concentration, but the tympanist must never weaken. Who could tell what surprises this performance would spring, what the music would conjure up? Perhaps nothing, absolutely nothing, and that would be the best way, simply to play numbly and keep time; such a music today's audience would understand best.

He waved a hand at Jirka: you'll have to help me today, I can't manage a performance like this singlehanded, and don't forget, in the last bars there's a change. Choir and orchestra fortissimo, and especially you, see to it! Three strokes short, one long!

He looked at his choir and soloists, and now he felt a little better; he knew every one of them, he knew what they could do, he could rely on them. His only fear was for Maruška; she had the most difficult task today, and to her alone he had spoken in advance. "You must not think of parents and brother and lover," he had told her, "remember the others, too, all those beaten and tormented and massacred, they will unite for you into one great mass, you will not even recognize individuals among them, and so much the more clearly you will be aware of the true face of the murderers. For today you will have the murderers before you. You must not show fear or weakness before them. Today you will be singing to the murderers, don't forget that."

The Jewish elder entered the auditorium and went straight to the conductor. They talked together agitatedly. Tonight's performance must not last more than an hour at the longest, so the Camp Commandant had just ordered. He would have to shorten the Requiem somehow, leave out some part of it.

Schächter stormed and gesticulated. "Scoundrels, villains," he shouted into the hum of the tuning instruments, "they ruin everything they touch, they can't even keep their hands off a work of art." This order hit him like a blow, but perhaps even that was just as well; let them all see what sort of an audience they had today.

Red in the face, he mounted his rostrum. "We're shortening the Requiem, by order of the Camp Commandant."

The orchestra fell silent, waiting confusedly for their conductor's decision.

We'll cut the beginning, thought Schächter, and begin somewhere in the middle. And already he knew where. "*Confutatis maledictis. . . .*" Yes, we'll begin there, damn you, that very verse we'll hurl into your faces. He longed to give the signal on the spot, but he hesitated. No, it wouldn't do; he couldn't begin like that. Better if they warmed up and sang themselves in first. He must not begin like that, he admitted on reflection; he was answerable for tonight's performance to the artists and their families. And Moese was here, and he understood music; there would be a terrible revenge for an insult so transparent. All the same, he wouldn't let them off that verse; he would yet throw it in their faces.

He heard the murmur of movement and voices from the auditorium, the penetrating announcement of the Commandant, and that was sign enough; in another moment the auditorium would be darkened and the curtains would swing apart. How should he begin? Whom should he choose, on whom should he call to stand up and be the first to overcome the paralyzing cold emanating from the dark auditorium?

"The *Recordare*," he whispered.

"Schächter's gone mad," muttered the choir. "He's chosen the women, he's beginning the same way as *that day!*"

The curtain parted, and uncovered menacing, repellent darkness. The footlights gleamed. The conductor stood erect, facing his choir. No one moved.

On the stage the Jewish elder entered. Thin and pale, he walked slowly to the edge of the stage. And bowed deeply.

"Weary he sank, seeking me."

The crucificial way of humanity.

Tonelessly, in a veiled voice, Maruška forced out the individual words; Betka joined her, and together they fixed their eyes fervently upon the conductor, seeking help and strength. He should have been guiding and directing them, but Schächter's face was white; he stood motionless, hardly living. You're singing accurately, only go on, go on numbly and keep step. So much they'll understand, those down there in the dark. Only go on and keep step.

The duet closed, the orchestra was hushed, and now came the tenor, beginning alone, without accompaniment. Rosenfeld was an experienced operatic singer; often in his career he had salvaged an unsuccessful performance. Calmly he stepped forward from the row of soloists, for this was his solo; his grand aria was beginning.

"Groaning 'neath my sins I languish, Lord, have mercy on my anguish . . ." the tenor's full voice rang, and Schächter listened attentively. You're not groaning, boy, he thought to himself, you're giving a brilliant performance of an operatic aria. That isn't how we rehearsed it. The orchestra suddenly felt where their conductor was leading them, and the singer amended his course. His voice softened and changed; he was praying passionately now.

"Spread Thy grace behind, before me
Lest the flames of hell devour me."

That isn't Rosenfeld singing, they marveled, that's someone else pleading and praying in deep penitence; his desperate groaning has penetrated even here out of the dark torture chamber under the earth. Your humble prayer didn't help you, child, Haindl got you, and he killed you—Haindl, who sprawls there now in his armchair, stupidly listening.

Schächter had drawn himself erect. He was conducting again; he was in command. Bass!

"*Confutatis maledictis*," thundered through the hall. Listen, you murderers there in the dark, damn you, you and those others a thousand times damned! Moaning could not move you, but soon now, soon, we shall speak to you in a language you'll understand better.

The singers were with him; they understood. The music exalted them; they drew deep, panting breaths, struggling to subdue their fierce passion, to hush their tormenting hatred. The tempo faltered; the orchestra waited. The storm was approaching. They yearned for it, waiting thirstily, until lightning slashed out of the baton, and the kettle drums thundered terribly.

The storm broke, but it did not sweep them away in its fury, for Schächter subdued it. He could not unleash the rage of elemental forces; his heart was constricted. There was one verse he had not remembered in time, but he thought of it now and his head reeled. *Lacrymosa!* He had not said one word of warning to Betka; he had forgotten her.

The storm passed, rolling away into the distance; already the last murmur died away in the violins. Silence fell. Even silence is music; it sharpens the awareness. Schächter fixed his eyes upon Betka, and saw no one else. The silence fettered and bound him; he could neither move nor speak. Feel my need, Betka, he implored, look at me, let me cry out to you, at least with a look, that you must not cry now, Betka, before them you must not!

But Betka did not look at him; she began the quartet of soloists alone. She stared into the darkness, straight before her, where danger was lurking. She was accustomed to danger; every day she looked into its face, always she lived and endured with the mad in their dark, closed cells. She felt the same perilous challenge now; something glittered there in the dark, and she had recognized it. Madmen! These were madmen she had before her, decked out in their tawdry finery, with jingling tinsel draped on their breasts, strutting out their fantasy as heroes.

Sharply she launched herself against them, and Schächter exulted:

yes, yes, that's how it should be pronounced, and now that hard "cry" again, and the broad "o," spit it in their faces, cast your lightnings at them. I need not teach you how to pronounce that word, you know best how you must sing.

The first part of the Requiem hushed to its close, but the director stretched out his hand at once, and bore his artists onward with him. The very music drove them forward now. Listen, you there in the dark, how solemnly the music cries, listen well to what the ancient book of humanity has been proclaiming for thousands of years.

I will multiply thy seed as the sands of the earth, I will bless him who blesseth thee, and curse him who curseth thee.

Do you hear, you there in the dark? You have marked us as the seed of Abraham, and now we, prisoners in a Jewish camp, exult before you. You have not broken us, you will not break us!

Joyfully they sang the glorious ode, but the conductor's gesture again calmed and silenced them.

The orchestra stilled, the choir was hushed. They drew a deep breath and watched with passionate concentration every move of the conductor's hand. The finale began.

"Libera me, Domine, de morte aeterna," sang the choir. As though indeed they prayed for the dead, Schächter thought to himself, and was not aware that he himself had willed it so. Dread had him in its grip now, and was draining the strength from him; he could not even lift his glance to gaze before him. Somewhere there Maruška stood; he was summoning her now to the inescapable moment when she would take her stand alone, fragile and slender, face to face with the inhuman murderers, as once, twice, three times before, in Munich, Vienna, and Prague.

The singing of the choir stilled into an awe-stricken whisper, and then even that died in a sudden, despairing cry. Schächter held his breath.

"Tremens factus sum," Maruška measured out coldly word after word, slowly pacing out her crucificial journey of terrible memories, and again transcending them. There was no one to help her, and she did not tremble. Slim and white she stood, erect, like a statue carved in marble; only her eyes burned, great, dilated eyes, seeing and sorrowing. Again she returned to the theme, again re-

peated it in a deep, chilling recitative. This was no longer song; this was an impartial judge pronouncing a stern and just judgment. And now the cello softly joined her, took up the melody and sang it in a grieved tremolo, quivering and afraid, Meisl's cello, which had earned bread for his four children and now lamented and wailed its desolation.

But enough of lamentation, the conductor's hand ordered, and he raised it high. Without the baton now, clenched into a fist. And struck.

The drum rolled, the kettle drums rattled, the brass blared, the singers yelled from full throats, the soloists giving voice with them; they could not be silent now. Schächter's fist held back the choir but could not hold back himself; he shouted aloud with the tumult. The last *Dies Irae!* The day of wrath is come, the day for which we have waited so long, and not in vain. Your armies are torn to pieces as you have torn and trampled us, streams of blood gush from your deep wounds, and your country is rent and tattered in the thunder and smoke of thousands of bursting bombs. And this is right and due, not for revenge, not for hatred, only for the sake of human justice.

The storm passed; passion and hatred were stilled. We are remembering you now, our dear ones, an eternal memorial to you who have died for us. And you, prisoners in the concentration camps, be strong and courageous in invincible faith and hope. They sang fervently now, their voices mingling in rich harmony and fusing into a mighty, sublime chorus that ceased abruptly. Deep silence. Their nerves were quivering with expectation.

Like the stroke of a bell, Maruška's crystal voice rang out: *"Libera me!"* Everywhere the bells pealed in answer. *"Libera me!"* resounded the voices of the choir. "Deliver us! Deliver us!" clamored altos and tenors, sopranos and basses, from all sides. "We want liberty!" the orchestra replied to them. And the kettle drums rolled and thundered: *"Libera nos! Libera nos!"*

Schächter started in consternation. No, not yet, Jirka, you're changing the rhythm, that's not here, what are you doing? But Jirka took no notice; he was directing the orchestra now.

"Li-be-ra nos! Li-be-ra nos!" he beat from the kettle drums. Understand, Raphael, three strokes short, one long; no one who has once heard it will ever forget it. Beethoven's strokes of fate!

Schächter drew himself to his full height.

"Libera me!" slashed Maruška's passionate cry.

"Libera nos!" thundered the gigantic choir for the last time.

The last roll of the tympani had ebbed away. The footlights outlined the conductor's figure sharply as he stood erect, his back turned upon his audience. Nothing stirred. Only the curtain slowly closed.

Eichmann sat crouched deep in his armchair, and strange thoughts tossed and eddied in his brain as strange as the music that had called them up. "Interesting, very interesting!" he observed to Moese.

"Unique. I've never before heard such a performance of the Requiem," Moese agreed.

Eichmann applauded. Not too lavishly, since the artists were Jews, not too faintly, for the performance had certainly been unique, and praise was due to the Camp Commandant, too, for the exemplary arrangements.

Eichmann was applauding, and that was a signal for the SS. Applause rang through the hall. Out before the curtain stepped the Jewish elder, thin and pale. And bowed deeply.

The summer drew to its close, and the time of the transports began again. The Command had promised that Schächter's company would not be separated. The promise was kept. All together they ascended into the first wagons of the first transport.

SECTION TWO

The Descent

Article IV: 1. A Jew cannot be a citizen of the Reich. He cannot exercise the right to vote. He cannot occupy public office.

Article V: 1. A Jew is anyone who is descended from at least three grandparents who were . . . Jews; or two grandparents if he is part of the Jewish community. . . .

THE NUREMBERG LAWS, 1933

INTRODUCTION

As WE BEGIN TO EXPLORE THE GEOGRAPHY OF NAZI GERMANY, our need for explanations becomes ever more pressing. It would be an impossible task for this volume to cover the many areas which attempt to provide partial answers. Psychology, economics, sociology, history, theology—each has its confrontation with Nazi Germany and the Holocaust. And as we enter the ambience of those days through literature, we must keep these other disciplines in mind.

In a way, this anthology is a historical study. It is the Jewish approach to history—*toldot*—which is the shared experience which passes from one generation to the next, and which is part of the process of existence and never becomes an abstraction. It is this shared experience which brings us to those days. Poetic fiction and scholarly reminiscences here join in an amalgam in which the various realms of our existence blend together in the anguished search for meaning.

We turn now to the 1930's and the early days of the Third Reich. We see how a criminal state perverts its citizens, how little persecutions in classrooms trained brown-shirted Pimpfe, members of the Hitler Youth Movement, into SS men at Dachau and Auschwitz. Facts, figures, tomes of psychology—these help us to understand.

But it is the poetic vision of the novelist that gains us entrance into the minds and hearts of children to whom good and evil are not yet abstractions but daily realities.

These were the early days of Nazi rule and the Jewish community was not a monolithic organization. But even after Jews had combined under a national association, each group went its own way and proposed its own solutions for dealing with the crisis. The determination to "wear the yellow badge with pride" was not the only answer; but it helped us to understand and to assess the German Jew under distress in those early Hitler years.

The questions we still must ask ourselves from the vantage point of our own day deal with the extent of the deception practiced upon the Jews by the Nazis. Was it possible for the Jews to see where these early attacks were leading? Could the Jews have done more to resist the Nazi effort? What were their failures and what did they achieve? In the essays of Leo Baeck and Salo Baron, the dimensions of Jewish history become clear. And, as we examine the early days of this first stage of the madness which was to engulf the world, we come to understand something of the nature of the twentieth century and its special brand of violence.

1. *THE LAST OF THE JUST*

ANDRÉ SCHWARZ-BART

As early as 1933, the Jews of Germany lived in a prison. The adults did not realize this clearly; the grown person has a marvelous capacity for self-deception and rationalization. But the Jewish children knew what was happening. They could not play in the parks. They could not go to the movies. And their playmates were encouraged to attack them. The author gives us a child's-eye view of life in those years. Schwarz-Bart saw Ernie Levy as one of the "thirty-six righteous men" of Jewish tradition for whose sake God permits the world to continue its existence. In *The Last of the Just,* the special function of the Levy family is to supply for every generation a "just man" who takes the sins and the suffering of the world upon himself. In this selection, Ernie, the last of the just men of the Levy family, takes the burden upon himself.

━━━

The new teacher burst in without ceremony. At five minutes after eight the door blew open and a short, square man sprang in like a jack-in-the-box. Paying no attention to the students, he went to the desk immediately and sat down, keeping a stiff attitude in order to lose nothing of the little height he had. The abruptness of his entrance was almost funny, but Ernie restrained himself because everyone seemed extremely serious. Herr Geek had a face of dried

From *The Last of the Just* by ANDRÉ SCHWARZ-BART. Copyright © 1960 by Atheneum House, Inc. Originally published in French under the title *Le dernier des justes* © 1959 by Editions du Seuil, Paris. Reprinted by permission of Atheneum Publishers. Translated by STEPHEN BECKER.

clay. Crevices lined it in all directions. The loose skin of his neck slightly overflowed his starched detachable collar. A strange smudge of mustache widened the yellow wings of his nostrils. "A peasant in his Sunday best," Ernie thought dryly.

But his joy lasted only a moment. Herr Geek was already pushing back his chair, standing at attention and proclaiming in an angry voice, "Attention! One, two, three, all rise!"

The tone was so aggressive, the voice so resolved to make itself heard that Ernie felt something like the bite of a whip at the base of his spine. He rose with a wild abruptness that surprised him, and as he stuck out his chest he noticed that Herr Geek's eyes were shining with a strange pallid glow under the heavy eyelids that bound them like dried cement.

At that moment Herr Geek clacked his heels, and his arm rose obliquely into the air in a single sudden motion, with the rigidity of a beam. "Heil Hitler!" he cried furiously.

Herr Geek's gesture was so sudden that the students responded without exception. Ernie himself, somewhere in the obscurity of his being, found the inspiration and the technique for a perfect clicking of heels. At the same moment he realized that he was crying at the top of his voice "Heil Hitler! Heil Hitler!" His voice was lost in the roaring of the whole class. Dumfounded, he discovered his arm pointed at the ceiling. Slowly, he brought it down and let it lie discreetly at his side, like a branch alien to his body.

"It is truly unbelievable," Herr Geek declared. His rural accent struck Ernie again. The thin lips stretched like leather thongs opened on a blackish mouth, and the words that escaped them were as if carved from some hard material, from wood—and brutally, by a machete. Ernie thought that neither the lips nor the teeth nor the shrubbery that served him for eyebrows nor the curious lawn of mustache nor the bumpy, rutted relief of wrinkles nor even, finally, the eyes, stagnant amid all that, like two shallow puddles of gray water—nothing of Herr Geek marked a teacher. One would have said, rather, a peasant come to barter in the church square, whose expression, depending on his mood, might be watery or earthy or cold, crushing, stony.

Suddenly Herr Geek's face tightened altogether, some eddy blurred his expression while his mouth twisted to form a hole at the right side of his nose. A thin stream of trembling, icy voice trickled out of the hole. "I thought—yes—they told me there were Jews in this class." And gesturing briefly at all the arms raised in the Hitlerite salute, "But I see only brave Germans who adore their Führer. Right, my boys?"

The triumphant laugh shook the ranks of Pimpfe in brown shirts. Hans Schliemann applauded enthusiastically. Herr Geek muttered in satisfaction, turned his glance toward Hans Schliemann and seemed to reflect for a moment. Then, spreading his enormous, blackish hand on the edge of the desk, he stepped calmly off the platform. At each step half his body sagged heavily to one side. His gait was that of a man carrying a burden. Ernie noted that he seemed to tap the ground with his foot first and then to place the full weight of his body upon it before swinging the other leg forward. But his left shoulder sloped lower than his right.

When Herr Geek had reached Hans Schliemann, he stood still and looked sympathetically at the boy's uniform. "There are only three Hitler Youth in this class?" he asked in a tone of pained astonishment. And then, as Hans Schliemann came to attention, he went on in a voice informed by severity, "The Hitler Youth must set an example of discipline." And without changing his benevolent expression, he slapped Hans Schliemann twice. The second slap drove the child's head against his desk and knocked him under his chair. Ernie was surprised to hear him shouting enthusiastically, "Yes, Herr Professor! Yes, Herr Professor!"

"That's what I like," Herr Geek declared suddenly.

In his heavy, slow step, his fat hands swinging against his thighs, he walked peacefully back to his desk. When he was on the platform again, he stiffened his neck, and taking up the pointer, he thrust it forward in a gesture of command. "And now," he cried in a raging tone, *"die Hunde, die Neger und die Juden, austreten!* Dogs, Negroes and Jews, step forward!"

For a moment Ernie Levy attributed those words to Herr Geek's incomprehensible sense of humor, but when the students did not laugh as the teacher stared furiously at Ernie's dark curls, the boy understood that the phrase was directed solely at the Jews. Immediately, he slipped to the side to take up his position as a Jew in the center of the aisle. Behind him, fat Simon Kotkowski was already sniffling.

"Jews!" Herr Geek cried. "When I give an order to the class in general, it means that I am addressing myself to the German students and not to their guests."

Rigid in his military posture, only his lower jaw moving, Herr Geek launched a confused, menacing diatribe at the "Jewish guests." These last, among others, were to know that Herr Geek would always find a way to make himself understood when he wished to address himself to them—for example, by beginning the phrase with the name of an animal.

When the guests, at the order of the master of the house, had retired to the last row in the classroom (isolated from the pure Aryans by a row of empty desks), Herr Geek relaxed and loosed a vast sigh of relief, answered by a vast burst of laughter from the Pimpfe. Finally, solemn again, he directed the rude language of truth to the German students—they had all been Jewified by their former professor, so all of them were to some degree suspect. He personally judged that Herr Kremer had some drops of Jewish blood in his veins, "or somewhere else," for a thoroughbred German would never have committed himself to such repugnant promiscuity. The hour of the Jews had struck—it was a funeral bell. The hour of authentic and pure Germans was beginning to sound in the heavens, and it was a victory bell, rung by him to whom we owe everything—Adolf Hitler. Finally, the students were not here *to play at learning* but to prepare the true grandeur of the Fatherland, for a day would come when the pen, transformed into a sword. . . .

Here Herr Geek stopped suddenly. In the first row it was noticed that the new teacher's face was pale. "Uh . . . on that day"—he continued with an effort—"you will all be men!"

Then a thin smile brushed his lips and a sudden gleam appeared in his small white eyes. "Hey, fat boy, back there," he called brutally, his arm stretched toward the back of the room. "Yes, you, what's your name?"

"Simon Kotkowski, sir," answered a fearful voice.

Herr Geek's sparkling steel ruler described a slashing orbit in space, finishing at the precise point where he wished to see the Jew take his position. "The Jew Simon Kotkowski, right here!"

Placid, resigned, huddled in his cheerful fat, the amiable Simon

Kotkowski approached the blackboard. The singularly Jewish shape of his nose had struck Herr Geek, who made it the subject of his first lesson. But sarcasms and comparisons, "typological" analyses and "biopolitical" commentaries seemed to bounce off Simon Kotkowski's elastic epidermis, lending a clear, lively pink tone to his expression.

"Jew," Herr Geek murmured, "you and your people, you're fighting for the domination of the universe, right?"

"I don't know, sir," the accused answered straightforwardly.

His arms crossed, his paunch cheerful, the hair frizzy on his low forehead, he presented a picture of the most total incomprehension. The bridge of his nose, like a carp's (like a vulture's beak, Herr Geek had said), rose and fell hesitantly. He seemed much intrigued.

"Do you hear?" Herr Geek said softly. "He says that he doesn't know. . . ." And leaning toward the child as if to underline the confidential character of the interview, "Jew, Jew," he exhaled, "isn't Germany your mortal enemy?"

"No . . . no. . . ."

"Jew, little Jew of my heart, how can I believe you, will you tell me?"

"It's true, sir," Simon answered, terrified.

"The strength of the Jews," Herr Geek went on without seeming to have heard him, "do you mean to say that it no longer lies in the suppleness of their spinal column?"

At that, Simon Kotkowski remained silent and Herr Geek took on an expression of extreme solemnity. In a voice that all the students guessed was broken by emotion, "Jew. Ah, little Jew, you who are still a child—tell us what fate you have reserved for us if"—here the tone of Herr Geek's voice thinned in terror—"if—ah, my God!—if we should emerge defeated from this fight to the death? *Von der Totenschlacht?* What will you do to us?"

And the Jewish child, fascinated, caught in the play of collective fear swirling about his person, the titanic struggle of the Jews and the poor Germans finishing as a sketch upon his eyeballs—Simon answered, with frightened good will, "We won't do anything to you, Herr Professor, we won't do anything to you. . . ."

Geek would have loved to take that incorrigible peon of a Kremer and cleave him in two before the whole class. A non-commissioned officer in the Imperial Army, recently promoted to the position of shock-instructor, Geek saw the purification of the class as a work worthy of the former leader of a mopping-up squad. From eight to ten in the morning he offered brilliant solutions to all pending problems, but the question of singing proved to be infinitely more delicate. . . .

Judging that the Jews would inevitably sing off key, he decided that they would not sing at all, "except," he added, "if they feel an irresistible urge. In that case, since cats meow, since dogs bark, and since pigs grunt, why shouldn't the Jews sing?"

That query split the class in two with the precision of a razor—those who laughed, and the Jews. But soon the teacher noticed that the Jews were not singing, that the Aryan pupils were, and that the result was a ridiculous double injustice. Four flat zeros in the record book did not console him for it, nor four seated interrogations, nor four kneeling punishments, lined up along the blackboard. The fact was unchallengeable—they were not singing.

The students launched the march of the Pimpfe, "Strike, pierce and kill"—the girls soprano, and the boys tenor in order to accelerate their change of voice—when the solution appeared to Herr Geek, simple, clear and natural.

"Halt!" he commanded, his arms scissoring the air. The chorus broke off cleanly.

Then Herr Geek, smiling: "It seems, my friends, that our guests are taking life a bit too easy. While you sing, what do they do? They listen tranquilly. They think themselves at a concert." Herr Geek was unable to resist pursing his lips at his little joke, and several students laughed boisterously. And yet he had to follow up on that felicitous phrase. Herr Geek wiped his eyes slowly, blew his nose into a handkerchief, took in a great breath and, thwarted, realized that the rest of his discourse was being awaited.

There was a considerable pause.

Twisting their heads in his direction, the four Jews themselves seemed crushed by the silence flowing from his lips, still half open, like lava immediately frozen into heavy, soft sheets on his face. And yet the suddenness of his attack surprised them. "Let the Jews sing," he growled, purple with indignation. "Let them give us a serenade!"

At which there was a new pause, but this was the pause of victory, the silence of the great German eagle, wings spread majestically, and already all were applauding but the Jews. . . .

Simon Kotkowski stood up, shook a cramped ankle and then stepped forward miserably to stand before the instructional pulpit. As soon as he had received the order, he rounded his mouth to a heart shape and with great good nature broke into the celebrated lament "There is no more beautiful death on earth," dedicated to the memory of the hero Horst Wessel. His eyes upon heaven and his pudgy hands lying delicately on his paunch, he had barely whispered "Unfurl the blood-soaked flag" when an atrocious laugh swept the class, sparing none of them, not even the three Jewish souls still on their knees.

The terrible interpreter serenely launched the second verse, "Arise! That which God made German. . . ." Herr Geek suddenly leaned across the lectern, screaming in Simon's ear to stop him, and striking him with the pointer to make his meaning clear. Himself in the grip of a nervous twitch, the teacher seemed highly shocked by such an interpretation, which was not a Jew's and yet not a German's. Simon Kotkowski went back to the blackboard, and immediately seeking the ideal position let himself fall backward, so as to rest his buttocks on his heels, then clasped his hands below his chubby abdomen as if to support himself better in his trial.

At a curt gesture, Moses Finkelstein rose with a fully submissive air. He stepped forward, repressing a birdlike hiccup. When he had arrived before the large lectern, a tear rolled from under his glasses, a tear of shame, of suppressed hilarity and of terror. No one really knew Moses Finkelstein—his father had abandoned his mother, who did housekeeping and breathed through the nostrils of her son, which is to say barely at all. Placing his hands flat against his chest in a vague gesture of defense, he broke into singsong in a sighing, nasal voice, almost a murmur. He was then sent back to his knees, broken, fearful, licking at his tears, tasting the dregs of shame.

"I don't want to sing," Marcus Rosenberg then said.

Standing, his back against the blackboard, he swaggered defiantly.

"Who is forcing you to sing?" Geek answered coldly.

Rather tall, with the thin, prominent neck of a young stag, Marcus Rosenberg could not bear humiliation. Often in the evening the Pimpfe organized a pack to bring him to earth. The scars all over his face announced the score of old defeats.

"No, I won't sing," he went on in a voice choked by his own surprise.

And as Geek limped heavily toward him, bending his adult back in order to bring his soothing gaze better to bear on Marcus Rosenberg's eyes, the latter retreated against the blackboard, which stopped him.

"But who is forcing you to sing, my friend?" Herr Geek repeated in a smooth, insinuating voice. "Where I come from people only sing for pleasure. Ask Moses Finkelstein. . . ." Then, taking him from behind, Geek threw the Jewish child to his knees, twisting his wrist in a hammer lock.

The aptness of the conception and the great good taste of his execution enchanted the Pimpfe, who applauded in silence.

"So it's that way? We have our pride?" Geek murmured affectionately, and he increased the pressure to force the child to groan. "But the pride of the Jew is made to be broken. And this is how," he added, and Marcus Rosenberg released a wail within himself without opening his tightened lips.

Geek's voice was syrupy sweet. "Come now, come now—*'wenn Judenblut'*, when Jewish blood . . .? When Jewish blood . . .?" At the end of five minutes, Marcus's lips were opening imperceptibly. When his mouth was wide open, a sudden drowned scream of music escaped it. The proof of Jewish ignominy was achieved. Herr Geek breathed delightedly, and flinging the child to the floor, he said, "Filth!"

And noticing a livid Ernie—"And that one, I almost forgot him."

Marcus Rosenberg stayed as he was—his face to the floor, hands over his skull, mute. The Pimpfe were rejoicing that his pride had been broken.

Two tears hung on Ernie's lashes. He managed nevertheless to make out his friend Ilse in the first row; her face, frozen in stony attention, implored him to sing.

"And when will this imbecile deign to begin?"

The child turned toward the teacher's desk, a thin wrinkle between his brows, his nose pink with grief. "Excuse me, sir," he stammered, rolling his eyes wildly. "I don't know yet if I ought to . . . oh. . . ." Then he brought an arm behind his back, offering himself without resistance to the extraordinary hold of the teacher. The class was silent. Intrigued, the pupils in the first row took in the snatches of speech escaping Ernie Levy's lips: "I don't know . . . I don't know. . . ."

Geek suspected a trap. He advanced one hand cautiously, guarding his face with the other, but when the child did not stir, he grabbed his wrist quickly and twisted it with such vigor that the boy gave a brief fishlike jump before falling back to his knees, imprisoned.

"You still don't know?"

But Ernie had taken his final stand right there. While Herr Geek went on with the cruel lesson, while the Aryans appreciated its clarity and the Jews its rigor, Ernie Levy was gliding at the height of a dove, crowned by the faces he would not assassinate in song—Mother Judith, the patriarch, Papa, Mama, Moritz and the little ones.

Herr Geek's comments bluntly confirmed the fact that Ernie had not sung.

But when the cruel excitement of the moment had passed, an immense majority of the students secretly refused to admit that he had not *wished* to sing, so that it was impossible to go on seeing an offense in Ernie's silence, and even more impossible to see a personal triumph or—as Geek had complained—the triumph of Jews in general. According to that secret majority, neither defeat nor victory was possible for the idiot. They felt that he had no wish to conquer anyone, and not being engaged in any combat, he could not undergo any defeat comparable to Marcus Rosenberg's. And yet deep within themselves that secret majority felt a hate for "the idiot" all the more lively in that it found no nourishment in his silence. The hatred of Marcus was a response to his permanent defiance, and Marcus vanquished inspired nothing more than the scorn he had wished to escape. But Ernie's silence had none of these motives, and several children suspected that he would willingly have sung if he had *been able to*. From then on their hatred of Ernie Levy was immeasurable, for it was aimed at the very gentleness that emanated from his person and that each of the children felt within himself, confusedly, buried like a taproot.

The Jews remained on their knees until the last Aryan had left, so that each might admire them in passing and express that admiration by word and deed. But there was not a glance for Ernie; the students turned away as they brushed by, as if they had been exposed to a subtle danger. Ilse could not help glancing sidewise at him. Surprised, she saw only a tangle of disheveled hair, for Ernie was staring at the floor, not in fear, but ashamed and grieving to have been irremediably separated from both the Aryans and the Jews.

The children dispersed with all the bustle and grace of a flight of sparrows. No group was formed to speed the departing Jews on their way. The Pimpfe themselves looked at the cripples joylessly. Simon Kotkowski swore never to come back to school—even if his father had to suffer harshly for that infraction of the law. Marcus Rosenberg sharpened an absolute revenge. Moses Finkelstein ran home. And with dragging steps, intoxicated by the afternoon sun, Ernie Levy went to meet his friend Ilse, who was waiting for him, as she did every day, beside the Schlosse, beyond the great block of houses, her blond hair sparkling in the sun. That day when he saw the beloved figure, the pain in his shoulder blinded him suddenly and tears leaped to his eyes. Ilse was standing in the middle of the street not far from the riverbank, motionless, her head set like a pretty apple above her black smock. Without the aching shoulder and the tears and that interminable approach over which each step increased his feeling of aloneness, he would doubtless never even have dreamed of kissing Ilse Bruckner on the cheek. He would doubtless not have dared. But had he only dreamed it? It seemed to him as he approached that Ilse shared his solitude and was offering her cheek, and he could not have said if he had kissed it before she offered it or if, on the contrary, Ilse had initiated that kiss —it all happened as if the two things were only one.

"You pig!" was the first shout from Hans Schliemann, camouflaged in the shrubbery on the bank. At that signal Hans's "men," surging out of the nearby houses or springing up from the reeds of the Schlosse, disclosed the ambush.

Ilse's eyes, gentle, blue, green, yellow, shone peacefully at him.

"Run!" Ernie cried, surrounded by the Pimpfe, smacked in the face, dragged against the naked wall of an apartment building. And as he worried about Ilse, he glimpsed her for a brief instant still in the middle of the street, in the sunlight, her arms hanging against her short pleated skirt, observing it all with a curious eye.

He heard a sharp voice, felt a tickling breath against the back of his neck. "That's the second time today he's sullied the honor of Germany," the voice announced in an extraordinarily solemn tone.

Yet Ernie felt that Hans Schliemann's voice was hollow, as empty as the display dumbbells the hardware man's children played with, the ones they lifted contorting themselves and turning red in a thousand imaginary tortures. So he decided that Hans Schliemann's voice merited a secret smile.

"Pig!" a Pimpf belched against Ernie's face. "I bet you've already kissed her on the mouth!"

"And maybe rubbed a titty or two!"

"Or stuck his hand in the little basket!"

Trembling in anger, the invisible voice of Hans Schliemann echoed against Ernie's neck. "Or maybe this little pig has already 'knocked her off'?"

Falling to his knees, Ernie felt the pain in his shoulder more acutely than ever. He was beaten without a fight by a single twist from Hans Schliemann.

The pain in his shoulder became sharper. Moisture blurred his eyes, then his forehead too was moist, and the little boy imagined confusedly (as the fire in his shoulder raged hotter) that all that abundant liquid leaking from his eyes and his skull, his neck and his trunk, and congealing in his throat, filtering through his lips drawn back by the mechanical pressure of his jaws and teeth, at the breaking point—the child imagined that all the liquid in his body was leaking away, fleeing the white-hot bar of his right shoulder.

"*Schweinhund!*" Hans Schliemann shouted, almost out of breath. "Have you decided to sing yet?"

Drunk on indignation, Hans Schliemann could only repeat incessantly, "*Hund*, dog, dog, dog," while the other Pimpfe spat in Ernie's face, stooping each in turn, bringing their rounded mouths to within an inch of him, spewing phlegm at him. His eyes closed, the little boy imagined that the sweat, the saliva, the tears and the phlegm in which he was bathing were simply one and the same substance, welling up from some spring deep within his being, splitting its envelope now and flowing in the sunlight. All those liquids emanated from his own interior substance, blue-green, shadowy, viscous, not composed normally of flesh and bone, as he had once thought. . . .

Time now seemed to him a bottomless sea.

Strangely, the floodgates opened and all the waters disappeared.

Opening his eyes, Ernie found himself kneeling on the hard, dry sidewalk. Some distance away, the Pimpfe were in a huddle. They seemed to be arguing a serious point, but Ernie was more aware of their expressions, concentrated and discouraged, than of the mysterious words they were exchanging, glaring at him sidewise from time to time. Between Wolfgang Oelendorff's solidly bowed legs Ernie discovered with delight the placid figure of his friend Ilse Bruckner, who seemed to be frozen in the same spot. Soon she directed her smooth, blue-green gaze between Oelendorff's legs, apparently without seeing Ernie, although her delicate features had contracted for a second, he thought he noticed, when their eyes met briefly.

"That Jew there," the redhead said, "he looks more Jewish than the others to me."

"I think we ought to strip him in front of Bruckner," Wolfgang Oelendorff said. "I hear their pricks are trimmed."

"No, no, not that!" the terrified redhead cried.

"Why not?" Hans Schliemann inquired calmly. *"We can pull the Devil by his tail."*

The group burst into strained laughter, every head turning toward Ilse, who seemed to have heard nothing—though her cheeks had colored—and whose eyes were taking on the light opacity of blind eyes, though she still stared in the direction of the boys, alternately at the Pimpfe, now silent, and at Ernie, still on his knees, accepting the caress of the sun between Wolfgang's legs. The heat comforted his shoulder.

All these things seen and heard seemed so unnatural that Ernie Levy believed the sun was approaching him, spinning on its axis like a wheel of fireworks only a few inches from his half-closed eyes. Yet a part of him was aware of the threat. Half rising, he propped himself sidewise against the wall of the house and opened his eyes still clogged by the sun, tears, the sweat running down his forehead, saliva and phlegm. Truly all these things were without precedent, and slowly becoming aware of the words spoken, the little boy took his eyes off Ilse Bruckner in vexation; she was still motionless in her black smock, and her face had become a pair of huge green eyes.

The Pimpfe surrounded him in silence. The little boy did not budge, staring at the spinning disc of the sun. These events concerned someone else. Nothing like them had ever happened to anyone. There was not the slightest allusion to any such phantasmagoria in the Legend of the Just Men. Desperately tense, Ernie searched his memories, hoping to find a clear path, a road to help him through that forest of strange circumstances, which did not seem entirely real though they bore a certain appearance of reality. . . . He found no road.

Hans Schliemann's arms bound him nonchalantly. Hans proceeded as if he had Ernie's complete agreement. The latter moved an elbow out of the way, allowing Hans to take a firm grip comfortably.

The redhead knelt and undid Ernie's suspenders.

Ernie Levy lowered his eyes and saw a head of red hair at the height of his belly.

With a sharp jerk, the redhead pulled Ernie's pants halfway down his thighs. Ernie noticed that his own legs were shaking violently, and as the redhead slipped two fingers between the skin and the elastic of the underwear, the little boy freed himself from Hans Schliemann's embrace in one jerk and raised his hands as high as he could. They fluttered in the air, up against the wheel of the sun, as if he did not know what to do with them and wished simply to testify to his own impotence.

Disturbed, the Pimpfe looked at those naked hands fluttering in the sunlight. But the redhead got back into the spirit of things immediately and pulled down the underwear, uncovering Ernie's sex, and it was at that moment that the beast a-borning rose to the little boy's throat, and he howled for the first time. He had already dropped to the redhead's feet, digging his teeth into the flesh of a calf and keeping them there. A flux of saliva rose to his mouth; his nails dug into the redhead's ankles.

Immediately Hans Schliemann set his knee against Ernie Levy's back and pulled the little boy backward violently, his hands reversed and his thumbs dug into the boy's eyes. Ernie let go, screamed again and hung by his teeth from one of Hans Schliemann's hands. Hans freed himself only after dragging the child for ten feet along the sidewalk. Hans Schliemann took a few steps more, as if he wanted to lengthen the distance between his hands and Ernie Levy's mouth. Then changing his mind, he saw that all the Pimpfe had suffered the same reflex and were on the defensive now, in a compact group, out of reach of Ernie Levy's teeth. Ernie had risen quickly to his feet and was standing, his back to the wall, facing them and growling in his throat like a dog while the tears sprang from his eyes like so many tiny, sharp knives.

"Dog shit," said the redhead.

"Jewish shit," said a Pimpf.

"Jewish dog," Hans Schliemann went on without conviction, and as he drew closer, he added in a forced tone, "Be careful, he may have rabies." The Pimpf spread out even more, but smiling to show that they did not take the remark seriously. They could not let Ernie Levy off, and yet no one felt like breaking the evil Jewish spell they had just witnessed. Hans Schliemann's little joke seemed to offer a way out.

"We'll take him to the furrier's," a Pimpf said. "He'll take him off our hands."

"How do they slaughter them?" a Pimpf asked.

"They give them injections," Hans Schliemann said, "and they die with their mouths open."

"Where do they do it?" a Pimpf laughed. "In the ass?"

"That depends," Hans answered in the manner of an expert, "that depends. . . . With Jewish dogs, they say it's in the prick."

And as if they had been waiting for that signal, the Pimpfe roared with laughter, shoving each other enthusiastically, slapping their thighs in such an excess of hilarity that they were suddenly conscious of evading the principal question and fell silent again. The redhead picked up a stone and threw it at Ernie Levy; several others followed him. In their anger, they aimed badly. Soon Hans Schliemann gave the signal to disperse.

"You coming?" he asked Ilse.

"You in a hurry?" she said dryly.

"You looking after your sweetie? Watch out, he's crazy."

"I'm not afraid of him," Ilse Bruckner said.

Turning toward Hans, she winked conspiratorially and whispered, "Go on, I'll catch up with you right away."

"At the corner by the school?" Hans asked.

And at her nod, he glanced strangely at her and turned his back slowly. Soon the gang reached the end of the street. A song rose in the distance. Their voices were fresh and cheerful.

The tears had dried. Slowly the spinning sun slipped back into its natural orbit. Finally it ceased spinning and was still, infinitely far away, like a candle in an enormous room. In the meadows a blackbird took up its song, and the Schlosse lapped among the reeds. Ernie noticed that his friend Ilse had not moved away. Her shoes had buttons instead of laces. She was wearing her pretty black smock, and her notebooks were on the ground, propped between her ankles. Ernie noticed that her moist eyes and all the glossiness in her hair and face gave her the look of a fish. At the school masquerade she had worn a long dress; she made it undulate like the tail of a little Chinese fish. There had also been many pretty things adorning her face and hands, with their marvelously pink fingers, but no one knew what all those things meant, no one knew what to call them. Ernie smiled at her in delight; her eyes were dilated in fascination and in a curiosity greater than herself. Abruptly all the green sparkle left her expression, the shadow of a smile passed fleetingly, raised her lip, reached a dimple, faded, disappeared. Now the little girl was staring at him from far off, as if at a stranger to be scorned and feared. Ernie started forward; she paled, stooped, picked up notebooks and fled like a graceful arrow in the track of the Pimpfe; twenty yards away she turned and applauded three times. The sun was so low that her silhouette, made sharper by her black smock, was like a sparkling insect in the path of its rays. And then there was nothing.

The sun began to spin again, faster and faster. Sparks leaped from the flaming wheel, shooting through the sky in multicolored spangles. Blond hairs too shot away. Ernie pulled up his pants. The beast in his heart was roaring so horribly that he was afraid he would die on the spot. As he mentally dug his teeth into the Pimpfe, he understood that he was feeling hate for the first time.

When he reached the bridge over the Schlosse, Ernie turned and saw that he was alone.

Quite small, chipped, humped, the stone bridge crossed the Schlosse with the rustic good nature of an old peasant. Tendrils of ivy gave it a flowered beard straggling down as far as the water. Now and then Ilse and Ernie had leaned upon it to watch time pass interminably between the banks. Carp and gudgeon followed the trail of the hours, and Ilse claimed that all fish disappeared into the sea—otherwise where would they go? Ernie never contradicted her, though he knew that certain delicate species—the bleaks, for example—stopped just at the border, at the frontier between fresh and salt water.

Today the Schlosse seemed frozen in its bed and the water as transparent and empty as air.

The little boy crossed the bridge and took the path that dropped to the river's edge to the left of the parapet, among the brambles, nettles and soft green tufts of grass on the bank, and the bouquets of yellow flowers blooming in the shadow of the reeds. Halfway down, the pass curved around the famous Rock of Woden, the Germanic god of war, of storm, of lords and kings. The boulder thrust upward from the bank ten or twelve feet high, like a cliff. Once, during the time of the republic, it was said that workingmen had dived from its summit every Sunday in summertime. It seemed so profoundly rooted in the earth that it was impossible to imagine it alone, isolated, reduced to itself like a simple huge stone; it was a granite tree, the stump of an oak, one might have said, still living with all its roots, decapitated but indestructible. Yet Herr Kremer had been positive: the ancestors of the Gentiles had brought it from the mountains, trimmed and chiseled it where it was, and used it as a slaughtering table where the throats of beasts and men were cut. The blood ran off into the Schlosse, which carried it as far as Taunus, where the witches of the Brocken came on Walpurgis Night and lapped it up—it was a *sacrificial altar.* . . . Some nights the Pimpfe and the adult members of the party burned tree trunks on it. People in the Riggenstrasse no longer said "the Stone" but "Woden's Rock"—with much respect. A professor from Berlin had found a swastika under the moss. The newspapers insisted that it was several thousand years old, and Ernie's father, shrewdly, that it was barely the age of a child in the cradle.

Ernie Levy stretched forth his arm and touched the rock with his index finger prudently, as if it were a sleeping animal. Then he went on down the slope and walked off ten yards or so in the late sunlight, out of reach of the fantastic shadow cast by the boulder. The rows of reeds thinnd out along a tiny sandy beach. Ernie Levy dropped to one knee and noticed that the shadow of the rock extended onto the surface of the Schlosse, carried along by the movement of the water so that threads of shadow were cast up on the beach. With one knee dug into the sand, he leaned gently to the left so that the two shadows, his and the rock's, became one. Leaning over the liquid shadow, from which muddy bubbles rose, he spread out his handkerchief like a raft. It drifted for a few seconds and then sank.

The ripples swirled. Ernie Levy wrung out his handkerchief slowly and proceeded to wipe off his forehead.

The slashing metal ruler had opened a gash; its lips were caked with dried blood. Ernie Levy swabbed it out with his handkerchief and then covered it with a nettle leaf. The wound seemed absolutely painless. Running his fingers over his skull, he noted with surprise that it was covered with swollen bumps. Yet he felt none of those bumps, nor even his jaw, simply numbed by Herr Geek's fist. If he was not suffering, it was because he would never again suffer; it was because the organs of suffering were abolished in him. Out of curiosity he bit into his palm, a deep bite that left toothmarks. In one of the depressions was a drop of blood, which caused him no perceptible pain. He could admire it as something pretty. "But the Just Men suffer," Ernie Levy murmured suddenly.

He cupped his hands and dipped up a little water with which he softened the blood dried on his face and on his naked chest. Then he scrubbed it with the wet handkerchief, rinsing it out afterward. The joint shadow of his body and the rock kept him from seeing the water redden; the tint was drowned quickly in the current. He rose and wiped off his sandy knee. Absolutely nothing stirred within him.

It was shortly afterward that Ernie had his first intuition of emptiness. Not wanting to go back along Woden's Trail, he pushed his way through the nettles on the bank, and from the height of the slope he contemplated the meadows for a moment before setting out across them calmly, in a ceremonious tread. . . . Some of the grass rose higher than his chin; the farther he pushed into the green, stagnant, infinitely divisible water of the meadow, the more it seemed to him that the waves of grass were rising about him as if they intended to drown him, or at least to imprison him by closing about him instantly, obliterating the wake of his random steps. He could not have said if the advancing waves were swelling to drown him or if, on the contrary, he was plunging step by step into that sea like someone deliberately abandoning the shore.

When the shore seemed far enough away, he stopped and saw by the immensity of the sky that Ernie Levy was a mote lost in the grass. At that moment he experienced emptiness, as if the earth had split beneath his feet, and while his eyes rejoiced in the immensity of the heavens, these words came sweetly to his lips: "I am nothing." The earth around him gave off its odors. All things were fixed, enveloped in the smells of the earth. The silence had that smell, and the exhalations of the sun, and the immutable blue of the sky. A grain of dust struck his cheek and stuck to it; he took it between index finger and thumb and submitted it to examination. It was a red ladybug dotted with black, its legs vibrating like tiny hairs. It might have been a jewel, a pinhead cut out of a ruby with tiny black dots inked in. With infinite gentleness, Ernie Levy set the ladybug on the end of his vertical thumb:

> *Ladybug, ladybug, fly away home,*
> *Your house is on fire, your children will burn,*
> *One,*
> *Two,*
> *Three!*

The childhood tradition demanded that when the word "three" was pronounced, one blew on the ladybug from behind. The little boy had rounded his lips, but changing his mind suddenly, he raised his index finger and squeezed it violently against his thumb. The insect's pulp crackled between his fingers. Ernie rolled the pulp into a soft, thin twist. Then, with a circular movement of his index finger, he transformed the ladybug into a tiny ball, the consistency of a bread crumb. It seemed to him that all the emptiness in his heart was there, pinched between those two fingers. But that was not enough: setting this atom of matter in the hollow of his hand, he rubbed it between his palms at great length until the ladybug was annihilated, leaving only a grayish stain.

Then, raising his head, he realized that the silence had just died. The meadow was alive with the rustling of wings, with the movement of grass, with that invisible, heavy quivering of life. The earth itself was seething defiantly. Ernie Levy noticed first a fragile grasshopper, perched on a sod, twitching its legs gently in a ray of sunlight. He leaned forward cautiously but the grasshopper seemed not at all upset by the menace, and the child saw that its mandibles recalled the industrious nibbling of a rabbit—even better, the alert tightening of an old woman's jaws. With that thought he shot a hand forward and caught what he could; the insect found himself imprisoned by a paw, between the palm and the index finger. Ernie Levy bent his thumb and crushed the grasshopper against his palm. Then he made a ball of it, a greenish color, abundant this time, which stained his fingers altogether.

The next victim proved to be a butterfly. . . . Rare are those who appreciate the butterfly at its true value. What generally lowers the butterfly in the eyes of the profane was for Ernie another reason to respect it—that it was born of the caterpillar and that its beauty was as dust. . . . Balthazar Klotz collected butterflies. He ran through the fields tilting the lance of his net, anesthetized the victim with a flagon of ether, executed it at home, in his own good time, with a pin driven through the geometric heart of the thorax. Balthazar Klotz's room was covered with fragile trophies. Examined with a magnifying glass, each of them proved to be a cathedral, and the beauty of the wings gave them a lifelike character, the illusion of being not yet dead. Ernie would have liked to hunt butterflies for pleasure, the pleasure of seeing them, but even if they were released it cost them a broken wing, a golden antenna forever extinguished, a radiance forever dead. So he settled for a silent approach to the wonder, stalking it cleverly, like an Indian, then contemplating it at leisure. He was rigid as stone; some of the butterflies fluttered about him, settling on his head or on a finger, like a ring—marvelous.

The martyr was a tiger swallowtail with wings like stained glass. The popular name swallowtail derives from the hind points of its wings, half an inch long—the immensity of its wingspread gives it the noble flight of a bird of prey.

The swallowtail landed on a violet. Ernie Levy enveloped the flower and the insect in his still moist handkerchief, and slipping a hand beneath it, he snatched at both things together, the butterfly and the violet, and then kneaded them between his already sticky palms. After the swallowtail came a dragonfly, a giant cricket, a beetle, a small butterfly with pearly-blue wings, other butterflies, other dragonflies, other grasshoppers. Ernie Levy ran through the meadow, arms spread wide, flapping his hands, gummy with vermin. . . .

Still, he was tired. Each insect death cost him more. Each death added its cortege of soft ordure, and now they were filling his stomach—viscid liquors on his palms but dismembered insects, seething and suffering, in his own belly. His heart heavy with these things, he stretched out and closed his eyes, his hands flat against the grass. His belly seemed to sprawl in all directions. In the imperfect night of his eyelids, its victims growled and swarmed. Profiting by the darkness, the thousand chitterings of the outside world entered his ears, flowing insidiously into that pouch where the butterflies and other insects were still suffering. His flattened hands were dead.

Ernie raised his eyelids and drowned in the fallen sky.

Soon the high grass formed a frame in the middle of which birds were gliding. The sky was swollen with them.

He tried to follow a bird with his eyes, hoping to reach it and to fly off with it. But the birds maneuvered scornfully, indifferent to his gaze, and the distance between him and them did not diminish. How could he have pretended to those heights, to the even greater heights of the Just Man—he, a puny, rapacious insect; he, crawling on a heavy, enormous belly swarming with its insect nourishment . . . ? *I was not a Just Man, I was nothing.*

As he thought, "I was nothing," the little boy buried his face against the earth and intoned his first cries. At the same instant he felt astonishment that his eyes should be empty of tears. For half an hour he cried out, his mouth against the earth. He seemed to be hailing someone far off, a being buried deep in the earth from whom he wanted only an echo. But his cries only exaggerated the silence, and the vermin remained lively in his belly. His mouth was full of grass and dirt. Finally he knew that nothing would answer his call, for that call was born of nothing: God could not hear it. It was precisely here that Ernie Levy, the little boy, felt burdened by his body and decided to let that burden fall.

2. *HEROD'S CHILDREN*

ILSE AICHINGER

Let us stay with the children for one more selection, capturing the terrible and sad beauty of their thoughts as they try to live in a world that has no room for them. Ilse Aichinger's poetic novel looks at the special world created by these children as they wander through the streets of Vienna, using their special logic as they try to cope with the illogic of the Nuremberg Laws. The problem of "the wrong grandmother" brings us into the world of the Holocaust where war was waged upon the smallest child. And we should know that there was no hope of survival for Ellen, the heroine of this story. She dies at the end of this book, just as Anne Frank died after the end of her book.

━━━

THE QUAY

"Let me play with you!"
"Go away!"
"Let me play with you!"
"Go on, go!"
"Let me play with you!"
"We're not playing."
"What are you doing?"

"We're waiting."

"For what?"

"We're waiting for a child to drown."

"Why?"

"We're going to save it."

"And then?"

"Then we'll have made good."

"Have you done something bad?"

"Our grandparents. It's our grandparents' fault."

"Oh. Have you been waiting long?"

"Seven weeks."

"Do a lot of children drown here?"

"No."

"And you want to wait till a baby comes floating down the canal?"

"Why not? We'll dry it off and bring it to the Mayor. And the Mayor'll say: Good, very good! Beginning tomorrow you may sit on any benches you want. We won't mention that matter about your grandparents any more. And we'll say, thank you, Mr. Mayor."

"Not at all, nice to have seen you. My regards to your grandparents!"

"Oh, you said that well! If you like, you can play the Mayor from now on."

"Again!"

"Here's a child, Mr. Mayor!"

"What about this child?"

"We've saved it."

"How did this happen?"

"We were sitting on the bank waiting for it—"

"No! You can't say that!"

"Well, then: We just happened to be sitting on the bank, and splash—in it fell!"

"And then what happened?"

"Well, it was all so fast, Mr. Mayor. But we did it all gladly, you know. Now may we sit on the benches again?"

"Yes. And you can play in the park again. We'll forget about your grandparents."

"Oh, thank you, Mr. Mayor!"

"Wait a minute! What shall I do with the child?"

"Oh, it's yours to keep."

"But I don't want to keep it!" Ellen shouted desperately. "It's an awful child! Its mother has emigrated and its father's in the service. When it meets its father, it's not allowed to talk about its mother. And wait a minute . . . there's something the matter with its grandparents: two are all right, but two are all wrong. Undetermined, no, that's the worst—that's too much!"

"What in the world are you saying?"

"This child belongs nowhere! It's good for nothing. Why did you save it? Take it back, for heaven's sake, take it back! And if it wants to play with you, then let it, for the love of God let it."

"Stay here!"

"Come, sit here beside us. What's your name?"

"Ellen."

"Wait for the child with us, Ellen."

"What are your names?"

"That's Bibi. She's got four wrong grandparents and a lipstick she's very proud of. She wants to go to dancing school. She thinks the Mayor will let her, after the baby's been saved.

"Over there, the third one, that's Kurt. He really thinks all this is ridiculous, waiting for the child. But still, he's waiting. After it's been saved he wants to play football again. He's got three wrong grandparents and he plays goalie.

"Leon's the oldest. He practices lifesaving with us, and wants to be a movie director. He's got four wrong grandparents and he knows all the ropes.

"Over there, that's Hannah. She wants to have seven children and a house on the Swedish coast. Her husband's going to be a parson, and she keeps sewing a tablecloth. Or maybe it's a curtain for the children's room in the new house. Isn't that so, Hannah? Too much sun is harmful. But she's waiting with the rest of us, and she never leaves this spot. She doesn't even go home at noontime, or a little upstream to where the gas reservoir throws some shade.

"Ruth—that's Ruth. She likes to sing, mostly songs about the silver lining whenever clouds appear. Even though her parents have been given notice for September, she's hoping for an apartment in heaven. The world's wide and wonderful—we all know that—and yet?. . . there's a catch in it, isn't there, Ruth? There's something that isn't as it ought to be.

"Herbert? Come over here. He's the little one, the youngest.

He's got a stiff leg and he's scared. Scared he won't be able to swim along with us when we save the child. But he practices all the time, and he'll make it. He's got three and a half wrong grandparents he loves very much and a red water ball he sometimes lends us. He's a very serious child."

"And you?"

"I'm George."

"The dragon-slayer?"

"Yes, I'm a kite flyer. They're dragons of sorts. Wait till it gets to be October! Then Ruth sings about letting your soul fly like a kite, or something like that. What else about me? I've got four wrong grandparents and a butterfly collection. You'll have to find out the rest by yourself."

"Slide in closer. See, Herbert has an old opera glass. Every now and then he scans the canal with it—Herbert's our lighthouse. Way over there's the streetcar stop. See it? And down there is moored an old boat; it'll take one of us at a time."

"If you walk a little farther, over there toward the mountains you come to a carrousel with flying swings."

"The flying swings are wonderful—you hold onto each other and then you let go—"

"You fly way, way out!"

"You keep your eyes closed."

"And if you're lucky the chains break. There's swing music and you can swing right to Manhattan, says the man in the shooting booth. If the chains break . . . but who's that lucky?"

"Every year some commissioner comes and checks the carrousel. No good, says the man in the shooting booth. Keeps people from flying. But they like to be stopped, says the man in the shooting booth."

"And then there's a kind of swing where you stand on your head!"

"Makes them finally realize they're standing on their heads, says the man in the shooting booth."

They were all talking at once.

"Do you ride on it often?" asked Ellen uneasily.

"Who, us?"

"Us, did you say?"

"We've never been."

"Never?"

"It isn't allowed; the chains might break."

"Our grandparents weigh too heavily."

"But sometimes the man comes out of the shooting booth and sits with us. He says it's better to be too heavy than too light. He says they're afraid of us."

"That's why we're not allowed to ride on the carrousel."

"Only after we've saved the child."

"What happens if no child falls into the water?"

"No child fall . . .?"

Fright settled on the children.

"There's still a lot of summer to come!"

"Why are you saying that? You don't belong to us!"

"Two wrong grandparents—that's not enough!"

"You don't understand. *You* don't have to save a child. You're allowed to sit on any bench you want. You're allowed to ride on the carrousel anyhow. Why are you crying?"

"I . . ." sobbed Ellen, "I was just thinking, it—it's going to be winter. And you'll all still be sitting here, one beside the other, waiting for the child. There'll be long icicles hanging from your ears and noses and eyes, and the opera glass will be frozen stiff. You'll be looking and looking, but the child you want to save hasn't drowned. The man from the shooting booth will have gone home long ago; the flying chains will be covered by boards, and the kites will all have flown away. Ruth'll want to sing. Ruth'll want to say: And yet . . . but she won't be able to open her mouth.

"Over there, the people in the warm, brightly lit streetcar press their cheeks against the cold windowpanes and say: Look, look over there! Over on the other side of the canal, where the streets are so quiet, to the right of the gas reservoir, above the ice floes. There's a little statue in the snow, isn't there? A statue? For whom?

"And then I'll say: 'A statue for the children with the wrong grandparents.' And then I'll say: 'I'm cold.' "

"Be quiet, Ellen."

"Don't worry about us. We're going to save that child."

A man was walking along the canal. The flowing water dissolved his mirrored image, folded it, pulled it apart and then left it for an instant itself.

The man looked down and laughed. "Life," he said, "is full of benign cruelty." And he spat wide across the dirty mirror.

Two old women stood on the bank, speaking excitedly.

They were talking so fast they might have been reciting a poem.

"Recognize yourself in the flowing water," said the man as he went by. "I think you look very odd indeed." He walked quickly and quietly.

When he saw the children, he began waving and walking still faster.

"I've traveled across the whole world—" Ruth and Hannah were singing in harmony. "The world is wide and wonderful." The rest of the children were silent. "And yet . . ." sang Ruth and Hannah. The boat rocked.

"And yet!" said the man loudly, and shook each child by the hand. "And yet—and yet—and yet?"

"This is Ellen," explained George quickly. "Two wrong grandparents and two right ones. Tie game."

"That are we all!" laughed the man, patting Ellen's shoulder with a large hand. "Be glad it's apparent."

"It is," said Ellen, hesitating.

"Be glad it's apparent," repeated the man. "If someone's laughing to your right and someone's crying to your left, to whom would you go?"

"The crying one," said Ellen.

"She wants to play with us!" shouted Herbert.

"Her mother's emigrated and her father's in the service."

"Where do you live?" asked the man sternly.

"With my wrong grandmother," Ellen answered uneasily. "But she's all right."

"Wait till you find out how wrong right is!" growled the man.

"Ellen's afraid," George said softly. "She's afraid the child we want to save will never fall into the water."

"How can you believe such a thing?" said the man angrily, shaking Ellen. "How can you believe such a thing? The child has got to fall into the water if it's going to be saved, don't you see?"

"Yes," Ellen replied. She was startled and she tried to get away.

"You don't understand anything!" said the man, growing angrier. "Nobody understands what happens to him. Everybody wants to be saved without ever falling into the water. But how can you be saved if you don't fall in the water?"

The old boat was still rocking. "It'll only carry one of us!" Bibi tried to distract the man.

"Just one," he said more calmly. "Always only one. And rightly so."

"It's a very weak boat," murmured Kurt.

"It's better than an ocean liner," the man replied. He sat down close to the children. The water slapped against the edge of the quay.

"What about you?" Ellen asked shyly. "I mean, your grandparents?"

"Four right ones and four wrong ones," replied the man, stretching his long legs into the gray grass.

"Not eight grandparents!" Ellen laughed.

"Four right ones and four wrong ones," repeated the man, unshaken, rolling himself a cigarette with three fingers. "Just like everybody else."

Birds crossed close to the stream. Tirelessly, Herbert searched the water with his opera glass.

"And besides that, I'm almost like God," explained the man. "I wanted a world and I've got a shooting gallery."

"I'm so sorry," said Ellen politely.

Silence fell over them again. The children stared alertly at the canal. The late sun gave them a deep light which may have held malice, but they didn't notice.

We're waiting for an unknown child; we'll save it from drowning and bring it to City Hall. Good of you, the Mayor'll say. Forget your grandparents. From tomorrow on, you can sit on the benches again. From tomorrow on, you can ride the carrousel again . . . tomorrow . . . tomorrow. . . .

"Fish leaping." Herbert laughed, letting the opera glass dance before his eyes.

"The lighthouse sees them, but they don't see the lighthouse," said Ruth thoughtfully. "You might say it's the wrong way around. And yet, that's what it says in one of the songs."

"And yet," said the man from the shooting gallery, suddenly jumping up, "you're going to ride on the carrousel today!"

"You can't mean that," said Hannah incredulously.

Bibi pulled up her socks very slowly.

"You know the price of the game?"

"There!" shouted Herbert suddenly. "The child! It's drowning!"

Leon snatched the opera glass from his hand. "It's a man," he said bitterly, "and he's swimming."

"Come on," said the shooting gallery man. "I'm not joking. My partner's away; it's your only chance. Nobody else wants to fly at this time. You'll be all alone."

"We'll stay alone," said George.

"Good!" shouted Bibi, and it sounded like a bird call. "And Ellen?"

"Ellen doesn't have to go today," said the man. "She can go any other time."

"I'll wait for you here," said Ellen, unruffled. She bore no opposition to this kind of justice. She watched them go.

The man from the shooting gallery was running ahead, and the children ran behind him, toward the mountains. Since the water flowed the other way, they seemed to be running even faster. They were holding tightly to one another's hands. Dogs barked and were left behind; couples rolled apart on the gray grass; stones splashed into the water.

The carrousel stood quietly in the late sun. The man unlocked the gates. There it stood, between the gas reservoirs, as far away and lost in reverie as a clown before he is painted. Long and silent, the chains hung down from the brightly colored roof. The swing seats were lacquered, and even sky and sun were suddenly lacquered.

The children laughed for no reason.

"You want music?" asked the man.

"Real music?" shouted Herbert excitedly.

"You're asking too much," replied the man.

The gas reservoirs looked blackly threatening.

"Music is dangerous," said George. "You can hear it a long way over water. And there's always the secret police."

"The water flows past," said the man darkly.

"Oh, if they knew we were riding on the carrousel!" Ruth shuddered.

The man was checking the seats silently. The sand glittered with threats.

"Music!"

"Suppose someone denounces you?"

"Do you know what that means?"

"No," said the man quietly, fastening the children into their seats. He set the carrousel in motion, as though to try it out. The seats began to move.

"Let's go!" shouted Bibi. "Music!"

The roof began to turn.

Herbert's stiff leg stuck out in terror into the empty air.

"Come back!" roared the loud-speaker over the quay wall.

"I want to get off!" screamed Herbert. Nobody heard him.

The children flew. They flew against the law of their heavy shoes and against the law of the secret police. They flew according to the law of centrifugal force.

All the gray-green was far below them, and colors ran into each other. Clear, blinding light flickered in praise of the unknown. The image melted to meaning.

Far below them, his arms crossed, stood the owner of the booth. He closed his eyes. For that moment he had exchanged his shooting gallery for the whole world.

The children screamed. They grabbed for each other again and again, the way people do so that they can fly still farther apart. Everything was exactly as they had imagined it.

"Come back!" roared the loud-speaker.

The children didn't hear it. They had been touched by the gleam of the farthest star.

A woman pushed a baby carriage across the bridge. The child in the carriage lay and slept and smiled. The child beside the carriage ran and cried loudly.

"Are you hungry?" asked the woman.

"No," cried the child.

"Are you thirsty?" asked the woman.

"No," cried the child.

"Does something hurt?" asked the woman.

The child cried still more loudly and didn't answer.

"Help me carry these things!" said the woman angrily.

Steps led diagonally to the water.

"Hold on tighter!" she snarled. "You hold everything too loosely."

The wind rose and tried to wave her stringy hair. The child

in the carriage began to cry. The child beside the carriage laughed.
They walked along the stream.

"Why are you laughing?" asked the woman.

The child laughed more loudly.

"We've got to find a place," she said. "A good place."

"Where there's a lot of wind," said the child. "And lots of ants."

"Where there's no wind," replied the woman. "And no ants."

"Where no one has lain. Where the grass is still high!" The child
laughed.

"Where the grass has been trodden down," said the woman.
"Where a lot of people have already lain, so it's easier to lie down."

The child grew silent. From far away came the voice of the loud-
speaker.

"Here," called the woman. "Here's a good place. Somebody must
just have been here."

"Who's been here?" asked the child.

The woman took a blanket from the carriage and spread it out
on the grass.

"Small footprints," she said. "Children."

"Children like me?" The child laughed.

"Now be quiet!" said the woman impatiently.

The child ran down to the water. He bent down, picked up a
stone and balanced it in his hand.

"Can a stone swim, Mother?"

"No."

"I'm going to make it swim anyway."

"Do what you want. I'm tired."

"What I want," repeated the child. The sun had disappeared.

"Mother, there's a boat, an old boat! And over there's a streetcar! It goes so fast, and its windows are so bright. Which shall I go
on, Mother? Which goes farther? The boat or the streetcar, Mother?
Are you asleep, Mother?"

The woman, exhausted, had laid her head on her arms and was
breathing regularly. Beside her, the infant lay with its open eyes
reflecting the sky.

The child ran back up the bank and leaned over the infant.
The baby carriage stood stiffly, blackly against the mist.

"Do you really want to keep riding in that?" asked the child.
"Don't you think it's much too slow?"

The infant smiled silently.

"Later you can transfer to the trolley. Only it stops too often."

The infant twisted its mouth anxiously.

"No, I can see you don't want that. Listen! There's a boat down there! Once you're in it, it never stops. It'll go on as long as you want. You'll never have to get off; nobody'll ever change your diapers. Want to? Come on!"

The woman breathed deeply and turned slowly to the other side. The boat swayed gently. Only a ragged rope bound it to the shore.

The child caught up the baby and ran down the embankment with it.

"Isn't it just like a cradle?"

The infant screamed. He lay at the stern of the boat like a trussed pilot.

"Wait—I'm coming!"

The child loosened the boat. He stood with both feet in the water.

"Why are you crying? Wait! Wait for me! Why can't you wait?"

The baby screamed still louder. Huge, dirty tears ran down its little face.

The boat drifted toward the middle of the stream. It turned, swayed, and seemed undecided. It was better than an ocean liner. Better than . . . .

Ellen blinked sleepily and raised her head above the quay wall. At just that moment the boat was taken by the main stream. It tipped.

"Come back!" The loud-speaker stopped with a little screech.

"Have you had enough?" The man from the shooting gallery laughed.

"Yes," replied the children, happily stupified.

He began to unstrap them.

"I'm not sick at all," said Herbert. "Really not."

"Thank you very much."

They all shook his hand. The man beamed.

"The same thing tomorrow?"

"No, never again," George said seriously. "Two kilometers down there's the secret police."

"Just be careful," said the man. "And if—I mean; there are always good friends. In any case, you've never been on a carrousel."

"We've never been on a carrousel," said Leon.

A tall boy was leaning against the exit.

"Why don't you pay?"

"We did before we went!" called the children, and they ran away.

Quickly, quickly! Only a few steps between them and their place. "There!"

Their arms fell to their sides. All the blood left their faces. They stood riveted to the edge of the stream, their silhouettes stiff and black against the summer evening.

What they saw surpassed by far their concept of the injustice of the world, and it surpassed their capacity to suffer: dripping, and with an infant in her arms, Ellen was wading to the edge of the canal.

This was the child for whom they had been waiting for seven weeks; the child they were going to save to exculpate themselves— their child—their child that was going to let them sit on the benches again.

Holding the older child by the hand, the mother was standing at the bank, screaming with fear and joy. People were running toward them from all sides; it was as though they were rising from the stream like specters, using this opportunity to show their sympathetic hearts.

Baffled, in the midst of it all, stood Ellen. Then she saw her friends at the edge of the slope.

The woman tried to hug Ellen, but she pushed her away. "I couldn't help it!" she called despairingly. "I couldn't help it. I wanted to call you, but you were too far away. I wanted—" she pushed people aside.

"Spare yourself the trouble!" Kurt said icily.

"Where's my opera glass?" called Herbert.

Hannah and Ruth were trying, not very successfully, to hold back their tears.

"We'll pay some other way," whispered Leon.

Pale and despairing, Ellen stood before them.

"Come on," George said quietly. He put his jacket around Ellen.

"Up there are some benches. We'll all go sit on a bench. We'll just do it."

Bootsteps crushed the gravel, purposeless and self-satisfied as are only the steps of those gone astray. The children jumped up in terror. The bench tipped over.

"Your identification!" demanded the voice. "Have you the right to sit here?"

That voice. Ellen turned her face into the dark.

"Yes," said George, his face stony with fright.

Hannah dug around in her coat pockets, looking for her card. But she found none. Leon, who was outside the circle of light, tried to slip away into the bushes. Herbert tried to follow him. His stiff leg made a dragging rustle. Both were pulled back.

The soldiers stood in stony calm. The one in the middle seemed to be an officer; his shoulder insignia had a silvery shine.

Bibi began crying, then stopped.

"All's lost," whispered Kurt.

For long seconds nobody moved.

The officer in the middle became impatient; he fingered his revolver angrily.

"I asked you—have you the right to sit here?"

Herbert swallowed loudly twice.

"Are you Aryan?"

Ellen still stood in the shadows, numb, trying to put a foot forward and twitching it back again. But when the officer repeated his question still more clearly and sharply, she stepped into the circle of light and slung her short hair out of her face with a movement she made often.

"You must know that, Father!"

Helmets seem to have been invented specifically to hide facial expressions. This fact has been authenticated on all fronts.

In that dusty little park there reigned a breathlessness, an unearthly noisy silence. The two soldiers to the left and to the right didn't understand at all, yet they had a feeling of nausea and dizziness, as though they had been refuted. The children all understood, and they stayed triumphantly in the dark.

This was the man who had asked Ellen to forget him. But can the word forget the lips that have spoken it? He had avoided thinking a thought to the end. Now it had come back to over-shadow and overpower him.

None of the children now considered flight. In the space of a second they were on the offensive; unknown powers had been given to their powerlessness. The tower of Babylon quivered with the still tremble of their breath. A damp, rain-filled wind came over the water from the west, the freeing breath of the world.

Ellen tried to smile. "Father!" She stretched her arms out to him. The man took a small step backward. He now stood a little behind his companions, so that his motions were invisible to them. His beseeching, bewildered eyes were fastened on the child. His right hand clutched his belt to stop its shaking. Silently, with all his might, he was trying to command Ellen.

But she was not to be stopped. Her confidence lifted her like a tornado from the midst of the pain and bitterness of her disappointment, and landed her in the wasteland of an unmasked country. With a leap she was at his throat, and she kissed him. Then he came to himself. Forcibly, he detached her hands from his shoulders with a brutal gesture and pushed her away.

"What are you doing here?" he asked sternly. "And what's this company you're keeping?"

"Oh," said Ellen, "pretty good company."

She turned, with an indulgent movement of her hand. "You can all go home now."

The bushes began to rustle quietly, then more and more loudly: leaves crackled apart; clothes were caught on thorns and torn loose with a rip. For a few seconds there was only Leon's whisper, the drag of Herbert's leg and quick, soft footsteps—then all was still.

The two soldiers had drawn back in amazement, but they received no orders, since Ellen held her father in an angry, purposeful embrace. She muffled him, kept him speechless. She clung to his shoulder straps like a little nuisance of an animal.

She was thinking, Herbert has a stiff leg, he needs more time. She thought of nothing else. She was crying, and her tears spotted his uniform. Her body was shaken by sobs, but in between the sobs she laughed, and before her father was able to free himself she bit him in the cheek.

He took out his handkerchief, tamped his mouth, and dried the spots on his jacket.

"You're sick," he said. "You must go now."

Ellen nodded.

"Will you find your way home?"

"Yes," she said quietly. "I think so." But she didn't mean the dirty section of the city where she lived with her grandmother, but the veiled, distant spaces that surrounded her.

"I'm on duty," he said, growing slowly calmer. He would be able to explain the whole thing to his superiors as a child's fevered hallucination.

"I don't want to keep you any longer," Ellen said politely.

He searched for a parting gesture, then raised a hesitant hand to the rim of his helmet. Ellen wanted to say something else, wanted to see his face once more, but she didn't move. The cone of light left her and she was in the dark.

She turned back toward the bench. "George!" she whispered.

George wasn't there. Nobody was there. They had all fled.

At that moment the wind pushed the clouds aside. Ellen ran down the steps and stood by the water. Like a bridge, the moon threw her shadow over to the other bank.

3. WEAR THE YELLOW BADGE
WITH PRIDE

ROBERT WELTSCH

The article here printed (in a translation by Harry Zohn) appeared on April, 1933, as an editorial in the prestigious Zionist periodical *Jüdische Rundschau* in Berlin. It brought a message of courage to the thousands of Jews who found themselves attacked and humiliated by the Nazi assumption of power. In the tradition of Jewish response to persecutions in the past, the editorial called for rededication, self-respect, and an acceptance of the challenge, so that the day designated by the Nazis to terrorize the Jew be turned "to a day of awakening and rebirth."

At the time, the "Yellow Badge" editorial gave inner strength to a shocked community. The new Jewish consciousness it created enabled German Jews to conduct their cultural affairs during the following ten years, as well as to organize emigration. In retrospect, however, Weltsch thinks "this article was based on a mistake"; it underestimated the true character and intentions of the enemy. One could not foresee that ten years after the appearance of the article the yellow badge would become a label for dispatch to concentration camps and gas chambers. Robert Weltsch was editor of the *Jüdische Rundschau* and is now editor of the Yearbooks of the Leo Baeck Institute (London).

NAHUM GLATZER

The first of April, 1933, will remain an important date in the history of German Jewry—indeed, in the history of the entire

Reprinted with permission of Beacon Press from *The Dynamics of Emancipation: The Jew in the Modern Age*, edited and introduced by NAHUM N. GLATZER. Copyright © 1965 by Nahum N. Glatzer.

Jewish people.[1] The events of that day have not only political and economic aspects, but moral and psychological ones as well. The political and economic implications have been widely discussed in the newspapers, although the requirements of agitation have frequently obscured an objective understanding of them. To speak about the moral aspects is our task. For no matter how often the Jewish question is discussed these days, we ourselves are the only ones who can express what is going on in the hearts of German Jews, what can be said about events from the Jewish point of view. Today Jews can speak only as Jews; anything else is utterly senseless. The spectre of the so-called "Jewish press" has been dispelled. The fatal misconception of many Jews that Jewish interests can be represented under some other cloak has been eliminated. On the first of April German Jewry was taught a lesson that goes much deeper than even its bitter and currently triumphant adversaries suppose.

Moaning is not our style. We leave it to those Jews of a bygone generation who have learned nothing and forgotten everything to react to events of such impact with sentimental twaddle. Today there must be a new note in the discussion of Jewish affairs. We live in a new era. The national revolution of the German people is a widely visible signal that the old world of concepts has collapsed. This may be painful for many, but only those who face realities can hold their own in this world. We are in the midst of a vast transformation of intellectual, political, social, and economic life. Our concern is: How does Jewry react?

The first of April, 1933, can be a day of Jewish awakening and Jewish rebirth—*if the Jews want it to be*; if the Jews are ripe for it and possess inner greatness; if the Jews are *not* as they are depicted by their adversaries.

Having been attacked, Jewry must avow its faith in itself.

Even on this day of extreme excitement, when the most tempestuous emotions fill our hearts in the face of the unprecedented phenomenon of the entire Jewish population of a great civilized country being universally outlawed, the one thing we must preserve is our composure. Even though we are staggered by the events of recent days, we must not be dismayed, but must take stock without self-deception. What should be recommended at this time is

---

1 Day of a violent boycott of Jewish businesses.

that the work which witnessed the infancy of Zionism, Theodor Herzl's *The Jewish State*,[2] be disseminated among Jews and non-Jews in hundreds of thousands of copies. If there is still left any feeling for greatness and nobility, gallantry and justice, then every National Socialist who looks into this book is bound to shudder at his own blind actions. Every Jew who reads it would also begin to understand and would be consoled and uplifted by it. Page after page of this booklet, which first appeared in 1896, would have to be copied to show that Theodor Herzl was the first Jew dispassionate enough to examine anti-Semitism in connection with the Jewish question. And he recognized that an improvement cannot be effected by ostrich-like behavior, but only by dealing with facts frankly and in full view of the world....

We Jews who have been raised in Theodor Herzl's spirit want to ask ourselves what our own guilt is, what sins we have committed. At times of crisis throughout its history, the Jewish people has faced the question of its own guilt. Our most important prayer says, "We were expelled from our country because of our sins." Only if we are critical toward ourselves shall we be just toward others.

Jewry bears a great guilt because it failed to heed Theodor Herzl's call and even mocked it in some instances. The Jews refused to acknowledge that "the Jewish question still exists." They thought the only important thing was not to be recognized as Jews. Today we are being reproached with having betrayed the German people; the National Socialist press calls us the "enemies of the nation," and there is nothing we can do about it. It is not true that the Jews have betrayed Germany. If they have betrayed anything, they have betrayed themselves and Judaism.

Because the Jews did not display their Jewishness with pride, because they wanted to shirk the Jewish question, they must share the blame for the degradation of Jewry....

The leaders of the boycott gave orders that signs "with a yellow badge against a black background" be affixed to the boycotted stores. Here is a powerful symbol. This measure is intended as an act of stigmatization, of disparagement. We accept it and propose to turn it into a badge of honor.

Many Jews had a shattering experience last Saturday. Suddenly

---

2 *See* chapter "The Jewish State" in this volume.

they were Jews—not out of inner conviction, nor out of pride in a magnificent heritage and contribution to mankind, but through the affixing of a red slip and a yellow badge. The squads went from house to house, pasting them on store fronts and business signs and painting them on windows; for twenty-four hours German Jews were put in a pillory, as it were. In addition to other marks and inscriptions one frequently saw on the shopwindows a large *Magen David*, the Shield of King David. This was supposed to be a disgrace. Jews, pick up the Shield of David and wear it honorably!

For—and this is the first task of our spiritual stock-taking—if today this shield is stained, it has not been entirely the work of our enemies. There have been many Jews whose undignified self-mockery knew no bounds. Judaism was regarded as something outmoded; people did not give it their serious attention; they wanted to free themselves of its tragic aspects by smiling. However, today there is a new type: the new, free Jew, a kind as yet unknown to the non-Jewish world. If today the National Socialist and German patriotic newspapers frequently refer to the type of the Jewish scribbler and the so-called Jewish press, if Jewry is held responsible for these factors, it must be pointed out again and again that they are not representative of Jewry, but at most have tried to derive a financial profit from the Jews. At a time of middle-class self-righteousness, these elements could expect acclamation from Jewish audiences . if they lampooned and made light of Jews and Judaism. Quite frequently these circles preached to us nationally oriented Jews the ideals of an abstract cosmopolitan in an effort to destroy all deeper values of Judaism. Upright Jews have always been indignant at the raillery and the caricature directed by Jewish buffoons against Jews to the same extent, or even a greater extent, than they aimed at Germans and others. Jewish audiences applauded their own degradation, and many attempted to create an alibi for themselves by joining in the mockery . . . .

As recently as thirty years ago it was considered objectionable in educated circles to discuss the Jewish question. In those days the Zionists were regarded as trouble-makers with an *idée fixe*. Now the Jewish question is so timely that every small child, every schoolboy as well as the man in the street have no other topic of conversation. All Jews throughout Germany were branded with the word "Jew" on April first. If there is a renewed boycott, the new directives of the boycott committee provide for a uniform designation of all shops: "German business" in the case of non-Jews, the simple word "Jew" for Jewish places. They know who is a Jew. There no longer is any evading or hiding it. The Jewish answer is clear. It is the brief sentence spoken by the prophet Jonah: *Ivri anochi*, I am a Hebrew. Yes, a Jew. The affirmation of our Jewishness—this is the moral significance of what is happening today. The times are too turbulent to use arguments in the discussion. Let us hope that a more tranquil time will come and that a movement which considers it a matter of pride to be recognized as the peacemaker of the national uprising will no longer derive pleasure from degrading others, even though it might feel that it must fight them. As for us Jews, we can defend our honor. We remember all those who were called Jews, stigmatized as Jews, over a period of five thousand years. We are being reminded that we are Jews. We affirm this and bear it with pride.

4. IN MEMORY OF
TWO OF OUR DEAD

LEO BAECK

Leo Baeck was the leader of German Jewry during its darkest hour. One of the great teachers of Judaism in our day, he lived his life according to his teachings. Baeck remained in Germany out of choice; he felt it was his duty. When he was sent to the concentration camp, he continued to teach and guide his people. In this short essay, written after his miraculous survival of the camp, Baeck looks at the early history of the Jewish community under the Nazis. Included in the selection is a prayer which the Nazis prohibited but which was nevertheless read in many synagogues during those early days of 1935.

—————

The political upheaval which came as a result of the First World War brought fundamental changes in German Jewry, both structural and in outlook and mental attitude. Areas where numerous and spiritually active communities had existed, in the East the Province of Posen and the greater part of West Prussia, went to Poland, and in the West Alsace and Lorraine, with their many flourishing, characteristic Jewish communities, returned to France. The Jews of Posen and West Prussia who felt bound to Germany by language, training and spirit almost all abandoned their homes to go to live

Reprinted with permission of East & West Library for The Leo Baeck Institute from *Year Book I.* Copyright 1956 Leo Baeck Institute.

in the new transformed Germany. The Jews in Alsace and Lorraine, who had their own linguistic and cultural milieu, and whose heart had long been with France, stayed in their places.

Thus the whole structure of German Jewry changed. To begin with, the number of Jews had diminished, the area of economic activity was restricted and, what was more significant, the number of communities was smaller. Those who had left Posen and West Prussia tried to find new homes mostly in the big cities; the number and the influence of the major communities increased. In addition, the migration from the small town to the big city, which had been determining the character of the German Jew since the last three decades of the nineteenth century continued. The Jew became mainly a city resident.

The trend of the new post-1918 Germany was to overcome the old particularism and to create a united, homogeneous State. The Jews of Germany were inspired by the same desire for unification. Attempts had been made decades before, through the *Deutsch-Israelitischen Gemeindebund*, to bring about a certain co-ordination among the Jews of Germany. But this collaboration that was started with great hopes extended only to a few minor activities. In the South-German lands, Bavaria, Wuerttemberg and Baden, the State legislation had achieved a united concentrated activity of the Jewish communities. The previous constitution in Hanover and Kurhessen had had a similar effect. Now the communities of Prussia tried to follow the example of the South-German States. The Prussian Federation of Jewish Communities (*Landesverband*) was formed. In contrast to the South-German Federations it was given a democratic basis, and a sort of Jewish Prussian Parliament was created.

This *Landesverband* found its financial support in the big wealthy Jewish communities. The big communities had their special interests and had organized their own circle to stand for the things they had in common, the *Konferenzgemeinschaft* of Jewish communities, to which the big communities of Berlin, Frankfort, Breslau and Cologne belonged. Its decisions—and they were decisions determined mostly by a sympathetic understanding for its objects—were then left not indeed formally, but in actual fact for the Prussian *Landesverband* only to ratify. This North-German Federation and the South-German Federations were in regular contact; in this way a kind of over-all representation of the Jewish communities in Germany came into being.

Much valuable work was done by the *Landesverbaende* as such, as well as by their co-operation. Special stress must be laid on the assistance rendered to the smaller communities, who were weakened by the departure of many of their members, particularly the more wealthy members. If conditions had continued quiet this development initiated by the *Landesverbaende* and by their joint consultations would have taken its normal course. When the rise of Nazism increasingly threatened the position of the Jews of Germany the demand became insistent for a representative body of the whole of German Jewry provided with adequate funds and powers.

The demand was most vocal in the two big organizations in which sections of German Jewry were divided, the Central Union of German Citizens of Jewish Faith (*Centralverein*) and the Zionist Federation of Germany. These two bodies more and more set the tone and indicated the line of thought. To them fell unmistakably the leadership—not outwardly, but because of their dynamic drive. The demand to concentrate the Jews all over Germany in a democratic form found in them increasing expression and emphasis. The leadership definitely passed from the big communities to these two bodies.

The events of January 1933 rendered abortive a plan from which much had been expected. After the 1918 Revolution the Prussian State had concluded a Concordat first with the Catholic and then with the Protestant Churches of Prussia. Responsible officials in the Prussian Education Ministry, the former Ministry of Cults, had entertained a plan of a "Jewish Concordat" inspired by the desire for official correctness and good order, but also urged on them by the Jews, who expressed the wish to have such a Concordat concluded by the Ministry with the Jews of Prussia as well. In particular, Ministerial-Direktor Trendelenburg, in whose Department the matter was dealt with, a man of strict Conservative principles, made an honest endeavour to see that this plan should be carried out. The preparatory work, which was conducted with the utmost fairness and open-mindedness, with the participation of the two Jewish experts at the Ministry, the present writer and Rabbi Dr. Esra Munk, a model of helpful co-operation, had succeeded to such an extent that by the end of 1932, at a joint conference of representatives of the Education Ministry and the Ministry of the Interior, which was also partly in charge of Jewish affairs, a bill had been drawn up for submission to the Prussian Parliament in January 1933. We have no information whether the relevant documents of the Prussian Ministry of Education have been preserved, and if so where they can be found. If they are ever brought to light it will be worthwhile to unravel the details of the history of this bill. From the writer's own experience it can be said that the officials of the Ministry, who had the assistance of State legal authorities, did a very important piece of work, which tried to create a completely new form of organizing the unification of the Jewish communities, which also provided for State assistance.

The events of 1933 found many Jews in Germany unprepared. They burst on them suddenly; it may perhaps be said that an enemy who was in retreat was handed the keys of the fortress by those who should have guarded it. But the Jews in Germany were much too optimistic about their future. At a meeting held in Allenstein at the end of the twenties for the purpose of winning support for the Keren Hayesod the present writer said that the day might come when the Homeland in the land of Israel would be needed not only for Jews from the existing areas of distress in Eastern Europe but also for the Jews of Germany. People were startled and incredulous.

The change was sudden, not only outwardly but within. The Prussian *Landesverband* and the representatives of the big Jewish communities seemed—understandably so—to be paralyzed; they did not know what to do. It was still hoped that those with whom we had worked together for decades in common activity and in common political life would be our allies, and that they would succeed in restoring sound relations. Hopes were placed in the non-Nazi members of the new Government, and the Vice-Chancellor Herr von Papen tried to foster such hopes. Even Boycott Day, 1st April, 1933, did not destroy this hope.

Realization came first in the two big organizations; through their publications, the *C. V. Zeitung* and especially the *Jüdische Rundschau*, they were able to speak to the Jews of Germany. The two papers rose in these fateful and disastrous days to the great occasion. These two organizations first came to understand that it was for us not only to become victims of the new policy of violence, but to develop and carry out our own ideas, both on the spot and in relation to the outside world, and above all to prepare our road, in conjunction with the Jews of other countries, especially Britain, the U.S.A. and Palestine. When, at a consultation of people connected with the *C.V.*, the present writer said that we could not hope for any change in the near future in the Nazi regime of violence, that we should therefore start taking our youth to other countries, and that the older folk should meanwhile stand fast and hold on to their positions as far as possible, in order to facilitate the youth emigration, one or two were dubious, but most, and the best of them, set themselves to the task. The Zionist Federation, which had the machinery already in existence in the Youth Aliyah for carrying out such a plan, did not wait for its approval. The *Hilfsverein der deutschen Juden*, which had valuable experience in this field and close relations for many years with the Jewish communities of other countries, was also an effective instrument for undertaking this work.

Moreover, it was becoming clear that the Jewish school children had to be removed from the public schools and that Jewish schools had to be provided for them. Impelled by the force of events and following on the growing realization of what was happening a provisional *Reichsvertretung* was created, which was however, in reality, only an enlarged Prussian *Landesverband,* or only an enlarged Board of the Berlin Jewish Community, and perhaps under the existing conditions that was all it could be. It was headed by the President of the Prussian *Landesverbaende* of Jewish Communities and the present writer. After a comparatively short time the latter resigned, when he saw there was no chance of carrying out the ideas that he considered essential. To say this is not intended to reproach anyone; a necessary development requires time.

But it soon appeared that a real *Reichsvertretung* of the Jews in Germany was indispensable. The two big organizations became increasingly insistent about it. Influential men like Max M. Warburg and Carl Melchior in Hamburg and Dr. Georg Hirschland in Essen offered their services. The real achievement however was that of the two big organizations. It was also due to them that people were won for the new activity. Rarely in history, perhaps never in Jewish history, has there been going on continually from month to month, such co-operation between people of different character, different ways of thought and different political convictions under such difficult conditions, with such mutual desire to understand each other, with so much trust and confidence, such recognition of what was essential and decisive, as in this small directing group. It had no real formal authority, only a moral authority and the sympathetic understanding of many of the people in the country.

Out of this small group two men who are no longer among the living must be mentioned above all, with deep gratitude, Otto Hirsch and Julius L. Seligsohn. Both came from a generation in whom the Jewish Renaissance that began at the end of the nineteenth century was alive. It was characteristic of this generation that it had definite political convictions, which were often openly expressed, yet not in party conceptions, but through a sharply impressed personality. All the ideologies which had previously separated them, like the question of 'nation or religious community' had ceased to be stubborn obsessions with them. They belonged to organized groups, but they would not let these cramp and narrow their thoughts and hopes. Otto Hirsch became the Executive Chairman of the *Reichsvertretung*, and Julius L. Seligsohn's task was to maintain the contact with the *Hilfsverein* and the Berlin Jewish Community. Both were men who could think clearly and calmly; they had nothing that was petty or biassed.

Otto Hirsch came from Wuerttemberg, a land that was in general rich as few other lands in Germany were in talent and even genius. It had produced Schiller, Hegel, and Robert Meyer. Otto Hirsch had much of the Swabian in his character and attitude, in his way of thinking, in his speech, and in his irrepressible humour. He was always proud of the land from which he came. He had a lavish ability to understand people and things. As a lawyer he had entered the administrative service of the country and had become a councillor in an important ministry, where he was entrusted especially with economic undertakings, like those connected with the construction of the Rhine-Danube Canal. He was a man who was secure in himself and therefore stood fast, a man who could be depended on. There was nothing false or faulty in him. Even when one had to contradict him, which was seldom, one had to love him. Without any desire to push himself forward he had made a name for himself in the Jewish world of Germany, and it was natural that he should conduct the business of the *Reichsvertretung*, and that the work of the *Reichsvertretung* should depend on his being there to conduct its affairs. In tireless effort, always ready to help, always ready to listen to people, he carried on for years the work of the *Reichsvertretung*. He never lost his courage. When the present writer after the burning of the Synagogues in November 1938 decided to go to the Reichs-Chancellery to make what proved a futile attempt to speak to the State Secretary, Dr. Meissner, Dr. Hirsch insisted on accompanying him to share in the danger. Soon after, but certainly unconnected with it, he was arrested with other leading officers of the *Reichsvertretung*. But since the authorities, for whatever reason, wanted to have a representative body of all the Jews in Germany, it was possible through talks with certain officials to secure his release after a few weeks. As his state of health required a carefully regulated way of life he must have suffered severely from the deprivations and hardships of imprisonment. But when he was again among us for the first time, though outwardly showing what he had endured, his personality had not changed. His first words to us were cheerful and jovial, as though he had only just returned from a journey. He went on with his work fearlessly, till he was sent to the concentration camp at Mauthausen and was tortured there to death. Shortly after he died his wife, who had been his constant, selfless companion in difficult times, consoled by their common love of music, was arrested, as she was preparing to take the plane to England; she was deported to the East and murdered. The present writer will never forget the last hours he spent with Otto Hirsch, nor the moment when his wife said goodbye to him, a heroine in her quiet way. His last words and hers were for their children, two daughters and a son, who, they were comforted to know, were abroad in safety.

Julius L. Seligsohn was born in Berlin, of a prominent family that had come from Posen, that small territory which had produced so much Jewish talent and ability—suffice it to mention but two such very different men as Heinrich Graetz and Eduard Lasker. The family belonged to the aristocracy of Jewish Berlin, an aristocracy whose distinction it was above all that it took full part in intellectual and in Jewish life. His father was one of the leading lawyers of Germany, the authority in the field of patent law. Julius L. Seligsohn had all the good qualities of the Berliner, especially the Jewish Berliner, acute reasoning, excellent wit, a sense of reality, and finally something that not many possessed, cheerful good humour, such as Otto Hirsch had. It softened and alleviated many difficulties that arose from differences of opinion. He was the conciliator, who kept up the necessary connections with the representatives of the old ways, and so removed many obstacles and cleared away many difficulties. He had a certain grace and charm; everybody loved him. He was often abroad on missions for the *Reichsvertretung*, the last time in America. He had succeeded in getting his family over there. It would have been easy for him to have stayed in the U.S.A., but his strong sense of duty brought him back to Germany.

The present writer must mention one personal experience with deep gratitude. He had been arrested in the autumn of 1935 and taken to the S.S. prison, because he had composed a prayer for the Jewish communities which tried to express Jewish pride before men and Jewish humility before God. Julius L. Seligsohn obtained a hearing from an authoritative Nazi official, an act of very great courage at that time, and, aided by foreign intervention, succeeded in securing his release. Otto Hirsch and Julius Seligsohn were both men of equal personal courage.

Julius L. Seligsohn too perished in a concentration camp, at Oranienburg. It was possible to bring his body to Berlin, where he was laid to rest in the old cemetery in the Schoenhauser Allee. At his grave the present writer was able to express something of what those who knew him felt about Julius L. Seligsohn. Is it possible that the text of what was said still exists somewhere?

Both Otto Hirsch and Julius L. Seligsohn were personally deeply religious. They were different in tone and manner, but both were full of warmth, and genuine, and a person who spoke to them often will never forget the words that penetrated to his soul.

Without Otto Hirsch and Julius L. Seligsohn the *Reichsvertretung* could never have survived the difficulties which it encountered from time to time and the dangers that threatened its work. When they were both taken from us it left a vacuum that could not be filled. As long as gratitude, perhaps the finest Jewish virtue, lives in the Jewish people these two men, who gave their lives for us, will always be remembered with loyalty and honour.

KOL NIDRE PRAYER

In this hour all Israel stands before God, the judge and the for-
giver.
In His presence let us all examine our ways, our deeds, and what
we have failed to do.
Where we transgressed, let us openly confess: "We have sinned!"
and, determined to return to God, let us pray: "Forgive us."
We stand before our God.
With the same fervor with which we confess our sins, the sins

of the individual and the sins of the community, do we, in indignation and abhorrence, express our contempt for the lies
concerning us and the defamation of our religion and its testimonies.

We have trust in our faith and in our future.

Who made known to the world the mystery of the Eternal, the
One God?

Who imparted to the world the comprehension of purity of conduct and purity of family life?

Who taught the world respect for man, created in the image of
God?

Who spoke of the commandment of righteousness, of social
justice?

In all this we see manifest the spirit of the prophets, the divine
revelation to the Jewish people. It grew out of our Judaism
and is still growing. By these facts we repel the insults flung at
us.

We stand before our God. On Him we rely. From Him issues
the truth and the glory of our history, our fortitude amidst
all change of fortune, our endurance in distress.

Our history is a history of nobility of soul, of human dignity. It
is history we have recourse to when attack and grievous wrong
are directed against us, when affliction and calamity befall us.

God has led our fathers from generation to generation. He will
guide us and our children through these days.

We stand before our God, strengthened by His commandment
that we fulfil. We bow to Him and stand erect before men.
We worship Him and remain firm in all vicissitudes. Humbly
we trust in Him and our path lies clear before us; we see our
future.

All Israel stands before her God in this hour. In our prayers, in
our hope, in our confession, we are one with all Jews on earth.
We look upon each other and know who we are; we look up to
our God and know what shall abide.

"Behold, He that keepeth Israel doth neither slumber nor sleep"
(Psalm 121:4).

"May He who maketh peace in His heights bring peace upon us
and upon all Israel" (Prayer book).

5. FROM A HISTORIAN'S NOTEBOOK
European Jewry Before and After Hitler

SALO W. BARON

During the trial of Adolf Eichmann, recurring questions arose concerning the origins of his crime. How could it have happened? Why in Germany? What were the real details of the tragedy? How many were killed —and why? Salo W. Baron, dean of Jewish historians, appeared at that time to give his testimony. He talked of the vanished community of Eastern Europe, and about the destruction of many things of which the world had been largely ignorant. Through the eyes of the historian, we come to see the full dimensions of the Holocaust and the greatness of our loss.

━━━

As a historian, not an eyewitness or a jurist, I shall concern myself with the historical situation of the Jewish people before, during, and after the Nazi onslaught—the greatest catastrophe in Jewish history, which has known many catastrophes.

A historian dealing with more or less contemporary problems confronts two major difficulties. The first is that historical perspective usually can be attained only after the passage of time. The second is that much relevant material is hidden away in archives and private collections, which are usually not open for inspection until several decades have passed. In this instance, however, the difficulties have been reduced. The world has been moving so fast

Reprinted with permission of SALO W. BARON from *American Jewish Year Book*, Volume 63, 1962.

since the end of World War II, and the situation of 1961 so little resembles that of the 1930's that one may consider the events of a quarter of a century ago as belonging almost to a bygone historic era, which the scholarly investigator can view with a modicum of detachment. In fact, a new generation has been growing up which "knew not Hitler." For its part, the older generation is often eager to forget the nightmare of the Nazi era. Hence that period has receded in the consciousness of man as if it had occurred long ago.

Furthermore, the amount of evidence available is quite extraordinary. The capture of many German archives by the Allied armies has opened up an enormous amount of information, of a kind not usually accessible until the passage of several decades. Many protagonists in the drama, moreover, have been extraordinarily articulate. Diaries, memoirs, and biographical records are so numerous that huge bibliographies would have to be compiled merely to list them. With respect to the Jewish tragedy alone, the more significant publications are abundant enough for Jacob Robinson and the late Philip Friedman to have initiated a lengthy series of specialized bibliographical guides, some of which are yet to appear. It is possible, therefore, to attempt within this brief compass a concise evaluation of the broad transformations in the life of European Jewry brought about by the twelve years of the Nazi regime, first in Germany and later in the other German-occupied areas.

EUROPEAN JEWRY IN THE 1930's

The general impression created by the Jewish people in Europe just before the Nazi era was one of extraordinary resourcefulness and vitality in the midst of a great world crisis and an equally severe crisis in Jewish life. The period between the First and Second World Wars in Europe generally resembled a prolonged armistice rather than genuine peace. The breakup of the established order; the rise of new states; the spread of Communist propaganda and the various Fascist and statist experiments in government; inflation, followed in 1929 by the Great Depression; the accelerating drive toward autarchy; the closing of frontiers to free migration; and, not least, the accompanying extremist doctrines in scholarship, letters, and the arts—all helped to keep Europe in a state of permanent tension. In Jewish life, the collapse of the oppressive tsarist empire, the international guarantees for both equality of rights and minority rights in most of the newly arisen states, and the Palestine Mandate had inspired hopes that contrasted sharply with the reality of ill-treatment in most of the territories of mass Jewish settlement, from the Baltic to the Aegean.

Such far-reaching transformations called for great ingenuity and a pioneering spirit. With courage and perseverance the Jewish people tried to adjust to the new situation not merely passively, but independently and creatively. Accustomed through the long history of their dispersion to such creative readjustments, they were able to develop during the interwar period certain new forms of communal and cultural living which fructified Jewish life throughout the world, contributed significantly to human civilization, and held out great promise for the future. All this was cut short by the Nazi attack, unprecedented in scope, geographic extension, and murderous intensity. . . .

Community Life

Emancipation and equality made great communal adjustment necessary. From ancient times the Jewish community had enjoyed much self-determination, not only in strictly religious matters but also in education, social welfare, and the administration of justice. Under Emancipation some of these prerogatives, originally supported by the European states themselves, had to be curtailed. The Jewish judiciary, in particular, lost much of its authority over the Jews in civil and criminal law, retaining jurisdiction mainly in religious and family affairs. Nevertheless, in Eastern and Central Europe many Jews continued, voluntarily, to submit their civil litigations to rabbinic courts, judging on the basis of Jewish law. Even in the 20th century legal problems were intensively studied by thousands of students of rabbinics both for theoretical reasons and for their practical application. Education, too, had to be shared now with the general school systems maintained by states and municipalities. However, as we shall see, the Jewish communities often maintained a ramified school system of their own, in supplementation to, or in substitution for, the public schools of the country. In social welfare, which until the modern development of the welfare state had always borne a predominantly denominational character, the Jewish communities strove, often with signal success, to take care of their own poor.

The Jewish communities revealed a remarkable adaptability to changing conditions. In France the reorganization of all Jewish communal life through the so-called consistorial system of the Napoleonic age was successfully maintained, with the necessary modifications, under the Napoleonic dictatorship, the Restoration, the Second Empire, and the Third Republic, despite the intimate relationships between the Jewish communal structure and the changing governmental controls. (Through most of that period the government actually defrayed a major part of the salaries of rabbis and other religious functionaries.) This structure was maintained on a voluntary basis after the separation of state and church in 1906. In the absence of governmental intervention, Jewish creativeness, especially during the interwar period, expressed itself in the formation of many new congregations, charitable associations, and cultural groupings, spontaneously organized by diverse immigrant groups. This rich and multicolored Jewish communal organization maintained a host of institutions serving the various needs of French Jewry and of Jews beyond the borders. On the other hand, Italian Jewry, which during the liberal era of united Italy from 1871 to the rise of the Fascist regime had experienced a certain degeneration and disorganization of communities rich in traditions hundreds of years old—if not, as in Rome, two thousand years old—succeeded in regaining some unity and central guidance in the interwar period. In 1929 Benito Mussolini and the Pope concluded the Lateran treaty, whereby the Catholic Church was reestablished as Italy's dominant religion; in 1931 Jews secured from the dictator a new communal law reorganizing the Jewish communal life of the entire country under the leadership of a centralized *Unione*. Whether in Italy or in France, such central organization did not interfere with the autonomous workings of the individual communal groups, including the numerous voluntary associations. The balance reflected the age-old compromise between centralized controls and local self-government, in force ever since the Babylonian Exile and the Graeco-Roman dispersion. The same unity within diversity was achieved also in Belgium, where the consistorial system along French lines had persisted throughout the interwar period, and in Holland, where since 1816 the Ashkenazi and Sephardi communities had central organizations in their "church associations." In particular, Amsterdam, that famous center of Jewish learning, had had a proliferation of Jewish voluntary associations as early as the 18th century. A characteristic will of an Amsterdam Jewish philanthropist, in the early years of the 19th century, provided bequests for over 200 charitable and educational societies.

Even more vigorous was Jewish community life in Germany and in the successor states of the Hapsburg empire. Although Prussia's community law of 1876 permitted the Jews to leave their community "for religious scruples," thus enabling some ultra-Orthodox Jews to form their independent congregations and others to leave the Jewish community altogether without joining another faith, the vast majority of Jews adhered to the traditional community, which was endowed by public law with the right of taxation for the support of its varied activities. In 1922 the Prussian communities organized a *Landesverband* to give these communal efforts a central direction, without interfering with the autonomy of the local groups. Similar *Landesverbände* were established in Bavaria and other states, while Baden and Württemberg had had such centralized guidance since the beginning of the 19th century. In the Austro-Hungarian empire, on the other hand, the diversity of its Jewries prevented the establishment of centralized authority, but the law of 1891 renewed, on a modern basis, the old public law recognition of Jewish communal autonomy and taxing powers. Here, too, many secularized Jews had a choice of leaving the community without converting to another faith, but, in contrast to Prussia, they had to declare publicly their secession on the ground that they were *konfessionslos* (professing no religion). In fact, the number of such professedly irreligious Jews was rather limited, the majority respecting the authority of their elected leaders in religious and cultural affairs. In interwar Austria the numerical preponderance of Viennese Jewry was so pronounced (in 1934, 176,000 of the 191,480 Austrian Jews lived in the capital) that the Viennese rabbis and lay leaders had *de facto* leadership over all Austrian Jewry, without formal authority. In Hungary, where 46 per cent of the Jewish population resided in Budapest, the struggle between Reform and Orthodoxy had led in the 19th century to a separation between Orthodox and liberal communities. A group of united or so-called *status quo* communities bridged the gap, and gained formal recognition from the Hungarian government in 1929. From 1928 on, rabbis of both the Orthodox and liberal wings sat in the upper chamber of the Hungarian parliament as representatives of the Jewish community. Czechoslovakia had a more diversified structure, with Bohemia, Moravia, and Silesia largely following the Austrian pattern, while Slovakia and Carpatho-Ruthenia, besides maintaining the communal structure inherited from prewar Hungary, differed from the others in mores, speech, and intensity of Orthodoxy. This diversity stimulated rather than hindered Jewish creativeness.

That creativeness was richest in interwar Poland and Lithuania. In Poland, although the government of the new republic effectively sabotaged some of the minority safeguards of the 1919 peace treaty, the Jewish communities before and after the community law of 1931 enjoyed a great measure of autonomy. Of course, there were important organizational differences between the provinces formerly under Austrian or Prussian domination and those formerly under Russian rule. In the former, Emancipation had been achieved decades before the First World War, and the Jewish community had a more circumscribed status. In the latter, to be sure, the Tsar had abolished the *Kahal* in 1844, but a partly voluntary communal structure was quite vigorous. The size of the Jewish population and the fact that in most Polish cities the Jews were a substantial minority, if not an outright majority, made communal autonomy doubly meaningful. Its extension into many secular cultural domains was often imposed by the will of the Jewish population against considerable governmental resistance. In fact, Orthodoxy, forming only one of many parties, was not even in control of most communities. Despite full governmental support for Orthodoxy, which also found expression in the community law of 1931, the electorate often preferred leadership from the more secular Zionist and socialist parties. In the elections of 1936 many communal boards actually included members of the Socialist Bund as the largest party. Communal elections were taken with the utmost seriousness, being regarded as not less important than the parliamentary elections, in which a strong Jewish representation carried on the constant uphill struggle for Jewish rights. In Lithuania, where the assimilatory pressures of the relatively young nationalism were far less intense, Jewish communal self-government was even more extensive. Of the 19,500 Jews in the Lithuanian school population in 1930, 16,000 were in all-Jewish schools. Lithuania also had for some time a special ministry of Jewish affairs. To a lesser extent that was true of Latvia and Estonia as well. . . .

It would take us too far afield to discuss the variegated functions of these communal groups in any detail. The communities and their subdivisions took care of the religious needs of their constituents. They maintained synagogues, large and small, to accommodate as few as ten and as many as thousands of adult male worshippers. Since traditionally Jewish law did not consider the synagogue building but rather the congregation as essential, any ten Jews meeting almost anywhere, even in a cave or an open field, were able to worship as effectively as those assembled in a monumental edifice. This made it possible for even the smallest community or movement in Jewry, meeting if necessary in a private home, to perform religious services wholly on a par with those of the most elaborate synagogues. Of course, wherever possible communities lavished of their bounty on building and decorating magnificent structures, within the limitations of the anti-imagery injunctions of biblical law. But the beautiful baroque structure of Leghorn or the magnificent Sephardi synagogue in Amsterdam were no more cherished than the small Rashi Chapel of Worms, which though not authentically going back to the times of the great 11th-century Bible commentator, was an important medieval monument of Jewish religious architecture. So was the *Altneuschul* in Prague, with its many memories of medieval Jewish life and with legends reaching back to pre-Christian antiquity. Similarly, the relatively small and inconspicuous wooden synagogues in certain Polish cities have long been recognized as genuine expressions of a peculiarly Polish Jewish architectural style, which added a significant chapter to the history of art. On the other hand, it was possible for the various chasidic groups, following their diverse leaders, to establish small conventicles of their own which, whether in their original East-Central European habitat or in their countries of immigration in Western Europe and the New World, readily developed into congregations of their own kind. But even this inherent diversity of rituals, rather than interfering with the basic unity of Jewish worship, merely kept the gate open to the creativity of poets, cantors, and preachers, which greatly enriched Jewish life.

From time immemorial these sacred structures stood under the protection of public law. Even in the pagan Roman empire any attack on a synagogue was considered as sacrilege. When, after the rise of Christianity to a dominant position in the Roman empire, some frenzied mobs tried to convert synagogues into churches, as a rule the emperors punished the evildoers, demanded restoration of the synagogues or, if it was too late, full compensation. One such incident led to the great controversy between Emperor Theodosius, himself rather unfriendly to the Jews, and St. Ambrose of Milan—one of the earliest recorded conflicts between state and church. Protection of Jewish houses of worship, indeed, was enjoined by canon and civil law and reiterated by popes, emperors, and kings throughout the Christian Middle Ages and early modern times. It was left to the Nazis during the *Kristallnacht* of November 9–10, 1938, to stage a wholesale destruction of synagogues as part of a well-thought-out "spontaneous" reaction of the German people. Two days later the infamous Reinhardt Heydrich rejoiced that in that night 101 synagogues had been destroyed and 76 others severely damaged, to the eternal "glory" of the Nazi party.

Similar vandalism affected the other major religious institution, the cemetery. For reasons which are perhaps not too difficult to explain, sadists of all ages often vented their spleen on the graves of deceased "enemies." In their so-called constitutions in favor of Roman Jewry, the popes found it necessary generation after generation to repeat their injunction against the violation of Jewish tombs. Secular legislation often followed suit, although many malefactors still found it possible to wreak vengeance on dead Jews, if they could not injure the living. Not surprisingly, during the interwar period hoodlums often attacked Jewish cemeteries in Germany and other countries. The Jewish communities tried to stave off such attacks, repaired the damages, and generally kept their "houses of eternity" in good order. This communal function was all the more important in the 20th century, as many Jews who otherwise maintained few contacts with the Jewish community nevertheless sought their resting place in a Jewish burial ground. Incidentally, cemeteries could also serve as vehicles of social justice. Not only were the egalitarian forms of burial apt to level some class distinctions, but also cemetery administrations were often able to tax wealthy but uncharitable members above the average, thus somewhat equal-izing the philanthropic and welfare burdens of their constituents.

Welfare activities were for the most part carried on by charitable associations acting under the supervision of the community at large. With the aid of philanthropically-minded individuals the community, directly or through its subdivisions, was able to establish a far-flung net of hospitals, orphanages, and homes for the aged; extend relief to the poor, in kind or money; take care of victims of fires and similar disasters; help the poor to educate their children or marry off their daughters, and create loan banks and otherwise help artisans and shopkeepers to embark upon new ventures or to weather a temporary emergency. Polish Jewry alone maintained 826 free-loan banks, with a capital of more than $2,000,000. The extent and ramifications of these activities were so great that hardly ever did a Jew die from actual starvation or lack of all medical care—through even in times of peace in the 20th century, famine and untreated disease still caused death in Europe. Jewish hospitals also helped to offset discrimination against Jewish physicians in general hospitals. They often also served as centers of medical research, the fruits of which accrued to the benefit of the world at large. Even where the separation between Jews and Gentiles had been traditionally very stringent, these hospitals and other Jewish charitable institutions often helped Christians. On the whole, despite the growth of social consciousness and governmental welfare programs, the Jewish philanthropies still performed a major function in the interwar period and added another justification to the traditional claim of the Jewish people of being *rahamanim bene rahamanim,* merciful sons of merciful sires.

Intellectual Life

Among the most important communal activities was Jewish education. The Jewish people had an age-old insistence upon learning as a great virtue in itself and a vital fulfillment of man's mission on earth. With pride the Jews remembered that they were the first to introduce publicly supported schools for the entire male population from the age of six or seven. This great educational reform had been introduced in the first century, at a time when even the great Graeco-Roman civilization was offering instruction only to a select few. It thus anticipated the modern public school by 17 centuries. Ever since, Jews cultivated the teaching of the youth as a major obligation of both the family and the community, while insisting also upon adult education to the end of one's life.

True to these traditions, interwar European Jewry maintained an elaborate school system and also provided extensive opportunities for self-instruction and adult education. It is truly remarkable with what creative elan the Jews of the newly independent Poland threw themselves into the task of building a novel system of education, corresponding to the different ideologies represented within the Jewish community. The Polish government, which sufficiently respected other minority rights to subsidize an extensive network of Ukrainian and German schools, evaded its responsibilities toward the independent Jewish school system, but the Jewish community was ready to expend its own money and effort. A large majority of the Orthodox population sent their children to the thousands of traditional *hadarim*, which either provided full-time instruction or gave supplementary Jewish education to the children attending the Polish public schools. In the 1930's 18,000 Jewish youth attended *yeshivot*, some of which were secondary schools up to college level. Besides these traditional schools were two major school systems, with Yiddish and Hebrew as languages of instruction. The Central Yiddish School Organization, the so-called CIShO, founded in 1921, drew its main support from the Bund and the Left Po'ale-Zion. Offering instruction in Yiddish, though using Polish history and geography, the CIShO schools had a secular curriculum with a predominantly socialist ideology. A statistical account for 1934-35, though incomplete, furnishes an idea of the size and extent of that system. The 86 schools listed gave instruction to 9,936 children, predominantly in the formerly Russian areas—45 of those schools, with 4,730 pupils, being concentrated in the provinces of Bialystok and Vilna alone. On the other hand, the central organization of Hebrew schools, called *Tarbut,* offered modern Hebrew instruction permeated with the Zionist ideology. In 1938 it had 70 school buildings and maintained 75 nurseries, 104 elementary schools, and 9 high schools, with an enrolment of 42,241 pupils and a staff of 1,350 teachers. Here again, most of those schools were in the eastern provinces of Bialystok, Vilna, Novogrodek, and Volhynia. (Polish culture attracted many more Jews in the ethnically Polish area of the old Kingdom of Poland and in Galicia than in the ethnically mixed eastern provinces, where the majority was Byelorussian or Ukrainian.) In all, it was estimated in 1934–37 that private Jewish schools had an enrolment of 81,895 in primary grades, 14,514 on the high-school level, and 7,821 in vocational institutions. Thus, while only 19.2 per cent of the Jewish primary-school population attended private Jewish schools, the rest going to public schools, the ratio rose to 50 per cent for high schools and 60 per cent for vocational schools. Some of the public schools maintained by the government, the so-called Sabbath schools, were set aside for Jewish children. These offered the regular public-school program but observed Saturday as the day of rest. There were also Jewish schools of higher learning, both of the *yeshivah* and the modern seminary types, particularly the rabbinical and teachers' seminary in Warsaw. The Yiddish Scientific Institute—YIOVO in Vilna, though also a training institution, was preeminently a research institute. At the same time, of course, Jews attended general universities and other schools of higher learning. Despite discouragement by the authorities and an often hostile reaction by fellow students, 5,682 Jewish students attended Polish universities in 1936–37, many other young Jewish men and women attending universities abroad. In short, interwar Poland reveals an intensity of Jewish educational effort which, in the absence of support by public taxation, was almost unparalleled in Europe's educational history.

Even more intensive was Jewish education in Lithuania, where fewer than 12 per cent of Jewish students attended non-Jewish institutions paralleled by Jewish schools. In 1938 there were 107 Jewish primary schools with 13,856 pupils and 14 Jewish high schools with about 3,000. Most of these Jewish schools, predominantly of the *Tarbut* type, received governmental subsidies. In neighboring Latvia, too, 85.5 per cent of Jewish schoolchildren attended Jewish schools in 1935–36, though the proportion was somewhat lower on the secondary-school level. As in other countries, the Jewish school system was divided between the Orthodox, Zionist, and Yiddishist groups, only the Orthodox being able to maintain two *yeshivot* giving instruction beyond high-school age.

It was in the Soviet Union, of course, that the secularization of the Jewish school was most pronounced. Among the tremendous adjustments enforced by the Revolution was a complete transformation of the Jewish educational structure, the old *hadarim, yeshivot,* and Zionist schools being replaced by a Yiddish school system extending from the primary grades to scientific institutes and sectors at the universities. With the temporary aid of the government, Yiddish teachers, writers and communal workers established schools in the Ukraine and White Russia which, within a decade, accommodated some 100,000 Jewish pupils. True, the Jewish content of these school programs was rather meager. After eliminating the Bible, Talmud, Hebrew literature, and most of Jewish history, all that remained was a bit of modern Yiddish literature and the history of a few decades. It made little difference whether the Communist Manifesto and Lenin's speeches were taught in Yiddish or in Russian. Like other schools of the totalitarian regime, these two were instruments for indoctrinating the youth. Nevertheless, an element of Jewish culture was retained which, under favorable conditions, might have developed a new approach to Jewish life, both in scholarship and in art. Unfortunately, here, as in Poland, the repercussions of the Nazi propaganda in the 1930's put an end to whatever auspicious beginnings had been made in the first 15 years after the Revolution.

Totally different was the development of Jewish schools in the older countries of Emancipation. In France, Belgium, and the Netherlands the large majority of Jewish schoolchildren attended general schools, both public and private. There were some special Jewish schools, serving immigrant families mostly. In 1939 France had 3 elementary Jewish day schools, 1 high school, 2 vocational boarding schools, 2 Talmud Torahs, 16 *hadarim,* and a number of part-time schools, some maintained by the Central Consistory. On a higher level there were some *yeshivot,* two teachers' seminaries, and the Ecole Rabbinique. The latter's antecedents went back to 1704, but it had been reorganized in Metz in 1829 and again in Paris in 1859. Simultaneously the Alliance Israélite Universelle made a valiant effort to spread Jewish, together with French, education through many countries of the Near East and North Africa. In 1931 it maintained 27 schools in the Balkans alone, with a school population of over 10,000.

Germany, Austria, and Hungary offered more intensive Jewish education. Among the day schools in Germany the Jewish Free School in Berlin, the Philanthropin in Frankfort on the Main, and the Talmud Torah in Hamburg dated back to the late 18th or early 19th century. In 1926–27, despite continuous attrition, 96 Jewish day schools still operated in Prussia, 25 in Bavaria, and 3 in Württemberg. In 1931, in Germany, 8,000 pupils attended 149 Jewish elementary schools and 2,000 attended 12 Jewish high schools, the two school systems employing 600 teachers—despite the tremendous attraction of the general school, and more broadly of German culture, for almost two centuries. In Austria the Viennese Chajes Realgymnasium, founded in 1919, had an international reputation. Several high schools in Budapest likewise offered excellent training to Jewish boys and girls, one of them being attached to the Francis Joseph Central Rabbinical Seminary, founded in 1867. This institution and its sister schools in Breslau (1854), in Berlin (the Hochschule für die Wissenschaft des Judentums, 1870, and the Rabbinerseminar, 1873), and Vienna (Israelitisch-Theologische Lehranstalt, 1893) were leading centers of modern Jewish scholarship, the *Wissenschaft des Judentums*. Between the two wars they provided rabbis and teachers not only for the Central European schools but also for the rest of Europe and many countries overseas. There also were several excellent teachers' seminaries, including the Jüdisches Pädagogium in Vienna, whose alumni served in schools all over the world.

It goes without saying that Jews also participated actively both as teachers and as students in general education. Anti-Semites often denounced the alleged Jewish domination of the German schools of higher learning. According to an early Nazi writer, Rudolf Jung, there were 937 Jews among the 3,140 teachers in the German institutions of higher learning in 1914. This figure seems to be exaggerated, but there is no question that the ratio of Jews in the academic profession rose in the liberal Weimar Republic. In Austria, Czechoslovakia, and Hungary, too, the number of Jewish professors was constantly on the rise, despite sharp discrimination against them by most universities and state authorities. Ignaz Goldziher, perhaps the greatest western student of Islamic history and thought, was forced to earn his living as a secretary of the Jewish community of Budapest because he was long refused an appointment to the university. After the First World War, to be sure, he had achieved a worldwide reputation and his presence on the faculty conferred much lustre on the University of Budapest. Where discrimination was almost wholly absent, as in interwar France and Italy, the ratio of Jewish professors was high.

Besides their schools, the Jewish communities often maintained major repositories for the cultural treasures accumulated over the centuries. Almost all well-organized Jewish communities had archives of their own, which were often many decades, and sometimes centuries, old. Among the most renowned Jewish archival collections were those of Rome, Mantua, Amsterdam, Frankfort, Berlin, Hamburg, and Vienna. To assure the preservation of documents of Jewish interest in Germany, particularly in smaller communities, the Gesamtarchiv der deutschen Juden, founded in Berlin in 1905, assembled them in its own building and regularly reported accessions in its *Mitteilungen,* of which six volumes appeared between 1909 and 1926. No such central organization operated in other countries, but YIVO in Vilna and other organizations made consistent efforts to keep alive the testimony of the Jewish past. Several Jewish communities and institutions also maintained splendid libraries and museums in which were housed significant collections of Hebraica and Judaica, including manuscripts and incunabula. Among the most renowned Jewish libraries were those of the five German, Austrian, and Hungarian seminaries, the Alliance in Paris, the Bibliotheca Montezinos in Amsterdam, the Tlomackie Street Library in Warsaw, the Straszun and YIVO libraries in Vilna, and several communal libraries in Russia, which were incorporated into major Soviet state libraries. Numerous private libraries likewise achieved great distinction, such as those of David Kaufmann, which ultimately found its way into the library of the Budapest Academy of Science, of Baron Günzburg, which was taken over by the Lenin Library in Moscow, and of David Simonsen, which became part of the National Library of Copenhagen. Many lesser communities maintained libraries of their own, some of a specialized character, like the Medem Farband's Yiddish collection in Paris. In addition, almost every larger synagogue and academy of learning had a library, sometimes of considerable size and distinction. They had also often assembled over the generations precious Torah scrolls and their accoutrements together with other objects, exemplars of Jewish art. Special museums, too, existed in major communities like Berlin, Frankfort, and Vienna. For some of the older communities, like Worms, it was a matter of pride to maintain a museum and archive which included such precious items as a two-volume *Mahzor* of 1272, imperial privileges dating from 1551 on, and many ceremonial objects of the 16th and 17th centuries. The *Tentative List of Jewish Cultural Treasures in Axis-Occupied Countries,* prepared under my direction by Dr. Hannah Arendt and associates and published by the Commission on European Jewish Cultural Reconstruction in New York in 1946, was able to list no fewer than 430 such institutions which had existed in the European countries before the Nazi occupation. Of course, there were also significant collections of Jewish books, documents, and art objects in general libraries, archives, and museums, many of which had come there from private Jewish collectors. No fewer than 274 important general repositories were likewise recorded in the *Tentative List.* Partly on the basis of that inventory, the Allied occupation forces in Germany were able to recover more than a million Jewish books of identifiable origin and nearly 500,000 volumes whose ownership could not be identified. Their distribution helped to enrich the cultural treasures of Israel and of many of the younger communities in the dispersion.

An astonishing number of Jewish periodicals appeared in Europe before the Nazi occupation. Even the small Jewish reading public in France had at its disposal 96 Jewish journals, including 2 Yiddish dailies and 6 French, 5 Yiddish, and 1 Russian weekly. The Netherlands had 21 Jewish periodicals, Austria 19, Hungary 21, Rumania 54, and Lithuania 15. Germany's 113 publications included 33 official *Gemeindeblätter,* issued by Jewish communities. Poland produced the astounding total of 30 Yiddish and 5 Polish dailies, besides 132 weeklies, 4 of them in Hebrew. There were also 224 fortnightlies, quarterlies, and the like. In all, the list of Jewish periodicals in Axis-occupied countries includes 854 items. Of course, some of these were merely ephemeral publications or otherwise little worthy of note. But some possessed great journalistic, scholarly, or literary value, and their influence extended far beyond the borders of their countries. Dailies like *Hajnt,* and *Nasz Przeglad* in Warsaw and *Chwila* in Lwów, a weekly like *Die jüdische Rundschau* in Berlin, and literary and scholarly journals such as the *Monatsschrift für Geschichte und Wissenschaft des Judentums,* published in Breslau from 1851 to 1939, the *Revue des études juives,* established in 1881 in Paris, *Magyar Zsidó Szemle* in Budapest, YIVO *Bleter* and *Ha-*

tekufah in Poland, had international importance. So had some journals devoted largely to the history and culture of particular countries, such as the yearbook published by the Czechoslovak Jewish Historical Society, the *Zeitschrift für die Geschichte der Juden in Deutschland*, the *Rassegna mensile di Israel* in Italy, and the *Tsaytshrift* in Minsk. Nor was there a lack of specialized journals for art, social welfare, crafts, and trades. Jewish journalism, starting with 17th century Amsterdam and including such weeklies as the *Allgemeine Zeitung des Judentums*, which was founded in Berlin in 1837 and continued for nearly a century, was a potent expression of the various cultural, social, and political movements within European Jewry. Even Greece had two Ladino dailies and one Ladino yearbook, as well as a Greek monthly, all attesting to the renaissance of the Sephardi world in the Balkans and its creative response to the impact of westernization on the Near Eastern Jewries.

Even more significant, in many ways, was the constant stream of books and pamphlets in Hebrew, Yiddish, Ladino, and nearly all local languages, produced by Jews (and some non-Jews) and relating to Jewish subjects. In no other domain can one so readily see the vitality of the European Jewish communities before the Catastrophe. Even in the Soviet Union, where the Revolution enforced a nearly total break with the past, Yiddish books on all sorts of political, historical, and scholarly subjects, as well as belles lettres, poured out of the government-owned presses. I vividly remember the pride with which the vice president of the White Russian Academy of Science announced to me in 1937 that his Academy was publishing a Yiddish scholarly book at an average rate of one a week.

When a short time thereafter I prepared a *Bibliography of Jewish Social Studies*, 1938–1939, I did not realize that those two years were to mark an end of the European epoch in Jewish history. I was able to list more than 5,000 publications of permanent interest during those two years. Unfortunately, too much space had to be assigned to anti-Semitic outpourings in Germany and elsewhere, as well as to a considerable number of apologias written in the defense of Jews and Judaism by both Jews and Christians. However, the overwhelming majority of the publications were devoted to the cultivation of traditional Jewish learning, modern Jewish scholarship, contemporary Jewish affairs, and critical analyses of Yiddish and Hebrew letters. I was amazed by the intensity which East and Central European Jewry gave to the production of "old-fashioned" responsa, homilies, ethical writings, and kabalistic, chasidic, and other works of *halachah* and *agadah*. It is no exaggeration to say that Polish Jewry alone produced in those two years more works of this traditional kind of Jewish scholarship than in any decade of the 17th or 18th century, the heyday of rabbinic learning. Many of these multi-volumed folio works had a sufficiently broad market to appear within a few years in third and fourth editions. Among them were works of outstanding scholarship, which, if written several hundred years earlier, would have earned for their authors distinguished places in the history of Jewish letters. As it was, they still appealed greatly to an enthusiastic following of millions of Jews not only in their home countries but also in Palestine, America, and elsewhere. Together with the educational work of the leading *yeshivot* in Lithuania, Poland, and Hungary, this literary output held out great promise for the continued flowering of rabbinic learning in Eastern and Central Europe and in its offshoots in other lands.

At the same time, European Jewry produced significant modern Hebrew and Yiddish literary studies and works in the various disciplines of the *Wissenschaft des Judentums*. Great poets, like Hayyim Nahman Bialik and Saul Tchernikhovsky in Hebrew, and David Pinski, Abraham Reisen, and Shalom Asch in Yiddish, may have been forced out of their native habitat; they had to transplant themselves at a mature age to Palestine, the United States, or other countries. But they had gifted disciples in both languages who carried on their work in Poland and the adjacent lands.

Apart from creative writing, much effort was devoted to the reconstruction of the Jewish past. Outstanding historians like Simon Dubnow, Majer Balaban, Ignaz Schipper, Philip Friedman, and Emanuel Ringelblum, writing predominantly in Russian and Polish but also in Yiddish and Hebrew, were joined by such western students of Jewish history as Eugen Täubler, Ismar Elbogen, Umberto Cassuto, Isaiah Sonne, and Ludwig Blau (a reasonably full list of names would occupy more space than can be allotted here), whose works originally appeared in German, Italian, or some other western language. The Berlin Academy's training of young scholars for the future was alone immensely productive. A few of its young re-search fellows, who subsequently became outstanding scholars, were Hanoch Albeck, Isaac Fritz Baer, Gershom Scholem, Selma Stern, and Leo Strauss. There were, of course, many other institutions of learning, particularly the seminaries, which gave their faculty mem-bers a chance to devote their lives to the scholarly investigation of Jewish life and letters in the past and the present. Apart from train-ing a multitude of rabbis and teachers, the seminaries also gave them sufficient scholarly training for a career at a university or a Jewish school of higher learning. Taken as a whole, the preoccupation of European Jewry with Jewish scholarship, arts, and letters exceeded in intensity that of any earlier modern generation.

All this did not keep Jews from contributing significantly to the science, literature, and art of the nations. Polish Jewry had been separated for centuries from Polish culture, yet Julian Tuwim and Antoni Slonimski belonged to the leading Polish poets of their generation. Jewish writers in Germany and Austria, such as Franz Kafka, Max Brod, Franz Werfel, Arthur Schnitzler, Richard Beer Hoffmann, Stefan and Arnold Zweig, and Jakob Wasserman achieved international reputations. Catulle Mendès, Henry Bern-stein, and André Spire were some of the important Jewish authors in 20th-century France. Soviet Jewry produced in Isaac Babel and Boris Pasternak two of the leading Russian writers of our time. In music the names are too many to list, and it is enough to mention the great composers Arnold Schönberg, Darius Milhaud, and Ernest Bloch. Painters include Max Liebermann, Lesser Ury, Soutine, Mo-digliani, Kisling, and Chagall; sculptors, Henryk (Enrico) Glicen-stein, and architects, Erich Mendelsohn and Julius Flegenheimer. What the generally anti-Jewish *Novoye Vremya* wrote in tsarist days about the painter Isaac Levitan could be applied as well to some Jewish artists in other lands: "This full-blooded Jew knew, as no other man, how to make us understand and love our plain and homely country scenes."

Among scientists and scholars there are no greater names than those of Albert Einstein and Sigmund Freud. Distinguished philos-ophers included Hermann Cohen, Emile Durkheim, Lucien Lévy-Bruhl, Ernst Cassirer, and Martin Buber. Many East European Jews would have achieved an international reputation if they had lived and worked in the west. Certainly, Emile Meyerson would not have been the renowned philosopher that he was if he had remained in his native Lublin. Some of the great Jewish thinkers and scholars, to be sure, found their way to the baptismal font, but, for one example, Henry Bergson, the son of a Warsaw Jew who toward the end of his life felt the strong attraction of Catholic mysticism, refused to be converted because, as he expressed it in his will of 1937, he had "seen in preparation for so many years this formidable wave to anti-Semitism which will soon overthrow the world. I wanted to remain among those who tomorrow will be the persecuted ones." While few of these thinkers immersed themselves in the Jewish tradition, Franz Rosenzweig, like Buber, not only drew much of his inspiration from Jewish sources, but also blazed new paths in Jewish philosophy and theology. To list the names of other eminent Jewish scientists and scholars, particularly in medicine and law, would require too much space. Before Hitler's rise to power Austro-German Jewry alone furnished the majority of the 17 Jewish Nobel Prize winners in 1907–30.

A mere enumeration of names, however distinguished, cannot begin to convey the richness and variety of these extraordinary minds and personalities. One had to have the good fortune of being befriended, as I was, by the great poet Bialik to feel the impact of his genius, which expressed itself not only in a series of immortal poems, but also in an endless outpouring of words of wisdom in any private conversation, however casual. It is a pity that only toward the end of his life did some disciples make an effort to record some of these for posterity. One had to know Chaim Weizmann well before one could assess the extraordinary combination of shrewdness and humor, statesmanlike realism and prophetic vision, of the man whom David Lloyd George styled the new Nehemiah of the Jewish people. Only close acquaintance could resolve in one's mind the apparent paradox of Albert Einstein—supreme mathematical genius together with unworldliness and an almost childlike humanity. Nor should we forget the multitude of anonymous saints, heroic in charity and self-sacrifice. The interwar generation seems to have produced more than the legendary thirty-six nameless righteous men, whose undetected and redemptive presence is said to sustain the world.

Of course, the Jewish people also had its sinners and idiots, thieves and lunatics. But on balance, future historians are likely to call the first third of the 20th century the golden age of Askenazi Jewry in Europe, just as they will see in it the beginning of a modern Sephardi renaissance.

The notable achievements by Jews provoked envy and resentment among unfriendly non-Jews, while at times filling some Jews with excessive pride. The reason for the ability of Jews to make such contributions is not difficult to ascertain. To the historian, the explanation is to be sought in the long history of the Jewish people and its position in contemporary society. As a permanent minority for some two thousand years, Jews were forced to seek the kinds of openings that were available to newcomers. As a rule, wherever they settled they found the established positions occupied by members of the majority. Hence they were forced to look for new opportunities. When they found and used such opportunities, they were working for both their own benefit and that of society as a whole. I have long believed that much of Jewish history ought to be rewritten in terms of the pioneering services which the Jews were forced to render by the particular circumstances of their history. Moreover, the Jews have always cherished learning above all other values. Even with respect to religious commandments, the ancient rabbis asserted that the study of Torah outweighed them all. Maimonides, the great philosopher, jurist, and physician, had advised the Jews to devote only three hours a day to earning a living, if at all possible, and at least nine hours more to the study of Jewish law. These counsels sank so deep into the mind of the people that most Jewish women through the ages dreamed of their sons becoming distinguished rabbis and scholars. With the modern secularization of life, those ambitions were directed to the arts and sciences. Finally, and ironically, the very anti-Semites who complained of Jewish over-representation in intellectual life, actually contributed to it. Precisely because discrimination against Jewish students, artists, and writers was so widely prevalent, they were forced to work doubly hard and often to do better than their neighbors if they wished to find a place in the sun. In short, it was no biological pre-disposition, but, rather an unusual concatenation of historic circumstances which accounted for this extraordinary intellectual and artistic fecundity of 20th-century European Jewry.

UNDER THE NAZI HEEL

It was in recognition of the cultural importance of the Jews that the Nazis almost immediately after achieving power sought to combat them intellectually. Quite early they established a special Jewish research division in their Reichsinstitut für Geschichte des neuen Deutschlands in Munich. This was followed by the Institut zur Erforschung der Judenfrage in Frankfort, the directorship of which was entrusted to the leading ideologist of the Nazi movement, Alfred Rosenberg. The Institut worked hard to assemble a library of Judaica and Hebraica which could be used for attacking the Jewish people and its religion. After confiscating many German and French collections, including the Rothschild archives and the library of the Alliance Israélite Universelle, the Frankfort institution brought together by 1941 some 350,000 volumes which could serve to support whatever distortions of the Jewish past were dictated by the Nazi ideology. Even the vulgar anti-Semite Julius Streicher, who needed no "scholarly" evidence for his pornographic attacks on the Jews, assembled a substantial collection of Hebraica, most of which is now in New York, on which he employed a number of so-called experts to find passages usable in his anti-Jewish propaganda. With the spread of the New Order, the Germans saw to it that similar institutes for the study of "the Jewish question" were also established in Paris, where it was affiliated with the Department of Jewish Affairs, and in Lodz. The Institut fur deutsche Ostarbeit, founded in Cracow in 1940, likewise concerned itself with Jewish matters, as did a special professorship in Jewish history and languages attached to the newly established University of Poznan in 1941. Under Nazi prompting, Italy made available in 1942 research facilities for the study of race and Jewish matters at the universities of Florence, Bologna, Milan and Trieste.

Otherwise, anti-intellectualism dominated Nazi ideology and greatly contributed to the sudden decline of the great German universities and research organizations. Typical of the new approach was the exclamation of Rudolf Tomaschek, director of the Institute of Physics in Dresden: "Modern physics is an instrument of Jewry for the destruction of Nordic science." Anti-intellectualism served domestically to undermine opposition to the Nazi regime, and externally, especially later in connection with the conquered territories, to suppress the native intelligentsias and thus make the masses more amenable to Nazi despotism. With the Jews too, Nazism first sought to undermine their cultural strength. The platform originally adopted by the Nazi party in 1920, within half a year after Adolf Hitler had assumed leadership, emphasized the denial of German citizenship to Jews. Yet when Hitler was appointed as chancellor of Germany on January 30, 1933, the Nazis took their time about the removal of the Jews' citizenship, starting with discrimination against Jewish civil servants, teachers, and lawyers. These early decrees of April 7, 1933, were followed two weeks later by the exclusion of Jewish physicians from panel practice and by a *numerus clausus* in German schools. Even the decrees of July 14 and 26, 1933, merely laid the basis for revoking the naturalization of East European Jews. It was not until the Nuremberg laws of September 15, 1935, that the German Jews, too, were deprived of their citizenship and made into mere subjects of the Reich. At the same time was enacted the law "for the protection of German blood and honor," which made of intermarriage and of extramarital sex relations between "Aryans" and "non-Aryans" a criminal offense.

This early Nazi legislation revealed the general procedures which Hitler and his associates were to use so successfully against Jews and other "enemies." Implicit in all the laws was the rationalization that the Nazis were only restoring the conditions of the pre-Emancipation era. It could be argued that just as medieval Jewry was segregated from the German people, enjoyed no political rights, and suffered from considerable disabilities, and yet managed to thrive culturally and religiously, so would Nazi legislation only renew the same situation in modern conditions. All that the German government intended to do, the semi-official commentators said, was to bring about a state of affairs in which "it will henceforth and for all future times be impossible for the Jews to mix with the German people and to meddle in the political, economic, and cultural management of the Reich."

The Branding of Europe

I am so weary that my pen can no longer write. "Man, strip off thy garments, cover thy head with ashes, run into the streets and dance in thy madness. . . ."

ANDRÉ SCHWARZ-BART: *The Last of the Just*

INTRODUCTION

DURING THE "FIRST STAGE," GERMANY PRESERVED SOME OUTWARD appearance of sanity, some semblance of law and order. Inwardly, it had already become a criminal state. And when it declared war against the world, it dropped all pretenses—the violence of war can give full outlet to the violence of the criminal. As the Nazis moved from country to country, they etched the virulence and criminality of their state upon the very flesh of the conquered people. The persecution of minority groups had been endemic in Europe; but now it became the order of the day.

Poland and Eastern Europe were not unacquainted with pogroms. But the Germans brought something new to this experience: a cold, scientific, systematic program of extermination. As we read the accounts of the victims—from Poland and the Warsaw Ghetto, from Hungary, from Italy—we are drawn to them with the deepest sympathy and love; their degradation becomes our agony. At the same time, we must analyze not only the crimes of the Nazis, but also the response of the victims. From accounts of the Warsaw Ghetto, we discern the values of Jewish community life. We read of those who crumbled and fell, those who bought extra hours of existence for themselves with the lives of others, those who withdrew from the community and were willing to survive as slaves. We can neither applaud nor condemn. We can only strive to understand. And when we fail to understand we must try to love. And when we cannot love we must learn that it is ourselves we confront—man in the utmost extremity.

1. *THE HOLOCAUST KINGDOM*

ALEXANDER DONAT

The story of the Warsaw Ghetto towers above all other incidents of those dark times. A number of accounts exist, and new material has recently been discovered. But Alexander Donat's story is written with a clarity and insight which sets it apart from the rest. In this selection, we note the pressure of the Nazi authorities as they keep pushing the Jews of the ghetto into a smaller and smaller area. We hear of Janus Korczak and his quiet heroism, and we listen to the anguish of self-appraisal as Donat asks himself the questions of life and death that reach us with their contemporary relevance.

━━━

ELI, ELI.

Vague rumors, dark hints, were the preliminary stage. Several members of the *Judenrat* had been arrested and were being held hostage; it was whispered that they had been executed. On Wednesday, July 22, 1942, the day before Tishah B'Av (the anniversary of the destruction of the ancient Temple in Jerusalem), the storm broke. It was a dark day to match our foreboding, with heavy clouds over a silent city. Shopkeepers closed their stores; streets were empty; even the beggars had disappeared. In the unnatural silence those who found themselves outdoors looked nervously behind them.

Early in the afternoon, black and white posters appeared all over the Ghetto:

1. By order of the German authorities all Jewish persons living in Warsaw, regardless of age or sex, are to be resettled in the East.

2. The following are exempt from resettlement:

a. All Jewish persons employed by the German authorities or German government agencies, who can produce adequate proof of their employment;

b. All Jewish persons who are members and employees of the Jewish Council [*Judenrat*] on the day this order is published;

c. All Jewish persons employed by German firms who can produce adequate proof of their employment;

d. *All Jews capable of work* who so far have not been included in the work process; these are to be barracked in the Jewish living quarter; [italics mine]

e. All Jewish persons belonging to the staff of Jewish hospitals or disinfection squads;

f. All Jewish persons belonging to the Jewish police;

g. All Jewish persons who belong to the immediate family of persons covered in a. through f. Only *wives and children* are considered members of the immediate family; [italics mine]

h. All Jewish persons who on the first day of resettlement are bedridden in one of the Jewish hospitals and not qualified for discharge. Such inability to leave the hospital must be attested to by a doctor appointed by the *Judenrat*.

3. Each Jewish resettler may take 15 kilograms (33 pounds) of personal belongings as baggage. All baggage exceeding 15 kilograms will be confiscated. All valuables such as gold, jewelry, money, etc., may be taken along. Enough food for three days should be brought.

4. Resettlement begins on July 22, 1942, at 11 A.M.

It was announced, too, that all administrative authorities in the Ghetto were now suspended and their powers assumed by a new Resettlement Agency.

The decree's final paragraph specified:

Failure to comply with the above decree will be punished by death. The *Judenrat* will be responsible for carrying out the above provisions and if they are not carried out to the letter, the hostages already under arrest will be shot. In carrying out its tasks, the *Judenrat* will choose a special committee whose head will be the Chairman of the *Judenrat* and his aide—the Commandant of the Jewish Police. Delivery of 6,000 Jews daily to assembly point at the Jewish Hospital in Stawki Street adjoining the *Umschlagplatz* is mandatory. For this purpose the hospital must be vacated immediately. All Jews presently employed must remain at their jobs. The *Judenrat* is responsible for the prompt burial of Jews who die in the course of the Resettlement Operation. Burial must be done on the day death occurs.

That document had reached the *Judenrat* in the morning. SS *Sturmbannführer* (Major) Hermann Hoefle appeared at the *Judenrat* offices with several high-ranking SS officers, declaring that he had been directed to initiate a Resettlement Operation by Odilo Globocnik, SS and Police Chief of the Lublin District. Globocnik was chief of resettlement for all German-occupied Poland and supervised all camps in Lublin province. The code name for this resettlement was "Operation Reinhard" in honor of former Security Police and SS Chief Reinhard Heydrich, the Nazi proconsul in Czechoslovakia who had just been assassinated by Czech patriots. Headquarters of the Resettlement Operation, the so-called *Befehlstelle* (command post), was at 101-103 Zelazna Street. In addition to Hoefle, the officers in charge were *Hauptsturmführer* (Captain) Michalsen, *Sturmführer* Mundt and the special SS unit *Treblinka*. The headquarters staff also included members transferred from the Warsaw Gestapo and other commissioned and noncommissioned officers of the SS.

To carry out the operation, detachments of Ukrainians, Latvians, and Lithuanians were brought in. The Jewish police also got a new chief, Jozef Szerynski, a convert to Christianity whose name had been Szenkman. A virulent anti-Semite, Szerynski had been an inspector in the Polish police force before the war. After the Ghetto was established, he was appointed commander of the Jewish police force. Subsequently, however, he was arrested by the Germans for complicity in the disappearance of a batch of the fur coats collected for the *Wehrmacht* on the Russian front, and his aide, Jakob Lejkin, took his place. At the inception of the Resettlement Operation, Szerynski was released from jail by the Germans and was to prove more zealous than ever in executing their orders, hoping thereby to regain some of his lost influence with the Nazis.

Once the posters were up, the strangely deserted streets were suddenly filled. Thousands gathered around them, studying them in silence, scrutinizing every word and letter. After the weeks of rumor and anxiety, the first feeling was relief. Whether this was the instinct of self-preservation, or the egotism of the strong, I don't know. One thing the posters made clear was that only those who were unable to work, who were a burden to society, were subject to resettlement. That was about 20 per cent of the Ghetto population. The remainder were evidently to be used in German businesses or military projects; that is, drafted for something much like forced labor. The intention of Operation Reinhard was painful and unmistakably cruel; it selected for resettlement those who were weakest and least able to look after themselves: the old, the sick, the crippled, the orphans. From the beginning of the war, however, resettlements and relocations of one sort or another had been everyday occurrences, so that no one thought that this one would be any different. True, Nazi brutality spoke in every line of the decree: there would be shootings, victimization of the weak, and beatings, but still everyone reassured himself, it *was* a resettlement.

Through their agents the Nazis did everything to maintain this illusion. Every few days the *Judenrat* was given official German reassurances on that score. The whole operation had been planned with military precision down to the last detail. There was, first, the element of surprise, to effect "psychological preparation" of the victims. The people were then divided against themselves in new ways and along new lines. New "privileged" groups were created. In fact, there seemed to be a logic in it: productive Jews would be put to work for the Germans, and the unproductive ones—well, weren't they the inevitable victims of war?

The first trainloads were to leave that day, July 22, and there were no difficulties in filling the quota. Prisoners from the Gesia Street prison and people from the refugee reception centers were loaded into horse-drawn carts and escorted by Jewish policemen to the *Umschlagplatz*. At the beginning no Germans participated in the actual details of the Resettlement Operation.

Everyone in the Ghetto frantically set about getting papers to prove employment. An *Ausweis* (work certificate) was a permit to live. As people rushed in search of them, streets were busier than usual. Instead of saying "Hello," or "How are you?" people now greeted each other with "Are you covered?" Unmarried girls were marrying members of the Jewish police with unusual haste and eagerness until scarcely a bachelor remained among them. German-owned and operated businesses were besieged.

In addition to the workshops already in existence, such as those of Toebbens or Schultz, a number of new German firms mushroomed in every branch of commerce. Some of these businesses were already in production when the decree appeared, but most were only in the planning stage. The *Befehlstelle* authorized each such business to employ a certain number of Jews, but the quotas were constantly fluctuating. Apartment houses adjacent to factories were vacated to provide living quarters for the factories' employees. Within a few days the face of the Ghetto was transformed beyond recognition. Wooden fences were erected around each of the German factories and shops, thus splitting the Ghetto into a number of isolated, fenced-off smaller ghettos. The Jewish managers of those workshops, in partnerships with the German owners, did a thriving business in selling work certificates to half-crazed Jews who had as yet found no employment. Often people used their last penny to buy an *Ausweis*. Firms were jammed with lines of applicants overflowing down stairways into the courtyards, weeping, swearing, screaming. Managers and their clerks worked until they dropped from weariness, taking money from the job applicants, answering questions, making out lists. The situation was a gold mine for every speculator and swindler. Not only were work certificates made up and sold to prove employment in nonexistent businesses, but *bona fide* work certificates were sold and resold several times over.

Within a few days everyone in the printing shops—owners and employees—received beautiful German work certificates made out by the office of the "trustee" for the industry. The approximately 300 people so affected exhibited their new documents proudly and for some time kept working happily. As with so many others in different fields, it seemed that so far as we were concerned the resettlement problem had been solved.

Lena, in her capacity as manager of a pharmacy, was in an even more secure position and she traveled to and from work daily without a qualm. Since our little Wlodek had two working parents, "obviously" he was also perfectly safe. Only our elderly Aunt Sarah and Wlodek's governess had as yet no "legal" basis for remaining in Warsaw. We hid them as long as we could, but they perished eventually anyway.

It rained all day July 23, Tishah B'Av, but the operation continued according to plan. Jewish policemen reinforced by *Judenrat* officials wearing white arm bands—the so-called soul-snatchers—continued their work of the preceding day, methodically emptying the refugee reception centers and the "death houses," buildings where there had been a very high mortality rate from hunger and typhus.

On this second day of Operation Reinhard the first of many blood-chilling roundups of street waifs began. These orphans resisted vigorously, biting and kicking Ghetto policemen, screaming at the top of their lungs when caught and carried away, but the well-fed police were bigger and stronger. In tribute to the homeless children of Warsaw it must be said that they were the first to *resist*, to put up a fight against the Jewish agents of the Nazis.

That second day, the large orphanage at 3 Dzika Street and the center for homeless children at 6 Gesia Street were evacuated. My kerchief-printing plant was located in the same building and the spectacle of Jewish police loading the children into wagons to be deported was enough to make the paving stones cry out.

Early on the morning of July 24, we heard the incredible news that Adam Czerniakow, *Obmann* of the *Judenrat*, had committed suicide. At 9:30 the previous night some Gestapo officers had called on him and shortly thereafter he took cyanide. On his desk lay a slip of paper containing only three words: "Till the last . . . ." Although the *Judenrat* was unpopular, Czerniakow had always been liked personally and respected as an honest man. His suicide shattered us. No one knew what his conversation with the Gestapo men had been about, and Czerniakow went to his grave with his secret. Had it been a demand to step up deportations to 10,000 a day? Had he learned the terrible truth about what the Resettlement Operation was? Was he so outraged by what had already occurred that he wished his death to serve as a protest? Or, having already delivered up the most defenseless people in the community for which he was responsible, did he choose death rather than sanction any further murder of his people? Whatever his motives or intention, his death did not help us. We felt it was desertion, not leadership. Czerniakow failed to sound the alarm and summon his people to resistance. If he had been given a glimpse of the bottomless abyss to which we were consigned, he did not pass his knowledge on to us. His suicide only intensified our despair and our panic. If it bore witness to his personal integrity, it did not attest to his greatness.

Marek Lichtenbaum was appointed to replace Czerniakow. An engineer by profession, he and his sons had made a fortune constructing the Ghetto walls. His reputation was that of a coarse, brutal man. Actual power was now in the hands of the Jewish Ghetto police who roamed the streets like wild beasts, seizing men, women, and children with increasing brutality.

The day after Czerniakow's suicide a group of SS officers called on the *Judenrat* to express their condolences and to give their word as officers that resettled Jews were in fact being resettled and not being mistreated in any way. That same day, July 24, the *Judenrat* announced that "the rumors circulating in the Ghetto about the Resettlement Operation" were false. Simultaneously, Gestapo agents spread a report—"based on reliable sources"—that only the poorest, least productive elements of the population would be resettled, that the entire operation would continue for no more than a few days, and certainly would be over by July 31. Letters supposedly written by people already deported were circulated; they were said to have been brought back by Polish policemen and railway workers who had accompanied the resettlement trains and reported that those resettled were doing well.

The following two days, a Saturday and Sunday, brought no letup. If anything, the operation gained momentum and the noose was drawn tighter around our necks. There was no time to think calmly and plan some kind of escape. The Ghetto was increasingly disorganized: stores closed down, bakeries stopped baking, smuggling ceased, and food became unobtainable. Famine stalked the city.

The roundup procedure began with cordoning off an apartment house. Ghetto police blocked all exits, and then fifteen or twenty of them, with an officer in charge, ordered all occupants into the courtyard. Here papers were checked; those who failed to pass muster were immediately loaded into a wagon. While this was going on, other policemen went through every apartment to make certain no one was hiding. At first, persons hiding had been able to escape when discovered by paying a small bribe, but the police were growing more brutal and callous.

Eventually whole streets were sealed off at one time and everyone on the street had to have his papers checked. In the early stages of the deportations every valid *Ausweis* was scrupulously respected; this was another German ruse to give Jews false confidence in documents, an illusion which led thousands to their deaths.

In our apartment house, roundups were under the command of my former lawyer, Henryk Lande, now a captain of the Ghetto police. On one roundup when I was stopped and produced my documents for him, Lande looked it over and said softly, "If I were you, I wouldn't feel so sure that this is enough. I'd get something better." I then learned that almost from the beginning there had been a special *Ausweis,* stamped *Einsatz Reinhard,* which bore the Nazi eagle and a swastika with the inscription, "Not subject to re-settlement." At that stage such an *Ausweis* was a guarantee of security.

I saw a young mother run downstairs into the street to get milk for her baby. Her husband, who worked at the *Ostbahn,* had as usual left earlier that morning. She had not bothered to dress, but was in bathrobe and slippers. An empty milk bottle in hand she was headed for a shop where, she knew, they sold milk under the counter. She walked into Operation Reinhard. The executioners demanded her *Ausweis.* "Upstairs ... *Ostbahn* ... work certificate. I'll bring it right away."

"We've heard that one before. Have you got an *Ausweis* with you, or haven't you?"

She was dragged protesting to the wagon, scarcely able to realize what was happening. "But my baby is all alone. Milk ..." she pro-tested. "My *Ausweis* is upstairs." Then, for the first time, she really looked at the men who were holding her and she saw where she was being dragged: to the gaping entrance at the back of a high boarded wagon with victims already jammed into it. With all her young mother's strength she wrenched herself free, and then two, and four policemen fell on her, hitting her, smashing her to the ground, picking her up again, and tossing her into the wagon like a sack. I can still hear her screaming in a half-crazed voice some-where between a sob of utter human despair and the howl of an animal.

Another young woman I knew after much trouble finally per-suaded a friend of her husband's, a man who managed a shop, to register her with his firm so that she could have an *Ausweis.* "I'm doing it for you because you're Leon's wife," the man told her, but it cost her every penny of what remained of the possessions she and her husband had owned when he had left in September 1939. "You know I'm not taking this for myself. You understand, don't you? It's because of the others. . . ." Then he explained to her how the very next day she must move to the shop area and bring her eight-year-old boy with her. There she would be safe. She needn't worry about having no money or about leaving her apartment; she must bring only the absolute necessities with her, no more than the apartment house janitor's wheelbarrow could carry in one trip; but everything would be all right.

And, indeed, she was reassured. Calmly she went about doing what she had to do, fighting for the life of her child. Her husband, she knew, would be proud of how well she had managed. Holding her little boy's hand, she told him, "Now, you mustn't be afraid. Mother is looking out for you." As she was turning the corner into the street where they lived, the little boy ran ahead as children do. He skipped around the corner before she got to it. Why had she let him do it? How could she have let her sense of danger relax even for an instant? The street seemed so calm. When she heard him scream, "Mama! Mama!" she sped around the corner and had just time enough to see a little body with a familiar striped sweater disappearing among the mass of other bodies in the wagon surrounded by police. She thanked God that she was in time to explain, that she had an *Ausweis*.

"But, Madam," the police said, "how can we be sure that this is *your* child?"

She had not, it seems, quite understood. No more than any of us did at first. And when she finally did understand, she was beaten brutally "for resisting the authorities," but not a sound, not a sob, escaped her. The policemen showed that they were not, after all, completely heartless. By surrendering her *Ausweis* to them—a commodity more valuable than gold at that point—she was permitted to get into the wagon, too, to accompany her son to the *Umschlagplatz* and what lay beyond.

As the wagon began to move away, anyone within earshot could hear the voice of an old woman coming from beyond the boards of the van, repeating monotonously, "Tell Zalme Katz his mother was taken away. . . . Tell Zalme Katz his mother was taken away.

. . . Tell Zalme Katz. . . ." And those who listened very carefully could also hear among the other sounds coming from the van the voice of an eight-year-old boy in a striped sweater crying, "O Daddy, why did you go away and leave us?"

All the wagons went to the *Umschlagplatz* near Stawki Street. Those selected for resettlement waited in the hospital in indescribable crowding and confusion. After a sufficient number of victims had been rounded up, usually by four or five in the afternoon, the hospital was emptied and the cattle cars filled. Gun butts and clubs drove the people into the square where two SS officers made the "final selection." The overwhelming majority, some with bundles over their shoulders and leading children by the hand, passed through the gate into the railhead proper and were then jammed into the railroad cars (capacity: 40 men or 8 horses) more than 100 people to a car; then the doors were shut and bolted from the outside.

Most able-bodied males were "rejected" by the SS officers and sent to the *Dulag* (transit camp) in Leszno Street where, if shop managers or supervisors intervened on their behalf, they were released. The very old and crippled were "rejected" too, but in another way; they were part of the German category of *Transportunfähig*, "unfit for transport," and were taken to the cemetery and shot. The entire procedure was run in a manner intended to reinforce the impression that the Resettlement Operation was genuine.

Because loading didn't usually begin before late afternoon, efforts were made to obtain the release of persons who had been rounded up during the day. Intervention by shop managers or the *Judenrat* officially, or unofficially by bribing Jewish policemen, were the methods and a well-organized network of corruption quickly grew up involving the Jewish police, Ukrainian and German guards. It was an enormously profitable business and one of the low points of Ghetto depravity, yet some individuals rounded up and taken to the *Umschlagplatz* were thus able to obtain their release as many as three or four times.

Many individuals carrying large amounts of money made no effort to buy their release when caught in the roundups. They firmly believed in the resettlement myth and felt they would need the money where they were going. I knew one man who had a contact with the police. Although penniless himself, he arranged to be released with his brother-in-law who had also been picked up and who was rich enough to pay for both of them. But the brother-in-law refused. "At a time like this," he said, "you don't spend your money on other people. I might need this money soon to save my own life." Later, I learned from a few men who managed to escape from the cattle cars, all of which went directly to Treblinka, that just before making their escape they were refused small sums of money by men who neither wished to escape themselves nor would aid those without money who did.

Much later, when I was in the concentration camp at Maidanek, Dr. Isaac Schipper, the historian, told me that at the beginning of Operation Reinhard a number of Jewish social and political leaders met secretly in order to discuss resistance, but the majority voted against active resistance in any form on the grounds that the operation would be concluded by July 31 and that resistance would merely give the Nazis a pretext for bloody reprisals.

Though the operation had been under way for a week, it did not stop; instead, it took on ever greater proportions. On my way home from work one day, I stopped at 24 Leszno Street to give Rachman my daily report. One of Biederman's lithographers rushed in, frantic. The Germans were conducting a terrible roundup in Gesia Street. All escape routes had been blocked off, everyone found in the street was being lined up and marched off to the *Umschlagplatz* whether or not he had an *Ausweis*. Because it was the time of day when people left work, the street had been very crowded and the roundup enormous. Up to that point roundups had taken place earlier in the day, the early morning and late afternoon hours being relatively safe. This was the first late-afternoon roundup and also the first operation *in which Ukrainian guards and German troops took part personally*. The Germans tore up work certificates and clubbed their owners with rifle butts and riding crops. Quickly the roundup became a street massacre. The screams of the wounded and the moans of the dying could be heard for blocks, and after the column of thousands was marched off to the *Umschlagplatz*, Gesia Street looked like a battlefield, bodies everywhere—dead, dying, wounded —lying in puddles of blood.

The next Sunday another bloody roundup took place, Ukrainians and Germans again participating. With the gunfire we heard shouts that we were to keep on hearing and remembering for a long time to come: *"Alles runter! Alle Juden runter!"* "Everything downstairs! All Jews downstairs!" The tone was bad enough, but the humiliating impersonality of that "Everything downstairs!" where normal speech called for "Everyone" was even more shocking.

The roundups taught us that our work certificates were a very precarious form of security after all. A number of printers and lithographers who had such documents, including the Biedermans, had been caught and "resettled." After long deliberation we decided that all things considered the "shops" offered the greatest security. The German businesses were still expanding. Toebbens, for example, had taken over chemical, electrical, metallurgical, and wood-working factories, as well as bakeries, pharmacies, barbershops and medical clinics, all part of a systematic looting of Jewish business. The most likely shop seemed to be the *Allgemeine Handelsgesellschaft Zimmermann,* colloquially known as the AHAGE, a Berlin firm which manufactured paper products. Before the Resettlement Operation, Dawid Krynski, a close friend of mine, had had frequent business dealings with the AHAGE and he was now put in charge of its hastily organized new Ghetto branch. AHAGE was a logical place for printers and lithographers, and Krynski and Fenigstein, the two managers, agreed to accept a limited number of printers for a fixed sum per person, presumably to be paid to the Polish managers outside of the Ghetto branch. Fortunately, I was one of the limited number accepted.

The food situation had grown worse as a result of the increased tempo of violence, large-scale roundups, and the reorganization of the Ghetto on a "shop basis." Food prices soared. Bakers and shopkeepers, unprotected by working papers, went into hiding. Smuggling was only sporadic, so that hunger gripped the Ghetto, and the Nazis were quick to exploit it. On July 29, 1942, a public announcement signed by Ghetto police chief Lejkin said that all who volunteered for resettlement would be given three kilos of bread and one of jam. The promise was repeated somewhat later with the added incentive that entire families who volunteered would not be separated. For days following there was a bitter spectacle in the Ghetto streets. Thousands of Jews, in families and sometimes larger groups, marched toward the *Umschlagplatz* of their own free will, having sold their lives for three kilos of bread and one kilo of jam. Children from families where the parents had already been resettled, and parents who had lost their children the same way, came forward voluntarily in the hope of "joining their families." Some days there were so many volunteers that people had to be turned away to wait for the next day's shipment.

Despite the volunteers, forced roundups continued unabated and a pattern began to emerge as the Great Pogrom rolled on. Round-ups began at eight in the morning and stopped at around six, after a morning and afternoon manhunt. Operations were directed by SS officers from the *Vernichtungskommando* who controlled several hundred Ukrainians, Latvians, and Lithuanians, as well as hundreds of Ghetto policemen. The procedure had been modified by now and made more ruthless. A house or street was surrounded. The deafening *"Alles runter! Alle Juden runter!"* resounded, echoed by the Jewish police's "Everything comes down!" in Polish. Doors were smashed in by boots or gun butts, and apartments searched. Anyone found hiding was killed on the spot—old, sick, or crippled included. Everything of value was stolen. Pillows and feather beds were slashed with bayonets in search of "hidden Jewish wealth." When the raiders had finished, it looked as if an earthquake had struck.

After several thousand people had been rounded up in the cor-doned-off streets, they were marched under guard to the *Umschlag-platz*. The horse-drawn wagons used in the early stages were soon abandoned and the victims driven on foot. For the slightest waver-ing in the ranks, the faintest suggestion of an effort to escape, shots rang out, and the route to the *Umschlagplatz* was consequently lined with corpses. Some hundred people a day lost their lives that way. Sometimes there was no pause at the *Umschlagplatz* and the vic-tims were loaded directly on to the cattle cars. No more document checking, no more *Ausweis* inspection: those who were not actually inside a shop, in the new Ghetto meaning of "shop," were doomed.

We made up our minds to spend nights from then on in the AHAGE area on Mila Street. We were assigned part of one room there, temporarily, and moved into it with only the absolute neces-sities. Nobody was left in our old Orla Street apartment, though occasionally I dropped in to see how things were going. My days were spent inside the printing shop at 24 Leszno Street, while Lena and Wlodek spent theirs at the pharmacy, which was only a block away from the AHAGE, and still considered a safe place. But Lena's life was complicated by having Wlodek constantly with her, and the responsibility began to prove too much for her. The pharmacy was on the corner of Zamenhof and Wolynska streets, where all the traffic to the *Umschlagplatz* had to pass. Through the windows, day after day, Lena witnessed the tragic procession of the doomed, the endless line of young and old, weak and strong, with and without bundles, with extinguished eyes and faces setting out on their journey to an unknown destination almost certain to bring them further suffering. The shouts of the SS men, the noise of gunfire, the thud of clubs on human flesh, the groans of the wounded and beaten, and the last *Shema Yisrael* (Hear, O Israel) of the dying punctuated the monotonous shuffling of weary feet on the pavement. To be forced to watch and listen to this day after day was enough to drive anyone out of her mind. The sight of children, who accounted for a large percentage of each "shipment to the East," was especially unnerving. Alone, or with their mothers, or in groups shepherded by teachers, they were ragged and unhappy, in short pants and skirts, barefoot or in sandals, most without knapsacks, food, or water, and with shaven heads.

Ukrainian guards, often very drunk, kept dropping into the pharmacy to ask for alcohol or some remedy or other. Wlodek was kept in a small room that served as an office, and it was sternly impressed on him that he must never come out into the store. When things looked especially dangerous, he was locked in a medicine cabinet. It was impossible for the child not to be affected by the nervousness around him. He was only four and a half and had been accustomed to constant care and attention; this new life frightened and bored him. He kept running out into the store, tormenting his mother with constant questions and requests. Lena's already frayed nerves had the added strain of not having a moment away from Wlodek. More and more often she spent the night at the pharmacy with him because it seemed the safest thing to do.

One day a Jewish policeman noticed Wlodek and asked whose child he was.

"Mine," Lena replied.

"Hide him in the closet!" the policeman yelled in an unnatural voice. "Haven't you got any brains? Put him in a closet!"

It was an easy thing to say, but how could a small, restless child be kept in a closet all day?

One morning, Lena's cousin, Izak Rubin, rushed into the pharmacy. Earlier in the day he had been caught in a roundup and was on his way to the *Umschlagplatz*. He had cast imploring glances at the pharmacy, hoping that Lena would notice him among the marchers. Even if she could do nothing, he would have liked a farewell look, a wave of the hand. Near Muranowska Street, just two blocks from the *Umschlagplatz*, he had been spotted among the victims by my brother-in-law, Mietek Haus, a policeman, who was on duty there at the time. Instantly, Mietek fell upon Izak and began to beat him with his rubber truncheon and kick him, at the same time carefully edging him toward the sidewalk. When the surprised escort asked what the matter was, Mietek pretended to be furiously angry and explained that this insolent fellow, Izak, had been trying to sneak into the ranks to join his wife. The Ukrainian guard smashed his rifle butt down on Izak, but Mietek had saved his life by that ruse. Unfortunately there were all too few such cases.

The Great Pogrom continued and more people were thrown to the Moloch. Until then policemen's parents had been exempt from resettlement and many a Jewish policeman had justified his ruthlessness toward other Jews by maintaining that he was, at least, protecting his own family. Now, however, even policemen's parents were to be deported. I knew policemen who gave their mothers overdoses of luminal or potassium cyanide rather than let them be deported. Others, weeping bitter tears, loaded their mothers onto the cattle cars themselves, then turned back to their task of fulfilling their daily quota of "five heads."

There was talk of policemen who committed suicide, and of some who "handed in their caps"—that is, resigned—but every man had to fulfill his daily quota of five victims, for failure meant death to those nearest and dearest to him. Those Jewish police who tried to avoid participating actively in the roundups were coerced; their colleagues saw that no one kept his hands clean. "What are you," they asked, "a virgin or something?" Policemen even beat up some of their more sensitive co-workers to emphasize the point. Those police whose parents were resettled grew more brutal and barbaric. "If *my* mother had to go, do you think I'm going to spare you?" was their refrain.

But it was the deportation of Janusz Korczak and the children in his care which made an enormous impression on the Ghetto and was a clear indication of the purpose and brutality of the resettlement program. Korczak was an unusual man. Not just an ordinary educator or writer, he had always been a symbol. Trained as a physician, he had devoted his entire life to children, and had been given the title "Father of Orphaned Children." He had replaced the humiliating name of *orphanage* with the more dignified "Child's Home."

It was Wednesday, August 5, 1942, when the Nazis came for the children in Korczak's charge. It was not clear whether Korczak told the children what they might expect or exactly where they were going, but his staff of teachers and nurses had the two hundred orphans ready for the Nazis when they raided the orphanage at 16 Sienna Street. The children had been bathed, given clean clothing, and provided with bread and water to take with them. The Nazis burst in, but the children, though frightened, did not cry out or run and hide. They clung to Korczak who stood between them and the Germans.

Bareheaded, he led the way, holding a child by each hand. Behind him were the rest of the two hundred children and a group of nurses clad in white aprons. They were surrounded by German and Ukrainian guards, and the Ghetto police. One could see how weak and undernourished the children were. But they marched to their deaths in exemplary order, without a single tear, in such a terrifying silence that it thundered with indictment and defiance.

When the *Judenrat* heard of what was happening in the orphanage, everyone there tried desperately to telephone, to do something, but they tried only to save Janusz Korczak, not the two hundred children. Korczak was told of their efforts in his behalf, but refused aid; instead, he chose to go with the children to the *Umschlagplatz*.

Other orphanages besides Korczak's, some of them larger, were liquidated by the Nazis in the very same manner, and there were many other nurses and teachers who refused to leave their charges but heroically went with them to their deaths. Korczak became a model of heroism and humanity in the night of barbarism.

Long before the time of murder, Korczak had written, "There is no greater mishap than to be born a man." He died, as he had lived, simply and with dignity. "Oh, how difficult is life, how easy death!" he wrote in his Ghetto diary, and in his death he became a monument to the 100,000 murdered Jewish children of Warsaw.

Their deaths also gave the Ghetto its first insight into the true significance of resettlement. Why had the *Judenrat* tried to save Korczak? If the two hundred children were really going to be re-settled somewhere in the East, wasn't it perfectly natural for their teacher and shepherd to go along with them? What we had suspected all along—but could not or did not want to believe—was now confirmed. What we had dismissed as the hysterical outpourings of morbid imaginations was now reality. This was not resettlement; this was deportation to death. Moreover, the *Judenrat* knew, the heads of the Jewish police knew, and they had not told us.

After the first sorrow came the soul-searching. How had it all come to pass? How could 300,000 people have let themselves be led to slaughter without putting up a fight? How could young healthy parents hand over their children without bashing in the criminal skulls of guards and executioners alike? Was it not a father's first, most elemental duty to save his child's life even at the cost of his own? Or for a son to die defending his mother? Why had we not lain in wait, axes in our hands, for the assassins? There is a time to live and a time to die, and when the time to die comes, we must stand up and accept death with dignity. Over and over, the Ghetto Jeremiahs asked each other aloud, "Why didn't we go out into the streets with whatever we could lay our hands on—axes, sticks, kitchen knives, stones? Why hadn't we poured boiling water on the murderers or thrown sulphuric acid? Why hadn't we broken out of the Ghetto walls and scattered all over Warsaw, all over Poland? Perhaps 20,000, even 50,000 of us would have been slain, but not 300,000! What a disgrace, what an unspeakable shame!"

It was an agonizing self-appraisal. We were bitter to the point of self-flagellation, profoundly ashamed of ourselves, and of the mis-fortunes we had endured. And those feelings intensified our sense of being abandoned alike by God and man. Above all we kept asking ourselves the age-old question: *why, why?* What was all that suffering for? What had we done to deserve this hurricane of evil, this avalanche of cruelty? Why had all the gates of Hell opened and spewed forth on us the furies of human vileness? What crimes had we committed for which this might have been calamitous punishment? Where, in what code of morals, human or divine, is there a crime so appalling that innocent women and children must expiate it with their lives in martyrdoms no Torquemada ever dreamed of?

In vain we looked at that cloudless September sky for some sign of God's wrath. The heavens were silent. In vain we waited to hear from the lips of the great ones of the world—the champions of light and justice, the Roosevelts, the Churchills, the Stalins—the words of thunder, the threat of massive retaliation that might have halted the executioner's axe. In vain we implored help from our Polish brothers with whom we had shared good and bad fortune alike for seven centuries, but they were utterly unmoved in our hour of anguish. They did not show even normal human compassion at our ordeal, let alone demonstrate Christian charity. They did not even let political good sense guide them; for after all we *were objectively allies* in a struggle against a common enemy. While we bled and died, their attitude was at best indifference, and all too often "friendly neutrality" to the Germans. "Let the Germans do this dirty work for us." And there were far too many cases of willing, active, enthusiastic Polish assistance to the Nazi murderers.

There was, of course, a handful of noble Poles, but nobody listened to them; their voices never carried over the barbaric yawp of hatred. Heroically they managed to save some individuals, but they could bring no mitigation of Nazi ferocity. The very bases of our faith had crumbled: the Polish fatherland whose children we had always considered ourselves; two thousand years of Christianity, silent in the face of Nazism; our own lie-ridden civilization. We were despairingly alone, stripped of all we had held sacred.

We hounded ourselves with our own guilt. Terrible as the pogrom was, had there been at any point a solution we had neglected out of ignorance, weakness, or cowardice? Could we have thought of something which might have saved us? Suppose that Czerniakow, before killing himself, had summoned the Ghetto to resistance. Would the Ghetto at that point have been capable of organized armed resistance? Not even the greatest optimist among us could answer that question affirmatively. We had lost our political and intellectual leaders. The majority of our young men, including the most militant, were in exile in the Soviet Union. Three years of hunger and epidemic had brought a sharp rise in male mortality, so that there were, when the Resettlement Operation began, four women to every three men. The Ghetto had been systematically ground down for three years, by savage Nazi discrimination and repression, by famine and disease, by traitors among us, by the Ghetto police, by the Gestapo, by the misgovernment of the *Judenrat,* and finally by the April and June massacres. No, at the time of Czerniakow's death, the Ghetto would not have been ready to offer mass armed resistance.

Militarily, the uprising of a single quarter in a great modern city—without a trained army or military organization, without arms or a chance of obtaining arms, without natural cover in which to hide, or means of retreat and maneuver—holds no prospect of the slightest success. Such a quarter could be promptly brought to its knees by cutting off food supplies, turning off the water. And it is much easier when the men rebelling are undernourished and heavily burdened with women and children.

There were other factors. Nothing in Jewish history had prepared the Ghetto for armed rising. The Ghetto Jews were not warriors. For more than two thousand years the Word had been more highly respected than the Sword. We were the descendants of that people who had created the image of the lion and wolf lying down with the lamb, of swords being beaten into ploughshares. The history of the Jews in Diaspora was a history of being driven from place to place, too often locked up in Ghettos, subjected to periodic persecution and pogrom, and it was not conducive to development of the military virtues. Heroic armed exploits by Jews in the Diaspora had been the exception, not the rule.

Not that Jews lacked courage. Jewish participation in the underground revolutionary movement in Tsarist Russia and in the political life of interwar Poland supplied abundant examples of bravery and dignity. The Sholom Aleichem *batlanim* and *luft-menschen,* Marc Chagall's surrealistic fiddlers, Franz Kafka's neurotic intelligentsia, and Martin Buber's exotic Chasidim were undergoing revolutionary change in the prewar years. They were becoming disciplined workers organized in trade unions, educated in the revolutionary traditions of the 1905 uprising, developing armed self-defense groups against pogroms, becoming a people of Zionist pioneers and toilers. But, despite all that, they were not prepared for military action against the Nazis. The unmerciful use of collective responsibility by the Germans kept even the most hotheaded in check. This use of terror had begun immediately after the occupation: on November 22, 1939, the Germans shot 53 Jews from the house at 9 Nalewki Street; in January, 1940, they shot 100 Jewish professionals—physicians, lawyers, and engineers; on April 17, 1942, they shot, in the street in the middle of the night, 52 people suspected of underground activities; on June 3, 1942, 110 Jews were executed in Babice.

The feeling we had for the Germans cannot be oversimplified into hatred. Hatred we felt, but the chief emotion was terror. We couldn't think of the Germans as human beings. They were mad dogs unaccountably loosed from the chains of history and morality. You don't hate a beast of prey, you feel loathing and terror. We feared the Germans with a dreadful, paralyzing panic stronger than the fear of our own deaths. During the final liquidation of the Ghetto, a Jewish woman, on her knees, begged a Polish policeman, "Shoot me! Shoot me. I'm more afraid of the Germans than of dying." One day a German came to take a Jewish child from its mother. When she pleaded for its life, he said, "If you can guess which of my eyes is artificial, I'll give you the child." She looked intently at him and said, "The right one." Astonished, the Nazi replied, "That's so, but how could you tell?" After hesitating for a moment, she told him, "It looks more human than the other one."

The basic factor in the Ghetto's lack of preparation for armed resistance was psychological; we did not at first believe the Resettlement Operation to be what in fact it was, systematic slaughter of the entire Jewish population. For generations East European Jews had looked to Berlin as the symbol of law, order, and culture. We could not now believe that the Third Reich was a government of gangsters embarked on a program of genocide "to solve the Jewish problem in Europe." We fell victim to our faith in mankind, our belief that humanity had set limits to the degradation and persecution of one's fellow man. This mentality underlay the behavior of the Jewish leadership at the very beginning of the Resettlement, when the overwhelming majority voted against armed resistance. Some felt we ought to wait for a joint rising with the Poles. Others were resigned to sacrificing 70,000 Jews rather than jeopardizing the entire community of 400,000—the Nazi policy of collective responsibility was very much alive in our memories. Still others were religious Jews, committed to the tradition of *Kiddush Hashem:*

that is, a martyr's death in the name of God. They believed that, when the enemy came for us, we should be dressed in our prayer shawls and phylacteries, poring over the holy books, all our thoughts concentrated on God. In that state of religious exaltation, we should simply ignore all Nazi orders with contempt and defiance; resistance, violence, only desecrated the majesty of martyrdom in sanctification of the Lord's name. I heard the following unexpected argument in favor of non-resistance.

"Try to imagine Jesus on the way to Golgotha suddenly stooping to pick up a stone and hurling it at one of the Roman legionnaires. After such an act, could he ever have become the Christ? Think of Gandhi and Tolstoy, too. For two thousand years we have served mankind with the Word, with the Book. Are we now to try to convince mankind that we are warriors? We shall never outdo them at that game."

Lastly, there was the fact that there can be no struggle without some hope. Why does the man unjustly condemned to death fail to turn on his guards as he is led to the gallows? Why did the three thousand Turkish prisoners Napoleon ordered drowned put up no resistance? Why did fifty thousand French Huguenots permit themselves to be slaughtered in a single night by French Catholics? And what of the Armenians?

There is no precedent for the eventual uprising of the Warsaw Ghetto because it was undertaken solely for death with dignity, and without the slightest hope of victory in life.

2. SCROLL OF AGONY

CHAIM A. KAPLAN

The last words in the Hebrew manuscript which Professor Abraham I. Katsh's translation now brings to us reads: "If my life ends—what will become of my diary?" Four months after writing these words, Chaim Kaplan died in Treblinka. But the diary was preserved, and it gives us a unique view of the final days and nights of the Warsaw Ghetto. Kaplan describes life from day to day—the decisions of the Jewish Council, the heroes and the villains, pathetic victims such as the "Hebrew-Christians"; and all the while he is dying of starvation. It is a scroll of agony; but it is also a record of greatness.

━━━━━

MAY 13, 1940

In the past few days the conquerors have been making the rounds of the schools for Polish children (Jewish children are still idle and are growing up wild) and taking them out of their classrooms to give blood—since they are elite, red-blooded Aryans born and bred—for use as plasma for the German soldiers. There is great turmoil among Polish parents, and many of them have stopped sending their children to school. The rich were affected first; after a while it became known to the masses, and then the real panic began. The school benches are becoming empty. When the oppressors began invading the children's homes as well, it became

Reprinted with permission of The Macmillan Company from *Scroll of Agony* by CHAIM A. KAPLAN, translated and edited by ABRAHAM I. KATSH. Copyright © Abraham I. Katsh 1965.

customary for the parents to send their Gentile children to spend the night in Jewish homes.

So anyone who says that the Jewish children are not to be envied because they were born in sin and are handicapped by their Semitism, is mistaken. They do envy us; they seek out our friendship—when they need us.

MAY 15, 1940

The Aryans have been learning much from bitter Jewish experience. They evade and avoid forced labor as much as they are able. They hide in their back rooms and don't go outside except when they must. The Aryan streets, too, are empty, and the silence of a desert is on every hand. The conquerors are not ashamed to make the rounds of their houses; still, as long as one is hidden in his apartment, the danger is not as great.

This week the conquerors did something so humorous that after the war it will furnish material for some theatrical sketch.

In Biala Street, a short, quiet side street, they caught three Jews. They stood them up near one of the buildings and ordered them to dance and sing self-derogatory songs. This mocking scene attracted a great crowd of Gentiles, who enjoyed the moral sufferings of the *Zyds*. While they laughed, they probably thought, Angels of doom don't go on two errands at once; when they are busy with the Jews they haven't time for Aryans. So they thought—but after the entire street had filled up with a crowd enjoying the spectacle of the sadistic game, the street was fenced off at both ends and the festive crowd was surrounded on all sides. They were thrown on trucks and taken away. The Gentiles were taken away as captives, and the three Jews were released and sent home. The entire fantastic business took place only to set a scene whose epilogue was the capture of Gentiles for forced labor.

Sometimes our work is done by schoolchildren. The children of our poor, with whom the streets of Warsaw are filled at all hours of the day, are not afraid even of the despotic conquerors. They remain as always—lively and mischievous. Their poverty and oppression serves to shield them from robberies and confiscations. No one will harm them. Even the conquerors' eye overlooks them: Let the Jewish weeds pine away in their iniquity. But these weeds watch every act of the conquerors and imitate the Nazis' manner of speech and their cruelty most successfully. For them this is nothing but good material for games and amusements. Childhood does much.

Once there came into the ghetto a certain Nazi from a province where the Jews are required to greet every Nazi soldier they encountered, removing their hats as they do. There is no such practice in Warsaw, but the "honored guest" wanted to be strict and force the rules of his place of origin on us. A great uproar arose suddenly in Jewish Karmelicka Street: Some psychopathic Nazi is demanding that every passerby take his hat off in his honor. Many fled, many hid, many were caught for their transgression and beaten and many were bursting with laughter. The little "wise guys," the true lords of the street, noticed what was going on and found great amusement in actually obeying the Nazi, and showing him great respect in a manner calculated to make a laughingstock out of the "great lord" in the eyes of all the passersby. They ran up to greet him a hundred and one times, taking off their hats in his honor. They gathered in great numbers, with an artificial look of awe on their faces, and wouldn't stop taking off their hats. Some did this with straight faces, while their friends stood behind them and laughed. Then these would leave, and others would approach, bowing before the Nazi with bare heads. There was no end to the laughter. Every one of the mischievous youths so directed his path as to appear before the Nazi several times, bowing before him in deepest respect. That wasn't all. Riffraff gathered for the fun, and they all made a noisy demonstration in honor of the Nazi with a resounding cheer.

This is Jewish revenge!

MAY 18, 1940

The military victories, which, though they may be exaggerated, nevertheless contain much of the truth, beat upon our heads like hailstones. Today it is Copenhagen, in which there is a Jewish community; the next day it is Amsterdam, The Hague, and Rotterdam, full of Jews who until now dwelt quietly and peacefully in their homeland. Just now the news has reached us that Brussels too has opened its gates to the Nazis. All the military activities of the past nine days prove that the earth trembles under the feet of the Nazis. It seems that these are not chance victories, but rather that the balance of power is such as to make these victories inevitable. Anyone with any perception can clearly see that the Western Powers are incapable of withstanding the military force of the Nazis. This is a gigantic military power in whose path there is no obstacle. And so the day after tomorrow Paris, too, will fall into their hands. And what then? In place of the Versailles Dictate there will be a Paris Dictate, but the dictator will be a different one. Can all this be possible? History is sometimes fond of oddities. It doesn't follow set rules; it moves by strange leaps and sometimes follows serpentine paths.

The conquerors have adopted a new tactic whose purpose is unknown to anyone. Even the mystics freely admit this time that it is an insoluble riddle. At almost every intersection that does not have trolley tracks, the *Judenrat* is putting up—by order of the conquerors, but at its own expense—a thick dividing wall which leaves no room to pass, thus stopping traffic from going from the one street to the other. Warsaw, like Noah's Ark in its day, is full of compartments and partitions that block the roads in the very places where up to now there was the most traffic. Thus for example on the corner of Nalewki and Nowolipki streets, a dividing wall has been made, and a man whose apartment is at Number 2 Nowolipki Street— a distance of only a few steps—is now forced to go around and around, via Nowolipki-Zamenhof-Gesia-Nalewki streets—a half hour's walk. The same is true of the corner of Rymarska-Leszno streets, and so too in all the other fenced-off streets.

It has become known to us that partitions of this sort were also erected in Prague, Czechoslovakia; and this gives support to the hypothesis that this is a military tactic, to diminish freedom of movement in the event of internal revolt. As I said, this is only a hypothesis, but it is a reasonable one.

In any case, beautiful Warsaw has become a jail made up of cell after cell, whose inhabitants are treated like prisoners.

MARCH 7, 1941

I skipped my entries for a day or two, not because there was a shortage of new events, but because there were too many.

The confusion of life has dulled our human sensibilities, and our hearts are not free for thoughts of revenge. But sometimes a time of calm comes, and anyone who thinks about one aspect or another of our strange lives feels the urge for revenge most adequately.

Since the time of the defeat there have been many apostates among Jews. For people educated in a foreign culture there is no reason for these tortures. Why should they risk their lives for something that is strange to them? Ossified Judaism did not furnish them with the strength necessary to continue their national lives, and even though they knew in advance that race would still be a handicap for them, it did not prevent them from taking the formal step of leaving Judaism. Even if they were not accepted into the foreign milieu at once, they would be after a while, when their entrance was forgotten—especially since priests were found who arranged not only the religious aspects but the racial aspects as well. Just as money purifies bastards, it purified the children of a foreign race. After the priest received a certain sum in cash, he simply wrote out a birth certificate stating that So-and-so is an Aryan from a long line of Aryans. These certificates are assumed to be genuine, and no one disputes their veracity. Those who knew such things say that "proper certificates" of this sort have been given to hundreds and thousands. The priests made fortunes, and these impoverished members of Polish Jewry enjoyed all the rights to which the Aryan race entitles its offspring. They remained outside the ghetto area legally and were treated as genuine Aryans.

Above this group was another category of "Jews," those who were born into Christianity. They were born to apostate parents, and so they don't have the slightest feeling for Judaism, either religiously or racially. But the conquerors checked and rechecked, and the family secrets were discovered. Maybe Jewish informers who were jealous of these Christians' peaceful existence were involved, or perhaps some Pole tipped the Nazis off about irregularities in the family trees of their coreligionists. At all events, the conquerors began a hunt for these *Pans* who originated from the Jewish race and who, in their eyes, are considered Jews in every respect. The Nazis brought a great caravan of them to the ghetto and turned them over to the president, Czerniakow, who was stunned to see them in their ruin. He had known them as the cream of Polish society, people who always showed their hatred for the Jews and who adhered closely to the customs they had adopted. Some of them are the descendants of financial and industrial titans, and some of Polish litterateurs, but neither wealth nor knowledge nor genealogy was of any consequence. Like members of the rabble caught in crime and sentenced to severe punishments, they were led back to the ghetto before the eyes of passersby among the ghetto dwellers. Huge crowds accompanied them to the gates of the *Judenrat*. Like unclean people who have no place in human society, they were removed suddenly from the environment in which they had been born and raised.

Who of them imagined that his origin was in the ghetto? Who of them dreamed that his ancestors stood on Mount Sinai? The good-for-nothing Czerniakow took them into his office with a great show of respect and commiserated with them. I cannot sympathize with their tribulations. One fate for all. I don't doubt that Czerniakow's heart bleeds for them, but fate has made him a leader in Israel, and it doesn't behoove him to spread his wings over apostates and the sons of apostates.

I don't know what their end will be, but one thing I know for a certainty. Their enmity to Israel will never cease . . . .

MAY 19, 1942

In Thy book all is inscribed!

When an individual is afflicted with a psychological illness it is a private matter for the doctor who is treating him. But when an entire community has been afflicted with a psychological illness it is a sign of the times, and is of interest to historians of the future as well. This I swear to: The Nazi is not a normal human being, and it is open to question whether he is human at all. Perhaps he is nothing but the missing link between man and the animals. Let me relate a psychopathic manifestation to which we were eye-witnesses today in the ghetto.

The goring of the Nazis is worse than that of a killer bull. People fear them as they would a lion. When a German appears in the streets of the ghetto, everyone crosses over to the opposite sidewalk, just as one keeps his distance from a beast of prey. And this, as a matter of fact, is not cowardice. When a Nazi meets a Jew, the outcome is harm, and if you escape your Jewish obligation of death by accepting a blow from a stick or a whiplash you are among the fortunate. Sometimes the Nazis invite you to follow them—and then your life is in danger. We know a basic rule: All those who are led to the Pawiak are being led to slaughter. Just yesterday an event of this sort occurred. Several killers went out hunting in the streets of the ghetto; a Jew was caught; and this morning he was taken out free—but dead. This is a basic rule: Every Nazi is a killer by nature, and when he is in Jewish surroundings he spreads death and destruction.

But today—wonder of wonders—at ten in the morning three trucks full of Nazis, laughing, friendly, with complete photographic equipment, stopped near Schultz's famous restaurant on the corner of Karmelicka-Nowolipki. It was evident that they hadn't come for murder and larceny this time. They behaved in a friendly manner toward whomever they met, and entered into personal conversations with the ghetto dwellers.

Why the difference today? Today they came to take photographs of the ghetto and its inhabitants, and the pictures must mirror the abundance and good fortune in the ghetto. And since in the ghetto there is poverty and famine, there is nothing to stop them from creating a temporary, artificial abundance and good fortune, made by the Nazis themselves. First they detained every beautiful virgin and every well-dressed woman, and even some who were not beautiful or well-dressed, but who were made up and somewhat elegant. The women were ordered to move around gaily and to look and sound animated. This was recorded on the film, so that the mouths of the liars and propagandists against Nazi cruelty will be stopped up. Behold life in the ghetto! How lighthearted and joyous it is!

Starving people are incapable of showing the laughter and light-heartedness that come from the zest of life and great good fortune. The Nazis detained every fat Jew and everyone with a potbelly which had not yet had a chance to cave in. Jews overloaded with flesh are almost nonexistent in the ghetto, but among tens of thousands of passersby even this kind may be found. Even plutocrats, those serious men so hated by the Führer, were good material for the film. On order, they crowd up and push their way into Schultz's while at the same time a waiter shoves them back because of lack of room. All the tables are taken, and other plutocrats sit around them eating rich meals and enjoying sweets and dainties. The Nazis are footing the bill because it is worth their while.

Thus nothing is lacking in the ghetto. On the contrary, every delight is enjoyed, for the Jews of the ghetto have attained paradise in this life.

Why did the Nazis do this? No one knows, but one can guess that it is for propaganda abroad. Before the Cracow Ghetto was created, they showed us how the happy Jews were running to the ghetto with gladness. Whoever saw them in the newspaper picture would say: These are people who are contented with their lot. And the same will be true this time. This is the way of the deceit, lies, and falsehoods of Nazism. Nazis distort the truths of life, and the unfortunate Jews are forced to help them.

A few days ago the Nazis came to the cemetery and ordered the Jews to make a circle and do a chasidic dance around a basket full of naked corpses. This too they recorded on film. All of these are segments of some anti-Semitic movie, which upon being spliced together will emerge as a gross falsification of the life of the Jews in the Warsaw Ghetto.

Just as Nazism itself is a lie and a distortion, so everything it produces is a lie and a distortion. All of Europe is fighting against England! Chasidic Jews dance around their dead!

MAY 20, 1942

A case of martyrdom.

Melech Czerniakower is a young man of thirty-eight, in his very prime. He dresses in chasidic garb because of his family origins, because of habit, and because of his trade, for he is a slaughterer. But this is done illegally and discreetly, because immediately upon their entry the Nazis banned Jewish ritual slaughtering. And for the very reason that it is a forbidden occupation, it brings in a handsome profit.

But under the Nazi regime no one's life is secure, least of all that of the "cursed Jew." Yesterday Czerniakower's luck brought him face to face with a Nazi whose blood boiled at the sight of his chasidic garb, and for no other reason he was arrested and brought to the Jewish prison in Gesia Street. There they searched him and found a ritual slaughter knife on his person—he had been on his way to slaughter an animal—and here the Nazis found a "legal" ground to accuse him of sabotage. Czerniakower was thus punished for the crime he hadn't committed; he was shot to death immediately, and today he was brought to burial. When a Jew transgresses, everything is done summarily on the basis of appearances with no judicial proceedings. The executed man left a wife and three children.

People say that Czerniakower was slaughtered with the knife they found on him. I do not vouch for this rumor.

JULY 26, 1942

The terrible events have engulfed me; the horrible deeds committed in the ghetto have so frightened and stunned me that I have not the power, either physical or spiritual, to review these events and perpetuate them with the pen of a scribe. I have no words to express what has happened to us since the day the expulsion was ordered. Those people who have gotten some notion of historical expulsions from books know nothing. We, the inhabitants of the Warsaw Ghetto, are now experiencing the reality. Our only good fortune is that our days are numbered—that we shall not have long to live under conditions like these, and that after our terrible sufferings and wanderings we shall come to eternal rest, which was denied us in life. Among ourselves we fully admit that this death which lurks behind our walls will be our salvation; but there is one thorn. We shall not be privileged to witness the downfall of the Nazis, which in the end will surely come to pass.

Some of my friends and acquaintances who know the secret of my diary urge me, in their despair, to stop writing. "Why? For what purpose? Will you live to see it published? Will these words of yours reach the ears of future generations? How? If you are deported you won't be able to take it with you because the Nazis will watch your every move, and even if you succeed in hiding it when you leave Warsaw, you will undoubtedly die on the way, for your strength is ebbing. And if you don't die from lack of strength, you will die by the Nazi sword. For not a single deportee will be able to hold out to the end of the war."

And yet in spite of it all I refuse to listen to them. I feel that continuing this diary to the very end of my physical and spiritual strength is a historical mission which must not be abandoned. My mind is still clear, my need to record unstilled, though it is now five days since any real food has passed my lips. Therefore I will not silence my diary!

We have a Jewish tradition that an evil law is foredoomed to defeat. This historical experience has caused us much trouble since the day we fell into the mouth of the Nazi whose dearest wish is to swallow us. It came to us from habit, this minimizing of all edicts with the common maxim, "It won't succeed." In this lay our undoing, and we made a bitter mistake. An evil decree made by the Nazis does not weaken in effect, it grows stronger. The mitigating paragraphs are increasingly overlooked and the more severe paragraphs intensified. At the beginning, the time of the "negotiations," a directive was issued to the *Judenrat* to deport 6,000 a day; in point of fact they are now deporting close to 10,000. The Jewish police, whose cruelty is no less than that of the Nazis, deliver to the "transfer point" on Stawki Street more than the quota to which the *Judenrat* obligated itself. Sometimes there are several thousand people waiting a day or two to be transported because of a shortage of railroad cars. Word has gotten around that the Nazis are satisfied that the extermination of the Jews is being carried out with all requisite efficiency. This deed is being done by the Jewish slaughterers.

The first victim of the deportation decree was the president, Adam Czerniakow, who committed suicide by poison in the *Judenrat* building. He perpetuated his name by his death more than by his life. His end proves conclusively that he worked and strove for the good of his people; that he wanted its welfare and continuity even though not everything done in his name was praiseworthy. The expulsion proclamation posted in the city streets on the afternoon of July 22 was not signed in the usual manner of *Judenrat* notices, "Head of the *Judenrat,* Certified Engineer Adam Czerniakow," but merely "*Judenrat.*" This innovation astonished those circles who examine bureaucratic changes in notices. After the president's death, the reason became clear. Czerniakow had refused to sign the expulsion order. He followed the talmudic law: If someone comes to kill me, using might and power, and turns a deaf ear to all my pleas, he can do to me whatever his heart desires, since he has the power, and strength always prevails. But to give my consent, to sign my own death warrant—this no power on earth can force me to do, not even the brutal force of the foul-souled Nazi.

A whole community with an ancient tradition, one that with all its faults was the very backbone of world Jewry, is going to destruction. First they took away its means of livelihood, then they stole its wares, then its houses and factories, and above all its human rights. It was left fair prey to every evildoer and sinner. It was locked into a ghetto. Food and drink was withheld from it; its fallen multiplied on every hand; and even after all this they were not content to let it dwell forever within its narrow, rotten ghetto, surrounded with its wall through which even bread could be brought in only by dangerous smuggling. Nor was this a ghetto of people who consume without producing, of speculators and profiteers. Most of its members were devoted to labor so that it became a productive legion. All that it produced, it produced for the benefit of those same soldiers who multiplied its fallen.

Yet all this was to no avail. There was only one decree—death. They came and divided the Warsaw Ghetto into two halves; one half was for sword, pestilence, and destruction; the other half for famine and slavery. The vigorous youth, the healthy and productive ones, were taken to work in the factories. The old people, the women, the children all were sent into exile.

The president, who had a spark of purity in his heart, found the only way out worthy of himself. Suicide! In the end the Nazis would have killed him anyhow, as is their custom in the areas from which they expel the Jewish population; nor would the president have been the last to be shot. From the moment of his refusal to sign the expulsion order he was a saboteur in the eyes of the Nazis and thus doomed to death. With a president one must be very exacting. In any event, he did well to anticipate the Nazis.

He did not have a good life, but he had a beautiful death. May his death atone for his wrongs against his people before becoming president. There are those who earn immortality in a single hour. The president, Adam Czerniakow, earned his immortality in a single instant.

3. *NIGHT OF THE MIST*

EUGENE HEIMLER

As the Germans moved on from their conquest in Poland to the rest of Europe, more Jews were caught in their nets. We turn now to an account from Hungary—with the knowledge that all roads lead to Auschwitz, Bergen-Belsen, or Buchenwald. Eugene Heimler was twenty-one and married when the Germans came. All of his family died in Auschwitz. Heimler survived Auschwitz and Buchenwald and is now a psychiatric social worker in London. His account of Auschwitz shows us the agonies of both body and spirit, how hard it is to love or hate when one is in the depths of hell.

━━━

The days which followed merged into an indistinct mass. I had completely lost my sense of time. Time in Auschwitz was not divided into minutes, hours and days. There the hour did not equal sixty minutes; the week did not consist of seven days. The only measure of time was one's ebbing vitality.

Back home each hour used to have its own hue and flavour. In the morning my father would stretch in his bed. I could hear his quiet yawn from next door. From the kitchen would come the clanging of pots and pans, as the noises of the morning filtered in from the staircase. Sleepy-eyed, my sister would rush in to breakfast: 'Oh, God, half-past seven, I'll be late for school.' Slowly the morning light flowed in through the curtains, washing the shadows

Reprinted with permission of The Bodley Head Ltd. from *Night of the Mist* by EUGENE HEIMLER. © Eugene Heimler 1959.

of night from the furniture. In my father's office, the typewriter would start up; round the corner, the blacksmith would be at his anvil.

In Auschwitz the sun rose crimson behind the electrified wire fence. The air was cold, yet it failed to bring colour into faces still drawn by the torments of the night. In the narrow yard between the barracks it mattered so little whether the sun was rising or setting—nights and days alike meant only weariness and exhaustion.

How clearly I could review the past from this cold and forbidding world of the barracks! I heard voices; fragments of insignificant conversations emerged in my memory while they were dishing out the uneatable concoction called 'lunch.' Five of us ate off one plate. If one of the five took one bite more than his due, we flew at one another and then literally licked up the food that spilled on the floor. There were even some who killed in their hunger. I had known these people at home. Once they had been respectable, cultured citizens, members of charitable societies and select clubs.

At home, lunch used to be ready at noon. While Mother served the meal, Father would bury himself in the paper.

'Here we sit happily, while all these horrors are taking place over there,' he said one day, pointing at the page.

'Are you thinking of Germany?' asked Mother. He nodded but said nothing. Then, with a little sigh, he started ladling out the soup. A wasp kept knocking against the window-pane. My sister opened the window, and the silly creature joyously flew out into the open. It was an oppressive afternoon, heavy with an approaching storm. The dull roll of thunder shook the far horizon.

'Yes, here we sit and eat our fill, while a nation is being locked into a cage. Well, don't we all share the guilt of it?' he demanded, still following the same train of thought. 'However, what we say won't help much.'

It was as if I were seeing the past reflected in a broken mirror. In the shattered fragments the world lived on. For the fragments of a mirror do not die.

My brain was humming as I lay in the slowly narrowing shadow of the barracks. During the hours of the morning they cast a wide shadow; but as the sun rose higher in the sky the shadows became ever narrower. I was giddy from the bromide which they mixed into our tea. At last the rays of the sun were pouring down upon me with scorching intensity. Blood-red crystals danced in front of my closed eyes; small rings of all hues of the rainbow flooded my vision. I imagined myself back home again, in the familiar old streets. I waved to someone, but the next moment the image faded away. Tatters of gipsy melodies wailed in my ears, and sank back into the abyss of oblivion before I could recognize them.

In the barracks which rose dark and forbidding on the other side of the road, a colony of gipsies had settled. Their 'Aryan' origin entitled them to special privileges: men and women could live together and even have children in the camp. In the years since they had been dragged here, little harm had been done to them. They lazed about in the elegant clothes of which we had been robbed by the SS; they did not have to work; in fact, they enjoyed quite a good time. All of us were very scared of the gipsies. They were dangerous: whenever they had a chance, they knocked us about.

I lay there next to the electrified fence, on the opposite side of the road to the gipsies, growing more and more lethargic. It was a strange kind of numbness. My eyelids felt heavy as lead, my limbs as though they were paralysed. With closed eyes, I lay inert in the sunshine. The noises of the camp sounded fainter and fainter. All at once everything became utterly silent. The suddenness with which this occurred threw me into a panic. Around me and within me, the moment became dumb and motionless. And then in the petrified darkness, it seemed as if someone started to walk towards me from a long way off. I longed to cry out, to scream, to break the silence with my voice, and the darkness, too, and to drive away the one who seemed to be approaching. But no sound came from my lips. The Unknown came nearer and nearer. I could almost hear his silent steps, the rustle of his clothes. 'What do you want?' the words shaped themselves in my mind. 'What do you want from me? Why won't you let me see your face?' And then, as if he understood my terror, he leaned forward and seemed to whisper in my ear: 'After the evening roll-call get away from Barrack No. 17. It is dangerous there. Dangerous. Danger!' His words reached me indistinct and distorted, as if echoed by dark mountains and divided by valleys across thousands of miles, as if in a dream.

I do not know whether it was only minutes or whole hours that passed before the darkness began to recede. I opened my eyes as the heat of the sun struck me with blinding force. I could not comprehend what had happened. I tried to stand up but my limbs seemed to be chained to the ground by fetters of lead. I leaned my head on my clenched fists. With the utmost concentration I tried to remember what had happened. But I could hear nothing except that unidentified voice: 'It is dangerous. Danger.'

While the whispered warning churned ceaselessly in my mind, I recalled a night in which a dream brought me a similar vision. Was there any connection between the two? The dream occurred on the night of 18th March, 1944. I dreamed that I was being transported somewhere on a lorry. Others were also in the lorry. The sky above was slowly turning the colour of blood: there was something strange even in the smell of the wind. The lorry took us to the military parade ground, where once I had learned to shoot. In my dream the field appeared deserted and terrifyingly silent. As we jumped off the lorries I suddenly froze with fright: a soldier wearing a swastika armband emerged from the driver's seat. With the others I was lined up in a long queue; among them I recognized childhood play-fellows, friends, relations. The crowd started to march towards a freshly dug pit. Beneath the blood-red sun the blade of a guillotine fell repeatedly with a dull thud, and into the pit in their thousands rolled an unending tide of human beings. Long after the blade had fallen the blood-stained headless corpses were still writhing.

In the meantime the soldier who had emerged from the driver's seat walked past the people in the queue, looking everyone in the eye. Whoever appeared intimidated by his glance was made to fall out of line and was directed towards the pit. As he approached me in my turn icy perspiration covered my brow—I felt that I was living through the most critical moments of my life. At last he was standing in front of me. His cold eyes bored into mine, trying to hypnotise me to death. I knew that this was a battle of wills between us, and that if but once I was caught up in the blue whirlpool of death in his eyes, I was lost. For a second I was winning, and then I felt that my strength was ebbing, that despite my will I was on the way to the pit in which heaved the dark sea of doomed bodies. There was a shovel in my hand, the kind that grave-diggers use in the cemetery. Slowly the thought came to me: 'You must die, you will die—but why die alone? The shovel in your hand is a weapon. You still have the strength to strike. If you must die, make certain that this murderer dies too.' I turned back, lifted up my shovel and with upraised arms ran towards him. Suddenly everything appeared to become formless, and fear shot through me. It even seemed as if this man, whose eyes had radiated such terror, was not a man at all but a figure of clay. With a face of clay he turned towards the sun which was setting behind the hills. For a moment I thought that he wanted to lure me into a trap, and that he had already fired the bullet carrying my death, but when my frenzied rush had brought me up to him I saw that it was indeed only an unarmed figure of clay which stared witlessly into the void. My onslaught was checked; my arm, raised to attack, was lowered without effect. I woke up. Looking at my watch, I saw that it was 3:30 in the morning.

The following morning, the 19th March, when my sister, deathly pale, announced to us the news that at 3:30 that morning the Germans had crossed the border and occupied our country, I was not even surprised.

The afternoon of my warning vision in the camp, a sudden commotion started up during the customary roll-call (the so-called 'Appel'). The road was emptied of traffic, sirens hooted, gongs were struck.

An SS patrol on motorcycles had arrived before our barrack. Their leader, a tall, blond officer, yelled from afar: *'Hauptschwein, antreten!'* With trembling limbs and knees knocking, the barrack commander moved towards him. 'Enough—stop there. Don't come any nearer, you filthy beast!' the SS man shouted at him, and went on to order him to report the number of 'carcasses'—that is, sick people—in the barrack. The SS man then started off towards the queues to ascertain personally the number of those unfit to work.

As the SS officer drew nearer, a flash of recognition struck me: this was the main figure in my dream on the night of the German invasion. The people who were there in my dream were with me now; I recognized the weird, dreamlike atmosphere. I began to shake with fear. Reality and dream were no longer distinct from each other. I knew what was coming. I knew that he would stand before me with eyes in which one might drown, and set me on the road to death. And while all this flashed through me, someone leaned towards me and whispered in my ear the same words I had heard from the apparition that morning: 'After the roll-call get away from Barrack No. 17. Danger. . . .'

The SS officer was now standing in front of me. I felt that even the wind had stopped blowing. In a thousandth fraction of that second strange images flitted through my mind. I felt as if I could see beyond the barracks, across space and time. Past, present and future converged to a point within me. He looked at me, and as if mesmerized I looked back deep into his eyes. I do not know how long we were staring at one another. I do not know how long he stood before me.

A harsh shout brought me back to my senses. The 'Appel' was over. People were slowly dispersing. I knew that something was about to happen, that I had to do something. Half-conscious, I stumbled towards the electrified fence.

A long ditch ran between the electric fence and the back entrance of the barracks. If someone could no longer bear his dreadful existence and deliberately touched the live wire or chanced to rush against it in a fit of nerves, his body, struck dead in an instant, fell into the ditch and lay there until the *'Sondercommando'* came to take it to the crematorium. It was in this ditch that I took refuge after the 'Appel' was over. Feigning death, I lay there motionless. Yet I did not understand myself why I did so: some unknown power seemed to have benumbed my senses, holding my thoughts and movements in suspension.

I had been lying there for a long time, watched only by the glassy stare of several corpses, when suddenly I became aware of a loud rumbling. Till then I seemed to have been in a coma, but this noise brought me back to full consciousness. I recognized it immediately—SS lorries were rolling into the camp. Almost at once they pulled up sharply before Barrack No. 17. The night was dark; only the headlamps of the lorries lit the scene. I held my breath and listened. Curt words of command were clearly audible. I knew what they meant: no one might leave the barracks.

With riflebutts, whips and bare fists they goaded my comrades from the barrack into the lorries. Now and again a shot echoed through the night. The minutes seemed endlessly long. Suddenly I sensed that someone was approaching the ditch.

'Well, what are we to do with these carcasses?' I could recognize the SS soldier by his voice as he addressed his companion. I did not dare to move my head or to look up out of the ditch. I lay there, my arms spread like the other dead bodies. His torch wavered over the corpses. 'Look, that one's still moving,' he yelled. 'He's moving, the stinking carcass.' Cold sweat broke out all over me. I knew that his machine-gun would be trained towards the ditch. I longed to cry out 'No, not this way—I don't want to die like this.' But I was paralysed. A single shot rang out, followed by a dull groan, then quiet again. He must have finished off someone not yet quite dead—perhaps one of those who had been thrown into the ditch in the afternoon after having been nearly beaten to death.

Minutes passed.

Then the steps receded. They would probably make a special trip for the corpses in the ditch later on.

It was only now that I became aware of the screams and cries that filled the night. One after the other the lorries started off, loaded with human cargo for their fiery destination. The whispered stories that I had heard from the older prisoners about the gas chambers now hit me with dreadful reality. It seemed to be true after all—a thing which even here had seemed unbelievable.

Slowly I lifted up my head as the last of the lorries was passing through the camp gates with its wailing load. Barrack No. 17 gaped wide open in terrible emptiness. I had to get away from it, forget I ever belonged to it, get into some other barrack.

'Away, away from here. . . . Quickly, quickly. . . .'

On all fours I began to crawl along the ditch. I knocked into dead bodies—I climbed over them. My hands were smeared with their blood. Each movement had to be made with care lest I touch the electrified fence. The searchlights on the watchtowers scanned the night, sweeping round the camp. As the beam came towards me I froze on the ground, arms spread out, eyes wide open, until the light had passed me. On, on. . . . The fire of the crematorium flared up, higher and higher. As though propelled by some super-human force, I crawled from barrack to barrack.

Near one of the barracks I clambered out of the ditch. Before the entrance there stood a few barrels, placed there as conveniences for the prisoners at night. Suddenly, with a single leap, I landed near one of them, and hid there. I did not have to wait long before it was opened from the inside. I pretended that I had just come out of that barrack; then I went in. Here, too, the overcrowding was as suffocating as it had been in No. 17. I had to find room for myself somewhere. I stumbled over human bodies—they struck out at me—I kicked back. It did not matter: nothing mattered any longer. I had to find room—just a little room to sit down.

'Go to . . . hell!' someone growled. 'What do you want here?' He kicked me so hard that my stomach turned: the tea adulterated with bromide, the single slice of bread, the half-ounce of margarine, the greenish concoction of soup rose in my gullet. . . .

'You disgusting, filthy swine, vomiting into our faces!'

I realized then that the only way to find some room and save my life was to pit force against force. And when, a few seconds later, I had recovered my wits, I kicked, smashed, and bit until I had obtained a bare foothold for myself in the darkness. At last I was able to sit down. But, though I was overwhelmed by exhaustion, I was unable to sleep. My mind was in a whirl as I thought of all that had happened, and I could not rest in the dreadful congestion, amid people tearing at each other's throats.

When the light of dawn began to trickle into the barrack, I glanced around to get my bearings. My neighbour seemed familiar. For a long time I stared dully at his pale face, puzzling at the way his eyebrows met in the middle. Gradually I placed him. It was Uncle Bert, our family doctor all through my childhood years—and now in this twilit dawn, amid death and terror and far from the old life, still the same old 'Uncle Bert' to me. This creature lying on the ground in his striped prison clothes had once shone his tiny torch into my throat on a winter evening. It was as he did so that I noticed his eyebrows met in the middle, which made a great impression on my childish mind. Neither I nor Mother, Father, nor even my sister could boast of such a thing. Now, as he lay there on the floor of the crowded barrack, I bent over him and had another look at those eyebrows which, on that long-past feverish winter evening, had made such an indelible imprint on my mind.

He used to be a rich man. A bit haughty, too, with a tendency to talk down to poor people who consulted him. It was difficult to tell whether he was serious or merely joking when he growled: 'Look, my boy, your boots are covered with mud, why don't you scrape them clean before you come in here?' And then the poor peasant would go back to the waiting-room to wipe his muddy feet. It paid them to win the favour of such an influential gentleman, for as chief medical officer of the municipality a great deal depended on him: free beds in the hospital, free medicine and the rest. He continued to be looked up to as a 'gentleman' even when the dark clouds were gathering in the sky for the rest of his race. The 'pillars of society' of the town remained friendly with Bert because—'Well, this Jew makes his money in an honest way.' Even when the Jews were herded into the ghetto, his social position remained the same: he became the physician of the ghetto. But by that time the Gentiles no longer showed any anxiety to be his friends.

After the German invasion, but still before the ghetto was set up, I had occasion to look up Uncle Bert in connection with my father's case when he was temporarily imprisoned in the municipal jail after his arrest. I went to see him to obtain a certificate concerning the heart disease from which my father had actually suffered. He was sitting with his family in his roof garden. They had just finished supper. The gramophone was playing; subdued lights created a pleasant atmosphere; glow-worms, cigars studded the semi-darkness. Husband and wife were cracking jokes, oblivious of the fact that elsewhere in the town the Germans were plotting a devastation unequalled in history, among whose victims they themselves were destined to be.

'Unfortunately there's nothing I can do for your dear father. I'm afraid—how shall I put it?—your father did involve himself . . . er . . . in certain Socialist connections with which I have no sympathy. I am sorry for your father because . . . er . . . I have always had a great personal regard for him. But a, what's-it-called, a certificate—that, I'm afraid, I cannot give you. . . .'

I tried to appeal to his heart. I recalled the years of my childhood when he used to be a daily caller at our house. I spoke of the affectionate help which my father had given him in legal matters. I told him that while my father was still in a Hungarian jail, with the help of such a certificate we might be able to get him into a prison hospital. I begged, I entreated—all in vain.

Dazed, in impotent rage, I descended the stairs. Long after I had stepped out into the street the slow rhythm of the gramophone was still throbbing in my ears.

Now he lay there, Uncle Bert, thin as a skeleton, in the midst of the whining, shouting, fighting multitude of the barrack. Gone were his home, his house with the roof garden, his 'gentleman's' attitude, his condescending manner; he lay helpless next to me. Slowly, he opened his eyes. He did not recognize me as, in a whimpering voice, he begged for some warm tea. Outside the barrack in the dawn light they were already beginning to dish out the drugged brew called tea. I went out and brought back a mugful of the steaming liquid. Some fever must have been burning within him; he drank with savage avidity. I felt that I really ought to have hated this man, if it had not been too much of an effort even to hate. But when, having drained the drink to the last drop, the former Medical Officer of Health looked up at me with childish gratitude shining from his eyes, I realized how hard it was to hate if one looked at the world through the eyes of childhood.

Until I met Marta that day in the barrack I had begun to forget that once emotion had vibrated like a melody within me, that I could be one in spirit with the lives of others, share in the unfolding of their joys and sorrows. But now this encounter brought down an avalanche of memories upon me, and the past was brought back into sharp relief. As I closed my eyes that night I distinctly heard the voices of old acquaintances walking along the streets, where I had so often met them—haughty ones who hardly acknowledged one's greeting and modest ones who would hail one first. Each with their familiar mannerisms, they came to meet me in the feverish night and then disappeared down the old street which, now, might well have been destroyed by bombs. Calmly they filed past as they had done before the war, and then they turned to face me once more, dark and distorted, their eyes sunk deep in their sockets—a terrifying apparition.

Many times in the night I started up, only to fall back again into this nightmare state. I was perched on a ledge which overlooked the dizzy chasm of insanity, down in whose depths my memories were revolving like so many hungry whirlpools, threatening to suck me down and down.

But the routine of camp life continued. For hours on end we stood during the morning roll-call and evening roll-call. Fewer and fewer of the old crowd were left, and the chimneys of the crematoria threw up their flames by night as if it were part of a firework display. Only in the gipsies' quarter did everything remain the same.

I spent every evening with Cara. By now I felt she was the only creature to whom I could talk and who could understand me. Was it love that developed between us during those slowly moving days? I do not know. If it was love, it was an Auschwitz brand of love. It was a mixture of numbness, suffering, hopelessness, death and the writhing agony of pleasure. I was little different from Cara now. Poetry, music and painting did not enter my thoughts any more. I, like the others, was only preoccupied with scheming how to grab a bigger chunk of bread, with rejoicing that it was not we who were being burnt that night. My brutality, my violence, the extinction of my moral sense no longer worried me. As if knocked on the head, my conscience lay unconscious somewhere in the deep recesses of my soul, no longer able to remind me of the eternal laws of humanity. The sight of people lying in their congealed blood in the ditch beneath the electrified fence had ceased to quicken my pulse. My fists were no longer itching to get at the murderers. I was a man of Auschwitz. Only rarely and that while dreaming, could I weep—and when I woke up I did not know why I had been crying.

I roamed aimlessly among the gipsy barracks. I saw their days and their nights, their embraces and the grunting expression of their delights. I recognized that their standard of living was a great deal better than our own, but I no longer asked myself why they deserved a more privileged lot. Nothing could make me wonder any more.

Not until a new horror took place one night. Everything happened as if in a nightmare. Afterwards I could only remember being blinded by the headlamps that shone into my eyes out of the darkness of the night, and hearing a sudden commotion and screaming from the gipsy quarter, as the SS lorries carried the gipsies out of the camp. And then I no longer felt Cara's body beside me.

I do not know how long it took them to liquidate the gipsies. But when at dawn I noticed the scattered pots, the torn garments before the empty barracks, at last I realized that I would never see Cara again. The fate of Auschwitz had overtaken the gipsies, too. I burst into tears. For hours I wept hysterically, as if all the tragedy

I had previously experienced, all the terror of days, weeks and months, had overwhelmed me in that one night. And in Cara's destruction I sensed my own.

A few days later, following a last sorting-out, we were herded into trucks again. We did not know until the very moment the train pulled out whether we were bound for the gas chambers or not. Then through the small, iron-grilled window I saw the barracks of Auschwitz becoming smaller and smaller in the distance: the smoke looming above the camp grew fainter also and at last merged into the grey sky. I dropped inert into a corner of the truck. 'I have survived Auschwitz—but what now?'

As I turned towards the wall of the truck, my hand hit something hard. It was a small album of photographs, left there probably by some other deportee, someone who might have arrived that day, or the day before, on the same train, from anywhere in Europe. A special squad was usually assigned to the task of emptying the trucks. Probably in their haste they had not noticed the small album.

I opened it. A woman in an out-moded dress stared at me from the first page. It was one of those typical photographs taken about the beginning of this century. The legend underneath the picture was merely: 'Mother, 1906.' On the next page a young girl was laughing into my eyes. She was sitting on the concrete edge of a swimming pool, her hair streaming with water. I could almost visualize her in front of me: how they threw her into the water, how she fell in with a little scream, how she climbed gaily out. . . . And now she was sitting there at the side of the pool, unaware that someone to whom she must have been dear had clicked the camera.

Another picture. A young lad's eyes smiled into the dimness of the truck. Underneath was written: 'To Mummy, from her loving Buksi.' There on the next page was the girl again, standing serenely in her bridal dress, a middle-aged man next to her. Another photograph—a big party in a garden. There they all are: mother, aunts, husband and wife. How sad this woman looks! What could have happened to her? A small bungalow. An elderly lady is leaning out of the window, and the outlines of a cat are visible through the curtain. And here is an old picture—isn't it funny?—Karoly the Fourth, last king of the monarchy, shaking hands with some soldiers standing in front of him. Well, now, if that isn't the husband! In the uniform of a captain, what a happy smile on his face! Then two snapshots: Quarnero, Italy, 1934. A young woman and a sun-tanned man are looking towards the lens. Hey, that one is Buksi again—how on earth did they get to Italy? Then Buksi in various poses: in the garden, picking some fruit off a tree, very conscious of being photographed, turning his head somewhat artificially towards the camera. Buksi in his study: judging by the instruments scattered on the drawing board, Buksi must be an engineer. An-other picture: 'To Dr. and Mrs. Ignac Szagola, very sincerely, Hen-rik Haber, art photographer.' Probably an extra copy ordered from the photographer. A woman lying in a clean, white bed, holding a small baby in her arms, beside her the husband, his face radiant —no Buksi anywhere—underneath the words: 'Csopi born on 7th September, 1942.' More pictures, pictures, pictures . . . the past coming to life, a family coming to life. People who had been strangers to me suddenly became acquaintances. An old lady, a young girl, Buksi, the husband, Dr. Szagola, where are you now, all of you? Where is that small baby, where the unknown woman leaning out of the window? Where is the sun that shone through the cracks of the shutters—where did the past vanish?

The truck was very quiet. People were lying about in a stupor as the train raced along. We were being carried to slave labour—somewhere.

As night fell the memories crept back again: they came, one after the other, in a weary, heavy-footed row. And the wheels of the carriage kept hammering out the rhythm: Hungary . . . Hungary . . . Hungary. . . . Sleep seemed reluctant to close my eyes. Shreds of talk from right and left drifted towards me in the dark truck.

'And then I told my wife,' somebody was saying, 'look dear, these shoes will be far too big for you. But she insisted on buying them. And then she complained that the shoes were too big. . . .'

People spoke about the past. Some tried to sleep.

Two SS soldiers were sitting in the middle of the truck, their weapons at the ready. One kept his eye on the left half of the truck, the other covered the right-hand half. Hungary . . . Hungary . . . Hungary . . . the rails reverberated. Like some tune which gets tangled up in one's mind and cannot be driven out, so did the name of my country whirl round my dizzy brain. And suddenly I saw before me my nursery room—the nursery with the little bed in which I used to sleep every night. I saw before me the flames of the open stove, lighting up the ceiling, forming moving shadows on the walls which, like so many fearsome devils, now stretched out, now withdrew their claws. Beyond the window was the night, and snow was falling in large, white flakes. I saw myself in the white featherbed. At times the fire crackled in a strange tongue. Someone turned on the tap in the kitchen.

'What use will it be if the Allies do win in the end?' I heard someone's voice coming from the depths of the reverberating truck, 'By then we shall all be dead.'

Hungary . . . Hungary . . . Hungary . . . the rails rattled beneath us.

The bed sat in the corner of the room like a little yellow prison. It was made of brass. When they put me to bed, they pulled up the wooden bars and fixed them with string, so that I should not fall out.

'Little Jancsi must go to sleep,' Mother said, 'All little boys ought to be asleep by now.'

'But I am not a little boy,' I whimpered.

When Mother had left me alone, silence prevailed. Then out of the silence came the voices: the voices of the fire, the voice of the wind, the voice of the water-tap, and last of all, the voice of silence itself—a strange, chirping, hissing, buzzing sound which I greatly feared. Terrified I lifted my head out of the featherbed.

All of a sudden, the screaming of air-raid sirens from the depths of the present night brought me to my senses. Like wounded beasts they wailed. Then silence returned, and once more the past unfolded. The carpet reached as far as the wardrobe: squares linked up with other squares in its pattern, like a number of trapped, wriggling crosses, or the slithering of snakes. A silvery key kept a melancholy vigil in the lock of the wardrobe, within which dwelt a world of whiteness—Daddy's shirts, Mummy's clothes, tablecloths and bedspreads. Hidden somewhere here was that many-layered black wallet with all sorts of leaflets and cards which Mother used to collect over the years tucked into it: I was allowed to play with them when I was ill. Here also was the small mahogany music box. When it was wound up for me I could watch the little disc revolving behind the glass and listen to the tinkling music.

Next to the wardrobe was the window, a double window. In summer flies crawled between the panes, seeking a way to the open air. And then there was the mirror, with its two folding wings. At a certain angle they would reflect a whole infinity of Me's. I played with it often. When they put me to bed I used to think of the innumerable little boys left inside the mirror—were they, too, put to bed by their mother? Next to the mirror came the bed, my parents' bed. In the mornings I frequently paid a visit to this bed. It was so wonderfully warm there, under Mummy's blanket. . . .

'Little Jancsi must sleep now,' I heard my Mother's voice from the distance. 'Little boys should be asleep by now.'

How clearly and sharply I saw myself, such a brief while ago, on this dreadful night! I was afraid not so much of the forces of the external world as of the powers of the universe within, the odd, mysterious universe of childhood, until, with bombs exploding in the distance, I became momentarily more aware of the peril which was now threatening from without. Then, for a long time, no images came at all . . . I just sat in the dark, my head bent over my knees. But later the darkness began to loosen up again, and in the slowly blinking twilight of this darkness fresh pictures arrived.

The park in the suburb, set beneath the cloister on the hillside. . . . Here stood the pavilion, a restaurant built of logs where on Sundays the stolid citizens, perched on benches, listened to the band. The wind was blowing from the direction of the river; Mother, sitting on a bench, was knitting a pullover. Further away some pensioners were sitting, savouring their pipes with slow puffs beneath their big moustaches. By the fountain a few children were playing. As the sun began to set, the rust-coloured rays lit up Mother's hair. 'How lovely you look, Mummy!' I said, and she smiled. In a little while, when the wind grew stronger and brought the chill of the north with it, we set out for home along the tree-lined road.

'Do you see those trees bending, Jancsi?' she asked. 'Do you know what makes them move?'

'The wind,' I answered proudly.

'Would you like to play the wind-game?'

The long road was quite deserted; hand in hand we started walking. The slow steps counted as a 'breeze,' we went faster when Mother said 'wind,' and then we ran as she shouted 'storm.' And then she picked me up high in the air, running as she held me.

'Whirlwind, whirlwind,' she whispered, exhausted by the effort. We reached the street. The bell of the near-by church rang its summons. A man riding a bicycle, holding a long pole, triggered the dim flames of the gas lamps into brightness under the evening sky . . . and . . . and I was thinking that one day I would grow up and not have Mother by my side any more. . . .

'Hungary . . . Hungary . . . Hungary . . .' the wheels of the truck wailed on. Large tears rolled down my cheeks. 'I did grow up, Mummy, I did grow up. . . .'

I was deathly tired by then. But my tormenting memories gave me no rest, as I looked back at the fearful pattern that had brought me to this time and place.

4. *IF THIS IS A MAN*

PRIMO LEVI

Another road leading to Auschwitz began in Italy. And, as Chaim Kaplan helped us understand Alexander Donat, so Levi adds new dimension to Heimler. They talk about the same camp. But here we are given isolated incidents, and case histories. Men like Elias, Henri, Alfred L., and Schepschel give us a clearer understanding of life at Auschwitz. And Dante's "Inferno" while strange literature in a concentration camp turns out to be most applicable.

THE DROWNED AND THE SAVED

What we have so far said and will say concerns the ambiguous life of the Lager. In our days many men have lived in this cruel manner, crushed against the bottom, but each for a relatively short period; so that we can perhaps ask ourselves if it is necessary or good to retain any memory of this exceptional human state.

To this question we feel that we have to reply in the affirmative. We are in fact convinced that no human experience is without meaning or unworthy of analysis, and that fundamental values, even if they are not positive, can be deduced from this particular world which we are describing. We would also like to consider that the Lager was pre-eminently a gigantic biological and social experiment.

Thousands of individuals, differing in age, condition, origin, language, culture and customs are enclosed within barbed wire: there they live a regular, controlled life which is identical for all and inadequate to all needs, and which is much more rigorous than any experimenter could have set up to establish what is essential and what adventitious to the conduct of the human animal in the struggle for life.

We do not believe in the most obvious and facile deduction: that man is fundamentally brutal, egoistic and stupid in his conduct once every civilized institution is taken away, and that the Häftling is consequently nothing but a man without inhibitions. We believe, rather, that the only conclusion to be drawn is that in the face of driving necessity and physical disabilities many social habits and instincts are reduced to silence.

But another fact seems to us worthy of attention: there comes to light the existence of two particularly well differentiated categories among men—the saved and the drowned. Other pairs of opposites (the good and the bad, the wise and the foolish, the cowards and the courageous, the unlucky and the fortunate) are considerably less distinct, they seem less essential, and above all they allow for more numerous and complex intermediary gradations.

This division is much less evident in ordinary life; for there it rarely happens that a man loses himself. A man is normally not alone, and in his rise or fall is tied to the destinies of his neighbors; so that it is exceptional for anyone to acquire unlimited power, or to fall by a succession of defeats into utter ruin. Moreover, everyone is normally in possession of such spiritual, physical and even financial resources that the probabilities of a shipwreck, of total inadequacy in the face of life, are relatively small. And one must take into account a definite cushioning effect exercised both by the law, and by the moral sense which constitutes a self-imposed law; for a country is considered the more civilized the more the wisdom and efficiency of its laws hinder a weak man from becoming too weak or a powerful one too powerful.

But in the Lager things are different: here the struggle to survive is without respite, because everyone is desperately and ferociously alone. If some Null Achtzehn vacillates, he will find no one to extend a helping hand; on the contrary, someone will knock him aside, because it is in no one's interest that there be one more "mussulman"[1] dragging himself to work every day; and if someone, by a miracle of savage patience and cunning, finds a new method of avoiding the hardest work, a new art which yields him an ounce of bread, he will try to keep his method secret, and he will be esteemed and respected for this, and will derive from it an exclusive, personal benefit; he will become stronger and so will be feared, and who is feared is, ipso facto, a candidate for survival.

In history and in life one sometimes seems to glimpse a ferocious law which states: "to he that has, will be given; to he that has not, will be taken away." In the Lager, where man is alone and where the struggle for life is reduced to its primordial mechanism, this unjust law is openly in force, is recognized by all. With the adaptable, the strong and astute individuals, even the leaders willingly keep contact, sometimes even friendly contact, because they hope later to perhaps derive some benefit. But with the mussulmans, the men in decay, it is not even worth speaking, because one knows already that they will complain and will speak about what they used to eat at home. Even less worthwhile is it to make friends with them, because they have no distinguished acquaintances in camp, they do not gain any extra rations, they do not work in profitable Kommandos and they know no secret method of organizing. And in any case, one knows that they are only here on a visit, that in a few weeks nothing will remain of them but a handful of ashes in some near-by field and a crossed-out number on a register. Although engulfed and swept along without rest by the innumerable crowd of those similar to them, they suffer and drag themselves along in an opaque intimate solitude, and in solitude they die or disappear, without leaving a trace in anyone's memory.

The result of this pitiless process of natural selection could be read in the statistics of Lager population movements. At Auschwitz, in 1944, of the old Jewish prisoners (we will not speak of the others here, as their condition was different), *"kleine Nummer,"* low numbers less than 150,000, only a few hundred had survived; not one was an ordinary Häftling, vegetating in the ordinary Kommandos, and subsisting on the normal ration. There remained only the doctors, tailors, shoemakers, musicians, cooks, young at-

---

[1] This word "mussulman," I do not know why, was used by the old ones of the camp to describe the weak, the inept, those doomed to selection.

tractive homosexuals, friends or compatriots of some authority in
the camp; or they were particularly pitiless, vigorous and inhuman
individuals, installed (following an investiture by the SS command,
which showed itself in such choices to possess satanic knowledge of
human beings) in the posts of Kapos, *Blockältester,* etc.; or finally,
those who, without fulfilling particular functions, had always succeeded through their astuteness and energy in successfully organizing, gaining in this way, besides material advantages and reputation, the indulgence and esteem of the powerful people in the
camp. Whosoever does not know how to become an "Organisator,"
"Kombinator," "Prominent" (the savage eloquence of these words!)
soon becomes a "mussulman." In life, a thrid way exists, and is in
fact the rule; it does not exist in the concentration camp.

To sink is the easiest of matters; it is enough to carry out all
the orders one receives, to eat only the ration, to observe the discipline of the work and the camp. Experience showed that only
exceptionally could one survive more than three months in this
way. All the mussulmans who finished in the gas chambers have the
same story, or more exactly, have no story; they followed the slope
down to the bottom, like streams that run down to the sea. On their
entry into the camp, through basic incapacity, or by misfortune, or
through some banal incident, they are overcome before they can
adapt themselves; they are beaten by time, they do not begin to
learn German, to disentangle the infernal knot of laws and prohibi-
tions until their body is already in decay, and nothing can save
them from selections or from death by exhaustion. Their life is
short, but their number is endless; they, the *Muselmänner,* the
drowned, form the backbone of the camp, an anonymous mass,
continually renewed and always identical, of non-men who march
and labor in silence, the divine spark dead within them, already
too empty to really suffer. One hesitates to call them living: one
hesitates to call their death death, in the face of which they have
no fear, as they are too tired to understand.

They crowd my memory with their faceless presences, and if
I could enclose all the evil of our time in one image, I would
choose this image which is familiar to me: an emaciated man, with
head dropped and shoulders curved, on whose face and in whose
eyes not a trace of a thought is to be seen.

If the drowned have no story, and single and broad is the path to perdition, the paths to salvation are many, difficult and improbable.

The most travelled road, as we have stated, is the *"Prominenz."* *"Prominenten"* is the name for the camp officials, from the Häftling-director *(Lagerältester)* to the Kapos, the cooks, the nurses, the night-guards, even to the hut-sweepers and to the *Scheissminister* and *Bademeister* (superintendents of the latrines and showers). We are more particularly interested in the Jewish prominents, because while the others are automatically invested with offices as they enter the camp in virtue of their natural supremacy, the Jews have to plot and struggle hard to gain them.

The Jewish prominents form a sad and notable human phenomenon. In them converge present, past and atavistic sufferings, and the tradition of hostility towards the stranger makes of them monsters of asociality and insensitivity.

They are the typical product of the structure of the German Lager: if one offers a position of privilege to a few individuals in a state of slavery, exacting in exchange the betrayal of a natural solidarity with their comrades, there will certainly be someone who will accept. He will be withdrawn from the common law and will become untouchable; the more power that he is given, the more he will be consequently hateful and hated. When he is given the command of a group of unfortunates, with the right of life or death over them, he will be cruel and tyrannical, because he will understand that if he is not sufficiently so, someone else, judged more suitable, will take over his post. Moreover, his capacity for hatred, unfulfilled in the direction of the oppressors, will double back, beyond all reason, on the oppressed; and he will only be satisfied when he has unloaded onto his underlings the injury received from above.

We are aware that this is very distant from the picture that is usually given of the oppressed who unite, if not in resistance, at least in suffering. We do not deny that this may be possible when oppression does not pass a certain limit, or perhaps when the oppressor, through inexperience or magnanimity, tolerates or favors it. But we state that in our days, in all countries in which a foreign people have set foot as invaders, an analogous position of rivalry and hatred among the subjected has been brought about; and this, like many other human characteristics, could be experienced in the Lager in the light of particularly cruel evidence.

About the non-Jewish prominents there is less to say, although they were far and away the most numerous (no "Aryan" Häftling was without a post, however modest). That they were stolid and bestial is natural when one thinks that the majority were ordinary criminals, chosen from the German prisons for the very purpose of their employment as superintendents of the camps for Jews; and we maintain that it was a very apt choice, because we refuse to believe that the squalid human specimens whom we saw at work were an average example, not of Germans in general, but even of German prisoners in particular. It is difficult to explain how in Auschwitz the political German, Polish and Russian prominents rivalled the ordinary convicts in brutality. But it is known that in Germany the qualification of political crime also applied to such acts as clandestine trade, illicit relations with Jewish women, theft from Party officials. The "real" politicals lived and died in other camps, with names now sadly famous, in notoriously hard conditions, which, however, in many aspects differed from those described here.

But besides the officials in the strict sense of the word, there is a vast category of prisoners, not initially favored by fate, who fight merely with their own strength to survive. One has to fight against the current; to battle every day and every hour against exhaustion, hunger, cold and the resulting inertia; to resist enemies and have no pity for rivals; to sharpen one's wits, build up one's patience, strengthen one's will-power. Or else, to throttle all dignity and kill all conscience, to climb down into the arena as a beast against other beasts, to let oneself be guided by those unsuspected subterranean forces which sustain families and individuals in cruel times. Many were the ways devised and put into effect by us in order not to die: as many as there are different human characters. All implied a weakening struggle of one against all, and a by no means small sum of aberrations and compromises. Survival without renunciation of any part of one's own moral world—apart from powerful and direct interventions by fortune—was conceded only to very few superior individuals, made of the stuff of martyrs and saints.

We will try to show in how many ways it was possible to reach salvation with the stories of Schepschel, Alfred L., Elias and Henri.

Schepschel has been living in the Lager for four years. He has seen the death of tens of thousands of those like him, beginning with the pogrom which had driven him from his village in Galicia. He had a wife and five children and a prosperous business as a saddler, but for a long time now he has grown accustomed to thinking of himself only as a sack which needs periodic refilling. Schepschel is not very robust, nor very courageous, nor very wicked; he is not even particularly astute, nor has he ever found a method which allows him a little respite, but he is reduced to small and occasional expedients, *"kombinacje"* as they are called here.

Every now and again he steals a broom in Buna and sells it to the *Blockältester,* when he manages to set aside a little bread-capital, he hires the tools of the cobbler in the Block, his compatriot, and works on his own account for a few hours; he knows how to make braces with interlaced electric wires. Sigi told me that he has seen him during the midday interval singing and dancing in front of the hut of the Slovak workers, who sometimes reward him with the remainders of their soup.

This said, one would be inclined to think of Schepschel with indulgent sympathy, as of a poor wretch who retains only a humble and elementary desire to live, and who bravely carries on his small struggle not to give way. But Schepschel was no exception, and when the opportunity showed itself, he did not hesitate to have Moischl, his accomplice in a theft from the kitchen, condemned to a flogging, in the mistaken hope of gaining favor in the eyes of the *Blockältester* and furthering his candidature for the position of *Kesselwäscher,* "vat-washer."

The story of engineer Alfred L. shows among other things how vain is the myth of original equality among men.

In his own country L. was the director of an extremely important factory of chemical products, and his name was (and is) well-known in industrial circles throughout Europe. He was a robust man of about fifty; I do not know how he had been arrested, but he entered the camp like all others: naked, alone and unknown. When I knew him he was very wasted away, but still showed on his face the signs of a disciplined and methodical energy; at that time, his privileges were limited to the daily cleaning of the Polish workers' pots; this work which he had gained in some manner as his exclusive monopoly, yielded him half a ladleful of soup per day. Certainly it was not enough to satisfy his hunger; nevertheless, no one had ever heard him complain. In fact, the few words that he let slip implied imposing secret resources, a solid and fruitful "organization."

This was confirmed by his appearance. L. had a "line": with his hands and face always perfectly clean, he had a rare self-denial to wash his shirt every fortnight, without waiting for the bi-monthly change (we would like to point out here that to wash a shirt meant finding soap, time and space in the overcrowded washroom; adapting oneself to carefully keep watch on the wet shirt without losing attention for a moment, and to put it on, naturally still wet, in the silence-hour when the lights are turned out); he owned a pair of wooden shoes to go to the shower, and even his striped suit was singularly adapted to his appearance, clean and new. L. had acquired in practice the whole appearance of a prominent considerably before becoming one; only a long time after did I find out that L. was able to earn all this show of prosperity with incredible tenacity, paying for his individual acquisitions and services with bread from his own ration, so imposing upon himself a regime of supplementary privations.

His plan was a long-term one, which is all the more notable as conceived in an environment dominated by a mentality of the provisional; and L. carried it out with rigid inner discipline without pity for himself or—with greater reason—for comrades who crossed his path. L. knew that the step was short from being judged powerful to effectively becoming so, and that everywhere, and especially in the midst of the general levelling of the Lager, a respectable appearance is the best guarantee of being respected. He took every care not to be confused with the mass; he worked with stubborn duty, even occasionally admonishing his lazy comrades in a persuasive and deprecatory tone of voice; he avoided the daily struggle for the best place in the queue for the ration, and prepared to take the first ration, notoriously the most liquid, every day, so as to be noticed by his *Blockältester* for his discipline. To complete the separation, he always behaved in his relations with his comrades with the maximum courtesy compatible with his egotism, which was absolute.

When the Chemical Kommando was formed, as will be described, L. knew that his hour had struck: he needed no more than his spruce suit and his emaciated and shaved face in the midst of the flock of his sordid and slovenly colleagues to at once convince both Kapo and *Arbeitsdienst* that he was one of the genuinely saved, a potential prominent; so that (to he who has, shall be given) he was without hesitation appointed "specialist," nominated technical head of the Kommando, and taken on by the Direction of the Buna as analyst in the laboratory of the styrene department. He was subsequently appointed to examine all the new intake to the Chemical Kommando, to judge their professional ability; which he always did with extreme severity, especially when faced with those in whom he smelled possible future rivals.

I do not know how his story continued; but I feel it is quite probable that he managed to escape death, and today is still living his cold life of the determined and joyless dominator.

Elias Lindzin, 141565, one day rained into the Chemical Kommando. He was a dwarf, not more than five feet high, but I have never seen muscles like his. When he is naked you can see every muscle taut under his skin, like a poised animal; his body, enlarged without alteration of proportions, would serve as a good model for a Hercules: but you must not look at his head.

Under his scalp, the skull sutures stand out immoderately. The cranium is massive and gives the impression of being made of metal or stone; the back limit of his shaven hair shows up barely a finger's width above his eyebrows. The nose, the chin, the forehead, the cheekbones are hard and compact, the whole face looks like a battering ram, an instrument made for butting. A sense of bestial vigor emanates from his body.

To see Elias work is a disconcerting spectacle; the Polish *Meister*, even the Germans sometimes stop to admire Elias at work. Nothing seems impossible to him. While we barely carry one sack of cement, Elias carries two, then three, then four, keeping them balanced no one knows how, and while he hurries along on his short, squat legs, he makes faces under the load, he laughs, curses, shouts and sings without pause, as if he had lungs made of bronze. Despite his wooden shoes Elias climbs like a monkey on to the scaffolding and runs safely on cross-beams poised over nothing; he carries six bricks at a time balanced on his head; he knows how to make a spoon from a piece of tin, and a knife from a scrap of steel; he finds dry paper, wood and coal everywhere and knows how to start a fire in a few moments even in the rain. He is a tailor, a carpenter, a cobbler, a barber; he can spit incredible distances; he sings, in a not unpleasant bass voice, Polish and Yiddish songs never heard before; he can ingest ten, fifteen, twenty pints of soup without vomiting and without having diarrhea, and begin work again immediately after. He knows how to make a big hump come out between his shoulders, and goes around the hut, bow-legged and mimicking, shouting and declaiming incomprehensibly, to the joy of the Prominents of the camp. I saw him fight a Pole a whole head taller than him and knock him down with a blow of his cranium into the stomach, as powerful and accurate as a catapult. I never saw him rest, I never saw him quiet or still, I never saw him injured or ill.

Of his life as a free man, no one knows anything; and in any case, to imagine Elias as a free man requires a great effort of fantasy and induction; he only speaks Yiddish, and the surly and deformed Yiddish of Warsaw; besides it is impossible to keep him to a coherent conversation. He might be twenty or forty years old; he usually says that he is thirty-three, and that he has begot seventeen children—which is not unlikely. He talks continuously on the most varied of subjects; always in a resounding voice, in an oratorical manner, with the violent mimicry of the deranged; as if he was always talking to a dense crowd—and, as is natural, he never lacks a public. Those who understand his language drink up his declamations, shaking with laughter; they pat him enthusiastically on the back—a back as hard as iron—inciting him to continue; while he, fierce and frowning, whirls around like a wild animal in the circle of his audience, apostrophizing now one, now another of them; he suddenly grabs hold of one by the chest with his small hooked paw, irresistibly drags him to himself, vomits into his face an incomprehensible invective, then throws him back like a piece of wood, and amidst the applause and laughter, with his arms reaching up to the heavens like some little prophetic monster, continues his raging and crazy speech.

His fame as an exceptional worker spread quite soon, and by the absurd law of the Lager, from then on he practically ceased to work. His help was requested directly by the *Meister* only for such work as required skill and special vigor. Apart from these services he insolently and violently supervised our daily, flat exhaustion, frequently disappearing on mysterious visits and adventures in who knows what recesses of the yard, from which he returned with large bulges in his pockets and often with his stomach visibly full.

Elias is naturally and innocently a thief: in this he shows the instinctive astuteness of wild animals. He is never caught in the act because he only steals when there is a good chance; but when this chance comes Elias steals as fatally and foreseeably as a stone drops. Apart from the fact that it is difficult to surprise him, it is obvious that it would be of no use punishing him for his thefts: to him they imply a vital act like breathing or sleeping.

We can now ask who is this man Elias. If he is a madman, incomprehensible and para-human, who ended in the Lager by chance. If he is an atavism, different from our modern world, and better adapted to the primordial conditions of camp life. Or if he is perhaps a product of the camp itself, what we will all become if we do not die in the camp, and if the camp itself does not end first.

There is some truth in all three suppositions. Elias has survived the destruction from outside, because he is physically indestructable; he has resisted the annihilation from within because he is insane. So, in the first place, he is a surviver: he is the most adaptable, the human type most suited to this way of living.

If Elias regains his liberty he will be confined to the fringes of human society, in a prison or a lunatic asylum. But here in Lager there are no criminals nor madmen; no criminals because there is no moral law to contravene, no madmen because we are wholly devoid of free will, as our every action is, in time and place, the only conceivable one.

In the Lager Elias prospers and is triumphant. He is a good worker and a good organizer, and for this double reason, he is safe from selections and respected by both leaders and comrades. For those who have no sound inner resources, for those who do not know how to draw from their own consciences sufficient force to cling to life, the only road to salvation leads to Elias: to insanity and to deceitful bestiality. All the other roads are dead-ends.

This said, one might perhaps be tempted to draw conclusions, and perhaps even rules for our daily life. Are there not all around us some Eliases, more or less in embryo? Do we not see individuals living without purpose, lacking all forms of self-control and conscience, who live not *in spite of* these defects, but like Elias precisely because of them?

The question is serious, but will not be further discussed as we want these to be stories of the Lager, while much has already been written on man outside the Lager. But one thing we would still like to add: Elias, as far as we could judge from outside, and as far as the phrase can have meaning, was probably a happy person.

Henri, on the other hand, is eminently civilized and sane, and possesses a complete and organic theory on the ways to survive in Lager. He is only twenty-two, he is extremely intelligent, speaks French, German, English and Russian, has an excellent scientific and classical culture.

His brother died in Buna last winter, and since then Henri has cut off every tie of affection; he has closed himself up, as if in armor and fights to live without distraction with all the resources that he can derive from his quick intellect and his refined education. According to Henri's theory, there are three methods open to man to escape extermination which still allow him to retain the name of man: organization, pity and theft.

He himself practices all three. There is no better strategist than Henri in seducing ("cultivating" he says) the English PoWs. In his hands they become real geese with golden eggs—if you remember that in exchange for a single English cigarette you can make enough in Lager not to starve for a day. Henri was once seen in the act of eating a real hard-boiled egg.

The traffic in products of English origin is Henri's monopoly, and this is all a matter of organization; but his instrument of penetration, with the English and with others, is pity. Henri has the delicate and subtly perverse body and face of Sodoma's San Sebastian: his eyes are deep and profound, he has no beard yet, he moves with a natural languid elegance (although when necessary he knows how to run and jump like a cat, while the capacity of his stomach is little inferior to that of Elias). Henri is perfectly aware of his natural gifts and exploits them with the cold competence of a physicist using a scientific instrument: the results are surprising. Basically it is a question of a discovery: Henri has discovered that pity, being a primary and instinctive sentiment, grows quite well if ably cultivated, particularly in the primitive minds of the brutes who command us, those very brutes who have no scruples about beating us up without a reason, or treading our faces into the ground; nor has the great practical importance of the discovery escaped him, and upon it he has built up his personal trade.

As the ichneumon paralyzes the great hairy caterpillar, wounding it in its only vulnerable ganglion, so Henri at a glance sizes up the subject, *"son type"*; he speaks to him briefly, to each with the appropriate language, and the *"type"* is conquered: he listens with increasing sympathy, he is moved by the fate of this unfortunate young man, and not much time is needed before he begins to yield returns.

There is no heart so hardened that Henri cannot breach it if he sets himself to it seriously. In the Lager, and in Buna as well, his protectors are very numerous: English soldiers, French Ukrainian, Polish civilian workers; German "politicals"; at least four *Blockältester,* a cook, even an SS man. But his favorite field is Ka-Be: Henri has free entry into Ka-Be; Doctor Citron and Doctor Weiss are more than his protectors, they are his friends and take him in whenever he wants and with the diagnosis he wants. This takes place especially immediately before selections, and in the periods of the most laborious work: "hibernation," as he says.

Possessing such conspicuous friendships, it is natural that Henri is rarely reduced to the third method, theft; on the other hand, he naturally does not talk much about this subject.

It is very pleasant to talk to Henri in moments of rest. It is also useful: there is nothing in the camp that he does not know and about which he has not reasoned in his close and coherent manner. Of his conquests, he speaks with educated modesty, as of prey of little worth, but he digresses willingly into an explanation of the calculation which led him to approach Hans asking him about his son at the front, and Otto instead showing him the scars on his shins.

To speak with Henri is useful and pleasant: one sometimes also feels him warm and near; communication, even affection seems possible. One seems to glimpse, behind his uncommon personality, a human soul, sorrowful and aware of itself. But the next moment his sad smile freezes into a cold grimace which seems studied at the mirror; Henri politely excuses himself (". . . j' ai quelque chose à faire," ". . . j' ai quelqu'un à voir") and here he is again, intent on his hunt and his struggle; hard and distant, enclosed in armor, the enemy of all, inhumanly cunning and incomprehensible like the Serpent in Genesis.

From all my talks with Henri, even the most cordial, I have always left with a slight taste of defeat; of also having been, somehow inadvertently, not a man to him, but an instrument in his hands.

I know that Henri is living today. I would give much to know his life as a free man, but I do not want to see him again.

THE CANTO OF ULYSSES

There were six of us, scraping and cleaning the inside of an underground petrol tank; the daylight only reached us through a small manhole. It was a luxury job because no one supervised us; but it was cold and damp. The powder of the rust burnt under our eyelids and coated our throats and mouths with a taste almost like blood.

The rope-ladder hanging from the manhole began to sway: someone was coming. Deutsch extinguished his cigarette, Goldner woke Sivadjan; we all began to vigorously scrape the resonant steelplate wall.

It was not the *Vorarbeiter*, it was only Jean, the Pikolo of our Kommando. Jean was an Alsatian student; although he was already twenty-four, he was the youngest Häftling of the Chemical Kommando. So that he was given the post of Pikolo, which meant the messenger-clerk, responsible for the cleaning of the hut, for the distribution of tools, for the washing of bowls, and for keeping record of the working hours of the Kommando.

Jean spoke French and German fluently; as soon as we recognized his shoes on the top step of the ladder we all stopped scraping.

"Also, Pikolo, was gibt es Neues?"

"Qu'est ce qu'il-y-a comme soupe aujourd'hui?"

. . . in what mood was the Kapo? And the affair of the twenty-five lashes given to Stern? What was the weather like outside? Had he read the newspaper? What smell was coming from the civilian kitchen? What was the time?

Jean was liked a great deal by the Kommando. One must realize that the post of Pikolo represented a quite high rank in the hierarchy of the Prominents: the Pikolo (who is usually no more than seventeen years old) does no manual work, has an absolute right to the remainder of the daily ration to be found on the bottom of the vat, and can stay all day near the stove. He "therefore" has the right to a supplementary half-ration and has a good chance of becoming the friend and confidant of the Kapo, from whom he officially receives discarded clothes and shoes. Now Jean was an exceptional Pikolo. He was shrewd and physically robust, and at the same time gentle and friendly: although he continued his secret individual struggle against the camp and against death, he did not neglect his human relationships with less privileged comrades; at the same time he had been so able and persevering that he had managed to establish himself in the confidence of Alex, the Kapo.

Alex had kept all his promises. He had shown himself a violent and unreliable rogue, with an armor of solid and compact ignorance and stupidity, always excepting his intuition and consummate technique as convict-keeper. He never let slip an opportunity of proclaiming his pride in his pure blood and his green triangle, and displayed a lofty contempt for his ragged and starving chemists: *"Ihr Doktoren! Ihr Intelligenten!"* he sneered every day, watching them crowd around with their bowls held out for the distribution of the ration. He was extremely compliant and servile before the civilian *Meister* and with the SS he kept up ties of cordial friendship.

He was clearly intimidated by the register of the Kommando and by the daily report of work, and this had been the path that Pikolo had chosen to make himself indispensable. It had been a long, cautious and subtle task which the entire Kommando had followed for a month with bated breath; but at the end the porcupine's defense was penetrated, and Pikolo confirmed in his office to the satisfaction of all concerned.

Although Jean had never abused his position, we had already been able to verify that a single word of his, said in the right tone of voice and at the right moment, had great power; many times already it had saved one of us from a whipping or from being denounced to the SS. We had been friends for a week: we discovered each other during the unusual occasion of an air-raid alarm, but then, swept by the fierce rhythm of the Lager, we had only been able to greet each other fleetingly, at the latrines, in the washroom. Hanging with one hand on the swaying ladder, he pointed to me:

"Aujourd'hui c'est Primo qui viendra avec moi chercher la soupe."

Until yesterday it had been Stern, the squinting Transylvanian; now he had fallen into disgrace for some story of brooms stolen from the store, and Pikolo had managed to support my candidature as assistant to the *"Essenholen,"* the daily corvée of the ration.

He climbed out and I followed him, blinking in the brightness of the day. It was warmish outside, the sun drew a faint smell of paint and tar from the greasy earth, which made me think of a holiday beach of my infancy. Pikolo gave me one of the two wooden poles, and we walked along under a clear June sky. I began to thank him, but he stopped me: it was not necessary. One could see the Carpathians covered in snow. I breathed in the fresh air, I felt unusually lighthearted.

"Tu es fou de marcher si vite. On a le temps, tu sais." The ration was collected half a mile away; one had to return with the pot weighing over a hundred pounds supported on the two poles. It was quite a tiring task, but it meant a pleasant walk there without a load, and the ever-welcome chance of going near the kitchens.

We slowed down. Pikolo was expert. He had chosen the path cleverly so that we would have to make a long detour, walking at least for an hour, without arousing suspicion. We spoke of our houses, of Strasbourg and Turin, of the books we had read, of what we had studied, of our mothers: how all mothers resemble each other! His mother too had scolded him for never knowing how much money he had in his pocket; his mother too would have been amazed if she had known that he had found his feet, that day by day he was finding his feet.

An SS man passed on a bicycle. It is Rudi, the *Blockführer*. Halt! Attention! Take off your beret! *"Sale brute, celui-là. Ein ganz gemeiner Hund."* Can he speak French and German with equal facility? Yes, he thinks indifferently in both languages. He spent a month in Liguria, he likes Italy, he would like to learn Italian. I would be pleased to teach him Italian: why not try? We can do it. Why not immediately, one thing is as good as another, the important thing is not to lose time, not to waste this hour.

Limentani from Rome walks by, dragging his feet, with a bowl hidden under his jacket. Pikolo listens carefully, picks up a few words of our conversation and repeats them smiling: *"Zup-pa, campo, acqua."*

Frenkl the spy passes. Quicken our pace, one never knows, he does evil for evil's sake.

. . . The canto of Ulysses. Who knows how or why it comes into my mind. But we have no time to change, this hour is already less than an hour. If Jean is intelligent he will understand. He *will* understand—today I feel capable of so much.

. . . Who is Dante? What is the Comedy? That curious sensation of novelty which one feels if one tries to explain briefly what is the *Divine Comedy*. How the "Inferno" is divided up, what are its punishments. Virgil is Reason, Beatrice is Theology.

Jean pays great attention, and I begin slowly and accurately:

> Then of that age-old fire the loftier horn
> Began to mutter and move, as a wavering flame
> Wrestles against the wind and is over-worn;
> And, like a speaking tongue vibrant to frame
> Language, the tip of it flickering to and fro
> Threw out a voice and answered: "When I came. . ."

Here I stop and try to translate. Disastrous—poor Dante and poor French! All the same, the experience seems to promise well: Jean admires the bizarre simile of the tongue and suggests the appropriate word to translate "age-old."

And after "When I came"? Nothing. A hole in my memory. "Before Aeneas ever named it so." Another hole. A fragment floats into my mind, not relevant: ". . . nor piety To my old father, nor the wedded love That should have comforted Penelope . . . ," is it correct?

". . . So on the open sea I set forth."

Of this I am certain, I am sure I can explain it to Pikolo, I can point out why "I set forth"[2] is not *"je me mis,"* it is much stronger and more audacious, it is a chain which has been broken, it is throwing oneself on the other side of a barrier, we know the impulse well. The open sea: Pikolo has travelled by sea, and knows what it means: it is when the horizon closes in on itself, free, straight ahead and simple, and there is nothing but the smell of the sea; sweet things, ferociously far away.

We have arrived at Kraftwerk, where the cable-laying Kommando works. Engineer Levi must be here. Here he is, one can only see his

---

2 "misi me" (Translator's note).

head above the trench. He waves to me, he is a brave man, I have never seen his morale low, he never speaks of eating.

"Open sea," "open sea." I know it rhymes with "left me": ". . . and that small band of comrades that had never left me," but I cannot remember if it comes before or after. And the journey as well, the foolhardy journey beyond the Pillars of Hercules, how sad, I have to tell it in prose—a sacrelegi. I have only rescued two lines, but they are worth stopping for:

> . . . that none should prove so hardy
> To venture the uncharted distances. . . .

"to venture"[3]: I had to come to the Lager to realize that it is the same expression as before "I set forth." But I say nothing to Jean, I am not sure that it is an important observation. How many things there are to say, and the sun is already high, midday is near. I am in a hurry, a terrible hurry.

Here, listen Pikolo, open your ears and your mind, you have to understand, for my sake:

> Think of your breed; for brutish ignorance
> Your mettle was not made; you were made men,
> To follow after knowledge and excellence.

As if I also was hearing it for the first time: like the blast of a trumpet, like the voice of God. For a moment I forget who I am and where I am.

Pikolo begs me to repeat it. How good Pikolo is, he is aware that it is doing me good. Or perhaps it is something more: perhaps, despite the wan translation and the pedestrian, rushed commentary, he has received the message, he has felt that it has to do with him, that it has to do with all men who toil, and with us in particular; and that it has to do with us two, who dare to reason of these things with the poles for the soup on our shoulders.

"My little speech made every one so keen . . ." . . . and I try, but in vain, to explain how many things this "keen" means. There is another lacuna here, this time irreparable. ". . . the light kindles and grows Beneath the moon" or something like it; but before it? . . . Not an idea, *"keine Ahnung"* as they say here. Forgive me, Pikolo, I have forgotten at least four triplets.

"Ça ne fait rien, vas-y tout de même."

> . . . When at last hove up a mountain, grey

---

3 "si metta" (Translator's note).

> With distance, and so lofty and so steep,
> I never had seen the like on any day.

Yes, yes, "so lofty and so steep," not "very steep,"[4] a consecutive prop-
osition. And the mountains when one sees them in the distance
. . . the mountains . . . oh, Pikolo, Pikolo, say something, speak, do
not let me think of my mountains which used to show up against
the dusk of evening as I returned by train from Milan to Turin!

Enough, one must go on, these are things that one thinks but does
not say. Pikolo waits and looks at me.

I would give today's soup to know how to connect "the like on
any day" to the last lines. I try to reconstruct it through the rhymes,
I close my eyes, I bite my fingers—but it is no use, the rest is silence.
Other verses dance in my head: ". . . The sodden ground belched
wind . . . ," no, it is something else. It is late, it is late, we have
reached the kitchen, I must finish:

> And three times round she went in roaring smother
> With all the waters; at the fourth the poop
> Rose, and the prow went down, as pleased Another.

I keep Pikolo back, it is vitally necessary and urgent that he listen,
that he understand this "as pleased Another" before it is too late;
tomorrow he or I might be dead, or we might never see each other
again, I must tell him, I must explain to him about the Middle
Ages, about the so human and so necessary and yet unexpected anach-
ronism, but still more, something gigantic that I myself have only
just seen, in a flask of intuition, perhaps the reason for our fate, for
our being here today . . . .

We are now in the soup queue, among the sordid, ragged crowd
of soup-carriers from other Kommandos. Those just arrived press
against our backs. *"Kraut und Rüben? Kraut und Rüben."* The
official announcement is made that the soup today is of cabbages
and turnips: *"Choux et navet. Kaposzta és répak."*

And over our heads the hollow seas closed up.

---

[4] "alta tanto," not "molto alta" (Translator's note).

5. *THE JANOWSKA ROAD*

LEON W. WELLS

Our final reading in this section comes from Leon W. Wells, who lived to testify against the Nazis at Nuremberg and at the Eichmann trial. It tells us of another aspect of the concentration camp—the story of the "Death Brigade." Once again, it is a story told without rancor and bitterness. But the unreal becomes real here; and we discover the qualities of a man like Wells who had the courage and determination to escape, time and again, from the innermost circle of hell.

===

THE DEATH BRIGADE

During this part of my imprisonment I was able to keep a diary. Thus I am able to give, to some extent, and as far as it proves useful here, a day-by-day account of what happened to me. Of course, if I had been caught keeping such a record I would have been shot. Later I shall explain how it happened that I was able to keep this journal of my experiences in what we inmates called the "Death Brigade"—that group of Jews the Germans forced to burn the bodies of their countless victims.

Perhaps I should say here that on my return I found Janowska Concentration Camp much larger and far more thoroughly organized for work than it had been when I had escaped. Now special work

Reprinted with permission of The Macmillan Company from *The Janowska Road* by LEON W. WELLS. Copyright © Leon W. Wells 1963.

brigades were sent into the city daily under complete guard to do all manner of work. These brigades were returned to the concentration camp each evening. Other brigades worked in shops within the camp. Instead of going to work, however, often a whole work brigade was taken out to be shot. There seemed to be no method or reason for such executions—work ill done, the members too weak to carry on, and so on. The Germans seemed to decide such matters completely arbitrarily. Every male individual in the camp never knew when he woke up in the morning whether he would be going to work or to death that day.

Only infants and children, the old, the sick and, for the most part, women, could be certain the Germans would kill them as soon as they arrived at Janowska. For these there was for the most part no respite.

But now to begin my diary, the step-by-step account of how I got into the "Death Brigade" and what happened therein.

JUNE 15TH, 1943

Reveille sounds at 4:00 A.M. This means getting dressed quickly and rushing out of the barracks where we sleep through the crowd of bedraggled, emaciated inmates. Everybody hurries because soon it will be time for formation. On the way voices call out in all directions; these are the voices of prisoners hawking their wares. They yell: "Hot coffee"; "Sugar"; "Salami"; "Bread." Because of the lack of money among the "business people" as well as among the customers, bread is sold in portions of about three ounces. This portion is the standard ration that an inmate received per day.

With the others, I am in a hurry to take care of the necessities. A long line has already formed at the toilets. The situation here is chaotic. It is a struggle to get in and a struggle to get out. At last I am able to get inside, where there is more confusion than at the entrance. There is a constant yelling: "Don't piss on me!" "Don't knock me over!"

Close to every temporary toilet occupant there is a long, disorderly line. Everybody who waits in line is holding his pants, ready to go. They quarrel over who came first. In unison they yell at the one who is squatting: "Hurry up; you can finish it later at work!" A few even threaten him: "If you don't get up right away, I'll push you right into it." Or, "If you don't get up right away, I'll piss right on you."

The next line is preparing to squat when someone suddenly says to the man in possession of a toilet hole, "I'll give you a piece of paper if you'll give me your place." An agreement is made, and the bickering starts anew.

Finally I manage to leave the latrine and begin pushing through the mob to the washroom. Here there is nothing but confusion. For a few groszys (pennies) one can buy a canteen of water from a ragged inmate who has managed to push through the mob at the camp's single water faucet several times to obtain an extra supply. He cannot keep this water for his own needs, but must sell it for the few pennies that it will bring him. Three ounces of bread and a quart of watery soup with a few beans in it daily are not enough to keep him in working condition, so he helps himself in this way. He is helped, too, by the fact that he works in one of the "camp brigades" (the people who work outside the camp and can smuggle things in to the inmates). When the man has a "good day," and gets his hands on five or six canteens of water and also finds customers with enough money, he can earn the price of a portion of bread.

I buy a canteen of water and wash myself. After washing, I buy a portion of coffee for half a zloty. Standing in line to get coffee is impossible. The very poor have monopolized this line, and it is necessary to buy from them. Even by passing near the kitchen one can get hit over the head by the camp police, who assume that you are trying to get to the kitchen window for the second time. The very poor are willing to run this risk.

Now I hurry to find the foreman of my work brigade to get my bread ration, since he is in charge of the supply for his whole group. I find the foreman (a prisoner like myself, of course) in the yard, where the inmates are formed into groups of five. Each brigade has its arranged place. The camp police, with rubber truncheons in their hands, herd the inmates to formation.

"Foreman, please, my bread portion," I say.

"You didn't get it yet?" He checks a piece of paper where he has the names of those who have received their portion—for some try to get a second helping.

I get into formation, and at the same time I start to eat. I hardly have the first bite in my mouth when an inmate begs me for some. He doesn't care that the formation has started and he is liable to get hit over the head with a club.

Finally the men are organized in formations. An ominous silence prevails. We are standing in fives, in separate brigades in the form of a U. Everybody is facing inward.

On the right side of each brigade a single inmate stands alone; each has a yellow, blue, red, or white armband on his left arm. These are the foremen of the different work brigades. From the faces and clothing of the men one can easily recognize where and what kind of work the brigade is doing. The brigade that is working on the *Ostbahn* (East Railroad) always looks black from the soot, and they are very lean. The work there is very arduous, and the men are constantly beaten. Because it is very hard to do any "business" on the railroad, they have no additional income and must subsist on the standard camp rations. Other brigades look better dressed and cleaner. They work some place or other in the city and under better circumstances. Impatiently we wait for the moment when we shall be leaving the camp.

Outside the gate music starts to play. Yes, we have an orchestra, made up of sixty men, all inmates. This orchestra, which has some known personalities in the music world in it, always plays when we are going to and from work or when the Germans take a group out to be shot. We know that for many, if not all, of us the music will someday play the "Death Tango," as we call it on such occasions.

At last the gate opens, and three SS men come in with Tommy guns on their left arms and whips in their right hands. They are accompanied by a large dog.

We hear the command "Attention! Hats off!" Like a precision drill team, we all take off our hats with our right hands and hold our breath, waiting for the next command. Everyone's face is frozen; for one motion or simply for a caprice of their own, these murderers can shoot tens or even hundreds of people.

Suddenly we hear the command, "Down!"

Everyone falls down. We are commanded to get up again. Then down. This is repeated many times. After this, there is a long pause, and we hear the call for the first brigade to march out. After the first comes the second, third, and so on.

Everyone is waiting impatiently to leave the gate behind him. At last we are in line, and we hear: "Left turn and forward march!" We march like soldiers. After we go through the gate, the brigade I am in hears, "Brigade, stop!" My brigade stops. The murderers are standing in front of us. There is ironic laughter on their faces.

Next to them the Askaris are standing in their black uniforms, looking into the face of the concentration-camp chief.

Wilhaus is still Chief of Janowska Camp. He still has the secret smile always on his face. At a given signal from Wilhaus, the Askaris may very well, for no reason at all, suddenly encircle a brigade and lead it off to be shot. They had done it to thousands before us.

We are lucky this time; it doesn't happen. Our foreman now reports the number of inmates in our group. One SS man checks to see if the number is correct, and we get our command to march forward. We march to the place where they assign us to work. There a few brigades are already waiting. I am one of seventy-five selected from all the waiting brigades. We are told to wait for a truck that will take us to build a road between the towns of Kulikov and Zolkiew. We wait for a few minutes, but the truck does not arrive. We get an order in the meantime, to carry bricks, and are instructed that when we hear the call, "Highway construction, Zolkiew," we must gather at a designated place. Our new foreman is a well-known heavyweight boxer named Gross; he has been saved from death several times by Wilhaus, who favors him.

It starts to drizzle.

I go to the plumbing shop where I usually work. The foreman allows me to work there instead of carrying bricks, but when the truck comes I will have to go on it to build the road. This is just a temporary respite.

Now I discuss with others in the shop the possibility that in telling us we are going to the town of Zolkiew to work the Nazis may be up to some kind of trick. I keep looking through the shop window where I can see the place we are to gather, but the truck does not arrive. Through the window I can see my comrades walking in a line with bowed heads and sad faces, each carrying five bricks. I can also see the hands of the clock, which hangs above the camp gate, moving slowly forward.

Time passes. The lunch hour is nearing, and it is still drizzling. The raindrops are falling on the faces of the men carrying the bricks, and they roll down their cheeks like tears. It looks as if nature is crying through these people.

It is twelve o'clock. The foreman gathers everybody for lunch, and we shuffle back toward the camp. Suddenly we hear the word *sechs*. It means an SS man is approaching. Within seconds, without turning our heads, we form groups of fives. We hear the voice of the foreman, "Attention! Hats off!" We take off our hats, and march like soldiers. After a short while we hear, "Hats on!" We put our hats back on, and for a while longer we march in formation until the SS man disappears.

Back at the gate through which we had gone earlier, the guard counts us and gives the foreman a slip with the number to be fed. We return to that part of the camp yard where we live and eat. It is clean everywhere. The barracks in which we live are surrounded by small gardens. Here and there one can see the cleaners; they carry sticks and are in charge of keeping the camp spic and span. One can hear the tread of our feet. The roads are made from headstones from the Jewish cemetery. You can see the lettering on these stones. The so-called *Friedhofskolonne* (Cemetery Brigade) works at the Jewish cemetery, bringing the gravestones that are used here for road construction.

We approach the building where the kitchen is. Here we line up in front of a window with our canteens in our hands. The foreman stands beside the window, checking each one so that nobody can return for a second helping. Everyone is staring at the cook's soupspoon to see if one is to get a bean or a piece of potato.

I have my soup now, and I am hurrying to see if I can buy a piece of bread. The soup is nothing but a pint of boiled water, but very few of us can afford to buy anything additional. Then, too, it is hard to get anything to buy. At last the Cemetery Brigade comes back. I buy a piece of bread from one of the marchers. In the meantime, my "soup" has cooled off. Like everyone else I sit down on the ground near the kitchen building, and eat. An inmate passes by who succeeded in getting a second portion of soup; he is looking for a customer who will buy his soup so that he in turn can buy a portion of bread. I finish eating my lunch and go to the washroom to wash the canteen. It is empty here now, too. I hang the clean canteen on my belt, as everyone else does. The half-hour lunch is over. We gather to leave again for work. We pass the gate. Here there is a tower that contains a guardhouse. Across one side of this guardhouse a boy about eighteen years old is spread-eagled. He is black and blue, and silent! He is tied so that his feet do not touch the ground; he hangs in the air. Before he was tied up he got twenty-five lashes. This is his end; as a result of his punishment he will be unable to work; he will be *kaput*, shot. Everybody goes back to his morning job; but before we leave, our foreman reminds us that when he calls us we should gather quickly so he will not have to wait for us.

I return to the plumbing shop. Here I discuss again what I should do, go with my group or not. Is this a trick? If they are going to take us to the "sands," why haven't they done it, as with everybody else, in the morning? Why do they need a truck, and couldn't we walk to the "sands" like everybody else?

Everyone advises me to go with my group because they know that at the first opportunity I intend to escape. They know me of old—I had escaped before. Leaving camp and the city, the truck will give me my best chance to escape.

While we are talking in the yard in front of the shop, two trucks arrive. Our brigade gathers and we start to board the trucks. I look out of the window of the plumbing shop; I can see what is happening, and again I ask myself, Should I go or not? I finally decide that if Gross, who has been saved from death so many times by Wilhaus, is going, I, too, can take the chance. It is a fateful decision.

I run out of the shop to where the trucks are loading, and board the same truck that Gross is on. A tall, slim SS man with the rank of Scharführer steps out of the cab and asks which one of us is a carpenter. Everyone raises his hand and yells what he is, a carpenter, bricklayer, a painter, and so on. From another side I hear a voice say, "Enough! Enough!" I look at the man who has spoken. He is a heavy, good-looking man with the rank of Untersturmführer. He is to be our future boss. He counts us, but instead of being seventy-five we are only forty-four. He says, however, that he has enough men for the time being and that tomorrow he will get more. He gets into the cab of the truck and we start to roll.

The heavy iron gate opens in front of us. We are now on the main road, but no one is certain whether we are actually going to Zolkiew. It is still drizzling. Everyone tries to figure out where the truck is taking us. At the approach of Pilichowsky Street, which leads to the "sands," the directional signal of the truck shows that we are turning into that street. We begin to stare at each other, and simultaneously say, "Let's jump!" Gross, our foreman, jumps first. After him a second man, then a third. I have one foot over the tailgate of the truck when out of nowhere a large truck appears carrying about eighty *Schupos* (German soldiers on police duty in occupied territories). We hear shots, and our truck stops. The two

men that jumped off the truck after Gross leap back on the truck.
I ask myself why they have come back when we are being taken to
the "sands" anyway? Isn't it better to be killed attempting to escape
than to get undressed and see in front of you the fire that consumed
the previous victims—for we know that the Germans burn our
bodies right after they shoot us. The truck moves forward, the
Scharführer standing on the step of the cab, pointing his pistols
over our heads. The truck with the Schupos follows. We are trapped.

Raise your head, man, and spit into the faces of these murderers!
Nobody does; it will bring only torture before death. Still, perhaps
one shouldn't give up so easily. Miracles do happen, and we may
be saved. Hundreds of thousands have waited for a miracle in the
past two years, but it never came. Stop hoping!

During the truck ride all kinds of thoughts go through my head.
What is my guilt that I have had to witness the deaths of my parents,
my brothers, and sisters first? Why didn't I go with my two little
brothers instead of now, all alone? Was I a coward, afraid of death?
Had I "saved" myself, watching as my two brothers undressed themselves to be shot, only to end up here, twelve days later?

Torturing questions. Yet, like everyone else around me, I bless
every moment that I am still alive, and hope each second for salvation.

It is still drizzling. The truck stops. We are at the "sands." The
Schupos and the SS men with machine guns surround us. The
Untersturmführer gives us the command, "Get off!" Everyone jumps
off the truck, and we fall into formations of five. A thick, greasy black
smoke rises from a deep ravine that is over a thousand feet long.
We look into the ravine. It contains an open mass grave with
thousands of bodies visible to us. On the side of the hill are large
piles of wooden logs. At the bottom of the ravine stands a machine,
operated by a Schupo in a black fatigue uniform. The machine is
connected by a hose to a barrel of oil. The machine pumps oil
through pipes into the fire. The fire is hissing. Perhaps the burning bodies are hissing? Perhaps they burn these people alive? In a
few minutes I shall know.

"Don't be afraid," the Untersturmführer begins his speech. "You
will work here, and when the work is finished you will go back to
camp."

We listen to him with mistrust. We know these speeches by now.
Weren't all those who were killed told they were on their way to

work? We are told that we must give up everything we have in our pockets except our handkerchiefs and cigarettes. They tell us that they know how to search and where people hide things. They advise us to give everything up and not to risk being shot. We throw everything on the ground in front of us, even our handkerchiefs and cigarettes, because we are sure that we are going to be killed. We are then asked, "Which one of you has been a foreman?" One young blond youth, Herches, in his twenties, our future *Oberjude* (Jewish brigade leader) steps out, and another man, named Lustman, about forty years of age, comes forward.

Who doesn't know the Germans' tricks? There are two fires. I am sure that one man will lead one group to one fire and the second to the other fire.

"Which one of you is a carpenter?" the Untersturmführer asks. Without thinking I raise my hand. I have nothing to lose. Maybe they will send me to Pelczynska Street, where the headquarters are, to work; dead bodies don't need a carpenter. Later on, I shall think about taking the next step. In any case I shall not be there long, as I shall attempt an escape at the first chance. A few of the other inmates raise their hands along with me. Because I am the tallest one in the group, the Germans choose me first and then select two others. Guarded by two Schupos and the Scharführer carrying a Tommy gun, we volunteers are led to the working place, leaving the others behind us. I have been wrong in volunteering, I suddenly realize. Nothing could be worse than this! Now it will be impossible to escape!

We stop.

"Here," explains the Untersturmführer, "we shall build the bunker where you will live."

The spot he indicates is near the edge of the ravine. Enclosing half of this spot are the sides of two very steep hills about fifty feet high. Flat terrain extends for a few thousand square feet between the two hills and the ravine.

When we get there we notice that somebody has already started to build; part of a bunker has been set up. There were three brigades here before us, but none of them had worked more than three days (I was told this in the concentration camp). Now I know exactly where I stand. The Scharführer tells us that we must build carefully because we shall have to live here. I know the whole truth now—we shall build as much as possible in three days and then we shall be burned to death. After us, a new brigade, new victims, will be told that they are going to Zolkiew or Boberik, and they, too, will end up in this accursed place.

We are issued tools and given general instructions by the Scharführer as to how the bunker should look. We look at one another, questioningly. Our looks say: Maybe you are a carpenter? It seems that everyone had the same thought in his mind when he volunteered: Perhaps the other man will be a carpenter and I'll be able to pass as a helper. But not one of us is a carpenter. Suddenly one of the men addresses the Scharführer, who has discovered by now that none of us has the slightest knowledge of carpentry. The man tells him that one of the other men in the brigade is a real carpenter. The German asks the name of the man, sends for him, and in a few minutes he arrives. Under his supervision we begin to build. The new man doesn't know too much about carpentry either, but somehow we make some progress. We are all curious to know what has happened to our other comrades, but we are afraid to ask since we are forbidden to speak. We hear the carpenter murmur, "It's hell back there in the ravine."

Suddenly the Scharführer tells us to interrupt our work and gather up the tools. We form a line, and under guard we go down to the ravine, to the huge open grave, in formations of fives. The fire is burning; the smoke stings our eyes and the smell chokes us. The fire crackles and sizzles. Some of the bodies in the fire have their hands extended. It looks as if they are pleading to be taken out. Many bodies are lying around with open mouths. Could they be trying to say: "We are your own mothers, fathers, who raised you and took care of you. Now you are burning us." If they could have spoken, maybe they would have said this, but they are forbidden to talk too—they are guarded. Maybe they would forgive us. They know that we are being forced to do this by the same murderers that killed them. We are under their whips and machine guns. They would forgive us, they are our fathers and mothers, who if they knew it would help their children. But what should we do?

> Father, if you came here
> Couldn't I have gone together with you
> And have everything behind me?
> I wouldn't have been standing alone on your grave
> And burning your body before my death.

We are standing between the bodies in puddles of blood. We wait, but for what? Perhaps we are waiting for death, or perhaps we shall be sent back to the "Death Cell" where we will sleep as the brigades before us have slept, waiting only for death.

On the hill the Schupos are standing with Tommy guns in their hands. They are armed as if they were waiting for an attack. We overhear one of them ask the other, "Do you have enough bullets?" We stare at one another. Do they mean this for us?

Our leader, the young blond boy Herches, reports how many of us there are. The number is forty-two. We hear the command "Right turn!" Everyone turns to the right. The turn is not so precise as in the concentration camp because of the bodies we are standing on.

There is a command, "Link arms!" In fives, we climb back up the steep, slippery ravine. They tell us if anyone releases the arm of the other he will be shot. In a little while we are at the top of the ravine where we were three hours before. Now, however, we have courage enough to breathe. The commander of the Schupos gives us instructions we must adhere to while walking. For the slightest error we can be shot.

1. Each must link arms with the other.
2. The distance between each group of five must not be more than one and a half feet.
3. It is forbidden to look around.
4. Everyone must walk with bowed head.
5. It is forbidden to talk.

The head of the Schupos reminds us again that for the slightest infraction of these regulations, or even any suspicion of it, we shall get a bullet.

Now we are counted again, and the head Schupo yells, "Forward!" He adds to it—"but slowly." We are walking with slow step, in fives, on the slippery clay and road. With bowed heads and arms linked we shuffle as if we were walking after a hearse. We are not going the same way as we came this noon, by truck. The road we are on is the one that connects the concentration camp with the "sands." The road is hilly, and contains puddles of water. The whole place is a mass grave.

We move forward. It is still drizzling. One can already see a camp tower on which an Askari stands. Maybe they are taking us back to sleep in the concentration camp? In that case they won't see me anymore—somehow I will escape.

We approach the concentration-camp yard. Here we find inmates sitting on the ground, sorting potatoes.

Among the inmates are some who were supposed to go to Zolkiew with us but had been smart enough to get out of it somehow.

We are told to turn our heads the other way. The Germans have forbidden anybody to see the faces of inmates who have seen the "sands."

We stop in front of the barbed-wire fence of the concentration camp. Then we are led into a special part where I had not been before. The barracks in this section are about three feet apart, all in one line. This is where the women prisoners live. They work in DAW (Deutsche Ausvuestungswerke—German Army Supplies) and in the laundry. Each barrack is about forty-five feet long and eighteen feet wide, and each in turn is divided into three sections. Each section has a door and three windows. The windows of the first barrack facing the gate through which we entered have gratings of iron bars. This is the so-called "Death Cell." The Jews caught in the city are brought here, where they wait until the next morning. Shooting usually takes place in the morning hours, and when enough people have been collected.

Anyone who lands in the "Death Cell' is certain to die. These barracks stand on pillars, so that there is about a twelve-inch separation between the floor and the ground. There is a space fifty feet long and ten feet wide between the barracks and the barbed wire. Here we are told to sit down on the ground, in the mud, with our feet tucked under us.

I think: Should I try to escape right now by crawling under the barracks? No. I decide to wait until late at night. I plan to pull out a piece of board from the barracks floor and crawl out in the space under the barracks. I hope that the guard won't stay with us all night and that they will lock us up and leave.

One Schupo leaves to get water so we can wash up. We sit and wait. From the second and third sections of the "Death Cell" barracks, frightened inmates, their eyes blackened, their faces swollen and with black and blue marks all over them, can be seen looking out through the iron bars of the windows. These are people brought in from the "Aryan side." (The whole city is now, in reality, the "Aryan side"—the Jewish side is now the concentration camp.) This means they had been caught hiding in Lvov, trying to pass as non-Jews. When captured they are brought to the concentration camp, where they are questioned and tortured until they lose consciousness. When the victim falls on the ground, nearly dead, the Germans revive him, and when he gains consciousness the torture resumes. The Germans want to find out if the victim knows where others are hiding. While we sit there one SS man, tall, slim, with only one arm, by the name of Heine, rank of Scharführer, brings over a tall, heavy-set prisoner. One can see that he had once been elegantly dressed—though his clothes are now in shreds and he has been beaten to a point beyond recognition. Heine is known by all as the worst sadist here. His greatest pleasure is derived from cutting people up with his dagger. He is the chief interrogator here.

The Schupo who had gone for the water returns. With him are two women carrying buckets of water for us. These are from the group who clean the women's barracks. They stop for a moment and stare at us, with that special look given new victims. We wash. While sitting, we strip from the waist up and in formations of five we go to the basins and wash. The second group of five does not approach the basin until the first group has finished and is seated.

Now we are finished washing. Our dinner arrives on a wagon. It is placed outside the barbed wire because the drivers are forbidden to come in. The dinner wagon leaves, and four of us go out, under guard, and bring the food back. One of the Schupos commands, "The fire tender and the tabulator will give out the food." I think to myself that I know practically all the occupations here, but I never heard the names of these two before. I am to find out.

Everybody receives half a gallon of soup, much thicker than the soup in the concentration camp, a five-ounce portion of bread, and a spoonful of marmalade.

We finish dinner and go into the third section of the "Death Cell" barrack. It is empty. The door is locked behind us.

Our cell is about seventeen feet wide and twenty feet long, and it has three iron-barred windows. Because the wooden partition dividing our cell from the one next to it doesn't reach the ceiling, it is possible to climb from one cell to the other. Around the walls are sacks filled with straw. Near the door are two buckets. Everyone rushes to the buckets, since none of us had taken care of his needs since lunchtime. We had been afraid to ask for permission. In a few minutes the buckets are overflowing, spilling all over the floor. The whole cell becomes one big puddle. We hear the voice of the Schupo: "What is happening here? Instant quiet!" Two shots are fired that hit the ceiling of our cell. "Everyone lie down immediately!" An ominous silence prevails in the cell. Two of us share one straw sack. We lie silently. From the other side of the wall we hear children crying. Perhaps they are crying because of thirst or hunger. We hear men and women moaning. They cannot sit, stand, or lie down because they have been beaten so badly. They have been in the cell for three days already, and now they are just waiting for the SS men to bring them to the "sands."

After a few minutes I begin to talk to my neighbor. He has a foul odor about him because of his work with the corpses. We can't even smell the stench from the buckets because the smell on the clothing of the people who work with the bodies is much stronger. (When we came into the cell we had heard from the neighboring cell: "Pfew, it smells!" "What smells so terribly here?")

I start a discussion with my neighbor with the question, How can we get out of here? Little by little we fill each other in on details of what had happened in the ravine. He had seen much that I had not, because I had worked on the construction on the top of the ravine.

"It was real hell," he says, and tells me that when his group had got to the bottom of the ravine two among them were called back up the hill. There was a truck, and on it was a corpse riddled with bullets. It was Gross, our foreman. Two of the prisoners were told to take Gross by the legs and pull him down the ravine and toss him in the flames. At the same time, my companion went on, a doctor who was in his group committed suicide by taking a capsule of cyanide. He died instantly. So of forty-four persons only forty-two were left.

They then were put to work in earnest, my neighbor now told me. One group worked with shovels—this meant digging out the bodies that had been buried or partly buried after former mass murders. Another group worked with the corpses directly....

The bodies were tossed into the fire, my neighbor says. On one side the fire tender was standing. (He was one of us prisoners, too.)

His work was to see that the bodies were put in right and that the fires burn at the right heat and are not extinguished. He must add wood and shovel away the ashes. On the other side of the fire the tabulator was standing. He held a piece of paper and a pencil in his hands. His task was to keep count of how many bodies were burned each day. This is a top-secret job. It is forbidden to tell even the Schupos how many are burned each day. In the evening the tabulator reports the exact number to the Untersturmführer. Even the tabulator must forget the amount after he reports to the Untersturmführer, my neighbor tells me. When the Untersturmführer asks him the next day, "How many bodies were burned yesterday?" the tabulator must answer, "I don't know."

The corpses are called "figures" here, my neighbor continues. To toss in the bodies one has practically to go into the fire oneself. Those on this job have their hands, face, and hair singed. Once the first body is thrown in the fire, they run for the next corpse, because even fast walking is dangerous here. Everyone is afraid of hearing the familiar phrase: "Faster! Why is the work going so slowly?"

"Another day like today and nobody will be able to endure it," my neighbor says. "They won't need to shoot us."

He falls silent. We look at each other. Neither one of us has the courage to interrupt our silence now or the other's thoughts. Perhaps he is thinking of his parents or family. These are always the last dreams of the doomed men. If the Germans were to ask any of us for a last wish, I am sure it would be to see once again our deceased father, mother, wife, children, brother, sister.

Mother . . . Mother, you who sold your gold teeth to buy food to send packages to the concentration camp so that your son might not hunger.

From a distance we can hear the sound of music. The Germans always play it for the inmates who are returning from work. Slowly one and then another of us gets up and quietly and carefully starts to move around the cell. Some of us cannot lie down any longer because we are starting to feel the pains from the whippings we had received that day. Nobody chases us away from the window. The head of the Schupos is gone. The Schupos, once they are alone, come near the windows. They look around to see if any of the SS men are watching them. They give us cigarettes and try to calm us down. They tell us not to worry, that we will not be killed.

Maybe they are telling us this to prevent us from trying to escape?

Across from our cell are the women's barracks. Women look out of their windows. They would like to pass something to us but are afraid of the Schupos. The Schupos notice this, and approach these women, asking if they want to give us bread. We indicate with our hands that we do not want any bread but that we would prefer cigarettes. Some of us call out our names. We want them to give our names to friends or relatives in other parts of the camp.

Night falls. Everybody lies down in his place. Two Schupos keep guard around our cell. Should I try to break through the door? They will start shooting. But there are only two guards and only some of us will be shot; the others will escape. But what will happen after we get out of the cell? We have the barbed wire to contend with. This barbed wire is closely woven, and about ten feet high. Two feet from the first fence is another identical fence. It would be hard to climb over it. Every six or seven feet there is a pole with a searchlight on it. And if one could break out of this section, there is still another where the workshops are located. It is very well lighted, and on each corner there are guard towers.

But we *have* to do something! For we are certainly going to go from this "Death Cell" to the "sands."

The two Schupos are still guarding us. Perhaps later they will leave. With these thoughts I fall asleep. I dream about my father and mother. They are crying because their last child is going to be killed by the same assassins that killed their other children. I awaken. I must try to escape. I approach the window and I hear the Schupos talking. I try to wake up my comrades, but they are sleeping soundly. Lying down again, I think about what could be done. After a while I fall asleep. I dream again about my parents, about my mother, when she was taken away to be killed. I dream about her telling that she is leaving seven children. In my dream I know it is eleven months later and that I am nearing the same end as all her other children. I dissolve in self-pity and I start to cry. I wake up and fall right back to sleep, continuing to dream about my mother, my father, my brothers, my sisters.

I wake up: day breaks. The night has passed—the night in which I had vowed to escape, the night that was my last hope. Now, surely, I am lost. Slowly everyone starts to wake up. One can hear moaning everywhere. Again the cursed day. Oh, God! What did we do to deserve this? If we could have died during the night!

It will be a day of new torture and surely a day of death.

I am near the window. Through its iron bars one can see the concentration-camp kitchen. The usual morning there. Ironically I think to myself: No more of those toilets, and no more reveilles. I don't have to be afraid of the "Death Gate" anymore. Today is the day I die. Of that I am certain.

It is seven o'clock. The doors are opening. We hear the voice of the head of the Schupos. "Out!" he yells. Everybody gets out. We sit down on the ground, as we did last night. The head of the Schupos counts us. The number checks. In front of us is a large container of coffee and bread. We receive a double portion of bread (about six ounces) and a quart of sweetened black coffee; as the proverb goes, "The sweetness before death." Breakfast is given out in the same manner as last night's dinner. We finish breakfast, and get up.

With arms linked we start marching, and the Schupos remind us of the regulations we have to obey while marching. We are forty-two, and the number of Schupos guarding us is forty. Every one of them carries a Tommy gun with a finger on the trigger ready to shoot.

We go through the small gate we used yesterday. On the other side we stop. We wait. From the direction of the concentration camp three Scharführers are coming. One of them is Heine, who manages to be present at every execution. Behind them a group of Askaris follows.

The people we saw last night in the second and third divisions of our cell join our group. The men are separated from the women and children. The guard is enlarged to about one hundred Schupos. Forty isn't enough?

Now we know that we are going to be killed, because women and children surely are not sent to work. Some take off their overcoats and jackets, dropping them on the ground, so that the undressing on the "sands" will be quicker. Perhaps in their fright they feel hampered by their clothing. We walk the same path as yesterday. About 150 feet before the ravine, the guards hold back the women and children, leaving them behind with the Askaris. The men, who number forty-three, are going with us.

These are newcomers from the city. They have just been arrested. Now they leave their wives, children, mothers, and other members of their families, with whom they had been hiding until now, behind them. Most of these new prisoners are from a concern called Feder und Daunen (Feather and Down) in Lvov. The director of the business had pretended he would hide them; he took away all their belongings, and afterward betrayed them to these executioners.

We go to the bottom of the ravine where we worked yesterday. The Schupos stay up on top encircling us. In the ravine we sit down on the corpses as if we were sitting on benches. We remain like this for a while. The putrid bodies wet our trousers. Presently two cars arrive in the ravine. Two SD* corporals step out of the cars along with one private, two sergeants, one warrant officer, and our chief, a second lieutenant.

We rise. They count us. We are eighty-five. The Scharführer who was in charge of the construction of the bunker yesterday calls us up and enlarges the group building the bunker to twenty inmates. We twenty are ordered to go up the hill in fives. We mount the hill and go over to the place where we worked yesterday. Today there is a good carpenter among us. The new carpenter explains to the Scharführer that our work yesterday was worthless, and it is decided to start the work anew. Under his supervision we take everything apart and we begin to build all over again.

Today a young fellow about nineteen years old, tall, blond, and in high boots, has joined us. He had been hiding, passing as an Aryan in the city. His first name is Marek. Because of his pleasant looks, the Untersturmführer, we learn, has ordered that Marek shouldn't be beaten. The Scharführer gives him cigarettes, bread and butter, and ham. Everybody likes this boy, and we all consider him one of the lucky ones. He tells us that whenever the Scharführer had asked him if he could help to find other hidden Jews, he would answer with the question: "If you, Herr Scharführer, were in my place, and knew that in any case you would be killed, would you give away your brothers?" He informs us that he will not fall into their trap.

The Scharführer is a little taller than average height, good-looking, slim, a builder by profession. He knows a little bit about ma-

---

* *Sicherheits Dienst*—Security Service, which outranked the SS.

chinery. He is not one of the worst sadists here, and he beats the inmates less than the others. His name is Jelitko. I believe that was
his Nazi-party name, not his real name. Like most of them here,
he originally came from Berlin. When any of his colleagues approaches, he pretends to be yelling at us.

Very often a Schupo named Koenig comes over to our group. He
is in charge of the oil-pumping machine. He beats everybody, regardless of whether they work or not. He looks very rough, is of
average height and on the heavy side, and comes from around
Berlin. He will spy even on his own colleagues and report them
to the SD, so that even the Schupos have become wary of him. All
the officers here belong to the SD.

During the morning I am carrying a beam about twenty feet
long, under the guard of Koenig. Two corporals, a sergeant, and the
second lieutenant are standing near the construction site. The beam
accidentally slips off my shoulder and falls close to two of these
officers. They let out an angry yell. I start to excuse myself, but
nothing helps. Each of them gives me ten lashes. I am sure they
will shoot me, but I don't care; I think: Let them get it over with.
Instead of hearing a shot, I hear, "Get up!" With what is left of
my strength I pull myself to the bunker under construction. Here
I take a piece of lumber in my hands so that it will appear that I am
handing it to the carpenter. By feigning work I get by until lunchtime, and save myself, for by then my strength has returned.

At twelve o'clock, at the command of the Scharführer, we stop
our work. We move into formation and are counted; the number
checks. We go to the ravine. The smell from the ravine gags us. It
is hard to imagine this overpowering odor. The neighboring villages,
a few miles away, had complained of the stench.

In the ravine the inmates also stop their work and prepare for
lunch.

The sweat is streaming down their faces like water. Their hands
are caked with the fluids from the corpses so that one cannot differentiate between the flesh of their hands and the flesh of the corpses.
From behind the thick, gray-looking layers of dried pus on their
hands one can see a patch here and there of their real skin.

The ravine workers stand in formation; we join them; we are
counted, and the number again checks. We are eighty-two. But, I
suddenly realize, the number does *not* agree. I remember that we

were eighty-five this morning. Maybe they forgot? It is none of my business, in any case. After they count us we are commanded to sit down. Ten people are summoned to go up the hill. The first two groups of fives go up. From a truck they unload containers of soup which had been brought over from the concentration camp. They bring the containers down, put them between the corpses. The same two who ladled out food last night do so today, too. One by one we get up and return with our soup. No one can wash his hands. They give us no water. It would be a mistake to think that at lunchtime we will be spared our beatings. Every so often someone is called up the hill and given a few lashes. We, as well as those who do the beating, never know the reason. We are beaten, and that is all. The object, I suppose, is to keep us under constant tension, constantly cowed.

One o'clock—lunchtime is over. We form into ranks again and are counted, and on the command of the Untersturmführer each group returns to its morning job. Our group, under the guard of eight Schupos, returns to our construction work, building the bunker we were told we would be living in from now on.

At five o'clock, on the command of the Scharführer, we stop work. Formation; counting; and under guard down to the ravine, where the others are already in formation. All are counted again—seventy-nine. We are told to sit down as we had during lunchtime. We sit and wait. What for? To be killed? What else? We sit on the corpses. There is the silence of the grave now, and no one moves. Everyone is as if dead already. Everyone has the same look on his face. With bowed heads, our eyes look inward. The impression is that nobody is thinking. We are sitting, and suddenly we hear "Get up!" We all rise, like automatons. No one raises his head. We get the command to go up the hill.

We stand on the top. We are counted again, and at the command of the Untersturmführer we start slowly to walk.

So today is not *the* day either.

We walk the same road as we did this morning. We arrive at the same place where we were last night. We wash up, receive our dinner, and the situation repeats itself. Tonight no one but us is in the barrack. The people who were brought over today from the city, who lived, with forged papers, as Aryans, have been herded into a field outside the wires under guard. In this place the Germans normally gather together large groups destined for death. The jail barrack is too small for them. This field was the place where the Nazis had collected the people during the liquidation of the ghetto two weeks before.

We enter yesterday's barrack, but today we are put into two cells. Forty inmates in one, the rest in the other. Our cell has been cleaned up. But again there is the same scramble for the pails. The mess is repeated, but no one minds it anymore. We lie down on the straw sacks. To my left lies a good-looking man who had been added to our brigade that morning. He is about forty-six years old, and graying at the temples. His name is Brill. Prior to the war he had a flourishing flour business, and lived on Lyczakowska Street. On my other side lies Roth, a young fellow, born, like me, in 1925. He is tall and slender. His birthplace was Bielsko, a city in western Poland. His father, a lawyer, was a representative of an American oil company in Poland. We lie quietly. The silence is interrupted only by the moans from the straw sacks.

I turn to Brill. "What are we going to do?"

"I would like to die," he says, and starts to tell me of the happenings of the day. He talks very slowly and haltingly—as if he were convincing himself that he, Brill, still existed. After each word he sighs "Oi." Often, in the middle of a sentence his voice trails off and he heaves a deep "Oi." Everything that has happened is beyond his belief, incredible. "I worked at the firm of Feder und Daunen at 5 Zrodlanej Street with my two daughters. One was seventeen, the other fifteen. After the liquidation of the ghetto we were hidden in the company's building. The director of this firm took everything away from us. Then the Gestapo came and brought us here; my two children and I." A long pause. "This was a few days ago. Today they took us, together with you, to the 'sands,' and I was separated from my two daughters." Pause.

He went on: "I, as everyone else, went down to the ravine. After a long time, about fifteen people were selected and taken to the place where we left the women and children in the morning." Pause. "And there—there" (in a terrible moaning voice) "all, and my two daughters among them, were lying dead . . . shot. What girls, beautiful, intelligent—what I wouldn't have done for them. . . . They told us to make a fire, and we threw all the bodies into it, my children, too."

He was saying something more, moaning, gesturing with his hands and feet, like an insane person. But I didn't listen any more. How could I help him? The tragedy was universal, not particular any more.

It is night, and outside it is pouring. It is dark. In the barrack it is quiet; everyone is asleep. In their sleep the inmates are moaning, "Oi," "Oi." From far off one can hear the muffled cry of children; they are sitting on the other side of the wires, waiting for death. I get up and go to the window. The rays from the searchlights are mixed with the streams of rain. Schupos are walking near the barracks, guarding us. I return to my place and ask Brill, "Maybe we should break out?"

"What for?" he answers. "I *want* to die."

After a while I start again. "If we break out we can die with honor."

"What is it to me, honor or no honor; it is all the same—I want to die."

Yes, yes, I thought to myself; yesterday this man thought differently; he thought about escaping. But he was afraid to risk the lives of his daughters. They preferred to die together. Tonight this man is not living; he is only existing. There is no way of winning; they have us.

Slowly I fall asleep. I dream about the Seder night. The whole family is sitting at the table. My mother serves the food, looks into the face of every child with a smile. The candles are throwing a beautiful glow. Father is asking us children different questions. But I don't answer. I am only smiling happily. . . .

I wake up. The rain is beating on the roof, and on the other side of the wire people are sitting in the rain with small children— we can hear their cries. They are waiting for their Savior . . . which will be death.

I fall asleep again. I dream about the place behind the wires. I am sitting there with my two brothers. I comfort my youngest brother, who cries because he is afraid. I try to make him understand that death takes only a short while, and afterward he will be together with Mother, Father, and his sisters.

He answers, "How much I would like that."

Dreams and reality merge. But here is a scene that is real—that actually happens that night.

The Schupos shoot a woman. The woman's child is sitting next to her in a puddle of blood with her head on her dead mother's breast, sleeping. An SS man wakes the child by whipping her. She must go with the other children to the "sands." The child screams in terror, "Mother, it hurts!" The child gets up and starts to run, and the SS man goes after her. The child yells, and the murderer decides to shoot her on the spot. He reaches for his pistol, and shoots.

The shot wakes me up. Later, we learn the story.

Day breaks and slowly everyone gets up. We move around the cell very slowly. We stop as the sound of music, the "Death Tango," reaches us. Surely, today they are playing for us. Today will be the third day, and from all previous experience of other groups which had worked with the corpses on the "sands" we know that it will be our last one.

The door opens. We hear, "Out!" We all step out and sit down as we had yesterday morning. We are counted, and the number checks. Now they release the people from the other cell. They sit down behind us. We have our breakfast, and after we finish, under heavy guard, march out to the "sands." At the "sands" forty-eight inmates are waiting for us; they have been added to our group. These people previously worked at H.K.P. (*Hepres Kraftfahrt Park* —Military Car Depot).

And so our brigade is enlarged to 129 inmates. The day passes as usual, and in the evening we return to the "Death Cells." This night one of the inmates hangs himself from a rafter with his belt. Now our brigade numbers 128. In the morning, when we leave for work, four inmates, following the command of the SS man, carry this man out and throw him behind the toilet. An hour later he is brought to the ravine with the other corpses from the concentration camp.

Thursday and Friday pass with hard work. Today our brigade is opening a mass grave that contains 1,450 bodies. Many of today's corpses don't have bullet holes in them. They have open mouths with projecting tongues. This would indicate that they had been buried alive.

In the evening my younger neighbor, Roth, tells me his story of the last days of the Jews in Lvov. Roth was caught on the

"Aryan side." He had been able to pass as an Aryan for the preceding ten months. Then one day he met an old school friend. The man immediately reported him to the Gestapo. They arrested him and his younger sister, who had also been passing herself off as an Aryan. Roth himself had tossed her body into the fire two days ago.

So passes the night. We talk, then sleep, and resume talking again. The topic of escape crops up. In order to clarify our situation and to describe how little chance we had for escape, I should like to describe the exact conditions and location of our working place.

In the western section of Lvov is Janowska Street. At the end of this street, as I've said, is a huge sandy area, called the Janowska "sands." These "sands" have high hills, deep ravines, and cover an area of approximately two and a half square miles. There are signs in Polish, German, and Ukrainian around the "sands": "To enter this place is strictly forbidden. Anyone nearing this site at a distance of less than 150 feet of the sign will be shot."

Every few hundred feet a Schupo stands guard in this area. On top of the highest sandhill stands the observation point. Here is a tent where the Schupos stay and where ammunition is kept. Here, too, is a telephone with a direct line to the concentration camp and the Gestapo's city headquarters. The houses in the "sands" area had been emptied and taken over by the Schupos. The Schupos, who number over one hundred, are divided into two groups. Each group has twenty-four hours on duty and twenty-four hours off. In addition to the Schupos there are quite a few SD men.

After a long discussion with Roth on how to escape, we fall asleep.

At six in the morning we are awakened. A new day of torture begins—perhaps our last one. Once again this day seems the most critical to us because it is the last day of the week.

It starts as usual. Everybody is at his job. From our brigade the carpenter and one of his assistants have been taken to one of the Schupos' houses to repair something. It is twelve o'clock—lunchtime. Our brigade as usual goes down to the ravine for lunch, but instead of twenty, we number only eighteen today because the two have not returned from the Schupo's house yet.

We are standing in formation waiting to be counted. We stand and wait. Why are they keeping us waiting? Probably to kill us. What else? We all know that today is the last working day in the week. We look straight into the fire—our destiny. Let's get it over with!

But nothing happens. Perhaps we are waiting for the others to join us. At last we see the Schupo and the carpenter arriving on top of the hill, but the carpenter's assistant is not with them. We see the two men are now approached by the second lieutenant, corporal, first lieutenant, and the private. They encircle the carpenter. The second lieutenant has a few words with the Schupo and afterward with the carpenter; he then reaches for his pistol and shoots the carpenter. We all surmise that the assistant must have escaped.

In a minute we hear the command, "Two men up!" Two of us run up the hill, carry the corpse down, and throw him into the fire. Now the second lieutenant himself comes down to the ravine. In silence, beckoning to us, he selects four inmates, most, but not all, of them elderly men, over fifty years of age, and he gestures to them to stand in one line. After that he asks, "Which of you complains?"

One man about thirty-five years old steps forward. "I do," he says. And then he adds, quietly, "Maybe at last I will rid myself of more tortures."

The Untersturmführer motions him to join the line, and picks out one more inmate. They now number six. They stand in front of the fire, looking at it; they are turned away from us.

Now the Untersturmführer begins his speech, directing it at us. "One of you escaped. Because of him these people will be shot. From now on, for everyone who tries to do the same, I will shoot twenty of you. If I find out that you are planning an escape, all of you will be shot."

After this speech he turns to the chosen six, and shoots one after another. Each is shot in the back of his head, and kicked so that the body won't fall toward the Untersturmführer. When he finishes, he calls for four of us to pick up the corpses and toss them into the fire.

While the bodies are being thrown into the fire, the Untersturmführer walks around us as if looking for someone else. Suddenly he points at Marek and says, *"Komm."*

Marek asks, *"Ich?"*

"Ja, du, du."

Tears appear in the boy's eyes. Walking toward the point where the other six stood a few minutes ago, Marek asks again, with a tearful voice, "Why me?"

"Don't babble so—turn around." Marek turns around, and a moment later he, too, is lying dead.

"Two men!" Two men toss him into the fire. Before he is tossed in, the Untersturmführer tells the two men to take off Marek's boots. "Let's not waste such a good pair of boots!"

Now we are counted—122 men. We have lunch. After lunch we march back to the barrack.

Today we work only half a day.

The only topic of conversation on Saturday afternoon and evening is the escape of the man and the death of Marek. Everyone prays the escapee will make it. Let one at least be saved from all those here, and live to tell the world what is happening to us. In any case, sooner or later, they will kill us all. We decide that anyone who gets the opportunity to escape should try it and not pay attention to what the Untersturmführer said about killing twenty other people. Marek is our symbol. Even if the lieutenant likes us, promises us a "long life," takes care that we get enough food, our end will be the same as Marek's—sudden death. If at this time we ask, as Marek had, "Why me?" each must tell himself, "Because I am a Jew!" We must not try to comfort ourselves with hope again.

Saturday and Sunday pass, and again we have before us a new week full of suffering and hard work. Who knows? Maybe not even a full week. Maybe only a few days or even a few hours. Again day, again night . . . .

MONDAY, JUNE 21, 1943

The day begins with breakfast, then we go over to the ravine. Everybody resumes his work of last week. At ten o'clock a truck arrives. We are called to unload it. The truck is carrying gravestones brought from the Jewish cemetery. They are very large and heavy, weighing 500 to 700 pounds apiece. Each of these stones must be carried to the bottom of the ravine. The SS men tell us that if we drop one, they will break our necks.

We carry the stones down somehow, and somehow without an accident. We are made to lay out all the stones in a square, and to fill the cracks with cement. Near this square we level off an area. Here we place the bones that were taken out of the fire—those not completely reduced to ashes. On the other side of the stone square we level another area for the ashes. On the third side we level a place for the bones which could not be crushed fine enough to pass through the sieve, and on the fourth side we build a bench. We have now created a new working place, where a special brigade will work, the Ash Brigade, *Asch Kolonne*.

The work of the Ash Brigade is to crush the bones that hadn't completely burned with heavy wooden poles to fine dust and pick out all the metallic items, for example, fillings of teeth, gold teeth, jewelry, and so on. These valuables are to be put into a sieve standing near the bench. In the evening the foreman is to bring the sieve up the hill, giving it to the Untersturmführer, who will then empty it into a linen bag which he then carries off with him.

The inmates working in the Ash Brigade come back at the end of the day blackened from head to foot by this terrible dust from the powdered human bones.

TUESDAY, JUNE 22ND

A prisoner sitting behind bars sees people on the outside, and grieves because he is not free; but it is worse for him if he is sent to an island and is completely cut off from the rest of the world. Here where we work, except for the bodies, our murderers, fires, hills, and sand, nothing exists. There is no connection with the community which exists in the concentration camp. One has a feeling that except for one another, and our assassins, we shall never see another living soul again. We, 122 inmates, share the same fate, work, and thoughts. Everyone thinks about being saved in order to revenge the death of our dear ones.

As on every other day, we leave our cells for work. But this is not going to end like every other day—though we do not know it then.

None of the SD's tell us that we shall not return to the "Death Cell" any more to sleep, but two of the Schupos disclose the secret. As usual our group goes over to the construction site. Today we finish encircling the bunker with barbed wire. Under tension we wait for four-thirty, the hour that the working day ends.

At four-thirty a wagon stops at the gate that leads to the bunker we have now finished, and one of the Schupos who normally guards us is on it. Our dinner has arrived, which means we are staying here.

We 122 members of the Death Brigade will live here in this bunker. That is now clear.

Our new quarters are about thirty-three feet long, twenty feet wide, and only five feet high. It seems as if the bunker were purposely built only five feet high so that our heads would be constantly bowed.

To enter the bunker one has to go down a few steps. One of the walls is a natural one—the side of the steep hill; the other three sides are wooden ones, and on the outside mud and sand are piled as high as the roof to secure the walls. From the main road six steps lead down to the yard where the bunker is situated. Our whole living area is encircled with barbed wire.

Directly in line with the gate is the entrance to the bunker. The distance is approximately seven feet, and from the other walls to the barbed wire it is about fifteen feet. The roof of the bunker contains three holes; when finished, these will give us our ventilation and light. The inside of the bunker is divided into two parts, one section twice the size of the other. These two parts are divided only by an aisle about ten inches wide. We are to sleep next to the walls and in the aisle.

We are commanded to enter our new abode. It is much too small. We quarrel over our sleeping places. At last we lie down. We are packed together like sardines; we have to lie sideways with our legs curled up. The openings in the roof have not been finished, and except for the open door there is no ventilation or light. We sweat and choke because of the lack of air. Owing to the limited space, some of the inmates must lie by the doorway, and no one can get in or out.

Fortunately the door is left open by our guards, and one can go to the toilet anytime, though we must report to the guard if we go out. The Schupos stand guard outside the barbed-wire fences. When one has to relieve himself, a guard keeps a light on him while he goes to the open toilet and returns. And he must walk close to the bunker wall and at no time is he to approach the wire fence. About a hundred feet from our bunker is a tent where the

Schupos stay when they change guard. The tent is also used to store extra ammunition.

WEDNESDAY, JUNE 23RD

At seven o'clock in the morning we have formation in our yard. We are counted, and Herches, the young man who had been appointed our leader, reports our number to the Schupos. After the report is given we scatter about the yard. Then breakfast arrives from the concentration camp by truck. Ten men go out to unload breakfast. In addition to our breakfast the truck is loaded with corpses, those who were killed yesterday in the concentration camp. And so, from now on, every morning with our breakfast we shall also receive corpses.

The men carry the bodies down to the fire without waiting for a command. The rest, in the meantime, bring the breakfast. It is given out; we finish it, and form up for our second counting. At eight o'clock the corporal and the lieutenant arrive. Our leader Herches again reports the number, and everyone leaves for his work. Our group, the construction unit, is now redistributed among other groups, except for one man, who has to finish the holes in the roof of the bunker.

Because I am very much afraid to work with the corpses, I start to move around so that I won't be assigned to any group. Without permission I stay around the bunker. I clean it up and put everything in order. What can they do to me? Shoot me? I am not afraid of that.

Twelve o'clock approaches. Today lunch isn't eaten in the ravine. Instead all the groups return to the bunker yard. We have formation, and Herches reports the number of inmates to the sergeant, who is second in position to the lieutenant. His name is Rauch. He is a slim man of medium height, about twenty-eight years old, and comes from Munich.

We finish our lunch. At one o'clock, formation, counting, and then everybody goes back to his morning job. A truck arrives with straw. This straw had been used to cover the potatoes in the concentration camp. It has a foul odor. A few people are called up from the ravine to unload the truck and to spread the straw in the bunker. The foul odor of the straw isn't as bad as the stench the people bring back from work. Their shoes are full of pus and decayed flesh. That terrible odor is absorbed at once by the straw, increasing it.

At five o'clock we finish our work. Again formation and counting. After that, we wash up. Today we receive buckets and basins. We have to fetch the water. Everyone would like to get washed up, but no one is willing to carry the water because the walk to the well is far and difficult and uphill. The foreman corrals ten young people, I among them, who fetch the water under guard. An hour later we return with twenty buckets. Everyone gets a quart of water, and drinks half of it. We are very thirsty. Dinner arrives—180 quarts of coffee, the same amount of soup, and seventy pounds of bread. Everyone gets his dinner and eats it sitting on the ground in the yard.

We sit around the yard until eight o'clock, at which time we again have formation and counting; then everyone goes into the bunker. Eight o'clock is curfew; we are forbidden to be in the yard after that time.

Now it starts to rain. Because of the open ventilation holes in the roof, the rain pours in. We all crouch together because the water is quite high. This is truly a calamity. We are drenched, exhausted, and sleepy. If, after a hard day's work, one does not get his rest at night, he will not have much strength left for the next day. Being weak, the chances of getting a beating are so much greater, and the probability of being shot increases. In the morning hours the rain stops and we drowse off.

THURSDAY, JUNE 24TH

The morning passes uneventfully. The Untersturmführer, satisfied with yesterday's work (over two thousand corpses were burned), makes a speech during our lunch.

He is a man of about forty, heavy-set, about five foot nine, with glassy, shifty eyes; he is always drunk but never rowdy. His name is Scherlack. He is originally from Berlin, but his family, his wife and a seven-year-old son, live here in Lvov. He is shrewd, and an excellent administrator.

He begins his speech with the words, which later become our motto, "Be decent and clean." By "clean" he means clean in conscience, too, because if one of us tries to escape, they will shoot twenty inmates. Thus the inmate who will cause the death of his comrades will not be "clean."

"If you will keep these two things in mind, you will live to be a hundred," he tells us—here he raises his hand and points his finger at us, his eyes narrowing, "I will care for you like a father for his children." He asks how we liked our breakfast, and last night's dinner, and assures us that this is nothing in comparison to what we will get in the near future. He promises us that we are going to get clothing and shoes so that we can change after work, and he will provide us with water so that we will not need to carry it so far. As for the holes in the bunker roof and the flooding when it rains —well, that we will have to learn to live with because, "unfortunately," he has no solution for it!

At the gate a large basin of water and Lysol is set up in order that we may wash our hands. A sprayer with pure Lysol is brought over to sprinkle our shoes before we enter the bunker. From now on we also spray the bunker every day.

The driver takes the empty coffee cans back to the truck. He is an SD man with the rank of sergeant. He, with his truck, was especially appointed to this command. His name is Ulmer. He wears glasses and is a bit rotund. He is a truck driver by trade. It is said that he belonged to the Nazi Party for twelve years; this means he belonged to it prior to 1933. When he beats one of us, he beats recklessly until his victim loses consciousness. At the sight of human blood his eyes glow. He is one of those who literally seem to thirst for blood.

An hour later Ulmer's truck brings water, and he tells me to distribute it before lunch and to keep part of it for dishwashing. From now on, we are going to have a routinized "household," and a manager is needed. I am that man.

Twelve o'clock: All the work brigades are returning for lunch. On the command of the Untersturmführer I stand with another boy at the gate stopping everyone, telling them to wash their hands in the basin of water and Lysol. After that, I tell them, they must go to the sprayer to spray their shoes. At the gate I had prepared a scraper, and everyone scraped off his shoes before entering the yard. In a few minutes everyone is standing in the yard in formation to be counted. After that, everyone washes his hands, rubbing them with sand. The stench of the bodies, however, cannot be removed so easily; washing with Lysol, chlorine, or gasoline still leaves one's hands with the stench of corpses upon them even the next day.

The Sturman checks us out today. Having the lowest rank here, he always likes to prove that he is a "good" SD man, which means that he is the worst one for us—the most sadistic. He is about thirty years old, and comes from Bolechow, Poland. He speaks Polish well and also Ukrainian—his name is Reiss.

After lunch the truck brings twelve containers of water that hold about a hundred gallons each, and everyone gets enough water this evening.

So passes Thursday, June 24, 1943.

Songs in the Night

the art and music
of the Shoah

INTRODUCTION

At a time when speech is stifled by darkness, songs live on. When writing fails to communicate, paint smeared on a canvas, crayons scrawled on a piece of dirty linen, or just an actor's gesture can convey a great deal.

The music and art of the Shoah should not be viewed as a direct communication to us, the next generation, to those who were outside the whirlwind of destruction. Those who suffered addressed only one another. Children expressed their puzzlement of a world that had suddenly grown dark and fearful. Musicians asserted the vitality of a folk music that was then reaching towards the stage

and concert halls, ready to make a significant contribution to Western civilization. Music and art were part of Jewish life. Why should they cease—until the last Jew was dead?

In Terezín, the musicians made their craft a means of expressing defiance. Art teachers worked with small children; poems and sketches of concentration camp life became interwoven and somehow endured as witnesses of what had happened. Outside of Terezín, there were the musical contests of the Vilna Ghetto; the children's choir of Warsaw; the singers and pianists, the composers and violinists—those who were known, the vast number never to become known.

When we sing their songs, read their poems, or look at the sketches they left behind, we once again enter into a world where the infinite breaks through into the darkness. In the imaginations of the little children, we celebrate the visions of man's goodness in an age of evil. And we hear the songs of the night that join together with the morning stars and sing of the crowning glory of God's creation: the human soul.

THE FIRST ONES

The first ones to be destroyed were the children,
little orphans, abandoned upon the face of the earth;
they who were the best in the world,
the acme of grace on the dark earth!
Oh, tender orphans!
From them, the bereaved of the world
in a house of shelter we drew consolation;
from the mournful faces, mute and dark,
we said the light of day will yet break upon us! . . .

Thus it was at the end of the winter, forty two,
in such a poor house of shelter,
I saw children just gathered from the street;
and I hid in a corner of corners,
I saw in the embrace of a nurse
a little girl less than two years old,
emaciated, thin, her face the pallor of death,
and her eyes so grave, so serious. . . .

I'D LIKE TO GO ALONE

I'd like to go away alone.
Where there are other, nicer people,
Somewhere into the far unknown,
There, where no one kills another.

Maybe more of us,
A thousand strong,
Will reach this goal
Before too long.

ALENA SYNKOVA

THE BUTTERFLY

The last, the very last,
So richly, brightly, dazzlingly yellow.
   Perhaps if the sun's tears would sing
   against a white stone . . .

Such, such a yellow
Is carried lightly 'way up high.
It went away I'm sure because it wished to
   kiss the world goodbye.

For seven weeks I've lived in here,
Penned up inside this ghetto
But I have found my people here.
The dandelions call to me
And the white chestnut candles in the court.
Only I never saw another butterfly.

That butterfly was the last one.
Butterflies don't live in here,
   In the ghetto.

PAVEL FRIEDMAN 4.6.1942

And I looked at her, I looked at this two year old crone;
like a grandma of a hundred years was this little girl in Israel;
the trouble and misery that her grandma had not seen even in a
nightmare, this little girl had seen fully awake.
And I wept and said to myself: Away with the tears!
The sorrow will cease but the graveness will remain! . . .

TEREZÍN

The heaviest wheel rolls across our foreheads
To bury itself deep somewhere inside our memories.

We've suffered here more than enough,
Here in this clot of grief and shame,
Wanting a badge of blindness
To be a proof for their own children.

A fourth year of waiting, like standing above a swamp
From which any moment might gush forth a spring.

Meanwhile, the rivers flow another way,
Another way,
Not letting you die, not letting you live.

And the cannons don't scream and the guns don't bark
And you don't see blood here.
Nothing, only silent hunger.
Children steal the bread here and ask and ask
                    and ask
And all would wish to sleep, keep silent and
        just to go to sleep again . . .

The heaviest wheel rolls across our foreheads
To bury itself deep somewhere inside our memories.

MIF 1944

(ANI MAMIN) I BELIEVE

I believe with perfect faith in the coming
of the Messiah. And even though he tarry,
still will I believe.

ANI MAMIN

The graveness will remain, it will seep into the well of the world,
into the well of life, and deepen it;
this Jewish earnestness will awaken,
will open the eyes of the blind,
will shine like the Torah to the whole world,
like a prophecy, like holy scriptures—
Do not cry, do not weep . . .
eighty million murderers will atone for one worried child in
  Israel! . . .

Do not cry . . .
At this station another girl I saw, about five years old;
she fed her younger brother and he cried,
the little one, he was sick;
into a diluted bit of jam she dipped tiny crusts of bread,
and skillfully she inserted them into his mouth . . .
This my eyes were privileged to see!

To see this mother, a mother of five years feeding her child,
to hear her soothing words—
My own mother, the best in the whole world
had not invented such a ruse.
But this one wiped his tears with a smile,
injected joy into his heart—A little girl in Israel!
Sholem Aleichem could not have improved upon her! . . .

They, the children of Israel, were the first in doom and disaster;
most of them without father and mother
were consumed by frost, starvation and lice;
holy messiahs sanctified in pain . . .
Say then, how have these lambs sinned?
Why in days of doom are they the first victims of wickedness,
the first in the trap of evil are they! . . .

I must be saving these days
(I have no money to save),
I must save health and strength,
Enough to last me for a long while.
I must save my nerves,
And my thoughts, and my mind
And the fire of my spirit;
I must be saving of tears that flow—
I shall need them for a long, long while.
I must save endurance these stormy days.

There is so much I need in my life:
Warmth of feeling and a kind heart—
These things I lack; of these I must be saving!
All these, the gifts of God,
I wish to keep.
How sad I should be
If I lost them quickly.

MARTHA

EINS, TZVEI, DREI

Es hot unz dos le-bn ge-ru-fn dos
le-bn fun zu-ni-ke teg hot ye-der in
land a-zoi mun-ter ge-shpant un ba-zun-der ge-
gan-gen zain veg tzu eins, tzvei, drei tzu
eins, tzvei, drei oif ar-bet in veg zich ge-lozt__
__ Ye-der trot hot zain klang ye-der veg zain ge-
zang ven du geist un du veist gut far-vos__

ONE, TWO, THREE

It is life which has come to call us,
Life from a sunnier sky.
And to all in the land
It is joy to be sent,
To walk singly into the new way.
To one, two, three,
To one, two, three,
To the work on the way which is bright.
Every step does belong,
Every way has its song,
When you go and you know what is right.

(GELE LATE) HONOR THE YELLOW BADGE

I held in trembling hand
A shred of yellow cloth;
It was besmirched and creased, a ragged wedge.
Bitter revulsion and nausea roared into my mouth:
There it is, there: The Jewish, yellow badge.

A blue flash caught my eye,
A point peeped from each fold.
Six points, all bent—the Star of David, blue.
A sudden pounding took me by my throat.
My blood streamed stronger, and hot words leaped out:
There it is—there: the badge of honor of the Jew.

And I repressed my sudden spurt of fear;
It seemed then that an outcry burst forth overhead

Which like a whirlwind tossed me, left me maimed.
And afterwards, throughout the night, till morn,
A pall took hold of me, imprisoning hand,
My body, all my limbs. And it proclaimed:

Give honor that the points are bent and twisted,
Give honor that the folds are wrapped and shifted
About the arms and shoulders of the Jew, God's pledge.
Give honor to the rag filled like a sponge
With desolation, sacred martyr's death, pogrom—
Proclaim and swear your love now to the yellow badge!

FEAR

Today the ghetto knows a different fear,
Close in its grip, Death wields an icy scythe.
An evil sickness spreads a terror in its wake,
The victims of its shadow weep and writhe.

Today a father's heartbeat tells his fright
And mothers bend their heads into their hands.
Now children choke and die with typhus here,
A bitter tax is taken from their bands.

My heart still beats inside my breast
While friends depart for other worlds.
Perhaps it's better—who can say?—
Than watching this, to die today?

No, no, my God, we want to live!
Not watch our numbers melt away.
We want to have a better world,
We want to work—we must not die!

EVA PICKOVA, 12 YEARS OLD, NYMBURK

IT BURNS

It burns, brothers, it burns.
The time of anguish—God forbid—now churns
When the village and you in one blow
Turns to ashes, to flames all aglow.
Nothing will remain at all—
Just a blackened wall—
And you look and you stand,
Each with folded hand.
And you look and you stand,
At burned village and land.

It burns, brothers, it burns,
To you alone this agony turns.
If you love your town, its name,
Take the vessels, quench the flame.
Quench it with your own blood too:
Show what you can do.
Brothers, do not look and stand,
Each with folded hand.
Brothers, do not look and stand
While town burns and land.

ES BRENT
(IT BURNS)

Andante

M. GEBIRTIG

Es brent bri - der es brent._
brent bri - der es brent._

S'ken cho - li - le ku - men der mo - ment._
Dos iz nor in aich a - lein ge - vendt._

Ven dos shte - tl mit aich tzu-za - men zol a - vek mit ash un fla - men
Ven dos shte - tl iz aich ta - ier nemt die kei - lim lesht dos fa - ier,

rit.

Blai - bn   zol   a   pus - ter   shliad   shvar-tze   pus - te   vent.
Lesht mit   ai - er   ei - gn   blut   ba - vaist   vos   ihr   kent.

Un   ihr   shteit   un   kukt   a - zoi   zich   mit   far - leig - te
Shteit   nit   bri - der   ot   a - zoi   zich   mit   far - leig - te

hent.   Un   ihr   shteit   un   kukt   a - zoi   zich   vie
hent.   Shteit   nit   bri - der   un   kukt   a - zoi   zich   vie

un - zer   shte - tl   brent.   Es
un - zer   shte - tl   brent.

3 times

Fine

From tomorrow on, I shall be sad—
From tomorrow on!
Today I will be gay.

What is the use of sadness—tell me that?—
Because these evil winds begin to blow?
Why should I grieve for tomorrow—today?
Tomorrow may be so good, so sunny,
Tomorrow the sun may shine for us again;
We shall no longer need to be sad.

From tomorrow on, I shall be sad—
From tomorrow on!
Not today; no! today I will be glad.
And every day, no matter how bitter it be,
I will say:
From tomorrow on, I shall be sad,
Not today!

                                        MOTELE

ZOG NIT KEINMOL
(SONG OF THE PARTISANS)

Words by
HIRSH GLIK

SONG OF THE PARTISANS

You must not say that you now walk the final way,
Because the darkened heavens hide the blue of day.
The time we've longed for will at last draw near,
And our steps, as drums, will sound that we are here.

From land all green with palms to lands all white with snow
We now arrive with all our pain and woe.
Where our blood sprayed out and came to touch the land,
There our courage and our manhood rise and stand.

The first were they detained for death,
the first into the wagons of slaughter;
they were thrown into the wagons, the huge wagons,
like heaps of refuse, like the ashes of the earth—
and they transported them,
killed them,
exterminated them
without remnant or remembrance . . .
The best of my children were all wiped out!
Oh woe unto me—
Doom and Desolation!

YITZHAK KATZENELSON

The poems appearing on pages 265-67, 275 and all the illustrations in this section were done by children in the Terezín Concentration Camp. They are reprinted here from *I Never Saw Another Butterfly*, by permission of McGraw-Hill Book Company and the State Jewish Museum in Prague. The poem, "The First Ones," by YITZHAK KATZENELSON, is reprinted by permission of the Jewish Education Committee Press from *The Flame and the Fury*. The poems on pages 271 and 279 are reprinted with permission from *Blessed Is the Match*, by MARIE SYRKIN.

The Great Silence

Am I my brother's keeper?

GENESIS 4:9

INTRODUCTION

W E ARE NOW IN THE INNERMOST CIRCLE OF HELL, WHERE CAIN
stands over the body of Abel. But the first fratricide is here multiplied a million times; all around, there are bystanders, witnesses
watching mutely, allowing murder and thus sharing in the crime.
A poisonous fog of silence shrouds the scene, shifted and shredded
by the winds of hell, with only an occasional patch of clear air.

The victims cried out to their neighbors. The neighbors had ears
but did not hear. They were listening to their own hatreds and
jealousies, to the insidious voices telling them that the Nazis were
acting out those dark dreams of hatred with which their own fan-
tasies had played from time to time. The neighbors had eyes but
did not see. Their minds were filled with visions of what might
happen to them if they interfered; they did not realize that it was
already happening. They had mouths but did not speak. And every
outcry silenced before it reached the lips weighed down the "tech-

nically innocent" neighbor until he was turned into another Cain, branded, residing in his special hell.

The victims cried out to the world. There have been so many victims, in so many centuries, who have appealed to the conscience of the world—Albigensians and Huguenots, Armenians and Vietnamese—and the world has been silent again and again. How many missions have been organized to appeal to the conscience of the world—and how many silences have turned the anguished outcry into a final prayer reaching towards the distant God!

Can God speak out if man is silent? When we believe in man, God speaks through man. And when our fellow man fashions the darkness of hell at Auschwitz—God hangs upon those gallows. Fellow man died at Auschwitz, and in every silence. But is the silence absolute? Can we still hear, at the outermost reaches of our awareness, a still small voice?

1. *THE TOWN BEYOND THE WALL*

ELIE WIESEL

The mystic soul of Elie Wiesel has many moods. In this novel, he is introspective, searching, almost gentle. Yet there is a terrifying passion underneath the quiet description of what happened the day a little girl turned to a bystander watching Jewish families being deported and said to him: I'm thirsty—and nothing happened. She remained thirsty. Soon, she died. The onlooker remained alive. And Wiesel's question reaches us with its full intensity: how shall we deal with those who participated in the crime of silence? Wiesel's answer is unusual in the literature of the Holocaust. But when we fully understand the question of the silence, we see how he arrived at his answer.

The sun retreated gently down the slope of the afternoon, igniting the clouds that barred its way. The water of the lake darkened, as if elements of the night were already part of it. Leaves rustled. I closed my eyes: sitting on the yellow grass, my back to a tree, I heard a voice call me by name. I looked around and knew that it was not a tree at my back, but my mother. I ask her, "Why have you come back?" She answers, "I was cold." I say, "Come; let's go back to the house." She answers, "I can't; don't you see that I'm a tree?"

From *The Town Beyond the Wall* by ELIE WIESEL. Copyright © 1964 by Elie Wiesel. Reprinted by permission of Atheneum Publishers. Translated from the French by STEPHEN BECKER.

My watch tells me it is after six. Time to leave, to go back to the city. On the way I experience a moment of worry: the man no longer lives in the same house! He's no longer alive! I hurry.

Crowded with people going home from work, the streets were like a forest tossed by the wind. They were all hurrying, rushing back to the warmth of the hearth.

I stopped in front of the house. The window was bright. The doorway was in the courtyard. I meditated for an instant: was this really an act of free will? I breathed deeply and pushed at the door without bothering to knock. It was open. In Szerencsevaros there was little need to lock doors, even at night. A corridor. At its end, the room that faced the street. In absolute silence I stepped that way. My heart pounded in spite of myself.

There he was.

Seated at a table, leaning on his elbows, his face in profile, he was reading a book. I'd have known him among a thousand. A heavy round head, completely bald. He hadn't changed. But now he was wearing glasses. A symbol of anonymity, the average man. I watched him in silence. A fly skipped along his skull: he didn't take notice. I stared at him without hate, without scorn. All I felt toward him was curiosity.

He sensed a presence suddenly. His eyes shifted toward the door; he saw me and started. "What do you want?"

On his feet, leaning against the table, he faced me. The features I had seen at the window. Large cold eyes, opaque as the ice that covered the river. A startling absence of eyebrows. Receding chin. Innocence itself: what does not exist is by definition innocent.

"I'm thirsty," my little sister said.

"Who are you?"

I did not answer. That was none of his business. I am here: let that be enough. I had no need to define myself in relation to him. I stepped forward, then walked about the room, as if the room interested me far more than his presence. Middle-class furnishings. Heavy, bulky pieces. Even the radio, big as a chest of drawers. On the walls, photographs of a soldier with drooping mustaches: his father, probably. A portrait in enamel, his mother as a girl. Hand beneath her chin, she smiled provocatively.

"I'm thirsty," my little sister said.

"Are you from the police?"

He kept his eyes on me. Pale, he was blinking. His lips trembled; he mumbled inaudibly. He took off his glasses to set them on the table, and almost dropped them. I looked again at the enamel portrait: my mother, too, had smiled, but there had been nothing provocative about her. On the contrary: she had been humble, reserved, shy.

She was thirsty, my mother said, but she was embarrassed to mention it.

"You're not from the police!"

He had guessed it from the way I was studying the smile his mother had left behind. The change in his attitude was abrupt. He was no longer afraid. He belonged in the category of people who fear only the police. I was not a policeman; from which it followed that there was no need to be afraid. On top of the radio was a mirror. With my day-old beard I looked gloomy and evil. But not like a policeman.

"What do you want?" he asked firmly.

"To humiliate you," I said.

"I'm thirsty," my little sister said.

She had the most beautiful hair in the world. The sun loved to carouse in it. But on that spring day—a Saturday—she wore a scarf on her head, as if she were old and a widow. She was eight years old. *"I'm so thirsty," she said.* I couldn't bring her water. The police were guarding the gates of the courtyard. We were forbidden to go out. And this man stood at the window and watched.

"I've come a long way," I said. "I've come to humiliate you."

I wanted to see him on his knees, licking the dust on my shoes. To make him taste the loneliness of cowards. To reduce him to shreds. To deprive him of any picture of himself, to decompose his identity, to scourge pride and self-esteem and countenance from him as one drives children away from a rotting cadaver.

"I'm thirsty," I told him. "Give me some wine."

He lumbered around the table, opened a cabinet, and brought out a bottle of Tokay and two glasses like inverted cones. He set them calmly on the table. I told him to fill the glasses. He did so. The bottle did not tremble in his hand. I took my glass in my right hand. He made as if to do the same. I stopped him. He nodded "All right," and waited. We stared at each other silently. Each gauged the other's strength. He sustained my glare. My fingers curled around the glass with near shattering force. I wanted to shout, "Lower your eyes, you scum! Crawl!" My expression shouted it. He did not give way. His opaque eyes reflected an inner winter, sheathed in ice, impenetrable, stiff. The silence grew heavier. The man betrayed not the slightest sign of weakness. He saw in me an enemy, in this confrontation a duel. Then, in a motion quite abrupt though carefully premeditated, I dashed the wine in his face. He narrowed his eyes. Heavy yellow drops trickled down his face, which remained impassive. I took the second glass and held it up for him to see: he did not look at it. His eyes never left mine. "Lower them! To the dust!" He received the contents of the second glass with the same calm.

"Fill them," I ordered him.

Without a word he did so again, but his face darkened. When they were full to the brim he pushed the glasses toward me, placing them within my reach.

"Let's talk," I said.

"About what?"

"A Saturday in spring. Nineteen forty-four. On one side, the Jews; on the other, you. Only the window—that window—between."

"I remember."

"With shame?"

"No."

"With remorse?"

"No."

"With sadness?"

"No. With nothing at all. There's no emotion attached to the memory."

I leaned forward slightly: "What did you feel then?"

"Nothing."

The muscles in my face tightened: "Outside, children were sick with thirst: what did you feel?"

"Outside, men were turning away so as not to see their children doubled up in pain: what did you feel?"

"Nothing." A silence; then: "Absolutely nothing. My wife was crying in the kitchen. Not me. She was sad and miserable. I wasn't." Another silence; then: "No, I tell you. I had a shocked feeling that I was a spectator at some sort of game—a game I didn't understand:

a game you had all begun playing, you on one side, the Germans and the police on the other. I had nothing to do with it."

A game! For the first time that evening anger rumbled in me. Because he was right. All the appearances of a game. Of course, we died for real, but that wasn't the point. The way in which we die is what counts. And we went at it as if we were playing a game. Without protesting, without fighting back, we let ourselves be cast as victims. A revolt, even badly organized, offered fair chances of success: it never broke out. Like a herd of sheep we allowed ourselves to be led. A game indeed! A Greek tragedy in which the characters are condemned in advance, long before the curtain rises. At Szerencsevaros, at Marmaroszighet, in a thousand other European cities, the Jews blindly obeyed the implacable instructions of an invisible director. Everywhere the first act was the same, and the second, and the last. A gesture, one only, a shout, one only—some interjection that was not in the script—and everything might have changed: the actors would have reverted to their own identities. That gesture, no one made; that shout, no one shouted. The victims were exemplary victims. Of course, they did not know. They did not know how the story went on, how it ended. They should have known. They could have known. There were a few who knew, who had seen. The others refused to listen to them. The others shut them up. Stopped their mouths. Were ready to stone them. Those were the rules of the game.

"I felt no sadness," the man went on. "I remember: the day after you left, I was walking around in the half-empty city. All your things were strewn in the streets as if the earth had spewed them up. Here and there people were singing and dancing, dead drunk. I didn't touch a thing. It was like being onstage an hour after the end of the show."

The blood beat in my temples. Remorse, shame, anger ebbed and flowed in me. Now I hated him. After all, I was not the defendant here. Even if he was right—and my heart said he was—that didn't justify his spectator's detachment. He too could have interrupted the game. If he had simply gone down to the courtyard of the synagogue and alerted the Jews: "Good people! Listen to me! Don't be fooled! Be careful! It's not a game!" He hadn't done it.

"Coward!" I shouted, and crashed my fist down on the table.

"You're a shameful coward! You haven't got the courage to do either good or evil. The role of spectator suited you to perfection. They killed? You had nothing to do with it. They looted the houses like vultures? You had nothing to do with it. Children were thirsty? You had nothing to do with it. Your conscience is clear. 'Not guilty, your honor!' You're a disgusting coward! You hedge: you want to be on the winning side no matter what! It's easy to say 'I am I and they are they and to hell with them'! It's comfortable to say 'It's all a fraud, they're only playing a game.' And who gave you the right to judge who's playing and who isn't, who's dying and who's just pretending? Who taught you so well to distinguish between suffering and the appearance of suffering?"

I turned my back to him and went to the window, to where he had stood years earlier. In the distance a voice: "Will you be back soon?" I didn't hear the answer. Anyway the ten thousand Jews of Szerencsevaros wouldn't be back. Not soon and not late. Not tonight and not tomorrow night. Their role is that of the absent. The favorite role of the dead. As death is the favorite game of the Jews.

There's the audience you performed for, Kalman. And you, Hersh-Leib and Menachem. And you, my little sister. What paltry performers you were! Not a tear in the audience, not a sigh, not a single gasp of horror. Nothing. A thousand times nothing. Martha, the old drunk, did better than you: at least she aroused fear, aroused shame. You—you aroused only indifference. The audience was disappointed. The play provoked no response. Nothing I tell you. No emotion, no alteration. In the kitchen his wife was crying. But he, front row center, remained dry-eyed and hard-hearted. You played badly! Were you thirsty, little sister? You performed badly. Your thirst was unconvincing.

"You hate me, don't you?"

I turned. His voice had suddenly taken on a human tone. A certain intensity showed in his face.

"No," I said. "I don't hate you." A pause; then: "I feel contempt for you. That's worse. The man who inspires hatred is still human; but not the man who inspires contempt. You don't feel contempt for the executioner; you hate him and you want him dead. You feel contempt only for cowards. People like you retreat to an ivory tower and say to themselves, 'All the world's a stage and all the men and women merely players. Ah, how pleasant when they make us shiver!' Hatred implies humanity: it has its coordinates, its motifs, its themes, its harmonics. Under certain conditions it can elevate men. But contempt has only one implication: decadence."

He paled perceptibly. His eyes were little more than slits. He stood erect, a hand on his stomach, as though he were sick.

"You won't do it," he said "You won't humiliate me. You're playing a game, and I won't go along. I refuse to play." He peered at me, and the cold glance grew harder, sharp as a sword: "You accuse me of cowardice. And you? What were you? A few policemen—not more than ten—led you all to the slaughterhouse: why didn't you seize their arms? Can you tell me why?"

"We didn't know," I said tightly. "We didn't know what was ahead of us."

"That's not true! There were some among you who knew, some who tried to warn you; you didn't listen. Why? Why? Can you tell me why you didn't listen?"

"What they were saying sounded too fantastic; nobody could really put much stock in it."

"You were afraid, you preferred the illusion to the bite of conscience, and the game to a show of courage!"

I contained my anger with difficulty. *You were thirsty, little sister.* And he dared to judge you, he the spectator. This man is accusing you of cowardice. My impulse was to charge him, to blind him, to kill him. A man like that had no right to live and to judge the dead.

"You're right; or rather you may be right. We too could have behaved differently. But you forget that we were victims: they had taken from us not only the right to live—and to drink when we were thirsty—but also any right to clarity. That doesn't apply to you: you weren't a victim. Your duty was clear: you had to choose. To fight us or to help. In the first case I would have hated you; in the second, loved. You never left your window: I have only contempt for you."

My voice was calm. It was important not to hate him. I concentrated my efforts to that end: to silence my hatred. Contempt was what he deserved. Hatred implied something of the human. The spectator has nothing of the human in him: he is a stone in the street, the cadaver of an animal, a pile of dead wood. He is there, he survives us, he is immobile. The spectator reduces himself to the level of an object. He is no longer he, you, or I: he is "it."

He wanted to say something, but I silenced him with a glance. I told him to join me at the window. He did so. We turned our backs to the room and looked out at the courtyard of the synagogue. It must have been close to midnight. The dead would never again come to pray.

"You won't humiliate me," he said.

I ignored his remark and said, "Do you remember the synagogue? Do you think it's destroyed forever? Wrong. It exists. A synagogue is like the Temple in Jerusalem. The wise men of Israel say that there is one on high and a second here below. The one here below can be reduced to ashes; it's been done twice. But the temple on high remains intact; its enemies cannot touch it. And this synagogue, too, exists. Only it's been transplanted. Every time you raise your eyes you'll see it. And you'll see it so often, so clearly, that you'll pray God to blind you."

"You won't humiliate me," he said.

I ignored him again; I went on, "You think you're living in peace and security, but in reality you're not living at all. People of your kind scuttle along the margins of existence. Far from men, from their struggles, which you no doubt consider stupid and senseless. You tell yourself that it's the only way to survive, to keep your head above water. You're afraid of drowning, so you never embark. You huddle on the beach, at the edge of the sea you fear so much, even to its spray. Let the ships sail without you! Whatever their flag—Communist, Nazi, Tartar, what difference does it make? You tell yourself, 'To link my life to other men's would be to diminish it, to set limits; so why do it?' You cling to your life. It's precious to you. You won't offer it to history or to country or to God. If living in peace means evolving in nothingness, you accept the nothingness. The Jews in the courtyard of the synagogue? Nothing. The shrieks of women gone mad in the cattle cars? Nothing. The silence of thirsty children? Nothing. All that's a game, you tell yourself. A movie! Fiction: seen and forgotten. I tell you, you're a machine for the fabrication of nothingness."

"I will not let myself be humiliated," he said.

And this time too I ignored him and said. "The dead Jews, the women gone mad, the mute children—I'm their messenger. And I tell you they haven't forgotten you. Someday they'll come marching, trampling you, spitting in your face. And at their shouts of contempt you'll pray God to deafen you."

A cool breeze flowed from the window and touched our faces, like the breath of a beast. Stars pursued one another across a very distant sky. A door squeaked. Murmured complaints. Far off the mountains had wrapped their secrets in a heavy cloak.

"I will not let myself be humiliated," the man said.

This time I answered: "Be quiet."

Suddenly I had no further desire to speak or listen. I was weary, as after a battle fought without conviction. I had come, I had seen, I had delivered the message: the wheel had come full circle. The act was consummated. Now I shall go. I shall return to the life they call normal. The past will have been exorcised. I'll live, I'll work, I'll love. I'll take a wife, I'll father a son, I'll fight to protect his future, his future happiness. The task is accomplished. No more concealed wrath, no more disguises. No more double life, lived on two levels. Now I am whole.

"Do you really feel contempt for me?"

I didn't answer. I'd talked enough. Everything had been said. I'll leave Szerencsevaros, the city of luck. I'll never come back.

"Come," I said.

We left the window. There was something bizarre about the two glasses of wine on the table.

"Let's drink," I said.

I took a glass and pushed the other across to him. He picked it up hesitantly, not knowing if I would insult him again. The lines around his mouth now revealed bitterness and bewilderment.

"Let's drink to the actors," I said. "To the actors destroyed in their own play."

We clinked glasses, and drained them.

"You don't hate me," he said.

"I told you. I don't hate you."

"But you must!" he cried hopelessly.

"I don't hate you," I said.

"I couldn't bear that! Your contempt would burn at my eyes; they'd never close again! You've got to hate me!"

"No," I said.

He stared at me for a moment and I thought he was going to

cry. If he had, I'd have thrown my arms around him. For the first time that night his face had quivered. The veins in his temples were swollen. He ran his tongue around his lips as if to absorb the last drops of wine. Then he smiled a curious, ironic smile, the meaning of which I understood only later.

"I feel sure you'll hate me," he said.

Now his suffering was obvious, as though an unseen hand had engraved it on his skin. He had become human again. Down deep, I thought, man is not only an executioner, not only a victim, not only a spectator: he is all three at once.

It was time to go. I said "Adieu" and without waiting for an answer turned and left, shrugging. The street was empty, asleep. I headed for Dr. Todor's house to see my father's friend. I intended to spend two days there, until the rendezvous.

But no man shouts his scorn and disgust at another with impunity. At the corner of the street running into the main square a car braked sharply at the curb; in the wink of an eye the door opened and two arms flashed out like lightning to drag me inside. In the front seat sat the spectator. I had barely left his house when he was off to warn the policeman on the corner. Our eyes met in the mirror: his were full of defiance, an anticipation of victory, saying, "Now you'll *have* to hate me!"

"Did you spit in his face?" Pedro asked.

"No."

"The man turned you in, and you didn't spit in his face?"

"No, my friend. I smiled at him. I smiled at the man to whom I had played God."

"That's crueler," Pedro said.

And he rubbed his forehead, absorbed; he always did that when he was moved.

Days and nights flowed by in the gloom that swallowed them up one after another. At first Michael found landmarks in the bread and the soup: bread was distributed in the morning, soup late in the afternoon. But Menachem soon disillusioned him. To confuse their minds the jailers sometimes amused themselves by reversing the schedule. So the prisoners were never quite sure whether it was day or night.

Michael felt his sanity dimming, extinguishing; its flame guttered low. His identity was dissolving in dead time.

Of his three companions, Menachem was the only one with whom he could converse. Naturally he too was touched by madness, but his had at least the virtue of being communicative, possessing its own poetic coherence.

"God is my caretaker," he liked to say. "Under bond, I give him all that I am and all that I have: at night, my soul; in the morning, my sanity. In the morning he returns my soul, and he will also restore my sanity."

"I refuse his services," Michael answered. "I'm poor. His prices are too high. I prefer to keep my baggage with me."

The other's handsome, Christlike face radiated compassion: "Don't blaspheme, my friend." He murmured a prayer, leaned forward, and spoke in a very gentle voice: "Are you sure that you are not already mad? Across the line? Are you absolutely convinced that madness wasn't behind your stubbornness? If faith is madness, why can't a lack of faith be the same?"

Not wanting to hurt him, Michael did not answer. One can prove one's sanity only to the sane.

"I grant you, I may be insane," Menachem went on. "It may be that we both are. If we aren't we will be. And yet, Michael, my friend, I prefer to be insane with God—or in Him—than without God, or far from Him."

"Now you're blaspheming," Michael answered.

"There, too, I prefer to blaspheme in God than far from Him."

Thanks to Menachem Michael managed not to founder for some time. When the Jew of Marmaroszighet saw him too sad—or not sad enough—he came over to chat with him, and it was as if he had offered an arm to lean on.

Menachem told him about his own crime against the state: he had organized clandestine classes in religion. At that time anti-Semitism was not only tolerated but encouraged in all countries behind the Iron Curtain. They arrested rabbis and students; they deported them to work camps so that they would not "contaminate" the minds of the young. He, Menachem, was neither a rabbi nor a teacher of religion. He was not even very pious. Often it happened that he transgressed the rigid Sabbath laws, and prayed less than three times a day. The change occurred one afternoon when his little boy came home from school and asked him, "Is it true that the Jews are the cancer of history? That they live off the past? That they invented

God just to humble man and stop progress?" Menachem went white beneath his beard. After several months of activity he was arrested. His torturers told him, "We'll make you forget God. You'll not only doubt the possibility of His existence, but also of your own." But he held out. He never ate without covering his head and reciting a prayer over the bread. Even for the daily housecleaning of the cell he had devised a special prayer that he muttered, weeping great tears that brightened his luminous gaze. "You ask me why I cry so much?" he said once. "I'll tell you: to survive. Do you know the story about the king's fool?"

"No, I don't," Michael said without thinking. He might have known it; he knew plenty of stories about kings and fools, playing their parts consciously or not. But he liked to hear his companion's voice. It pulled him out of his stupor.

"One day the king sent for his favorite jester and told him, 'I feel melancholy. I need to laugh. Make me laugh, or you will not see the sun rise again.' Panic-stricken, the fool forgot his art. As if accursed, he could remember no grimace, no dance, no song that normally loosed laughter among the court. Knowing himself doomed, he broke into convulsive sobs. Now, it is well known that fools cannot weep. Their tears are unconvincing; everyone knows they are false tears. As he wept, the fool looked so comical that the king slapped his fat belly and a sufficient roar of laughter escaped him."

"That's a cruel story," Michael said.

"All stories about fools are cruel."

"Are you the fool, Menachem?"

"Maybe."

"Then the king is God. Do you want to make God laugh?"

"God is the king, and I am only a fool. But He is not a king like other kings, and I am not a fool like other fools. All he asks is to weep with us. Within us. For that our tears must remain pure and whole. Their source is the source of life."

"And what lies beyond tears? Do you know?"

"Yes. God. God awaits us beyond all things. Let yourself go, my friend. Weep and you will find the crust of existence less thick, less hard."

His thoughts far away, Michael smiled: in heaven, near the Celestial Throne, there is a special chalice into which all our tears are poured. When it is full, the Messiah will come. The poet Frug made a song of it, and cried out, "Has that cup no bottom?"

But Menachem never wrung a single tear from his friend. The discussion lasted several days and nights. Michael refused to yield.

One night he woke with a start: he heard strange choking gasps. Michael opened his eyes and was horrified for a moment. The man he had nicknamed "The Impatient One" was strangling the pious Jew. In one bound Michael was upon him, and pushed him back to his corner.

"He's the one who took my letter," the other shouted. "I want it back! I'll kill him!"

Menachem was exhausted. He was rubbing his neck and breathing with difficulty. He seemed sad and distant. Michael knelt beside him, worried.

"Are you all right?" he asked.

"All right."

They were silent for several moments, and then Menachem gave him a look so full of affection that Michael trembled. "Thank you, my friend," Menachem said feebly.

"Be quiet," Michael answered.

He went back to his corner and there, sure of privacy, he wept his first tear. It brought him a sense of relief mingled with shame. A few days later—or was it a few weeks? a few months?—he gave in to it a second time.

It was morning. The guard, entering the cell, bore only three rations of bread. "You," he said to Menachem. "Come with me. You're transferred."

Michael gasped. He had not expected this. He had never imagined that they might be separated. Through a dream he saw Menachem pick up his blanket, his spoon, and his jacket, an indefinable smile on his lips. Passing Michael, he stopped to embrace him fondly. He repeated the same benediction several times: "God be with you, God be with you!"

"No, Menachem. You'll need Him more than I will."

Menachem embraced him tightly and left him abruptly. Michael saw only his back, beyond the doorway; he heard the footsteps trail off in the interminable corridor. He listened closely: nothing more.

Then, so suddenly impoverished, he leaned his head against the wall and broke into sobs, at the end of his tether. Neither the

Impatient One nor the Silent One paid any attention. The one searched for his letter, the other no longer sought anything. The Silent One stared fixedly before him, not even noticing that Menachem—the body which for months had filled his field of vision —was no longer there.

Michael felt himself slipping downward. His loneliness grew thicker, heavier. To rise for soup, or to clean the cell, or to urinate in the bucket close at hand, was an almost insurmountable effort. The center of the earth was dragging him down.

Sometimes he tried to remember Pedro, to speak to him, but he felt that his friend was not listening. Cloaked in fog and forgetfulness, Spain was far away, beyond the horizon.

Ah, to do something that one cannot do, that one must not do! To fling oneself beneath a moving automobile, to cut off one's own tongue or ear, to attack one's own sanity, to dig oneself a grave in heaven, an opening in the clouds, and to contemplate oneself in the sun!

Once in an elevator in Paris Michael had stood behind a woman of whom he could see only the nape of the neck. He had no idea whether she was young or old, pretty or homely. Suddenly a thought —a need—crossed his mind: what if I kissed her, right there, on the nape of the neck?

In a bus, another time, his seatmate was a fat burgher who sat twiddling an unlighted cigar. Suddenly Michael hated him. He wanted to shout "You son of a bitch!" and strangle him.

And still another time he was walking down a street when a beggar in a tattered coat got down on his knees to grub for a cigarette butt. Michael felt like lifting him by the collar and asking him, "Why do you hate me? What have I done?"

For Michael madness was a door opening onto a forest, onto the liberty in which anything is permitted, anything is possible. There A does not precede B, children are born dotards, fire produces cold, and snow becomes the source of desire. There, animals are gifted with human intelligence and demons display a sense of humor. There, all is impulse, passion, and chaos. There, the laws are abolished and those who promulgated them removed from office. The universe frees itself from the order in which it was imprisoned. Appearance snaps its ties with reality. A chair is no longer a chair, the king no longer king, the fool ceases to be a fool, or to cry.

To go mad: why not? All he had to do now was adapt to the Impatient One's system: to read him the letter he never ceased calling for. Or to construct a system for himself alone: he would surely not lack ideas. Should he let go? Isn't a bird at the edge of the nest better off beating toward the heights? He'll plummet to earth? So what?

A character from Shakespeare obsessed him: that old man enraged by the neglect of others, who falls to his knees and murmurs despairingly, "O fool, I shall go mad!" There was a man who preferred suffering at the hands of men to flight into a trackless desert. There was a man who could have immunized himself against the treason of friends and the cowardice of enemies and who yet chose the least easy solution: he faced them directly. He opened his mind to them, exposed his sensibilities to them, and told them, "I am here and nowhere else!"

Yet Michael remained furious at the old man: idiot that you are, bloody fool! What are you trying to prove when you cling to others' values, others' judgments? That you're courageous? That you're human? That you aren't afraid of pain or injustice? That you insist on sanity? To whom are you justifying yourself? Of whom are you asking understanding or forgiveness? Why do you fear madness? Accept it, and rouse fear in others! Rouse fear in God himself! Accept madness, old man, take it, embrace it: that will be your protest against pain and injustice! Come, old man: Spit in their faces! Tell them, "If that's how you see life—thank you, but it's not for me!" Tell them, "If that's the sanity, the intelligence you're so proud of—not for me!" Go on, hopeless old man! Tell them what hurts! Are you afraid to leave them? Ashamed, perhaps?

But the old man lay prostrate and refused to listen.

Michael was awakened again one night by an attempted murder: the Impatient One had attacked the Silent One and was throttling him furiously. "Give me that letter! I know you've got it! That's why you don't talk! Give it to me!"

The boy was blue in the face, and his eyes were popping. He was not defending himself, and made no effort to struggle free. If Michael had awakened two minutes later he'd have found him dead. With surprising strength he leaped up and tried to separate them. But the Impatient One had the strength of a bloodthirsty animal. His fingers were clenched around the boy's neck like a pair of tongs: impossible to pry them open. With no time to waste, Michael grabbed his neck and squeezed; squeezed harder, still harder, and finally saw the killer release his prey.

Michael should have relaxed his own hold then, but for a fraction of a second he went on squeezing: his fingers refused to obey. He snapped out of it then and let the unconscious man fall.

That night Michael did not sleep. Pedro came to visit. He seemed more melancholy than usual. A bit more worried. He is dead or arrested, Michael thought.

"You saved a human life, little brother. I'm proud of you."

"I saved a body. A body with a sleeping mind and a dead soul. I'm not proud."

"Save his soul. You can do it."

"No, Pedro. I can't. I'm sinking fast too. A little while ago I almost killed a man. My own soul is blotting up madness and night. The whole universe has gone mad. Here and everywhere."

Pedro smiled: he was remembering something.

"You're smiling, Pedro, and I'm going mad. I have no strength left. I'm at the end of the line. I can't do any more. I'm alone. To stay sane I've got to have someone across from me. Otherwise my mind will rot, and smell of decay, and twist like the serpent that feels the earth and death."

Pedro went on smiling: "That's exactly what I want you to do: re-create the universe. Restore that boy's sanity. Cure him. He'll save you."

Pedro had come without his pipe. He was probably arrested or dead, and that was why he hadn't brought it. Ask him directly? I was afraid to. I didn't want to hear him say, "I've been arrested," or "I'm dead." I let him talk and didn't interrupt. He was saying, "The only valuable protest, or attitude, is one rooted in the uncertain soil of humanity. Remaining human—in spite of all temptations and humiliations—is the only way to hold your own against the Other, whatever it may be. Your Impatient One, waiting for a letter that no one will ever send him—what is he proving? Nothing at all. His behavior—however tragic—is as futile, as sterile, as a machine running in neutral. To see liberty only in madness is wrong: liberation, yes; liberty, no."

Michael welcomed the dawn as a new man. His strength flowed

back. He was suddenly responsible for a life that was an inseparable part of the life of mankind. He would fight. He would resume the creation of the world from the void. God of Adam and of Abraham, this time, I beg You, don't be against us!

The Impatient One was transferred to another cell and Michael remained alone with his protégé. He changed corners immediately; now he was living where Manachem had lived.

During the first days he communicated only in gestures, and then by expressions; finally he used words too. The important thing was to establish an exchange, a rapport, of whatever kind.

In the morning—or the evening—he waited until the boy had drunk his coffee, and then offered his own. Absently the boy took the bowl and drained it. On the fourth or fifth day Michael, holding his breath, withheld the second bowl and waited: failure or success? It worked. The other, like a blind man, extended a hand and groped for something that belonged to him. The gesture moved Michael profoundly.

A few days later he pushed the experiment further: when the guard brought the two rations of coffee Michael took them both and hid them behind his back. The boy extended his right hand, then his left. Michael did not stir. He watched: would life suffuse that face, that stare? For a moment nothing happened. Absolute immobility. The earth ceased to turn, the blood to flow, the heart to beat.

And then the ice broke. A gleam—the first—split the opacity of those eyes. Michael glimpsed human thirst, human suffering, a human question: "Why are you torturing me?"

Tears in his eyes, Michael proffered the still-warm drink.

He repeated the trick with bread, with water, with soup. The boy's reflexes grew fuller and quicker. After a time his body responded: Yes, I'm thirsty; yes, I'm hungry; yes, I need you so that I can eat and drink. It was language on an animal level, physical, but Michael was full of hope: the rest would come. He had broken down one wall, that of the senses: the boy was aware of his presence. As a first result, that was not negligible. But the battle was far from finished; it would be full of difficulties and Michael had only himself to call upon.

At times he was on the verge of despondency: Will I one day pierce that wall, dispel those murky shadows? This boy has a past; will I ever know about it? His silence veils joys, fears, hopes, women's kisses, humiliations inflicted by "grownups"; will it shatter for me? Michael knew nothing save what those eyes could tell him: was he at least capable of speech, or understanding? Did he have a name? Had he ever had an identity? Relentlessly he persevered. The means at his disposition were poor: the cave man had had better. Not even a scrap of iron or a sharp stone for drawing pictures on the walls. Michael did not lose heart. I have nothing? No matter. I can push back the night with my bare hands. I'll kill the black spider in prey of our silence.

As soon as he was sure that the boy was seeing him, he became a changed man.

To set the boy an example he danced, laughed, clapped hands, scratched himself with his dirty nails, made faces, stuck out his tongue: he had to show the boy that being a man meant all this.

Now he talked all day long, sang through endless evenings. He told sad stories and let his tears run freely: when a man is troubled, he weeps. He told erotic stories, even obscene stories, while his cheeks flamed like torches at twilight: desire is fire and strength. He reported funny adventures he had lived through or heard about, and laughed in great gusts: laughter is a weapon.

The boy listened silently, immobile as a statue, resisting all assaults. Words, tears, Michael's funny faces were flung up against him and fell back like dead birds.

Michael lost his temper often; then, his face wrathful, his eyes flashing sparks, he struck the boy violently or shook him by the shoulders until they were both out of breath.

"Wake up, for God's sake! It's our only chance! One of us will win, and if it isn't me we're both lost! Do you hear me?"

Futile. The shaggy boy kept silence, breathing the air of another world.

Michael wept in impotent rage: "Help me, you bloody cretin! Make an effort! Snap out of it!"

Imperturbable, the other stared, as if all this were no concern of his.

Once Michael opened the boy's mouth by main strength, pulling at his jaws with both hands: "Say something! Speak! One word, just one! Speak up!"

The other did not react. If he was in pain, he gave no sign. His eyes gazed through Michael as if they saw nothing.

"At least tell me your name!" Michael shouted, and gritted

his teeth. "I am Michael. Are you listening? Michael! Pay attention, watch my lips: Mi-chael! And who are you? What's your name? Help me. It's silly, I know, but that's how it is. You're crazy, and I'm not, but only you can get us out of this. Give me some help, for God's sake! What's your name?"

Futile efforts, vain furies. The boy lived in a kingdom barred to Michael. Where he lived, tortures and caresses were of little effect. Michael therefore armed himself with fresh patience. He had to persevere at any cost.

The day when the boy suddenly began sketching arabesques in the air was one of the happiest of Michael's life. His eyes dimmed with tears. Then all was not inexorably lost and barren. He felt like dropping to his knees and offering thanks to God. He did not; but took the boy's hand in his own, squeezed it hard, very hard, and murmured gently. "Thank you, little one, thank you." His intelligence and personality were still dim, barely flickering, but Michael took heart.

Now he talked more, as if wishing to store ideas and values in the boy for his moment of awakening. Michael compared himself to a farmer: months separated the planting and the harvest. For the moment, he was planting.

"Right at this instant, little one, there are couples all over the world who think they're embracing, and some who really are; there are hearts hammering because they want to be beside someone who has just departed; and in the wild countryside of some country just awakening or just falling asleep there is a woman, some woman, being stoned for a reason, some reason, and nothing can save her from human beings; and there is a man, some man, being deserted, whatever his desires, and he can expect nothing more from human beings. And yet I tell you: affection exists; it is created and transmitted like a secret formula from heart to heart and from mouth to ear.

"I know: the paths of the soul, overgrown, often know only the night, a very vast, very barren night, without landscapes. And yet I tell you: we'll get out. The most glorious works of man are born of that night.

"I know, little one: it isn't easy to live always under a question mark. But who says that the essential question has an answer? The essence of man is to be a question, and the essence of the question is to be without answer.

"But to say, 'What is God? What is the world? What is my friend?' is to say that I have someone to talk to, someone to ask a direction of. The depth, the meaning, the very salt of man is his constant desire to ask the question ever deeper within himself, to feel ever more intimately the existence of an unknowable answer.

"Man has the right to risk life, his own life; he does not need to submerge himself in destiny in order to maintain his deep significance. He must risk, he can risk, a confrontation with destiny, he must try to seize what he demands, to ask the great questions and ask them again, to look up at another, a friend, and to look up again: if two questions stand face to face, that's at least something. It's at least a victory. The question, the demand, the outcry, the sickness in the soul or in the eyes—they never die.

"What I say to you, pass on to you, little one, I learned from a friend—the only one I had. He's dead, or in prison. He taught me the art and the necessity of clinging to humanity, never deserting humanity. The man who tries to be an angel only succeeds in making faces.

"It's in humanity itself that we find both our question and strength to keep it within limits—or on the contrary to make it universal. To flee to a sort of Nirvana—whether through a considered indifference or through a sick apathy—is to oppose humanity in the most absurd, useless, and comfortable manner possible. A man is a man only when he is among men. It's harder to remain human than to try to leap beyond humanity. Accept that difficulty. Tell yourself that even God admits His weakness before the image He has created.

"To be indifferent—for whatever reason—is to deny not only the validity of existence, but also its beauty. Betray, and you are a man; torture your neighbor, you're still a man. Evil is human, weakness is human; indifference is not.

"They'll probably tell you that it's all only a play, that the actors are in disguise. So what? Jump onto the stage, mingle with the actors, and perform, you too. Don't stay at the window. Get out of the nest, but never try to reach the heights by flying away from thirsty children and mothers with milkless breasts. The real heights are like the real depths: you find them at your own level, in simple and honest conversation, in glances heavy with existence.

"One day the ice will break and you'll begin to smile: for me that will be a proof of our strength, of our compact. Then you'll shake yourself and the shadows will fall away from you as the fever leaves a sick man: you'll open your eyes and you'll say to yourself, 'I feel better, the sickness is gone, I'm different.' You'll tell me your name and you'll ask me, 'Who are you?' and I'll answer, 'I'm Pedro.' And that will be a proof that man survives, that he passes himself along. Later, in another prison, someone will ask your name and you'll say, 'I'm Michael.' And then you will know the taste of the most genuine of victories."

Michael had come to the end of his strength. Before him the night was receding, as on a mountain before dawn.

The other bore the biblical name of Eliezer, which means, *God has granted my prayer.*

Legend tells us that one day man spoke to God in this wise:

"Let us change about. You be man, and I will be God. For only one second."

God smiled gently and asked him, "Aren't you afraid?"

"No. And you?"

"Yes, I am," God said.

Nevertheless he granted man's desire. He became a man, and the man took his place and immediately availed himself of his omnipotence: he refused to revert to his previous state. So neither God nor man was ever again what he seemed to be.

Years passed, centuries, perhaps eternities. And suddenly the drama quickened. The past for one, and the present for the other, were too heavy to be borne.

As the liberation of the one was bound to the liberation of the other, they renewed the ancient dialogue whose echoes come to us in the night, charged with hatred, with remorse, and most of all, with infinite yearning.

2. *THE MISSION*

HANS HABE

In July of 1938, shortly after Hitler annexed Austria, Franklin Delano Roosevelt convened the International Conference on Refugees. The meeting took place at Evian-les-Bains, a French resort on the Swiss border. Thirty-two nations agreed to attend the conference, together with representatives of Jewish organizations, Vatican observers, and others. With the best of intentions, they failed to do anything to help those caught by Hitler or threatened by his plans for extermination. At that point— and much later, according to the testimony given at the Eichmann trial —a "deal" could have been made with Hitler; Europe's Jews might have been ransomed. Hans Habe was a reporter at that conference; and the novel he wrote describes what happened when moral and political questions clashed.

In addition to Colombia, the committee was made up of Belgium, Ecuador, Bolivia, Brazil, Norway, Switzerland and Great Britain. Bolivia was represented by an ambassador, Brazil by an envoy, Belgium by the Brussels chief of police, Ecuador by a chargé d'affaires, Norway by a highly placed judge, Switzerland by the Bern police chief, Great Britain by the deputy leader of the delegation, a minister plenipotentiary.

Heinrich von Benda had to wait in the hotel lobby until he was called. He had placed his briefcase on his knees; it contained for the most part statistical data and excerpts from German newspapers. Were these the written proofs for the defense or was it the required reading for an examination, the Professor asked himself; and he himself—was he an accused man to be brought to trial, or an examination candidate about to appear before his professors? He had often sat on the other side of the table. How many students, anxiously aware of their shortcomings, had waited to be called before him to convince him of their knowledge or delude him as to their lack of it—if only he asks me this, if only he doesn't touch on that subject, if only it were over ... ! He had been invited from one hour to the next, he was unprepared, and perhaps it was fortunate that at least now he had some time to collect his thoughts. The Colombian Minister had informed his colleagues about the German ultimatum, but had concealed from them the fact that Germany was demanding money to release the forty thousand Jews; soon the Professor would have to decide whether also to remain silent or to speak the truth. If he did not mention the demand, how were the ten millions to be raised, and would Germany let the forty thousand go without receiving the ransom money they demanded? But if he revealed the number, if he named the price besides the ultimatum, he would be stabbing the Colombian, his only friend, in the back, would perhaps make it easy for the members of the committee to draw back totally and finally with moral self-satisfaction, with horror, indignation and anger. He would have to leave the decision to the impulse, the inspiration of the moment, the spark struck by contact. What sort of contact would it be? Before anyone else could examine him, Heinrich von Benda examined himself, and he was surprised to note that he felt no humiliation, not even anger at the length of time he was kept waiting, at the slowly passing hour. Everything was an examination, whether you were a defendant or a student, whether you were arming yourself for a joust or embracing a woman, whether you were going to an operation or receiving guests, whether you were delivering a lecture or embarking on a journey, but there were examinations in which only the examiners could fail. He had to prevent his judges from being condemned—it was not so strange, after all, that he felt no humiliation.

The Hôtel Royal was too small for the numerous committees and subcommittees that were meeting here simultaneously, so that the Colombian's committee had established itself in the hotel bar.

As he entered, the delegates rose; the chairman introduced the Professor to them. The Professor had had time to study their titles; now he tried to harmonize the names and titles with the men, but the introductions went too quickly and only two or three people impressed themselves upon him—the overostentatiously dressed young delegate from Ecuador, the cumbersome, bucolic figure of the Swiss police chief, the little man with dark glasses whom he knew to be representing the Republic of Brazil.

They sat down at the green conference table, which, to be more exact, consisted of three tables, forming as it were an open gate. To the Professor's left sat the representatives of Great Britain, Brazil, Belgium and Switzerland; to his right the chairman, next to the representatives of Bolivia, Norway and Ecuador; but he was alone on the long side of the table, an isolated object of attention. At the moment, however, the delegates were still discussing a question that had evidently been preoccupying them before the Professor's entry; an intimacy from which he was excluded prevailed among them. Only the interpreter, a blond young Frenchman with curly hair, and the shorthand typist, a sad little creature, looked at him with a certain curiosity.

The Colombian Minister opened the proceedings by introducing the guest in flattering terms. The Conference, he said, intended to hear several delegates of private defense and aid organizations, but it was not by chance that Professor von Benda was the first to be invited, for he possessed information which it was the Conference's task, indeed urgent duty, to hear. Perhaps it would be helpful and would expedite matters, said the Minister, if he himself asked the first questions—and he immediately turned to the witness. "How many Jews, Professor, are still living in Austria now?"

"Between a hundred and eighty thousand and two hundred thousand," replied the Professor. "But it is impossible to say with certainty. The number of those regarded as Jews is rising daily, since the Nuremberg Laws are being applied more and more rigorously. It is said that in the whole Reich half a million Catholics are to be included under them."

"How many Jews have so far left what used to be Austria?" the Belgian police chief asked.

What used to be Austria, thought the Professor—of course, that which has been conquered has ceased to be.

"About fifty thousand," he said.

"Have these people taken any possessions with them?"

"The Austrians hardly. Up to the end of last year German Jews who had at least thirty thousand Reichsmarks, or a family of two who could together produce fifty thousand Reichsmarks, were allowed to take a modest proportion of their capital with them. The rest of the confiscated capital was supposed to be paid into a fund that would make certain loans to emigrating Jews."

"What do you mean by loans?"

"The loans are without practical significance. They are what is called 'demonstration money.' When an emigrant applies for a visa, the country he wishes to enter in almost all cases demands proof of a certain capital. Sometimes the German Government places this sum at his disposal, but the emigrant is not allowed to retain the money; it is taken away from him again after he has obtained the visa but before he has left the country."

Although he knew French, the Professor had been speaking in English; now the interpreter translated his answer into French. No sooner had he done so than the delegate from Ecuador—the over-elegantly dressed young man, lithe as a Spanish dancer—burst out: "That is blatant fraud!"

"Undoubtedly." The Professor nodded. "The fund that is supposed to contain many millions of pounds of confiscated capital serves the purpose of fraud."

"That's not what I meant," the Ecuadorian chargé d'affaires said, turning to his colleagues. "The fraud is practiced on a single victim, the credulous host country, but it is practiced by two accomplices—or are you going to tell us, Professor, that the Jewish emigrant who produces the counterfeit coin knows nothing about the fraud?"

"*Monsieur le chargé d'affaires,*" the Professor replied with restrained exasperation, "the victims are the Jewish emigrants who have been robbed of their property, people in danger of their lives, and the fraud, if you want to use the word, is forced upon them."

He thought of Elisabeth. The Vorarlberg peasant was on his way back to his village with a thousand marks, and if the Lord who ruled over mountains, valleys and frontier patrols willed, tomorrow night, with His help but in disregard of the host country's laws, Elisabeth would cross the frontier into free Switzerland. She wouldn't even be able to show a counterfeit coin and would bring nothing with her but four hungry mouths.

"Has your own property been confiscated?" the Ecuadorian chargé d'affaires asked from the other end of the table.

"Apart from very small sums belonging to my wife my accounts have been blocked," the Professor replied and his face went red. He noticed that the delegates were smoking, and lit a cigarette. After the first deep inhalations he felt calmer; today as an exception—the thought passed through his head—since abstinence was bound to increase his nervous tension, he would not restrict his smoking.

"Gentlemen," he heard the chairman say, "we are not here to ask personal questions, but to gain information about the situation of the Jews in Germany." When he turned to the Professor there was the same sly yet encouraging twinkle in his eyes that Heinrich von Benda had noticed during their first encounter. "On what conditions do the Germans issue emigration permits?"

"In the case of a Jew whom they are prepared to let out at all, it depends in the first place upon his being able to produce an entry permit for another country."

"Assuming that a Jew cannot obtain such papers and makes his way to one of the German frontiers—say the Belgian, Dutch or Swiss. Do the Germans let him pass—I mean, do they turn a blind eye if the refugee tries to leave his homeland illegally and enter a neighboring country equally illegally?"

The Professor thought he knew what the Colombian was after. "On the contrary," he replied. "They hunt down illegal emigrants and, if they catch them, they put them in prisons and concentration camps."

"Do you know of any instance where the Germans have sent large transports of Jews to one of the frontiers?"

"On the contrary, all places on the frontier are closed areas to Jews."

"What do you conclude from that?"

"The conclusion is obvious," the Professor said. "But before discussing it, I should like to show the committee these cuttings from German newspapers. The *Völkischer Beobachter* of yesterday declares that the 'Jew Conference' is 'a Satanic game of political agitation,' but 'thanks to the attitude of countries like Argentina, who repudiate interference in their internal affairs, it is condemned to failure.' The Vienna edition of the *Völkischer Beobachter* headlines its report 'No One Wants the Riff-raff' and writes: 'Most of the government representatives refuse to open the gates of their own countries to a gang who have caused Germany's ruin.' The *Hitler-Jugend*, Munich, writes: 'One thing alone has emerged from this meeting of the unwanted. The Jews' lackey in the White House was making a mistake when he speculated on the participants' tear ducts.' I believe that these excerpts are the best answer to the chairman's question. If Germany's sole purpose was to get rid of its Jews, then the German Government would be bound to welcome this Conference and do all it could to assist Jewish emigration. Germany does not want to get rid of the Jews but to exterminate them."

The gray-haired delegate of Norway, who was also President of the Nansen Office, raised his hand. "I should not like to allow Professor von Benda's conclusions to go uncontradicted," he said in a low voice, but with sovereign emphasis. "The expulsion of half a million Jews, even the attempt to smuggle them out of the country, would on the one hand place before the world the most serious problems and, on the other, would lead to very serious international complications for Germany. The fact that Germany does nothing of the sort indicates a willingness to work together with other countries and by no means proves what the delegate of the Jewish Community, in his understandable excitement, has asserted. We have no reason to suppose that Germany intends to 'exterminate' the Jews—it is a long way from material persecution and even occasional acts of violence, regrettable as they may be, to 'extermination'; we should guard against regarding the latter as a fact, as an established certainty."

While he was asking himself whether it was merely apathy and lack of imagination, or the premeditated intention of turning this great hour into a quickly forgotten episode that was speaking out of the mouth of the Norwegian, Heinrich von Benda felt a heaviness in his left arm that began to weigh on his shoulders and oppress his heart. This time, it seemed to him, the cramp had not started in the immediate vicinity of the heart, had not spread from there; the pain was creeping in the opposite direction, from the shoulder over the chest toward the heart. The pain stretched out its claws toward the heart, drew them in again, stretched them out again. Like an anatomist bending over a body that has been cut open and dissected, he saw his heart, saw the calcified corona of arteries, saw the ring gripping his heart tighter and tighter, saw it open up only to close all the more tightly. He slipped his hand into his trouser pocket, found the box of nitroglycerin pills, opened it in his pocket, took out one pill, careful all the time not to betray himself with his gesture. This time he would not wait until he had no choice and had to take the pills; he would take them before an attack robbed him of his breath. Seized with panic, he noticed that his breath was becoming shorter and shorter. On the two sides of the table at which the delegates were sitting there stood a carafe of water with glasses, and in front of him too there stood a glass, but he would have had to lean over the table, would have to ask for the carafe, could probably not swallow the pill unnoticed. He did not want to arouse pity, must not do so, and who could tell whether in fact he would rouse pity at all, whether one or other of the delegates would not imagine that he was playing a mean game with the delegates' sympathy. The two carafes grew before his eyes, grew out of themselves and became gigantic, glassy mirages. He straightened up because, although experience should have taught him the contrary, he hoped that the pain would abate; the pain did not abate, but his glance fell on a carafe which, although it bore the advertisement of a whisky firm, was filled with clear water—the carafe stood on the bar just to his right, only a step from his chair. He rose, walked to the bar, poured water into one of the glasses standing in a row by the carafe, and standing with his back to the conference table, he managed to bring the pill that he was holding in the palm of his hand unnoticed to his mouth. As he turned around and returned to his place the carafes had been held out to him from both sides, but he merely said thank you with a smile and acted as though nothing had happened. He stubbed out the smoldering cigarette in the ashtray.

A murmur of approval had greeted the Norwegian judge's words; now the Brazilian with the green glasses turned to the Professor.

"Has there ever been any mention in the Jewish Community's discussions with the German Government," asked the Ambassador, "of whether such emigrants as the Evian member states would accept would be given more than ten marks, that is to say a sum at least halfway sufficient to provide them with a means of livelihood?"

The Professor looked for help at the Colombian chairman. Not a word had yet been said about the German ultimatum, the forty thousand had not yet been mentioned; any informed official of the League of Nations could have answered the questions so far asked. Why had he been called to appear before this forum, why was he here? Hitler was demanding two hundred and fifty dollars for every Jew, and around the green table at Evian people seemed to be interested only in how much each Jew was worth in hellers and pfennigs, or rather in dollars, and how they could close the frontiers to every Jew who was not worth anything.

"There is absolutely no possibility," the Professor said, "of the German Government departing from its ten-mark principle; for the last two months or so it has ceased even to provide so-called 'demonstration money.' "

The next question came from the left; there, at the end of the table, sat the Swiss police chief, who looked like any policeman, in Switzerland or elsewhere.

"What do the Jews plan to do," he asked, "after they have left the country entirely without means?"

"They want to work."

"You obviously haven't heard of unemployment," the delegate from Ecuador interposed.

"How high is the percentage of intellectuals among the Austrian Jews?" asked the Belgian, who looked like any policeman, in Belgium or elsewhere.

"About fifty percent."

"Have you counted businessmen as intellectuals?"

"No."

"In other words, the number of **manual** laborers is negligible?"

"Probably."

"And probably the number of young Jews is equally small?"

"It probably isn't high, because the young people were the first to leave the country. The older people are, the more attached they are to their homeland, the less able to believe what is happening in Germany and Austria."

The pain in Heinrich von Benda's chest began to give way to a dull weariness. He was familiar with the sensation he was experiencing now: first a warmth spread in which the pain became submerged, then a weariness that swallowed up the warmth.

As though from far away, he heard the voice of the Swiss delegate backing up his Belgian colleague. "At least eighty percent of the refugees would become a burden on public charity."

The Professor looked around. The Colombian Minister had immersed himself in his papers, as though he were looking there for the open sesame that would unlock hearts, or as though he were afraid to look at the Professor. There was the frank but worried face of the Bolivian, the pinched bureaucrat's face of the Belgian, the red petty-bourgeois face of the Swiss, there was the closed expression of the Englishman, who had not yet uttered a word, there were the veiled eyes of the Brazilian, and the cold eyes of the Norwegian, there was the provocative gaze of the delegate of Ecuador. To become a burden on public charity! Let not thy left hand know what thy right hand doeth. Charity that feels charity to be a burden. And how far what the gentlemen felt to be charity was from the demand that was going to be made on their charity!

At last the chairman raised his head, at last he said, "Is it correct, Professor von Benda, that forty thousand Austrian Jews are threatened with immediate arrest?"

"Such is my information, and it is undoubtedly correct."

"Where did your information come from?" the Brazilian asked.

"From the Gestapo."

"For what purpose did the Gestapo tell you this?"

"So that I might inform the Conference."

"Just a moment," the Bolivian Ambassador interrupted. "As far as I know, Professor von Benda has been accredited to the Conference by the Jewish Community of Austria. Is the Professor speaking in the name of the Community or of the Gestapo?"

"In the name of the Community," the Colombian interrupted quickly. "But the Gestapo did not give Professor von Benda an exit permit out of pure humanity, but because they think that at least over one point the interests of the German Government and the interests of the Jews coincide."

"Then it isn't true," the Ecuadorian delegate interjected, "that Germany wants to exterminate the Jews. Germany simply wants to dump them on other countries."

So this is the result of a half-truth, thought the Professor. The delegates were sitting at an inn on the edge of the jungle; every now and then someone appeared out of the jungle, but his stories sounded like lies and wild exaggerations; every now and then they heard the roaring of the beasts in the jungle, but in the inn they were sitting at copiously laden tables—"No one can be anyone else's comrade here." The Colombian's plan was bound to fail. If they didn't say that Germany wanted to sell the Jews, to sell or exterminate them, then the young man from Ecuador was right, it almost looked as though the interests of Germany and of the Jews were identical.

The Professor was about to speak when the Bolivian turned to him. "Do you think Germany would dare to carry out such a mass arrest?"

The Bolivian—a dapper little man with gray temples, one of the early champions of the League of Nations, as the Professor now remembered—had intelligent, kind eyes: if you were a Jew you knew how to read other people's eyes. He had probably asked the question about the Gestapo to help the Professor.

"Yes," Heinrich von Benda replied. "Germany will dare that and more. Germany has kidnapped emigrants abroad and taken them back to Germany. The German Nobel Peace Prize winner, who by the way isn't a Jew, is dying from the aftereffects of maltreatment. Tens of thousands are being beaten and tortured in concentration camps—" He broke off. What was the use of repeating the unbelievable? "Why do you doubt," he asked, "that this regime is capable of arresting forty thousand innocent people—tomorrow forty thousand, the day after four hundred thousand, the day after that, if it can, four million?"

A look from the chairman told him that he had said too much. Evil must be presented on a reduced scale; in its true proportions it appears incredible.

"So to let in the forty thousand Jews," interrupted the Swiss delegate, "would be only a drop in the ocean." His hands lay on the conference table like two stones broken out of a column. "So our compassion is to be put to the test. If we go a step further, tomorrow Germany will indeed send us four hundred thousand Jews and the day after perhaps four million. I'm not a professional diplomat, I'm only a simple man who is used to speaking the truth. Reasonable compassion is one thing, the weakness of not being able to say no another. Germany is probably counting on our weakness and the emigrants who are illegally flooding the neighboring countries are certainly counting on it."

Only the delegate from Ecuador said, "Quite right!" Otherwise there was silence. Outside it had long ago stopped raining. A beam of sunlight came in through the heavily curtained windows and was caught up by the colored bottles standing on the bar. An elephant had crashed through the china shop and left it in smithereens. That had not been the idea. You could smash the china, the glasses, the bottles, the mirrors one by one, slowly, carefully, one at a time; it was not only superfluous, it was also contrary to diplomatic practice to smash all the china, all the glasses, all the bottles, all the mirrors at once.

"I should like to point out to the honorable representative of the Confédération Helvétique," the Colombian said, "that we have not reached the stage of drawing conclusions. We are here to put questions to Professor von Benda."

"Very well," the Swiss rejoined, offended. "In that case I should like to inquire whether Professor von Benda negotiated with the Gestapo on Swiss or on French soil."

"I happen to know that the Professor negotiated with the Gestapo in Vienna," the chairman declared.

"Is it true that you yourself were in prison?" the Belgian asked, coming to his Swiss colleague's aid.

"Yes."

"Were you maltreated?"

"No. I was released in response to the intervention of the Duke of Windsor. A man was beaten to death in the next cell. He wasn't lucky enough to have treated His Royal Highness."

"Did the Gestapo get in touch with you after your release?" the delegate of Ecuador asked.

"Yes."

"Did you have the impression that you were released in order to be entrusted with this mission?"

"I have already told you that the Duke of Windsor . . ."

"Have you a family, Professor?" the Belgian asked.

"Yes."

"Are they in Austria?"

"Yes."

"Did the Gestapo supply you with foreign currency?" the Swiss asked.

Heinrich von Benda's gaze fell upon his hands. His hands were white and they were trembling. He hid them under the table. He heard the Colombian say, "I cannot permit that question. It goes without saying that the German authorities had to issue a currency permit."

Heinrich von Benda heard this only as though from a great distance. He began to speak and he now spoke without looking to right or left, all he saw was occasionally the blond head of the interpreter and the mouse-colored head of the typist. At first he spoke in a low voice, then louder and finally loud. He felt no fatigue and no pain, like the wounded or shot, who may perhaps be dying but who feel no fatigue and no pain; no one tried to interrupt him, but he wouldn't have heard if anyone had tried to interrupt him.

"Gentlemen," he said, "I did not come here to answer questions that might just as well have been put to me by the Gestapo, but I am grateful to you for asking them because they teach me that the sickness that has fallen upon my fatherland is infectious; suspicion, ill will and prejudice need no passport, no visa and no foreign currency. Inhumanity, it seems, has no flag. A few days ago, when I set out on my journey to Evian, I seriously believed that I held the key to the salvation of hundreds of thousands of victims of undeserved persecution, illegal imprisonment, inhuman torture, hundreds of thousands of people marked off for death. I learned to be modest. Germany, I was told, would release forty thousand Jews in return for ten million dollars. I wanted to beg these ten million of you. Every day ten million dollars are spent on building roads —where are these roads to lead to, if we are approaching the abyss? Every day ships are built costing more than ten million dollars— are they to be ships without human freight? Every day ten million dollars are invested in agricultural projects—can the earth be fruitful if it is fertilized with corpses?"

Now he was resolved to betray his only friend in this circle; he had to betray him if he was not to betray forty thousand men, women and children.

"I was told here in Evian," he went on, "that I must say nothing about the price of the Jews, for in Evian people only want to know how much money the Jews can bring with them, why they don't go to another country, how strong the hands are that they bring with them, and how young the blood is that flows in their veins. Perhaps my friends are right, perhaps it would be wrong to yield to blackmail, perhaps not a single dollar is needed, perhaps a single act of mercy can open the prison gates. But one thing you must know. If this Conference breaks up without having opened a harbor of refuge to forty thousand people, then on the first of August forty thousand people will set out on the march to death."

For a moment he could not go on speaking, he could feel his heart growing weak, but greater than his fear of a fresh attack was his fear that he would be dismissed before he had said everything.

"How can I prove it to you?" he said. "Is there really nothing standing between life and death but my inability to make myself intelligible to you?" He drew a deep breath. "I have come here in the cause of the persecuted. To share my knowledge with you and, if necessary, to implore you on my knees. But I believe I am only acting in your own cause. The President of the United States has called you together here. You have heard his call. Nothing can ever erase the Evian Conference from the annals of history. When you entered your names in the register of the Hôtel Royal in Evian you unsuspectingly entered your names in the book of history. The pages will turn yellow, but they will not disappear. Evian will go down in history—as the place where good either laid down its arms or took them up. All evil takes place with the tacit connivance of the good; if they did not remain silent it would not happen. Nothing devilish in human history has ever happened without the Devil first testing the ground, stretching out his feelers, making sure of the complicity of the good. I have nothing more to say, no more questions to answer. I have only to ask you whether you want to share in the guilt."

The silence that followed the Professor's words had so many faces that it had no face. No one, and he least of all, could have said whether it was a silence of emotion or of disapproval, of reflection or of hostility, of understanding or of refusal to understand.

At last the chairman looked up. "I should like to thank Professor von Benda for his information," he said.

And the Professor rose, nodded awkwardly, turned and walked out of the silence. . . .

The Professor had spent the evening after his questioning in gloomy thoughts, as one does when one knows that one has disappointed a friend and is not sure whether there will be an opportunity to explain the compelling reasons for one's behavior. He had not expected a call, had actually feared that he would never again be received by the Colombian; he therefore felt it to be a double gift when the Minister assured him that although he had not approved of the Professor's impulsive utterances he had understood them. "I'm afraid that in your position and under these terrible circumstances I should have acted just the same," the Minister said, but his call proved that nothing final, nothing irrevocable, had happened. He was not empowered to inform the Professor of the committee's reactions, continued the Minister, but that same evening the full assembly had set up a committee of four to consider the problem of the forty thousand Austrian Jews and report back direct to the Chairman of the Conference. "Don't indulge in happy illusions," admonished the Colombian. "You have made matters incomparably more difficult for yourself and for me. We must talk about that before the committee meets tomorrow—by the way, it is made up of Canada, Holland, Sweden and Colombia." The Professor wanted to ask what favorable recommendations the new committee might make, whether it meant anything, what real, practical value it had and what influence it could exercise on the Conference, but he forebore to overdraw the bow and merely listened with gratitude to an invitation to dinner. This, however, he had to refuse, because he could not possibly get back from Geneva in time, which brought him once more into conflict with his conscience; he had not come to Evian on private business and this evening discussion with his understanding friend might have been of great, perhaps decisive importance. However, this morning must have been exceptionally blessed, for the Minister showed neither surprise nor anger. He invited the Professor to breakfast with him the following morning. This second invitation the Professor dared not refuse; he resolved to return from Geneva under all circumstances, even if it were late at night.

By the time he had bathed and breakfasted—at last at peace again and with a certain tranquil gaiety—it was ten o'clock, just time to go to the hotel lobby and keep the appointment with a prominent rabbi from New York, Samuel Milestone, which he had made the previous day. The elevator was continually out of order, so the Professor walked downstairs with a light step; his thoughts were circling round his reunion with Elisabeth and the children, especially with fourteen-year-old Marianne, his declared favorite, and if he had to stop to listen to his irregular heartbeat, it was only because he remembered Fräulein Selig's promise. She was going to try to arrange a conversation with Bettina, which might perhaps be possible from Geneva—it was asking too much, certainly, but he must at all costs share with Bettina his happiness at having found Elisabeth. The happy turn of events had restored his self-confidence, for confidence in oneself is fundamentally merely confidence in the alliance one has made with destiny, a confirmation of the mutual love between destiny and oneself; also his relationship to Elisabeth had always been a touchstone, her trust was his responsibility, not to have disappointed it his happiness.

The next few hours, however, did not live up to the augury of the day; the promise of the stars had not been binding.

He had seen the New York rabbi several times fleetingly, but it had never occurred to him how little this American corresponded to the ideas one has in Europe of a Jewish preacher. Although there were probably just as many young rabbis in Europe as in the New World, people were accustomed to seeing in the Jewish rabbi a wise man, a miracle worker. Rabbi Milestone, on the other hand, was not only a young man, he also adopted the most youthful, indeed fashionably athletic appearance; with his black hair, large nose and black-rimmed spectacles he certainly looked what would be described as a Jewish type, but he was no less an American type. The collar buttoned down at the tips, the sloppy ready-made suit and the tie clip were as American as the free and easy gestures and the accent peculiar to the inhabitants of New York's East Side.

At this period circumstances had caused the world to enter into an entirely new relationship with the Jews, to acquire entirely new ideas about them—more absurd perhaps than it had anyway. More remarkable than this, however, was the fact that Jews developed new relationships among themselves and met one another with new, more conscious, and thus more prejudiced, preconceptions. The rabbi, an American Jew of East European origins, had his own preconceived ideas of what a Jew should be—an idea to which the completely Europeanized, completely Western Jew Heinrich von Benda in no way corresponded; and in Heinrich von Benda there was reawakened the old aversion to the emphasizing of an almost professional Jewishness. No wonder then that from the outset the Viennese professor and the New York rabbi could find little fellow feeling and even less common ground between them. Nevertheless, they would soon have overcome their spontaneous, instinctive, almost anachronistic prejudices if the subject that had brought them together had not at the same time formed an unbridgeable gulf between them.

In his matter-of-fact way—it was an unctuous matter-of-factness, a contradiction that the Professor found disturbing—the rabbi came straight to the point as soon as they had sat down under the chestnuts on the gravel terrace, or rather he spoke of the "Benda Mission," which, he said, was known in every detail to the Jewish organizations represented in Evian.

Heinrich von Benda remained silent. He had realized that his mission, of which a good dozen of the participants in the Conference were informed, could not remain entirely secret, but if the secret became generally known and was dragged through all the corridors, the press was bound sooner or later to get hold of it; this would finally destroy all prospect of a successful outcome.

The Conference, said the rabbi, had decided to hear the views of the most important Jewish organizations, in particular the World Jewish Congress, the Jewish Agency for Palestine and the American Joint Distribution Committee. He considered it incumbent upon him not only in the name of fair play, but also of Jewish solidarity, to warn and inform the Professor that, if asked, all the organizations would strongly oppose the "Vienna Project." Solidarity— this brought him, he continued, close to the heart of the matter. The fault did not lie with the Professor, who after all had devoted his whole life to science, but rather with the Jewish Community in Vienna. They ought to have had enough sense not to address the Conference over the heads of the existing organizations. The German and Austrian Jews possessed no overall picture; they didn't know, or didn't want to know, that for years the Jewish organizations had been working closely with foreign governments, the High Commissioner for Refugees, the Nansen Office and the League of Nations, that they had saved tens of thousands of Jews and ensured them a new life—work which the "Vienna Project" was likely to disrupt, if not to destroy. Understandably, the Professor had no idea of the complexity of the problem—"understandably," he said, interspersing his diatribe with mitigating phrases: "understandably" or "as I can well understand" or "which I don't blame you for at all." How could the Professor know that it was not only the German and Austrian Jews who were involved, but no less those of Czechoslovakia, Hungary, Rumania and Poland; that the prospects of saving the latter were far better, so that discussion must not be confined to the Germans and Austrians; that the name of the port of refuge was Palestine and that this had to be made safe before the ships in distress could be steered thither; that neither the financial means of the Jews nor the readiness of the various countries to accept refugees were inexhaustible, so that only negotiations between the governments and the whole body of Jewish organizations were capable of achieving a just distribution.

Like an icy wind blowing from the quarter from which one least expects it—that was how the rabbi's words affected Heinrich von Benda. Only because he hoped in the course of an urbane discussion to persuade the rabbi to act with discretion, did he speak politely and with restraint. "You mentioned solidarity, Rabbi," he said, "but I should like to know who is supposed to maintain solidarity with whom. Are half a million Jews in danger of their lives to worry about sparing the Jewish organizations unpleasantness? Ought not the Jewish organizations to cast aside all other considerations in order to save the Jews whose lives are directly threatened?"

"I'm afraid you've misunderstood me, Professor," rejoined the rabbi. "The aim is to save all our brothers. But as to the means, only those Jews can decide who are in safety and see the situation clearly."

"I can think of nothing more likely to blur vision than safety."

"I can understand your holding that view, but it is wrong. Just picture what would happen if the Jewish organizations backed your mission! How could we ever again criticize the relations of the civilized world with Hitler Germany, how could we call for a boycott of German goods, if at the same time we implored the governments to trade with Germany in human beings? I don't want to use big words like human dignity, although we shouldn't forget that either. Let the Christians trade in Jews among themselves—only the slave who acknowledges his servitude is really enslaved. But we needn't think so far ahead; let us think in practical terms! The task of the Jewish organizations consists primarily in arousing the conscience of the world. If the Evian governments ransomed ten or twenty thousand Jews they would pacify their consciences; they would have the feeling that they had done enough and more than enough—hundreds of thousands of our brothers would perish miserably."

The logic of these words filled the Professor with mounting disquiet. The whole world—Christians and Jews, ministers of state and simple people, men and women, warmhearted friends and cold egotists—it was impossible that everyone should be wrong and he alone right. And yet perhaps they were all wrong, because they had one thing in common, something outside religion, sex, status and character, something apparently insignificant and yet essential: their geographical position. They were all outside, and those whose desperate cause he represented were inside.

"Do you know," he said, "that the SA and SS will carry forty thousand people off to concentration camps if the Evian states do not take them over?"

"We are here to see that Germany does not dare to take this step. Have you read the German papers?"

"That is precisely what I have done."

"But, understandably, you have misinterpreted them. Don't you see that Germany is afraid of Evian? A proclamation of human solidarity—thirty-two states, Professor, among them the most powerful in the world!—would strike the murder weapon from Germany's hand. If we acknowledge the legality of the anti-Semitic measures, even indirectly, we are lost. Instead of rewarding Germany for her crimes we must call for a boycott of German goods, an embargo on deliveries to Germany, a boycott and embargo against all countries that trade with Germany. Yes—the world will negotiate with Germany, but only when Germany appears as a supplicant. Then we shall be able to lead not only the German and Austrian Jews out of Hitler's power, but the majority of our brothers—"

"All who are still alive, that is," the Professor interrupted him. "I used to think that only lack of imagination was dangerous, but it seems to me now that too much imagination may be just as critical. Has the course of the Conference so far—I'm told it is to be concluded in three or four days—convinced you that a proclamation of human solidarity is being prepared? What illusions you give yourself up to, Rabbi Milestone! And what makes you think that the psychology of the mass murderer is the same as yours and mine? If National Socialism cared about the opinion of the world, it would have strangled itself in the cradle. Are you a realist or are the men of the Vienna Jewish Community realists? Hitler cares nothing for the opinion of the world, the only things he does care about are dollars and cents."

The Professor's sharp tone angered the rabbi. He had always felt a distrust toward this famous surgeon, not so much because the emigrants had pointed out the links between the Professor and the Gestapo, perhaps the outcome of necessity, nor because the Professor was said to be married to a Christian, the daughter of an Austrian national painter, but above all because the rabbi had little liking for the species *Chamaeleo judaicus,* so common in Western Europe. It was remarkable that this old man, who imagined that he was sacrificing himself for the Jews, was not a good Jew, if a Jew at all; he had discovered his Jewishness late and under the pressure of events, like those who became God-fearing only during a storm; he was probably one of those German and Austrian Jews who, if Hitler had not prevented them, would have remained the most blatant nationalists—naturally such a man could have no relationship to Zionism, knew nothing of the common interest of the Jews, in fact had no idea that he would have acted just as enthusiastically in the cause of suppressed and persecuted protestants, Negroes, liberals or Botocudos. The rabbi pondered whether to retort to sharpness with sharpness or to appeal to the understanding of the blind Jew, but finally settled for a middle way.

"I requested this meeting," he said, "because it would have made an extremely bad impression if you had heard from a third party that the Jewish organizations were going to oppose the Vienna Project. But that doesn't mean"—he smiled warmly and leaned closer to the Professor—"that your mission is bound to have been in vain. If you could make up your mind to remain outside, one or more of our Jewish organizations would call a press conference at which you would disclose the monstrous commission with which you were entrusted. No one would doubt the word of Professor Heinrich von Benda. Your story would arouse a storm of indignation . . ."

"And the Jews in Hitler's hands?"

"That we are hostile to Germany, which has forced us to be so, is nothing new to Hitler. It is too late for compromise; strength is the only language the Germans understand."

This was what the rabbi was saying when the porter appeared in the hotel door, came over to the Professor and informed him that a car had just arrived from Geneva and was waiting for him.

Like his interlocutor, Heinrich von Benda too now asked himself whether he should say openly what he thought, should flatly reject the proposal that had obviously been carefully considered, prepared at length and finally uttered, or whether he should choose the diplomatic path. It would no doubt have been easier to tell the rabbi, who certainly knew it already, that he, Professor von Benda, quite apart from his convictions, had no choice, that he had a wife and child, but what did the rabbi care about the Christian wife and the little child? Or the Professor too could have said that he "well understood" the standpoint of the Jewish organizations and "didn't in the least blame them." But the bitterness that had overcome him was of a special making and different from anything he had felt before. Anyone who held a passport, even if he were a Jew, could not understand a Jew without a passport so that the great inside and outside separated Jews from one another just as much as they were separated from other people; not even the blood-stained regime had succeeded in welding together the Jews, who were said to stick together like glue; there were German Jews and Palestinian Jews and Jews who had only been made into Jews by Hitler, and Jews who thought they represented all Jews; prejudices, differences of interests and convictions and methods made the Jews forget that the only thing that mattered now was to bring help to the drowning, without consideration for a future which only the shortsighted were sure they could see. Nevertheless the fear that a brusque refusal might lead to a conflict moved him to assure the rabbi that he would carefully consider the arguments he had just heard, would pass on to the Jewish Community in Vienna the objections that had been raised, although he did not agree with them, and would base his own attitude entirely on the instructions he received from Vienna—but he must make it a condition, and this was in their mutual interest, that both sides should exercise extreme discretion.

The rabbi assured him that, as up to now, he would naturally deal with the matter in confidence, but he seemed to have seen through the Professor's intentions, because he insisted on continuing the conversation, tomorrow afternoon at the latest, since the hearing of the first Jewish organizations was fixed for a secret session during the night.

As Heinrich von Benda walked toward the hotel door where a chauffeur was waiting for him, he had the feeling that the eyes of the rabbi were following him with searching interest. Probably Rabbi Milestone was asking himself what sort of car it was that had come to fetch the Professor, what the Professor had to do in Geneva and how it had been made possible for him to cross the Swiss frontier without difficulty. He could no more tell the representative of the Jews the truth than anyone else. He thought of little Herr Steiner at the Basel frontier station.

3. *BLOOD FROM THE SKY*

PIOTR RAWICZ

This major French novel with its original and savage detachment is the
story of a Jew who attempts to conceal his Judaism and who tries to
hide among his fellow men. Arrested on suspicion of being Jewish, he
finds that his fellow prisoners try to help the Germans in trapping him.
Their hate and prejudice surround him. Like any good lesson, this selection raises many more questions than it answers.

━━━━━

Bare cold days, like scales, formed an armor plating around Boris.

Since he persisted in denying his origins, he was transferred to
another cell—this one inhabited by people who were not doomed
to immediate extermination. Among them was a village shoemaker,
a weak and sentimental man, who had killed his wife in a drunken
fit. He would cry bitterly and relate the lives of a number of saints
who seldom figured in the history of the Church. His huge
head, bald and sickly-colored, shed a sad autumnal light in the
cell. He was a just and upright man who wouldn't normally have
hurt a hair on anybody's head, but he hated lies; it was he who,
after Boris's arrival, was first to call a spade a spade: "You aren't
one of us. What's the use of trying to hide it? Tell your judges the

Reprinted with permission of Harcourt, Brace & World, Inc., from *Blood from the
Sky* by PIOTR RAWICZ. © 1964 by Harcourt, Brace & World, Inc. Translated from the
French by PETER WILES.

truth, and you will be granted an easy death. Which is more than my own death will be."

The second shoemaker, a wiry, venomous man, nodded his head in approval: "There was one just like him back home in the village," he said. "He was blond and blue-eyed; you could have taken him for one of the local boys. He was hiding with the Count's family, up at the manor house. They gave him food and drink. He pretended he had been an officer. He gave English lessons to the Count's children. And then suddenly he started to get fresh. He came out of hiding, he went riding through the fields with His Lordship's daughter, he was high and mighty to good Christian people—thinking they would never know who they were dealing with. But these things show, they have a stink of their own, you sniff them. Some of the village organized a hunt. We went after him with pitchforks. How he struggled when we caught up with him, poor devil! How he struck out with his fists and feet. . . ."

A peasant charged with illegal slaughter of pigs (which, under the law of the times, might cost him his life) treated Boris with unbounded contempt: "If God permits your kind to be killed, it's because you are all bloodsuckers and filthy sinners. The measure of your sins is filled to overflowing. It's because of you this war broke out, because of you that the blood of Christians is flowing in torrents. You provoked it, you brought it about. In the prophecies of the Queen of Sheba, it's written that the Beast will devour not only the Just, but its own children as well. You are the children of the Beast. To celebrate your Sabbaths, you used to drink our babies' blood. Today, the Beast clamors for YOUR blood, in preparation for its own Great Sabbath. You're an educated man, I can see that. You'll have heard and read about what I'm saying. . . ."

A fair-haired boy of sixteen—shy and nice to everyone, even to Boris—was awaiting trial for escaping from a forced labor camp. He knew an old peasant fairy tale and would start telling it, monotonously, every night. "In a faraway country there lived a bird with golden feathers. By means of spells that he had learned from a witch, the poorest peasant in the neighborhood summoned the bird, who offered him one of his feathers. This golden feather, inlaid with precious stones, was worth a king's ransom. But, in exchange, the bird demanded an object of his own choice from his debtor's mean hovel. The peasant quickly agreed to this condition, thinking it innocent enough, and immediately the bird flew off, clutching in its beak an old iron cross that the peasant's little daughter used to wear around her neck. From then on, one disaster followed another, striking not only the peasant, but the village and the entire province as well. Children died, fires and Tatars ravaged the countryside. A strange illness broke out, carrying off the cattle and wiping out the happiness in men's hearts. . . . The peasant set off in search of the bird, hoping to get his cross back. After many adventures, he came to a land where cannibalism was considered the highest of virtues and the greatest of privileges. Where children were taught false swearing at school, as elsewhere they are taught multiplication tables. The king of this land was an infidel bird with golden feathers. . . ."

At this point in the story, the audience's eyes would invariably turn toward Boris, fastening the whole burden of the crimes attributed to the bird and its subjects on him. The treatment inflicted on Boris by his cellmates was caused by the imperative need they all felt to re-establish the moral equilibrium upset by the bird's treacherous carryings on.

A highway robber, arrested on a charge of murder, relieved Boris of his shirt and socks, insisting on his rights as one who was going to survive, as opposed to the absence of rights of one who was soon to depart this life anyway.

A notary, who, as the one representative of the "intelligentsia," enjoyed considerable prestige in the cell, would enliven the hours of forced leisure with regular lectures analyzing the baneful role that Boris's race had played in the nation's economy and politics and culture:

"They are now, gentlemen, reaping the rewards that they have richly deserved for their age-long abuse of our all too generous hospitality. They led us into unclean ways. Their money-grabbing nearly poisoned the spirit of our splendid race. They contaminated our young people by the example of debauchery which they had exalted to an ideal and to a system. They repaid our endless kindnesses with the blackest ingratitude. But luckily God is with us, gentlemen, and now they are brought low. Which is consoling and irrefutable proof that heavenly justice is no idle phrase. Isn't that so, Mr. . . . ,Mr. . . . (oh dear, I keep forgetting what name you go under!), Mr. Yuri Goletz—is that it? What's your opinion? You say nothing, and yet this is a subject on which you must be bursting with knowledge . . . .

"Just look at him, gentlemen, he's shaking, he's as white as a sheet. Between ourselves—and heaven knows there should be complete trust between companions in misfortune—allow me to confess that I don't believe a single word of our Mr. Goletz's story. In my humble opinion, his name is certainly neither Goletz nor Yuri, and he has never been a farm hand. . . .

"You ought to be ashamed of your lies, young man. At a pinch, I could understand your continuing to pull the wool over the eyes of the police—although I, for one, don't believe in lying. . . . But here, in this cell, you are among decent folk who are not informers. Unless you think the opposite? If you do, say so and we shall behave accordingly."

The peasants were staggered by the notary's elegant turns of phrase. They would endeavor to imitate him. A collective protest was even organized against Boris's presence in the cell—"occupied, Mr. Prison Governor, by persons who are certainly on the wrong side of the law, which can happen to anyone, but whose blood is pure and whose origins are beyond dispute."

There were collective lessons, too: fifteen overseers set about teaching Boris how to sweep the floor of the cell, how to hold the broom, how to clean—without implement of any kind, with his bare hands—the pail full of excrement and urine. All that was left of the broom was the handle, but the floor had to shine. The cleaning of the pail had been entrusted exclusively to Boris. He began to love shit: a patient substance, humble and completely unaggressive.

The inmates were summoned to the interrogation room. They returned with swollen faces and with lilac weals on their skin. Some were shot, others released. Night and morning they chanted solemn, weighty prayers in chorus, prayers that rippled like a wheatfield.

New tenants would arrive in the cell where Boris had become the oldest piece of furniture, a kind of pail or spittoon. Occasionally his companions would receive food parcels from their families and ceremoniously share them out, without tossing so much as a crumb in Boris's direction. Hunger became an obsession; it was like a tangible substance. The hungry went on and on about food, so much so that their conversation resembled a weird and wonderful cookery book. Their dreams were devoid of fresh air and open skies, but were crammed with bacon. In their dreams, they wandered in unknown climes strewn with chapels and churches whose walls were built of this fat, silvery and universal fat.

Rinsed in waters clear and waters turbid, tall, rather stooping, with a face that retained a constant, animal attentiveness, even though its sensitivity and curiosity in things seemed to have been quite washed away, Humeniuk sported the invader's uniform the way some people sport celestial grace, grace sent from heaven a little too late. Doubtless he had greater density, a higher specific weight than Lesch, who had summoned him, but it was in Lesch that the power of life and death resided, and Humeniuk could only bow to the other man's congenital superiority.

All the same, the natural and supernatural gulf between the conqueror and his native-born assistants was not a thing that could properly be displayed in front of such a shady character—especially one suspected of impure origins, and consequently doomed to extermination. The two gentlemen therefore exchanged courteous salutes (though they didn't, it's true, shake hands) and even a knowing smile. But something whispered to Boris that there was a crack at the bottom of his smile.

Was a fellow feeling between men of the great plain, between heirs of the Scythians, developing between Boris and Humeniuk the Horsy? If so, Boris said to himself, it will be against my will, without my seeking. And yet, may not Humeniuk's forefathers have worked on the estates of the princes to whom my own forefathers lent money? Or again, when the opportunity presented itself, did they not slaughter my ancestors, whose children they fondled, in the good old days when pogroms, cruel though they were, were at least not final and conclusive? Be that as it may, I know you, my good Humeniuk. I know the landscape that molded and nourished you. I know the songs that surrounded your cradle and the colors of the ceremonial costumes worn by your mother and your peasant grandmothers. Likewise, I know the road that led you from the stable to the palace antechamber, and from there to the lecture room and to the cheap lodgings you had as a hungry and painfully earnest student. I can picture your winter afternoons in a strange town, which to you seemed immense and inhuman, and your evenings in shabby, unheated rooms, and your humiliations and your longings. And the latest stage in your journey, the one that brought you here to this room, in their pay. You can scent yourself as much as you like with that ghastly eau de Cologne for which junior officers trade their coupons, but you will never be able to dispel that smell of hayricks and stables which is yours and which it is impossible for me not to love, just as I love your past daydreams and love this love—such a delicate vibration, as though it already belonged to the past, to A past. . . .

Lesch broke in upon the silence: "My dear Humeniuk, I explained the situation to you over the phone. You are exactly the kind of Ukrainian intellectual by whom this Jew-boy asked to be confronted. Question him, wear him down, hit him, do as you like to him, but let's get it over. I'm hungry and I've really had enough of this case!"

Humeniuk did not even glance up at Boris. Clenching his teeth, he flung out a question like a sour village schoolteacher, displeased with his pupil's answer even before he hears it:

"Who is the greatest Ukrainian poet?"

It was then that the game began to amuse Boris. His brain was working as it hadn't worked for a long time. He thought: If a man wishes to prove he is an Englishman, and a well-educated Englishman, he will prove nothing by answering "Shakespeare" or "Byron" to such a question. Of course not, for everyone has heard of Shakespeare and Byron, whether English or not. On the contrary, what he must do is imply, and get his interrogator to acknowledge the implication, that it is unthinkable he should be asked such a question. He must immediately mention some such figure as Eliot or Edith Sitwell. In the same situation, a Frenchman, a REAL, well-educated Frenchman, could not possibly answer "Ronsard" or "Victor Hugo." In that way, he would be proving nothing. It is only by alluding to a Lautréamont or a Milosz that he would give proof, if not of his French origins, at least of his degree of initiation in matters pertaining to France. Well now, in asking me who is the greatest Ukrainian poet, our friend is expecting me to voice one name and one name only: that of their bard, Tara Shevchenko. . . . But everybody here—not just the Ukrainians, but the Russians, Poles, and Jews living in the Ukraine—knows that this singer of the serfs' hardships and of Cossack pride IS the glory of your nation. That's stale. If I were to cite Shevchenko, I'd please you, my good

Humeniuk, but I wouldn't appeal to your imagination and, most important of all, I wouldn't prove anything to you. I need, or rather YOU need, something quite different.

And Boris named an avant-garde poet who had died not long before, at the age of twenty-nine, an old friend of his, known and loved by perhaps two hundred readers. Like a Horace aiming to transplant Hellenic rhythms onto the soil of Italy, this man—Ihor Hranich—had tried to graft surrealist shoots onto the tree of young Ukrainian poetry. Much good did it do him. Shortly before the war, he succumbed to the inevitable and proverbial tragic tuberculosis, in his parents' cottage. Massive and inconsolable was their grief at the death of this son, whom they had raised and educated at such cost to themselves and who, had he only followed their heartfelt wishes, might have made a good country priest, and perhaps even a bishop.

My poor Ihor, Boris said to himself, to think that I should be using your name—the name of somebody dead and buried, of somebody I loved—as a life line. It deserved a better fate, as we both know.

Humeniuk leapt up in protest: "What else could I have expected from a gallows-bird like you! You have the nerve to say that Hranich, poor twisted devil, is our greatest poet! That he is a poet at all! Why, you're joking! I knew friend Hranich, he used to make me feel sorry for him. To be frank, I've never understood a word he wrote, and I don't think there is anything to understand. . . . His work is a crazy quilt of gibberish just about on the level of a child of four. . . ."

"That may be your opinion," said Boris, "but it isn't mine. You asked me a question, and I answered it as honestly as I could."

"Honestly, honestly . . . ." Humeniuk was entering more and more fully into his role as a schoolmaster called upon to examine a pupil, who might be brilliant but who was also alarming and eccentric.

"Well, we don't see eye to eye on that score. Not by a long shot. We'd better forget about poets and turn to more down-to-earth matters."

The Ukrainian in which Huemeniuk was expressing himself was somewhat artificial. A sensitive ear would have detected traces of the years he had spent in non-Slav countries. But his usage was correct, elegant even. As for Boris, he was familiar with every refinement of his tongue, which for him was filled with the scent of summer evenings on the banks of the Dniester: marsh tongue, steppe tongue, twilight tongue, water tongue.

Humeniuk was proceeding with his task: Name the leading prewar Ukrainian newspapers.

Name the chief political parties.

This examination was a witches' Sabbath, a Walpurgis Night. But Boris was in supreme control of its successive starts and finishes. Like a turn performed by white mice, intoxicated by drink yet obeying the finger and eye of him who holds the threads, who prompts and checks their every leap, their every trick, their every skilled entrechat—this discussion, down to every detail, was going exactly as Boris's will intended. He gave the wires another jerk, and the conversation degenerated, just as he had wished, into a quarrel. They wrangled. They raised their voices. Poor Lesch, quite forgotten, looked on—dumb as an oyster—at this tussle between two men of the East, conducted in a language that he couldn't understand. And even if he had understood it, he would have been quite lost in this welter of claims and counterclaims, of recriminations mortal and venial. Humeniuk wasn't cheating. He was defending, with all his heart, his opinion that it had been only right for the sons of an oppressed nation, which had been prevented for hundreds of years from becoming a state, to don the uniform of the conquering power. Boris, on his side, was arguing: "But can't you see they are leading us by the nose? They aren't letting us enjoy the fruits of a victory which may be short-lived. Which WILL be short-lived. But if they meet with defeat, we shall be associated with it. Our young men are fighting under foreign banners, yet though he promised us our independence, the invader wouldn't even proclaim Kiev the state capital. A gesture that would have cost him nothing, since the real power remains in his hands anyway, for as long as the war continues. He didn't even deign to recognize the government which we had prepared, even though it would have been his staunchest ally. As for our ministers, you know as well as I do what he did with them. It hurts me to speak of such an outrage. Your bosses want everything for themselves. In the end, they will be left empty-handed."

Boris's nationalism was pure and wholly messianic. He loathed compromising.

Humeniuk: "You are unrealistic, young man. With your insane intransigence, you and your likes are going to rob us of the only opportunity that has come our way in decades. Partnership with them, whatever our private feelings, is our one hope of achieving anything real, anything tangible. We mustn't besot ourselves with big words like independence and sovereignty. We must begin with small concrete tasks. This is the first time our generation has had a say, a small say, in the running of this country—which is, after all, our own. They are ridding our land of the Jewish pestilence. To do so, they need our help, for without it they would be incapable of tracking down and unmasking and identifying those Jews who are in hiding. True, we would rather they began with the Poles, but for political reasons which are theirs and not ours they will not or cannot. Not yet, at least. What is our role in all this? Are we to sulk and hang back because their timing of events doesn't entirely coincide with our wishes? No, and no again! We must make ourselves useful and indispensable. We must learn whatever we can from them. Away with false ambitions. We must accept any particle of power that is offered to us, irrespective of its size and origin. How are you to know that, once the Jewish chapter is closed, we won't be called upon to rid this country of Poles and Russians and gypsies . . . ? And if that happens, then whatever the outcome of the present military campaign we shall have a homogeneous territory, truly our own. Call it what you like: independence, autonomy, or protectorate. There are plenty of dependences that end in freedom, and plenty of independences that get further and further away from it. What difference does it make to us? Our goal is still the same. And if they help us to draw even an inch closer to that goal, it is only right for us to co-operate. And that is our SOLE duty at the moment."

He looked Boris straight in the eye. It was Boris's turn to ask a question:

"Do you know Kiev, Mr. Humeniuk? Have you ever been to our former capital . . . ? I've lived there."

He was scanning Humeniuk's face. That face in flight, that flight of a face. Once, while he was still only a child, Boris had seen the body of a hare that had been killed by an eagle. This hare had lain on the roadside for three whole days, devoured by the ants and washed by the rain. Humeniuk's face was at this moment the very image of the dead little animal's.

Humeniuk was stupefied. Could he have misheard Boris's question, a question so incongruous and astonishing?

"Kiev?" he said. "Kiev?"

"Well, Mr. Humeniuk, I've been to Kiev and I've stayed there. It is the most beautiful town in the world. A miracle. THE miracle of humility. When spring comes to its outlying districts, the smell of the earth isn't something vague and fleeting; it is yearning and the object of that yearning, passion and its appeasement. It is love-sickness and its remedy. At first, you feel a yearning. Then you are no longer capable of that, and all you feel is a yearning for your own yearning, and so on. That is the path that leads away from life. But what if we turned our scale of values upside down . . . . What if yearning became more precious than its object, and yearning for a yearning became purer and more precious than the original after-image? There, perhaps, lies the enigma, the immortality of Kiev. I have watched the current of the Dnieper in March, full of ice and uprooted willows. The whole scene is gray, but I wouldn't swap its universe-containing grayness for even the loveliest girl or the most radiant landscape. Kiev is the stained-glass window of a cathedral which no one has ever yet dared to build. I know the caves and the underground passages which, as used to be thought in the old days, and as I still think, lead directly to Mount Athos, to Jerusalem, to Paradise.

"There are little wooden cottages in pink and green, quite clearly reflected in the river. In a procession around you are cherry trees —yes, miraculous cherry trees, the equal of those in Japan. It was in this town—all river, all honey, all fresh breezes—that our destiny took root, twelve centuries ago. The town where our spirit was born . . . . They stole it from us. They arrested the members of the government which we had constituted there and which was, as it were, the heart of a free man. They didn't even shoot them. That, presumably, would have been too noble, too chivalrous. They transported them, ignominiously, with common criminals, with Jews, with the very worst kind of riffraff; they made them peel potatoes and polish boots. Their boots. That was the ultimate outrage. All we asked was to be their allies, to die for the common cause. They spat on the fraternity that we had offered them.

"And after all that, Humeniuk, you strut about in their uniform and feel happy when they entrust their dirty little jobs to you. . . ."

At this point, Boris ran out of breath. His spirit was appeased.

He had just thought of his uncle Zachariah, who had been dead for years. Zachariah would neither have lied nor have made a speech like Boris's. He would have remained silent. Can it be, he wondered, that our only real betrayal is the one we commit against silence?

Meanwhile, Humeniuk seemed to be searching desperately for a reply; but it was not forthcoming. The time for arguing had passed. Now was the time for bidding, for rivalry between two loves, and Boris's was the stronger.

Humeniuk stammered: "I know Kiev, too. . . ."

Then, in a voice turned suddenly furious: "But what has that to do with it? You stand accused of . . . you know what. You've got yourself in a fine mess. You're all the same, when it comes to the point. You're irresponsible. You're criminals. Look at my uniform and look at your rags. . . ."

So this is his only argument, thought Boris. He has no other. And he knows it. He will try to save me. Otherwise, he won't be able to return to his rut. My love for the town, his town and mine, is more convincing than his instinct, than reality. . . . As for his rage, he loves me really, he loves me already. My words have sunk in like a seed. There will be no peace of mind for him after this. I've turned a policeman into a knight-errant in a cause that isn't my own. Not quite my own . . . ."

Humeniuk looked up. He shouted hoarsely at the sentries: "Get this heap of dung out of here, and be quick about it!"

And, turning to Lesch: "That's no Jew. Take my word for it, he couldn't be. He's trash, of course. Politically, I wouldn't trust him an inch. But as for being a Ukrainian—alas, he is. . . ."

"Good God!" said Lesch. "I'd never have believed it. You mean to say even a turd like that can entertain political ideas? Why, how absurd. . . . You amaze me, my dear Humeniuk. . . ."

The observation was ambiguous. It could be aimed equally well at Goletz and at his compatriot, who had just been having such a heated argument with him. The shaft went home, yet Humeniuk continued, imperturbably: "As I said: politically, I wouldn't trust him an inch. A pernicious character, on quite the wrong side of the fence. But he isn't a Jew. No question of that. He speaks our language too well, he knows too much about our history, our literature, our way of life. . . ."

Lesch: "But he is circumcised."

Humeniuk: "True—I'd forgotten that! But it makes no difference. We must ask him how it happened. His circumcision amazes me every bit as much as it does you. But as for his being a Jew, I'll never accept that. Not in a thousand years. I'm not mistaken. I cannot be mistaken. . . ."

4. *THE WHOLE LAND BRIMSTONE*

ANNA LANGFUS

The Whole Land Brimstone is a novel which takes us back to Poland at the time of the Nazi invasion. Anna Langfus' heroine comes to discover the new world in which the friendships between Jew and non-Jew are attenuated and broken as the Nazi poison seeps into the atmosphere of the city. Man betrays man. This time, there was no escape from Sodom and Gomorrah; the whole land was turned into brimstone. Miss Langfus was awarded one of France's most important literary prizes for this work.

The sun was making game of the walls. It hung over the streets and houses and over our heads. I was walking aimlessly. My summer dress clung to my skin and beads of sweat trickled slowly down my arms. I was caught up in the crowd, jostled by the people plodding behind me and the people coming the other way, against the stream, and the people emerging from the narrow side-streets and trying to turn right or left, trying to embed themselves, to insinuate themselves, in this slack, halting, chaotic surge. A very elegant young woman passed me and I caught a strong whiff of scent. I knew the scent but could not think what it was called. Its name might have been *L'Approche,* or *Ombre,* or *Présage,* or possibly *Dernier Parfum.*

I walked with my head slightly averted so as not to see *them*. But they were there just the same, still propped against the walls in their rags, holding out their hands, sexless creatures whose avid eyes pursued one. One shrank away lest the hands that they were holding out should clutch one, one gave one's mind to other things so as not to understand the words issuing from those lips, so as not to admit that they spoke the same language as oneself. Some of them were so thin that their bones seemed on the point of piercing the skin. These, more than any, had to be avoided. There was still an unsuspected strength in their bony fingers, and when they closed on one's dress or arm, a pair of well-nourished hands had a job to make them let go. One had to remember not to go near them, not to look at them . . . not to glance down, so as not to see those who were no longer able to stand and who were sitting against the wall with their pale, puffy faces—the fat cheeks now flabby and sagging—and their bare, swollen legs stretched out on the pavement, sitting like people who had eaten too much and were lying there in post-prandial stupor. *Their* eyes did not strain after one; sunk in the white, flaccid skin, they were quite expressionless. They sat against the wall, never moving; even in the sunshine they seemed to be in some dark, dank cellar far below ground, and to have been there for a long time—sickly, abnormal outgrowths. How long was it since they had tasted the smallest scrap of food, these hearty eaters now bloated with hunger? And there they sat, till the end came.

Afterwards they were covered over with a thick sheet of paper, held down by a stone at each corner, before being taken away so as to make room for others. People who were in a hurry would jump over them to save two or three steps. But sometimes the wind would pluck the paper away and reveal the bloated white thighs and the enormous heads that seemed to revive and grin at the passers-by. People would still step over them, without breaking off a conversation. Here, the death of others did not prompt fear. Each man had his own death following him, keeping watch over him, ready to pounce, and pouncing anywhere, in the most un-expected places. One had to be on one's toes to escape it. Some people considered that the best way was to ignore it. Even if one felt it close at hand, really close at hand, the thing to do was to feign ignorance, remain indifferent as though it had nothing to do with one. At the last moment one could always step aside: someone else might take one's place. Death was not so discerning, it would not spot the mistake. All men look alike from the back. Naturally, one must not allow oneself to be distracted by the death of others.

A weighty hand fell on my shoulder. I jumped.

"Hullo, Princess."

He was standing beside me in his policeman's cap with his truncheon slung from his belt. He was handsomer and more engaging than ever. It was Marc. He had been a student, like myself and Jan. He talked to me of the university, of our old friends, reminded me of this fact and that detail ("Do you remember, sweetie?") and repeated the words that had been said, echoed the old laughs, and singled out such-and-such a day, during so-and-so's lecture, X was there, and Y. . . . ("Do you remember?" "Yes, I remember.") In a flash he restored a vanished world, bringing back the memories of another life like precious objects previously tucked away in a drawer of which I had lost the key. Gratefully I gave him my hand. In his eyes danced the small flame of satisfaction that always lights up in the eyes of men with the gift of charm. He took my arm and pressed it to his side. We had walked like this once before, one night in Belgium, on our way home from a ball.

"I am still as much in love with you as ever, you know," he said, stooping towards me.

"You're wasting your time," I said with a laugh. "I don't like cops. What are you doing, walking about in that ridiculous get-up?"

The pressure of his hand on my arm eased.

"Not many people are going to come out of this alive. I am doing what I can to tilt the balance in my favour. For the time being they need me. They will need me for a long time to come—so long as people are left here."

"Why?" I asked stupidly. "To maintain law and order?" He let go of my arm and I amended: "To carry out German orders?"

He replied coldly: "Precisely. Well, somebody has to."

We walked in silence for a few yards, then he took my arm again and became once more as I had known him, gay and carefree, instinctively adjusting his manner to that of any good-looking young man, a manner that he knew to be his own. He did this as one might adjust the angle of light falling on a statue, sadness or bitterness seeming to him first and foremost a breach of good taste.

"Do you realise that there are already six of us in here? Henry, Tadek, Felix, you, me and Jan. We must get together one night. I promise to bring some champagne. We'll really raise the roof. Is it a deal?"

Without waiting for my answer, as though he knew it in advance, he plunged back into the world of memory and I followed him. He mimicked our lecturers' voices and gestures to perfection, and we laughed like mad. It was then that one of the scraggy hands reaching out from the wall clutched my dress. Before I had time to do anything, Marc's truncheon crashed down on the hand, which retracted like one of those animal plants on the ocean bed that suddenly vanish into a hole in the rocks if touched or approached by an enemy. We were pursued by a mixture of groans and curses. Marc tried to resume the conversation, but I was not listening now. He noticed.

"Well, I shall expect to see you soon."

Mechanically I held out my hand. He took it and said: "You'll be less squeamish before long. We all go through that stage at the beginning."

I went on my way alone. I was very careful not to go near the wall. A cart was coming along the road, drawn by a woman. In it lay two small children with swollen bellies. The wheels creaked, the cart wobbled on the roadway, and from time to time the children's heads would clash together. Beside them walked a man of appalling thinness. Pointing at the cart, he was chanting an endless, monotonous chant, as though unwinding a thread in some dark labyrinth, the shadows of which filled his haunted eyes: "Brother Jews, have pity on a poor woman dragging her dying children. A scrap of bread, a small scrap of bread. . . ." I took the first side street. "Dragging her dying children. A scrap of bread, a small scrap of bread. . . ." I took another turning, then another. When I slowed down there was nothing to be heard.

The short street down which I was walking ended in a square. I recognised the spot. In the middle a huge chestnut-tree shed its soothing shade. Opposite rose the church. For a moment I stood staring at the house of the Christians' God in the kingdom of the Jews. Right at the top of the steeple, which stood outlined against the sky of the ghetto, a dark cross spread its rigid arms above the Jewish people. Lower down, four white angels faced the four points of the compass. As I drew nearer, I saw that their wings were secured by stout rope. I had not noticed it before. Had they been fastened lest they should ascend and speed from this hell into which their purity had strayed? Perhaps they were being held as witnesses. Or why not simply for their edification? Angels with choir-boy faces. . . . Pure white against the blue of the sky. Not high enough, though, for this stench down here not to reach your stone nostrils. What does it matter? There will always be enough incense in heaven and earth to hide the smell of charnel-houses. Crane your neck, turn your head a little. . . . The angel facing south had a small bit of wing missing: nothing to speak of, yet the fact of being slightly chipped in this way was sufficient to give it a touch of humanity, to turn it into something fragile, perishable, arousing sympathy. There are times when one needs to have one's heart wrung by the sight of a piece of stone crumbling away.

I was within three paces of the heavy door of the church when it opened and a tall black figure appeared in front of me. I was no less astonished than on the first occasion on which I had encountered it. True, one learned here to be astonished at nothing. I said: "Good afternoon, Father."

He smiled at me. "Come inside, my child."

The sunshine illumined the saints on the stained-glass windows. We made our way silently along the Stations of the Cross. Jesus stared down at us from his many faces, his eyes dilated with pain. His executioners stood round him, leering. But Mary Magdalen was there, and she was wiping up the blood and spittle with her hair. And I reflected that, outside, there were too many people dying against the walls for even a whore to show them pity.

We went through a low door and along a dark passage to a bright, pretty, comfortable room. The priest told me to sit down and I obeyed him, just as I had obeyed him a long time, a very long time, ago. He too belonged to my past, but a more distant past than the one to which Marc had just carried me back. I had only to look at this priest to feel again the weight of my school satchel crammed with books, to re-experience the excitement that always preceded examinations, and my shyness and embarrassment with teachers. After classes the Father had often stopped me and slipped me a holy picture. Now he was sitting facing me and his hair was as white, his face as pink as ever.

On my first visit I had asked him: "But what are you doing

here, Father?" And he had shaken his head and said with a sigh: "It appears my grandparents were Jews, which was something I did not know myself. And since, according to them, one is Jewish to the third generation. . . ." He had given me a gentle smile: "There are Christian souls here who need me." Whereupon I had stupidly repeated my question: "What are you doing here, Father?" "I am doing what a priest has to do, my child. I am praying."

And now again he was shaking his head and smiling and sighing. His sister came in, just as she had before, while we were chatting. She extended a small, plump, white hand and at once suggested that I join them for tea. I knew that it would be real tea, not hot water with colouring matter. "It is the faithful imprisoned here like ourselves who provide us with food," she had explained to me one day. "From time to time they bring us some little extra."

We had our tea and chatted. The Father and I talked about old times. His sister gazed dotingly at him: "Do drink your tea, dear, it will get cold . . . . Another slice?" He took it all without a murmur, having long since grown used to being coddled by her. We drank our tea, somewhere outside time, among the lace napkins and the soft gleam of the highly polished furniture. On the wall Christ drooped from an ivory crucifix. The teaspoons tinkled discreetly, voices were unsubdued, words died away without disturbing anything in the room, without hurting anyone. It was like being in a velvet-lined tomb.

The priest rose.

"Forgive me, my child, it's time for Benediction, the congregation will be waiting for me. Come and see us again soon."

I made to leave too, but his sister stopped me.

"Stay with me for a while. We are so lonely here. To us this church is like a ship on an unknown, hostile sea. We never leave it. Do you know, I have never gone farther than the tree in the square? How dreadful it is to be cooped up here. There is no need to tell you that all that nonsense about Jewish grandparents was a piece of base personal vengeance. And do you know who was behind it?"

She drew her chair closer to mine and lowered her voice.

"It was the same people who crucified Jesus Christ—the Jews. They smote my brother, that saintly man, just as they smote Our Lord."

I could feel her breath on my cheek now.

"I know who did it. It was that scoundrel Rosenthal, the child's father. And after my brother had risked his life to save that child. . . . I'm not complaining for myself, of course; of what account is the life of a poor old woman? Another cup of tea? Oh, do . . . I know how hard it is to get. And sugar . . . that's very scarce too, isn't it? Oh, do take another lump, you mustn't be shy, and it is such a pleasure for me to be able to offer you some. Please. . . ."

From a long way off came the sound of the priest conducting the service.

"Does the tea taste good? I am going to tell you the whole story, but you must promise never to breathe a word of it to my brother. If I hide certain things from him, it is to avoid making things even harder for him than they are. He has always sacrificed himself for others. It is a good thing I am here to remind him that even saints have mortal bodies that must be fed and cared for. Otherwise he would have departed this life long ago. Oh, I am so glad to be able to tell you about it. There are times, you know, when one *has* to speak out, when one *has* to open one's heart. This loneliness is so painfully hard to bear. Not that I regret anything, you understand. I have nothing to reproach myself with. I did it out of love for him. He is like a child, so helpless in his innocence; I have to protect him against himself.

"I think I told you before that we left Lublin in January to settle in Bozewo. We could have lived quietly down there, in that little town, till the end of the war. It was the Jews who were our undoing, the Jews and my brother's saintly goodness. There were not many of them in Bozewo but naturally they owned the best shops in town. For centuries we have nourished them; for centuries they have been a kind of abscess in our flesh, an abscess that we can never quite lance. There were some poor ones in Bozewo too, or quite possibly they were only pretending to be poor. My brother got to know one of those ragamuffin families who somehow manage to live crowded together in a single room, surrounded by filth and stench, and my brother had the courage to call on them. Can you imagine? It turns my stomach just to think of it. You would think Our Lord would keep bad smells from his nostrils.

"Anyway, when the Germans ordered the Jews to be evicted and taken somewhere or other, one of the women in that family came to our house after dark; she was holding a little boy by the hand.

As ill-luck would have it, my brother opened the door to her. He shut himself away with her and the child and I could hear the woman crying. She left ten minutes later. She was leaving the child with us. 'We are going to look after him,' my brother told me. 'If anyone notices his presence we can easily say he is one of the family.' Dear Jesus! He is as naive as he is goodhearted. You had only to look at the child with his white face and his long nose and his dark round eyes and his thin, stooping little body to guess the rest. But the Father is stubborn, saintly though he is. So I looked after the child. I cut his long, black, filthy hair, I washed his head, but that only made his nose and his jutting ears stand out more. I had to keep him in a little dark room and forbid him to leave it. And do you know, he obeyed me. He always obeyed me. Very docile, I must admit. He could stand in the same spot for hour after hour, without moving. After a time I wondered whether he were not a bit afraid of me. For example, when I took him food he always recoiled slightly, as though to hide himself. Yet I spoke to him nicely and I fed him well. How he could eat! And never a word of thanks, not even a smile. I like children, I love them, but who could have grown attached to a little creature like that? That did not prevent me from doing everything that had to be done for him. But my brother thought he looked pale. So I had to let him out in the yard for a while each day. The Father would go and talk to him, and—just to show you what a saintly man can achieve—he began to soften a little. One day he even asked me whether his mother would be coming for him soon. It brought the tears to my eyes. He was a child after all.

"But then—well, people noticed him and started asking me questions. It is hard to lie when you are not used to it and I could see quite well they did not believe me: how could anyone believe that unlikely story dreamed up by my brother? And one day the grocer's wife said to me—there were several people in the shop—'Is it true you are hiding a little Jew-boy at home?' I had to act fast if I wanted to save my brother. That very day he had gone to pay a call on a priest in one of the neighbouring parishes. Towards evening I took the child into the forest. I walked him round and round the tiny paths, then I plunged deep into the woods. I had filled his hands with sweets."

I forgot to drink my tea, real tea, so scarce and delicious. I listened to the woman and I said to myself: It is not true. This is *Tom Thumb* I'm listening to. She stopped for a moment and her eyes grew misty.

"I stopped my ears so as not to hear him. He was calling from where I had left him. He hadn't moved, for I had told him to stand still and wait for me. He was just calling out and crying. God forgive me, I did it to save my brother. When he came home I told him an uncle had come for the child. And then three months later the child's father returned, having escaped from one of those places where they put Jews. I was in town at the time. My brother was working in the garden; it was a neighbour who told me what happened. That man Rosenthal came charging at him and calling him a blackguard; he threatened him; he would get his own back, he said, we would pay for what we had done. When I got home my brother said to me: 'If you got rid of the child, God have pity on you.'"

By now the tears were running down her cheeks.

"God forgive him his cruelty to me. It was for him that I forfeited my soul. He should not have said that to me. No, he should not. . . . I can see that you, at least, understand me. Come and see us again, come often. You must have tea with us. But whatever happens—you promised—not a word to my brother."

The priest's distant voice reached us again.

"You are not obliged to go through the church," said the woman, opening another door for me.

I cannot recall saying a word. I walked round the outside of the church, and as I passed the door I heard the priest's voice intoning, "*Ora pro nobis.*" And a few scattered voices responded, "*Ora pro nobis.*"

I found the three of them—my parents and Jan—standing outside the house, beside themselves with worry. They questioned me and I shrugged. Where had I been? Well, one could not go far, could one? I was tired. I lay down in the small kitchen where Jan and I slept.

From my bed I could see the yard where my parents and husband were talking to some neighbours. A child cried a long way off, then there was silence. I stared at the trees. Suddenly a wind sprang up from nowhere and bore down on their branches and Jan and my parents vanished behind them. I jumped out of the window to join them, but they were gone. I called. My voice did not carry. It was lost in the folds of the foliage now motionless right above my head. I could feel a tremendous weight of greenery pressing down on me. A dim light was blurring the shapes of things; everything was as in a neglected tapestry in some shadowy room. I tried to run . . . I stumbled over roots and the trees rose up before me. They barred my way. They multiplied into dense colonnades, almost without perspective, dissolving into twilit depths, becoming ever denser, more persistent, more malevolent. I tried guile . . . I would choose one of them, pretend to walk towards it, then side-step it at the last moment, trying to surprise it, to slip past it, to bound forward . . . only to collide with some other obstacle which appeared to be secreted by this depthless void. I kept calling out all the time this peculiar game was going on, but my voice barely disturbed the silence. I felt caught in the folds of a heavy tapestry, suffocating, entangled. My throat was no longer obeying and the cries knotted themselves into a painful lump. Had night come? How could one tell in this dull half-light in which shapes wavered uncertainly? The trees were all round me. They were coming still closer . . . . Their branches were spreading round my shoulders, gripping my knees, scratching my face. I could no longer make the slightest movement, pinioned, paralysed as much by horror as by my bonds. I sensed that I ought to try and free my hands . . . . Inexorably the bark's grip tightened. I was getting no air, I was suffocating . . . . I told myself that I ought to struggle, to free first one hand, then . . . . All that was needed was a sudden exertion. But I did not make that exertion. I could not make it. I stayed quite still, terrorised, my fingers clutching the sweets that filled my hands. How could I wrest myself free of this entanglement if I did not unclench my hands? If I did not make up my mind to leave go of these few sticky, inexplicable sweets? I knew that I had to hold on to them whatever happened. I knew nothing else. My thoughts were crumbling away . . . . I could no longer distinguish between my body and the tough wood gripping it. And still this absurd conviction that I must not loosen my fingers. All light had gone. I was petrified. Now there was nothing. . . . Nothing but this growing feeling of something creeping up on me. *They* were there, between the trees, and the trees were parting, guiding them, leading them to me as I waited there, speechless and powerless. Gently, implacably they approached. I knew the look they wore, their wary tread, the way they carried their sub-machine-guns in front of them. They had closed in on me for ever. At this, my throat relaxed and the scream broke loose, delivering me . . . . The warm, salt blood filled my mouth . . . . I was emptying and growing light, light, light . . . . Nothing was left but my two hands closed on the sweets. . . .

5. *RESCUE IN DENMARK*

HAROLD FLENDER

Sometimes, the call came to man and man listened to the cry for help. Denmark provides one of the great examples of man discovering his own greatness. There are other instances, notably in the case of Bulgaria, where a captive population refused to do the Nazis' will; but the Danish action touches us with a warmness unique in our time. These two short chapters are from Harold Flender's sober and straightforward account of how the Danes replied to the great question of that time—they *were* their brothers' keeper.

FLIGHT

Then steal away, give little warning,
Choose thine own time;
Say not "Good night," but in some
brighter clime,
Bid me "Good morning."
— ANNA LETITIA BARBAULD

There was only one way for the Danish Jews to get to Sweden— by boat. However, several days before the raid of October 1 the Germans had ordered that all Danish boats be taken out of the water and brought at least 1,000 feet inland. There was only one exception to this order—the fishing boats.

Immediately after Sweden's publicly announced offer of refuge to the Danish Jews, several hundred of them in hiding made a beeline to the coastal towns where they hoped to find fishermen who would be willing to ferry them across the sound to Sweden. While most of the Danish Jews were fearful of coming out of hiding to attempt to reach the coastal towns, these several hundred piled into taxicabs and headed for Elsinore, Snekkersten, Stevns and

Reprinted with permission of Simon and Schuster from *Rescue in Denmark* by HAROLD FLENDER. Copyright, ©, 1963, by Harold Flender.

Dragør. A high official in the Danish foreign ministry, active at the time in the Socialist Youth Movement, reported the flight.[1] "It was interesting to see on the road at the time many taxis loaded with Jews headed for the seacoast towns. In many cases the taxi drivers were well paid for their services, but, still, they were taking an awful chance, for it was illegal to help the Jews to escape. I've heard it said that some Germans, particularly members of the Wehrmacht as opposed to the Gestapo, looked aside, closed one eye, and let the Jews escape, but I don't believe this to be true. Rather, it all happened so fast that they were taken by surprise and fooled. They became quite angry, and, as a matter of fact, did everything they could to stop the refugees."

Snekkersten and Elsinore, where the sound separating Denmark from Sweden is only two and half miles wide, received the majority of these refugees. The local inhabitants cooperated in putting them up in hotels, inns, farms, garages and private homes. Werner Christiansen, owner of a coastal resort inn at Rødvig, turned his entire establishment over to them, and placed the overflow with local townspeople and farmers. Not one of the scores of local inhabitants he approached turned him down when he asked them to hide the Jews.

The flight to the coastal towns during these first days of October was disorganized and chaotic. The majority of the 472 Danish Jews caught by the Germans were captured during this time.

The absent-minded Jewish editor of the Danish newspaper *Politiken* was arrested during this period.[2] When stopped on the street after curfew by German soldiers who asked him what he was doing carrying a valise, he replied, "I'm fleeing."

"What do you mean?" asked one of the soldiers.

"You see," said the editor, "I'm Jewish and Sweden has said she will accept all Danish Jews. So I'm fleeing to Snekkersten."

During this first week in October, a short, fifty-year-old tailor showed up at the house of one of his customers, Stig Hansen, a civil engineer.[3] Hansen was shocked to see him.

"My God, what are you doing here? Haven't you heard..."

"Yes, yes," interrupted the tailor, "I've heard all about it. You owe me money."

---

[1] As reported to the author by Per Haekkerup, now Foreign Minister of Denmark.
[2] Archives, Danish Resistance Museum.
[3] As told to the author by Stig Hansen's daughter Ingrid.

"Are you crazy?" asked Hansen. "You should be in hiding!"

"I can't afford it. I've heard Sweden is going to take us in if we can get there and I need some money for the fare. The only way we can get there is by fishing boats, and the fishermen will probably charge an arm and a leg."

"I'll lend you the money," said Hansen.

The tailor raised his chin proudly. "I have made it a lifelong principle never to borrow money."

"But this is an exceptional circumstance," said Hansen. "You can pay me back when this mess is over."

"No, no," said the tailor. "I'll go around to all the customers who owe me money, and if all of them pay me what they owe me, perhaps then my wife and I will be able to afford to go."

"You'll never make it that way," protested Hansen. "You'll be picked up by the Gestapo. Take the money from me."

The tailor hesitated. "I never borrow money," he repeated.

Hansen paid him what he owed him. The tailor stood holding the money in one hand, scratching his head with the other.

"Yes?" asked Hansen. "What are you thinking about?"

"My wife has a fur coat," said the tailor. "Does your wife need a fur coat? I could sell it to you cheap."

Hansen accompanied the tailor to his house. He and his wife lived rather poorly. It was obvious to Hansen that he earned barely enough to make ends meet, and if there was any profit it was undoubtedly spent on the large collection of books scattered about the house. The fur coat he showed Hansen was moth-eaten. Nevertheless, Hansen offered him the equivalent of seventy-five dollars for it. He looked around the apartment. The furniture was old and seedy.

"You know," said Hansen, "I could use some of these pieces of furniture. I don't want you to think I'm trying to take advantage of you, but how about selling me these two chairs for another seventy-five dollars?"

The tailor agreed.

"Now you have a hundred and fifty dollars," said Hansen. "That should be enough for the fare to Sweden."

"Yes," agreed the tailor, "but I don't know anyone to take us there."

Hansen took the tailor and his wife to the estate of his friend A. P. Møller, a shipbuilder in Hellerup. Møller promised to see to it that somehow or other the tailor and his wife would get to Sweden.

It was also during this period of haphazard attempts to flee to the coastal towns that several of the fishermen contacted to take the Jews across to Sweden charged exorbitant fees.[4] It cannot be denied that in making the trip they were risking not only their boats but their very lives. However, this was still no excuse for those instances where mercenary fishermen milked the desperate refugees for every cent they could. During the first week of October, some fishermen demanded and received as much as five thousand dollars per passenger. It must be pointed out that the charging of exorbitant rates was confined only to relatively few fishermen. Later on, the average crossing cost sixty dollars per passenger. Also, there were many fishermen who took the refugees across for nothing. There is not a single case on record of a refugee failing to reach Sweden because he lacked the fare, and many of the refugees had no money to pay. For every fisherman who overcharged the Jews, there were a dozen who ferried them across out of a genuine desire to be of help.

Peder Christopher Hansen[5] was among those who did it out of idealism. His actions in transporting Danish Jews and resistance people to Sweden earned him honors and citations from the American as well as Danish governments. His first brush with the Germans occurred at 7 A.M. on April 9, 1940. Hansen was returning to port with 5,000 kilos of cod in the hold of his boat, when he was stopped by an armed German trawler. Four German soldiers hopped on board.

"We want some fish," said one of the Germans.

"What the hell do you mean you want some fish! Are you pirates?"

"No," replied the soldier, "we'll pay for it."

"Even if you're willing to pay, you krauts have no right to be here. These are Danish territorial waters."

"Haven't you heard?" asked the soldier, laughing. "We're at war with you!"

At that moment, German planes appeared overhead. "Those

---

[4] As reported to the author by refugees and resistance people who had contact with these fishermen.

[5] As reported to the author by fisherman Peder Christopher Hansen.

are our bombers," said the soldier. "They're on their way to Copenhagen."

"They will be shot down," said Hansen.

"No they won't," replied the soldier.

"If we're at war, they'll be shot down."

"No, they won't," insisted the soldier. "It isn't much of a war you Danes are fighting. There have been a few shots at the frontier, but that's all. In Copenhagen the government has already capitulated."

The Germans paid Hansen for the fish they took, and departed. Hansen was so disgusted with the fact that the Danes had not fought back that he changed the course of his boat and headed for Sweden. The heavy ice floes forced him to return, but did not cool him off.

During the first week of October 1943, Hansen was tying up his boat in the harbor of Rødvig, when he was approached by a sixty-year-old stranger.

"Can I speak to you in confidence?" whispered the man.

"What is it?" asked Hansen.

"I have to get my two sons to Sweden. We're Jewish and the Germans have started arresting all Danish Jews. Could you take them to Sweden? I'm willing to stay here and take a chance, but I must get my sons over."

"Yes," said Hansen. "I can take them. And I can take you, too."

"There are quite a few of us hiding here," said the man. "About how many others can you take?"

"How many are you?" asked Hansen.

"There are about fifty others hiding with my sons," said the man.

"I'll take them all," said Hansen. "I'll have to make more than one trip, but I'll take them all."

"Wonderful," said the man. "And don't worry. We're prepared to pay you for it."

"I don't give a damn about the money," said Hansen.

That night, Hansen made two trips to Sweden to get the fifty refugees across. It was his first illegal action against the Germans.

Two days later, a fisherman friend approached Hansen, saying, "Look, you have a daughter, so I know you can appreciate my situation. There are two young Jewish girls staying with me. Their parents have disappeared. Would you take them over to Sweden?"

"Yes," replied Hansen.

"They have no money."

"I don't care," said Hansen. "Anything I can do against the Germans is fine with me."

"Have you room for some other refugees in addition to the two girls? My own boat is full."

"Sure," said Hansen.

That night, at 1 A.M., Hansen let the two young girls and eight other Jewish refugees into the hold of his ship. Just as he was about to pull out, a spotlight hit the deck, and he was told to stand by. Ten German sailors boarded his ship.

"What are you doing at this hour of the night?" demanded the petty officer in charge.

"What does it look like I'm doing?" asked Hansen. "I'm setting out to fish. Now get the hell off my ship."

The German sailors were standing on top of the hold directly under which were hidden the ten Jewish refugees.

"I have the feeling," said the petty officer, "that you're involved in something else. I think we ought to search the ship."

Hansen decided to take a wild chance.

"You do that," he screamed, "and they'll hear about it at the German Naval Station at Korsør! What have you sons of bitches come to Denmark for? You're supposed to be here to protect us, not to bother us. Now get the hell off my ship or I'll sail with you on board right over to your commanding officer at Korsør, who happens to be a personal friend of mine, and I'll tell him what a hard time you've been giving me!"

The Germans left the ship and Hansen took the refugees over to Trelleborg in Sweden.

A week later, Hansen was contacted by resort-owner Werner Christiansen.

"I hear you've been taking Jewish refugees over to Sweden," said Christiansen.

"I've made a couple of trips," replied Hansen.

"Would you like to take some more over?"

"How many?"

"Four hundred."

"Four hundred!" exclaimed Hansen. "How big do you think my boat is?"

"And after you get those four hundred over, there may be others."

"What about my codfish?" asked Hansen. "Oh, hell, human beings are more important than codfish. Okay, I'll do whatever I can."

Another fisherman who acted out of idealism and was extremely active during the first week of flight was Axel Olsen.[6] He and his wife hated the Germans from the very first day they set foot in Denmark. On April 9, 1940, Olsen was on his way by bicycle to the docks when he noticed German planes overhead dropping leaflets. It was by picking up and reading one of them that he learned of Denmark's surrender to Germany. He turned his bicycle around and rode home to his wife and five-year-old son. His wife was still in bed sleeping, and when he awakened her to tell her what happened, she said simply, "It's a lie. I don't believe it. We wouldn't let them come in just like that without putting up a struggle." He showed her the leaflet, and, after reading it, she jumped out of bed, went into her son's room, gathered up his toy boats which had been made in Germany, threw them into the kitchen stove and burned them.

Olsen harbored resentment against the Germans from that time on, but it wasn't until the first week of October 1943 that he had an opportunity to put his resentment into concrete action. During the early part of that week, Olsen dragged up in his fishing net, in addition to dozens of cod, a dead man. The body was badly bloated, having been in the water for several weeks, but from its clothes, Olsen could see that it was the body of a Danish fisherman. He pulled it up on the boat and brought it to shore. The German soldiers at the nearby police station examined the corpse, questioned Olsen superficially and for only a few minutes, and apparently convinced that there was nothing more to the story than he told, released him. Outside the prison, Olsen expressed to an Austrian guard his relief and astonishment over the dispatch with which he had been released.

"I thought they'd hold me much longer," said Olsen. "And I thought they'd give me a much harder time. After all, it's not every day that a fisherman brings up in his net a dead body."

---

[6] As reported to the author by fisherman Axel Olsen.

"You're lucky," said the Austrian guard, "that they don't have time to bother with you today. They're all involved because of the failure of the raids during the past two nights."

"What raids?" asked Olsen.

"To arrest the Danish Jews," said the Austrian soldier. "From what I hear, they hardly caught any at all. They were all in hiding. Now they're trying to find out *where* they're hiding."

Walking toward his boat from the prison, Olsen was wondering what he could do to help the Jews in hiding when he bumped into a young baker's apprentice he knew. He thought it odd to see the boy walking down the middle of the street in his white clothes and hat, his hands and arms covered white with flour.

"What are you doing here?" asked Olsen. "Shouldn't you be in the bakery?"

Suddenly the boy broke down and cried.

"What's the matter?" asked Olsen.

"Haven't you heard of the German raids against the Danish Jews during the past few nights?" asked the boy.

"I just learned about it," said Olsen. "But what has that to do with you?"

"I'm Jewish."

"I never knew it," said Olsen.

"Nobody around here knows it," said the boy. "That's why I didn't go into hiding like the rest. But now I'm scared the Germans will find out. Several of the Jews in the town are trying to get to Sweden, but I have no money. I don't make much as an apprentice. In fact, I have only ten kroner."

Olsen got the boy to stop crying, took him to his house, fed him, dressed him in fisherman's clothes and took him to his boat. He had him remain in hiding at the bottom of the boat until after dark, and then took him over to Sweden.

Several days later, after an arduous fishing trip, Olsen was resting on his living room couch when Erik Beck, a friend who was a criminal lawyer, entered and told him that he was hiding the local police commissioner, Aage Lothinga, who was Jewish. Did Olsen, wondered Beck, know a fisherman who might be willing to take Lothinga over to Sweden? Olsen agreed to do the job himself. From that day until the war's end, Olsen was involved in the illegal transport of refugees.

Among those who attempted the flight to Sweden during the first week of October were Rabbi Melchior and his family.[7] The son of Reverend Hans Kildeby, pastor of the church of Ørslev, made arrangements with a young fisherman to take Rabbi Melchior and his family to Sweden. By 7 P.M., when the Melchiors started out, the night was pitch-black. They left from the island of Falster, south of Zealand, and the trip in the small boat was to take six hours. Twelve hours later they were still at sea. As dawn broke, land appeared ahead of them. Melchior recognized the town of Gedser, a Danish town not far from the German frontier. The young fisherman, who had been behaving strangely all evening, confessed that because he was afraid of running into German patrol boats, all he had done throughout the long night was to circle about and finally bring them back to the Danish shore at a point not far from the German border. Melchior angrily knocked down the young fisherman, and, although he had never before steered a boat, grabbed the rudder and managed to turn the boat around in the direction of Sweden. He held the boat on course for six hours until they were safe in Swedish waters.

Within a matter of days it became evident to the Danes that if the exodus of Danish Jews to Sweden was to be successful, capricious acts of individual daring had to be replaced by some form of organized action. At the beginning, there had been no planning, no organization. But the challenge of saving the lives of eight thousand countrymen gave the Danes an enormous impetus to band together to prove that if the will was there, the Germans, could be thwarted in their plan to exterminate Denmark's Jewry.

No Customers Wanted

Fortune favors the brave
—Terence

Until September 12, 1943, Mogens Staffeldt's bookshop was located in Dagmarhus, the same building used by the Gestapo as its

---

[7]As reported to the author by Rabbi Melchior.

Copenhagen headquarters. On that date the Gestapo took posses-sion of the entire building and Mogens Staffeldt was forced to find new quarters. He moved into a store across the street. It was in the empty back room of this new store that a group of under-ground men met during the first week of October. They included Staffeldt, his younger brother Jørgen, Jens Lillelund and Sven Truelsen, a lawyer. Their purpose was to try to figure out an organized way of smuggling Denmark's Jews to Sweden.[1] They knew that individual attempts to get over were too dangerous. About two hundred of the refugees had attempted it during the past few days and had been caught. What was needed was an or-ganized method of getting the refugees from their places of hiding to various collection points, and later handing them over to fisher-men willing to take them across the sound to Sweden. It was also necessary to get the fishermen to set a uniform price. Lillelund suggested that the group speak to a fisherman he knew by the name of Nielsen. He was certain that Nielsen would put them in touch with key members of the Fishermen's Association who would be cooperative in getting the fishermen to adopt a low, uniform price.

When the meeting ended, the underground group had decided to use as collection points the various hospitals in Copenhagen where there were already thousands of Jews in hiding. Ambu-lances and taxis were selected as the best means of transportation to take the refugees to the boats. Mogens Staffeldt suggested that the back of his bookstore be used as one of the collection points. At first there was some opposition to this suggestion, but Danes are known for their sense of humor, and, upon reflection, the idea of using a store across the street from Gestapo Headquarters as a collection point for the Jewish refugees struck the younger Staffeldt, Lillelund, and even Truelsen, as an amusing challenge. They agreed to use the bookstore.

One of the first groups of refugees brought to the store con-sisted of twenty Danish Jews, about half of whom were young children.[2] Lillelund brought them there from the cellar of a friend's house, where they had been hiding. All of them were ex-tremely frightened, and at about 1 A.M. one of the children broke

---

[1] As reported to the author by Staffeldt, Lillelund, and Truelsen.
[2] As reported to the author by Lillelund.

into a fit of hysteria which became contagious. In a matter of minutes, half a dozen of the children were screaming at the tops of their lungs, and the parents could do nothing to calm them.

"He's very nervous," said the mother of the child who had started the ruckus. "We usually give him a sedative when he gets like this, but we're all out of them now."

"They could all use sedatives," said one of the other mothers.

Lillelund knew that he had to get something to quiet the children or the entire group would be discovered. His own physician was in Sweden, and the only other physicians he knew were located far from the bookstore. He quickly consulted the telephone directory and picked out the name of an unknown physician who lived only a few blocks away. Because it was well after curfew, he had to sneak along in the shadows of the buildings to avoid being picked up by German soldiers.

The physician appeared at the door in his nightshirt.

"Can I come in?" asked Lillelund.

"Who are you? What do you want?"

"It's an emergency."

The doctor was suspicious and did not budge. Lillelund knew in what contempt practically all of Denmark's physicians held the Germans, and without hesitation he quickly explained the situation. "So if you could just give me a bottle of sedatives or sleeping pills for the children, I'd appreciate it ever so much."

"Nonsense," said the doctor. "A thing like that needs a physician. I'll have to take care of it myself. If you take me to the children, I'll get them to keep quiet. Now come in while I get dressed."

"We don't have much time," warned Lillelund.

"All right," said the doctor. "Let me at least put an overcoat over my pajamas."

Hurriedly throwing an overcoat over his shoulders and grabbing his medical bag, the physician followed Lillelund to the back of Staffeldt's bookstore. The parents were frantic. The children were still screaming.

Working as quickly as he could, the doctor injected all of the children with a sedative that made them unconscious. They looked dead. Their parents turned white with apprehension. Lillelund found himself trembling.

"I know," said the doctor. "They look dead. But don't worry, they're not. If you look closely, you can see they're breathing."

Lillelund and the parents examined the children. They were breathing.

"They'll remain unconscious like that for from six to eight hours," explained the doctor.

Lillelund couldn't take his eyes off the children. Continuing to stare at them, he addressed the doctor: "What's your fee?"

"None," said the physician. He packed up his medical bag, threw his overcoat over his pajamas and left.

No one spoke. The parents of the unconscious children were deathly silent. Like Lillelund, they could not take their eyes off the children.

"I'm sure the doctor knew what he was doing," said Lillelund. "It's much better this way. Now nobody will hear them. And, as the doctor said, they'll snap out of it in from six to eight hours. We won't be going to the fishing boats before then."

"What if they start screaming again when they wake up?" asked one of the refugees. "What if they start screaming on the way to the boats?"

"They'll have to be injected again," replied Lillelund. "Maybe it's a good idea to inject them again just before leaving for the boats. They can be carried down to the boats. It'll be a lot safer that way."

One of the fathers, holding his unconscious son in his arms, began to sob.

"What have they done to deserve this?" he asked. "What do the Germans want with them? They're only children. Children . . . ."

Lillelund hurriedly walked out of the back room into the book-store proper. He could barely see as there was practically no light coming in from the blacked-out street. Somehow he made his way past the bookstacks to Staffeldt's desk. He sat down, buried his head in his arms, and then Jens Lillelund, a tough saboteur, cried.

Out of Lillelund's grim experience with the refugees whose hysterical children had to be drugged into unconsciousness came a valuable and regularly employed procedure, the sedation of all of the refugee children during the transportation to the boats and on the sea crossing to Sweden. In addition to the injections, the physicians often gagged and taped the mouths of the children, so that should the trip take longer than anticipated and the effect of the injections wear off, the children would still be quiet.

Word spread that Mogens Staffeldt's bookstore was a collecting point for the Jewish refugees, and, in addition to those Danish Jews who were brought into the store by members of Staffeldt's underground unit, many started coming in on their own. This resulted in a larger influx of refugees than had been anticipated, and for assistance, Staffeldt enlisted the aid of his five employees. A signal had been decided upon to announce that the store was free of Germans. If a copy of Kaj Munk's poems was in the window, it meant the coast was clear. The absence of the book from the window meant that it was dangerous for Jews to enter the store. Arrangements were made with a number of dependable fishermen in Copenhagen Harbor. The Fishermen's Association got them to agree on a uniform price—about sixty dollars per passenger. During the day, the refugees were brought, or came themselves, into the store, and at night they were taken by ambulance from the store to small wooden shacks and warehouses near the docks south of Copenhagen. They usually left for Sweden the same night that they were taken to the docks, but, occasionally, when German patrols in the area were unusually heavy, the refugees had to remain hidden in the wooden shacks and warehouses for as long as two or three days. Whenever this occurred, it meant that Staffeldt's group had the additional problem of feeding the refugees.

For the Staffeldt group, not all of the incidents in getting the Jews to the boats were as disturbing as Lillelund's initial experience with the children who had to be drugged.

One night Staffeldt's group was asked to cooperate with another underground unit which had forty refugees it wanted to get to Sweden.[3] Lillelund and Staffeldt's younger brother Jørgen were taken by an agent from the other underground unit to an empty summerhouse on a beach south of Copenhagen. The agent informed them that after he left they were to remain hidden in the house for exactly half an hour, and were then to report to the rendezvous on the beach to which he would bring the refugees. The agent further explained that because of the German patrols

---

[3] As reported to the author by Lillelund.

on the beach, exact timing was of the utmost importance. Lillelund and Jørgen had to be at the appointed rendezvous *in exactly half an hour.*

After the agent departed, Lillelund looked at his watch and noticed that it had stopped running. He wound it and shook it to no avail.

"What time have you got?" he asked Jørgen. "My watch is broken." Jørgen felt his wrist.

"I forgot to take my watch," he said.

"Oh Jesus," said Lillelund. "How the hell will we know when the half-hour is up? Let's look around, maybe there's a clock somewhere in this summer house."

They desperately scampered around the house until Lillelund heard Jørgen cry out from the kitchen: "Our worries are over."

Lillelund ran into the kitchen, where he saw Jørgen gulping down a bottle of beer.

"Did you find a clock?" asked Lillelund.

"No," replied Jørgen. He held the bottle in the air. "But I found this."

"A fine time to drink beer," exploded Lillelund. "We need a watch and you—"

"This is just as good," interrupted Jørgen. He gulped down the remainder of the beer and smiled. "Have you ever seen me drink beer before?" he asked.

Now that Lillelund thought about it, he had never seen him drink beer.

"Do you know why?" asked Jørgen. "Because I seem to have some sort of allergy to it. Drinking beer is embarrassing to me because it gives me an uncontrollable urge to pee. My brother and I once timed it and we found this uncontrollable, irresistible urge came on exactly half an hour after I'd have a bottle. Believe me, it works like clockwork."

Lillelund and Jørgen went into the living room, where they sat in the dark and waited.

"Now?" asked Lillelund.

"Not yet," said Jørgen. "I can pee if I want to, but it's not that uncontrollable, irresistible urge."

After a few minutes, Jørgen jumped to his feet. "Now!" he said. "Let's go!"

They raced to the rendezvous on the beach. The forty refugees were also arriving at that precise moment, and Lillelund and Jørgen, with time out for Jørgen's call of nature, got them to the boats on schedule.

Several days after the incident on the beach, Staffeldt's group was involved in another episode with humorous overtones.[4] Arrangements had been made with a large fishing boat to take fourteen Jewish refugees to Sweden. Lillelund transferred them from the bookstore to a house in Nyhavn, the tough sailors' section on the Copenhagen docks. When he went to see the ship's captain to verify last-minute details, the captain unexpectedly expressed a fear: "I've got two new crew members," he said, "and I don't know if I can trust them."

"But you've about ten other crew members on board," pointed out Lillelund. "If the two start anything, the rest of you should be able to handle them."

"It's not that," said the captain. "I'm not worried about handling them during the trip. But what happens if after the trip they squeal to the Germans about what I've done? It'll mean my neck."

"But how can you back out at the last minute?" asked Lillelund. "You'll be jeopardizing the lives of fourteen people."

"I didn't say I wanted to back out," said the captain. "I've another scheme. The normal run of this boat is down to Germany. Instead of starting out for Sweden, what if I tell the crew that we're going to Germany, as usual. But then, once we get halfway there, suppose some of the refugees break out of the hold as though they were stowed away? I can arrange for them to get into the hold before any of the crew come on board."

"Then what?" asked Lillelund.

"Well, then they'll hold us up with guns, forcing us to take them to Sweden. In other words, it'll look like they're hijacking the ship."

"Do you really think all of that play acting is necessary?" asked Lillelund.

"Absolutely," replied the captain. "Then, in case the two new men turn out to be informers and inform on me, I can always say that I was forced to go to Sweden at gunpoint."

"But those Jews are a mild-mannered, gentle lot," pointed out

---

[4] As reported to the author by Lillelund.

Lillelund. "They don't know anything about weapons. Hell, they wouldn't even know at which end to hold a revolver."

"You could teach them," said the captain. "We've an hour before we sail. Teach them how to hold a gun and how to say 'Hands up!' You'll have to do it fast because I want them on board and hidden before the crew arrives."

"What if the crew tries to disarm them?" asked Lillelund.

"Don't worry," said the captain. "I'll brief the whole crew on what's happening so they'll cooperate. I mean I'll tell the whole crew except for the two new men. Okay?"

Lillelund hesitated for a moment, then said, "Okay. If that's the only way you'll sail, okay."

He started to walk away when the captain called out, "Oh, one more thing." He ambled up to Lillelund and whispered; "Make sure there are no cartridges in the guns. I don't want those refugees getting nervous and shooting me."

Lillelund raced back to the store, got two pistols from Staffeldt, emptied them, and forced two unwilling refugees to learn how to hold them and shout "Hands up!"

The boat set sail on schedule, and several hours out of port, as planned, the two refugees came out of their places of hiding in the hold. The captain and the crew—except for the two new crew members—were expecting them, and, before the two refugees had a chance to draw their pistols or to say anything, the captain and his men had their hands high in the air and the captain was saying, "Don't shoot! We'll take you to Sweden, we'll do anything you want! Only don't shoot!" This was followed by the two nervous refugees drawing their pistols and stammering, "H-h-hands up!"

Several hours later, all fourteen Danish Jews were safe in Sweden. It turned out that the two new crew members were sympathetic to the plight of the refugees and eager to do everything they could to help them. All subsequent illegal trips this particular boat made to Sweden were without theatrics.

The members of Staffeldt's group admit that their work would not have been as effective as it was had it not been for the cooperation received from almost everyone with whom they came into contact. For example, at one time Lillelund was assigned to pick up four Danish Jews at the railroad station and bring them to the bookstore. In this particular operation an ambulance would have been too conspicuous, and so he decided to use a taxicab. Taxis were extremely scarce at that time, and when he and the refugees reached the street in front of the station they noticed that there were several people ahead of them who were also waiting for cabs. Finally, a taxi showed up and the man first in line approached it. The taxi driver, sensing somehow from their nervousness that the four people with Lillelund were Jews, turned to the man who was rightfully his passenger and said, "You were here first, so you can have the cab if you want it, but I think that the gentleman at the end of the line has a more urgent need for a taxi than you." The man took one look at the frightened refugees with Lillelund, sized up the situation, opened the door of the taxi and motioned for Lillelund and his charges to hurry in. There was not a single complaint from any of the other people on the line; instead, they nodded their approval.

Staffeldt's group had little or no contact with the other underground groups. This was deliberate, so that if one group was caught, its members could not be tortured by the Germans into revealing the membership and whereabouts of any of the other groups.

All in all the members of Staffeldt's group had nothing but complete respect for the way the Danish Jews behaved during their period of escape. According to Lillelund, they were all frightened, but, at the same time, they were courageous and often noble. The only times they became difficult, according to Lillelund, were on those occasions when there was not enough room for all of the members of a particular group in a single boat. Then the trouble would arise not because of a dearth of volunteers to stay behind, but, because nearly all of the adult members of the group would insist on remaining in Denmark while their fellow refugees went on ahead to Sweden. On one such occasion, an elderly man told Lillelund: "I'm seventy. Why should I go now? Maybe I'll die next year. This man is forty. Let him go in my place."

No accurate records were kept of the number of Jews who passed through Mogens Staffeldt's bookstore on their way to Sweden, but it is estimated that there were at least six hundred of them.

There were so many refugees passing through Mogens Staffeldt's shop during the October exodus that it resembled a travel agency more than it did a bookstore. In fact, during those days Staffeldt and his brother became quite annoyed and suspicious whenever someone entered who actually wanted to buy a book. It was the first and only time for Staffeldt since he had become a bookseller that no customers were wanted.

When asked why he helped the Jews to escape, Staffeldt replied: "I never think of a man as a Jew or not. It makes no difference to me. At that time I was helping people in trouble. I did the same for the Jews as I did for Allied fliers, saboteurs and others who had to get to Sweden."

6. *THE DEPUTY*

ROLF HOCHHUTH

The Deputy has created a worldwide controversy which continues to occupy men's minds. Hochhuth, a young German Protestant, became convinced that the Catholic Church, and Pope Pius XII in particular, had not responded to the cry addressed to mankind. The Pope had been silent, Hochhuth decided. Mankind had been silent. And God—had He not been silent as well? And so Hochhuth created a stage play in which Riccardo, a young Catholic priest, identifies himself with the fate of the Jews and tries to convince his church hierarchy to intervene on their behalf. He fails, and goes to Auschwitz of his own free will. There he is confronted by the camp doctor, a figure patterned after the infamous camp doctor Mengele; and the doctor, representative of all evil, challenges the man of religion and the God who seems to have withdrawn from the world.

════

HELGA *quickly goes across the garden. She turns to the left around the hut, her head briefly appearing behind the window, and then disappears. The* DOCTOR, *tapping his swagger stick against one of his extremely smart, supple riding boots, looks at* RICCARDO *who stands with Signora* LUCCANI, *her father-in-law and the children.* RICCARDO *can just barely be discerned. We hear the sharp noise of an approaching truck. The oppressive "light," the gaseous smoke and the glow of fire, concentrate the gaze upon the* DOCTOR *who stands with his back to the audience, legs wide apart, but neverthe-*

Reprinted with permission of Grove Press, Inc. from *The Deputy* by ROLF HOCHHUTH. Copyright © 1964 by Grove Press, Inc. Translated from the German by RICHARD and CLARA WINSTON.

less graceful. He stares fixedly at RICCARDO, *who glances over once shyly and timidly, as though he felt the look, and then quickly takes the Luccanis' small daughter in his arms.*

DOCTOR: You there! Your Holiness.
The one in black over there—come here.

Signora LUCCANI *draws her son closer to her. All the deportees look at the* DOCTOR *except* RICCARDO. *It has become very quiet.*

Get a move on, come here!

Impatiently he goes upstage, left, toward the group, beckoning to RICCARDO, *who can now no longer evade him. Carrying the little girl in his arms,* RICCARDO *hesitantly steps forward out of the line. The* DOCTOR *silently retraces his steps, going as far as possible downstage, right, signing to* RICCARDO *to follow him. Uncertainly,* RICCARDO *follows. Signora* LUCCANI *watches him walking away with her child and screams wildly.*

JULIA: Don't go away. Stay here, stay with us!

She weeps. Her father-in-law takes her arm reassuringly and talks to her. At her scream, RICCARDO *stands still and looks back. He is frightened.*

DOCTOR (*threateningly, as if speaking to a dog*) : Come here, I say.

RICCARDO *again follows him a short distance. They now stand face to face, far downstage.* RICCARDO's *forehead and face are bleeding. He has been beaten.*

DOCTOR (*in a sarcastically friendly tone*) :
That pretty brat your own?
RICCARDO (*with pent fury*) : The Germans beat her father to death.
They thought it funny because he wore glasses.
DOCTOR: Such brutes, these Germans.

With his stick, which he handles with the air of a dandy, he gives RICCARDO *a brief and almost comradely tap on the chest.*

Where is your yellow star?

RICCARDO: I threw it away because I wanted to escape.

DOCTOR: What's this about your not being a Jew?
On the railroad platform, I am told, you claimed
the Pope assigned you to care for the Jews.

RICCARDO: I said that only to escape.
They believed me and let me go.
I am a Jew like the others.

DOCTOR: Congratulations. A subtle Jesuit trick.
How is it they caught up with you again?

RICCARDO (*contemptuously*) : Nobody caught me.
I joined my companions of my own accord,
when nobody was looking.

DOCTOR (*scornfully*) : My, how noble!
We've needed volunteers. Priests too.
Just in case someone should die here.
The climate can be nasty in Auschwitz.
Of course you're not a Jew. . . .

RICCARDO *does not answer. The* DOCTOR *sits down on the bench. He says sarcastically:*

A martyr, then.
If that's the case, why did you run away?

RICCARDO: Wouldn't you be afraid if you were sent here?

DOCTOR: Afraid of what? An internment camp.
Why should a man so close to God as you
be afraid!

RICCARDO (*insistently*): *People* are being burned here. . . .
The smell of burning flesh and hair—

DOCTOR (*addressing him more as an equal*) :
What foolish ideas you have.
What you see here is only industry.
The smell comes from lubricating oil and horsehair,
drugs and nitrates, rubber and sulphur.
A second Ruhr is growing up here.
I. G. Farben, Buna, have built branches here.
Krupp will be coming soon.
Air raids don't bother us.
Labor is cheap.

RICCARDO: I've known for a year what this place is used for.
Only my imagination was too feeble.
And today I no longer had the courage—to go along.
DOCTOR: Ah, then you know about it. Very well.
I understand your ambition to be crucified,
but in the name of God the Father,
the Son and the Holy Ghost,
I intend to have a little sport
deflating your self-importance.
I have something quite different in mind for you.

RICCARDO *has placed the child he was carrying at his side. She snuggles close to him.*

DOCTOR (*to the child*): Uncle Doctor has some candy for you.
Come here!

He takes a bag from his pocket. The child reaches out eagerly.

THE GIRL (*shyly*): Thank you.

The DOCTOR *picks up the little girl and attempts to seat her on the bench. But the child scrambles off and clings to* RICCARDO.

DOCTOR (*scornfully*): So affectionate!
(*Pleasantly, to the child.*) What's your name?

The child does not answer.

A pity the little girl has no twin brother.
Research on twins is my special hobby.
Other children here never live
more than six hours, even when we're rushed.
Nor their mothers either—we have enough workhorses
and we're sufficiently accommodating
to gas children under fifteen
together with their mothers.
It saves a lot of screaming. What's wrong?
You did say you knew what we do here.
RICCARDO (*hoarse from horror*): Get it over with.

DOCTOR: Don't tell me you want to die right now!
   You'd like that, wouldn't you:
   inhaling for fifteen minutes, and then
   sitting at God's right hand as saint! No!
   I cannot give you such preferential treatment
   while so many others
   go up in smoke without that consolation.
   As long as you can *believe,* my dear priest,
   dying is just a joke.

A scuffle in the background; the deportees are being made to move forward. The line advances. Signora LUCCANI *tries to break out of it, to go to* RICCARDO. *She screams:*

JULIA: Let us stay together.
   I won't.—My child!

A Kapo runs up and tries to push her back into the line. LUC-
CANI *clumsily intervenes.*

LUCCANI: Don't! Don't hit the women. Don't hit their children.

The little GIRL *tries to pull* RICCARDO *over to her mother.* RICCARDO
hesitates. The DOCTOR *interferes.*

DOCTOR: Let her go!
   (*To* JULIA.) What's this weeping over a brief separation?

The deportees move forward; old LUCCANI *tries to stay back, is pushed on. He calls out in a feeble voice:*

LUCCANI: Julia—Julia—I'm waiting—do come.

He is pushed out of sight. The whole group, including the MANU-
FACTURER, *who is supporting old* LUCCANI, *and a pregnant woman, disappear off right. The back of the stage is left empty. Soon the cement mixer falls silent.*

JULIA (*pleading with the* DOCTOR):
   Let us stay with the priest! You can see
   how attached the child is to him.

He calmed us so on the train. Please,
let us die together, the priest and us—
DOCTOR (*to* JULIA): Now, now, nobody's dying here.
(*To* RICCARDO.) Tell the woman the truth!
That those are factory chimneys over there.
You'll have to turn out work here, work hard.
But nobody will do you any harm.
(*He strokes the little boy's hair reassuringly.*)
Come along, my boy. It's time for lunch,
and there's pudding for dessert.
JULIA (*a moment before half-mad with fear, is now full of
confidence in the* DOCTOR):
Do you know where my husband is?
Where my husband was taken to?
DOCTOR: Run along now. Here, take your sister with you.
Your husband? Still in Rome, I think.
Or perhaps in another camp.
I don't know everybody here.
(*To* RICCARDO.) Let go—give the woman her child!
(*To* JULIA.) Here, take your little girl.
The priest and I have some things to discuss.
JULIA (*to* RICCARDO): Stay with us, please stay!
You disappeared so suddenly this morning,
were gone so long.
I was so relieved when you returned.
RICCARDO (*strokes the little girl, kisses her and gives her to her
mother*) : I'll come afterwards—I'll come,
as surely as God is with us.
DOCTOR: Please, now—in fifteen minutes
your friend will be with you again.

He beckons to the Kapo, who herds the family along.

Those who don't keep up
get nothing more to eat.
Hurry—move on!

All go out except the DOCTOR *and* RICCARDO. RICCARDO *sways. The*
DOCTOR *addresses him patronizingly:*

You're very tired, I see.
Do sit down.

*He points to the bench and walks back and forth with little tripping
steps.* RICCARDO, *exhausted, sits down.*

RICCARDO: What a devil you are!
DOCTOR (*extremely pleased*): Devil—wonderful! I am the devil.
And you will be my private chaplain.
It's a deal: save my soul.
But first I must see to those scratches.
Oh dear—however did it happen?

While the DOCTOR *goes into the hut,* RICCARDO *remains seated
on the bench, holding the bloodstained handkerchief to his forehead to check the flow. The* DOCTOR, *in the doorway, calls:*

Come here, I have great plans for you,
Chaplain.
RICCARDO: What do you want of me?
DOCTOR: I mean my offer seriously.
Do you really know what awaits you otherwise?

He goes inside the hut, and is rummaging in a medicine chest.
RICCARDO *has dragged himself up the steps. He drops into the
nearest chair. The* DOCTOR *applies a dressing and adhesive tape
to his wounds, meanwhile saying reassuringly, and almost seriously:*

Not long ago the brutal idiots here
had their fun with a certain Polish priest
who said he wanted to die in place
of another prisoner—a man with a family.
A voluntary offering, in short, like yours.
They kept him in a starvation cell ten days,
then even put a barbed wire crown on him.
Oh well, he had what he wanted, what your kind wants:
suffering in Christ—and Rome
will surely canonize him some day.
He died as an individual,
a fine, old-fashioned, personal death.

You, my dear friend, would be merely gassed.
Quite simply gassed, and *no one,*
no man, Pope or God, will ever find out.
At best you may be missed
like an enlisted man on the Volga,
or a U-boat sailor in the Atlantic.
If you insist on it, you'll die here
like a snail crushed under an auto tire—
die as the heroes of today do die, namelessly,
snuffed out by powers they have never known,
let alone can fight. In other words, meaninglessly.

RICCARDO (*scornfully*) :
Do you think God would overlook a sacrifice,
merely because the killing is done
without pomp and circumstance?
Your ideas can't be as primitive as that!

DOCTOR: Aha, you think God does not overlook
the sacrifice! Really?
You know, at bottom all my work's concerned
entirely with this one question. Really, now,
I'm doing all I can.
Since July of '42, for fifteen months,
weekdays and Sabbath, I've been sending people to God.
Do you think He's made the slightest acknowledgement?
He has not even directed
a bolt of lightning against me.
Can you understand that? *You* ought to know.
Nine thousand in one day a while back.

RICCARDO (*groans, says against his better knowledge*) :
That isn't true, it can't be. . . .

DOCTOR (*calmly*) : Nine thousand in one day. Pretty little
vermin, like that child you were holding.
All the same, in an hour they're unconscious or dead.
At any rate ready for the furnace.
Young children often go into the furnaces
still alive, though unconscious. An
interesting phenomenon. Infants, especially.
A remarkable fact: the gas doesn't always kill them.

RICCARDO *covers his face with his hand. Then he rushes to the door. Laughing, the* DOCTOR *pulls him back.*

DOCTOR: You cannot always run away.
　　Stop trembling like that. My word of honor,
　　I'll let you *live.* . . . What difference does it make
　　to me, one item more or less
　　puffing up the chimney.
RICCARDO (*screams*): Live—to be *your* prisoner!
DOCTOR: Not my prisoner. My partner.
RICCARDO: I assure you leaving a world
　　in which you and Auschwitz are possible,
　　is scarcely harder than to live in it.
DOCTOR: The martyr always prefers dying to thinking.
　　Paul Valery was right. The angel,
　　he said—who knows, you may be an angel—
　　(*laughs*) is distinguishable from me, the devil,
　　only by the act of thought that still awaits him.
　　I shall expose you to the task of thinking
　　like a swimmer to the ocean.
　　If your cassock keeps you above water
　　then I promise I'll let you fetch me
　　back home into the bosom of Christ's Church.
　　(*Laughs.*) Who knows, who knows. But first you have to
　　　practice
　　the celebrated patience of Negation.
　　First you can watch me for a year or so
　　conducting this, the boldest experiment
　　that man has ever undertaken.
　　Only a theological mind like my own—
　　(*he taps* RICCARDO's *clerical collar*)
　　I too once wore the iron collar for a while—
　　could risk loading himself with
　　such a burden of sacrilege.
RICCARDO (*beating his forehead in despair, cries*):
　　Why . . . why? Why do you do it?
DOCTOR: Because I wanted an answer!
　　And so I've ventured what no man

has ever ventured since the beginning of the world.
I took the vow to challenge the Old Gent,
to provoke Him so limitlessly
that He would have to give an answer.
Even if only the negative answer
which can be His sole excuse, as
Stendhal put it: that He doesn't exist.

RICCARDO (*bitingly*) : A medical student's joke—for which millions
are paying with their lives. Can it be
that you are not even a criminal?
Are you only a lunatic? As primitive
as Virchow when he said he had dissected
ten thousand cadavers and never found a soul?

DOCTOR (*offended*): Soul! Now *that's* what I call primitive!
What utter flippancy to be forever
taking cover behind such empty words!
(*He imitates a priest praying.*)
Credo quia absurdum est—still?
(*Seriously.*) Well, hear the answer: not a peep
came from Heaven, not a peep
for fifteen months,
not once since I've been giving tourists
tickets to Paradise.

RICCARDO (*ironically*) : So much sheer cruelty—merely to do
what every harmless schoolmaster manages
without all this effort,
if he happens to be stupid enough
to want to prove that the Incomprehensible
isn't there.

DOCTOR: Then do you find it more acceptable
that God in person is turning the human race
on the spit of history?
History! The final vindication
of God's ways to man? Really?
(*He laughs like a torturer.*)
History: dust and altars, misery and rape,
and all glory a mockery of its victims.
The truth is, Auschwitz refutes
creator, creation, and the creature.

Life as an idea is dead.
This may well be the beginning
of a great new era,
a redemption from suffering.
From this point of view only one crime
remains: cursed be he who creates life.
I cremate life. That is modern
humanitarianism—the sole salvation from the future.
I mean that seriously, even on the personal level.
Out of pity, I have always buried
my own children right away—in condoms.
RICCARDO (*attempts mockery, but shouts in order to keep himself
from weeping*) : Redemption from suffering! A lecture
on humanism from a homicidal maniac!
Save someone—save just a single child!
DOCTOR (*calmly*) : What gives priests the right to look down on
the SS?
We are the Dominicans of the technological age.
It is no accident that so many of my kind,
the leaders, come from good Catholic homes.
Heydrich was a Jew—all right.
Eichmann and Göring are Protestants.
But Hitler, Goebbels, Bormann, Kaltenbrunner. . . ?
Höss, our commandant, studied for the priesthood.
And Himmler's uncle, who stood godfather to him,
is nothing less than Suffragan Bishop in Bamberg!
(*He laughs.*) The Allies have solemnly sworn
to hang us all if they should catch us.
So after the war, it's only logical,
the SS tunic will become
a shroud for gallows birds.
The Church, however, after centuries
of killing heretics throughout the West
now sets itself up as the exclusive
moral authority of this Continent.
Absurd! Saint Thomas Aquinas, a mystic,
a god-crazed visionary like Heinrich Himmler,
who also babbles well-meant nonsense,
Thomas condemned the innocent for heresy

just as these morons here condemn the Jews . . . .
But you do not cast him out of your temple!
The readers that they use in German schools
in centuries to come may well reprint
the speeches Himmler made in honor of
the mothers of large families—why not?
(*He is royally amused.*)
A civilization that commits
its children's souls into the safeguard
of a Church responsible for the Inquisition
comes to the end that it deserves
when for its funeral pyres it plucks
the brands from our furnaces for human bodies.
Do you admit that? Of course not.
(*Spits and pours a glass of brandy for himself.*)
One of us is honest—the other credulous.
(*Malignantly.*)
Your Church was the first to show
that you can burn men just like coke.
In Spain alone, without the benefit of crematoria,
you turned to ashes three hundred and fifty thousand
human beings, most of them while alive, mind you.
Such an achievement surely needs the help of Christ.

RICCARDO (*furious, loudly*) :
I know as well as you—or I would not be here—
how many times the Church has been guilty,
as it is again today. I have nothing more to say
if you make God responsible
for the crimes of His Church.
God does not stand *above* history.
He shares the fate of the natural order.
In Him all man's anguish is contained.

DOCTOR (*interrupting*): Oh yes, I also learned that drivel once.
His suffering in the world fetters the evil principle.
Prove it. Where—when have I ever been fettered?
Luther did not fool himself so badly.
Not man, he said, but God
hangs, tortures, strangles, wars. . . .

Laughing, he slaps RICCARDO *on the back.* RICCARDO *shrinks from him.*

Your anger amuses me—you'll make a good partner.
I saw that right off. You'll help in the laboratory,
and at night we'll wrangle
about that product of neurosis
which for the present you call God
or about some other philosophical rot.

RICCARDO: I don't intend to act your court jester,
to cheer the hours when you are
face to face with your own self.
I have never seen a man so wretched,
for you know what you do. . . .

DOCTOR (*painfully jarred*) :
Then I must disappoint you once again.
Just as your whole faith is self-deception
and desperation, so is your hope
that I feel wretched. Of course
boredom has always plagued me.
That is why I find our dispute so refreshing,
and why you are to stay alive.
But wretched? No. At present I
am studying *homo sapiens*. Yesterday I watched
one of the workers at the crematorium.
As he was chopping up the cadavers
to get them through the furnace doors
he discovered the body of his wife.
How did he react?

RICCARDO: You do not look as if this study
made you especially cheerful . . . .
I think you too feel
no easier than that worker.

DOCTOR: Don't I? Well then, I still have my books.
Napoleon, as you know, remarked to Metternich
he did not give a damn about
the death of a million men. I've just been
investigating how long it was before

that scoundrel became the idol of posterity.
Quite relevant, in view of Hitler's. . . .
Of course, that disgusting vegetarian has not,
like Napoleon, seduced all of his sisters.
He's quite devoid of such endearing traits.
All the same I find him more likable—

He picks up a book; the name "Hegel" is on the cover.

than the philosophers who squeeze
the horrors of world history
through countless convolutions of their brains,
until at last they look acceptable.
I was recently rereading Nietzsche,
that eternal schoolboy, because a colleague of mine
had the honor of delivering to Mussolini
Herr Hitler's present on his sixtieth birthday.

Laughs piercingly.

Just think: The complete works of Nietzsche
on *Bible* paper.
RICCARDO: Is Nietzsche to blame
if weak-headed visionaries, brutes and murderers
have stolen his legacy?
Only madmen take him literally. . . .
DOCTOR: Right, only madmen, men of action.
It suits *them* perfectly that Nietzsche
looked to the beasts of prey for his criterion
of manly virtues—
presumably because he himself
had so little of the beast in him,
not even enough to lay a girl.
Grosteque: the Blond Beast, or,
The Consequences of Crippling Inhibitions,
comes down to: a massacre of millions.
(He chuckles.)
No, what captivated Hitler was certainly not
the finest critical mind in Europe.

What Hitler fell for was the Beast, the
beautiful beast of prey.
No wonder, when the inventor of that monstrosity
wrote in language so intoxicated,
and with such sovereign arrogance, it seemed
he had champagne instead of ink in his pen.
(Abruptly.)
You can have champagne here too, and girls.
This afternoon when those people there,
the ones you came with,
burn up in smoke,
I shall be burning up myself
between the legs of a nineteen-year-old girl.
That's one amenity that beats your faith
because it's something a fellow really has,
with heart, mouth and hands.
And has it here on earth, where we need such things.
But of course you know all that. . . .

RICCARDO *(casually)*: Oh yes, a fine amenity . . .
only it doesn't last too long.

DOCTOR *(draws on his gloves, smiles with something close to
triumph)*: We understand each other splendidly.
You'll have two nice girls in the laboratory.
I suppose the newest books will interest you more.
Habent sua fata divini—the saints
fall on their faces.
The light of reason falls on the Gospels.
I made a pilgrimage last year to Marburg,
to hear Bultmann. Daring, for a theologian,
the way he throws out the clutter in the New Testament.
Even evangelism no longer asks men to believe
the mythical cosmogony of the past.

*During these last sentences the rumble of the cement mixer resumes.
As yet, no more deportees are visible. But upstage, far right, the
glare of a mighty fire rises once more, high and menacing. Shrill
whistles.* RICCARDO *has leaped to his feet. He wrenches the door
open and runs outside. He points to the underworld light and cries
out contemptuously, as the* DOCTOR *slowly follows him—*

RICCARDO: Here—there—I'm in the midst of it.
What need have I of believing
in Heaven or Hell.

He comes closer to the DOCTOR, *speaks in a lower voice.*

You know that. You know that even St. John
did not see the Last Judgment as a cosmic event.

Loudly, flinging the insult at the DOCTOR.

Your hideous face
composed of lust and filth and gibberish
sweeps all doubts away—all. Since
the devil exists, God also exists.
Otherwise *you* would have won a long time ago.
DOCTOR *(grips his arms, laughs ebulliently):*
That's the way I like you. The idealist's St. Vitus dance.

He grips him by both arms as RICCARDO *attempts to run off to another group of deportees who have appeared and are now stand-ing silently, with only a* KAPO *prowling around them. The* DOCTOR *forces* RICCARDO, *whose strength quickly deserts him, down on the bench.* RICCARDO *covers his face with his hands, resting his fore-arms on his knees. The* DOCTOR *places his foot on the bench beside* RICCARDO *and says chummily:*

All tensed up. You're trembling. So scared
you can't stand on your feet.
RICCARDO *(shrinks back because the* DOCTOR's *face has come too close to him. Sick at heart, he says):*
I never said that I was not afraid.
Courage or not—in the end
that is only a question of vanity.
DOCTOR *(while* RICCARDO *scarcely listens, for he has his eyes fixed on the waiting victims):*
I gave my word that nothing would be done to you.
I need you for a purpose of my own . . . .
The war is lost; the Allies will hang me.

You find me a refuge in Rome, a monastery.
The Commandant will even thank me
if I personally return to Rome
the Holy Father's guest, whom we
did not exactly invite to come here. Agreed?
One moment.

He goes toward the hut, looks around.

RICCARDO *(as in a dream):* To Rome? I am—to go back to Rome?
DOCTOR: We'll have a fine drive to Breslau.

He goes to the telephone in the hut, dials, listens, hangs up, meanwhile saying, half to RICCARDO, *half into the receiver:*

With a girl as blond as sunlight
and our own personal deputy of Christ.
Helga, hello! Helga? Asleep already . . . .
And you'll be back with Pius.

He leaves the hut. RICCARDO *is shaking with emotion.*

RICCARDO: No—never! You only want me to try to run away.
I would not get a hundred yards. You want
to say I was shot trying to escape.
DOCTOR *(takes out his wallet and shows him a passport):*
Only natural for you to mistrust my offer.
But look at this. Is this a passport from the Holy See?
RICCARDO: So it is—where did it come from?
DOCTOR: Only the personal data are missing.
I'll fill those out as needed. Now our agreement:
You find me a place to stay in Rome
until I can escape to South America.
RICCARDO: How can you hope to desert?
Rome is occupied by the German army.
DOCTOR: For that very reason it's so easy
for me to make a pilgrimage there.
With a perfectly legitimate travel order.
I'll be there in a week—then with your help
I go underground. Agreed?

RICCARDO *remains silent.*

DOCTOR *(impatiently, insistently, persuasively):*
   Why—are you still thinking only of yourself,
   of your soul, as you call it?
   Go to Rome and hang your message
   on St. Peter's bell.
RICCARDO *(haltingly):* How could I tell the Pope anything new?
   Details, of course. But that the Jews
   are being gassed in Poland—the whole world
   has known that for a year.
DOCTOR: Yes—but the Deputy of Christ
   should speak out. Why is he silent?
   (Eagerly.) You couldn't yet have heard the news:
   last week two or three bombs
   which killed nobody, fell in the Vatican gardens.
   For days that's been the great sensation
   all over the world!
   The Americans, the British, and the Germans
   are all desperately trying to prove
   that they could not have been the culprits.
   There you have it again: the Pope is sacred
   even to heretics. Make use of that.
   Demand that he—what's wrong with you?
   Sit down.

He grips RICCARDO's *shoulder.* RICCARDO *has collapsed on to the bench.*

You're whiter than the walls of a gas chamber.

Pause.

RICCARDO *(on the bench, with effort):*
   I *have* already asked the Pope to protest.
   But he is playing politics.
   My father stood by me—my father.
DOCTOR *(with infernal laughter):*
   Politics! Yes, that's what he's good for,
   the windbag.

RICCARDO *(for a moment seems to be elsewhere. Then,*
still lost in thought): Let us not judge him.

During these last sentences the cement mixer has stopped. Upstage
right, from the direction of the fires, comes the shrilling of whistles.
The KAPO *drives the waiting victims off to the right—the procedure*
should be exactly the same as the last walk of the Luccanis and
the other Italians. The DOCTOR *blows his whistle to summon the*
KAPO; the deportees have vanished down the ramp; the reflection
of the flames leaps very high.

KAPO *(comes back, stands at attention):* Major!
DOCTOR *(indicating* RICCARDO):
  This fellow goes along to the crematorium.
  No jokes with him, understand.
  He is my personal patient.
  He's to work there.
  (Ironically, to RICCARDO.)
  I will not forget you, Father.
  You'll have plenty to eat,
  and a normal workday of about nine hours.
  You can engage in studies there,
  theological studies. Find out about God.
  In two weeks I'll take you into the laboratory,
  as my assistant, if you wish.
  I'm sure you will.
  (To the KAPO.) On your ashes: not a hair,
  not a hair of his head is to be touched.
  I'll talk to your superior later.
  Now beat it.
KAPO: *Jawohl, Sturmbannführer!*

He goes off, right, with RICCARDO, *down the ramp. The* DOCTOR
stands motionlessly watching them.

7. *YOSSEL RAKOVER'S*
APPEAL TO GOD

ZVI KOLITZ

Zvi Kolitz, who co-produced Hochhuth's *The Deputy* in New York, has studied the Shoah and its implications for many years. In his quest for meaning, he came to know the story of the Rakovers, a family of Chasidim who were wiped out by the Nazis. And he wondered: How would a Chasid, a pious Jew of Eastern Europe filled with the spirit of men like Levi Yitzchak of Berditchev—how would such a Jew address himself to God at this time? There is no actual document written by Yossel Rakover. But there was a Yossel Rakover who died in the flames. And there is the tradition of those who trust in God though He slay them. And Kolitz's reconstruction of the last thoughts of a pious Jew has become a small classic which has been utilized in the Yom Kippur liturgy of university students at Yale and elsewhere. If we say with Zvi Kolitz that Jews did pray in this manner in those final days, one question remains: Can we, the survivors, pray in the same manner?

In the ruins of the Ghetto of Warsaw, among heaps of charred rubbish, there was found, packed tightly into a small bottle, the following testament, written during the ghetto's last hours by a Jew named Yossel Rakover.

WARSAW, APRIL 28, 1943

I, Yossel, son of David Rakover of Tarnopol, a Chasid of the Rabbi of Ger and a descendant of the great and pious families of Rakover

Reprinted by permission of the author.

and Meisel, inscribe these lines as the houses of the Warsaw Ghetto go up in flames. The house I am in is one of the last unburnt houses remaining. For several hours an unusually heavy artillery barrage has been crashing down on us, and the walls are disintegrating under the fire. It will not be long before the house I am in is transformed, like almost every other house of the ghetto, into a grave for its defenders. By the dagger-sharp, unusually crimson rays of the sun that strikes through the small, half-walled-up window of my room through which I have been shooting at the enemy day and night, I see that it must now be late afternoon, just before sundown, and I cannot regret that this is the last sun that I shall see. All of our notions and emotions have been altered. Death, swift and immediate, seems to us a liberator, sundering our shackles, and beasts of the field, even if their freedom exceeds their gentleness, seem to me to be so lovable and dear that I feel deep pain whenever I hear the evil fiends that lord it over Europe referred to as beasts. It is untrue that the tyrant who rules Europe now has something of the beast in him. Oh, No! He is a typical child of modern man; mankind as whole spawned him and reared him. He is merely frankest expression of its innermost, most deeply buried instincts.

In a forest where I once hid, I encountered a dog one night, sick and hungry, his tail between his legs. Both of us immediately felt the kinship of our situation. He cuddled up to me, buried his head in my lap, and licked my hands. I do not know if I ever cried so much as that night. I threw my arms around his neck, crying like a baby. If I say that I envied the animals at that moment, it would not be remarkable. But what I felt was more than envy. It was shame. I felt ashamed before the dog to be a man. That is how matters stand. That is the spiritual level to which we have sunk. Life is a tragedy, death a savior; man a calamity, the beast an ideal; the day a horror, the night—relief.

When my wife, my children and I—six in all—hid in the forest, it was the night and the night alone that concealed us in its bosom. The day turned us over to our persecutors and murderers. I remember with the most painful clarity the day when the Germans raked with a hail of fire the thousands of refugees on the highway from Grodno to Warsaw. As the sun rose, the airplanes zoomed over us and the whole day long they murdered us. In this massacre, my wife with our seven months old child in her arms perished. Two of my five remaining children also disappeared that day without a trace. Their names were David and Yehuda, one was four years old, the other six.

At sunset, the handful of survivors continued their journey in the direction of Warsaw, and I, with my three remaining children, started out to comb the fields and woods at the site of the massacre in search of the children. The entire night we called for them, but only echoes replied. I never saw my two children again, and later, in a dream, I was told that they were in God's hands.

My other three children died in the space of a single year in the Warsaw Ghetto. Rachel, my daughter of ten, heard that it was possible to find scraps of bread in the public dump outside the ghetto walls. The ghetto was starving at the time, and the people who died of starvation lay in the streets like heaps of rags. The people of the ghetto were prepared to face any death but the death of hunger. Against no death did they struggle so fiercely as against death by starvation.

My daughter, Rachel, told me nothing of her plan to steal out of the ghetto, which was punishable by death. She and a girl friend of the same age started out on the perilous journey. She left home under cover of darkness, and at sunrise she and her friend were caught outside the ghetto walls. Nazi ghetto guards, together with dozens of their Polish underlings, at once started in pursuit of those two Jewish children who dared to venture out to hunt for a piece of bread in a garbage can. People witnessing the chase could not believe their eyes. It was unusual even in the ghetto. It looked like a pursuit of dangerous criminals. A horde of fiends run amok in pursuit of a pair of starved ten year old children did not endure very long in the unequal match. One of them, my child, running with her last ounce of strength, fell exhausted to the ground and the Nazis put a bullet through her head. The other child saved herself, but, driven out of her mind, died two weeks later.

The fifth child, Yacob, a boy of thirteen, died on his Bar Mitzvah day of tuberculosis. The last child, my fifteen-year old daughter, Chaya, perished during a Kinderaktion—a children's operation—that began at sunrise last Rosh Hashanah and ended at sundown. That day, before sunset, hundreds of Jewish families lost their children.

Now my time has come. And like Job, I can say of myself, nor am I the only one that can say it, that I return to the soil naked, as naked as the day of my birth.

I am forty-three years old, and when I look back on the past I can assert confidently, as confident as a man can be of himself, that I have lived a respectable, upstanding life, my heart full of love for God. I was once blessed with success, but never boasted of it. My possessions were extensive. My house was open to the needy. I served God enthusiastically, and my single request to Him was that He should allow me to worship Him with all my heart, and all my soul, and all my strength.

I cannot say that my relationship to God has remained unchanged after everything I have lived through, but I can say with absolute certainty that my belief in Him has not changed by a hair's breadth. Previously, when I was happy and well off, my relation to God was as to one who granted me a favor for nothing, and I was eternally obliged to Him for it. Now my relations to Him are as to one who owes me something, too, who owes me very much in fact, and since I feel so, I believe I have the right to demand it of Him. But I do not say like Job that God should point out my sin with His finger so that I may know why I deserve this; for greater and saintlier men than I are now firmly convinced that it is not a question of punishing sinners: something entirely different is taking place in the world. It is, namely, a time when God has veiled His Countenance from the world, sacrificing mankind to its wild instincts. This, however, does not mean that the pious members of my people should justify the edict, saying that God and His judgments are correct. For to say that we deserve the blows we have received is to malign ourselves, to desecrate the Holy Name of God's children. And those who desecrate our name desecrate the Name of the Lord; God is maligned by our self-deprecation.

In a situation like this, I naturally expect no miracles, nor do I ask Him, my Lord, to show me mercy. May He treat me with the same indifference with which He treated millions of His people. I am no exception, and I expect no special treatment. I will no longer attempt to save myself, nor flee anymore. I will facilitate the work of the fire by moistening my clothing with gasoline. I have three bottles of gasoline left after having emptied several scores over the heads of the murderers. It was one of the finest moments of my life when I did this, and I was shaken with laughter by it. I never dreamed that the death of people, even of enemies—even such enemies—could cause me such great pleasure. Foolish humanists may say what they choose. Vengeance was and always will be the last means of waging just battles and the greatest spiritual release of the oppressed. I had never until now understood the precise meaning of the expression in the Talmud which states that, Vengeance is sacred because it is mentioned between two of God's names: A God of Vengeance is the Lord. I understand it now. I know now, moreover, why my heart is so overjoyed at remembering that for thousands of years we have been calling our Lord a God of Vengeance: A God of Vengeance is our Lord! We have had only a few opportunities to witness true vengeance. When we did, however, it was so good, so worthwhile, I felt such profound happiness, so terribly fortunate—that for a moment it seemed an entirely new life was springing up in me. A tank had suddenly broken in our street. It was bombarded with flying bottles of gasoline from all the embattled houses. They failed to hit their target, however, and the tank continued to approach. My friends and I waited until the tank was almost upon us. Then, through the half bricked-up window, we suddenly attacked. The tank soon burst into flames, and six blazing Nazis jumped out. Ah, how they burned! They burned like the Jews they had set on fire. But they shrieked more. Jews do not shriek. They welcome death like a savior. The Warsaw Ghetto perishes in battle. It is going down shooting, struggling, blazing, but not shrieking!

I have three more bottles of gasoline. They are as precious to me as wine to a drunkard. After pouring one over my clothes, I will place the paper on which I write these lines in the empty bottle and hide it among the bricks filling the window of this room. If anyone ever finds it and reads it, he will, perhaps, understand the emotions of a Jew, one of millions, who died forsaken by the God in Whom he believed unshakably. I will let the two other bottles explode on the heads of the murderers when my last moment comes.

There were twelve of us in this room at the outbreak of the rebellion. For nine days we battled against the enemy. All eleven of my comrades have fallen, dying silently in battle, including the small boy of about five—who came here only God knows how and who now lies dead near me, with his face wearing the kind of smile that appears on children's faces when dreaming peacefully—even this child died with the same epic calm as his older comrades. It happened early this morning. Most of us were dead already. The boy scaled the heap of corpses to catch a glimpse of the outside world through the window. He stood beside me in that position for several minutes. Suddenly he fell backwards, rolling down the pile of corpses, and lay like a stone. On his small, pale forehead, between the locks of black hair, there was a spattering of blood.

Up until yesterday morning, when the enemy launched a concentrated barrage against this stronghold, one of the last in the ghetto, every one of us was still alive, although five were wounded. During yesterday and today, all the rest fell, one after the other, one on top of the other, watching and firing until shot to death. I have no more ammunition, apart from the three bottles of gasoline. From the floors of the house above still come frequent shots, but they can hold out no more hope for them, for by all signs the stairway has been razed by the shell fire, and I think the house is about to collapse. I write these lines lying on the floor. Around me lie my dead comrades. I look into their faces, and it seems to me that a quiet but mocking irony animates them, as if they were saying to me, 'A little patience, you foolish man, another few minutes and everything will become clear to you too.' This irony is particularly noticeable on the face of the small boy lying near my right hand as if he were asleep. His small mouth is drawn into a smile exactly as if he were laughing, and I, who still live and feel and think—it seems to me that he is laughing at me. He laughs with that quiet but eloquent laughter so characteristic of the wise speaking of knowledge with the ignorant who believe, as ignorants always do, they know everything. Yes, he is omniscient now. Everything is clear to the boy now. He even knows why he was born, but had to die so soon—why he died only five years after his birth. And even if he does not know why, he knows at least that it is entirely unimportant and insignificant whether or not he knows it, in the light of that Godly majesty which shines over him in the better world he now inhabits, and in the arms of his murdered parents to whom he has returned. In an hour or two I will make the same discovery. Unless my face is eaten by the flames, a similar smile may rest on it after my death. Meanwhile, I still live, and before my death I wish to speak to my Lord as a living man, a simple, living person who had the great but tragic honor of being a Jew.

I am proud that I am a Jew not in spite of the world's treatment of us, but precisely because of this treatment. I should be ashamed to belong to the people who spawned and raised the criminals who are responsible for the deeds that have been perpetrated against us or to any people who tolerated these deeds.

I am proud to be a Jew because it is an art to be a Jew. It is no art to be an Englishman, an American or a Frenchman. It may be easier, more comfortable to be one of them, but not more honorable. Yes, it is an honor, a terrible honor to be a Jew!

I believe that to be a Jew means to be a fighter, an everlasting swimmer against the turbulent human current. The Jew is a hero, a martyr, a saint. You, our evil enemies, declare that we are bad. I believe that we are better and finer than you, but even if we were worse, I should like to see how you would look in our place!

I am happy to belong to the unhappiest of all peoples of the world, whose precepts represent the loftiest and most beautiful of all morality and laws. These immortal precepts which we possess have now been even more sanctified and immortalized by the fact that they have been so debased and insulted by the enemies of the Lord.

I believe that to be a Jew is an inborn trait. One is born a Jew exactly as one is born an artist. It is impossible to be released from being a Jew. That is our Godly attribute that has made us a chosen people. Those who do not understand this will never understand the higher meaning of our martyrdom. If I ever doubted that God once designated us as the chosen people, I would believe now that our tribulations have made us the chosen one.

I believe in You, God of Israel, even though You have done everything to stop me from believing in You. I believe in Your laws even if I cannot excuse Your actions. My relationship to You is not the relationship of a slave to his master but rather that of a pupil to his teacher. I bow my head before Your greatness, but I will not kiss the lash with which You strike me.

You say, I know, that we have sinned, O Lord. It must surely be true! And therefore we are punished? I can understand that too! But I should like You to tell me whether *there is any sin in the world deserving of such a punishment as the punishment we have received?*

You assert that you will yet repay our enemies? I am convinced of it! Repay them without mercy? I have no doubt of that either! I should like You to tell me, however—*is there any punishment in the world capable of compensating for the crimes that have been committed against us?*

You say, I know, that it is no longer a question of sin and punishment, but rather a situation in which Your countenance is veiled, in which humanity is abandoned to its evil instincts. But I should like to ask You, O Lord—and this question burns in me like a consuming fire—*what more, O, what more must transpire before You unveil Your countenance again to the world?*

I want to say to You that now, more than in any previous period of our eternal path of agony, we, we the tortured, the humiliated, the buried alive and burned alive, we the insulted, the mocked, the lonely, the forsaken by God and man—we have the right to know *what are the limits of Your forebearance?*

I should like to say something more: Do not put the rope under too much strain, lest, alas, it snaps! The test to which You have put us is so severe, so unbearably severe, that You should—You must—forgive those members of Your people who, in their misery, have turned from You.

Forgive those who have turned from You in their misery, but also those who have turned from You in their happiness. You have transformed our life into such a frightful, perpetual ordeal that the cowards among us have been forced to flee from it; and what is happiness but a place of refuge for cowards? Do not chastise them for it. One does not strike cowards, but has mercy on them. Have mercy on *them,* rather than *us,* O Lord.

Forgive those who have desecrated Your name, who have gone over to the service of other gods, who have become indifferent to You. You have castigated them so severely that they no longer believe that You are their Father, that they have any Father at all.

I tell You this because I do believe in You, because I believe in You more strongly than ever, because now I know that You are my Lord, because after all You are not, You cannot possibly be after all the God of those whose deeds are the most horrible expression of ungodliness!

If You are not *my* Lord, then whose Lord are You? The Lord of the murderers?

If those that hate me and murder me are so benighted, so evil, what then am I if not he who relects something of Your light, of Your goodness?

I cannot extol You for the deeds that You tolerate. I bless You and extol You, however, for the very fact of Your existence, for Your awesome mightiness!

The murderers themselves have already passed sentence on themselves and will never escape it, but may You carry out a doubly severe sentence on those who are condoning the murder.

Those who condemn murder orally, but rejoice at it in their hearts . . . . Those who meditate in their foul hearts: It is fitting, after all, to say that he is evil, the tyrant, but he carries out a bit of work for us for which we will always be grateful to him!

It is written in Your Torah that a thief should be punished more severely than a brigand, in spite of the fact that the thief does not attack his victim physically and merely attempts to take his possessions stealthily.

The reason for this is that a robber by attacking his victim in broad daylight shows no more fear of man than of God. The thief, on the other hand, fears man, but not God. His punishment, therefore, is greater.

I should be satisfied if You dealt with the murderers as with brigands, for their attitude towards You and towards us is the same.

But those who are silent in the face of murder, those who have no fears of You but fear what people might say (Fools! They are unaware that the people will say nothing!), those who express their sympathy with the drowning man but refuse to rescue him though they can swim—punish them, O Lord, punish them, I implore You, like the thief, with a doubly severe sentence!

Death can wait no longer. From the floors above me, the firing becomes weaker by the minute. The last defenders of this stronghold are now falling, and with them falls and perishes the great, beautiful, and God-fearing Jewish part of Warsaw. The sun is about to set, and I thank God that I will never see it again. Fire lights my small window, and the bit of sky that I can see is flooded with red like a waterfall of blood. In about an hour at the most I will be with the rest of my family and with the millions of other stricken members of my people in that better world where there are no more questions.

I die peacefully, but not complacently; persecuted, but not enslaved; embittered, but not cynical; a believer, but not a supplicant; a lover of God, but no blind amen-sayer of His.

I have followed Him even when He rejected me. I have followed His commandments even when He castigated me for it; I have loved Him and I love Him even when He hurls me to the earth, tortures me to death, makes me an object of shame and ridicule.

My rabbi would frequently tell the story of a Jew who fled from the Spanish Inquisition with his wife and child, striking out in a small boat over the stormy sea until he reached a rocky island where a flash of lightning killed his wife; a storm rose and hurled his son into the sea. Then, as lonely as a stone, naked, barefoot, lashed by the storm and terrified by the thunder and the lightning, hands turned up to God, the Jew, setting out on his journey through the wastes of the island, turned to his Maker with the following words:

God of Israel, I have fled to this place in order to worship You without molestation, to obey Your commandments and sanctify Your name. You, however, have done everything to make me stop believing in You. Now lest it seem to You that You will succeed by these tribulations to drive me from the right path, I notify You, my God and the God of my father, *that it will not avail You in the least!* You may insult me, You may castigate me, You may take from me all that I cherish and hold dear in the world, You may torture me to death—I shall believe in *You,* I shall love You no matter what You do to test me!

And these are my last words to You, my wrathful God: nothing will avail You in the least. You have done everything to make me renounce You, to make me lose my faith in You, but I die exactly as I have lived, a *believer!*

Eternally praised be the God of the dead, the God of vengeance, of truth and of law, Who will soon show His face to the world again and shake its foundations with His almighty voice.

Hear, O Israel, the Lord our God the Lord is One.

Into your hands, O Lord, I consign my soul.

8. *NIGHT*

ELIE WIESEL

From the light of day, we turn back to the night of Auschwitz. Of all the witnesses, Elie Wiesel is the most sensitive one, with the most accurate vision and the clearest recall. And there came a time at Auschwitz, as it came to all other places inside the Holocaust, that the question had to be asked: Where is God? Wiesel answered: He is hanging on the gallows.

———

There were two boys attached to our group: Yossi and Tibi, two brothers. They were Czechs whose parents had been exterminated at Birkenau. They lived, body and soul, for each other.

They and I very soon became friends. Having once belonged to a Zionist youth organization, they knew innumerable Hebrew chants. Thus we would often hum tunes evoking the calm waters of Jordan and the majestic sanctity of Jerusalem. And we would often talk of Palestine. Their parents, like mine, had lacked the courage to wind up their affairs and emigrate while there was still time. We decided that, if we were granted our lives until the liberation, we would not stay in Europe a day longer. We would take the first boat for Haifa.

Still lost in his cabbalistic dreams, Akiba Drumer had discovered a verse in the Bible which, interpreted in terms of numerology, en-

From *Night* by ELIE WIESEL, translated by STELLA RODWAY. Copyright © 1960 by MacGibbon & Kee. Copyright renewed © 1988 by The Collins Publishing Group. Reprinted by permission of Hill and Wang, a division of Farrar, Straus & Giroux, Inc.

abled him to predict that the deliverance was due within the coming weeks. We had left the tents for the musicians' block. We were entitled to a blanket, a wash bowl, and a bar of soap. The head of the block was a German Jew.

It was good to be under a Jew. He was called Alphonse. A young man with an extraordinarily aged face, he was entirely devoted to the cause of "his" block. Whenever he could, he would organize a cauldron of soup for the young ones, the weak, all those who were dreaming more about an extra plateful than of liberty.

One day when we had just come back from the warehouse, I was sent for by the secretary of the block.

"A-7713?"

"That's me."

"After eating, you're to go to the dentist."

"But I haven't got toothache."

"After eating. Without fail."

I went to the hospital block. There were about twenty prisoners waiting in a queue in front of the door. It did not take long to discover why we had been summoned: it was for the extraction of our gold teeth.

The dentist, a Jew from Czechoslovakia, had a face like a death mask. When he opened his mouth, there was a horrible sight of yellow, decaying teeth. I sat in the chair and asked him humbly: "Please, what are you going to do?"

"Simply take out your gold crown," he replied, indifferently.

I had the idea of pretending to be ill.

"You couldn't wait a few days, Doctor? I don't feel very well. I've got a temperature . . . ."

He wrinkled his brow, thought for a moment, and took my pulse.

"All right, son. When you feel better, come back and see me. But don't wait till I send for you!"

I went to see him a week later. With the same excuse: I still did not feel any better. He did not seem to show any surprise, and I do not know if he believed me. He was probably glad to see that I had come back of my own accord, as I had promised. He gave me another reprieve.

A few days after this visit of mine, they closed the dentist's surgery, and he was thrown into prison. He was going to be hanged. It was alleged that he had been running a private traffic of his own in the prisoners' gold teeth. I did not feel any pity for him. I was even pleased about what had happened. I had saved my gold crown. It might be useful to me one day to buy something— bread or life. I now took little interest in anything except my daily plate of soup and my crust of stale bread. Bread, soup— these were my whole life. I was a body. Perhaps less than that even: a starved stomach. The stomach alone was aware of the passage of time.

At the warehouse I often worked next to a young French girl. We did not speak to one another, since she knew no German and I did not understand French.

She seemed to me to be a Jewess, though here she passed as Aryan. She was a forced labor deportee.

One day when Idek was seized with one of his fits of frenzy, I got in his way. He leapt on me, like a wild animal, hitting me in the chest, on the head, throwing me down and pulling me up again, his blows growing more and more violent, until I was covered with blood. As I was biting my lips to stop myself from screaming with pain, he must have taken my silence for defiance, for he went on hitting me even harder.

Suddenly he calmed down. As if nothing had happened, he sent me back to work. It was as though we had been taking part together in some game where we each had our role to play.

I dragged myself to my corner. I ached all over. I felt a cool hand wiping my blood-stained forehead. It was the French girl. She gave me her mournful smile and slipped a bit of bread into my hand. She looked into my eyes. I felt that she wanted to say something but was choked by fear. For a long moment she stayed like that, then her face cleared and she said to me in almost perfect German:

"Bite your lip, little brother. . . . Don't cry. Keep your anger and hatred for another day, for later on. The day will come, but not now. . . .Wait. Grit your teeth and wait. . . ."

Many years later, in Paris, I was reading my paper in the Metro. Facing me was a very beautiful woman with black hair and dreamy yes. I had seen those eyes before somewhere. It was she.

"You don't recognize me?"

"I don't know you."

"In 1944 you were in Germany, at Buna, weren't you?"

"Yes. . . ."

"You used to work in the electrical warehouse. . . ."

"Yes," she said, somewhat disturbed. And then, after a moment's silence: "Wait a minute. . . I do remember. . . ."

"Idek, the Kapo . . . the little Jewish boy . . . your kind words. . . ."

We left the Metro together to sit down on the terrace of a cafe. We spent the whole evening reminiscing.

Before I parted from her, I asked her: "May I ask you a question?"

"I know what it will be—go on."

"What?"

"Am I Jewish . . .? Yes, I am Jewish. From a religious family. During the occupation I obtained forged papers and passed myself off as an Aryan. That's how I was enlisted in the forced labor groups, and when I was deported to Germany, I escaped the concentration camp. At the warehouse, no one knew I could speak German. That would have aroused suspicions. Saying those few words to you was risky: but I knew you wouldn't give me away. . . ."

Another time we had to load Diesel engines onto trains supervised by German soldiers. Idek's nerves were on edge. He was restraining himself with great difficulty. Suddenly, his frenzy broke out. The victim was my father.

"You lazy old devil!" Idek began to yell. "Do you call that work?"

And he began to beat him with an iron bar. At first my father crouched under the blows, then he broke in two, like a dry tree struck by lightning, and collapsed.

I had watched the whole scene without moving. I kept quiet. In fact I was thinking of how to get farther away so that I would not be hit myself. What is more, any anger I felt at that moment was directed, not against the Kapo, but against my father. I was angry with him, for not knowing how to avoid Idek's outbreak. That is what concentration camp life had made of me.

Franek, the foreman, one day noticed the gold-crowned tooth in my mouth.

"Give me your crown, kid."

I told him it was impossible, that I could not eat without it.

"What do they give you to eat, anyway?"

I found another answer: the crown had been put down on a list after the medical inspection. This could bring trouble on us both.

"If you don't give me your crown, you'll pay for it even more."

This sympathetic, intelligent youth was suddenly no longer the same person. His eyes gleamed with desire. I told him I had to ask my father's advice.

"Ask your father, kid. But I want an answer by tomorrow."

When I spoke to my father about it, he turned pale, was silent a long while, and then said:

"No, son, you mustn't do it."

"He'll take it out on us!"

"He won't dare."

But alas, Franek knew where to touch me; he knew my weak point. My father had never done military service, and he never succeeded in marching in step. Here, every time we moved from one place to another in a body, we marched in strict rhythm. This was Franek's chance to torment my father and to thrash him savagely every day. Left, right: punch! Left, right: clout!

I decided to give my father lessons myself, to teach him to change step, and to keep to the rhythm. We began to do exercises in front of our block. I would give the commands: "Left, right!" and my father would practice. Some of the prisoners began to laugh at us.

"Look at this little officer teaching the old chap to march. . . . Hey, general, how many rations of bread does the old boy give you for this?"

But my father's progress was still inadequate, and blows continued to rain down on him.

"So you still can't march in step, you lazy old devil?"

These scenes were repeated for two weeks. We could not stand any more. We had to give in. When the day came, Franek burst into wild laughter.

"I knew it, I knew quite well I would win. Better late than never. And because you've made me wait, that's going to cost you a ration of bread. A ration of bread for one of my pals, a famous dentist from Warsaw, so that he can take your crown out."

"What? *My* ration of bread so that you can have *my* crown?"

Franek grinned.

"What would you like then? Shall I break your teeth with my fist?"

That same evening, in the lavatory the dentist from Warsaw pulled out my crowned tooth with the aid of a rusty spoon.

Franek grew kinder. Occasionally, he even gave me extra soup. But that did not last long. A fortnight later, all the Poles were transferred to another camp. I had lost my crown for nothing.

A few days before the Poles left, I had a new experience.

It was a Sunday morning. Our unit did not need to go to work that day. But all the same Idek would not hear of our staying in the camp. We had to go to the warehouse. This sudden enthusiasm for work left us stunned.

At the warehouse, Idek handed us over to Franek, saying, "Do what you like. But do something. If not, you'll hear from me. . . ."

And he disappeared.

We did not know what to do. Tired of squatting down, we each in turn went for a walk through the warehouse, looking for a bit of bread some civilian might have left behind.

When I came to the back of the building, I heard a noise coming from a little room next door. I went up and saw Idek with a young Polish girl, half-naked, on a mattress. Then I understood why Idek had refused to let us stay in the camp. Moving a hundred prisoners so that he could lie with a girl! It struck me as so funny that I burst out laughing.

Idek leapt up, turned around, and saw me, while the girl tried to cover up her breasts. I wanted to run away, but my legs were glued to the ground. Idek seized me by the throat.

Speaking in a low voice, he said, "You wait and see, kid. . . .You'll soon find out what leaving your work's going to cost you. . . .You're going to pay for this pretty soon. . . .And now, go back to your place."

Half an hour before work usually ended, the Kapo collected together the whole unit. Roll call. Nobody knew what had happened. Roll call at this time of day? Here? But I knew. The Kapo gave a short speech.

"An ordinary prisoner has no right to meddle in other people's affairs. One of you does not seem to have understood this. I'm obliged, therefore, to make it very clear to him once and for all."

I felt the sweat run down my back.

"A-7713!"

I came forward.

"A box!" he ordered.

They brought him a box.

"Lie down on it! On your stomach!"

I obeyed.

Then I was aware of nothing but the strokes of the whip.

"One . . . two . . .," he counted.

He took his time between each stroke. Only the first ones really hurt me. I could hear him counting:

"Ten . . . eleven. . ."

His voice was calm and reached me as through a thick wall.

"Twenty-three. . ."

Two more, I thought, half conscious. The Kapo waited.

"Twenty-four . . . twenty-five!"

It was over. But I did not realize it, for I had fainted. I felt myself come round as a bucket of cold water was thrown over me. I was still lying on the box. I could just vaguely make out the wet ground surrounding me. Then I heard someone cry out. It must have been the Kapo. I began to distinguish the words he was shouting.

"Get up!"

I probably made some movement to raise myself, because I felt myself falling back onto the box. How I longed to get up!

"Get up!" he yelled more loudly.

If only I could have answered him, at least; if only I could have told him that I could not move! But I could not manage to open my lips.

At Idek's command, two prisoners lifted me up and led me in front of him.

"Look me in the eye!"

I looked at him without seeing him. I was thinking of my father. He must have suffered more than I did.

"Listen to me, you bastard!" said Idek, coldly. "That's for your curiosity. You'll get five times more if you dare tell anyone what you saw! Understand?"

I nodded my head, once, ten times. I nodded ceaselessly, as if my head had decided to say yes without ever stopping.

One Sunday, when half of us—including my father—were at work, the rest—including myself—were in the block, taking advantage of the chance to stay in bed late in the morning.

At about ten o'clock, the air-raid sirens began to wail. An alert.

The leaders of the block ran to assemble us inside, while the SS took refuge in the shelters. As it was relatively easy to escape during a warning—the guards left their lookout posts and the electric current was cut off in the barbed-wire fences—the SS had orders to kill anyone found outside the blocks.

Within a few minutes, the camp looked like an abandoned ship. Not a living soul on the paths. Near the kitchen, two cauldrons of steaming hot soup had been left, half full. Two cauldrons of soup, right in the middle of the path, with no one guarding them! A feast for kings, abandoned, supreme temptation! Hundreds of eyes looked at them, sparkling with desire. Two lambs, with a hundred wolves lying in wait for them. Two lambs without a shepherd— a gift. But who would dare?

Terror was stronger than hunger. Suddenly, we saw the door of Block 37 open imperceptibly. A man appeared, crawling like a worm in the direction of the cauldrons.

Hundreds of eyes followed his movements. Hundreds of men crawled with him, scraping their knees with his on the gravel. Every heart trembled, but with envy above all. This man had dared.

He reached the first cauldron. Hearts raced: he had succeeded. Jealousy consumed us, burned us up like straw. We never thought for a moment of admiring him. Poor hero, committing suicide for a ration of soup! In our thoughts we were murdering him.

Stretched out by the cauldron, he was now trying to raise himself up to the edge. Either from weakness or fear he stayed there, trying, no doubt, to muster up the last of his strength. At last he succeeded in hoisting himself onto the edge of the pot. For a moment, he seemed to be looking at himself, seeking his ghostlike reflection in the soup. Then, for no apparent reason, he let out a terrible cry, a rattle such as I had never heard before, and, his mouth open, thrust his head toward the still steaming liquid. We jumped at the explosion. Falling back onto the ground, his face stained with soup, the man writhed for a few seconds at the foot of the cauldron, then he moved no more.

Then we began to hear the airplanes. Almost at once, the barracks began to shake.

"They're bombing Buna!" someone shouted.

I thought of my father. But I was glad all the same. To see the whole works go up in fire—what revenge! We had heard so much talk about the defeats of German troops on various fronts, but we did not know how much to believe. This, today, was real!

We were not afraid. And yet, if a bomb had fallen on the blocks, it alone would have claimed hundreds of victims on the spot. But we were no longer afraid of death; at any rate, not of that death. Every bomb that exploded filled us with joy and gave us new confidence in life.

The raid lasted over an hour. If it could only have lasted ten times ten hours! . . . Then silence fell once more. The last sound of an American plane was lost on the wind, and we found ourselves back again in the cemetery. A great trail of black smoke was rising up on the horizon. The sirens began to wail once more. It was the end of the alert.

Everyone came out of the blocks. We filled our lungs with the fire- and smoke-laden air, and our eyes shone with hope. A bomb had fallen in the middle of the camp, near the assembly point, but it had not gone off. We had to take it outside the camp.

The head of the camp, accompanied by his assistant and the chief Kapo, made a tour of inspection along the paths. The raid had left traces of terror on his face.

Right in the middle of the camp lay the body of the man with the soup-stained face, the only victim. The cauldrons were taken back into the kitchen.

The SS had gone back to their lookout posts, behind their machine guns. The interlude was over.

At the end of an hour, we saw the units come back, in step, as usual. Joyfully, I caught sight of my father.

"Several buildings have been flattened right out," he said, "but the warehouse hasn't suffered."

In the afternoon we went cheerfully to clear away the ruins.

A week later, on the way back from work, we noticed in the center of the camp, at the assembly place, a black gallows.

We were told that soup would not be distributed until after roll call. This took longer than usual. The orders were given in a sharper manner than on other days, and in the air there were strange undertones.

"Bare your heads!" yelled the head of the camp, suddenly.

Ten thousand caps were simultaneously removed.

"Cover your heads!"

Ten thousands caps went back onto their skulls, as quick as lightning.

The gate to the camp opened. An SS section appeared and surrounded us: one SS at every three paces. On the lookout towers the machine guns were trained on the assembly place.

"They fear trouble," whispered Juliek.

Two SS men had gone to the cells. They came back with the condemned man between them. He was a youth from Warsaw. He had three years of concentration camp life behind him. He was a strong, well-built boy, a giant in comparison with me.

His back to the gallows, his face turned toward his judge, who was the head of the camp, the boy was pale, but seemed more moved than afraid. His manacled hands did not tremble. His eyes gazed coldly at the hundreds of SS guards, the thousands of prisoners who surrounded him.

The head of the camp began to read his verdict, hammering out each phrase:

"In the name of Himmler . . . prisoner Number . . . stole during the alert. . . .According to the law . . . paragraph . . . prisoner Number . . . is condemned to death. May this be a warning and an example to all prisoners."

No one moved.

I could hear my heart beating. The thousands who had died daily at Auschwitz and at Birkenau in the crematory ovens no longer troubled me. But this one, leaning against his gallows—he overwhelmed me.

"Do you think this ceremony'll be over soon? I'm hungry. . . ." whispered Juliek.

At a sign from the head of the camp, the Lagerkapo advanced toward the condemned man. Two prisoners helped him in his task—for two plates of soup.

The Kapo wanted to bandage the victim's eyes, but he refused.

After a long moment of waiting, the executioner put the rope round his neck. He was on the point of motioning to his assistants to draw the chair away from the prisoner's feet, when the latter cried, in a calm, strong voice:

"Long live liberty! A curse upon Germany! A curse. . .! A cur—"

The executioners had completed their task.

A command cleft the air like a sword.

"Bare your heads."

Ten thousand prisoners paid their last respects.

"Cover your heads!"

Then the whole camp, block after block, had to march past the hanged man and stare at the dimmed eyes, the lolling tongue of death. The Kapos and heads of each block forced everyone to look him full in the face.

After the march, we were given permission to return to the blocks for our meal.

I remember that I found the soup excellent that evening. . . .

I witnessed other hangings. I never saw a single one of the victims weep. For a long time those dried-up bodies had forgotten the bitter taste of tears.

Except once. The Oberkapo of the fifty-second cable unit was a Dutchman, a giant, well over six feet. Seven hundred prisoners worked under his orders, and they all loved him like a brother. No one had ever received a blow at his hands, nor an insult from his lips.

He had a young boy under him, a *pipel*, as they were called—a child with a refined and beautiful face, unheard of in this camp.

(At Buna, the *pipel* were loathed; they were often crueller than adults. I once saw one of thirteen beating his father because the latter had not made his bed properly. The old man was crying softly while the boy shouted: "If you don't stop crying at once I shan't bring you any more bread. Do you understand?" But the Dutchman's little servant was loved by all. He had the face of a sad angel.)

One day, the electric power station at Buna was blown up. The Gestapo, summoned to the spot, suspected sabotage. They found a trail. It eventually led to the Dutch Oberkapo. And there, after a search, they found an important stock of arms.

The Oberkapo was arrested immediately. He was tortured for a period of weeks, but in vain. He would not give a single name. He was transferred to Auschwitz. We never heard of him again.

But his little servant had been left behind in the camp in prison. Also put to torture, he too would not speak. Then the SS sentenced him to death, with two other prisoners who had been discovered with arms.

One day when we came back from work, we saw three gallows

rearing up in the assembly place, three black crows. Roll call. SS all around us, machine guns trained: the traditional ceremony. Three victims in chains—and one of them, the little servant, the sad-eyed angel.

The SS seemed more preoccupied, more disturbed than usual. To hang a young boy in front of thousands of spectators was no light matter. The head of the camp read the verdict. All eyes were on the child. He was lividly pale, almost calm, biting his lips. The gallows threw its shadow over him.

This time the Lagerkapo refused to act as executioner. Three SS replaced him.

The three victims mounted together onto the chairs.

The three necks were placed at the same moment within the nooses.

"Long live liberty!" cried the two adults.

But the child was silent.

"Where is God? Where is He?" someone behind me asked.

At a sign from the head of the camp, the three chairs tipped over.

Total silence throughout the camp. On the horizon, the sun was setting.

"Bare your heads!" yelled the head of the camp. His voice was raucous. We were weeping.

"Cover your heads!"

Then the march past began. The two adults were no longer alive. Their tongues hung swollen, blue-tinged. But the third rope was still moving; being so light, the child was still alive. . . .

For more than half an hour he stayed there, struggling between life and death, dying in slow agony under our eyes. And we had to look him full in the face. He was still alive when I passed in front of him. His tongue was still red, his eyes were not yet glazed.

Behind me, I heard the same man asking:

"Where is God now?"

And I heard a voice within me answer him:

"Where is He? Here He is—He is hanging here on this gallows. . . ."

That night the soup tasted of corpses.

The Road Back

*You must not say you now walk the final
    way,*
*Because the darkened heavens hide the blue
    of day.*
*The time we've longed for will at last draw
    near,*
*And our steps, as drums, will sound that we
    are here.*

SONG OF THE PARTISANS

INTRODUCTION

A REMNANT WAS LEFT—THE TINIEST, MOST PITIFUL REMNANT conceivable—emphasizing by its presence the absence of the 6,000,000 who had been murdered. And yet, in the lives of the survivors, there came to flower a new story of human achievement, a story which can be found in marvelous detail in works such as Marie Syrkin's *Blessed Is the Match*, a pioneer work which traces the story of Jewish resistance through the days of the Shoah until it merges with the story of Eretz Yisrael. But that is the present and the future. In this section, we still deal with the past—what happened when *Goetterdaemmerung* came, when the pagan hell built by the Nazis collapsed upon itself?

Out of the rubble and the smoking ruins, there emerged the survivors. By their very presence, they shamed neighbors who had not helped them, who had turned away and now only wanted to forget. But the survivors looked past their neighbors, looked for one another, looked for the miracles which might have spared other members of their families—what else was there left in this world?

We are here to listen to those witnesses who came back out of the furnaces, who give testimony by their very existence. Once the survivors discovered how few were willing to listen to their testimony, they turned to the task of reconstructing their own lives. For many, the road back led to Israel. If we repeat that this is another story we must also indicate that in that story we find the present anguish of Eastern European Jewry, of America's shortcomings, of the achievements and the disappointments of Israel. But a dream and its fulfillment should not distract us from the harsh testimony of those who sought a road back to the world from which they had been taken, and who discovered that the Shoah was not a unique break with inhuman history, but rather a clear expression of certain conditions of man's existence.

1. *THE HOLOCAUST KINGDOM*

ALEXANDER DONAT

We return to the end of the story which took the Donat family through every province of the Holocaust kingdom. In some ways, nothing was harder than finding their child alive—and filled with the virus of anti-Semitism. The reconstruction of life which marked the beginning of the road back for the survivors had to begin within their own homes; and it was a hard and arduous task.

═══

THE REMNANT THAT WAS SAVED
(The end of the story as Lena and Wlodek saw it.)

At daybreak the next day we took the train for Otwock. I still had enough of the money Berlowicz had given me to buy tickets with. When Maria and I walked up the street, there was a big villa, typical of the country houses around Otwock. It had a wooden fence around it, a few small frame buildings, and some pine trees on the grounds. The superintendent recognized Maria and greeted her warmly. "This is Wlodek's mother," Maria introduced us. It took them a long time to find Wlodek.

Miss Olenka called me and said, "Hide in the bushes, Wlodek.

From *The Holocaust Kingdom* by ALEXANDER DONAT. Copyright © 1963, 1965 by Alexander Donat. Reprinted by permission of Holt, Rinehart and Winston, Inc.

Some Jewess has come for you." I had a couple of potatoes under my jacket which I had taken from the cart. I ran to the bushes right away but I began to wonder. Who had come for me? Had they brought something to eat? So I sneaked out to where I could look, and I saw Auntie Maria with some other lady. I walked over to them with the other boys.

When Wlodek finally came, I didn't recognize him. They all stood there, in dreadful rags, barefoot, with close-cropped heads. They all looked alike, every face pinched with hunger; I couldn't have picked my own child from among them. Not until he ran up to Maria and threw his arms around her did I see the two hollows at his temples, the marks made by the forceps when he was brought into the world.

"Do you know who this lady is?" Maria asked him.

"I think I know. Let me guess," he replied. He looked me over apprehensively. His feet were covered with monstrous sores. My experienced eyes immediately diagnosed scabies. Could this little starveling, this ragged creature, frightened to death and looking like a hunted animal, could this be the pampered little boy I had longed for night after terrible night in Auschwitz? My poor baby! How he must have suffered to be in such a pitiful state. Even Maria had not expected anything like that, and she burst into sobs.

I did not say anything, I did not cry. After a little, I went closer to him and stroked his head lightly. He did not move away. When the other boys went away, he took a couple of potatoes out from under his jacket. "Come with me, my little boy," I said, "I'll buy you something to eat. Do you know where I can get food around here?"

"Of course." He was more animated now and I recognized his voice. "There's a grocery store just around the corner."

I bought him a big roll. We sat on the empty porch and he began to eat it, biting off big pieces and swallowing them without chewing. I could hardly hold back my tears.

"That was good," he said when he had finished. He looked at me more closely.

I bought him some ice cream. "Do you recognize me now?" I asked him gently.

"Yes, I do. But Mama had curly hair, now it's straight."

So he had preserved some image of me through those years. I edged closer to him.

"Wlodek, would you like to come with me and stay with me forever?"

"No, I want to stay with the boys," he said, his eyes glistening with tears. Then something occurred to him. "Mama, if I come with you, will I never be hungry again?"

"I swear to you that never, never as long as you live, will you ever be hungry again."

He huddled closer to me and squeezed me. "Well, then, I suppose I'll come."

I asked Maria to tell the superintendent at once. She got busy, and was going to have his things brought from the laundry. But I didn't want his things; I didn't want to wait. I took him as he was and would not let go of his hand.

The train was crowded and we lost Maria. Only after the train started did I burst into tears, whether from my own happiness, because of the pitiful little creature who was my son, or my own sudden exhaustion. I realized that I had no place to sleep, no money, and no one in the world except this boy to whom I had just solemnly promised that he would never go hungry again. Wlodek was excited, too. He couldn't stop talking for a minute, and soon all our fellow passengers knew that his mother had come back from a camp, that his father had not come back, and that he had just been taken from the orphanage. He looked so miserable that one passenger, with tears in his eyes, thrust a banknote into Wlodek's hand. I came to my senses just in time. Not that, not while I was alive.

I decided to go back to the Berlowiczes, and on my way, ran into Sarenka. When she saw us, she drew back as if frightened, as if she had seen a ghost. She held her head in her hands, and stared goggle-eyed. "You found him!" she cried out. And then she told me that never for a moment had she believed that my son would be alive, nor had any one of the others. They had looked on my faith as harmless madness, to be humored because it helped me to survive.

The Berlowiczes received us warmly, and we spent the night on an armchair. Wlodek could not sleep. Because he was so excited or had eaten too much, he had diarrhea. The next day the Berlowiczes showed great energy. They found me a tiny, dirty room in Zabkowska Street, but to me it seemed like a palace. And Dr. Berlowicz also got me a job. I was to organize a pharmacy for the Jewish Committee with the medicines it had received from America, from Palestine and from the Polish government. I had a place to sleep, the Jewish Committee would give me breakfast and dinner, food for Wlodek and a little money as well. My life took on meaning and purpose once more.

It didn't take long to get rid of Wlodek's scabies; cleanliness, better food, and some medical treatment worked wonders. But I had more trouble with his mind, which had become warped. He was a regular guttersnipe who talked the language of the streets. And he had also been infected with rabid anti-Semitism; he hated everything Jewish. I shed bitter tears over this child of mine. I knew it would take all the love and devotion I had to get him straightened out. The greatest tact would be necessary if he was to grow up without serious emotional difficulties. I had no particular theories on the score; I simply trusted my feelings.

The day after we moved into the little place in Zabkowska Street, where, under the name of Jakubowska, I occupied one room and an elderly Gentile woman the other, Wlodek said prayers from morning to night, on his knees. I pretended that it didn't bother me, but even my neighbor was surprised by such excessive religious zeal. "Wlodek," she remarked to him, "not even priests pray that much. Just say an 'Our Father,' that's quite enough."

To wipe out the memory of the past few years, I sang the lullabies I used to sing him when he was a child and I was happy when he joined in. "I want you to remember these lullabies," I said to him. "When you grow up and have children of your own, you'll sing them the same songs your mother sang to you."

"I won't have children," he replied, quite serious. "I want to be a priest. But if you want to have grandchildren, try to have a little girl. And do it quickly, before Daddy comes back, so he'll have a surprise."

He would ask me in the middle of the day, "May I pray to the Lord Jesus?" I never said no.

One day when I came home from work—I had to leave Wlodek alone during the day—he handed me a letter he had written which was addressed to "Miss Olenka." "Please put a stamp on it and put in the mailbox," he said. "But you mustn't read it. It's secret."

The letter read: "Dear Miss Olenka, I am well, Mother is very good to me, and I am never hungry. Mother even bought me a red radish once. And *what we talked about*—it's all right for now." He wrote several such letters. Later, he told me that "what we talked about" referred to his prayers. He had agreed with Miss Olenka that he would run away and go back to her if his mother did not let him pray.

I was not too upset by Wlodek's Catholicism. My own Jewishness was rooted in tradition rather than religion, and I was ready, if that was necessary, to pay for Wlodek's rescue with his conversion to Christianity. The world needs true Christians as it needs true Jews. But after the ordeal we had lived through, simply for being Jewish, I could not endure the hatred my child had been taught. His was no true Christianity based on love of his fellow man; instead, his mind had been poisoned by a medieval distortion of Christianity, a fanatic version of Catholicism impregnated with hatred for his own people. I was deeply hurt by his anti-Semitic songs and chatter. When he repeated them out of childish spite, they made me wince. "All Jews are thieves and swindlers," he would say, with firm conviction. "They killed the Lord Jesus and now they kill Christian children to mix their blood in the matzot." Sometimes he hummed a song which made fun of Jewish speech and habits, and explained, "You see, Mommy, that's how Jews pray."

One day I had had it. "Look here, Wlodek," I said, "we've got to talk about this once and for all. You're Catholic, I'm Jewish. You may pray to God the way you want to and as often as you want to. I won't tease you about it. But don't you dare to make fun of my religion, or the way I say my prayers."

"But you never pray!"

"I don't have to kneel two hours a day and fold my hands in order to pray. I pray in my mind and God can hear and understand me. I could make fun of you, too, because you have to kneel, and fold your hands, and pray for hours on end. But I don't. And I don't want you to do it either. Then we can be friends."

That stopped him for good.

He often asked me to take him to church, and I would walk with him as far as the door and tell him, "Go in, say your prayers. I'll wait outside."

"Please come in with me."

"No. I'm Jewish. I won't go in, but I promise not to budge from this spot until you come out."

He never went in alone, he was afraid to. For many years he was to be pursued by the fear that he would suddenly find himself deserted by everyone.

Every day at 6 A.M. a woman would come by with milk and I always ran to get some for Wlodek. Once I bought him an egg, hard-boiled it, and sliced an onion into it so he would get the vitamins. When he saw the onion, he burst into tears and bitterly reproached me: "Why did you have to spoil a nice egg like that? Onions stink. Only Jews eat onions." But he couldn't resist the temptation and so he ate the Jewish dish with great relish. "You know," he said, "it's not so bad after all. . . ."

He could be very cruel, with all the cruelty of children. One time he told me that I was not his real mother because otherwise I wouldn't forbid him to do anything he wanted to do.

"Now, what makes you say that?" I asked. "Don't you see that I know all kinds of things about you and I sing your old lullabies for you?"

"That's nothing. You were in camp with my real mother. She told you all about me. And you promised her you'd take care of me. But you're not my real mother."

Though I wept about such things, they grew rarer and he became increasingly attached to me. Once he cuddled up to me and said pensively, as if talking to himself, "All Jews can't be bad. You're Jewish and you're not bad at all. . . ."

Wlodek had not been sick for two years, but now his whole organism seemed to be making up for all that time. The moment his scabies disappeared, he had stomach troubles; then bronchitis. Though I had a job, I didn't earn enough to buy him shoes and he went around barefoot. I still wore my heavy ski boots and he had nothing. One day it was raining when I took him to the doctor and that was when a cold became bronchitis. The doctor, a woman, examined him and filled out the usual form. "Name? Address?" When she asked about his father, I said, "His father has not come back yet."

"What do you mean? Have you heard from him?"

"No. I have not heard from him, but he has not yet come back."

The doctor looked at me strangely, but asked no further questions. As for me, I had not the slightest doubt he would come back. My Michal would not disappoint me; he'd be back. I waited for him impassively, just as I had waited for the moment of reunion with Wlodek. Hundreds of people came to the Committee, pored over the records, hoping against hope. Then they turned away, sagging, apathetic, hopeless. I kept very much to myself, putting people off with, "Wait until my husband returns." People around me thought my experiences had unbalanced me, that I was a victim of a kind of madness. My unflinching faith shocked many. How could one be so self-centered in an epoch of universal disaster, and refuse even in one's innermost thoughts to let go of something one had possessed? But I believed in Michal. When people tried to bring the subject up, I would reply, "Until someone comes and tells me that he saw Michal die with his own eyes, Michal is alive as far as I am concerned, and I shall wait for him."

Early in July a stranger who came to the Committee offices suddenly threw himself into my arms and began to kiss me. It was Melcer. "Send someone to the city gates to tell your husband you're alive. He is convinced that you're dead. If he sees you suddenly like this, he'll drop dead on the spot." But I sent no one. And I was not a bit surprised when Michal appeared in the doorway, in an old German uniform, emaciated and white as chalk. I felt strong and calm. I pushed him gently away from me and said over and over again, "Now, now, calm down," but everything in me sang. The dingy Committee offices were suddenly bathed in light. I had my husband back, I had my son. Life had the promise of new happiness. We were not only liberated, we were saved.

Strangers crowded around us. Everyone wept. They wept not only because they had witnessed an incomprehensible miracle, an improbable joy. Their tears were also a terrible lament. They wept for the millions who would never come back, who for all ages will remind us. . . .

2. *THE TRUCE*

PRIMO LEVI

Primo Levi's *If This Is a Man* told of his efforts to remain a human being in the concentration camp. In this later work, he gives an account of the road back to the world of man once the barbed wires came down. His home was in Italy; and the homeward journey was a long one. The new freedom still seemed a thousand years away; and the old oppressors lined the road to it.

———

The first Russian patrol came in sight of the camp about midday on 27th January 1945. Charles and I were the first to see them: we were carrying Sómogyi's body to the common grave, the first of our roommates to die. We tipped the stretcher on to the defiled snow, as the pit was now full, and no other grave was at hand: Charles took off his beret as a salute to both the living and the dead.

They were four young soldiers on horseback, who advanced along the road that marked the limits of the camp, cautiously holding their sten-guns. When they reached the barbed wire, they stopped to look, exchanging a few timid words, and throwing strangely embarrassed glances at the sprawling bodies, at the battered huts, and at us few still alive.

Reprinted with permission of The Bodley Head Ltd. from *The Truce* by PRIMO LEVI. English translation © The Bodley Head 1965. Translated from the Italian by STUART WOOLF.

To us they seemed wonderfully concrete and real, perched on their enormous horses, between the grey of the snow and the grey of the sky, immobile beneath the gusts of damp wind which threatened a thaw.

It seemed to us, and so it was, that the nothing full of death in which we had wandered like spent stars for ten days had found its own solid centre, a nucleus of condensation; four men, armed, but not against us: four messengers of peace, with rough and boyish faces beneath their heavy fur hats.

They did not greet us, nor did they smile; they seemed oppressed not only by compassion but by a confused restraint, which sealed their lips and bound their eyes to the funeral scene. It was that shame we knew so well, the shame that drowned us after the selections, and every time we had to watch, or submit to, some outrage: the shame the Germans did not know, that the just man experiences at another man's crime; the feeling of guilt that such a crime should exist, that it should have been introduced irrevocably into the world of things that exist, and that his will for good should have proved too weak or null, and should not have availed in defence.

So for us even the hour of liberty rang out grave and muffled, and filled our souls with joy and yet with a painful sense of pudency, so that we should have liked to wash our consciences and our memories clean from the foulness that lay upon them; and also with anguish, because we felt that this should never happen, that now nothing could ever happen good and pure enough to rub out our past, and that the scars of the outrage would remain within us for ever, and in the memories of those who saw it, and in the places where it occurred, and in the stories that we should tell of it. Because, and this is the awful privilege of our generation and of my people, no one better than us has ever been able to grasp the incurable nature of the offence, that spreads like a contagion. It is foolish to think that human justice can eradicate it. It is an inexhaustible fount of evil; it breaks the body and the spirit of the submerged, it stifles them and renders them abject; it returns as ignominy upon the oppressors, it perpetuates itself as hatred among the survivors, and swarms around in a thousand ways, against the very will of all, as a thirst for revenge, as a moral capitulation, as denial, as weariness, as renunciation.

These things, at that time blurred, and felt by most as no more than an unexpected attack of mortal fatigue, accompanied the joy of liberation for us. This is why few among us ran to greet our saviours, few fell in prayer. Charles and I remained standing beside the pit overflowing with discoloured limbs, while others knocked down the barbed wire; then we returned with the empty stretcher to break the news to our companions.

The morning brought us the first signs of liberty. Some twenty Polish men and women, clearly summoned by the Russians, arrived and with little enthusiasm began to fumble around, attempting to bring some order and cleanliness into the huts and to clear away the bodies. About midday a frightened child appeared, dragging a cow by the halter; he made us understand that it was for us, that the Russians had sent it, then he abandoned the beast and fled like a bolt. . . . I don't know how, but within a few minutes the poor animal was slaughtered, gutted and quartered, and its remains distributed to all the corners of the camp where survivors nestled.

During the following days, we saw more Polish girls wander around the camp, pale with disgust and pity: they cleaned the patients and tended to their sores as best they could. They also lit an enormous fire in the middle of the camp, which they fed with planks from broken-down huts, and on which they cooked soup in whatever pots came to hand. Finally, on the third day, we saw a cart enter the camp led joyfully by Yankel, a Häftling*: he was a young Russian Jew, perhaps the only Russian among the survivors, and as such he naturally found himself acting as interpreter and liaison officer with the Soviet H.Q. Between resounding cracks of his whip, he announced that he had the task of carrying all the survivors, in small groups of thirty or forty a day, beginning with the most seriously ill, to the central Lager of Auschwitz, now transformed into a gigantic lazaret.

In the meantime, the thaw we had been fearing for so many days had started, and as the snow slowly disappeared, the camp began to change into a squalid bog. The bodies and the filth made the misty, muggy air impossible to breathe. Nor had death ceased to take its toll: the sick died in their cold bunks by the dozen, and here and there along the muddy roads, as if suddenly struck down,

---

* A concentration-camp internee.

died the greediest of the survivors, those who had followed
blindly the imperious command of our age-old hunger and had
stuffed themselves with the rations of meat that the Russians, still
engaged in fighting, sent irregularly to the camp: sometimes little,
sometimes nothing, sometimes in crazy abundance.

But I was aware of what was going on around me in only a disconnected and hazy manner. It seemed as if the weariness and the
illness, like ferocious and cowardly beasts, had waited in ambush
for the moment when I dismantled my defences, in order to attack
me from behind. I lay in a feverish torpor, semi-conscious, tended
fraternally by Charles, and tormented by thirst and acute pains in
my joints. There were no doctors or drugs. I also had a sore throat,
and half my face had swollen; my skin had become red and rough
and hurt me like a burn; perhaps I was suffering from more than
one illness at the same time. When it was my turn to climb on to
Yankel's cart, I was no longer able to stand on my feet.

I was hoisted on to the cart by Charles and Arthur, together with
a load of dying men, from whom I did not feel very different. It was
drizzling, and the sky was low and gloomy. While the slow steps
of Yankel's horses drew me towards remote liberty, for the last time
there filed before my eyes the huts where I had suffered and matured,
the Roll-call square where the gallows and the gigantic Christmas
tree still towered side by side, and the gate to slavery, on which
one could still read the three, now hollow, words of derision:
'*Arbeit Macht Frei*,' 'Work Gives Freedom.'

It was in fact a dramatic sight. When we threw open the doors in
the early morning, a surprisingly domestic scene opened out before
our eyes; no longer a deserted, geological steppe, but the green
hills of Moldavia, with farms, haystacks and rows of vines; no longer
enigmatic Cyrillic signs, but, right in front of our truck, a decrepit
hovel, blue-green with verdigris, with clear writing on it, curiously
similar to the Italian words: '*Paine, Lapte, Vin, Carnaciuri de
Purcel*,' bread, milk, wine, pork sausages. And in fact, in front of
the hovel there was a woman, who was pulling an enormously long
sausage out of a basket at her feet, and measuring it by lengths
like string.

We saw peasants like our own, with broiled faces and pale foreheads, dressed in black, with jackets and waistcoats and watch-chains

over their bellies; girls on foot or on bicycles, dressed almost like ours, whom we could have mistaken for Venetian or Abruzzese peasant girls. There were goats, sheep, cows, pigs, chickens. But, standing at a railway crossing, to act as a check to any precocious illusion of home, was a camel, driving us back into another world; a worn-out, grey woolly camel, laden with sacks, exhaling haughtiness and stupid solemnity from his prehistoric leporine muzzle. The language of the place sounded equally mixed to our ears; well-known roots and terminations, but entangled and contaminated in a millenary common growth, could be heard alongside others, of a strange wild sound; a speech familiar in its music, hermetic in its sense.

At the frontier took place the complicated and difficult ceremony of transference from the ramshackle trucks of Soviet-gauge lines to others, equally ramshackle, with a western gauge; and soon after we entered the station of Iasi, where the train was laboriously broken up into three parts; a sign that the halt would last for many hours. . . .

As the halt at Iasi threatened to last all day, we left the station and wandered through the deserted streets, between low mud-coloured houses. A single, minute, archaic tram ran from one end of the city to the other; the ticket collector stood at a terminal; he spoke Yiddish, he was a Jew. With some effort we managed to understand each other. He informed me that other trainloads of ex-prisoners had passed through Iasi, of all races, French, English, Greek, Italian, Dutch, American. In many of these there had been Jews in need of assistance; so the local Jewish community had formed a relief centre. If we had one or two hours to spare, he counselled us to go as a delegation to the centre; we should be given advice and help. In fact, as his tram was about to leave, he told us to climb on, he would put us down at the right stop and would take care of the tickets.

Leonardo, Mr. Unverdorben and I went; we crossed the dead city and reached a squalid, crumbling building, with temporary boarding in place of the doors and windows. Two old patriarchs, with a scarcely more opulent or flourishing air than ours, received us in a gloomy, dusty office; but they were full of affectionate kindness and good intentions, they made us sit on the only three chairs, over-whelmed us with attention and precipitately recounted to us, in Yiddish and French, the terrible trials which they and a few others had survived. They were prone to tears and laughter; at the moment of departure, they invited us peremptorily to drink a toast with terrible rectified alcohol, and gave us a basket of grapes to distribute among the Jews on the train. They also emptied all the drawers and their own pockets, and raked together a sum of *lei* which on the spot seemed to us astronomical; but, later, after we had divided it, and taken into account the inflation, we realised that its value was principally symbolic.

Austria borders on Italy, and St. Valentin is only 180 miles from Tarvisio; but on 15th October, the thirty-first day of our journey, we crossed a new frontier and entered Munich, prey to a disconsolate railway tiredness, a permanent loathing for trains, for snatches of sleep on wooden floors, for jolting and for stations; so that familiar smells, common to all the railways of the world, the sharp smell of impregnated sleepers, hot brakes, burning fuel, inspired in us a deep disgust. We were tired of everything, tired in particular of perforating useless frontiers.

But from another point of view, the fact of feeling a piece of Germany under our feet for the first time, not a piece of Upper Silesia or of Austria, but of Germany itself, overlaid our tiredness with a complex attitude composed of intolerance, frustration and tension. We felt we had something to say, enormous things to say, to every single German, and we felt that every German should have something to say to us; we felt an urgent need to settle our accounts, to ask, explain and comment, like chess players at the end of a game. Did 'they' know about Auschwitz, about the silent daily massacre, a step away from their doors? If they did, how could they walk about, return home and look at their children, cross the threshold of a church? If they did not, they ought, as a sacred duty, to listen, to learn everything, immediately, from us, from me; I felt the tattooed number on my arm burning like a sore.

As I wandered around the streets of Munich, full of ruins, near the station where our train lay stranded once more, I felt I was moving among throngs of insolvent debtors, as if everybody owed me something, and refused to pay. I was among them, in the enemy camp, among the *Herrenvolk;* but the men were few, many were mutilated, many dressed in rags like us. I felt that everybody should interrogate

us, read in our faces who we were, and listen to our tale in humility.
But no one looked us in the eyes, no one accepted the challenge;
they were deaf, blind and dumb, imprisoned in their ruins, as in a
fortress of wilful ignorance, still strong, still capable of hatred and
contempt, still prisoners of their old tangle of pride and guilt.

I found myself searching among them, among that anonymous
crowd of sealed faces, for other faces, clearly stamped in my memory,
many bearing a name: the name of someone who could not but
know, remember, reply; who had commanded and obeyed, killed,
humiliated, corrupted. A vain and foolish search; because not they,
but others, the few just ones, would reply for them.

If we had taken one guest on board at Szób, after Munich we
realised that we had taken on board an entire contingent: our train
consisted no longer of sixty, but of sixty-one trucks. A new truck
was travelling with us towards Italy at the end of our train, crammed
with young Jews, boys and girls, coming from all the countries of
Eastern Europe. None of them seemed more than twenty years
old, but they were extremely self-confident and resolute people; they
were young Zionists, on their way to Israel, travelling where they
were able to, and finding a path where they could. A ship was waiting for them at Bari; they had purchased their truck, and it had
proved the simplest thing in the world to attach it to our train:
they had not asked anybody's permission, but had hooked it on, and
that was that. I was amazed, but they laughed at my amazement:
'Hitler's dead, isn't he?' replied their leader, with his intense hawk-
like glance. They felt immensely free and strong, lords of the world
and of their destinies.

We passed through Garmisch-Partenkirchen and in the evening
reached the fantastically disordered transit camp of Mittenwald, in
the mountains, on the Austrian border. We spent the night there,
and it was our last night of cold. The following day the train ran
down to Innsbruck, where it filled up with Italian smugglers, who
brought us the greetings of our homeland, in the absence of official
authorities, and generously distributed chocolate, grappa and tobacco.

As the train, more tired than us, climbed towards the Italian
frontier it snapped in two like an overtaut cable; there were several
injuries, but this was the last adventure. Late at night we crossed

the Brenner, which we had passed in our exile twenty months before; our less tired companions celebrated with a cheerful uproar; Leonardo and I remained lost in a silence crowded with memories. Of 650, our number when we had left, three of us were returning. And how much had we lost, in those twenty months? What should we find at home? How much of ourselves had been eroded, extinguished? Were we returning richer or poorer, stronger or emptier? We did not know; but we knew that on the thresholds of our homes, for good or ill, a trial awaited us, and we anticipated it with fear. We felt in our veins the poison of Auschwitz, flowing together with our thin blood; where should we find the strength to begin our lives again, to break down the barriers, the brushwood which grows up spontaneously in all absences, around every deserted house, every empty refuge? Soon, tomorrow, we should have to give battle, against enemies still unknown, outside ourselves and inside; with what weapons, what energies, what will power? We felt the weight of centuries on our shoulders, we felt oppressed by a year of ferocious memories; we felt emptied and defenceless. The months just past, although hard, of wandering on the margins of civilisation now seemed to us like a truce, a parenthesis of unlimited availability, a providential but unrepeatable gift of fate.

With these thoughts, which kept us from sleep, we passed our first night in Italy, as the train slowly descended the deserted, dark Adige Valley. On 17th October, we reached the camp of Pescantina, near Verona, and here we split up, everyone following his own destiny; but no train left in the direction of Turin until the evening of the following day. In the confused vortex of thousands of refugees and displaced persons, we glimpsed Pista, who had already found his path; he wore the white and yellow armband of the Pontifical Organization of Assistance, and collaborated briskly and cheerfully in the life of the camp. And then we saw advance towards us a figure, a well-known face, a full head higher than the crowd, the Moor of Verona. He had come to say goodbye to us, to Leonardo and me; he had reached his home, the first of all of us, for Avesa, his village, was only a few miles away. And he blessed us, the old blasphemer: he raised two enormous knobbly fingers, and blessed us with the solemn gesture of a Pontiff, wishing us a good return and a happy future.

I reached Turin on 19th October, after thirty-five days of travel;

my house was still standing, all my family was alive, no one was expecting me. I was swollen, bearded and in rags, and had difficulty in making myself recognised. I found my friends full of life, the warmth of secure meals, the solidity of daily work, the liberating joy of recounting my story. I found a large clean bed, which in the evening (a moment of terror) yielded softly under my weight. But only after many months did I lose the habit of walking with my glance fixed to the ground, as if searching for something to eat or to pocket hastily or to sell for bread; and a dream full of horror has still not ceased to visit me, at sometimes frequent, sometimes longer, intervals.

It is a dream within a dream, varied in detail, one in substance. I am sitting at a table with my family, or with friends, or at work, or in the green countryside; in short, in a peaceful relaxed environment, apparently without tension or affliction; yet I feel a deep and subtle anguish, the definite sensation of an impending threat. And in fact, as the dream proceeds, slowly or brutally, each time in a different way, everything collapses and disintegrates around me, the scenery, the walls, the people, while the anguish becomes more intense and more precise. Now everything has changed to chaos; I am alone in the centre of a grey and turbid nothing, and now, I *know* what this thing means, and I also know that I have always known it; I am in the Lager once more, and nothing is true outside the Lager. All the rest was a brief pause, a deception of the senses, a dream; my family, nature in flower, my home. Now this inner dream, this dream of peace, is over, and in the outer dream, which continues, gelid, a well-known voice resounds: a single word, not imperious, but brief and subdued. It is the dawn command of Auschwitz, a foreign word, feared and expected: get up, '*Wstawàch.*'

3. *THE HUNTER*

TUVIAH FRIEDMAN

There are some scholars who feel that Tuviah Friedman tends to overstate his case as a hunter of Nazi criminals. Yet all agreed that he has made significant contributions to this work, that he has been a relentless, dedicated, and dogged pursuer of the murderers of his people. Whether or not Friedman is to be given the major credit for the capture of Eichmann, his work in documenting Nazi crimes, ferreting out the criminals, and bringing them to (an often lax) justice deserves full recognition. And our understanding of the road back from Auschwitz and Bergen-Belsen is incomplete if we do not see it through the eyes of the victim whose sense of justice becomes the absolute purpose of his days from that point on, who wants to see justice, wants to see it now, wants it as a necessary foundation of any future.

━━━

I had made up my mind.

Poland held too many bitter memories for me. I despised the resentment of the people toward the pitiful handful of Jews who had survived the Hitler period, and I was sickened by the attitude of the Polish Government officials, who pretended that anti-Jewish sentiment did not exist. For me, a homeland for the Jews seemed the only possible answer. I did not then—or now—wish to be tolerated. Tolerance is no substitute for respect.

From *The Hunter* by TUVIAH FRIEDMAN. Copyright © 1961 by Towia Frydman. Reprinted by permission of Doubleday & Company, Inc. Edited and translated by DAVID C. GROSS.

At the Security Service offices, my request for an honorable severance from my government job was met with raised eyebrows. Some people thought I had abandoned my reason; others were more suspicious of my motives. My friends and immediate superiors tried to dissuade me from my decision, but I was steadfast and determined in my desire to leave Poland, to reach Palestine, and to join with Jews from all over the world in working—and fighting—for a homeland for my people.

Colonel Korczynski greeted my decision calmly, and with understanding. He told me he was sorry to see me leave his office, complimented me on my work, and wished that I would find the fulfillment I was obviously seeking. He expedited my application for a voluntary resignation, which had to be approved in Warsaw.

I toured the Danzig prison one evening before my final departure for Lodz, where I was to meet with the Kibbutz leaders and await instructions for my departure for Palestine. The emigration of Jews from Poland was discouraged by the government, and would-be Palestinians were compelled to leave the country via illegal routes. When I left Danzig, I took off my Polish uniform; and with it, I think, a certain sense of kinship with millions of other Poles. In my new street clothing, I felt Jasinski fade away and Friedman replace him. I was once again a Polish Jew, a member of an unrooted minority, preparing to take my wanderer's staff in hand and go on . . . only this time to return to a small area on the shores of the Mediterranean, from whence my forefathers had been forcibly separated nearly two millennia ago.

Bella had in the meantime returned to Radom; we had decided that she would wait there until I left Poland and sent for her. I contacted the Kibbutz headquarters in Lodz, and was sent to Cracow to await further instructions. Our small group of Palestine-bound Jews was housed in Cracow for two weeks; impatiently we waited for the signal to move. Quietly, in groups of two and three, we proceeded by rail and bus to Wroclaw, closer to the Czech border, and waited two more weeks. Most of the time we remained indoors, playing cards, reading, talking. We learned patience under the most trying conditions—not an easy virtue, you may be sure.

Finally, one late afternoon our Kibbutz leader arrived from Lodz and told us we were leaving that same night. He brought with him about a dozen elderly couples—men and women in their sixties who were attached to our group, of whom no one was more than twenty-seven or twenty-eight years of age. We were told that we were to help these oldsters, and under no circumstances were we to allow them to falter in the difficult journey that lay ahead. The older people carried heavy suitcases secured with strong rope. Most of us bore knapsacks that seldom weighed more than ten pounds.

Shortly after midnight we boarded a large truck fitted with rough benches and drove to the border. The road ended and we left the truck, moving deeper into a small wood. No one spoke, although I am sure that some of the oldsters must have been reciting snatches of prayer as we left the woods and began to ascend the first heights of the Matras mountains. All eyes were on our mountaineer guide, a sturdy, sure-footed Pole who was at the head of our procession of nighttime mountain climbers.

We had been descending on the other side of the mountain for nearly an hour, when the first light of the new day arose from the East. Our guide ordered us to halt and to rest. As we sat on the cold ground, in the early morning of March 31, 1946, he told us that we were now in Czechoslovakia, that we had crossed the border.

I looked behind me, at Poland. My father and his father were buried there. Jews had lived in Poland for a thousand years, their condition fluctuating like the fever of a malaria patient. One hour back, I thought, is the country in which I was born, to which I had shown allegiance, which I had tried to love; now, here, with a packful of clothing, happy that I had succeeded in crossing its frontier, I sat catching my breath, gathering up my strength for an unknown future.

I had perhaps a total of ten dollars, and some socks and shirts and underclothing.

Everything else was in my heart.

Our leader signaled for us to continue our journey; we were to be lodged in a farmer's home before going on to cross the Czech border into Austria, and then to Vienna, our immediate destination. It was still very early, and we wanted to avoid any Czech frontier patrols. Our elderly fellow travelers had begun to tire, and we picked up their suitcases and helped them on.

We entered a tiny picture-postcard hamlet of perhaps twenty houses at the same time that the first roosters began to crow. The "ku-ku-ri-ku" of the roosters sounded, to me, like a clarion call to freedom.

The farmer in whose house we were warmly welcomed gave us freshly baked bread and hot milk. We lay down on mats of straw and took off our shoes. The old-fashioned hearth gave off a glow that radiated throughout the simple house; none of us could speak Czech, and our only exchanges were made up of smiles of gratitude and handclasps of thanks.

Later that day, accompanied by our farmer friend, we boarded an antiquated train that wound its way through the countryside, toward Prague. There we were taken in hand by a group of Jewish community officials who had already arranged rooms for us at a secluded hotel. We toured the beautiful city, where the legend of the Golem was born, and early the next morning we took a train for Bratislava. We had practically an entire car to ourselves, and our trip soon took on the air of an outing. We sang Hebrew songs, songs of Jerusalem and Galilee, of building a country—and of being rebuilt in the process. Our spirits rose; we were on our way to a new life, in which we would stand erect, as free men.

In Bratislava we were taken to a house that belonged to the Bricha organization—the escape arm established by the Palestine Jewish community to aid Jews from Europe to reach the Promised Land. We waited two days for another group to arrive from Poland; the plan was for all of us to cross into Austria together.

Early in the morning all of us—we were now more than 125 people—boarded trucks-converted-into-buses and drove to the Austrian frontier. We had been instructed not to speak Yiddish or Polish, to destroy all our credentials, and if questioned, to answer in Hebrew—a language that could not readily be distinguished from Greek, we hoped. We were crossing into Austria as a group of Greek nationals who had been freed from German concentration camps and were now en route home.

At the border, our Bricha leaders were warmly greeted by the Czech guards. We could see them exchanging pleasantries, drinking each other's good health and wishing each other well; I learned later that it was also customary to make substantial monetary gifts to the guards. After a polite interval, the guards ordered the barriers raised, and we "Greeks" crossed into Austria. We were stunned when the Austrian border police greeted us warmly, in German. We had forgotten the sound of this language, drowning out of our memory the harsh and strident tones of Nazi commands and German curses. Now the German words fell on unattuned ears—"welcome," the words said; Austria welcomes you. We heard, but did not immediately understand.

For us, German had become the language of death and destruction.

Soon after we crossed into Austria, we were seated in a large mess hall, where sandwiches and wonderful coffee and cigarettes were distributed freely. I had never before seen such bounty. I asked our leaders where it all came from.

"From America," he said, "from the Joint Distribution Committee. The American Jews are sending help to the Jews in Europe."

I ate and drank my fill, and smoked my first American cigarette.

It was a wonderful feeling to know that they were worried about us. My sense of being alone, a pitiful handful of people all alone, was gone; in far-off America, people cared. It made me want to laugh.

We set off for Vienna, remembering what our guides had told us: that it was a beautiful city, that we would not quickly want to leave it, that we should stay out of trouble, and not lose sight of our eventual goal.

The trip for me was beginning to take on new dimensions. I began to feel keenly interested in Vienna, in the world of music and art, in what life had to offer in the future.

A sense of excitement and enthusiasm gripped me; I had not known before how cold and contemptuous I had become.

I suddenly felt myself young, a free man, still in my early twenties.

We entered Vienna, borne by three heavy trucks, knapsacks and suitcases at our feet, our eyes straining to catch a glimpse of everything. The city was enchanting, soft, gentle, a far cry from the foreboding Slavic tones to which most of us were accustomed. We looked and we marveled. Our guides pointed out the Russian zone, through which we were passing, and then the American zone, to which we were going.

We stopped and alighted in front of the Rothschild Hospital, which the American occupation authorities had converted into a giant transit hostel for the thousands of Jewish refugees passing through Vienna en route to Western Europe. Several thousands of Jews were housed in the building, all of them waiting for their final papers to France and Italy, and from there to America and Palestine, the latter through "illegal" channels. The former hospital, built by the Rothschild family, was a microcosm of European Jewry in the year 1946.

The director of the Rothschild Hospital was a Polish Jew, Bronislaw Teichholz, who had taken over the job of supervising the building's activities a few days after V-E Day. The flood tide of East European Jews who poured into Vienna on their way to new homes across the sea taxed the limited facilities of the Rothschild Hospital, and the American occupation authorities had taken over four former German school buildings, which had been converted into additional refugee centers. Our group was assigned to one of these buildings, on Robertus Street.

Large rooms had been transformed into army-style barracks, with double-tiered bunks. One side of our room was set aside for men, another for women, and still another for married couples. The girls hung up sheets around their section of the room while they dressed and undressed. We men were less careful with such amenities, and would merely pretend that we were in our own private bedroom. There were many amusing moments in our common bedroom.

Like people who had for a long time been denied even the simplest of life's pleasures, we seized every opportunity to taste everything in Vienna. I suppose we were a little like children let loose in a carnival with pockets full of coins. We ran around to the theaters, the opera performances, the concerts, the movies. Everything was enjoyable, everything made us laugh. We were, I am sure, trying to catch up on lost years, years when we had known little else but anguish.

All of our pleasures were not only of the stage and the screen. We soon got to know the laughing, friendly Viennese girls. They laughed at our "strange German," which we said was that of an outlandish section of Austria, not caring at the moment to admit that we were talking Yiddish. It was all so pleasant, those first few weeks in Vienna. The girls would tell us that we were sports and that the local Vienna youths were tightwads, unwilling to spend even a few measly pfennigs to treat a girl to a movie or a café. What is more, they told us, in the midst of laughter and soft music that every coffee house featured, we were from a far place, we were more interesting, worldly, even cosmopolitan.

The Jewish girls in our group, waiting like the rest of us for the orders to move on to Italy, thence to Palestine, looked at our behavior with disapproval.

We received food parcels from the Joint people, plus a little pocket money for fares and the like, and we waited.

April turned to May, and all Vienna seemed to know that this was the first peaceful May in Europe in a long, long time.

Some of the young men in our group had too much of Vienna; for others, they never had enough. They converted their food parcels into ready cash, and paraded from café to café, filled with an almost mad hunger for life's pleasures.

One afternoon as I was walking on a main street, restless and listless, someone called from across the heavily trafficked street, "Tuviah! Tuviah!" I looked and looked but could see no one. I was now known by nearly everyone as "Tadek" Friedman; who could be calling me by my old given name, which I had not heard spoken in so many months?

Traffic came to a standstill, and I could see a heavy-set man swinging a briefcase and hailing me. Not until he came right up to me did I recognize him. He was fat now, and breathing heavily from the brief dash across the street, but there was no mistaking Heinrich Rakocz, from Radom. We embraced and clapped each other's backs heartily. I was amazed to find myself so deeply happy to see this old face from my hometown. We sat down in the nearest coffee house, and I remembered him as he looked in the Szkolna Street camp, sharing a bunk in our barracks with me.

His was an unusual case. He had been born in Poland, but had lived in Vienna for twenty-five years, until the Anschluss, in 1938. The Nazis had quickly returned him to Radom, where he had been imprisoned in a camp, like the rest of us. He told me that after he was liberated, he returned to Vienna, married a Christian woman and now managed his own shoe store. He had not seen me since my escape, and I told him now of what had happened to me. He was, it seemed to me, most impressed by my work in Danzig. He interrupted me excitedly.

"Tuviah, it's a miracle that we met just now." He looked about him, and bent closer toward me.

"You remember Buchmayer, the S.S. man who murdered so many

Jews in Radom? I saw him here, in Vienna. Three months ago I walked past his store."

I felt a charge of excitement pass through me.

"What did you do?" I asked him, as calmly as I could.

"Do? I walked past there a second time, and I didn't see him any more. It was too much excitement for me, Tuviah. Even now, when I think of it, my heart begins to pound."

I waited until my voice would not betray me.

"Take me there, Rakocz," I asked him, "to the store where Buchmayer is."

He did not demur, to my pleasant surprise. We took the trolley and rode to Weiringer Street. Halfway down the block was a large sign in front of a pork store: Konrad Buchmayer. This was the same Buchmayer, I thought, who used to run around in the camp with a heavy club, beating prisoners, clubbing them on the head until they collapsed, or died.

We peered through the store window, and could see only a woman and a young employee slicing pork chops for their waiting customers. I proposed to Rakocz that we go upstairs to the apartment above the store. "If there is a housekeeper," I said, "you speak to her, with your Viennese accent. Say we're old friends, and would like to see our old friend Buchmayer," I added. I was amazed at my coolness.

The housekeeper said she knew nothing, that Buchmayer had not been seen or heard from in many months, and that she believed he was in the Russian zone of Austria.

I took Rakocz to the Vienna police headquarters, and told our story to a high police official who had himself been interned in a concentration camp, for "political reasons." He suggested that the Buchmayer family's mail be watched, and promised to contact us just as soon as anything developed. Within three days he summoned me to his office and said that Buchmayer was interested in an American prisoner-of-war camp for S.S. men, near Salzburg.

I asked the inspector for his support, explaining that if Buchmayer were returned to Poland, he would be tried as a war criminal and receive his just punishment. In American hands, he might be set free.

The inspector said he would help. Within two days I had received from him a transit pass allowing me to cross through the

Russian zone, and a letter to the American authorities at the war-prisoner camp which explained that I wished to find a certain Buchmayer, who was a Nazi war criminal wanted by the Polish Government.

The trip by train took twelve hours. The Russian passengers sang and played musical instruments throughout the journey, while the Austrians sat quietly, their faces expressionless, looking neither to the left nor to the right. At one control point, a Russian sergeant examined my papers.

"You're a Pole, aren't you?" he asked, a sly inflection in his voice.

"No, I'm a Jew," I answered.

"Yes, yes, you're a Pole—why don't you go back to Poland and rebuild your country?"

I repeated that I was a Jew and that I had received permission from the Austrian police authorities to travel to Salzburg on a special mission. The sergeant did not like my answer. He summoned his commanding officer, a young lieutenant, and handed my papers to him.

"According to these documents," the Soviet officer said, "you are looking for a Nazi war criminal in an American war-prisoner camp. Is that correct?"

I assured the Russian that that was the sole purpose of my trip. He looked hard and long at me and at my papers and then, with a shrug, handed the papers to his sergeant, ordering him to affix his approval.

"This is the first time I've ever heard of a Jew looking for a Nazi criminal," the Russian lieutenant said to me. With a smile and a brief salute, he wished me success.

Soon afterward we crossed the demarcation line and entered the American zone. An amazing transformation took place among the Austrian passengers. Almost all of them began to talk to one another, and to walk up and down the aisle; I could hear many of them cursing the Russians. A number of the Austrians offered to share their chocolate and other goodies with me; they acted like people at a celebration.

I arrived in Salzburg, Mozart's city, tired but determined to lose no time. The American camp was near a small town called Hollein. There was a bus that passed the camp and I asked the driver to drop me nearby.

"Sure," he said. He looked at me for a few minutes while we waited for the other passengers to board. He leaned toward me, and asked in a low voice:

"You bringing someone a little food?"

I smiled. "Not food," I said. "A little present."

The American sergeant at the prison headquarters took my papers and asked me to wait. In a few minutes I was seated in front of the camp commandant, a major in his early fifties, whose hair was short and steel-gray, and who spoke to me in perfect German.

"According to these documents, you're looking for a Nazi war criminal in our camp," he began. "Tell me a little about this man and about yourself."

I told him about Buchmayer, about the countless murders he had committed in my hometown of Radom, and assured the American major that I could single out this S.S. man from among 10,000 prisoners. The American listened carefully and reflectively. It seemed to me that his blue eyes now looked sharp and tough. He paced his office for a few minutes, and then turned to me.

"All right, let's do it. Your German is very good, Friedman. I'll let you into the camp for a few hours. Look around, and if you see him, don't say a word, just come back here and we'll do the rest. You won't be disappointed," he added.

I was given a POW shirt and a pair of old khaki trousers. An S.S. jacket from which all emblems and insignia had been removed completed my uniform. I followed the sergeant into the heart of the prison camp, feeling like a stray dog in a pack of wolves.

I strolled through two empty barracks, noticing the comfortable accommodations that the S.S. prisoners were given. In the third barrack, an S.S. prisoner lounging on his bunk called out to me:

"Hey, comrade, are you new here? Did they just pick you up?"

"Yes," I replied. "Yesterday."

"Well, you can stay here with us, there are two empty bunks."

I looked about carefully. There were pictures and changes of clothing hanging on the wall. The beds were made and looked clean. I told the lounging prisoner that I would look around a little more.

"All right, you look around, and if you decide to come here, I'm sure you'll like it. We'll be eating lunch soon and then we all take a nap on the grass." He sat up and asked me eagerly, "Do you play soccer? We can use some good players. There's a game every afternoon at three." My host was delighted with me when I assured him that I was a fairly good player, and once again urged me to stay in his barracks.

"You know," he said, "it's not too bad here. We take it easy all day long and nobody has to work. There's a game every afternoon. The Yanks are very decent to us, and the food's good too. Nobody ever tries to escape. What for? In a few months they'll give us a clean bill of health and we'll be released from here. And then everybody will have a chance for a job and a normal life. After all, the war's over."

I sat down on the bunk opposite him, listening attentively. He continued.

"There are a couple of no-good bastards in the camp. You know, they get packages from home but they never share anything. But you'll like it here, you'll see."

When he asked me where I was from, I said that I was from Danzig and that I had been working in a print shop in Linz. I told him things had been fine in Linz and that I had not hidden the fact from the other people in the shop that I had been an active member of the Danzig Gestapo. Sure enough, I said, in a few days several American C.I.C. agents arrested me in the middle of my work, and brought me here.

My S.S. friend expressed surprise that I had decided to work in Linz, since that was where Kaltenbrunner, the chief of the Nazi security police, was from, and in fact that was where many of the Nazis came from. We talked some more, and my new companion, who was from Munich, expressed strong sentiments about the Austrians.

"When we had captured all of Europe," he explained, "the Austrians called themselves Germans. But when the war ended, they pleaded that they were Austrians and had never supported us Germans."

Our discussion was interrupted by the signal for lunch. I found a set of eating utensils and was advised to wash them thoroughly, since the previous owner had been hospitalized with TB. Utensils in hand, I walked outside to find a faucet, and rinsed my things thoroughly. My eyes darted from side to side, looking for the familiar face of Buchmayer.

I found a seat on a long bench near Hanssi, my new camp guide, and spooned up the thick soup hungrily. Hanssi was talking with every swallow.

"It's a good thing the Americans caught us, not the Russians. You know, our S.S. men made sure the Americans and the British would capture them, not the Russians. Those Wehrmacht troops, they're in Siberia right now."

I finished lunch and promised Hanssi I would return to the barracks for a blanket, for the after-lunch nap. I was washing my utensils again when I saw Buchmayer approaching, headed straight for the faucet. He walked with a carefree air, whistling a tune. I averted my face, and watched him. When he returned to his barracks, apparently for his blanket, I saw that he was housed in barracks number eleven.

Hastily, I returned to the camp headquarters. I was brought before the major. When I told him of my discovery, he thumbed through a prisoner's list and found Buchmayer's name listed in its proper alphabetical order. I smiled. The Nazis in their arrogant confidence had not, for the most part, even bothered to change their names.

Within the hour I had changed back to my own clothing and joined the major and a number of other camp officers in a large interrogation room. Buchmayer was brought in and, with a smart salute, clicked his heels and stood at attention, inspecting the faces of the American military officers. His eyes never fell on me. He looked as though he had been summoned to be told that he was being released from camp.

The commandant spoke first. "Buchmayer, do you know this man?" he asked, pointing to me.

The Nazi looked in my direction, and answered politely, "No, sir, I do not."

I stood up and said to the prisoner, "But Buchmayer, how could you forget me? We were in Radom together."

"Oh, in Radom?" he asked. "Were you in the S.S. in Radom, too?"

"No, I was not," I replied. "I was one of the Jews who worked under you, Buchmayer."

The man's face turned white; his eyes seemed transfixed.

"Don't you remember?" I pressed on. "You used to love to run around with a heavy club, beating us until the blood covered our entire bodies. You even had nurses with you who used to bandage us up so that you could beat us again later on."

His lips trembling, Buchmayer said to me, "But—but I wasn't the worst one in Radom, was I?"

The Americans laughed at this and urged me to question him further.

"Do you remember, Buchmayer, how you pulled the small children from the Radom Ghetto into Bialla Street and shot them?" I asked.

"But that was an order from General Botscher," he protested. "I merely took the children into the street and the other S.S. men did the shooting. It wasn't I. Why did you pick me as your victim? I was only a corporal. Why don't you find the general of the S.S.? He was the one who gave the orders in Radom."

Buchmayer did not see the daily soccer game that afternoon. The American major ordered his transfer to solitary imprisonment, and proceedings were begun to have him removed to Vienna, en route to Poland, where he would stand trial. I thanked the Americans for their help, and returned to Vienna. I reported the results of my trip to the police inspector and to Rakocz. The three of us felt happy, as only former inmates of a concentration camp can feel in learning of the arrest of a Nazi criminal.

About a week later Rokocz confided that he knew of another Nazi who was probably in Vienna, and when he told me his name, I felt my skin crawl. He said that Richard Schoegl was in Vienna; this was the same S.S. officer who had deported thousands of Jews from Radom to the extermination center in Treblinka; among them, my mother and my sister Itka.

Rakocz explained that his wife did not want him to bother about finding Nazis. "You know, Tuviah," he said, "she says the Nazis are coming back to power and that they'll throw me into a concentration camp again."

"Well, which do you think is better?" I asked him: "to wait for the Nazis to return to power, or should we go after these mice now and poison them?

"You couldn't take another imprisonment in a camp anyway. Look, you lost your entire family to the Nazis. Stop being afraid.

Every Nazi, every S.S. man, every Gestapo man who is caught and put away is one less menace to the whole world."

I went back to my Austrian police inspector, and learned that Schoegl had been imprisoned and released for lack of evidence. He told me that we would face a similar problem after Buchmayer was brought to Vienna, unless there were sworn statements from eyewitnesses to the crimes that had been committed in Radom.

I realized then that there was only one thing to do. A group of Radom survivors had settled temporarily in Stuttgart, Germany, and had in fact been given housing accommodations in a separate quarter of the city by the Allied commander-in-chief, General Eisenhower. I told the Austrian police inspector that I would bring him the eyewitness testimony that he needed, and hurried to the Rothschild Hospital. On the basis of my own testimony—which was taken by a police secretary in the inspector's office—Schoegl was arrested that very night.

I knew that Bricha representatives were wandering all over Europe, working to bring Jewish survivors to Palestine. To enter Germany and reach Stuttgart was no mean feat; but with the Bricha organization's support, I knew that it could be done.

At the hospital, I waited until Teichholz, the overworked director, could see me. While I waited, I watched him working, talking to assistants, shouting into the telephone, signing papers, all the time urging me to be patient with him. His was no easy task. Originally from Lwow, he had escaped from the ghetto there and hid out during the war in Budapest.

When he was finally free, I told him that I wanted to see the chief of the Haganah and Bricha organization, a mysterious person known only as "Arthur." He hesitated for a while, then, his back to me, he dialed a number. He told the mysterious Arthur that Tuviah "Tadek" Friedman—one of the young men awaiting early transport to Palestine—wished to see him on a confidential matter.

Teichholz replaced the receiver, and said that Arthur would be along presently.

"He told me that you had been an officer in the Polish security service," he added, obviously surprised.

"Yes, that's true."

We shook hands and I went outside to wait for Arthur. In ten minutes he drove up in a rather large sedan, smoking a cigar. He called to me, "Friedman?"

Together we drove to his office. Arthur was tall, a few years older than I, rather ebullient. If someone had pointed him out as one of the Rothschild heirs, I would have believed it. He seemed calm, relaxed, almost fully content. As we drove, we talked of Vienna, and I told him I was anxious to be on my way to Palestine.

Arthur laughed when I said that. "And we're anxious to get you there, believe me. I'm a Kibbutz member myself, and we need healthy young men like you, Tadek." He laughed some more; it surprised me that he called me "Tadek."

Two flights up on Frank Street was the Bricha organization's headquarters. There were five or six rooms, filled with people in a hurry, most of whom seemed to be trying to get a few moments with Arthur. He instructed his secretary to keep everyone out of his office for a half-hour; the only calls he would take would be those from abroad.

We sat down and Arthur lit a fresh cigar. I took a proffered cigarette. We smoked, looking at one another. He asked what it was I wanted. I told him I had to get to Stuttgart to take sworn testimony to be used against two Nazi murderers who had killed thousands of my fellow Jews in Radom.

"What are their names?" he asked.

"Konrad Buchmayer and Richard Schoegl," I replied.

From his desk drawer, Arthur took out a small notebook. "Buchmayer?" he said, thumbing the pages. "Yes, he's listed." He turned several more pages. "There's a Gestapo officer named Schokl in Radom. That must be your man, Schoegl."

With a red pencil he checked both names. He held the notebook in front of me, and said:

"This little notebook, Tadek, is the result of two years of hard work in Palestine. Very hard work." He paused, and bent closer to me. "Tadek, a few weeks ago the leader of your Kibbutz group told me about you, and about your work in Danzig."

He replaced the notebook in his drawer, and stood up. He drew a chair closer to me and continued. "In 1943 the Executive of the Jewish Agency in Jerusalem issued orders that we should begin to assemble evidence against the German murderers who took part in the executions of Jewish populations in Europe. Our little notebook has the names of Buchmayer and Schoegl, and also Botscher and Blum, who were also active in Radom. We have the names of thousands of lesser and major Nazi officials, given to us by Jews who reached Palestine from concentration camps and labor camps and ghettos. This evidence was taken through long hours of questioning, in Haifa, in Tel Aviv, in Jerusalem. We created quite an archive of these murderers, so that they can be brought to trial and punished for their crimes against our people."

Actually, he continued, this was the original reason why he had been sent to Austria from his Kibbutz in Palestine, to establish a group of dedicated volunteers who would track down the S.S. and Gestapo murderers in Germany and Austria. But, he said, he had been unable to initiate this work because of his other duties. "Every minute of the day we are bringing people to Palestine, and we also must do some work for the Haganah people, to get them some arms," he added. "Austria has seven borders, and groups of Jews are coming to us across all of them, begging for help to get to Palestine. We have transit camps filled with people, in Vienna, in Salzburg, in Linz, in Innsbruck, all waiting for us to bring them to Eretz Yisrael. And you know, Tadek, the situation in Palestine is far from good. The British are against us, the Arabs are against us. We cannot send Jews to Palestine who have never held a gun in their hands. They must be trained before we send them over. And to get people across the borders is not easy, as you know, I am sure. Meanwhile, our young people are becoming demoralized with the waiting, and we cannot do anything until they have been trained, and until the moment is right to cross the border to Italy and board one of our ships. And Jews keep coming here from every corner of Europe."

He paused and looked at me, his eyes hard and serious.

"This is not an easy job. None of us here works for money. We are all together, like members of a Kibbutz.

"I tell you all this, Tadek, so that you'll understand why I have not even been able to begin the work of tracking Nazi criminals. I know that you're experienced in this kind of work, and I am asking you, when you return from Stuttgart, to undertake this job for us, to establish a special Haganah group to find these murderers, to hunt them down and to find the greatest murderer of them all, Adolf Eichmann."

Arthur's words had electrified me. I felt somehow that destiny had guided me from Radom to Danzig, across Czechoslovakia, to Vienna, to this small room, to Arthur.

"Did you ever hear of Eichmann?" Arthur asked me.

I felt stupid, ashamed almost. "Everybody has heard of Hitler, Himmler, Heydrich, Goering, Kaltenbrunner, Goebbels, Rosenberg, Streicher, Ribbentrop," I said. "But I never heard the name Eichmann."

Very calmly, very seriously, Arthur said to me, "Friedman, you must find Eichmann. I will say it to you again: *you must find Eichmann.*"

4. *FORGIVE THEM NOT, FOR THEY KNEW WHAT THEY DID*

A. M. ROSENTHAL

When Mr. Rosenthal published this article in the *New York Times* magazine, an indignant reader of German background wrote a letter of complaint, comparing the often-mentioned destruction of Warsaw's Ghetto with the burning of Dresden by allied fliers. Others wrote in praise of Rosenthal's perceptive recognition of current anti-Semitism in Poland and Germany. More than assigning responsibilities for the past, Rosenthal leads us into the consideration of the present.

━━━

The first night we were together in Warsaw my wife and I went to a small cellar restaurant called "Manikin," and there we met a young writer and we had something to eat and a bit to drink and it was noisy and gay. Then the young writer said he would show us Warsaw.

It was early in the morning, about 2 or 3 o'clock, and he took us out of the old part of town into a terrible emptiness. I said, "What is it?" and he said it was the ghetto. There were some apartment buildings on the edges of the emptiness and they seemed awkward and strange, standing on what looked like mounds.

I said, "Why are they built like that?" and he said they were built

on the remains of buildings and bodies and rubble of the ghetto, because it was cheaper that way. The emptiness and realization of
what lay beneath the buildings made us cold and clammy, though
it was July, and my wife wept and, of course, so did I. The young
writer wept, too.

We walked back to our rooms at the Hotel Bristol, which was
our first home during my newspaper assignment to Warsaw. Our
children were sleeping there and my wife wept again. We talked
with the young writer for an hour or two more and then he left.
He told us he was not a Jew. But he was. His friends told us that
later, and then a long time afterwards he told us so, too.

I cannot remember now a great deal about how the ghetto
looked, though it was only about six years ago that I saw it last.
I do remember a monument to the Jewish dead in the midst of the
rubble, and how one day an East German delegation placed a
wreath there and how it was taken away later, because that was too
much.

I remember Richard Nixon, then Vice President, visiting the
ghetto and posing in a ruin for pictures and saying a few words,
and how pale and drawn he looked and how I felt a sympathy for
this man confronting the unspeakable for the first time. I remember
taking my three sons to the ghetto and trying to tell them what it
was and why, and not wanting to hurt or frighten them too much,
but how my oldest boy, who was then 8, did understand and was
filled with fears I did not know how to assuage.

These are my memories of the ghetto. Perhaps there are others,
but I do not wish to search for them, though I am ashamed of my
cowardice. I did not visit the ghetto very often in the year and a
half we spent in Poland. I do not know what the ghetto looks like
now and I do not really wish to know. Every man must have his
hiding place, though he be ashamed of it.

Why speak of these things now? Only because this is the time
of the 25th anniversary of the creation by the German Government
and German mind of that particular hell called the Warsaw Ghetto.
A time of anniversary is a time of remembrance or of mourning—at
least of remembrance—and in courtesy a man should say something.
A time of anniversary and what is there to say?

At least it can be known and said that the Jews of the Warsaw
Ghetto, and their wives and their children, at last fought the demons

unleashed upon them from out of the black and killed a goodly number of them before they all finally perished. Praise be to those Jews of the ghetto for that final act of cleansing amidst the imprisoning filth of the demons' evil.

Warsaw before the war was the most Jewish of European cities: There were some 400,000 Jews in the city when, on October 16, 1940, the Germans began rounding them up and packing them into the 100 square city blocks between the main railway station, the Saxon Gardens and the Danzig railroad terminal. The Germans built red brick walls and fences of barbed wire and caged their Jews, at first to starve, then to be rounded up neatly, plucked out and murdered by the tens of thousands in the magnificently engineered ovens.

Later, in 1943, those Jews who were left rose and fought and died, but took Germans with them into death. That was the uprising of the Warsaw Ghetto. (In 1959, when I was riding from West to East Berlin to return to Warsaw, the German driver of the car shook his head gloomily at the thought of the city. He told me he had been a Wehrmacht captain in Warsaw throughout the war and that it had been terrible, hideous. "You have no idea how many Germans were killed!" he said. I tipped him well, perhaps at the thought.)

And of the living? Now it is more than 20 years later and Poland lives on and Jews live in Poland.

There was once a Jewish tang to Warsaw, a ferment, a bustle, a shrill wonderment, a shrug, a yearning, that every Jew recognizes as the taste of Eastern European Jewry, and of which every Jew is rather abashedly fond, no matter how assimilated or unbelieving or sanitized his Jewishness is.

The taste still lingers. One day the pianist, Artur Rubinstein, came back to Poland after 20 years of absence and Warsaw wept in joy for him. At a party for the pianist, I asked a famous Polish poet just how people in Warsaw regarded Rubinstein—as a Pole, or an American, or a Jew, or what?

The poet said: "He is the best, so of course he is a Pole."

I thought the poet was a Pole and dutifully recorded the remark in a story, quite impressed with Polish nationalism. I found out later that the poet was a Jew, and by that time I knew a little about Poland, and I laughed and laughed and still laugh when I think of how he so solemnly mocked Rubinstein and me and himself and

Poles and all people who need labels—mocked us so solemnly, so lovingly.

The taste still lingers, but faintly. There are Jews in Poland, some 20,000 of them, who live with their Jewishness, and some few thousand more who try to forget it, but no real flavor of Warsaw's Jewishness survives the fire.

And what of their lives years later? Looking back, trying to cut away emotionalism, which is difficult, trying to get at root truths about what has followed the holocaust for the Jews of Poland, I think there are two.

The first is that the present Communist Government of Poland has neither stirred up public anti-Semitism nor condoned it, which is more than can be said about almost any other Government in Poland's history.

Of course, all Communist governments are "officially" against anti-Semitism. This becomes deeply sickening when basic policy, as so often in the Soviet Union, has been a mask for inspired anti-Semitism.

But so far as I was aware during my year and a half in Poland, the Communist Government itself never raked the ghetto's ashes to find living coals of evil. As a matter of fact, quietly and secretly the Government, at considerable risk of displeasure from Moscow and the Arab states, permitted Polish Jews and Jews returning from Russia to move on to Israel if they wished.

Perhaps there were motivations other than mere kindliness. Some Jews thought so, suggesting that the Government was also eager to rid itself of whatever Jewishness remained in Poland. But nobody who wanted to leave inquired too closely.

My relations with the Government before I was expelled in 1959 were hardly brotherly. But only once or twice did the Polish Communists ask me officially to treat a specific story delicately. And one was the story of the Jews leaving for Israel; the Polish Foreign Office felt that at that time publicity would make the Russians force the Poles to close the doors.

But this is the second truth: To the measure that the Jews of the ghetto died to save future Polish Jews from anti-Semitism in Poland, to that measure they died in vain.

It was the Germans, not the Poles who killed the Jews of the ghetto during the first years of the war and in the final uprising. But those Jews who died in the ghetto had lived their lives amidst the heavy stench of Polish anti-Semitism. That stench is lighter, now and again perfumed with guilt, but I believe it still hangs over Poland like a miasma.

I write of Poland as it was when I knew it. But I have shown this memoir to Poles and foreigners fresh from Warsaw and have talked with them of how things stand now with the Poles and the Jews, and they say nothing has changed, that it is still true.

It is a strange country, Poland, a schizophrenic country of wild ecstatic gaiety and deep brooding, great bravery and great cruelty. All countries have all these opposites, but in Poland they exist in more startling contrast than in any other country I know.

It was in Poland that one of the fiercest records of underground resistance to the German Gestapo was written. And it was in Warsaw and Lvov and Cracow that Polish gangs of "Jew catchers" roamed the streets, turning over to the Gestapo those helpless souls who could not pay ransom.

I do not really know why so many Poles dislike "their" Jews—to foreign Jews they are usually entirely correct—and I really do not care to know any more. I am weary to death of all the mincing sociological explanations that Jews were once money lenders or that some of them were Communists or that they were an economic threat to the Polish tradesmen. Weary, as a Negro in Alabama or Harlem must be weary, of being told that he simply must understand the *motivations* of people who try to cage him within the narrowness of their own inadequacies.

In Warsaw, almost a quarter of a century after the ghetto uprising, the Jews who remain are free to walk and talk—but only among the Poles, not of them. In Warsaw a Pole remains a Pole, a Jew a Jew.

There is a story told in Warsaw about a Jewish diplomat of the Polish Foreign Office. I know the man well. It goes this way: 25 per cent of the people hate him because he is a Communist; 25 per cent of the people hate him because he is a Jew; the rest hate him because he is a Jewish Communist.

It would be terribly unfair to believe that all Poles hate Jews. There are Poles who died to save Jews. There are also Jews who died to save Poles. But it would be naive not to understand that years after the wrenching agony of the Warsaw Ghetto, anti-Semitism still is part of Poland's marrow.

Some Jews try to escape reality. My young writer friend was one.

And one night another Polish friend took me to a restaurant out of town. The unshaven owner sat down with us and told us a story which my friend and newspaper clippings reported was true—that he was a Christian and wore one of the Government's highest medals for his acts of bravery in rescuing Jews from the ghetto.

"I am not a Jew, you know," he assured me. "But it makes me proud to get packages from some of the people of the ghetto now in Israel or in America."

We had a few drinks on that, and the owner went on drinking and drinking. Then he leaned his vodka breath on me, looked carefully around to see that his fat Russian wife was out of range, and whispered:

"It's a lie, a lie. My wife doesn't know it and my son doesn't know, but I am a Jew, a Jew. I don't look like one, do I? The Germans didn't know it and these Poles don't know it but it is true. On the Torah, it is true."

I had another friend who one day was arrested because he was politically disliked by the Government. I was worried, but a mutual friend who was a newspaperman and a colonel in the secret police, and quite a decent fellow, told me not to worry too much because "the jailers know Alex has friends and they won't treat him too roughly even though he is a Jew."

Another Jewish friend was a member of the Central Committee of the Communist party. One day after lunch I asked him whether there was any anti-Semitism within the party. He looked at me in astonishment and in scorn, and as I recall, said: "Rosenthal, you've been in this country almost a year and a half and apparently you haven't learned a damned thing."

Then he told me what it was to be a Jewish Communist. The Government did not want to encourage public anti-Semitism, he said, but inside the party it had to "take account of the realities of Polish life and not antagonize the people." That meant, he said, that Jews in the party kept as much as possible in the background so as "not to irritate people."

"I need a secretary, but I could never hire a Jewish girl," he said as I remember the conversation. "People would talk."

There was a priest who came to our house in Warsaw fairly often and I knew him quite well. One night I asked him about anti-Semitism in Poland. Could it possibly exist after Poles and Jews had suffered so much at the hands of Germans who had made anti-Semitism their crusade? Quietly he said he did not wish to make me sad, and so perhaps we should talk of other things, which we did.

These are my thoughts and memories at the 25th anniversary of the beginning of the Warsaw Ghetto, and they are not such as to lift men's hearts.

I speak only of a microcosm of the small Polish world. Perhaps other men can truthfully find in Poland or elsewhere richer meaning and hope in the lessons men and nations have drawn from the martyred ghetto. I pray so.

Then why speak of these things? Only because 25 years later I simply cannot tell myself nor my sons that it cannot happen again. I can only tell them that there was a time of madness and that some of the Jews of the ghetto fought the mad beast and died like men. And if it does happen again, even if there are faint dark signs that it might happen again, that most terrible of all prayers will rise, from myself, my sons and from men in all parts of the earth: "Forgive them not, Father, for they knew what they did."

The Questions after the Storm

Man, where art Thou? GEN. 3:9

They say to me: "Where is thy God?" PS. 42:4

INTRODUCTION

T HROUGHOUT THIS ANTHOLOGY, WE HAVE PARTICIPATED IN THE experience of the Shoah. Great literature—both fiction and fact—has guided us through the geography of hell, beyond the first stage, into the burning furnace, and out again into life. We now know what happened; and knowing this, we are prepared to ask why.

Why did it happen? A partial answer is contained in the selections presented in previous units. They bring us to a fuller knowledge of man—to the depths of his potential for evil, to the heights of his potential for good. These selections are not meant to be used as a parochial recounting of various horrors experienced by one people at one moment in history. The events of the Holocaust are only one terrible avenue leading into the abyss of human evil, and the twentieth century has many pathways leading into that abyss—Graveyards and camps in Russia testifying to the Stalin purges, the rain of death which covered the countryside of Hiroshima and Nagasaki, hundreds of thousands slain within one week in Indonesia, famine in India in a world of plenty; we learn of evil in many ways. Out of this knowledge comes the realization that there is in man's nature that which destroys, that the world is etched in the acid of man's deeds. Some take this as the full answer—as Sartre's assertion that man is condemned to be free is a courageous attempt to accept man in his evil, to live in a world without meaning, still striving to assert aspects of man's nobility with the full knowledge of the futility of his action. Others, using the same facts, arrive at the opposite conclusions—that man's goodness can overcome all evil. Though confronted with man's evil deeds, they, nonetheless, feel that man can renounce this path and advance into a better world which is his to create. Both of these answers are generally given outside the framework of religion. The question of evil is asked of man and not of God. But our selections examine the dimensions of evil as they manifested themselves in the Shoah, an event which decimated the covenant people Israel, the people who have affirmed God and have been His witness. And so, religion enters. And we confront God with the question, "Why is there evil in Your world?"

A century and a half ago, the poet Heinrich Heine viewed the religion of his era as a tottering business establishment "which cannot maintain itself for much longer. The checks it has written out on philosophy come back marked 'insufficient funds.' Even now, it is going into bankruptcy. . . ." Somehow, the various establishments of religion are still around. Yet, there are many who feel that religion has simply neglected to notify the public of its bankrupt condition. Today, when the demands made upon religion are so much clearer and more urgent—the Shoah simply puts old questions into the sharpest possible form—religion must make some response or close its doors.

There are religious answers. We have encountered some of them in our readings. And can we lightly say that the most traditional answers are invalid and have no force? If there were those who prayed in the final moments of torture, if there were those who saw themselves as witnesses of a faith which would ultimately prevail, if there were those who believed in resurrection and the Messiah—if there were these, can we deny the validity and strength of their solutions? Although we may not be prepared to admit it, our own existence is built upon a heritage of belief in a God who both loves and metes out punishment; it may well be that we are free to doubt because they were ready to believe.

Our generation is a doubting one; and we must explore those avenues of twentieth century thought which reach out towards answers through which our own generation may confront God. At the very least, we need a new language in this attempt. The Reverend William Hamilton, one of the prominent "God is dead" theologians, once said, "God died at Auschwitz, with the death of six million Jews." For Hamilton and others, the crimes of the Nazis and the anguish of the twentieth century shattered all previously held notions about a God whose moral system guides the world towards perfection. Rabbi Richard Rubenstein, who views himself in the mainstream of God-is-dead theology, has written: "My own way of facing the question of God and the death camps has been to regard life as arriving out of God's Nothingness and ultimately returning to that same Nothingness. My view of existence is not optimistic. The ironies and tragedies of life can only be overcome by a return to God's Nothingness. Auschwitz is part of the terrible price we have to pay for the human condition." Doubt and moral anguish here lead to a post-Auschwitz nihilism which sees the evil of man as the prime fact of life.

Other answers are given. There are the actions of those days which speak to us—a father leads his child into the gas chamber, bending down to whisper final words of comfort. The novelist Maurice Samuel has pointed out that this father had more important things to do than to pick up a gun and shoot a Nazi; he had to give solace to his child in those last moments. There were those who prayed. There were those who cursed. Some were struck dumb. At times, the human body gave its own answer—Eugene Heimler reports that women did not have menstrual periods once they had entered the camps. All of this speaks to us; and we have to listen.

The teachers of our time have their own answers. In this final section, we turn to contemporary thinkers and pose our questions about the nature of God and man after Auschwitz. Their answers conflict with one another. Hans Jonas begins with an involved myth and uses it to shatter most of the religious framework which we possess. Jack Bemporad is a young liberal theologian who applies Jonas' insight to the concept of man in Jewish life today. By contrast, Abraham Joshua Heschel gives a traditional answer touched by poetry and mysticism. Emil Fackenheim then surveys all of the theological scene today—the secular atmosphere, radical theology, Jewish thought from Buber to Wiesel; both rabbi and philosopher, he arrives at his answer. The outer environment speaks to us once more through the wisdom of Paul Tillich, one of the great Christian thinkers of our time. Finally, we come to Leo Baeck—Judaism anchored in philosophy. He speaks for the tradition, but out of the experience of the twentieth century. Starting with man and the human experience, he terminates in the awareness of the Unconditional, the Infinite. In defining man, Baeck discovers God.

Somehow, in one of these answers, in all of them, in none but in our own, we have to discover ourselves—post-Auschwitz man.

1. THE CONCEPT OF GOD AFTER AUSCHWITZ

HANS JONAS

Professor Hans Jonas teaches philosophy at the New School for Social Research. He is a provocative thinker with an enormous span of knowledge; more than an authority on contemporary philosophy, he is also one of the world authorities on gnosticism and gnostic religion. In this selection, he enlarges upon a concept of God first presented in his Harvard University Ingersoll lecture on "Immortality and the Modern Temper,"[1] which created a stir among religious thinkers. In the course of its argument, Professor Jonas employed the Platonic device of a "myth," that is, a symbolic tale, to adumbrate a possible view of things which by their transcendent nature elude the grasp of direct rational discourse. The following presentation combines excerpts from this myth with a discussion of some of its theological implications.

━━━

In the beginning, for unknowable reasons, the ground of being, or the divine, chose to give itself over to the chance and risk and endless variety of becoming. And wholly so: entering into the adventure of space and time, the deity held back nothing of itself: no uncommitted or unimpaired part remained to direct, correct, and ultimately guarantee the devious working-out of its destiny in

---

[1] First published in the *Harvard Theological Review,* Vol. 55 (1962), pp. 1–20, and now forming the concluding essay in Jonas' book *The Phenomenon of Life: Toward a Philosophical Biology,* New York: Harper and Row, 1966.

creation. On this unconditional immanence the modern temper insists. It is its courage or despair, in any case its bitter honesty, to take our being-in-the-world seriously: to view the world as left to itself, its laws as brooking no interference, and the rigor of our belonging to it as not softened by extramundane providence. The same our myth postulates for God's being in the world . . . . In order that the world might be, and be for itself, God renounced His own being, divesting Himself of His deity—to receive it back from the Odyssey of time weighted with the chance harvest of unforeseeable temporal experience: transfigured or possibly even disfigured by it. In such self-forfeiture of divine integrity for the sake of un-prejudiced becoming, no other foreknowledge can be admitted than that of *possibilities* which cosmic being offers in its own terms: to these, God committed His cause in effacing Himself for the world.

And for aeons God's cause is safe in the slow hands of cosmic chance and probability—while all the time we may surmise a patient memory of the gyrations of matter to accumulate into an ever more expectant accompaniment of eternity to the labors of time—a hesitant emergence of transcendence from the opaqueness of immanence.

And then the first stirring of *life*—a new language of the world: and with it a tremendous quickening of concern in the eternal realm and a sudden leap in its growth toward recovery of its pleni-tude. It is the world-accident for which becoming deity had waited and with which its prodigal stake begins to show signs of being re-deemed. From the infinite swell of feeling, sensing, striving and acting, which ever more varied and intense rises above the mute eddyings of matter, eternity gains strength, filling with content after content of self-affirmation, and the awakening God can first pro-nounce creation to be good.

But note that with life together came death, and that mortality is the price which the new possibility of being had to pay for it-self . . . . If, then, mortality is the very condition of the separate self-hood which in the instinct of self-preservation shows itself so highly prized throughout the organic world, and if the yield of this mortal-ity is the food of eternity, it is unreasonable to demand for its appointed executants, the self-affirming selves—immortality. The instinct of self-preservation indeed acknowledges this, for it implies the premise of extinction in its straining each time to ward it off for the nonce.

Note also this that with life's innocence before the advent of knowledge God's cause cannot go wrong. Whatever variety evolution brings forth adds to the possibilities of feeling and acting, and thus enriches the self-experiencing of the ground of being. . . . The ever more sharpened keenness of appetite and fear, pleasure and pain, triumph and anguish, love and even cruelty—their very edge is the deity's gain. Their countless, yet never blunted incidence—hence the necessity of death and new birth—supplies the tempered essence from which the Godhead reconstitutes itself. All this, evolution provides in the mere lavishness of its play and the sternness of its spur. Its creatures, by merely fulfilling themselves in pursuit of their lives, vindicate the divine venture. Even their suffering deepens the fullness of the symphony. Thus, this side of good and evil, God cannot lose in the great evolutionary game.

Nor yet can He fully win in the shelter of its innocence, and a new expectancy grows in Him in answer to the direction which the unconscious drift of immanence gradually takes.

And then He trembles as the thrust of evolution, carried by its own momentum, passes the threshold where innocence ceases and an entirely new criterion of success and failure takes hold of the divine stake. The advent of man means the advent of knowledge and freedom, and with this supremely double-edged gift the innocence of the mere subject of self-fulfilling life has given way to the charge of responsibility under the disjunction of good and evil. To the promise and risk of this agency the divine cause, revealed at last, henceforth finds itself committed; and its issue trembles in the balance. The image of God, haltingly begun by the universe, for so long worked upon—and left undecided—in the wide and then narrowing spirals of prehuman life, passes with this last twist, and with a dramatic quickening of the movement, into man's precarious trust, to be completed, saved, or spoiled by what he will do to himself and the world. And in this awesome impact of his deeds on God's destiny, on the very complexion of eternal being, lies the immortality of man.

With the appearance of man, transcendence awakened to itself and henceforth accompanies his doings with the bated breath of suspense, hoping and beckoning, rejoicing and grieving, approving and frowning—and, I dare say, making itself felt to him even while not intervening in the dynamics of his worldly scene: for could it not be that by the reflection of its own state as it wavers with the record of man, the transcendent casts light and shadow over the human landscape?

Such is the tentative myth which I propose for consideration. There are a number of theological implications in this myth of mine, but—as a matter of biographical fact—the myth really came first, and the theological or conceptual translation to which it lends itself has only slowly emerged for me. It is still in the process of emerging. I will treat here some of the more obvious concepts involved, in the hope to connect what must seem a strange and rather willful personal fantasy with the more responsible tradition of Jewish religious thought. By this means I try to redeem the irresponsibility of my tentative, groping speculation.

First, and most obviously, I have been speaking of a *suffering God* —which immediately seems to clash with the biblical conception of divine majesty. There is, of course, a Christian connotation of the term "suffering God," with which my myth must not be confounded; it does not speak, as does the former, of a special act by which the deity at one time, and for the special purpose of saving man, sends part of itself into a particular situation of suffering (the incarnation and crucifixion). If anything in what I said makes sense, then the sense is that the relation of God to the world *from the moment of creation,* and certainly from the creation of man on, involves suffering on the part of God. It involves, to be sure, suffering on the part of the creature too, but this truism has always been recognized in every theology. Not so the idea of God's suffering with creation, and of this I said that prima facie it clashes with the biblical conception of divine majesty. But does it really clash so extremely as it seems at first glance? Don't we also in the Bible encounter God as slighted and rejected by man and grieving over him? Don't we encounter Him as ruing that He created man, and suffering from the disappointment He experiences with him—and with His chosen people in particular? We remember the prophet Hosea.

Then, the myth suggests the picture of a *becoming God*. It is a God emerging in time instead of possessing a completed being that remains identical with itself throughout eternity. Such an idea of divine becoming is surely at variance with the Greek, Platonic-

Aristotelian tradition of philosophical theology which, since its incorporation into the Jewish and Christian theological tradition, has somehow usurped to itself an authority to which it is not at all entitled by authentic Jewish (and Christian) standards. Trans-temporality, impassibility, immutability have been taken to be necessary attributes of God. And the ontological opposition maintained by classical thought between being and becoming, with the latter characteristic of the lower, sensible world, excluded every shadow of becoming from the pure, absolute being of the Godhead. But this Hellenic concept has never accorded well with the spirit and language of the Bible; and the concept of divine becoming can actually be better reconciled with it.

For what does the becoming God mean? Even if we do not go as far as our myth suggests, that much at least we must concede of "becoming" in God as lies in the mere fact that He is affected by what happens in the world, and "affected" means altered, made different. Even apart from the fact that creation as such was after all a decisive change in the condition of God himself, His continuous *relation* (if only of knowledge, let alone of interest) to the creation, once it exists and moves in the flux of becoming, means that He experiences something with the world, that His own being is affected by what goes on in it. Thus if God is in any relation to the world—which is the cardinal assumption of religion—then by that token alone the Eternal has "temporalized" Himself and progressively becomes different through the actualizations of the world process.

One incidental consequence of the idea of the becoming God is that it destroys the idea of an eternal recurrence of the same. This was Nietzsche's alternative to Christian metaphysics, which in this case is the same as Jewish metaphysics. It is indeed the extreme symbol of the turn to unconditional temporality and of the complete negation of any transcendence which could keep a memory of what happens in time, to assume that by the mere exhaustion of the possible combinations and recombinations of material elements it must come to pass that an "initial" configuration recurs and the whole cycle starts over again; and if once, then innumerable times—Nietzsche's "ring of rings, the ring of eternal recurrence." However, if we assume that eternity is not unaffected by what happens in time, there can never be a recurrence of the same, because God will not be the same after He has gone through the experience of a world process. Any new world coming after the end of one will carry, as it were, in its own heritage the memory of what has gone before; or in other words, there will not be an indifferent and dead eternity, but an eternity that grows with the accumulating harvest of time.

Bound up with the concepts of a suffering and a becoming God is that of a *caring God*—a God not remote and detached and self-contained but involved with what He cares for. Whatever the "prim-ordial" condition of the Godhead, He ceased to be self-contained once He let Himself in for the existence of a world by creating such a world or letting it come to be. God's caring about His creatures is, of course, among the most familiar tenets of Jewish faith. But my myth stresses the less familiar aspect that this caring God is not a sorcerer who in the act of caring also provides the fulfillment of His concern: He has left something for other agents to do and thereby made His care dependent upon them. He is therefore also an en-dangered God, a God who risks something. Clearly that must be so, or else the world would be in a condition of permanent perfection. The fact that it is not bespeaks one of two things: that either there is no God at all, or there is a God who has given a chance and au-thority to something other than Himself about that which is a con-cern of His. This is why I said that the caring God is not a sorcerer. Somehow He has, by an act of either inscrutable wisdom or love or whatever else the divine motive may have been, foregone the guar-anteeing of His self-satisfaction by His own power.

And therewith we come to what is perhaps the most critical point in our speculative, theological venture: this is not an omnipotent God. We argue indeed that, for the sake of our image of God and our whole relation to the divine, for the sake of any viable theology, we cannot uphold the time-honored (medieval) doctrine of absolute, unlimited divine power.

Let me argue this first, on a purely logical plane, by pointing out the paradox in the idea of absolute power. The logical situation in-deed is by no means that divine omnipotence is the rationally plaus-ible and somehow self-recommending doctrine, while that of its limitation is wayward and in need of defense. Quite the opposite. From the very concept of power it follows that omnipotence is a self-contradictory, self-destructive, indeed senseless concept. Abso-lute, total power means power not limited by anything, not even by the mere existence of something other than the possessor of that power; for the very existence of such another would already constitute a limitation, and the one would have to annihilate it so as to save its absoluteness. Absolute power then, in its solitude, has no object on which to act. But as objectless power it is a powerless power, canceling itself out: "all" equals "zero" here. In order for it to act there must be something else, and as soon as there is, the one is not all-powerful any more, even though in any comparison its power may be superior by any degree you please to imagine. The existence of another object limits the power of the most powerful agent at the same time that it allows it to be an agent. In brief, power as such is a relational concept and requires relation.

Again, power meeting no resistance in its relatum is equal to no-power-at-all: power is exercised only in relation to something which itself has power. Power, unless otiose, consists in the capacity to overcome something; and something's existence as such is enough to provide this condition. For existence means resistance and thus opposing force. That, therefore, upon which power acts must have a power of its own, even if that power derives from the first and was initially granted to it, as one with its existence, by a self-renunciation of limitless power—i.e., in the act of creation.

In short, it cannot be that all power is on the side of one agent only. Power must be divided so that there be any power at all.

But beside this logical and ontological, there is a more theological, genuinely religious objection to the idea of absolute and unlimited divine omnipotence. We can have divine omnipotence together with divine goodness only at the price of complete divine inscrutability. Seeing the existence of evil in the world, we must sacrifice intelligibility in God to the combination of the other two attributes. Only a completely unintelligible God can be said to be absolutely good and absolutely powerful, and yet tolerate the world as it is. Now, which of the three attributes at stake, the conjunction of any two of which excludes the third, are truly integral to our concept of God, and which, being of lesser force, must give way to their superior claim? Surely, goodness is inalienable from the concept of God and not open to qualification. Intelligibility, related to both God's nature and man's limitation, is on the latter count indeed subject to qualification, but on no account to complete elimination. The *Deus absconditus*, the hidden God, is a profoundly un-Jewish conception. Our teaching holds that we can understand God, not completely, to be sure, but something of Him—of His will, intentions, and even nature, because He has told us. There has been revelation, we have His commandments and His law, and He has directly communicated with some. Thus, a completely hidden God is not an acceptable concept by Jewish norms.

But He would have to be precisely that if together with being good He were conceived as all-powerful. After Auschwitz, we can assert with greater force than ever before that an omnipotent deity would have to be either not good or totally unintelligible. But if God is to be intelligible in some manner and to some extent (and to this we must hold), then His goodness must be compatible with the existence of evil, and this it is only if He is not *all*-powerful. Only then can we uphold that He is intelligible and good, and there is yet evil in the world. And since we have found the concept of omnipotence to be doubtful anyway, it is this which has to give way.

So far, our argument about omnipotence has done no more than lay it down as a principle for any acceptable theology somehow continuous with the Jewish heritage that God's power be seen limited by something whose being in its own right and whose power to act on its own authority He himself acknowledges.[2] We may well consider that this is a voluntary concession on God's part which He has the power to revoke at will. My own suggestion as presented in the "myth" goes further. For reasons decisively prompted by contemporary experience I entertain the idea of a God who for a time—the time of the ongoing world process—has divested Himself of any power to interfere with the physical course of things, and Who responds to the impact on His being of worldly events—not *beyad chazakah uzeroah netuyah*, but with the mutely insistent appeal of His unfulfilled aim.

This I will not further elaborate. In any case, the elimination of divine omnipotence which follows from our discussion of power leaves us with the alternatives of either some preexistent—theological or ontological—dualism, or of God's own self-limitation through the creation from nothing. The first alternative might take

---

[2] The same principle has been argued, with a slightly different reasoning, by Rabbi J. Bemporad, "Toward a New Jewish Theology," *American Judaism*, Winter 1964–65, pp. 9 ff.

the Manichaean form of an active force of evil opposing the divine purpose in the universal scheme of things (a two-god theology), or the Platonic form of a passive medium imposing imperfection, no less universally, on the embodiment of the ideal in the world (a form-matter dualism). The first is plainly unacceptable to Judaism. The second answers at best the problem of imperfection and natural necessity, but not that of positive evil which implies a freedom empowered by its own authority over and against God; and it is the fact and success of evil rather than the inflictions of blind, natural causality—the use of the latter in the hands of responsible agents (Auschwitz rather than the earthquake of Lisbon)—with which Jewish theology has to contend at this hour. Only with creation from nothing do we have the oneness of the divine principle combined with that self-limitation which then permits (gives "room" to) the existence and autonomy of a world. Creation was that act of absolute sovereignty with which it consented, for the sake of self-determined finitude, to be absolute no more. My myth merely pushes further the old Jewish idea of the *tzimtzum,* the contraction of divine being as the condition for the being of a world. The enormous enhancement of this being in the light of modern knowledge, viz., of the irrefrangible, self-sufficient, creative powers of Nature—and of the share appropriable of them by man—must needs radicalize the concept of *tzimtzum* to a point never imagined before.

Certain ethical conclusions follow from the myth and its adumbrations. The first is the transcendent importance of our deeds, of how we live our lives. If man, as our tale has it, was created "for" the image of God, rather than "in" His image; if our lives become lines in the divine countenance—then our responsibility is not defined in mundane terms alone, by which often it is inconsequential enough, but registers in a dimension where efficacy follows transcausal norms of inner essence. Further, as transcendence grows with the terribly ambiguous harvest of deeds, our impact on eternity is for good *and* for evil—we can build and we can destroy, we can heal and we can hurt, we can nourish and we can starve divinity, we can perfect and we can disfigure its image—and the scars of one are as enduring as the lustre of the other. Thus the immortality of our deeds is no cause for vain rejoicing—what most often ought to be wished for is rather their leaving no trace. But this is not granted;

they have traced their line. Not, however, as the individual's destiny. The individual is by nature temporal, not eternal; and the person in particular, mortal trustee of an immortal cause, has the enjoyment of selfhood for the moment of time as the means by which eternity lays itself open to the decisions of time. As enacted in the medium of becoming, that is, as transient, are personal selves eternity's stake. Thus it is that in the irrepeatable occasions of finite lives the issue must be decided time and again; infinite duration would blunt the point of the issue and rob occasion of its urgent call.

Nor, apart from this ontological consideration, does man have a moral claim to the gift of immortality. Availing himself of the enjoyment of selfhood, he has endorsed the terms on which it is offered, and rather than having it as a title for more he owes thanks for the grant of existence as such—and for that which made it possible. For there is no necessity of there being a world at all. Why there is something rather than nothing—this unanswerable question of metaphysics should protect us from taking existence for an axiom, and its finiteness for a blemish on it or a curtailment of its right. Rather is the fact of existence the mystery of mysteries —which our myth has tried to reflect in a symbol. By foregoing its own inviolateness the eternal ground allowed the world to be. To this self-denial all creature owes its existence, and with it has received all there is to receive from beyond. Having given Himself whole to the becoming world, God has no more to give; it is man's now to give to Him. And he may give by seeing to it in the ways of his life that it does not happen, or not happen too often, and not on his account, that "it repented the Lord" (Gen. 6:6-7) to have made the world. This may well be the secret of the "thirty-six righteous ones" whom, according to Jewish tradition, the world shall never lack (Sanhedrin 97b, Sukkah 45b): that with the superior valency of good over evil, which, we hope, obtains in the non-causal logic of things there, their hidden holiness can outweigh countless guilt, redress the balance of a generation and secure the serenity of the invisible realm.

But does that serenity, or its contrary, matter to our life on earth? Does it touch it? Let me join this question with another one, in conclusion of my groping journey. What about those who never could inscribe themselves in the Book of Life with deeds either good or evil, great or small, because their lives were cut off before they had their chance, or their humanity was destroyed in degradations most cruel and most thorough such as no humanity can survive? I am thinking of the gassed and burnt children of Auschwitz, of the defaced, de-humanized phantoms of the camps, and of all the other, numberless victims of the other man-made holocausts of our time. Among men, their sufferings will soon be forgotten, and their names even sooner. Another chance is not given them, and eternity has no compensation for what has been missed in time. Are they, then, debarred from an immortality which even their tormentors and murderers obtain because they could act—abominably, yet accountably, thus leaving their sinister mark on eternity's face? This I refuse to believe. And this I like to believe: that there was weeping in the heights at the waste and despoilment of humanity; that a groan answered the rising shout of ignoble suffering, and wrath—the terrible wrong done to the reality and possibility of each life thus wantonly victimized, each one a thwarted attempt of God. "The voice of thy brother's blood cries unto me from the ground": Should we not believe that the immense chorus of such cries that has risen up in our lifetime now hangs over our world as a dark, mournful, and accusing cloud? That eternity looks down upon us with a frown, wounded itself and perturbed in its depths? And might we not even feel it? If the secret sympathy that connects our being with the transcendent condition works both ways (as in some manner it must, or else there would not even be that inward testimony for us to invoke on which our whole case for the eternal was grounded[3]), then there will always be some resonance to that condition in ours—sometimes felt, though mostly not, and presently felt, perhaps, in a general malaise, in the profound distemper of the contemporary mind. Things human do not prosper under our hands. Happiness eludes our pursuit, and meaning mocks our desperate need. Could it not be that superinduced upon the many-levelled, but never completely explaining causes from within our historical existence, also the disturbance of the transcendent order which we have caused thus reverberates in the spiritual mood of men—and thus the modern temper paradoxically might itself reflect the immor-

---

[3] Refers to an earlier part of the Ingersoll lecture, not included here. See *Phenomenon of Life,* pp. 268 f.

tality which it disowns? It would be fitting—more I dare not say—if the slaughtered had that share in immortality, and on their account a great effort were asked of those alive to lift the shadow from our brow and gain for those after us a new chance of serenity by restoring it to the invisible world.

But even if not their shadow, certainly the shadow of the Bomb is there to remind us that the image of God is in danger as never before, and on most unequivocal, terrestrial terms. That in these terms an eternal issue is at stake together with the temporal one—this aspect of our responsibility can be our guard against the temptation of fatalistic acquiescence or the worse treason of "après nous le déluge." We literally hold in our faltering hands the future of the divine adventure and must not fail Him, even if we would fail ourselves.

Thus in the dim light at the end of our wandering we may discern a twofold responsibility of man: one in terms of worldly causality, by which the effect of his deed extends for some greater or shorter length into a future where it eventually dissipates; and a simultaneous one in terms of its impact on the eternal realm, where it never dissipates. The one, with our limited foresight and the complexity of worldly things, is much at the mercy of luck and chance; the other goes by knowable norms which, in the Bible's words (Deut. 30:14), are not far from our hearts. There might even be, as I indicated, a third dimension to our responsibility in terms of the impalpably reciprocal way in which Eternity, without intervening in the physical course of things, will communicate its spiritual state as a pervading mood to a generation which will have to live with it.

But the first two are more than enough to summon us to our task. Although the hereafter is not ours, nor eternal recurrence of the here, we can have immortality at heart when in our brief span we serve our threatened mortal affairs and help the suffering immortal God.

2. *THE CONCEPT OF MAN AFTER AUSCHWITZ*

JACK BEMPORAD

Jack Bemporad, director of worship for the Union of American Hebrew Congregations, assesses the vitality of Jewish thought and its relevance to the problems of the day, its ability to speak to the new generation who come in or stay out of synagogues. In a very real way, he functions as a "Socratic gadfly." In this essay, he asks disturbing questions which deserve answers from the spokesmen of organized religion.

———

Serene optimism and staunch belief in the inevitability of progress —these are the key attitudes that characterize late-nineteenth century thinking; thinking that was the result of a unique combination of doctrines which maintained that man was essentially a rational being, that the only serious evil was ignorance, and that the combined forces of science, technology, and man's innate goodness and rationality could lead to progress and social fulfillment. Science, it was believed, could unveil the secrets of reality and, through technology, would be the means by which man would triumph as lord of creation.

In this optimistic spirit, there was Einstein attempting to work out a unified field theory which would integrate and set forth the final stage in the progress of physics which began with Galileo. And there was Freud who hoped that through the development of psychoanalysis, the last dark clouds of ignorance and irrationality that hovered over man could be illuminated by the light of science and rationality. If there were some like Nietzsche and Burkhardt who sounded a note of warning, still, the nineteenth century maintained its dogmatic belief in the progress and fulfillment of man.

But the nineteenth century all too quickly became the twentieth, and now it is all so different. Today we have the bomb and have learned such words as failsafe and overkill. We have the awesome power to destroy our planet and with it the process of creation. Today we are much less sanguine about the limits of science as well as its triumphs. We are uncertain and uneasy in the face of the colossal expansion of twentieth century technology. We are living in the midst of transformations that stagger the imagination. So much that will happen is unimaginable but also so much that has happened was also and continues to be unimaginable.

We have managed to forget Auschwitz and Buchenwald; perhaps we could never really believe or understand them in the first place. They seem to have been some horrifying intrusion, a prolonged nightmare that we have suppressed and prefer not to discuss. And yet it happened and it can happen again or worse.

There are some like Elie Wiesel who live among us as ghosts, who ask us how we can live and forget and still be human. What we seem to forget is the real issue that our humanity is at stake. The real issue is to question man himself, his dimensions, his destructiveness, his demonism, his awesome power for evil.

The holocaust has given rise to a temper of absolute despair—despair because man has used his most precious knowledge, his reason, science, and technology, the achievements of the scientific spirit, for genocide, for mass murder. And yet this surrender to despair is much too facile; it does not adequately account for the value of what has been lost. The holocaust has shaken us not because it shows that nothing has meaning—in such a situation, the loss of the meaningless and useless is no cause for dismay. The tragedy is that so very much that had so much meaning could be lost—and was lost. It demonstrates for us the possibility of the perversion of all that is dear. It indicates to us the potential demonism in man, and it has awakened us from the optimistic slumber of the nineteenth century.

The holocaust has taught us a great deal about the nature of man —psychologically, philosophically, and theologically.

On the psychological level, the holocaust has shown us the effects a totalitarian system has on its subjects—both persecuted and persecutor. The concentration camp provides an agonizingly clear example of how a totalitarian state can deform and depersonalize all people under its rule.

The Nazis depersonalized and dehumanized their victims in a variety of ways, beginning with mass arrests, often awakening and terrorizing victims at night, herding them by the hundreds and thousands into stifling cattle cars, taking away all their belongings, shaving their heads, and assigning them numbers in place of names. The list goes on and on. Suffice it to say that any attempt at individuality and spontaneity was immediately and ruthlessly punished. The camp was geared to reducing man to a purely sub-human animal existence, an animal existence with but one aim—to survive at any cost, and the final result of the process of dehumanization and depersonalization was that in time, those who did survive often adopted Nazi attitudes, identifying themselves with their persecutors, judging themselves by Nazi standards.

Bruno Bettelheim points this out when he writes:

> A prisoner had reached the final stage of adjustment to the camp situation when he had changed his personality so as to accept as his own the values of the Gestapo .... Can one imagine a greater triumph for any system than this adoption of its values and behavior by its powerless victims?

The process of dehumanization and depersonalization was not limited to the victims; it affected the persecutors, too. Certain eyewitness reports vividly demonstrate this. This can be seen in a description of the Elite Guards' destruction of the little French town of Oradour-sur-Glane:

> "The peak of horror," said the Swiss informant, Ernst von Schenck, "is not reached by the fact, that as an act of revenge, a whole town has been reduced to ashes, the entire male population shot and all women and children locked up and burned in the church. If such a thing had been done in a delirium

of hatred, aroused by a savage fight, it would have been grue-some enough, but somehow humanly understandable . . . . But the Elite Guards who had received this order . . . carried it out with utter calmness and placidity (*seelenruhig*). They assembled the women and children with pronounced kind-ness. The mothers were moved by so much tender care on the part of these dreaded men who were hugging and fondling the children, playing and joking with them, taking them gently into their arms or putting them carefully into the perambulators. Their behavior was such that the mothers followed them confidently into the church as if they all went to some feast of atonement. After all the women and children had gathered in the church the doors were closed and the mass murder began.

"I am convinced," Mr. Von Schenck continues, "that these Elite Guards did not feel the slightest shade of hatred against the French children when they held them in their arms. Some of them, in this moment, might even have thought of home and might have toyed with the idea of fondling their own child. And I am equally convinced that, if a counter order had arrived . . . they would have continued to play daddy . . . but, an order is an order. What kind of human beings are these? . . ." Mr. Von Schenck shudderingly asks. "Here a limit has been reached where no analogy can be found in the be-havior of any other people up to this time and, let us hope—from now on."

Eric Kahler, in his book, *The Tower and the Abyss*, illustrates the schizophrenic quality characteristic of the Nazi doctors and others who engaged in experiments on human guinea pigs. They observed all the health regulations so that conditions would be hygienic while the actual activities engaged in were barbarically inhuman. I believe Kahler correctly evaluates the psychological character of this process when he writes:

The same phenomenon that we observed here in specific cases of actual human behavior may also be found residual in common practices of the Third Reich. The interrogation of terrified Jews as a feature of the radio, the mailing of the ashes of murdered people by parcel post, the use of human bones, fats and hair for the manufacturing of fertilizers, soap and mattresses, of tattooed human skin for lampshades and handbags, the setting up of advertising posters next to the extermination camps by the firms which furnished installa-tions—all such combinations of things human, of death and suffering which, throughout history, have been surrounded by awe and ritual cultivation, with the mechanized processes of modern industry and technology and the exploitation of matter which they imply—all this reflects the same weirdly incoherent form of human behavior, which, I contend made its first appearance in our epoch. . . . The frightening new feature in modern atrocities is exactly the lack of such personal focus in which conflicting faculties can still cohere. The split in the personality reaches into unfathomable depths, it is total, it is consummate schizophrenia. While formerly the divergent parts of the personality, being somewhere and somehow deeply connected, both belonged in the orbit of the individual psyche and, therefore, retained some ultimate homogeneity—they were both still human in that they were personal—today these parts are utterly heterogeneous; the part that commits atrocities seems wholly impersonal and, accordingly, inhuman in the literal sense of the word; indeed, we should rather call it a-human. Even inhuman behavior, brutality or cruelty derives from impulses which are human. These Nazi acts and practices did not evolve from genuine cruelty or brutal rage (they were not particularly enjoyed, nor were they abhorred) ; they were done without pleasure but also without repugnance. They were not done personally at all—no feeling whatsoever was involved. They were done functionally on order with extreme factuality in a thoroughly businesslike manner.

The depersonalization and dehumanization characteristic of the Nazis (and also practiced by the Russian and Chinese Communists) was the culmination of a process whose roots went back to the sixteenth century. Implicit in the triumph of modern science and the dualism that ensued between matter and mind concomitant with its rejection of teleology, the universe became completely divorced from any reference to human ends. The world functioned on the basis of purely mechanical laws. Professor Hans Jonas points this out when he states:

> The indifference of nature also means that nature has no reference to ends. With the ejection of teleology from the system of natural causes, nature, itself purposeless, ceased to provide any sanction to possible human purposes. A universe without an intrinsic hierarchy of being, as the Copernican universe is, leaves values ontologically unsupported, and the self is thrown back entirely upon itself in its quest for meaning and value. Meaning is no longer found but is "conferred."

> Values are no longer beheld in the vision of objective reality, but are posited as feats of valuation. As functions of the will, ends are solely my own creation. Will replaces vision; temporality of the act ousts the eternity of the "good in itself." This is the Nietzschean phase of the situation in which European nihilism breaks the surface. Now man is alone with himself.

Left alone with his own will without any reference to a physical or spiritual cosmos, man simply becomes a creature of desires, of needs and passions. This philosophical result fits in well with the triumph of Darwinism which viewed man as a high grade animal whose reason in no way elevated him or separated him from the rest of the animal kingdom. Reason in evolutionary thought was viewed as an instrument for survival and became a tool of the life process. It thus became a means and once reason becomes merely a means, all ends are irrational. Once man is seen to be devoid of any connection with objective values, and as merely a high grade animal completely alien to nature, then one reaches what Jonas has called the true abyss. As Jonas states, "that nature does not care one way or the other is the true abyss. That only man cares, in his finitude facing nothing but death, alone with his contingency and the objective meaninglessness of his projecting meanings is a truly unprecedented situation." There is very little question that the holocaust could have occurred only through such a devaluation of all that man cherished. Only through the wide acceptance that man had no special dignity and meaning that nothing mattered except survival on the most animalistic level.

For some it appears that this human condition, this general malaise whose ultimate expression culminated in the holocaust reinforces the Augustinian Christian belief in original sin: man is by nature corrupt and through his own devices can only destroy himself. The only hope is an otherworldly salvation. Only a depraved being, this view maintains, born with original sin could have committed such heinous crimes.

It seems that we have gone full circle from the rational optimistic doctrine of man rooted in Greek and Enlightenment thought to an irrationalist pessimism rooted in classic Augustinian, Lutheran Christianity conjoined with some aspects of contemporary biology.

The holocaust has indeed demonstrated that man can destroy

himself. It has shown that man in a dehumanized state is capable of doing untold and unbelievable harm. It has also shown that man is not by nature good. It has not, however, demonstrated that man is by nature evil. It has shown us that his awesome potentialities are for both good and for evil. It forces us to look at what contemporaneously is leading to dehumanization and depersonalization, and to do our best to prevent its coming to be. We must emphasize all those aspects which stress man's spirituality as a being with dignity and value related to an objective structure of values at the basis of his existence. We must strive to preserve man's integrity and foster those personal and social elements that make for human integration. We must strenuously reject those doctrines that see man as merely a creature of needs and desires—a complicated or high grade animal and nothing more. I believe that no one would deny that man has passions and needs, that he is inclined to self-centeredness and egotism, to idolatry and that he can often be manipulated and used inhumanly especially in a conformist and totalitarian social structure so that he is alienated from that element within him that can respond to the true, the good and the beautiful, to the sacred and the holy. A view that sees man as a high grade animal sees only part of the truth. The other aspect is that man is also responsive and related to a world of values and rationality that leaves far behind his animal status. It is in fact only because of the impact of bifurcationist theories that such a dualistic view of man has become prevalent. Man is indeed not an animal and only by abstracting certain aspects of his nature can one see him in this aspect. Man is a human living being whose humanity which is represented by his capacity to symbolize, to think, to be self-conscious, to project the future, to transcend himself, qualifies his animal status. All those elements that one identifies with animal are completely transmuted in human beings since they are conjoined with man's symbolic self-transcending nature. Once we recognize that man is by nature neither good nor evil and that both his good and his evil are human qualities and that man has the freedom to actualize either good or evil, then we are able to recognize the traditional Jewish teaching with respect to the nature of man.

It is important to note, however, that both the view that man is essentially good and that he is essentially evil have had negative social and historical consequences. If man is seen as essentially good, then it is believed that social progress comes about merely by taking away all those elements that impede the realization of this goodness. Thus, the social order is geared negatively. The philosophy of the Enlightenment clearly demonstrates this fact. If all that society must do is merely to prevent ignorance and maintain a "laissez-faire" attitude since by giving man utmost freedom he will by nature realize goodness, then no real thought is given to social planning and to achieving the task of realizing the spiritual potential within man.

The Marxist-Leninist view is especially vulnerable in this respect. So much thought was given to achieving a socialist society that once Lenin had the reins of power he had great difficulty realizing his program since his whole orientation was to eliminate the evil and the good would spring forth automatically. Because of this dogmatic view of the innate goodness of man, society has not really developed the kind of social planning that makes for spiritual realization.

If, on the other hand, one assumes that man is by nature evil, then social planning again becomes useless since man by his nature can only bring about evil and needs some external power or leader graced by God to bring about social cohesiveness. This makes man excessively passive and also puts him at the mercy of an authoritarian type society.

Judaism points to the twofoldedness of human nature. Once we recognize that man is by nature neither good nor evil and that both his good and evil are human qualities and that man has the freedom to actualize either good or evil, then we are able to recognize the traditional Jewish teaching with respect to the nature of man.

Judaism recognized that man has much power for good and for evil. It recognizes that man can destroy himself or bring about the Messianic Age. The prophetic doctrine which announces the consequences of destruction through the bold admonition of a day that was darkness and not light also spoke of a day of peace and justice. Judaism believes that man has within him the power to bring about the one or the other. In the book of Deuteronomy Moses spoke to the people and said, "I have set before thee life and death, the blessing and the curse. Choose life that you may live." But the blessing and the curse are not in God's hands. It is not something that God is going to take care of for man. Man is to choose and realize life or death, blessing or curse, the Messianic Age or the bomb.

The Midrash to Genesis relates that when God was about to create man, the angels of the service were divided. Love said let him be created for he will do loving deeds. But Truth said let him not be created for he will be all lies. Righteousness said let him be created for he will do righteous deeds. Peace said let him not be created for he will be all quarrelsomeness and discord. What did God do? He took hold of Truth and cast him to the earth. The angels then said, "Lord of the World, why do You despise the Angel of Truth? Let Truth arise from the earth. As it is said, Truth shall spring from the earth."

Judaism recognizes that it is man's task to bring forth truth and justice and righteousness and peace. It is a mistake to believe that man is by nature good or evil. Man has the capacity for both and the holocaust has shown that he can in fact actualize great evil.

This has important contemporary consequences. We can no longer maintain that man is inherently good and thus take it for granted. We can no longer avoid the task of guaranteeing man's goodness through realizing in man and society those values and institutions that make for survival, peace and fulfillment. This means that the ideal of truth should be dominant. Science should be directed towards the understanding of the nature of the universe and not be merely interested in technological exploitation and control. Too much of our study of man is motivated by propagandistic and exploitative reasons. Our age is concerned not so much with truth but with propaganda, not with genuine communication but with manipulation. The rise of mass media has completely redefined and distorted the nature of discussion and the general character of the marketplace for ideas. When propaganda and advertising become total, when all the mass media are used so as to hold back knowledge and truth, where the power of science and technology is used for manipulating man and where what comes to the fore are not questions of inner worth but of acceptability, then we are indeed in danger of mass dehumanization and depersonalization. What we must concern ourselves with is the strengthening of the spiritual forces that oppose those factors that would make a recurrence of the holocaust, or even worse, possible. What must be reaffirmed is man's rationality not as a biological means to voluntaristic ends but as that faculty which can differentiate between manipulation and truth, illusion and reality. Man has the possibility of redeeming himself, and bringing about the Messianic Age or he has the possibility of destroying himself. God hasn't arranged that one will happen and the other won't. Man must ultimately make that decision; and it is only a concept of man that gives him this kind of power to deal with his life that really takes man seriously. A view of man that shows him continually doing evil, which makes him purely a high-grade animal, which shows him as strictly satisfying his lusts and desires doesn't really take man seriously. To take man seriously you have to see the great tragedy of man's life, to see that he can become in fact a little lower than the angels or that he can become a Hitler. That the potentiality is there for both and we cannot simply say that man is wonderful, that man is good, that man is born good, or that man is terrible and was born evil. Judaism says man is born with a creative capacity that creates good or bad.

The School of Hillel and the School of Shammai fought for many years and there was one question which they fought over very seriously. This question was: Would it have been better for man to have been created, or not to have been created? The School of Shammai said, it would have been better for man not to have been created, and the School of Hillel said, it was better for man to have been created. After all, the Shammaites must have argued, looked at all the suffering and tragedy; all that is horrible in the world, it is better off for man not to have been created. So they debated and debated and couldn't agree. After two years of debate they took a vote and the Shammaites won. So they decided that man should examine his past deeds and future deeds. There is a hint as to the meaning of this statement in the Tosafist's comment on this passage and we might expand it as follows: Before a person is born you don't know if it is better if he were created or not. For instance, it certainly would have been much better for Hitler and Stalin never to have been created, and each one of us is never sure whether it would have been better not to be created. Therefore, we interpret the passage to mean, live your life in such a way so that you will be worthy of having been created. This is an important concept. It doesn't mean that when one is born, he is born in a state of original sin, that anything he does will be bad. It doesn't mean that he is born with reason and goodness, and it is only through sheer error that he does anything bad. No, it means that the individual is born with both a potentiality for doing great good and with the potentiality for doing great evil, and it is up to him whether he does one or the other, whether he chooses life and the blessing, or whether he chooses death and the curse. Let us choose life, that we may live.

3. *THE MEANING OF THIS HOUR*

ABRAHAM JOSHUA HESCHEL

A. J. Heschel (born 1907) is one of the most significant religious philosophers and interpreters of Judaism today. As author of numerous
books and studies, as professor of Jewish ethics and mysticism at the
Jewish Theological Seminary of America, as a tireless lecturer from
coast to coast, Heschel enunciates the relevance of religion, and expounds
the teachings of Judaism—prophetic, rabbinic, philosophical, mystical—
the faith of scholars, saints, martyrs, poets, Messianists, and of the simple
pious worshipper. In Heschel's thinking, in which immense learning is
paired with the sensitivity of a true artist, these various strains form a
coherent, integrated whole. What moves him to speak and to write is a
keen awareness of the precarious situation of modern man and deep
belief that faith is the answer. A faith that is not a set pattern, form,
convention, but a "living in a holy dimension," in which traditional
rituals and creeds are transformed into elements of a "spiritual order."

Heschel calls his method "depth theology," a theology that speaks for
the individual, that "seeks to meet the person in moments in which the
whole person is involved." Religion understands man's life as an answer
to God's question, addressed to him, a fulfillment of God's eternal expectation. "God is in search of man" and the Bible is the revelation of
that search.

Emblazoned over the gates of the world in which we live is the es-
cutcheon of the demons. The mark of Cain in the face of man has
come to overshadow the likeness of God. There has never been so

much guilt and distress, agony, and terror. At no time has the earth been so soaked with blood. Fellow men turned out to be evil ghosts, monstrous and weird. Ashamed and dismayed, we ask: Who is responsible?

History is a pyramid of efforts and errors; yet at times it is the Holy Mountain on which God holds judgment over the nations. Few are privileged to discern God's judgment in history. But all may be guided by the words of the Baal Shem: If a man has beheld evil, he may know that it was shown to him in order that he learn his own guilt and repent; for what is shown to him is also within him.

We have trifled with the name of God. We have taken the ideals in vain. We have called for the Lord. He came. And was ignored. We have preached but eluded Him. We have praised but defied Him. Now we reap the fruits of our failure. Through centuries His voice cried in the wilderness. How skillfully it was trapped and imprisoned in the temples! How often it was drowned or distorted! Now we behold how it gradually withdraws, abandoning one people after another, departing from their souls, despising their wisdom. The taste for the good has all but gone from the earth. Men heap spite upon cruelty, malice upon atrocity.

The horrors of our time fill our souls with reproach and everlasting shame. We have profaned the word of God, and we have given the wealth of our land, the ingenuity of our minds and the dear lives of our youth to tragedy and perdition. There has never been more reason for man to be ashamed than now. Silence hovers mercilessly over many dreadful lands. The day of the Lord is a day without the Lord. Where is God? Why didst Thou not halt the trains loaded with Jews being led to slaughter? It is so hard to rear a child, to nourish and to educate. Why dost Thou make it so easy to kill? Like Moses, we hide our face; for we are afraid to look upon *Elohim,* upon His power of judgment.[1] Indeed, where were we when men learned to hate in the days of starvation? When raving madmen were sowing wrath in the hearts of the unemployed?

Let modern dictatorship not serve as an alibi for our conscience. We have failed to fight for right, for justice, for goodness; as a result

---

1 The reference is to Exodus 3:6. In Jewish tradition, *Elohim* is the name of God denoting the attribute of judgment (while the name YHVH denotes mercy).

we must fight *against* wrong, *against* injustice, *against* evil. We have failed to offer sacrifices on the altar of peace; thus we offered sacrifices on the altar of war. A tale is told of a band of inexperienced mountain climbers. Without guides, they struck recklessly into the wilderness. Suddenly a rocky ledge gave way beneath their feet and they tumbled headlong into a dismal pit. In the darkness of the pit they recovered from their shock only to find themselves set upon by a swarm of angry snakes. For each snake the desperate men slew, ten more seemed to lash out in its place. Strangely enough, one man seemed to stand aside from the fight. When indignant voices of his struggling companions reproached him for not fighting, he called back: "If we remain here, we shall be dead before the snakes. I am searching for a way of escape from the pit for all of us."

Our world seems not unlike a pit of snakes. We did not sink into the pit in 1939, or even in 1933. We had descended into it generations ago, and the snakes have sent their venom into the bloodstream of humanity, gradually paralyzing us, numbing nerve after nerve, dulling our minds, darkening our vision. Good and evil, that were once as real as day and night, have become a blurred mist. In our everyday life we worshiped force, despised compassion, and obeyed no law but our unappeasable appetite. The vision of the sacred has all but died in the soul of man. And when greed, envy and the reckless will to power came to maturity, the serpents cherished in the bosom of our civilization broke out of their dens to fall upon the helpless nations.

The outbreak of war was no surprise. It came as a long expected sequel to a spiritual disaster. Instilled with the gospel that truth is mere advantage and reverence weakness, people succumbed to the bigger advantage of a lie—"the Jew is our misfortune"—and to the power of arrogance—"tomorrow the whole world shall be ours," "the peoples' democracies must depend upon force." The roar of bombers over Rotterdam, Warsaw, London, was but the echo of thoughts bred for years by individual brains, and later applauded by entire nations. It was through our failure that people started to suspect that science is a device for exploitation, parliaments pulpits for hypocrisy, and religion a pretext for a bad conscience. In the tantalized souls of those who had faith in ideals, suspicion became a dogma and contempt the only solace. Mistaking the abortions of their conscience for intellectual heroism, many thinkers employ clever pens to scold and to scorn the reverence for life, the awe for truth, the loyalty to justice. Man, about to hang himself, discovers it is easier to hang others.

The conscience of the world was destroyed by those who were wont to blame others rather than themselves. Let us remember. We revered the instincts but distrusted the prophets. We labored to perfect engines and let our inner life go to wreck. We ridiculed superstition until we lost our ability to believe. We have helped to extinguish the light our fathers had kindled. We have bartered holiness for convenience, loyalty for success, love for power, wisdom for information, tradition for fashion.

We cannot dwell at ease under the sun of our civilization as our ancestors thought we could. What was in the minds of our martyred brothers in their last hours? They died with disdain and scorn for a civilization in which the killing of civilians could become a carnival of fun, for a civilization which gave us mastery over the forces of nature but lost control over the forces of our self.

Tanks and planes cannot redeem humanity, nor the discovery of guilt by association nor suspicion. A man with a gun is like a beast without a gun. The killing of snakes will save us for the moment but not forever. The war has outlasted the victory of arms as we failed to conquer the infamy of the soul: the indifference to crime, when committed against others. For evil is indivisible. It is the same in thought and in speech, in private and in social life. The greatest task of our time is to take the souls of men out of the pit. The world has experienced that God is involved. Let us forever remember that the sense for the sacred is as vital to us as the light of the sun. There can be no nature without spirit, no world without the Torah, no brotherhood without a father, no humanity without attachment to God.

God will return to us when we shall be willing to let Him in— into our banks and factories, into our Congress and clubs, into our courts and investigating committees, into our homes and theaters. For God is everywhere or nowhere, the Father of all men or no man, concerned about everything or nothing. Only in His presence shall we learn that the glory of man is not in his will to power, but in his power of compassion. Man reflects either the image of His presence or that of a beast.

Soldiers in the horror of battle offer solemn testimony that life is not a hunt for pleasure, but an engagement for service; that there are things more valuable than life; that the world is not a vacuum. Either we make it an altar for God or it is invaded by demons. There can be no neutrality. Either we are ministers of the sacred or slaves of evil. Let the blasphemy of our time not become an eternal scandal. Let future generations not loathe us for having failed to preserve what prophets and saints, martyrs and scholars have created in thousands of years. The apostles of force have shown that they are great in evil. Let us reveal that we can be as great in goodness. We will survive if we shall be as fine and sacrificial in our homes and offices, in our Congress and clubs, as our soldiers are on the fields of battle.

There is a divine dream which the prophets and rabbis have cherished and which fills our prayers, and permeates the acts of true piety. It is the dream of a world, rid of evil by the grace of God as well as by the efforts of man, by his dedication to the task of establishing the kingship of God in the world. God is waiting for us to redeem the world. We should not spend our life hunting for trivial satisfactions while God is waiting constantly and keenly for our effort and devotion.

The Almighty has not created the universe that we may have opportunities to satisfy our greed, envy and ambition. We have not survived that we may waste our years in vulgar vanities. The martyrdom of millions demands that we consecrate ourselves to the fulfillment of God's dream of salvation. Israel did not accept the Torah of their own free will. When Israel approached Sinai, God lifted up the mountain and held it over their heads, saying: "Either you accept the Torah or be crushed beneath the mountain."[2]

The mountain of history is over our heads again. Shall we renew the covenant with God?

---

2 Babli, Shabbat 88a.

4. ON FAITH IN
THE SECULAR WORLD

EMIL L. FACKENHEIM

Professor Fackenheim teaches philosophy at the University of Toronto. Born in Germany he was trained for the rabbinate at the Berlin Lehranstalt. In a rare way, he combines a profound knowledge of Judaism with the mastery of modern philosophy. Kant, Hegel, Nietzsche and Kirkegaard here enter into a presentation of modern theology which takes issue with secularity, Christian radical theology, and certain Jewish thinkers. In the end, Emil L. Fackenheim finds the beginnings of his answer in Elie Wiesel, the novelist who teaches both rabbis and theologians in our time.

———

Ever since the Jew became modern, he has existed, as it were, between Christianity and secularist liberalism. If a believer, he has shared with Christianity the Biblical God; and if not, at least a regard for a religious tradition to which he owes his survival. With secularist liberalism he has shared the ideals that have produced democracy and his own emancipation; so far as these are concerned, even orthodox Jews are secularist liberals. The conflict that came to exist between these two forms of modern belief and life has contributed to a religious-secularist conflict within Jewish existence.

The one conflict still exists, and so does the other. In any contemporary reversal of traditional fronts, the Jew is obviously not an impartial bystander but rather a participant; his stance, whatever its nature, is informed by his Jewish situation.[1]

This first experience has been joined, if not overshadowed and dwarfed, by another in this generation. The one experience the Jew has lived with and assimilated for nearly two centuries; the other is, as yet, wholly unassimilable. *The events that are associated with the dread name of Auschwitz still pass human comprehension. But they have shaken Jewish existence to the core, even when they are uncomprehended.* They call everything into question: for the believing Jew, for the unbelieving Jew, for the Jew who is neither believer nor unbeliever but merely asks unanswered or unanswerable questions. Only one thing is as yet clear. The Jew may not authentically think about religion, or its modern crisis, or the goods and ills of the modern-secular world as though Auschwitz had not happened.

There are differences in the post-Auschwitz Christian world. To the extent that they affect us, we must study them.

The present reversal of traditional fronts in Protestantism may be said to originate with Dietrich Bonhoeffer's *Letters and Papers from Prison*,[2] written in a Nazi jail and concentration camp in 1943–44 prior to his execution. This is an oversimplification historically, but not poetically. These documents were written in a country which, once the heart of Western Christendom, was then in the grip of demonic, anti-Christian powers; and by a member of a church which, alone among German churches, clearly opposed these powers, in the name not of modern humanism but rather of the ancient gospel, brought by neo-orthodox theology to new life. The man who wrote these documents did not only die a martyr; he suffered this death because he had given his Christian witness a political expression by participating in a plot on Hitler's life. No more dramatic example

---

[1] I have attempted to view the confrontation of Christianity and secularist liberalism from the standpoint of contemporary Jewish experience and faith in "A Jew Looks at Christianity and Secularist Liberalism," *The Restless Church*, ed. Wm. Kilbourn, Toronto, 1966, pp. 86ff.

[2] Dietrich Bonhoeffer, *Letters and Papers from Prison*, London, 1953.

can be found in this century of what has since come to be the basic issue at stake in the current reversal of traditional fronts: the radical religious—in this case, Christian—self-exposure to the modern-secular world and all its works. The example is all the more compelling because it occurred in a country in which Christianity, since Luther, has been prone to cut off the "inner" world reserved for Christian conscience from the "outer" world, handed over to Machiavellian princes and autocrats.

No less dramatic than the occasion and the author of the *Letters and Papers from Prison* are those of its passages—terse, radical, though, as will be seen, in the end profoundly problematical—which were destined to be the most influential. The confrontation between Christianity and the modern-secular world demanded in these passages is indeed radical. The modern-secular world is taken as it takes itself, and as such confronted; and what it is confronted with is not weak, diluted apologetics, but rather the pristine Christian gospel.

For the present purpose, Bonhoeffer's crucial passages may be summed up in four basic affirmations. First, the modern-secular world has "come of age." Its science, politics, morality, even its philosophy and religion stand in no need of God as a "working hypothesis," in terms of which they must be explained.

Secondly, the "autonomy" of the modern-secular world rules out any honest Christian recourse to "the so-called ultimate questions— death, guilt—on which only 'God' can furnish an answer." Thus is rejected any Christian use of "the existentialist philosopher and the psychotherapist" who "make it their object first of all to drive man to inward despair, and then it is all theirs." For "whom [do such efforts] . . . touch? A small number of intellectuals, of degenerates. . . . The ordinary man who spends his everyday life at work, and with his family . . . is not affected. . . ." Modern-secular man exists "*etsi Deus non daretur.*"

Yet, thirdly, while even the Christian ought to live in this godless world, he lives in it "before God." God is no longer needed as a crutch. Everywhere he is confronted by faith and love.

Fourthly and finally, to confront God in faith is to find Him in the midst of life, not merely at such of its margins as guilt and death. And to speak of Him to secular man is not to "speak ill of . . . his worldliness" but to "confront him with God at his strongest" rather than at his weakest point. Far from letting "this world be written off prematurely," the Biblical God—in the New as well as in the Old Testament—focuses his primary concern not on otherworldly salvation, but on this-wordly life.[3]

Their radicalism lends these affirmations a tremendous liberating power. Swept aside is all apologetic nineteenth-century halfheartedness—toward the scientist, the secularist reformer, the agnostic moralist, each of whom used to be told that he stood in need of religion, no matter how much his thought and his life gave the lie to this story; it was to be replaced by a radically honest self-exposure. Swept aside, too, is the half-hearted Christian testimony that used to define itself in alien terms—the terms of a world for which it could still perform some useful function, or the terms of philosophies still left with a gap of some kind. This was to be replaced by a testimony to a God who, ever-present to man, can confront modern-secular man as surely as his less secular ancestors. Radical, modern-secular honesty is united with radical Biblical authenticity.

A Jew's Jewish affirmations may differ from Bonhoeffer's Christian ones. Yet the Jew is bound to be moved by them and, indeed, become deeply involved. For one thing, the profane-sacred, temporal-eternal dichotomy has always been alien to Judaism and Jewish existence; and Bonhoeffer opposes it because of Hebraic inspiration. For another (as has been said), modern Jewish existence has been exposed to special strains because of the modern conflict between secularist liberalism and Christianity. But, when more closely considered, Bonhoeffer's affirmations are, in the end, profoundly problematical; and, as will be seen, what is problematical about them is augmented in the thought of his disciples.

Two questions are left hanging in mid-air. First, who is the God to be confronted, and how is he related to the "God-hypothesis" to be discarded, the hypothesis through which things were once explained? Although this may seem an abstract theoretical question, it is, nevertheless, inescapable. What if Bonhoeffer's modern-secular man were to reject—indeed, were in all honesty obliged to reject— the God with whom Christian testimony confronts him as a mere myth of bygone ages, now in need of demythologization? As will be seen, this question haunts Bonhoeffer's theological disciples.

---

[3] *Ibid.*, pp. 146ff., 157ff., 160, 163ff.

The second question is even on the surface not abstract and theoretical only. Who is Bonhoeffer's "man-come-of-age," happy in his secularity and free of guilt? Is he an ideal man as pictured by Spinoza, Kant, or Hegel? But that man is himself only an ideal. Or is he an actually existing man? Doubtless he is this latter, for he alone is an "ordinary man who spends his everyday life at work, and with his family." *It is a tragic irony, however, that Bonhoeffer should have cleared this man of guilt at the precise time when he became implicated, all around him, in a guilt without historical precedent*: not only when his "work" was to drive gas-chamber trucks or to fight Hitler's war, but also when it was merely to clean the streets—and hold his peace. Bonhoeffer aimed at two great goals: a gospel found in the midst of life and joy rather than merely in death and guilt; and the protection of the secular man against religion-inspired slander. A nearly incredible lack of realism made him fail to rise to what would have been not slander but judgment —of "ordinary" Christians and secularists alike.

Clear-sighted witness, apostle of Christian self-exposure to the secular world and himself martyr to his cause, Bonhoeffer nevertheless failed wholly to grasp—almost no one to this day has succeeded in wholly grasping—the monstrous evil in the actual world about him. This painful truth, in retrospect inescapable, cannot escape his Jewish reader. In a concentration camp filled with Jews subjected to every imaginable form of torture, Bonhoeffer writes that Protestants must learn about suffering from Catholics.[4] No mention is made in the *Letters and Papers* of Jewish martyrdom. . . .

Jews and Christians now live together in the "secular city."

Only in recent decades have Jews had occasion to realize fully the bonds they have with Christianity as well as with secularist liberalism. In the heyday of nineteenth-century optimism, the Western Jew was apt to throw in his destiny wholly with secularist liberalism "abroad" even if he remained an orthodox Jew "at home,"[5] and to

---

[4] *Ibid.*, p. 111.

[5] Here and *infra*, I allude to a famous post-France Revolution slogan, according to which the Jew was to be permitted to remain a Jew "at home"—in the privacy of a purely religious conscience—on condition that he become "a man abroad," that he purge all remnants of Jewish national-cultural life from his public-secular existence. In pluralistic North America this artificial and illiberal dichotomy never took hold.

have no very positive relation to the forces of Christianity except insofar as these, too, threw their weight behind liberal ideals. But what if secularist liberalism were to become wholly omnipotent? Would it remain liberal? Could it be counted on to respect the Jew's right to his Jewishness, of which it had little appreciation, and to his Judaism, of which it had less? Might it, in fact, even be perverted into a demonic pseudo-religion and deny the Jew's very humanity?

Some of these questions have *in abstracto* been present ever since, after the French Revolution, the Jew was requested to surrender his public Jewishness "abroad" (if not his private Jewish faith "at home") as the price of his emancipation. In the mid-twentieth century, these questions have assumed a reality of which no wild imagination could have dreamed in the nineteenth. Soviet secularism seems bent on a policy designed to dissipate both Jewish culture "abroad" and Jewish faith "at home." And the Nazi secularist pseudo-religion of blood and soil has succeeded in the physical destruction of one third of the world's Jewish population. These two events must, under no circumstances, be viewed as in the same class, and can be so viewed only by indiscriminate cold-war warriors. They have, nevertheless, had the common effect of making many Jews view secularism with newly critical eyes. The modern Jew has been obliged to look to secularist liberalism for the recognition of his humanity in the past. The momentous and fearsome events of the present have made him wonder whether if to anyone, it is not to the Christian that he must look for the recognition of his singled-out Jewish condition.[6] Indeed, may contemporary

---

[6] This statement is not, I think, the product of mere romantic optimism. I must, however, mention in passing that during the thirties Jews then in Germany, this writer included, were wont to make a saint of any Christian showing the slightest signs of resistance to Nazism; for example, of so questionable a figure as Cardinal Faulhaber, solely because he spoke up in behalf of Old Testament Patriarchs. (Cf. G. Lewy, *The Catholic Church and Nazi Germany*, New York, 1965, pp. 111, 276.) In those dark days it was a simple human impossibility to recognize enemies on *all* sides; and it would appear to be no accident that it took twenty years for works to appear that fully document the grim truth that while Nazi anti-Semitism is, of course, anti-Christian in essence, both this anti-Semitism and the attempted genocide in which it culminated would have been impossible except for centuries of Christian anti-Semitism; indeed, without considerable cooperation of Christians not all of whom were nominal. I trust I am not uttering a Jewish view only when I assert that the confrontation of this grim truth, now begun in some Christian quarters, is one of the major tasks of Christian thought in this generation.

events not indicate that secularist liberalism itself stands in secret need of Biblical inspiration for its liberalism? If bereft of this inspiration, or subjugating and thus perverting it, may secularism not become illiberal and totalitarian, or even a demonic pseudo-religion?

Such fears are obviously not felt by those Jews who grasp the opportunities offered by the secular city for surrendering their Jewishness in the faith that such a surrender will make them "simply human." But despite statistics concerning assimilation and inter-marriage, their response to the secular city does not represent what must be called mid-twentieth-century American Jewish normative behavior. To the astonishment of many, the normative American Jewish response to the events of this century has been a reaffirmation, if not of Judaism, at least of Jewish group-survival. (In the light of the dynamics of present Jewish life, it is the Jewish intellectuals whose intellectualism has led them to surrender their Jewishness who are out of step, not the community which they have abandoned.) The causes of this reaffirmation are complex: among others, a flight from the anonymous society of megalopolis to the community—such as it is—of suburbia; loyalty to the martyred European millions which, once aroused by plain need, refuses to vanish; a new seriousness about Judaism among formerly perfunctory believers; and even a new openness to Jewish religious resources among formerly confirmed secularists. All these responses, from a minimal commitment to Jewishness to a maximal commitment to Judaism, imply some degree of criticism of the modern-secular world where before there was little or none.

In the light of this experience, how will a Jewish reader react to such a work as *The Secular City?* [7] ...

The Secular City justifies caution. No single item of the work will strike a Jewish reader more forcefully than its failure—twenty years after—to come to grips with Nazism. The work warns in a general way against the dangers of the modern-secular world; yet such is the degree of its infatuation that it has no room for Nazism in that world. Nazism is a mere "throwback to a lost tribalism." What an insult to any tribe ever in existence. And what a staggering

---

[7] Harvey Cox, *The Secular City*, New York, 1965.

failure to grasp that Nazism, far from being a mere falling-out-of-step innocuous to all who are *in* step, is, alas, a distinctly modern phenomenon. How, except for modern anonymity and modern technological quantification, could Nazism have engaged in its grisly mathematics of mass-murder? So blithely is *The Secular City* in love with the virtues of modern secularity that it is able to commit this enormous tautology: "When a political leader makes religious or totalitarian claims, when a Hitler or Stalin tries once again to assert himself as the pure expression of the *Zeitgeist* or the dialectic, free [sic] men recognize this as an affront to their deepest convictions about politics."[8] As if the question raised by Nazism were not precisely why Germans preferred slavery to freedom, and even "thought they were free"[9] when in fact they were slaves. Moreover, for long and crucial years, even "free" Western leaders—both Christian and secularist—appeased Hitler not only as the lesser evil to war but also as the savior of Western civilization from Communism.

Harvey Cox's Christian statement of modern life, *The Secular City*, comes to grief over Nazism not because of moral blindness but rather because like Bonhoeffer, it fights on one front and ignores the simultaneous need to fight on another. It fights for the recognition of the challenge of the liberal secular-city dweller to the religious believer, in particular to the rural believer. It fights, too, against all religious efforts to reduce the former to a guilt or despair for which there is neither need nor cause. It ignores the real grounds for despair and guilt—among secularists and believers alike. Is there no guilt in an America well-fed in the midst of world-wide starvation and with enough arms to destroy the human race? And no despair in the secular city even if guilt can be shut out? Not if those novelists are to be believed who discover meaninglessness in busy suburbia as well as in the slums. American "pragmatic man" may waste "little time thinking about 'ultimate' or 'religious' questions," and be able to live "with highly provisional solutions."[10] But only the idolization of pragmatism can shut out those ultimate moral dilemmas of the present time in the light of which all the

---

[8] *Ibid.*, pp. 3, 26ff.

[9] This is the title of a book by Milton Mayer (Chicago, 1955) which gives a portrait of ten Germans, all of them decent people and Nazis.

[10] Cox, *op. cit.*, p. 63.

provisional solutions must be groped for; or fail to notice that it is precisely when his actual needs are filled that pragmatic man falls either to restlessly inventing ever-new unneeded needs or to asking the desperate and utterly unpragmatic question: "What is the use of use?" [11]

The secularist must find his own way out of the dilemmas of the secular city. The believer—Jewish and Christian—must surely seek the word of the ancient Biblical God as it applies to the modern-secular world. Such a search, if it remains for the Biblical God, will not result in a surrender to secularism, if only because the Biblical God *judges* the world—the modern-secular world as much as any other—even as he accepts it in love.

The Secular City, to be sure, does not surrender. It culminates in the attempt to speak "in a secular fashion" of God, sociologically, politically, and even theologically. It is, however, virtually left without speech. So deeply is the work impressed with the novelty of modern-secular man as to see virtually no continuity between him and the whole preceding human species. Hence, it cannot hear a divine voice from the past in the present and is faced with a future that is wholly open.[12]

Less reliance on sociology and more metaphysical discipline might have prevented such a hollow outcome. Following an old and shop-worn doctrine harking back to Auguste Comte, *The Secular City* views metaphysics as primitive guesswork about the universe, the necessity of which disappears with the rise of science. In fact and at its best, metaphysics is radical thinking about the totality of human experience. As such, it helps see in perspective all changes, including those in the human social condition and those that the believer may affirm about the Divine. The famous passage (Exodus 3:14) that *The Secular City* translates as "I will do what I will do" [13] assuredly contains no ontological information about the divine nature. But neither does it command an openness to the future so total

---

[11] An expression used by the nineteenth-century Jewish Hegelian Samuel Hirsch, in his critique of the utilitarian destruction of Roman religion in the later Roman Empire. With respect to religious pragmatism, there is an uncomfortable resemblance between the modern-secular world and the Roman Empire as viewed by Hegel himself: uncomfortable because Hegel sees Rome's all-encompassing utilitarianism as the source of its destruction.

[12] Cox, *op. cit.*, Part IV.

[13] *Ibid.*, p. 268.

as to fragment the One God of Israel into as many "moment-gods" [14] as there are historical moments. The Hebraic believer confronts the future with a present knowledge coming from the past; the word from the past is judging justice and accepting love. He who revealed Himself to Moses as "I shall be who I shall be" may disclose Himself in the future by yet unknown names. He will be the same already-known "I."

On the "Death" of God

But what if a truly uncompromising self-exposure of faith to the modern-secular world *ipso facto* is surrender to secularism? We have noted Bonhoeffer's failure to clarify the relation between the "God-hypothesis" that is to be discarded, and the Biblical God who is to be confronted. Its nemeses are the current so-called "God-is-dead" theologies.

The expression covers a variety of different and possibly incompatible assertions. The first is purely metaphorical: not God is dead in our time but merely human belief in him. This latter is dead not so much because men no longer, in fact, believe, but rather because the legitimacy of belief would have vanished even if belief were still widely alive.[15] Modern science has demythologized the world of fact, thus disposing of the need for a God-hypothesis; and modern philosophy—it is linguistic empiricism, mostly Oxford-inspired—has reduced the meaning of the word *God*, as employed by the believer, to a mere expression of emotion. The believer imagines that the assertion "God exists," although not necessarily demonstrable, nevertheless refers to an objective truth. Philosophy disposes of this illusion. The believer's statement is not "about the world," but merely about his own attitude toward the world.

The philosopher may or may not find this attitude legitimate; on his part, he is clearly incapable of himself adopting it. How, having acquired knowledge, can he return to innocence? How, having

---

14 Cf. Martin Buber, *Between Man and Man*, Boston, 1955, p. 15. For the interpretation of the Exodus passage, cf. Buber's *The Prophetic Faith*, New York, 1949, pp. 28ff., and his *Moses*, New York, 1958, pp. 52ff.

15 The claim that belief can no longer be genuinely alive is logically distinct from the claim that it is no longer intellectually legitimate. The latter claim is presently under review; the former will be discussed in the following section of this essay.

unmasked the word *God* as a mere projection upon the world, can he ever again adopt an attitude dependent on the belief that a truth beyond his mere attitude is disclosed in it? Belief in God, then, is dead among the scientifically and philosophically enlightened; and it would never have been alive among previous generations had they been blessed with our present enlightenment. As for God himself, He is not dead. He was never alive.

There is nothing either new or startling about these assertions—except that they should be made in a theological work, *The Secular Meaning of the Gospel. . . .* [16]

In its self-exposure to the modern-secular world, can Christian faith come upon deeper challenges than those faced by *The Secular Meaning of the Gospel*? Is it faced not only with the long-obvious threat of externally opposing forces, but also with a threat from within? Or, to stay with the previously used image, is Christian faith challenged not only to *abandon* its own circle for the secularist circle external to it, but also to *transfigure* itself radically, so as to become absorbed by the secularist circle without remainder? With this question we come upon a far more profound Christian self-exposure to the modern-secular world, and at the same time one far more dangerous. *The Secular Meaning of the Gospel* merely abandons the Biblical God for an atheistic humanism. *The Gospel of Christian Atheism* [17] literally affirms and indeed wills the death of the Biblical God; and its affirming and willing produces the spectre of idolatry.

The Gospel of Christian Atheism revels in sweeping generalizations and unsubstantiated assertions, [18] as well as in a dialectic which, while at times the Hegelian movement of spirit which transfigures what it negates, is at other times merely incoherence made into a theological virtue. But rather than pounce on such vices, one must attend to its central virtue, a radicalism than which one bolder and more extreme it would be difficult to imagine. Here the central

---

[16] Paul Van Buren, *The Secular Meaning of the Gospel*, New York, 1963; paperback edition, 1966.

[17] Thomas J. J. Altizer, *The Gospel of Christian Atheism*, Philadelphia, 1966. Cf. also *Radical Theology and the Death of God*, by Thomas J. J. Altizer and William Hamilton; referred to as RT, *infra*.

[18] Cf., for example, RT, p. 95: "We shall *simply assume* the truth of Nietzsche's proclamation of the death of God. . ." (italics ours).

theological issue left hanging in mid-air since Bonhoeffer is confronted head-on and dealt with in a manner that leaves no room for ambiguity or compromise. *The Gospel of Christian Atheism* is a work which itself must be confronted head-on, if only to be uncompromisingly rejected.

For all its lack of intellectual discipline, the work states its central thesis with admirable clarity. The spirit of the modern-secular world is most clearly expressed in modern speculative philosophy; this is neither simply indifferent to Christianity nor simply hostile to it. Modern speculative philosophy—and the whole modern-secular world—are the dialectical result of Christianity, as well as its dialectical negation. Its result: only the Christian God incarnate in the world has made possible "profane" modern worldliness. Its negation: only as modern worldliness negates the transcendent otherness of the Biblical God, so as to appropriate it into total immanence, does it, *qua* worldliness, become complete. This movement is already, in principle, complete in modern philosophy—above all, in Hegel and Nietzsche; for here the "death" of the transcendent God is effected by means of an immanent self-elevation of thought toward divinity. If the movement is as yet incomplete in the modern-secular world as a whole—if at the present time there is a chaos in which the old Christian values have already vanished while new, post-Christian values have not yet emerged, it is in large measure because Christian theology has opposed modern autonomous-godless thought in the name of the transcendent God, when to transfigure itself into just that mode of thought, and hence to accept the death of the transcendent God, is in truth its inescapable destiny. Christian theology must therefore accept and even "will" the death of God—anyhow occurring in the midst of Christendom "in our time, in our history, in our existence," [19] and in effect write a third testament. The Old Testament knew only the alien, transcendent, externally commanding Father. He became the Son, incarnate and immanent, in the New Testament. It will be left for the third testament to come dialectically to deny the Son's resurrection to transcendence, and along with it the Father who makes this resurrection possible. This step will lay "faith . . . open to the most terrible darkness"; yet in precisely that darkness will it "be recep-

---

[19] RT, p. 95.

tive of the most redemptive light." And the redemption-to-come
will be the "full and actual presence of the Christ who is a totally
incarnate love." [20]

Such, in brief, is *The Gospel of Christian Atheism*. In this essay,
it calls for both a philosophical and a Jewish response. This response
must begin with noting the work's totally inadequate grasp of
Hegel, more obviously even than Nietzsche, its philosophical patron
saint. Hegel does transfigure Christian faith into autonomous philosophical thought. He does not in the process produce the death
either of God or of the Christian faith. Hegel's philosophy rests
on two crucial presuppositions: on the one hand, the faith which
receives the descent of God into Christ; on the other, the ascent
of modern secularity to freedom and autonomy. Its task is to reconcile these two presuppositions in the form of philosophical thought,
and yet so to reconcile them as not to destroy them. Thought
transfigures secular and religious life into a union of thought but it
also reinstates them in that creative difference in which they exist
in life.[21] If taken at his full word rather than selectively made use of,
Hegel lends no support to *The Gospel of Christian Atheism*. On
the contrary, he anticipates the move taken in that work and rejects it.

But there is, of course, ample precedent for the kind of selective
reading of Hegel that takes a left-wing turn and denies transcendence. It is instructive to consider the fate of nineteenth-century
left-wing Hegelians. Their denial of Hegelian transcendence led
them to seek an absoluteness immanent in actual humanity; yet
in the process of this search virtually every left-wing Hegelian accused his predecessor of dissipating concrete man into an unreal
abstraction. This process may be said to have culminated in Marx
and Nietzsche, both left-wing Hegelians in a wider sense. Scorning
the spurious "freedom" of Feuerbach's "abstract" humanity, as well
as the "mere idealism" of "utopian" socialists, both men sought an
actual humanity absolutely free, in the one case in the future class-
less society; in the other, in the future "Overman." But with what
success? In retrospect, Marx's dialectical socialism is far more utopian

---

20 RT, pp. 20ff., 157.
21 This is argued in detail in my forthcoming book, tentatively entitled *Peace Between Faith and Philosophy: The Religious Dimension in Hegel's Thought*, Indiana
University Press.

than "utopian" socialism. As for Nietzsche's Overman, he is a mere myth, and one far more unreal—and dangerous—than all those transcendent deities that he was meant to replace.

Nietzsche assuredly is not a proto-fascist. He is, however, a reckless and apocalyptic mythmaker, divorced from reality as all apocalyptic mythmakers are. Americans have only lately discovered Nietzsche. Now that some American theologians idolize him, they stand in need of a warning from someone who never has had to discover him behind false stereotypes. Karl Loewith, lifelong German student of Nietzsche and author of a classic study of him as far back as in 1935, writes in 1956:

> He is still close to us, yet already quite remote. . . . [In his case] the question of . . . the historic responsibility of all public thought, speech and writing is inescapable. For in the case of Nietzsche it is undeniable that he wished from the beginning to be effective through his writing and be as philosopher a "physician of culture." Thus in the end he sketched a world-historical program designed for "great politics." . . . And he coined maxims with an unheard of harshness and recklessness of which in his personal life he never was capable, maxims which entered into public consciousness and then were practised for twelve years. Among these were the maxim of the dangerous life, of contempt for sympathy . . . of a decisive nihilism of action, according to which that which already falls is yet to be pushed down.[22]

What responsible secular philosopher of the age of Auschwitz and Hiroshima would utter the Nietzsche-style demand to "abandon all those moral laws which the Christian Church has sanctioned"?[23] It seems strange that theologians should embrace Nietzschean apocalypticism when secular philosophers—Sartre and Camus come to mind—have abandoned all reckless human aspirations to an immanent divinity, leaving man with a responsible but finite freedom.

But perhaps this is not strange. Theologians, after all, cannot let go of infinity and divinity, even if the search for these is at the cost of a reckless antinomian disregard for morality. Is this disregard necessary? And is the search successful? It is tempting to contrast the goal of *The Gospel of Christian Atheism* (which is to lay hold of concrete present worldliness) with its actual result (which is the

---

[22] *Gesammelte Abhandlungen*, Stuttgart, 1960, pp. 127, 129, 130.
[23] Altizer, *The Gospel of Christian Atheism*, p. 147.

apocalyptic dissipation of everything concrete and present into what Hegel would have called a "night in which all cows are black"). One is all the more tempted to dwell on this result because apocalyptic nihilism is not uncommon among present post-Christian writers, who respond to our present despairs with the indiscriminate surrender of all those things in the present which must under no circumstances be surrendered, but, on the contrary, loved and nurtured.[24] We must turn at once to what in the context of this essay is the crucial theological issue: between any possible form of Jewish faith and this Christian (or post-Christian) theology—possibly the most radically anti-Judaic theology ever nurtured in the bosom of the Christian church.

Why must *The Gospel of Christian Atheism* accept and even "will" the death of God? Not because modern belief in God is no longer genuine; the work would attack it as reactionary even when it was genuine. Nor because God is ruled out by modern science and empiricist philosophy; the work cares little about science and less about empirical evidence. The death of God must be willed because "God ... is the transcendent enemy of the fulness and the passion of man's life in the world, and only through God's death can humanity be liberated from that repression which is the real ruler of history."[25] In short, it is the Lord of Israel whose otherness—and hence lordship and divinity—is the enemy; and only as Christianity rids itself of this Jewish element can it consummate the salvation aimed at ever since the time of its origin, but until now unconsummated because of its failure to emancipate itself from Judaism.[26]

Such views must produce from a Jew one fundamental question. Who is this hostile God, foe of human freedom and source of every repression? He is not and never has been the authentic God of Israel: not in the Hebrew Bible, not in the rabbinic writings, not

---

24 Cf. Robert Alter, "The Apocalyptic Temper," *Commentary*, June, 1966, pp. 61ff. Alter's article is an outstanding critique of the "savagely comical apocalypse in vogue in American fiction."

25 Altizer, *The Gospel of Christian Atheism*, p. 22.

26 In fairness, it must be added that *The Gospel of Christian Atheism* in no way follows the kind of crude anti-Jewish line that attributes whatever is found inconvenient in Christian ethics and theology to Jewish influence. Cf. Altizer, *op. cit.*, p. 45: "It is ... Christianity that has reduced human existence to sin and guilt, confronting a broken humanity with a wholly other God who demands total submission to his numinous and judgmental power." If the "wholly other" God is Jewish then this Jewish God has been essential to Christianity until the time of his "death."

in the history of Jewish religious thought until this day. He is not the God of the psalmist when he "delights" in the divine commandments (Ps. 119:47); not the God of the rabbinic sage who declares that "when the Torah came into the world freedom came into the world" (*Midrash Genesis Rabba, Wayyera* LIII 7); not the God of the ordinary Jewish worshiper who daily proclaims that it is in his love that God gave commandments to Israel. The enemy-God is a caricature. The authentic God of Israel is He who in His transcendent otherness does not need man and yet chooses to need him; Who in His love makes man free and responsible, and thus as commanding demands a free response. He is, in short, a God of grace. But must a Jew tell a Christian about grace?

From time to time this would appear to be necessary. In the perspective of Judaism, Nietzsche's titanic war on the Biblical God is not a modern necessity, inevitably waged in behalf of human freedom. It is the nemesis manifested in this parson's son of an age-old Christian—or is it pseudo-Christian?—blindness to a grace that is manifest in the commandments, to a grace that does not diminish or vanquish human freedom but rather augments and, indeed, establishes it. This same nemesis is manifest in *The Gospel of Christian Atheism*.[27]

On the "Eclipse" of God

Philosophers have always been demythologizers.[28] More to the present point, the Bible demythologizes when it reduces nature to the undivine product of a divine Creator that is intended for human

---

[27] The section just concluded is not intended as a comprehensive critique of the "God-is-dead" theology. I may, however, say in passing that I am puzzled to find William Hamilton in close association with Altizer. His ethically inspired optimism (and consequent repudiation of such writers as Ezra Pound); his intense concern with actual human suffering; his stance of "waiting for God": these and other themes would appear to associate him far more closely, on the one hand, with *The Secular City* and, on the other, with the doctrine of the "eclipse" of God (cf. *infra,* Section V); they would also appear to make the expression "death of God" in his case not readily intelligible. Cf. for example, RT, pp. 37ff., 157ff.; also William Hamilton, *The New Essence of Christianity*, New York, 1966, especially pp. 44ff.

[28] On the theme of this section, cf. also my "On the Eclipse of God," *Commentary*, June, 1964, pp. 55ff., reprinted in *The Star and the Cross*, ed. K. T. Hargrove, R.S.C.J., Milwaukee, 1966, pp. 227ff.

use. (It has been plausibly argued that modern science and technology are Biblical in inspiration when, rather than contemplate nature with a religious awe, they subject it to experimental "torture" and technological control.) But while the Bible demythologizes the creation, it does not demythologize a divine word that may enter into it, in order to be present for man in and through it. It is the possibility of just this presence that the modern-secular world calls radically into question; and when the question is given an unequivocally negative answer, modern secularity has turned into secularism.

The essence of secularism may be formulated as an answer to one of the questions left hanging by Bonhoeffer. Suppose a secularist experienced, with or without the witness of a Bonhoeffer, the presence of the "confronting" God: Would he believe in Him? If he were an unrepentant secularist, he would "explain" the confronting God as the mere unconscious projection of his subjective "experience." This explanation, moreover, would encompass in principle all similar experiences throughout human history. Secularist man may or may not deny "the existence of God." He is, in any case, cut off from His presence. According to his lights, man—every man —is radically and inescapably alone.

Faith does not radically expose itself to the modern-secular world if it avoids the challenge of secularism. Yet self-exposure to secularism involves a risk without precedent in the history of faith. When faced with false prophets, an ancient prophet recognized the possibility and the risk that he himself might be false. When faced with secularism, modern faith recognizes the vastly more shattering possibility that all human witnessing to a divine presence ever made might have been based on a radical illusion: the possibility that man is, as secularism holds him to be, radically alone.

The modern believer dare not ignore this possibility, lest his self-exposure to the modern-secular world fail precisely when it is most serious. Yet dare he embrace the possibility as actuality? This would be to surrender to secularism. The modern believer walks on the "narrow ridge" of total risk.

On this ridge the great modern theologians have been walking for nearly half a century. To give one example, whatever questions may be asked about the "positivism" of Karl Barth's neo-orthodoxy,[29] it does not ignore secularism but arises from self-exposure to it.[30] To give another, Martin Buber's *I and Thou*[31] is not a mere homily that expresses its author's experience of a "divine Thou" and ignores the secularist objection that such experiences are in principle illusory. It confronts the secularist objection and repudiates it. *I and Thou* does not refute a Feuerbachian secularism that makes all I-Thou relations human. Faith can neither refute secularism nor itself be proved. The work does bring about, however, a significant confrontation; from this, it emerges that Biblical openness to a divine presence and the unyielding solitariness of secularism are both equally unprovable and irrefutable. They are, in this sense, rival faiths.

Secularist unbelief dissipates the present divine Other into a projection of human feeling. Belief on its part takes human feeling as the mere by-product of an actual encounter with Divinity: Only if man is "withdrawn" from the encounter is he left with mere feeling. Secularism asserts that belief deifies the projection of feeling. Faith retorts that secularism deifies its withdrawal from God; it holds that to repent of his secularism a man must not in his withdrawn state cast about for "religious experiences," but rather "turn" away from his self-absorption and toward the God who speaks.

This self-exposure is in principle adequate;[32] it bears witness to the "confronting" God while, self-exposed to a secularism that would "explain" away belief in this God, walking on the narrow ridge of risk. It falls short, however, in at least one crucial particular. Committed to the thesis that God speaks constantly,[33] *I and Thou* stakes all responsibility for "hearing" on a human "turning." But the weight of such a responsibility was too great even in Biblical times. In the modern-secular world it is intolerable.

But perhaps the greatest achievement of Buber's career is the

---

[29] Cf. Bonhoeffer, *op. cit.*, pp. 126, 148.

[30] Those currently inclined to dismiss Barth's neo-orthodoxy as being in the end merely old-fashioned orthodoxy might find instructive his *From Rousseau to Ritschl* (London, 1959), a work showing a far deeper penetration of Hegel than is shown by those who invoke Hegel in their argument for the death of God.

[31] Martin Buber, *I and Thou*, New York, 1958.

[32] The brief summary of Buber's teaching just given is based, as well as on *I and Thou*, on other writings, notably those collected in *Between Man and Man*. The adequacy of Buber's teaching, here merely asserted, is argued for in my "Buber's Concept of Revelation," in the forthcoming *The Philosophy of Martin Buber*, eds. Schilpp and Friedman, La Salle, Illinois.

[33] Buber, *I and Thou*, pp. 75, 77, 99, 118ff.

steadfastness with which it moves from an original resort to romantic illusions toward an ever-greater realism. About thirty years after
I and Thou, Buber writes:

> Let us ask whether it may not literally be true that God
> formerly spoke to us and is now silent, and whether this is
> not to be understood as the Hebrew Bible understands it,
> namely, that the living God is not only a self-revealing but
> also a self-concealing God. Let us realize what it means to live
> in the age of such a concealment, such a divine silence. . . .
> It would be worthier not to explain it to oneself in sensa-
> tional and incompetent sayings, such as that of the death
> of God, but to endure it as it is and at the same time move
> existentially toward a new happening, toward that event in
> which the word between heaven and earth will again be
> heard.[34]

This statement is made in direct response to Sartre's atheism, but
in indirect response to all modern secularism and, in anticipation,
to all the "God-is-dead" theologies. Faith stands here self-exposed
to all the evidence that secularist unbelief might cite against it in
the contemporary world; yet it remains faith because it continues
to listen to God even if, there being no hearing, there may be an
"eclipse of God." An eclipse does not destroy the sun; moreover,
it is temporary. A faith which accepts a divine eclipse listens even
in a time of silence, in the trust that the divine word will again be
heard.[35]

Can such a faith endure in the present age? This is an as-yet unanswered question. The contradictions in which this endurance
must prove itself today are nearly nowhere confronted. In this age,
there is celebration of the freedoms of the secular city, coupled with
dread of its emptiness. Democratic tolerance coexists with unpre-

---

34 Martin Buber, *Eclipse of God*, New York, 1952, pp. 89, 91.

35 Altizer refers to the possibility of a divine eclipse (RT, pp. 10, 107, 126); but
despite much pondering, I cannot conclude that he has seriously considered it. Cf.
RT, p. 126: "Buber asserts that the Jew can be safe in a time of God's eclipse because he exists in an eternal covenant that cannot be annulled by an act of man. The
contemporary Jew can experience the contradiction of our existence as a theophany.
However, not existing in an eternal covenant with God—if only because he exists in
an Incarnate Word—the Christian cannot know the death of God as a theophany."
Is the Jew "safe," and does Buber consider him so? Is a divine eclipse a theophany?
Is not the Christian too in a covenant, the question of the "death" of God being
precisely what is at issue? Finally, can Christian and Jew be as infinitely apart as
is here asserted?

cedented violence and with the spectre of universal disaster. Modern man is torn between an at-homeness in a secular world exalting human autonomy, and flights from both into an apocalyptic nihilism. The listening endurance of faith will have to exist steadfast in this world, exposed at once to its marvels and terrors.

The Jew is singled out for special contradictions. In America he enjoys a freedom and security unparalleled in his history; yet he is but twenty years separated from the greatest and as yet uncomprehended Jewish catastrophe. His trust and joy in the modern-secular world cannot but coexist with radical distrust and profound sorrow. Authentic Jewish religious witness in this age must both face up to Auschwitz and yet refuse a despair of this world which, wholly contrary to Judaism, would hand still another victory to the forces of radical evil. Insofar as he is committed to Jewish survival, the Jew has already taken a stand against these forces. But survival-for-survival's-sake is an inadequate stand. The Jew can go beyond it only if he can reopen the quest of Jeremiah and Job, who for all their agony refused to despair either of God or the world.

Despair, Silence, Waiting, Interrogation

Is there an authentic Jewish enduring of the contradictions of present Jewish existence? Is it giving rise to a quest, to a listening, indeed, to an interrogation of God which, born of faith, may itself bespeak a Presence while as yet no voice is heard? Perhaps one must not look to philosophers or even theologians. Perhaps one must look to a novelist whose heaven-storming shatters conventions and literary forms.[36] Elie Wiesel's *Night* is no mere speculation upon imagined darkness. It is an eye-witness account of the most terrible actual darkness, by a man who experienced it when he was a four-

---

[36] At a recent symposium "Toward Jewish Unity," S. Schwarzschild said: "The . . . point which I want to make . . . is a reference to an experience which many of us here shared last summer. . . . It was a gathering in the Canadian Province of Quebec . . . where a number of us, from all over the spectrum of Jewish life, gathered for a week's intensive study and conversation. . . . We discovered something at the end of the week . . . , namely, that the one man who spoke and protested and stormed the heavens and implicated Israel most tellingly for our generation and for our hearts, and for our hopes, and for our tragedy, was not a theologian, nor a professor, nor even a rabbi. The *de facto* High Priest of our generation turned out to be Elie Wiesel." (Judaism, Vol. 15, No. 2, Spring, 1966, p. 157.)

teen-year-old boy. In this document—the document of our time of the impact of radical evil on Jewish faith—we read:

> One day when we came back from work, we saw three gallows rearing up in the assembly place, three black crows. Roll Call. SS all round us, machine guns trained: the traditional ceremony. Three victims in chains—and one of them, the little servant, the sad-eyed angel.
>
> The SS seemed more preoccupied, more disturbed than usual. To hang a young boy in front of thousands of spectators was no light matter. The head of the camp read the verdict. All eyes were on the child. He was lividly pale, almost calm, biting his lips. The gallows threw its shadow over him. . . .
>
> The three victims mounted together onto the chairs.
>
> The three necks were placed at the same moment within the nooses.
>
> "Long live liberty!" cried the two adults.
>
> But the child was silent.
>
> "Where is God? Where is He?" someone behind me asked.
>
> At a sign from the head of the camp, the three chairs tipped over. . . .
>
> I heard a voice within me answer . . . :
>
> "Where is He? Here He is—He is hanging here on this gallows. . . ."[37]

The hero of *The Accident* has listened to Sarah, former "SS whore" who has been forced into every degradation conceivable by a satanic imagination.

> I shouldn't have listened. I should have fled. . . . Whoever listens to Sarah and doesn't change, whoever enters Sarah's world and doesn't invent new gods and new religions, deserves death and destruction. Sarah alone had the right to decide what is good and what is evil, the right to differentiate what is true from what usurps the appearance of truth.[38]

The Town Beyond the Wall ends with a legend. Man once was granted by God his request for a temporary exchange of places. The request granted, he immediately assumed omnipotence and refused to return to his place. In the years or centuries or eternities following:

---

37 Elie Wiesel, *Night*, New York, 1961, pp. 70f.
38 Elie Wiesel, *The Accident*, New York, 1962, pp. 90ff.

The past for one, the present for the other, were too heavy to be borne. As the liberation of one was bound to the liberation of the other, they renewed the ancient dialogue whose echoes come to us in the night, charged with hatred, with remorse, and most of all, with infinite yearning.[39]

In *The Gates of the Forest*, Gregor remains in an inconclusive argument with the chasidic rabbi.

Gregor was angry. "After what has happened to us, how can you believe in God?" With an understanding smile on his lips the Rebbe answered, "How can you not believe in God after what has happened?"[40]

Yet Gregor reaches an affirmation, or the fragment of an affirmation, or the fragment of a fragment.

"Whether or not the Messiah comes doesn't matter; we'll manage without him. It is because it is too late that we are commanded to hope. . . . The Messiah isn't one man, Clara, he's all men. As long as there are men there will be a Messiah. One day you'll sing, and he will sing in you. . . ."

At the appropriate moments Gregor recited the *Kaddish*, that solemn affirmation, filled with grandeur and serenity, by which man returns God his crown and sceptre. He recited it slowly, concentrating on every sentence, every word, every syllable of praise. His voice trembled, timid, like that of the orphan suddenly made aware of the relationship between death and eternity, between eternity and the word.[41]

---

[39] Elie Wiesel, *The Town Beyond the Wall*, New York, 1964, p. 179.
[40] Elie Wiesel, *The Gates of the Forest*, New York, 1966, p. 194.
[41] *Ibid.*, pp. 225ff.

5. *A FINAL CONVERSATION*
WITH PAUL TILLICH

ALBERT H. FRIEDLANDER

In August of 1965, shortly before his death, Professor Tillich discussed some of the moral and theological implications of the Shoah at his home in East Hampton, Long Island. The theological discourse of the past forty years is based upon Paul Tillich and his teachings; and his impact extends far beyond the area of Christian thought. In this conversation with one of the profound thinkers of our time, new dimensions of the problem of human suffering and of evil appear to us; and there is a redemptive quality in this encounter with a great Christian who was always known for his actions as well as his teachings.

———

The Life of Intellect is discipleship. "Take thyself a teacher" is a basic aspect of Jewish study; and the links in the chain of tradition are the great men of each generation. This summer has been a poignant reminder that students must also become teachers, as the great teachers of our times have quietly closed their lecture notes and have left the academy of life: Martin Buber, Albert Schweitzer, and now—Paul Tillich. Their disciples will continue their work.

Reprinted with permission of the Jewish Reconstructionist Foundation, Inc., from the *Reconstructionist*, Vol. XXXI, No. 14. Copyright by Albert Hoschander Friedlander, 1965.

Our scholars will assess their lasting contribution to dialogue, to civilization, to issues of ultimate concern. But there will also be the special memories drawn out of lives of encounter: as all great teachers, these three men taught by their lives as much as by their books. Here, then, is one of these special memories: a discussion with Paul Tillich, shortly before his death, dealing with the problems of the holocaust and the nature of Jewish destiny.

Paul Tillich was a familiar figure in East Hampton, at the very end of Long Island. Even during the summer, there are vast stretches of beach that remain isolated and lonely, with only sand, sea, the sea gulls, and an occasional wanderer such as Paul Tillich, walking for mile after mile, alone with his thoughts. But most of his visitors came to his home on Woods Lane. It had once been a potato farm, and Dr. Tillich showed them around the place with a great deal of pride. All of the trees, bushes, and arbors had been planted by him; and over the past twenty years, the bleak bareness of the farm had been transformed into a wooded retreat, a place of quietness and beauty. And it was here, sitting under his grape arbor, that we talked about the Shoah.

How To Teach the Holocaust

"Shoah—a fascinating word," said Dr. Tillich. "I did not realize that there is already a technical vocabulary about what happened in those days: holocaust and Shoah. It is a Biblical word, of course: 'a devastating storm.' But you know, it is only one storm in the whole history of Jewish life. You must teach it as part of the other persecutions: the Inquisition, the Middle Ages—they are all part of the story."

Dr. Tillich was offering me advice on a projected book that would try to teach aspects of the holocaust to Jewish high school students; and he was intensely interested in all phases of the project. We had first met at a civil rights rally in East Hampton; and the proximity of the synagogues to the Tillich place had made further conversations possible.

"But *why* is this all part of the Jewish story?" I asked Dr. Tillich. "When our high school students turn to you as a friend—and as a

Christian theologian viewing Jewish history—how will you answer their question: why did it happen to *us?*"

We sat quietly for a while, pondering the question. Then, Tillich broke the silence.

"I've been asked that question before," he said. "One of the judges in the Eichmann trial came to me when it was all over. He spent the whole day with me, asking the question in countless different ways. Week after week, he had been plowing through the material dealing with the destruction of European Jewry. And he felt the need for an answer that was not really mine to give."

A Question for Theology

"You see," said Paul Tillich, "you cannot just ask: why did it happen to *us?* It happens to all, and it is still taking place. We do have particular questions about the nature of the world in which we live. And philosophy helps us analyze the structures of being which we encounter in every meeting with reality. But you asked an ultimate question. You asked about the meaning of this reality for us; and that is a question for theology. Now, there is the revelation in Judaism that gives you an answer; and there is the revelation in Christianity that helps me in understanding what happened. But we each have to reach our own answers; and while they will agree, your students must discover the answer of Judaism. Nevertheless, there are some answers that I can give, and that I have given before. They deal with the fact that Hitler represented everything to which Judaism was opposed, that Judaism simply had to be the opponent of the false nationalism which we find in National Socialism. Stephen Wise once asked me to talk about this and I gave a public lecture at the Jewish Institute of Religion on the struggle between the gods of time and space. You could look this up in Volume 6 of my *Gesammelte Werke. . . .*"

Briefly, Paul Tillich talked about the contents of that lecture. He had written about space and time, and how they fight against one another in the world. They belong together: we measure time through space and space within time; and we exist in both. But pagans make space the ultimate value; their gods are tied to space which they defend against other gods. They do not believe in one God, because they cannot believe in a unique God. And belief in space leads to belief in blood and race and nation. It also leads to war: nations who believe in themselves live next to other nations —and space wants to expand. While it is good to believe in one's self and land, if that becomes the most important belief, it leads to a tragic existence that always remains imprisoned in space.

The Victory of Time Over Space

Then came the Jews and announced the victory of time over space. The command to Abraham to leave the land of his fathers and his father's home meant giving up the gods of blood and soil, of tribe and nation. For Judaism did not teach that its God was more powerful, that He ruled over all gods. It taught that God was unique; that there are no other gods; that God is not bound to any place in the world and space, but that He ruled time. The Temple could be destroyed, Palestine could cease to be a Jewish state—God was not affected by this, and His people were not destroyed by it. And the God of time is the God of history, who has given history a goal and a purpose, and who has given a task to Israel: to fight the belief in the gods of space. For Judaism teaches ethical monotheism; and ethical monotheism means universal justice—one justice, One God, one humanity.

The Jewish people, said Tillich, is uniquely the people of time. It represents the eternal fight between time and space. It stayed alive even when living space was constantly taken from it by the other nations of the world. Seen just as a people in space, it has had a tragic history; but seen as the people of time, it stands beyond tragedy, for it is an eternal people. It will always be persecuted (this applies also to the true Christian in the Church who fights the battle of time over space), because its mere existence challenges those pagan gods found within might, imperialism, injustice, demonic ecstasy—personified by the Nazi and similar groups. There will always be those who hate and fear the One God and those who follow Him. And there will always be the need for Israel to be the witness of the One God.

"Are you then saying," I asked Paul Tillich, "that Jews will always be persecuted? That this is God's will?"

Dr. Tillich shook his head.

"Remember what I said before: it happened to all, and it is still taking place. All Jews and Christians who believe in the One God and in universal justice have to confront this evil in the world. Church and synagogue must be united here in fighting for the realization of God's justice in history. Sometimes I talk about God's providence, by which I understand God's creative activity. And when I talk about God's justice, I mean this in the Hebrew sense: the word *tzedakah* must be understood as creative justice and not in the Aristotelian sense."

For some reason, we started to continue the discussion in German; perhaps, because Tillich was upset by the way in which the term "God" is used in any language.

God as the Ground of All Being

"So many people," said Paul Tillich, "talk about *'der liebe Gott'* as though he were just a super-human figure who could do everything possible or impossible. There is so much primitive, perverted thinking about God by people who insist on seeing Him in man's image. God is not a kindly father-figure. He is the ground of all being, and His imprint is upon everything. *'Der liebe Gott'* who is all powerful does not exist: man's freedom is a limitation here that must be recognized if man is to assert himself and is to gain his victory over space. We should not ask: why does God permit suffering? Instead, we should recognize that there is that in the depth of our being which will enable us to challenge evil, to overcome suffering, to work for the fulfillment of the ultimate goal which is the goal of history. And part of Jewish suffering, and part of Jewish greatness, is that the Jew has historically aligned himself with universal justice, and has been the great opponent of evil. But have your students read the prophets: let them read Second Isaiah and Jeremiah."

And so we talked about the prophets; about the greatness of Jewish history; about Jewish life in every age. But always, we came back to the history of the holocaust, to the Shoah. And once more, I had a question for Dr. Tillich: "How can we evaluate the details of that history? How can we judge what happened in the concentration camps?"

The Greatness Revealed in the Concentration Camps

"We cannot fully judge what happened there," said Tillich. "We were not inside the camps. And so I cannot accept some scholars' indictment of Jewish leaders. Of course there were some who faltered. But when I think of the greatness that was revealed there. . . ."

We talked about the great Jews of our time whom he had met. Tillich had known Leo Baeck. He had been in Frankfurt in time to know and to appreciate Martin Buber; and he deeply regretted that Franz Rosenzweig was already dying at that time, and was not accessible to him. Rosenzweig's friend Rosenstock-Heussy had been also a close friend of Tillich's. But there were differences:

"He believed in converting the Jews; and this is something that I cannot accept. I have never tried to convert Jews; we have a common task, and synagogue and church can and must work together."

Talking about Leo Baeck, Tillich expressed his conviction that Baeck's actions were always examples of true goodness in action: the greatness of his ministry to the Jewish community, his heroism in staying when he could have left—these were "true testimony."

On Leo Baeck and Buber's Zionism

"There is one point where I might have disagreed with Baeck," said Tillich, "if I had been in his place, in the concentration camp. But I was not there. I might have shared the last iota of information, the fact that the way of those railroad tracks to Auschwitz led to certain death. The full existential truth should always be made available. But the concentration camp was a special place, outside our knowledge; and nothing could be done inside that place to change the fate of those imprisoned there. It's hard to judge. In the same way, I believe that the incurable patient should *always* be told the full truth. But no one can judge that situation from this distance, and with hindsight. One can only act in the full awareness of the place and the time in which one stands. Baeck was there; and he acted nobly."

Our meeting was drawing to its close. We had left the arbor—the grapes still hard and green but showing promise of a good harvest—and walked back and forth among the trees. Tillich talked about Israel, about his conviction that Martin Buber's approach to Zionism held the greatest promise for the Jewish future. Tillich was still concerned that Judaism should not be captured by space, but should continue to fight the battle of time against space, against nationalist limitations. Then Mrs. Tillich joined us and the talk shifted to family matters. The Tillichs were driving to town and could drop me at the synagogue. I took my leave. At the very end, there was a return to the topic, an encouragement to teach the past to young students:

"A book on the holocaust—on that devastating storm you call Shoah—is vital; it should be written. And what is more: it should be read."

For Paul Tillich, great theologian of Christianity, this was not just a matter that concerned the Jewish community; he saw it as a challenge to all humanity. And if his voice is no longer among us, admonishing and teaching, his writings remain, speaking to Christians and Jews.

6. *THIS PEOPLE ISRAEL*

LEO BAECK

"Every people is a question which God addresses to humanity . . ." and Leo Baeck reminds us that just as man questions God, God also questions man. In the pages that follow, the final section of his last work, Baeck comes to view history as theology as God is approached through the total experience of man. Baeck's vision was never crowded. In the poisonous miasma of the concentration camp, and in the post-Auschwitz darkness of our own days, he acknowledged all aspects of human suffering. But he found in them also pathways, and these pathways led to the mystery, to the hope, to the task of man. Aware of the fullness of man's inadequacies, moving through the realm of human experience, Baeck reminds us of the ultimate dimensions of humanity which reach through the Holocaust and encounter the mystery of God. Despite all that happened, man can still act ethically.

The Tension of Jewish History

The history of this people is also a history of boundaries, of eras that divided it deeply, of domains and areas that created manners, of spheres of history within the one history. At times there existed a tension between the parts, but the parts never broke apart. In the

From *This People Israel* by Leo Baeck. Translated by ALBERT H. FRIEDLANDER. Copyright © 1964 by the Union of American Hebrew Congregations. Reprinted by permission of Holt, Rinehart and Winston, Inc.

end, the tension had the strength to create strength. The unity always endured.

It will endure, and blessing will stream from the whole to the parts and from the parts to the whole, as long as there are beings here who exist, and constantly arise again, who "live by their faith," so that the faith lives through them. Rabbi Simlai, who hearkened to both East and West, has said that the summation of all the commandments is that "the righteous shall live by his faith."

Everything declares itself in faith which, as certainty and experience, from the very beginning, had its earthly place within this people: the certainty of the covenant of God, of human freedom, of the revelation, of the reconciliation, of the soil and the community, of the readiness and the renunciation, of the will to Torah, to the message, to the contemporary and the coming, to work, and to the Sabbath, and the certainty of the gift of prayer and expectation. Faith appears as something manifold, but is one. In this totality, in this unity, and through this unity and totality, this people lived generation after generation, for the sake of the generations—"from Egypt even until now" (Num. 14:19). Thus, thus alone, will it continue to live.

"From Egypt even until now." Until this time, in which mankind is once more changing, its parts striving to separate, this people, participating in or drawn into everything, is yet to remain within its individuality in order to recognize and fulfill new tasks. Until this time, when once again focal points shifted or were displaced, when this people came to experience all the displacement in itself, it held fast to its own enduring focal point. Until this time, when the New World, which had become great, became the land of most of this people, and when in the Old World, nations were awakening, a new life had grown for this people upon the soil of the Promised Land. Until this time, when there arises, among peoples and religions, an almost undreamed of understanding for this people and its religion, and also a previously unknown adversary, this people is to be prepared and work willingly that "righteousness and peace may come together." Until this time, when mankind searches for itself and yet cannot find itself, this people is to cling fast to the fact that it has its existence in humanity and for the sake of humanity. "From Egypt even until now."

Moses once pleaded with God for his people that had gone

astray: "Pardon, I pray Thee, the iniquity of this people according unto the greatness of Thy lovingkindness, and according as Thou hast forgiven this people, from Egypt even until now" (Num. 14:19). When this people prays for forgiveness year after year on the Day of Atonement, it utters these words. He who considers the future of this people finds these words forcing themselves to his lips and into his heart.

What will a later generation see when it looks about? What must it recognize, what may it recognize when it looks at itself? These are questions which the generation that lives today must address to itself, just as they were addressed to every previous generation, whether it heard them or not. Every generation by choosing its way, its present way, at the same time chooses an essential part of the future, the way of its children. Perhaps the children will turn from the eternal way, but in this, too, they will be determined by the direction of their parents. The responsibility to those who follow after us is included in the responsibility to ourselves. The way of the children, whether accepting or rejecting the direction, emanates from our way. Ways bind, wind, and wander.

Nevertheless, ever again a child is born; an individual, a promise of the likeness of the image of God; the great miracle within humanity is reborn. With the birth of a human being the whole problem of humanity is raised anew. The great possibility, the message to humanity, the annunciation of the confidence that must never end, is brought anew into life through the child. It always re-enters humanity in the sequence of the generations, and in history.

When people or peoples assume that they can fit history into a personally fixed pattern, they delude themselves. They want to make things easy for themselves. Responsibility in which freedom turns to freedom is so much harder. But all strivings and endeavors to bind history are in vain. An inheritance cannot be fabricated, let alone forced; it can only be assumed by a freedom that has the ability to build on it. The work of the clever and the mighty, who think they have established a lasting inheritance, breaks down so much easier, generally, than the work of the simple and the insignificant. The shrewd think they are securing the future; and one day, often very near, they or those who follow them stand before ruins. The question is raised, and many questions join in it: Is an

inheritance possible, that can endure from generation to generation, not in its forms, but in its power (for the nature of form is
change), that remains in its blessing, in order to endure any fate?
When this people raises this question, it raises the question of its
existence.

In all of the declines of history in which humanity apparently
destroys itself or seems to refute itself, one thing surely endured
and experienced renewal. That which was searched out and formed
by the spirit arose out of ruins and beyond ruins; it wandered from
land to land. It could speak to men everywhere; it could engage
them in dialogue. The history of these rebirths encounters the works
of the spirit—and in the spirit, in its best and ultimate forms, lies
an essential part of the actual history of humanity. What would
humanity be without it? Would it exist without it? The many
things the tool built, the tool then destroyed in many ways. That
which spirit has fashioned is indestructible. It endures, even when
it is rejected. In the Bible, the word "spirit" has the sound of holiness. The spirit comes from God, and in it, too, man can sanctify
himself.

The Encounter with God

One thing leads still higher, to something even more encompassing
than the encounter with man's spirit. It is "nearness to God," the
meeting with God. It is the greatest aspect of human existence. In
it, "man gains his world, his eternity, in the span of an hour";
such is the daring expression of an ancient teacher. Thus, in an
all-encompassing piety, the Psalmist prayed: "But as for me, the
nearness of God is my good" (Ps. 73:28). Previously, this man of
prayer said: "Whom have I in heaven but Thee? And beside Thee
I desire none upon earth" (Ps. 73:25). This nearness is this people's
inheritance through which alone it could and will endure, on
whatever ground it may live. This people's true history is a history
of encounters with God. It has this history for its own sake and
for the sake of humanity. It bears it and is borne by it.

Every people is a question which God addresses to humanity; and
every people, from its place, with its special talents and possibilities,
must answer for its own sake and for the sake of humanity. Any

people cannot, may not, be without humanity or beyond humanity. Humanity cannot be without all peoples nor beyond any people. God questions humanity through the peoples. Humanity lives only through these peoples, those that have come into being and those that are in the process of becoming. Every people is thus responsible for the fact that humanity exists. For the sake of a responsibility which it has before God, through the question which God poses, a people exists, just as the individual exists only when he is conscious of responsibility and finds his life in it. A man and a people are thus a question of God; or, as the wonderful image of an ancient teacher dared: they are a resignation made by God. Beyond all of the special questions, stands the one question which is life itself, the question from God.

Jewish Existence

This people Israel developed and grew in one millennium and formed the question that rests within it. It has kept arising ever again, through rebirths, in new epochs, for more than two millennia now. Through its prophets, its poets, its teachers, its righteous ones, Israel was able to learn how to listen to the question which God addressed to it. Its question proved, in Israel's experience, to be the deepest of all questions which live within and form humanity. This people's hope is, therefore, the greatest of all hopes; it is the great expectation to which the way of all ways leads. The iniquity of this people is, therefore, deeper iniquity than any other. And offenses against this people signify more than other offenses. Both need "God's reconciliation." This people is "a covenant for the nations," a law for the peoples.

On the "Day of Judgment" and the "Days of Penitence," this people knows, in its prayers that lift it anew to God, that it stands in court before God. The sin within this people reverberates through these prayers. Only because atonement is in God's hands, can this people appear before God. The prayer continues: "A court also sits in judgment on the nations." These words seem to express the question to the nations: "What have you done to My people, to this Jewish people?" But the reverence in which all, the peoples and the nations, may find themselves united, penetrates these prayers too: "So be it: Grant reverence of He-Who-Is our God, to all Thy creatures, and honor of Thee to all whom Thou hast created; and all creatures will revere Thee, and all creatures will bow before Thee; and out of them will come *one* covenant, to do Thy will with a perfect heart."* The great expectation speaks here, the hope for the reconciliation in which all reconciliations join together.

The Great Readiness for God

The great task of dark days, and the greater one of bright hours, was to keep faith with the expectation. Man waits for God, and God waits for man. The promise and the demand speak here, both in one: the grace of the commandment and the commandment of grace. Both are one in the One God. Around the One God there is the concealment. He does not reveal Himself, but He reveals the commandment and the grace. And He, the Eternal One, has given mortal man freedom of will and has shown him a goal for his will. But the ultimate remains concealed from man. Thus the prophet announced the word of God: "For My thoughts are not your thoughts, neither are your ways My ways, saith He-Who-Is" (Is. 55:8). The great reverence was exalted in this, and it always clung to this, even when men assumed that God's thoughts were their thoughts, and when men dared the supposition that their ways were God's ways. The mystery surrounds God. He is not the revealed God, but He is the revealing God. Wherever the great reverence lives in a man and the great readiness for God rises out of it, there and then, man is near to God.

Men near to God existed in this people in all its days. They are this people's "holy ground." This people is sustained by them alone. Through two sentences of Moses, this people declared itself for God and for itself by becoming conscious of God and of itself: "Hear, O Israel: He-Who-Is our God He-Who-Is is one. And thou shalt love Him-Who-Is thy God with all thy heart, and with all thy soul, and with all thy might" (Deut. 6:4-5). The first sentence tells of the great reverence, in which the certainty of the belief dwells; and the second, of the great readiness, in which man

---

* See *High Holiday Prayer* Book, ed. M. Silverman, p. 11.

declares himself for God. That God is our God, is the promise, the grace, upon which the commandment is founded. To love Him thy God, is the commandment out of which new grace flows to men. The man who fulfills the commandment has encountered God. These two sentences are not just sentences, they are the history of this people. This history, after all, is the history of encounters with God. Whoever wishes to see, sees this.

Man and the Mystery

We live in a clearness surrounded by mystery. This, our earth, courses around its sun, one of the many myriads of stars. Are there, upon any of these stars, beings like ourselves? Beings descended from a mother and father, who desire to live on through their children, beings who search and roam, who get lost in their days between birth and death, who doubt, who fear, who hope, who sin, and who can yet be reconciled?

Whatever the case, we are these men upon this earth. It is our home, and its circumference includes us. Upon it, we are born, generation after generation; and upon it, we die, grave after grave. For the earth exists in many years, and we, in but the few. It existed before us, it will exist after us. It carries us and reaches out to us. It holds fast to everything upon it by the strength of its attracting power.

But a miracle exists upon it, exists in human beings who live upon it. The miracle leads outward and upward and is stronger than everything terrestrial. It is the miracle of the spirit, of the created human who becomes creative, fashioning within the fashioned.

It is a miracle of the thinking human being. The spirit of men who dwell upon the earth, upon this star, travels into the All and takes up its foundation there. There, man cogitates. He takes space and time, which embrace all the stars, and makes them his tool. Comparing and measuring, investigating and counting, contemplating that which has come out of the thoughts of a higher power, he determines passage and duration. He recognizes the rule of the law, the constantly returning sanction of the enduring. A great definiteness, a great clarity appears before him; and he moves forward, from definiteness to definiteness, from clarity to clarity. He stands in the All and walks in the All. Such is the miracle of the thinking spirit.

But a greater miracle reveals itself to him here. For behind every certainty there stands a concealment, behind every new clarity a new mystery is revealed. All the certainties, all the concealments and the searching spirit itself that traveled out into them, all are embraced by something unfathomable, by the miracle of all miracles. Behind all of them, above all of them, and beneath all of them is the great mystery which is beyond space and time, which exists through itself and which exists through everything that is. No man's mind has fathomed it or will be able to fathom it. But reverence, that reverence without which love does not live and faithfulness does not endure, may approach it. And it hears the voice out of the mystery: "I AM THAT I AM, thy God."

And another great miracle is within the human being upon this earth. It is the miracle in which the artistic spirit awakens. This spirit does not gaze outward but gains perspective. It steps back to view a totality, to hear a totality, to understand a totality—this totality in which the particular receives meaning and gains its place and its right. Thus, man also stands above the earth, above its constant change. He takes his position in the higher domain, that of ideas. Seeing, or hearing, or pondering, he wants to grasp a unity, a totality, a harmony there where he sees lines beside lines, hears sounds beside sounds, where he experiences thoughts beside thoughts. He, earthly man, has lifted himself above earth. He, the created man, begins as if by a miracle to be creative. Clarities, certainties approach him; and through him they appear to the days which come after him.

But here too the concealed once again emerged behind the definite; the mystery stood behind every clarity. Something which existed behind the presentations, behind the appearances, a unity, a totality, a harmony had opened itself; and behind it, in the hidden, a still wider totality, a more comprehensive unity, a deeper harmony, was surmised. Appearances were merely a reflection of an infinite mystery which had revealed itself. The reverence without which the truly artistic cannot exist could sense this. To it also, out of that unfathomable, the word sounded: "I AM THAT I AM, thy God."

Still another miracle exists, which develops and can then grant even greater power to the others: the miracle of the moral in the human being. The moral is the great contradiction of everything which earthly existence seems to indicate. Everything upon this earth bespeaks a battle of all against all, in which one being, in order not to be conquered, strives to conquer another. Existence upon earth seems to be an existence of self-seeking; self-seeking appears as the "natural." The other man is either the subjugated or excluded one, or he is the enemy. Now the great miracle fulfills itself within the spirit: men discover their true selves in selflessness, so that they begin to understand themselves. In the "thou" they discover the "I," and the other man becomes their "other one," placed near them, entrusted to them. A definiteness, a clarity has entered into being, into life. Now, not the drive for the desires of the hour directs or oppresses man; but something steadfast, enduring, a strength out of the strength of the law has come to exist within him, like a miracle. It is there to make him strong, to lead him, to order his life. Now there is something creative within him; he can form his self, he can give shape to his life. He, the created man, can become a creator. He can be free inwardly, free by reason of the commandment. He is allowed to be more than the earth upon which he was born and upon which he dies. The great commandment, which never ceases and never changes, this miracle—it renders it thus for him. This miracle of morality makes him truly man.

The Task

When man thus forms his life, he begins to create community. He is not only born into community as if by fate, but he has now been called to the task of molding it. He stands within it as a figure of freedom. The encounters between the "I" and "thou," the "we" and the "you" attain the possibility of good. He, the created man, creates freedom and peace. Human beings enter and depart, generations come and go, but the commandment endures; ever new, everywhere, it brings men together, toward peace, toward the peace of the community. What was confused becomes definite; clarity pre-empts what had been confused. The man of this earth works for something to come into being which this earth itself does not give.

Thus the mystery again stands behind the clarity here. The certainty can only ascertain itself by drawing upon it. That which comes from the earth, which presents itself as "the natural," contradicts the creative power within human beings. It contradicts the fact that man rises above the earth by heeding something within himself which is above the earth, that is, the commandment, thus forming freedom within himself and community around himself. The earth does not answer when he asks for the fundamental reason. It only shows him battle and subjugation, the force which rises and then crumbles into itself. Perhaps it presents reasons of utility to him, for the sake of which it pays to act right, in peace and within the community. But useful things only possess their limited moment, in which they assume definition. Sooner or later they break apart and speak to displace one another or to destroy one another. Where is the fundamental basis for the commandment which endures, for the freedom and the community which endure? This is only revealed out of the mystery. The commandment has its roots in the mystery, out of which it gathers its strength, in order to give the mystery its meaning upon earth. Around the clarity there is concealment, the concealed around what it conceals; but from concealment comes the answer in which there is certainty and from which confidence emanates. The reverence learns this and meets the other, this higher world. The distant reaches become the nearness, and man hears the word: "I am He-Who-Is thy God. Thou shalt . . . ." The "Kingdom of God," which has been promised to man and has been assigned as his task, has approached him.

And now, what of this people, in the midst of peoples that are upon this earth, with them on one star amidst stars? Around every people, each in its way and each in its place, there is something hidden. But around this people there is more of the mystery than there is around others. Here there is mystery rising out of the eternal mystery. When the poets and the prophets, the teachers and the thinkers who arose from this people's midst, came to think about their people—each in his time and in his way—they contemplated the unending worlds, the harmony of the spheres, the "heavens which declare the glory of God." Then they spoke of their people, of its way and its hope, of the commandment which it must follow in order to encounter peace. Only one whose soul has opened to the great mystery which dwells in all, whether he stands within or sees from without, will be able to understand the reason why this people is to exist and why it does exist.

Every people can be chosen for a history, for a share in the history of humanity. Each is a question which God has asked, and each people must answer. But more history has been assigned to this people than to any other people. God's question speaks stronger here. Many peoples turned toward the commandments of idols, and, in that, they lost the history which had been promised them. The word of the One God penetrated this people from its beginning. When the commandment of God awakes in man, freedom also opens its eyes; and where freedom commences, history begins. A difficult task was assigned this people in its history. It is so easy to listen to the voices of idols, and it is so hard to receive the word of the One God into oneself. It is so easy to remain a slave, and it is so difficult to become a free man. But this people can only exist in the full seriousness of its task. It can only exist in this freedom which reaches beyond all other freedoms. Its history began when it heard the word, rising out of the mystery, and emerging into clarity: "I am He-Who-Is thy God, who brought thee out of the land of Egypt, out of the house of bondage" (Ex. 20:2).

This is the basic foundation and the goal, this is the revelation and the expectation. And confidence then approaches the soul of man, so that the best within him will enter there, where the nearness to God, the encounter with God, will become new truth. Only the reverence, in which alone is belief, can hear such a thing.

Man lives within the universe and within history. This people understood that history and universe testify to a oneness, and reveal a totality and order. One word has dared to be the one expression for that which keeps everything together: "covenant"—"the enduring," the covenant of the One God. It is the covenant of God with the universe, and therefore with the earth; the covenant of God with humanity and therefore with this people contained in it; the covenant with history and therefore with every one within it; the covenant with the fathers and therefore with the children; the covenant with days which were and therefore with days which are to come. "As true as My covenant is"—this was the word of the Eternal One heard by the prophet when he thought about his people in a time of oppression and dark destiny, and certainty entered him. The question of all questions, that of the entrance of the eternal, the unending, the one, into the domain of the many, the terrestrial, the passing, this question in which the searching, the thinking, the hope of this people has always lived, in which it once grew and in which it was ever reborn—this question itself possesses the answer: "As true as My covenant is."

This people traveled through the history of humanity, century after century, millennium after millennium. Its very history became divine guidance for it. Once Moses and the children of Israel sang this song to Him-Who-Is, and said: "Thou in Thy love hast led the people that Thou hast redeemed" (Ex. 15:13). And confidence, whenever it looked backward or forward, then said: "Once they sang unto Him-Who-Is; so will they yet sing unto Him-Who-Is."

Looking Back

Never shall I forget these things, even if I am condemned to live as long as God himself. Never.

ELIE WIESEL: *Night*

1. *BADENHEIM 1939*

AHARON APPELFELD

In 1939, still a time of ignorance, many Jews vacationed in the small resort towns of Germany and Austria. Even today, the old inhabitants will point out the former "Jewish" hotels. Appelfeld's novel shows us such a town near Vienna, where the Jewish visitors—musicians, scholars, businessmen, and their families—live out the fateful time before their "resettlement to the East." They rationalize every threatening event, unaware that each one is a step closer to deportation and death. Appelfeld himself escaped a labor camp at the age of eight and hid in the forests until he was found by the Red Army. Today he is one of the great Israeli writers of our age.

The town was full of strangers. The shadows of the forest returned to the town and spread themselves over the paving stones of the Imperial Square. Mountain breezes blew in the alleys and there was a smell of moss. Sally and Gertie stood at their gate and offered the strangers mugs of soup.

"What is this place?" someone asked, as if waking from a troubled sleep.

"The holiday resort of Badenheim, the Music Festival city."

"Where do the concerts take place?"

"In the hall."

At the sound of these words the man seemed to come alive again.

In the late afternoon the people would gather next to the hotel entrance and Dr. Pappenheim would speak to them. How his face had

changed over the past few months! He would tell them about Poland.
About the wonderful world to which they were going. "Here we have no
life left," he would say. "Here everything has become empty."

Only a few days before, they had been sitting in their warm houses,
busy with their flourishing practices. Now they were sitting here, without shelter. Everything had been taken from them; it was like a bad dream.
Someone asked for details about housing conditions, employment, trans-
ferring foreign currency, and a man who had lost his wife on the way
asked if she had perhaps gone on ahead and was already in Poland.

"Will we have a chance to hear the twins?" someone asked in the dissolving darkness.

Salo was happy. His stay here would cost the company a fortune.
Everything was at their expense, even the journey to Poland. The musicians liked him and called him "the agent." And Salo, used to words and
soliciting for trade, sat in the armchair and held forth: a man should broad-
en his horizons. Ever since he was a boy he had loved traveling. "You
should make Dr. Pappenheim sign Form 101. He's sure to have it, every
employer does. Travel by all means, but like me, at the company's
expense."

"Form 101, what's that? I've never heard of it," said one of the musicians.

"I've been using it for years, it's an official form. I discovered it immediately. It's brought me a good bit of indirect income, I can tell you."

One of the strangers invaded the hotel and threatened to murder the
owner. "*Ostjuden*, you're to blame!"

"I'm not to blame for anything." The hotel owner stood next to the
stranger like a prisoner.

The man shouted and waved his fists, and since he was in the grip of
madness, people approached him and tried to explain that things weren't
as bad as they looked. A board of appeals would surely exempt him.

Every committee had a board of appeals, that was a well-known fact.
No committee could simply do as it pleased. There was a question of procedure, after all. And if the lower courts made a mistake, then the higher
courts were always there to remedy it. There was no need to get upset.

"If you're right, where does the board of appeals sit?" asked the man, a
little appeased.

"They'll probably make an announcement soon."

"I don't understand," said the man. "Am I a criminal to be thrown out
of my house? You tell me, please."

"It's not a question of crime, but of a misunderstanding. We, too, to a certain extent, are the victims of a misunderstanding."

The words *procedure* and *appeal* seemed to satisfy him. He had apparently once studied law. He calmed down a little. The contact with the old words restored him to his sanity.

Since the hotel owner saw that the old words had a good effect on the agitated soul of the stranger, he continued to use the same tone with him. The board of appeals would surely start hearing the appeals soon. They would be sure to discover plenty of flaws in these hasty procedures. Someone had probably made a mistake. There were empty beds upstairs. He could rest a little. Tomorrow they would probably know more.

The man was embarrassed, ashamed. "I didn't know," he said. "I'm sorry. Suddenly everything was taken away from me. They drove me here on the grounds that I'm a Jew. They must have meant the *Ostjuden*. And I'm like you, an Austrian. My forefathers? I don't know. Maybe, who knows. What does it matter who my forefathers were?"

Then he turned to the hotel owner and said loudly: "Please accept my apologies." The latter hurried to assist him as if he were an honored guest. They went upstairs.

"Why don't you sleep? You've been through a hard time," said the hotel owner. "Here are some pajamas, a towel."

The stranger, chastened, took off his sweater and shoes and said—as he was perhaps accustomed to saying to his wife—"Please wake me early in the morning."

Gray days settled on the town. In the hotel they stopped serving meals. Everyone stood in line to get their lunch—barley soup and dry bread. The musicians opened their suitcases. A smell of sawdust and open roads swept through the long corridors.

Suddenly the old rabbi appeared in the street. Many years ago they had brought him to Badenheim from the east. For a few years he had officiated in the local synagogue—or to tell the truth, the old-age home. When the old men died, the place was left empty. The rabbi had a paralytic stroke. In the town they were sure that he had died along with the other old men. [...]

The rabbi asked questions and the people answered. The many years of isolation had made him forget the language, and he spoke a mixture of Yiddish and Hebrew. A number of musicians appeared in the doorway, suitcases in their hands.

From the station they could still see Badenheim: a low hill cut like a cone, with the roofs of the houses like little pieces of folded cardboard. Only the hotel and bell tower seemed real. The kiosk owner was delighted to see all the people, and their eyes lit up at the sight of the lemonade, the newspapers, and journals—a testimony to the life that was still going on around them. Dr. Langmann bought the financial weekly and studied it like a man returning to a beloved city after years of absence. His eye fell on some ridiculous item and he laughed out loud. Sally and Gertie equipped themselves with two big parcels—one of cigarettes and one of sweets. The yanuka dirtied his suit and they busied themselves with cleaning it.

The skeptical bitterness did not leave the rabbi's lips. He placed no faith in these delusions. He had seen much in his life and all that was left in him was suspicion, and in this transition too his suspicions did not cease but only grew more intense. The headwaiter bought sausages. The dog liked sausages. The headwaiter's happiness knew no bounds.

The musicians crowded together in a corner, in the shade. Some of the plates had been broken on the way, and they had to unpack their cases and pack them again. This annoying necessity, which gave rise to anger and mutual recriminations, marred the festive atmosphere a little. Strangely enough, Mandelbaum did not despise them. He asked them how they were and inquired about the resorts they played in. His questions relaxed the tension a little.

The people did not forget Samitzky and bought him some bottles of vodka. Samitzky sat on a bench and did not utter a word. "When are we leaving?" asked a woman's voice. Another woman stood next to the closed ticket office and made herself up. Salo put on his old expression again, his traveling salesman's expression. At any moment, it seemed, he would open his medium-sized suitcase and offer his samples for sale. From here the carriages would pick the people up and there was always the same fragrance in the air, the fragrance of the transition from the town to the country, and from the station to the enchanted Badenheim. There were no carriages now, but the fragrance still lingered in the air, mingled with an intoxicating dampness.

And suddenly the sky opened and light broke out of the heavens. The valley in all its glory and the hills scattered about filled with the abundance, and even the trembling, leafless trees standing wretchedly at the edge of the station seemed to breathe a sigh of relief.

"What did I tell you?" exclaimed Dr. Pappenheim, opening his arms in an expansive gesture that seemed too big for him. Tears of joy came into his eyes. All the misery of the days of confinement suddenly burst inside him.

Sally and Gertie wrapped the yanuka up warmly. Karl took the sweater off the bottle: two little fish were already dead and the rest floated limply and listlessly in the water. "Can no one help me?" cried Karl despairingly.

The light poured down from the low hills directly onto the station platform. There was nowhere to hide. "Come and see, everybody!" Mitzi suddenly cried, in an affected feminine voice. A little distance away, as if on an illuminated tray, a man was walking with two armed policemen behind him. They came closer as if they were being borne on the light.

"Peter, Peter!" shouted the hotel owner in relief.

Peter.

But their amazement was cut short. An engine, an engine coupled to four filthy freight cars, emerged from the hills and stopped at the station. Its appearance was as sudden as if it had risen from a pit in the ground. "Get in!" yelled invisible voices. And the people were sucked in. Even those who were standing with a bottle of lemonade in their hands, a bar of chocolate, the headwaiter with his dog—they were all sucked in as easily as grains of wheat poured into a funnel. Nevertheless Dr. Pappenheim found time to make the following remark: "If the coaches are so dirty, it must mean that we have not far to go."

2. JEAN-CHRISTOPHE

IDA FINK

The poignant story of young girls on a labor detail in the forest shows them surrounded by the beauty of nature, by their memories, and by their dreams. Fearfully they listen for the sound of trains, knowing that these trains may be taking their loved ones from the ghetto to the death camps. Uncertain of their future, they are aware that they may never see the promise of their youth. Ida Fink was born in Poland, lived in a ghetto and then in hiding until the end of the war. She emigrated from Poland to Israel in 1957. This story appears in her volume of collected stories, *A Scrap of Time*.

━━━

We are working on the Ostbahn. It was a good work assignment because our *Aufseherin* was a girl we knew; we had gone to school with her. She was pretty then, roundfaced, with curly dark hair. She used to sleep with the clerks in the district office, and now she slept with the Germans, but she was a good girl—she only slept with them, that's all. It was a good assignment: planting embankments wasn't hard work, and we were in the woods, in a beautiful forest some five or maybe eight kilometers outside of town, amid the silence of the trees. Also, this *Aufseherin* didn't much care what we did or how we worked. She just sat under a tree, bored. She would have loved to talk to us, but she was probably afraid of losing her

From *A Scrap of Time* by IDA FINK. Copyright © by IDA FINK. Translation copyright © by Random House, Inc. Reprinted by arrangement with Liepman AG, c/o Joan Daves Agency as agent for the proprietor. Translated from the Polish by MADELINE LEVINE and FRANCINE PROSE.

job. She wasn't pretty anymore; she had grown heavy and her complexion was blotchy.

Sometimes, during our dinner break, she would sit near us and say, "This is a lovely forest, isn't it?"

"It *is* lovely," we would reply.

It was obvious that she was sensitive.

On the day of the action in town she was tactful enough not to ask why we weren't working, why our shovels and hoes lay under the tree. She sat at the edge of the clearing with her back to us. We were lying on the grass, not saying a word, waiting for the thundering of the train, because then we know it was all over—though not, of course who was on the train, who had been taken and who had been spared.

We lay on the grass, not saying a word, as if our voices could have drowned out the thundering of the train, which would pass near the edge of the forest, not far from where we were working. Only one girl was crying. She wasn't the youngest, and, in fact, she was the only one of us who had no one left in the town, who was all alone. She cried quietly, moaning every once in a while. No one tried to comfort her. Another girl was braiding wreaths—large clumps of bluebells grew everywhere—but every time she finished one she would rip it apart and begin all over again. She pulled up every bluebell in the clearing. Another girl was gnawing on some bread; she chewed it slowly, thoughtfully, and when she had eaten her ration, she grabbed someone else's bread and kept chewing. The oldest girl kept putting her ear to the ground.

It was silent in the forest. There were no birds, but the smell of the trees and flowers was magnificent. We couldn't hear anything. There was nothing to hear. The silence was horrifying because we knew that there was shooting going on and people screaming and crying, that it was a slaughterhouse out there. But here there were bluebells, hazelwood, daisies, and other flowers, very pretty, very colorful. That was what was so horrifying—just as horrifying as waiting for the thundering of the train, as horrifying as wondering whom they had taken.

One of us, a thin, dark-haired girl, had moved slightly away from the group and lay in the shade of the hazel trees. She alone wasn't straining to hear anything; she just lay on her stomach, reading a book. We could hear the soft, steady rustle of pages being turned. Not once did she lift her head and look at us. The book was thick; it was falling apart. When a strong wind blew up in the afternoon—the train still had not thundered past—several pages were suddenly whipped into the air. And as they fluttered over us like doves, she ran around, crying, "Catch them!" Then she gathered up the pages, put the book back together, lay down on her stomach, propped herself up on her elbows, and began to read again.

The girl who had been crying was now sobbing louder; all of us were aware that every passing minute brought the train's thunder nearer, that any moment now we would hear death riding down the tracks. One girl cried "Mama!" and then other voices cried "Mama!" because there was an echo in the woods.

Our *Aufseherin* finished hemming a kerchief, tossed her empty cigarette box into the bushes, stood up, and began pacing. Once she stopped beside the thin, dark-haired girl, obviously wanting to ask her something; instead, she walked away, humming softly and repeatedly checking her watch.

But the next time she passed near the girl, she couldn't help herself. "What are you reading?" she asked.

With great reluctance, the girl tore herself away from her book and looked up.

"*Jean-Christophe.*"

"*Jean-Christophe?*" The *Aufseherin* was surprised. "The title's just *Jean-Christophe*?"

"*Jean-Christophe,*" the girl replied.

"Is it good?"

She nodded.

"Is it about love?"

The girl thought for a moment. She was very thin, she wore a man's jacket instead of a blouse, and she looked very ugly. She answered seriously, "Love? That too."

"About love!" The *Aufseherin* burst out laughing. Maybe she laughed because she liked love. "Will you lend it to me when you're done?"

"Why not?" she answered. "I'll give it to you to keep."

"No, not to keep; lend it to me and I'll return it." She thought for a moment. "It must be good—you've been reading it all day; and especially on a day like this when they're taking your people away."

"I have to hurry," said the girl. "I want to make sure I finish it in time. There's one more section, and I'm afraid I won't be able to finish it." She looked carefully at the book to see how many pages she had left. "I'm afraid I won't have time to finish it," she repeated, to herself now, but the *Aufseherin* heard her.

"It must be *very* good. What's it called? I forget . . ."

"*Jean-Christophe.*"

"*Jean-Christophe,*" she repeated several times and explained, "If you're not around to lend it to me, I'll look for it in the library."

Then she felt sorry and added, "But I'm sure you'll finish it. Its not *that* long."

The girl who had been crying began sobbing still louder. It wasn't weeping anymore, it was lamentation. The oldest one of us knelt down and placed her ear to the earth. But the earth was still silent.

3. *MILENA*

MARGARETE BUBER-NEUMANN

At Ravensbrück, a women's camp for political prisoners outside of Berlin, Margarete Buber-Neumann met Milena Jesenská, a non-Jewish Czech journalist imprisoned for anti-Nazi writings. Buber-Neumann, who was formerly imprisoned in the Soviet Union and disillusioned with the Soviet experiment, was shunned by the pro-Soviet Communist prisoners who wielded a great deal of power within the camp. In this narrative, she describes her relief and joy in finding a true friend. "Under these circumstances," she writes, "the feeling that one was necessary to another human being was a source of supreme happiness, made life worth living, and gave one the strength to survive." In her tribute to Milena, who died at Ravensbrück, she describes the friendship that sustained them spiritually and emotionally.

———

I received Milena's first letter on October 21, 1940; someone slipped it into my hand while I was walking on the camp street. We had known each other for only a few days. But what can days mean when time is counted not in hours and minutes, but in heartbeats?

We met at the women's concentration camp at Ravensbrück. Milena had heard about me from a German woman who had arrived at the camp in the same shipment as herself. The journalist Milena Jesenská wanted to talk to me; she wished to know if it was true that the Soviet Union had

From *Milena: The Story of a Remarkable Friendship* by MARGARETE BUBER-NEUMANN. Copyright © 1977 by Albert Langen-Georg Müller Verlag. Translation copyright © 1988 by Seaver Books. Reprinted by permission of Seaver Books. Translated from the German by RALPH MANHEIM.

really handed over antifascist refugees to Hitler. Milena approached me during the newcomers' exercise period on the narrow path between the backs of the barracks and the high wall topped with electrified barbed wire. "Milena from Prague," she said by way of introduction. Her native city meant more to her than her surname. I shall never forget the strength and grace of the gesture with which she gave me her hand. When her hand was in mine, she said with a tinge of irony, "Please don't give me one of your German handshakes. My fingers are sore." Her face was prison-gray, marked with suffering. But my impression of illness was dissipated by the light in her eyes and the force of her movements. Milena was a tall woman with broad, straight shoulders and fine features. Her eyes and chin revealed energy and her beautifully curved lips a superabundance of emotion.

The path was narrow and we were in the way, obstructing the other prisoners in their movements to and fro. Muttering angrily, they kept trying to push us forward. I wanted nothing more than to get our greetings over with as quickly as possible and fall back into the prescribed "exercise" rhythm. In years of imprisonment I had adapted to these herd movements. Of this, Milena was utterly incapable. Here in the concentration camp she behaved exactly as if we had been introduced on a boulevard in some peaceful city. Carried away by the pleasure of making a new acquaintance or perhaps by the curiosity of the born reporter, she ignored the grumbling all around us and prolonged our amenities as much as possible. At first her insouciance infuriated me. But soon I was fascinated and delighted. Here was an unbroken spirit, a free woman in the midst of the insulted and injured.

After that we walked along with the others, back and forth at the foot of the "Wailing Wall" (as Milena called it), while the dust raised by our wooden clogs swirled all around us. When you meet someone under normal conditions, the way he is dressed usually tells you something about him. "Milena from Prague" was wearing the same long, striped, bulky dress as I, the same blue apron and regulation headscarf. I knew nothing about her except that she was a Czech journalist. She spoke with a slight Czech accent, but her German was otherwise perfect.

After a few parting words and the usual *Auf Wiedersehen* I went back to my barracks. All the rest of the day I was blind and deaf to everything. I was full of the name "Milena," drunk on the sound of it.

My feelings can only be appreciated by one who has been lonely in the midst of a great crowd. I had been shipped to Ravensbrück early in

August 1940. Behind me I had years of terror in the Soviet Union. Arrested in Moscow by the NKVD and sentenced to five years at forced labor, I was taken to Karaganda, a concentration camp in Kazakhstan. Then in 1940 the Russian state police handed me over to the Gestapo, who questioned me for months before sending me to Ravensbrück. On the third day of my stay at Ravensbrück, my Communist fellow prisoners subjected me to a third degree. They knew that I was Heinz Neumann's companion and that I had made no secret of our bitter experience in the Soviet Union. When they were through, they claimed I had been spreading lies about the Soviet Union and branded me a traitor. As the Communist women enjoyed considerable prestige among the inmates, their ostracism had the desired effect; from then on, my fellow politicals made a point of avoiding me. Milena Jesenská was the first among the political prisoners who not only spoke to me but showed that she trusted me.

Ravensbrück is in Mecklenburg, fifty miles north of Berlin. In 1940 the Gestapo interned five thousand women there, political offenders, Jews, members of proscribed religious groups, Gypsies, criminals, and so-called asocials. By the end of the war there were roughly twenty-five thousand women in the camp. At first there were sixteen ground-level barracks. Others were built little by little, and in the end there were thirty-two. Apart from the criminals and the asocials, the prisoners were from all walks of life. They differed widely from one another, but all in all they were very much like women at freedom. With the exception of the German, Polish, and Czech politicals and the Jehovah's Witnesses, there were relatively few conscious political oppositionists at the start. Later on, their numbers were swelled by members of the resistance movements in all the countries occupied by Hitler.

The politicals found it easier than others to adapt to conditions in the camp. Their being sent to a camp proved they were regarded as a threat to National Socialism, and that increased their self-respect. But most of the inmates were harmless innocents who had no idea why they had been sent to that ghastly place or for how long.

Every one of these women lived in thoughts of the life she had been wrenched away from, of her children, her husband, her parents. And now they were drilled like recruits and hadn't a minute of the day or night to themselves. At every step they were surrounded by others as unhappy as themselves. In every barracks an individual might be attracted to one or two others, but she was sure to find the vast majority unbearable in every way. The SS members, of both sexes, who ran the camp saw to it that the inmates were permanently cold and hungry, worked them like dogs, and even beat them.[...]

In the course of his or her confinement, every prisoner must go through different stages. One of the gravest dangers is inability to surmount the first shock of arrival at the camp. To survive, the prisoner had somehow to adapt to this extreme situation and give meaning to the new life, terrible as it was. Only a few succeeded by a great effort of the will in finding a new balance. Though ill on her arrival, Milena was one of these. Even in the first bewildering days of her stay, she took a keen interest in her fellow prisoners. In other words, she kept her grip on live.

Deep friendship is always a great gift. But if such good fortune is experienced in the desolation of a concentration camp, it can become the content of a life. During our time together Milena and I succeeded in defeating the unbearable reality. And because it was so strong, because it filled our whole beings, our friendship became something more, an open protest against the humiliations imposed on us. The SS could prohibit everything, they could treat us like disembodied numbers, threaten us with death, enslave us—in our feeling for each other we remained free and unassailable. It was toward the end of November, during our evening exercise, that we dared for the first time to walk arm in arm. This was strictly forbidden in Ravensbrück. It was dark, and we walked in silence, with strangely long steps as though dancing, peering into the milky moonlight. Not a breath of wind. Somewhere far away, far from our world, the wooden clogs of the other inmates shuffled and crunched. For me nothing existed but Milena's hand on my arm and the wish that this walk might never end. And then the siren howled: Time to turn in. All the others ran to their barracks. But we hesitated, holding each other tight, unwilling to part. The bellowing voice of an overseer came closer. Milena whispered, "Come to the Wailing Wall later. So we can be alone for just a few minutes." Then we parted. Someone shouted, "Damn bitches!" That was us.

At the appointed time I slipped away from the bustling crowd in the barracks. It didn't even occur to me that this meeting might end with a flogging or solitary confinement or even death. It didn't cross my mind that someone might see me. I ran past the lighted windows, came to the path beside the Wailing Wall. It was pitch-dark and I couldn't see a thing. To muffle the sound of my wooden clogs, I groped my way to the edge of the path and continued on the grass. I saw something bright behind the leafless bushes that bordered the windowless wall of the second barracks. In my haste and excitement I tripped over a stump and fell into Milena's arms.

Because of her work in the infirmary, Milena was automatically assigned to No. 1 Barracks, the best in the camp, that of the "old" politicals, interned for their "subversive opinions." One of its main advantages was that it was less crowded than the other barracks. At that time, as I've already said, I was *Blockälteste* of Barracks No. 3, that of the Jehovah's Witnesses. Each barracks had an orderly room for the SS overseer, to which the *Blockälteste* also had access. It was the only room in which a certain privacy was possible. The SS overseer spent a few hours a day there, but at night the room was empty.

Sometimes Milena risked coming to see me, when she knew the SS overseer wouldn't be there. As she was employed in the infirmary, she was able to enter the barracks during working hours on various errands. When that happened, I took her to the orderly room, and we were able to talk for a few minutes undisturbed. But that too was dangerous; the overseer was a permanent threat.

Our longing to spend more time together became more and more imperious. One evening during exercise period—it was autumn by then, and the nights were dark and stormy—Milena informed me of her plan. Half an hour after the SS guards made their night round, she would climb out of her barracks window and cross the camp street—where trained wolfhounds were let loose at night—to mine. I was to open the window for her. At the thought of the terrible danger she would be incurring, my heart skipped a beat. But her determination shamed me, and I agreed. Half an hour after the night round, I opened my barracks door and listened. I couldn't see my hand before my face and it was pouring rain. As I listened for footsteps, my tense nerves made me hear menacing sounds on all sides: SS boots crunching on gravel, shots on the camp street. But this was a time of great activity in the barracks, and I had to avoid being seen. Every few minutes one of the three hundred occupants would go to the toilet, and then I had to hurry away from my listening post.

Suddenly the door was opened from the outside, and in stepped Milena, whistling softly *It's a long way to Tipperary, it's a long way to go....* I seized her by the arm and pulled her into the orderly room.

Her hair was dripping, the slippers she had put on to avoid making noise were soaked through. But what did it matter? She had made it. We sat down by the warm stove, which I had lit beforehand, and felt as if we had escaped from jail. We would be free for a whole night.

4. *NEW YORK 1942–43: DEATH WATCH*

LUCY S. DAWIDOWICZ

New York-born historian Lucy S. Dawidowicz went to Vilna in 1938 for a year of study at the YIVO Institute, then the premier institute for the study of Yiddish. She grew to love the city and her many friends and acquaintances there. Later, back in New York and working at the New York branch of YIVO, she learned more, or perhaps understood more, than most American Jews about what was taking place in Europe. Dawidowicz describes her anguish and rage and that of her associates as news of the European slaughter poured in relentlessly throughout the war years in her memoir, *From That Place and Time.*

At the war's end, Dawidowicz returned to Europe for the JDC (Joint Distribution Committee) to work with refugees in the DP ("displaced persons") camps. In Offenbach, Germany, she stumbled across the remains of YIVO's library, which had been shipped there from Vilna; she sifted through its volumes, sending those of value on to YIVO in New York, realizing that "whatever [she] rescued from oblivion was all that could ever be rescued from the ruins of Vilna."

Years later, she wrote The War Against the Jews," a landmark study of the Nazi genocide and its centrality in Germany's agenda.

———

Hatred for the Germans consumed me that summer of 1942, as news about massacres and murders of the European Jews swelled. I read the papers even more obsessively than I had in 1939—the *New York Times* regularly, the New York *Herald Tribune* occasionally, and *PM,* a lively, brash, left-liberal paper that had begun to appear in New York in June 1940. In the YIVO, we read all the Yiddish papers, even the Communist *Freiheit.* [...] Being at the YIVO, I probably knew more than most other American Jews about what was happening to the European Jews.

Early in June 1942, the most definitive news yet reached us about what was happening to the Polish Jews. It was a report which the underground Bund in Warsaw had sent through clandestine channels to the Polish Government-in-Exile in London. The two Jewish members of the Polish National Council, Shmuel Arthur Zygielbaum, who not long before had left New York, and Ignacy Schwarzbart, a leading Polish Zionist, transmitted the contents of the report to General Wladyslaw Sikorski, the Polish prime minister, and also to British government authorities and the BBC. On June 10 a summary appeared in the *New York Times.* More than thirty years later, I included that report in a book of mine, *A Holocaust Reader,* a collection of basic documents about the murder of the European Jews.

The report estimated that at the time of writing—May 1942—the Germans had murdered 700,000 Polish Jews since June 1941, when they had invaded Soviet-held Poland. Cities where the Jewish population had been slaughtered were enumerated with the local statistics of murder. In Vilna, 50,000 Jews were said to have been murdered in November 1941; only 12,000 remained. The report also told of the annihilation of the Jews in that part of Poland which the Germans had occupied since 1939. In a place called Chelmno, people were being gassed, ninety at a time, in vans equipped with gas chambers. Later we learned that those were mobile gassing units with which the Germans were still experimenting. In Lublin, some 25,000 Jews were taken away in sealed railroad cars to an "unknown destination." Not a single Jew was said to have remained in Lublin. In Warsaw, on the night of April 17–18, the Gestapo had "organized a blood bath in the ghetto," seizing more than fifty Jewish men and women from their homes and murdering them on their doorsteps.

The German government was fulfilling Hitler's prophecy to annihilate all the European Jews, the report's authors wrote. They asked the Polish government to urge the Allied powers to adopt a policy of retribution against German citizens and fifth columnists living in their countries. "This is the only possibility," they concluded, "of rescuing millions of Jews from certain annihilation."

Within a few weeks, those terrible tidings were printed and reprinted in England, the United States and Canada, and in Palestine. We heard skeptical voices; people suspected the statistics were exaggerated. Their enormity made it hard for us to grasp their full implications, but I believed the figures. Still, my refugee friends continued to think—how could they not?—that their families and friends were still alive. I, too, thinking of Rivele and Kalmanovich and my other friends in the Vilna ghetto, visualized them suffering cold, hunger, sickness, gripped by fear and despondency. I didn't have so luridly inventive an imagination as to envision anything beyond the misfortunes which the history of earlier wars and enemy occupations had made familiar.

Nor did we try to make sense of the incoming information. No one I knew could understand why or how these murders were being committed. In the midst of a war, why should the Germans distract themselves with the Jews? We had known for years that the Germans were fanatical anti-Semites. But we hadn't known, until now, that they were murderers, mass murderers. The terrible news about the Jews fueled the explosive energy of my rage against the Germans. It was past my fathoming how even fanatical anti-Semites could become mass murderers, freeing themselves from the moral and religious restraints that had somehow held killer instincts in check.

Whether or not American Jews believed the statistics of murder, everyone acknowledged that Jews were being massacred on an unprecedented scale. Jewish organizations deliberated about what to do. A mass meeting at Madison Square Garden on July 11, sponsored by the American Jewish Congress, drew an overflow crowd of some 20,000. The big-name speakers included Governor Herbert H. Lehman, Mayor Fiorello LaGuardia, Senator Henry Cabot, William Green of the AFL, and Bishop Francis J. McConnell, besides Rabbi Stephen S. Wise and other Jewish spokesmen. Messages came from Churchill and Roosevelt. Roosevelt declared that the American people would "hold the perpetrators of these crimes to strict accountability in a day of reckoning which will surely come." Demonstrations and meetings were held also in Los Angeles, Boston, Chicago, Cleveland, and St. Paul, and probably in other places I hadn't read about. Rabbis called for fast days and memorial services.

Thereafter, the stream of terrible news about the Jews in German-occupied countries flowed relentlessly. From Soviet sources we learned that German SS troops, shortly after their invasion of Soviet-held territory in June 1941, had murdered thousands upon thousands of Jews in

Minsk, Vitebsk, Kiev, Kharkov, Riga, Vilna, and countless other cities. These accounts corroborated the authenticity of the Bund report of June.

In July devastating news began to arrive about Warsaw. It was reported that old people were being killed, while able-bodied Jews were being deported "eastward to build fortifications for the Germans." Two weeks later, we read that Adam Czerniaków, head of Judenrat in the Warsaw ghetto, had committed suicide, because he had refused to approve the deportation of 100,000 Jews. It would take a long time before we realized that "deportation to the East" was a euphemism, that those hundreds of thousands of "deported" Jews had been sent to their deaths in specially constructed killing sites. We didn't yet know the name of Treblinka, where most of the Warsaw Jews were gassed. Nor had we yet heard of Auschwitz, Belzec, or Majdanek.

On August 21, 1942, Roosevelt opened his press conference by reading a warning to the enemy nations. Obviously in response to the avalanche of news about the German crimes against the Jews, he reiterated a declaration which nine occupied European nations had issued the previous January. They had then stated that one of their principal war aims would be the punishment of the Germans for the barbaric crimes which they were committing against civilian populations. To this Roosevelt added that the United States had been aware of these crimes and welcomed further reports "from any trustworthy source" as evidence of such crimes. After the Allied victory, the United States would make appropriate use of this evidence against the Germans: "It seems only fair that they should have this warning: that the time will come when they shall have to stand in courts of law, in the very countries which they are now oppressing, and answer for their acts."

My friends and I were not impressed. We didn't think the German barbarians deserved fair warning or trials in courts of law. They were not entitled to be treated as members of a civilized society. I burned with an unquenchable passion for revenge. I wanted to see Germany bombed to dust, its cities obliterated, its people ravaged with fire and sword.

In September and October the bad news continued to pour in. Only 100,000 Jews were said to have remained in Warsaw. We learned from Shlomo Mendelsohn that Menahem Linder, my friend from Warsaw, had been murdered in Warsaw in April. There was no other information. He was the first person murdered by the Germans with a name and a face I could identify. I tortured myself with the thought that I, the last one of us at the YIVO to have seen him, had left him there to be murdered. Much later we learned that he had been one of some fifty Jews seized by the Gestapo late Friday night, April 17, 1942, in the "blood bath" mentioned in the Bund report released in London last June. On that bloody Friday, the Gestapo had rounded up printers and journalists who they suspected of producing the ghetto's underground press. Menahem had been shot in front of his house on Leszno 50. We knew nothing of the fate of his wife, Mira.

On November 24, the Polish Government-in-Exile released the substance of a firsthand report it had received from a trusted courier of the Polish underground state. His name, we later learned, was Jan Karski. He had told them that one million Polish Jews had already been murdered and that Himmler had ordered the annihilation of half of the surviving Jews in Poland by the end of 1942. As of October, when he had left Poland, only 40,000 Jews remained in the Warsaw ghetto, a terrible place to which he had been taken by two leaders of the Jewish underground. Other cities no longer had any Jews at all. The courier brought the first news of a death camp located at Belzec, about 100 miles east of Warsaw. There the Jews were brought to be murdered in mass by quicklime and asphyxiation. The day after Karski's report was released, another report was released, which had come via Switzerland, to the effect that Hitler planned to murder some three and a half million to four million Jews in territory occupied by the Germans "to resolve once for all the Jewish question."

Those last days in November and early December were like a protracted Yom Kippur, a time of fasting and mourning which we all observed. It was as if the Jews in the United States were reenacting the events in the Book of Esther, when the Jews learned of the king's decree to destroy them: "there was great mourning among the Jews, and fasting, and weeping, and wailing; and many lay in sackcloth and ashes." Memorial services were held in synagogues and churches all over the country and on radio networks. The rabbis decreed a fast day. Across the nation, two-minute periods of silence were observed. In New York, half a million workers stopped work for ten minutes.

On December 8, 1942, a delegation from six Jewish organizations saw Roosevelt and left with him a memorandum describing the atrocities the Germans had committed against the European Jews. They asked him to do what he had already said he would do: hold the Germans to strict accountability for their crimes and set up a commission to gather and study the evidence of such crimes. On December 16, Premier Sikorski, then in the United States, visited Roosevelt and presented him with the Polish government's report on the German massacres of Jews and Poles.

I sorrowed for the murdered European Jews, even if I didn't know the names of the people for whom I was mourning. Still the sorrow I felt did not interfere with the discharge of my family obligations or dilute the devotion I lavished on my work, nor was my personal life without its joys and pleasures even in those days of communal sadness. Somehow I felt as if I were living in disconnected universes—in a real world of normal obligations and pastimes and in a phantasmagoric world of my fevered imagination, in which I partook of its agony and death as if it were my real world.

The flow of bad news did not let up during those months. Every day the papers brought fresh statistics of death and destruction. Every day we learned that towns and cities which Jews had once populated in Poland, Lithuania, Russia, the Ukraine, Rumania no longer had any Jews left at all. It was hard to assimilate this information, to absorb the statistics of anonymous masses slaughtered. We couldn't grasp how so many people could have been killed. Nor could we understand why. What use was it to the Germans?

Early in February 1943 the Bund in New York received information that the Bund in the Warsaw ghetto together with several Zionist groups had formed a resistance organization, that they had obtained weapons, and had actually battled the Germans in the ghetto in January. The news electrified us. Yet I saw it then as a sign of ultimate despair, an evocation of Masada. There, in 73 C.E., the beleaguered Jewish fighters against Rome chose mass suicide instead of captivity. In 1943, the Western Allies, with the enormous resources of the United States, didn't yet dare to take on the entrenched strength of the Germans on the European continent. What chance did the ghetto Jews have? About a month later, Zygielbaum in London released a report from the Warsaw underground sent after that January battle. It was published in the *Forverts:* "Alarm the world. Appeal to the Pope. The few hundred thousand surviving Jews in Poland are in danger of being annihilated soon. Only you can save us."

At times, when I woke after a fitful night, I thought that the news about the European Jews was only a bad dream, a hallucination. Other times, I'd be seized by the irrational notion that we were witnessing the end of the world. Not our world here in New York, but the world from which I had fled in 1939. In those moments, I'd try to imagine the emptiness of Vilna's Jewish quarter with its crooked little streets. Vilna had never in its history had a ghetto, but the Germans had made one in those little streets. I tried to picture warfare in the streets of the Warsaw ghetto. Instead I summoned up the memory of the bustle on Warsaw's Jewish streets, as I had seen them aswarm with people, buying and selling, bargaining, shouting, laughing. The end of that world had come without portents or prophecies, without visions or revelations. None of us had seen the heavens turn black, but in Europe I knew the earth was red with Jewish blood.

At the YIVO, we were deep in preparations for our annual conference to be held from January 7 to 9, 1944. At the closing session, Shlomo Mendelsohn read a paper on resistance in the Warsaw ghetto. The hall was jam-packed with several hundred listeners. People stood in the back and against the side walls. Mendelsohn began by enumerating and qualifying his sources—the underground Jewish and Polish reports to the Polish Government-in-Exile and to the Bund's representative in the Polish National Council (Zygielbaum's place had already been filled), the underground Polish press, documents issued by the Jewish resistance organization, even several eyewitnesses who had escaped from Poland. Then he described conditions in the ghetto up to 1942.

When he spoke about Czerniaków's suicide and the terrible deportations of the Jews from the Warsaw ghetto during the summer of 1942, the tension in the hall heightened. He spoke about the trains that brought the Jews to the gas chambers in Treblinka. Though he had no information about how the Jewish Combat Organization had come into being, he had reports of the Polish government and of the Polish underground press about the actual battles the Jews fought against the Germans. He quoted an appeal issued on the fifth day of the fighting by the Jewish Combat Organization to the Polish population:

> ...every threshold in the ghetto has been and will continue to be a fortress. We may all perish in this struggle, but we will not surrender. Like you, we breathe with the desire for revenge and punishment for all the crimes of our common foe.
>
> This is a battle for our and your freedom.

In the crowded hall you heard only Mendelsohn's voice, punctuated by occasional sharp gasps among the audience, quick intakes of breath. The atmosphere was heavy with grief. When he finished, the hall was hushed. No one applauded. Spontaneously everyone arose to honor the fallen Jews of the Warsaw ghetto. Then someone said: "Let's recite Kaddish." From the other end of the room, a man began to intone the Jewish prayer for the dead. Everyone joined in, amid a surge of sobbing.

5. *SHAME*

PRIMO LEVI

Primo Levi, the Italian chemist and writer, is well known for his memoirs on the nature of life in the camps. (An excerpt from his first memoir, *If This Is a Man*—subsequently reissued as *Survival in Auschwitz*—appears earlier in this anthology.) Towards the end of this great writer's life, his essays became more meditative, a more focused quest to understand.

In his last published book, he explores the phenomenon of shame: "That many (including me) experienced 'shame,' that is, a feeling of guilt during the imprisonment and afterward, is an ascertained fact confirmed by numerous testimonies. It may seem absurd, but it is a fact." Here Levi takes up the issue of survivor guilt. Levi rejects theological interpretations to explain why some survived and others did not, convinced that the best died; many perished "not despite their valor, but because of it." Shame, he argues from his strongly humanistic point of view, is part of the concentrationary universe in which the spirit of man is absent or extinguished.

———

Few survivors feel guilty about having deliberately damaged, robbed, or beaten a companion. Those who did so (the *Kapos*, but not only they) block out the memory. By contrast, however, almost everybody feels guilty of having omitted to offer help. The presence at your side of a

From *The Drowned and the Saved* by Primo Levi. Translated by Raymond Rosenthal. Copyright © 1986 by Guilio Einaudi Editore, Spa, Torino. English translation copyright © 1988 by Simon & Schuster, Inc.

weaker—or less cunning, or older, or too young—companion, hounding you with his demands for help or with his simple presence, in itself an entreaty, is a constant in the life of the Lager. The demand for solidarity, for a human word, advice, even just a listening ear, was permanent and universal but rarely satisfied. There was no time, space, privacy, patience, strength; most often, the person to whom the request was addressed found himself in his turn in a state of need, entitled to comfort.

I remember with a certain relief that I once tried to give courage (at a moment when I felt I had some) to an eighteen-year-old Italian who had just arrived, who was floundering in the bottomless despair of his first days in camp. I forget what I told him, certainly words of hope, perhaps a few lies, acceptable to a "new arrival," expressed with the authority of my twenty-five years and my three months of seniority; at any rate, I made him the gift of a momentary attention. But I also remember, with disquiet, that much more often I shrugged my shoulders impatiently at other requests, and this precisely when I had been in camp for almost a year and so had accumulated a good store of experience: but I had also deeply assimilated the principal rule of the place, which made it mandatory that you take care of yourself first of all. I never found this rule expressed with as much frankness as in *Prisoners of Fear* by Ella Lingens-Reiner (where, however, the woman doctor, regardless of her own statement, proved to be generous and brave and saved many lives): "How was I able to survive in Auschwitz? My principle is: I come first, second, and third. Then nothing, then again I; and then all the others."

In August of 1944 it was very hot in Auschwitz. A torrid, tropical wind lifted clouds of dust from the buildings wrecked by the air raids, dried the sweat on our skin, and thickened the blood in our veins. My squad had been sent into a cellar to clear out the plaster rubble, and we all suffered from thirst: a new suffering, which was added to, indeed, multiplied by the old one of hunger. There was no drinkable water in the camp or often on the work site; in those days there was often no water in the wash trough either, undrinkable but good enough to freshen up and clean off the dust. As a rule, the evening soup and the ersatz coffee distributed around ten o'clock were abundantly sufficient to quench our thirst, but now they were no longer enough and thirst tormented us. Thirst is more imperative than hunger: hunger obeys the nerves, grants remission, can be temporarily obliterated by an emotion, a pain, a fear (we had realized this during our journey by train from Italy); not so with thirst, which does not give respite. Hunger exhausts, thirst enrages; in those days it accompanied us day and night: by day, on the work site, whose order (our enemy, but nevertheless order, a place of logic and certainty) was transformed into a chaos of shattered constructions; by night, in the hut without ventilation, as we gasped the air breathed a hundred times before.

The corner of the cellar that had been assigned to me by the *Kapo* and where I was to remove the rubble was next to a large room filled with chemical equipment in the process of being installed but already damaged by the bombs. Along the vertical wall ran a two-inch pipe, which ended in a spigot just above the floor. A water pipe? I took a chance and tried to open it. I was alone, nobody saw me. It was blocked, but using a stone for a hammer I managed to shift it a few millimeters. A few drops came out, they had no odor, I caught them on my fingers: it really seemed water. I had no receptacle, and the drops came out slowly, without pressure: the pipe must be only half full, perhaps less. I stretched out on the floor with my mouth under the spigot, not trying to open it further: it was water made tepid by the sun, insipid, perhaps distilled or the result of condensation; at any rate, a delight.

How much water can a two-inch pipe one or two meters high contain? A liter, perhaps not even that. I could have drunk all of it immediately; that would have been the safest way. Or save a bit for the next day. Or share half of it with Alberto. Or reveal the secret to the whole squad. I chose the third path, that of selfishness extended to the person closest to you, which in distant times a friend of mine appropriately called us-ism. We drank all the water, in small, avaricious gulps, changing places under the spigot, just the two of us. On the sly. But on the march back to camp at my side I found Daniele, all gray with cement dust, his lips cracked and his eyes feverish, and I felt guilty. I exchanged a look with Alberto; we understood each other immediately and hoped nobody had seen us. But Daniele had caught a glimpse of us in that strange position, supine near the wall among the rubble, and had suspected something, and then had guessed. He curtly told me so many months later, in Byelorussia, after the Liberation: Why the two of you and not I? It was the "civilian" moral code surfacing again. [...] Is this belated shame justified or not? I was not able to decide then and I am not able to decide even now, but shame there was and is, concrete, heavy, perennial. Daniele is dead now, but in our meetings as survivors, fraternal, affectionate, the veil of that act of omission, that unshared glass of water, stood between us, transparent, not expressed, but perceptible and "costly."

Changing moral codes is always costly: all heretics, apostates, and dissidents know this. We cannot judge our behavior or that of others, driven at that time by the code of that time, on the basis of today's code; but the anger that pervades us when one of the "others" feels entitled to consider us "apostates," or, more precisely, reconverted, seems right to me.

Are you ashamed because you are alive in place of another? And, in particular, of a man more generous, more sensitive, more useful, wiser, worthier of living than you? You cannot block out such feelings: you examine yourself, you review your memories, hoping to find them all, and that none of them are masked or disguised. No. you find no obvious transgressions, you did not usurp anyone's place, you did not beat anyone (but would you have had the strength to do so?), you did not accept positions (but none were offered to you . . .), you did not steal anyone's bread; nevertheless you cannot exclude it. It is no more than a supposition, indeed the shadow of a suspicion: that each man is his brother's Cain, that each one of us (but this time I say "us" in a much vaster, indeed, universal sense) has usurped his neighbor's place and lived in his stead. It is a supposition, but it gnaws at us; it has nestled deeply like a woodworm; although unseen from the outside, it gnaws and rasps.

After my return from imprisonment I was visited by a friend older than myself, mild and intransigent, the cultivator of a personal religion, which, however, always seemed to me severe and serious. He was glad to find me alive and basically unhurt, perhaps matured and fortified, certainly enriched. He told me that my having survived could not be the work of chance, of an accumulation of fortunate circumstances (as I did then and still do maintain) but rather of Providence. I bore the mark, I was an elect: I, the nonbeliever, and even less of a believer after the season of Auschwitz, was a person touched by Grace, a saved man. And why me? It is impossible to know, he answered. Perhaps because I had to write, and by writing bear witness: Wasn't I in fact then, in 1946, writing a book about my imprisonment?

Such an opinion seemed monstrous to me. It pained me as when one touches an exposed nerve, and kindled the doubt I spoke of before: I might be alive in the place of another, at the expense of another; I might have usurped, that is, in fact, killed. The "saved" of the Lager were not the best, those predestined to do good, the bearers of a message: what I had seen and lived through proved the exact contrary. Preferably the worst survived, the selfish, the violent, the insensitive, the collaborators of the "gray zone," the spies. It was not a certain rule (there were none, nor are there certain rules in human matters), but it was nevertheless a rule. I felt innocent, yes, but enrolled among the saved and therefore in permanent search of a justification in my own eyes and those of others. The worst survived, that is, the fittest; the best all died.

Chaim died, a watchmaker from Krakow, a pious Jew who despite the language difficulties made an effort to understand and be understood, and explained to me, the foreigner, the essential rules for survival during the first crucial days of captivity; Szabo died, the taciturn Hungarian peasant who was almost two meters tall and so was the hungriest of all, and yet, as long as he had the strength, did not hesitate to help his weaker companions to pull and push; and Robert, a professor at the Sorbonne who spread courage and trust all around him, spoke five languages, wore himself out recording everything in his prodigious memory, and had he lived would have answered the questions which I do not know how to answer; and Baruch died, a longshoreman from Livorno, immediately, on the first day, because he had answered the first punch he had received with punches and was massacred by three *Kapos* in coalition. These, and innumerable others, died not despite their valor but because of it.

My religious friend had told me that I survived so that I could bear witness. I have done so, as best I could, and I also could not have done so; and I am still doing so, whenever the opportunity presents itself; but the thought that this testifying of mine could by itself gain for me the privilege of surviving and living for many years without serious problems troubles me because I cannot see any proportion between the privilege and its outcome.

I must repeat: we, the survivors, are not the true witnesses. This is an uncomfortable notion of which I have become conscious little by little, reading the memoirs of others and reading mine at a distance of years. We survivors are not only an exiguous but also an anomalous minority: we are those who by their prevarications or abilities or good luck did not touch bottom. Those who did so, those who saw the Gorgon, have not returned to tell about it or have returned mute, but they are the "Muslims," the submerged, the complete witnesses, the ones whose deposition would have a general significance. They are the rule, we are the exception. Under another sky, and returned from a similar and diverse slavery, Solzhenitsyn also noted: "Almost all those who served a long sentence and whom you congratulate because they are survivors are unquestionably *pridurki* or were such during the greater part of their imprisonment. Because Lagers are meant for extermination, this should not be forgotten."

In the language of that other concentrationary universe, the *pridurki* are the prisoners who, in one way or another, won a position of privilege, those we called the Prominent.

We who were favored by fate tried, with more or less wisdom, to recount not only our fate but also that of the others, indeed of the drowned; but this was a discourse "on behalf of third parties," the story of things seen at close hand, not experienced personally. The destruction brought to an end, the job completed, was not told by anyone, just as no one ever returned to describe his own death. Even if they had paper and pen, the drowned would not have testified because their death had begun before that of their body. Weeks and months before being snuffed out, they had already lost the ability to observe, to remember, to compare and express themselves. We speak in their stead, by proxy.

I could not say whether we did or do so out of a kind of moral obligation toward those who were silenced or in order to free ourselves of their memory; certainly we do it because of a strong and durable impulse. I do not believe that psychoanalysts (who have pounced upon our tangles with professional avidity) are competent to explain this impulse. Their knowledge has been built up and tested "outside," in the world that, for the sake of simplicity, we call civilian: psychoanalysis traces its phenomenology and tries to explain it; studies its deviations and tries to heal them. Their interpretations, even those of someone like Bruno Bettelheim, who went through the trials of the Lager, seem to me approximate and simplified, as if someone wished to apply the theorems of plane geometry to the solution of spheric triangles. The mental mechanisms of the *Häftlinge* were different from ours; curiously, and in parallel, different also were their physiology and pathology. In the Lager colds and influenza were unknown, but one died, at times suddenly, from illnesses that the doctors never had an opportunity to study. Gastric ulcers and mental illnesses were healed (or became asymptomatic), but everyone suffered from an unceasing discomfort that polluted sleep and was nameless. To define this as a "neurosis" is reductive and ridiculous. Perhaps it would be more correct to see in it an atavistic anguish whose echo one hears in the second verse of Genesis: the anguish inscribed in everyone of the "tohu-bohu" of a deserted and empty universe crushed under the spirit of God but from which the spirit of man is absent: not yet born or already extinguished.

6. *ALL AROUND ATLANTIS*

DEBORAH EISENBERG

In Deborah Eisenberg's short story, Anna, a child of survivors, describes what it was like growing up with her mother, Lili, her mother's companion, Sándor, and the community of immigrants that filled their New York apartment. Lili and her guests never talked directly about their wartime experiences, but Holocaust memories dwelt in their household like a charged presence threatening to erupt at any moment. Looking back at herself as a child, Anna shares her memories with Peter, an old family acquaintance.

———

Were you aware, Peter, how Sándor responded to Mrs. Spiegel's admiration? Were you aware how completely insane it drove him? "The genius," as she sometimes referred to him. He could detect her footfall with absolute accuracy, as if the two of them were in the forest, and he'd fade instantly into his room for hours, to write, or to read his Thoreau or Dickens or Auden or Stevens, while Mrs. Spiegel chattered on emptily with Lili in the kitchen, stalling. "Did I hear something?" she'd say, glancing over her shoulder. "No."

Oh, Peter. How he hated to hear her go on about his "brilliance," his "originality," his "place in European letters"! Even when his work was available in German, I once heard him say to Lili, could Mrs. Spiegel have—in any meaningful sense of the word—"read" any? The woman's brain, unfortunately, was a Möbius strip of clichés; things went in, he assumed, in working order, but emulsified there, through a continuous, twisting process of Mrs. Spiegelization. Besides, *what* place in European letters? No Europe, no letters, no place. He had no place anywhere but in our apartment, thank you, he added to me. And that was the only place he wanted.

I remember the way Lili patted his arm and smiled the lazy, inscrutable smile that kept all those men prisoner on our sofa or tamed them to the yoke of irksome tasks and errands, like picking up groceries or fixing the lamp or taking me to the playground.

When you first met us, were you flabbergasted that Lili never became irritable with Mrs. Spiegel? That Lili always had time for Mrs. Spiegel? Did you realize that Lili actually chided me for mimicking the irresistibly mimicable Mrs. Spiegel? Did you marvel how the two of them used to sit at the kitchen table over interminable tea and cookies?

When I was little I used to sit there at Lili's side, supplied with cookies, myself, and a teacup filled with milk. It made me truly sick, Peter, it made me furious, to look at Mrs. Spiegel's arm, just lying there casually on the table—her sleeve riding up over the blue brand that looked so similar to the numbers stamped on the meat at the grocery store: Did Mrs. Spiegel want to be a human being, or did she prefer to be a slab of meat? The truth is, it was as though that dark number of hers could activate Lili's, even under the "decent" (as I felt) cover of her clothing or bracelets.

They never spoke about the past, really, either, those two. At least when I was around, they never, to use Neil's formula, had "a normal conversation" about their "past situation."

And what do you suppose he *meant* by that, Peter? *A normal conversation about her past situation*—It seems to be one of those things words can construct independently of meaning, doesn't it? Because how could there have been such a thing?

In fact, I don't remember anything that sounded particularly like "a normal conversation" about *anything!* Mr. Korda's arthritis, what the hairdresser said about her son's girlfriend—no subject was sufficiently mundane to resist a septic influence.

I submit to you, Peter, this example: The day Lili found Walden Tócska in the street and brought him home. Well, as you would imagine, Mrs. Spiegel was simply horrified. "But, darling!" she said. "The beast is filthy!"

Not so, Lili said. That very morning, we'd gone to the vet, where Tócska had received numerous shots and his leg was bound up; we'd bathed and deflead him all afternoon.

But there was no telling where an animal like that had been! What habits it had acquired, or what secret diseases, clever enough to evade the vet's medications, it might be harboring, to spread among us at any instant!

Absurd, Lili said; not scientific. Besides, every child should have a pet, and clearly—she shot a guilty look at me—Anna already adored this dog.

Adored, Mrs. Spiegel protested—though I'd steeled myself to pat, illustratively, the great, snoring, quivering heap of hair—it was completely obvious that, on the contrary, the child was terrified!

Lili inhaled deeply, and put her palms down on the table in front of her. "Lise, are you saying that poor dog should be . . ."

No, but of course no! Mein Gott! (And both women, Peter, had gone absolutely white.) Mrs. Spiegel hadn't meant . . . She had only meant . . . She had meant only . . .

And then, Peter, there was just a long, long silence, which Lili brought to a close with a sign, and that was that.

I mean, *Lili* allowed something terrible to develop? It was *Lili* who created an atmosphere of violence and danger? *Lili* was responsible for an atmosphere of violence and danger?

If the silences around our household were vivid and eloquent, was that Lili's fault? Look, I said to Neil, we were all careful back then. And wouldn't you have been, in my place? It was as if Lili were sleepwalking over the abyss of her own life. What if she were to wake? What if I were to wake her?

7. *RECONCEIVING CENTRAL ASPECTS OF THE HOLOCAUST*

DANIEL JONAH GOLDHAGEN

Hitler's Willing Executioners, Goldhagen's powerful and controversial study, adds to the work of other Holocaust historians in dispelling the myth of few murderers and many innocent onlookers. His research focuses on the perpetrators, which included members of the police battalions, who served in killing squads massacring thousands of Jews, and camp guards, who led the death marches up to the last days of the war. These were not SS men but "ordinary Germans." Why were these individuals willing to collaborate in genocide?

Goldhagen argues that the prime motivating factor was anti-Semitism and asserts that a particularly virulent strain of anti-Semitism in German society enabled "ordinary Germans" to become murderers. Parts of Goldhagen's conclusions have been criticized by other historians in heated scholarly debates. Some fault him for indicting an entire generation. Nevertheless, his book has had a major impact in reopening the issue. Its publication generated international debate, culminating in a lecture tour in Germany that spurred a postwar generation of Germans to confront its history. He was awarded the Democracy Prize in Germany.

━━━

Captain Wolfgang Hoffmann was a zealous executioner of Jews. As the commander of one of the three companies of Police Battalion 101, he and his fellow officers led their men, who were not SS men but ordinary Germans, in the deportation and gruesome slaughter in Poland of tens of thousands of Jewish men, women, and children. Yet this same man, in the midst of his genocidal activities, once stridently disobeyed a superior order that he deemed morally objectionable.

From *Hitler's Willing Executioners* by DANIEL JONAH GOLDHAGEN. Copyright © 1996 by DANIEL JONAH GOLDHAGEN. Reprinted by permission of Alfred A. Knopf Inc.

The order commanded that members of his company sign a declaration that had been sent to them. Hoffmann began his written refusal by saying that upon reading it, he had thought that an error had been made, "because it appeared to me a piece of impertinence to demand of a decent German soldier to sign a declaration in which he obligates himself not to steal, not to plunder, and not to buy without paying. . . ." He continued by describing how unnecessary such a demand was, since his men, of proper ideological conviction, were fully aware that such activities were punishable offenses. He also pronounced to his superiors his judgment of his men's character and actions, including, presumably, their slaughtering of Jews. He wrote that his men's adherence to German norms of morality and conduct "derives from their own free will and is not caused by a craving for advantages or fear of punishment." Hoffmann then declared defiantly: "As an officer I regret, however, that I must set my view against that of the battalion commander and am not able to carry out the order, since I feel injured in my sense of honor. I must decline to sign a general declaration."

Hoffmann's letter is astonishing and instructive for a number of reasons. Here is an officer who had already led his men in the genocidal slaughter of tens of thousands of Jews, yet who deemed it an effrontery that anyone might suppose that he and his men would steal food from Poles! The genocidal killer's honor was wounded, and wounded doubly, for he was both a soldier and a German. His conception of the obligations that Germans owed the "subhuman" Poles must have been immeasurably greater than those owed Jews. Hoffmann also understood his parent institution to be so tolerant that he was willing to refuse a direct order and even to record his brazen insubordination in writing. His judgment of his men—a judgment based, no doubt, on the compass of their activities, including their genocidal ones—was that they acted not out of fear of punishment, but with willing assent; they acted from conviction, according to their inner beliefs.

Hoffmann's written refusal sets in sharp relief important, neglected aspects of the Holocaust—such as the laxness of many of the institutions of killing, the capacity of the perpetrators to refuse orders (even orders to kill), and, not least of all, their moral autonomy—and provides insight into the unusual mind-set of the perpetrators, including their motivation for killing. It should force us to ask long-ignored questions about the sort of worldview and the institutional context that could produce such a letter which, though on a tangential subject and seemingly bizarre, reveals a host of typical features of the Germans' perpetration of the Holocaust. Understanding the actions and mind-set of the tens of thousands of ordinary Germans who, like Captain Hoffmann, became genocidal killers is the subject of [my] book.

During the Holocaust, Germans extinguished the lives of six million Jews and, had Germany not been defeated, would have annihilated millions more. The Holocaust was also the defining feature of German politics and political culture during the Nazi period, the most shocking event of the twentieth century, and the most difficult event to understand in all of German history. The Germans' persecution of the Jews culminating in the Holocaust is thus the central feature of Germany during the Nazi period. It is so not because we are retrospectively shocked by the most shocking event of the century, but because of what it meant to Germans at the time and why so many of them contributed to it. It marked their departure from the community of "civilized peoples." This departure needs to be explained.

Explaining the Holocaust is the central intellectual problem for understanding Germany during the Nazi period. All the other problems combined are comparatively simple. How the Nazis came to power, how they suppressed the left, how they revived the economy, how the state was structured and functioned, how they made and waged war are all more or less ordinary, "normal" events, easily enough understood. But the Holocaust and the change in sensibilities that it involved "defies" explanation. There is no comparable event in the twentieth century, indeed in modern European history. Whatever the remaining debates, every other major event of nineteenth- and twentieth-century German history and political development is, in comparison to the Holocaust, transparently clear in its genesis. Explaining how the Holocaust happened is a daunting task empirically and even more so theoretically, so much so that some have argued, in my view erroneously, that it is "inexplicable." The theoretical difficulty is shown by its utterly new nature, by the inability of social theory (or what passed for common sense) preceding it to provide a hint not only that it would happen but also that it was even possible. Retrospective theory has not done much better, shedding but modest light in the darkness. [...]

Foremost among the three subjects that must be reconceived are the perpetrators of the Holocaust. Few readers will have failed to give some thought to the question of what impelled the perpetrators of the Holocaust to kill. Few have neglected to provide for themselves an answer to the question, an answer that necessarily derives usually not from any intimate knowledge of the perpetrators and their deeds, but greatly from the individual's conception of human nature and social life. Few would probably disagree with the notion that the perpetrators should be studied.

Yet until now the perpetrators, the most important group of people responsible for the slaughter of European Jewry, excepting the Nazi leadership itself, have received little concerted attention in the literature that describes the events and purports to explain them. Surprisingly, the vast literature on the Holocaust contains little on the people who were its executors. Little is known of who the perpetrators were, the details of their actions, the circumstances of many of their deeds, let alone their motivations. A decent estimate of how many people contributed to the genocide, of how many perpetrators there were, has never been made. Certain institutions of killing and the people who manned them have been hardly treated or not at all. As a consequence of this general lack of knowledge, all kinds of misunderstandings and myths about the perpetrators abound. These misconceptions, moreover, have broader implications for the way in which the Holocaust and Germany during the Nazi period are conceived and understood.

We must therefore refocus our attention, our intellectual energy, which has overwhelmingly been devoted elsewhere, onto the perpetrators, namely the men and women who in some intimate way knowingly contributed to the slaughter of Jews. We must investigate their deeds in detail and explain their actions. It is not sufficient to treat the institutions of killing collectively or singly as internally uncomplicated instruments of the Nazi leadership's will, as well-lubricated machines that the regime activated, as if by the flick of a switch, to do its bidding, whatever it might have been. The study of the men and women who collectively gave life to the inert institutional forms, who peopled the institutions of genocidal killing must be set at the focus of scholarship on the Holocaust and become as central to investigations of the genocide as they were to its commission.

These people were overwhelmingly and most importantly Germans. While members of other national groups aided the Germans in their slaughter of Jews, the commission of the Holocaust was primarily a German undertaking. Non-Germans were not essential to the perpetration of the genocide, and they did not supply the drive and initiative that pushed it forward. To be sure, had the Germans not found European (especially, eastern European) helpers, then the Holocaust would have unfolded somewhat differently, and the Germans would likely not have succeeded in killing as many Jews. Still, this was above all a German enterprise; the decisions, plans, organizational resources, and the majority of its executors were German. Comprehension and explanation of the perpetration of the Holocaust therefore requires an explanation of the *Germans'* drive to kill Jews. Because what can be said about the Germans cannot be said about any other nationality or about all of the other nationalities combined—namely no Germans, no Holocaust—the focus here is appropriately on the German perpetrators.

The first task in restoring the perpetrators to the center of our understanding of the Holocaust is to restore to them their identities, grammatically by using not the passive but the active voice in order to ensure that they, the actors, are not absent from their own deeds (as in, "five hundred Jews were killed in city X on date Y"), and by eschewing convenient, yet often inappropriate and obfuscating labels, like "Nazis" and "SS men," and calling them what they were, "Germans." The most appropriate, indeed the only appropriate *general* proper name for the Germans who perpetrated the Holocaust is "Germans." They were Germans acting in the name of Germany and its highly popular leader, Adolf Hitler. Some were "Nazis," either by reason of the Nazi Party membership or according to ideological conviction; some were not. Some were SS men; some were not. The perpetrators killed and made their other genocidal contributions under the auspices of many institutions other than the SS. Their chief common denominator was that they were all Germans pursuing German national political goals—in this case, the genocidal killing of Jews. To be sure, it is sometimes appropriate to use institutional or occupational names or roles and the generic terms "perpetrators" or "killers" to describe the perpetrators, yet this must be done only in the understood context that these men and women were German first, and SS men, policemen, or camp guards second. [...]

The study of the perpetrators further demands a reconsideration, indeed a reconceiving, of the character of German society during its Nazi period and before. The Holocaust was the defining aspect of Nazism, but not only of Nazism. It was also the defining feature of German society during its Nazi period. No significant aspect of German society was untouched by anti-Jewish policy; from the economy, to society, to politics, to culture, from cattle farmers, to merchants, to the organization of small towns, to lawyers, doctors, physicists, and professors. No analysis of German society, no understanding or characterization of it, can be made without placing the persecution and extermination of the Jews at its center. The program's first parts, namely the systematic exclusion of Jews from German economic and social life, were carried out in the open, under approving eyes, and with the complicity of virtually all sectors of German society, from the legal, medical, and teaching professions, to the churches, both Catholic and Protestant, to the gamut of economic, social, and cultural groups and associations. Hundreds of thousands of Germans contributed to the genocide and the still larger system of subjugation that was the vast concentration camp system. Despite the regime's half-hearted attempts to keep the genocide beyond the view of most Germans, millions knew of the mass slaughters. Hitler announced many times, emphatically, that the war would end in the extermination of the Jews. The killings met with general understanding, if not approval. No other policy (of similar or greater scope) was carried out with more persistence and zeal, and with fewer difficulties, than the genocide, except perhaps the war itself. [...]

Explaining why the Holocaust occurred requires a radical revision of what has until now been written. This revision calls for us to acknowledge what has for so long been generally denied or obscured by academic and non-academic interpreters alike: Germans' antisemitic beliefs about Jews were the central causal agent of the Holocaust. They were the central causal agent not only of Hitler's decision to annihilate European Jewry (which is accepted by many) but also of the perpetrators' willingness to kill and to brutalize Jews. The conclusion of this book is that antisemitism moved many thousands of "ordinary" Germans—and would have moved millions more, had they been appropriately positioned—to slaughter Jews. Not economic hardship, not the coercive means of a totalitarian state, not social psychological pressure, not invariable psychological propensities, but ideas about Jews that were pervasive in Germany, and had been for decades, induced ordinary Germans to kill unarmed, defenseless Jewish men, women, and children by the thousands, systematically and without pity.

8. *THE READER*

BERNHARD SCHLINK

Looking at the "second generation," it is helpful to see the total picture, which includes young Germans trying to cope with their nation's shame. Bernhard Schlink, born in 1944, captures the questions of this generation in his novel, *The Reader*, a coming-of-age story of a German youth introduced to love by an older woman. Later, as a law student, he attends the trial of concentration camp guards and discovers this woman in the dock. He resists coming to the defense of a woman he once loved, silenced by the weight of her generation's guilt.

━━━

I did not miss a single day of the trial. The other students were surprised. The professor was pleased that one of us was making sure that the next group learned what the last one had heard and seen.

Only once did Hanna look at the spectators and over at me. Usually she was brought in by a guard and took her place and then kept her eyes fixed on the bench throughout the day's proceedings. It appeared arrogant, as did the fact that she didn't talk to the other defendants and almost never with her lawyer either. However, as the trial went on, the other defendants talked less among themselves too. When there were breaks in the proceedings, they stood with relatives and friends, and in the mornings they waved and called hello to them when they saw them in the public benches. During the breaks Hanna remained in her seat.

So I watched her from behind. I saw her head, her neck, her shoulders. I decoded her head, her neck, her shoulders. When she was being discussed, she held her head very erect. When she felt she was being unjustly treated, slandered, or attacked and she was struggling to respond, she rolled her shoulders forward and her neck swelled, showing the play of muscles. The objections were regularly overruled, and her shoulders regularly sank. She never shrugged, and she never shook her head. She was too keyed up to allow herself anything as casual as a shrug or a shake of the head. Nor did she allow herself to hold her head at an angle, or to let it fall, or to lean her chin on her hand. She sat as if frozen. It must have hurt to sit that way.

Sometimes strands of hair slipped out of the tight knot, began to curl, lay on the back of her neck, and moved gently against it in the draft. Sometimes Hanna wore a dress with a neckline low enough to reveal the birthmark high on her left shoulder. Then I remembered how I had blown the hair away from that neck and how I had kissed that birthmark and that neck. But the memory was like a retrieved file. I felt nothing.

During the weeks of the trial, I felt nothing: my feelings were numbed. Sometimes I poked at them, and imagined Hanna doing what she was accused of doing as clearly as I could, and also doing what the hair on her neck and the birthmark on her shoulder recalled to my mind. It was like a hand pinching an arm numbed by an injection. The arm doesn't register that it is being pinched by the hand, the hand registers that it is pinching the arm, and at first the mind cannot tell the two of them apart. But a moment later it distinguishes them quite clearly. Perhaps the hand has pinched so hard that the flesh stays white for a while. Then the blood flows back and the spot regains its color. But that does not bring back sensation.

Who had given me the injection? Had I done it myself, because I couldn't manage without anesthesia? The anesthetic functioned not only in the courtroom, and not only to allow me to see Hanna as if it was someone else who had loved and desired her, someone I knew well but who wasn't me. In every part of my life, too, I stood outside myself and watched; I saw myself functioning at the university, with my parents and brother and sister and my friends, but inwardly I felt no involvement.

After a time I thought I could detect a similar numbness in other people. Not in the lawyers, who carried on throughout the trial with the same rhetorical legalistic pugnacity, jabbing pedantry, or loud, calculated truculence, depending on their personalities and their political standpoint.

Admittedly the trial proceedings exhausted them; in the evenings they were tired and got more shrill. But overnight they recharged or reinflated themselves and droned and hissed away the next morning just as they had twenty-four hours before. The prosecutors made an effort to keep up and display the same level of attack day after day. But they didn't succeed, at first because the facts and their outcome as laid out at the trial horrified them so much, and later because the numbness began to take hold. The effect was strongest on the judges and the lay members of the court. During the first weeks of the trial they took in the horrors—sometimes recounted in tears, sometimes in choking voices, sometimes in agitated or broken sentences—with visible shock or obvious efforts at self-control. Later their faces returned to normal; they could smile and whisper to one another or even show traces of impatience when a witness lost the thread while testifying. When going to Israel to question a witness was discussed, they started getting the travel bug. The other students kept being horrified all over again. They only came to the trial once a week, and each time the same thing happened: the intrusion of horror into daily life. I, who was in court every day, observed their reactions with detachment.

It was like being a prisoner in the death camps who survives month after month and becomes accustomed to the life, while he registers with an objective eye the horror of the new arrivals: registers it with the same numbness that he brings to the murders and deaths themselves. All survivor literature talks about this numbness, in which life's functions are reduced to a minimum, behavior becomes completely selfish and indifferent to others, and gassing and burning are everyday occurrences. In the rare accounts by perpetrators, too, the gas chambers and ovens become ordinary scenery, the perpetrators reduced to their few functions and exhibiting a mental paralysis and indifference, a dullness that makes them seem drugged or drunk. The defendants seemed to me to be trapped still, and forever, in this drugged state, in a sense petrified in it.

Even then, when I was preoccupied by this general numbness, and by the fact that it had taken hold not only of the perpetrators and victims, but of all of us, judges and lay members of the court, prosecutors and recorders, who had to deal with these events now; when I likened perpetrators, victims, the dead, the living, survivors, and their descendants to each other, I didn't feel good about it and I still don't.

Can one see them all as linked in this way? When I began to make such comparisons in discussions, I always emphasized that the linkage was not meant to relativize the difference between being forced into the world of the death camps and entering it voluntarily, between enduring suffering and imposing it on others, and that this difference was of the greatest, most critical importance. But I met with shock and indignation when I said this not in reaction to the others' objections, but before they had even had the chance to demur.

At the same time I ask myself, as I had already begun to ask myself back then: What should our second generation have done, what should it do with the knowledge of the horrors of the extermination of the Jews? We should not believe we can comprehend the incomprehensible, we may not compare the incomparable, we may not inquire because to inquire is to make the horrors an object of discussion, even if the horrors themselves are not questioned, instead of accepting them as something in the face of which we can only fall silent in revulsion, shame, and guilt. Should we only fall silent in revulsion, shame, and guilt? To what purpose? It was not that I had lost my eagerness to explore and cast light on things which had filled the seminar, once the trial got under way. But that some few would be convicted and punished while we of the second generation were silenced by revulsion, shame, and guilt—was that all there was to it now?

9. *MAUS*

ART SPIEGELMAN

The unique format of Spiegelman's *Maus,* shaped by today's images, techniques, and language, speaks for the second generation, the children of survivors. The son tries to deal with a father scarred by the Holocaust experience, and nothing is "prettified": the horrors, the flaws within the victims, acts of betrayal and of courage are shown with an honesty that few Holocaust writers have matched. The Jews are drawn as mice, the Germans as cats, and it is amazing how quickly we accept this presentation. The images bring us closer to an understanding of what the parents experienced and how it affected the next generation. Scenes from his father's history are interspersed with scenes of their relationship today. Here, the father recalls the last days of the ghetto in Srodula.

MILOCH-TAKE CARE OF COUSIN VLADEK.

GLADLY

BEN HERE CAN SHOW YOU HOW TO RESOLE THE GERMAN BOOTS.

HASKEL HAD 2 BROTHERS, PESACH AND MILOCH. PESACH WAS ALSO A *KOMBINATOR*. BUT MILOCH, HE WAS A FINE FELLOW.

WE'LL RESERVE THIS WORKBENCH FOR YOU...

YOU DON'T HAVE TO SIT HERE ALL THE TIME, BUT WHENEVER THE GERMAN COMMISSION COMES TO INSPECT, JUST SIT THERE AND LOOK BUSY...

FROM TIME TO TIME I HAD OTHER JOBS ALSO TO DO AROUND THE GHETTO...

YES! THIS REMINDS ME SOMETHING NOW...

REMEMBER THIS GUY WHAT I TOLD YOU GAVE US OUT OF OUR BUNKER?...

WELL, YOU KNOW, I BURIED HIM...

HEY! THIS IS THE RAT THAT TURNED MY FAMILY OVER TO THE GESTAPO.

HE WAS SHOT!

HASKEL HAD ARRANGED HE WOULD BE KILLED.

BUT IF HE'S DEAD WHY ARE HIS EYES STILL WIDE OPEN?

HE WAS STRUGGLING TO SURVIVE.

IT HAPPENED I WAS ON THE WORK DETAIL, SO ... I BURIED HIM.

I TOLD HASKEL AND MILOCH LATER ABOUT THIS.

YOU WERE VERY LUCKY, VLADEK...

THEY CALL HIM "THE SHOOTER". EVERY DAY HE KILLS SOME POOR JEW, JUST FOR FUN.

HEY! AREN'T YOU GOING OVER TO PESACH'S TO BUY SOME CAKE?

CAKE?

FOR YEARS WE DIDN'T SEE ANY CAKE. HARDLY EVEN BREAD WE SAW!

IT'S IMPOSSIBLE! HE'S JOKING! CAKE!

BUT COUSIN PESACH WAS REALLY SELLING CAKE! EVERYONE WHAT COULD AFFORD IT STOOD ON LINE TO BUY A PIECE...

IT LOOKS DELICIOUS.

HOW DID YOU MANAGE IT, PESACH?

WHEN PEOPLE ARE SENT TO AUSCHWITZ, MY MEN SEARCH THEIR HOUSES.

PESACH WAS LIKE HASKEL, PART OF THE JEWISH POLICE.

THEY FIND A LITTLE FLOUR HERE, A FEW GRAMS OF SUGAR THERE...I SAVED IT!

HE WAS YOUNGER FROM HASKEL, BUT ALSO A "KOMBINATOR".

YOU KNOW WHAT A COOK MY RIFKA IS... TRY IT! ONLY 95 ZLOTYS A SLICE.

I HAD STILL SAVINGS, SO I GOT FOR ANJA AND ME SOME CAKE.

BUT, THE WHOLE GHETTO, WE WERE SO SICK LATER, YOU CAN'T IMAGINE...

SOME OF THE FLOUR PESACH FOUND—IT WASN'T REALLY FLOUR, ONLY LAUNDRY SOAP, WHAT HE PUT IN THE CAKE BY MISTAKE.

OW! GROAN OY! OUCH!

...WE WERE, ALL OF US, SICK LIKE DOGS.

BY THE END OF 1943 THE VANS WENT EVERY WEDNESDAY WITH MORE AND MORE AND MORE PEOPLE FROM SRODULA TO AUSCHWITZ UNTIL IT WAS VERY FEW LEFT.

IT COULD BE OUR TURN SOON, EH VLADEK?

LET'S HOPE NOT, MILOCH.

HASKEL HEARD THAT ANY DAY NOW THEY INTEND TO DEPORT EVERYONE THAT'S STILL LEFT HERE.

MILOCH TOOK ME TO THE SHOE SHOP

IT WAS EARLY AND NOBODY WAS THERE...

HASKEL MADE PLANS TO SMUGGLE HIMSELF OUT OF THE GHETTO.

PESACH AND I HAVE A PLAN ALSO...

HE MOVED A FEW SHOES FROM A PILE HIGH TO THE CEILING...

...AND TOOK ME INSIDE A TUNNEL...

DON'T TELL ANYONE ABOUT THIS EXCEPT ANJA AND YOUR NEPHEW.

...A TUNNEL MADE FROM SHOES!

WE CAME OUT TO A BUNKER...

BE PREPARED TO BRING THEM ON A MOMENT'S NOTICE!

INCREDIBLE!

EVERYTHING WAS READY HERE SO 15 OR 16 PEOPLE COULD HIDE,

10. *RETURN TO KONIN*

THEO RICHMOND

Konin is the name of a shtetl, a small town in eastern Poland. It is the place where Theo Richmond's parents were born, and the place they always talked about after they emigrated to London. Discovering a large memorial book ("a *yizker* book") for the town, written in Yiddish with hand-drawn maps and photographs, Richmond began a quest to recover memories of the town. He sought out members of Konin's far-flung diaspora, learned Yiddish, and finally visited the town on a trip to Poland with Izzy Hahn, a Holocaust survivor who last saw Konin in 1945.

One of the people Richmond wanted most to see was a Polish Catholic veterinarian who had been in the Polish Resistance and imprisoned at Mauthausen. He had witnessed the massacre of Konin's Jews in the nearby forest of Kazimierz and had testified at the war crimes trials. Now deaf and forgotten, this aged vet is the last to remember the Jews of Konin.

In the end, Richmond leaves Konin without emotion: "The town was releasing me from its grip, for I knew now that it was not the place that held meaning for me but the people who once lived here. Their Konin would stay with me always."

———

On our first evening in Konin, Izzy had asked Feliks and his wife to join us for dinner. They chose the venue, an inn run by a cooperative a few miles outside the town that displayed the sign of the Konin white horse.

It was situated in a forest clearing close to the road, and maybe it was this that turned my thoughts to the forest at Kazimierz. As always, it was not only the Jews or their killers who stayed in my mind but also the Polish witness who lived to tell the tale—the Konin "veterinary surgeon, with no criminal record, a Pole and a Catholic," born on Christmas Day 1910. The murdered ones lived on in me because of him. I heard their last cries because of him. Now that I was so close to Kazimierz, my curiosity about him sharpened. I wondered what became of him after he returned to the forest and gave his testimony, standing on the very spot where, four years previously, he had stuffed rags into his ears to silence the screams. Might he still be alive and living in the area?

We ate and talked our way through the meatball soup and the greasy roast chicken. Then came a lull in the chatter. I became conscious of my self-absorption, as did the kindly Feliks, who smiled at me encouragingly from across the table. I handed him a piece of paper on which I had written the vet's name. He shook his head blankly. I showed it to his wife, who said something to Izzy. "She knows him," Izzy said. "She says he used to be a vet." One moment I was half-asleep, the next as though doused by cold water. "Is he still living?" I asked. Primo Levi has commented on the disparity between time as measured by a chronometer, and subjective time. One objective minute spent waiting at a red traffic light, he observed, equals eight subjective minutes. I waited several years while Izzy interpreted my question and listened to her reply: "So far as she knows, he's still alive." "Does she know where he lives?" The answer: "Somewhere in Kronin." My excitement needed no interpreter. The couple conferred briefly. Izzy said, "They are going to try to find him for you."

Less than twenty-four hours later I was standing outside the vet's door in the old town. His house lay back from the road behind a thickly screened front garden with a door in the garden wall. We rang the bell and waited. Through a hedge we caught a glimpse of the house, a mellow, single-story building set in a rambling, slightly overgrown garden of bushes, hollyhocks, and old apple trees. Dappled light fell on a white wooden table and rickety chair planted in the tall grass, waiting for an Impressionist painter.

We rang the bell again. We had been warned that the vet was rather deaf. Perhaps his wife was out and he could not hear the bell. A more worrying thought: perhaps they were both away and would not be back before we departed from Kronin. The door was locked and we could not get closer to the house. We rang a third time, then gave up.

That night Izzy dined in Feliks's home in one of the concrete apartment towers in new Kronin. Feliks's wife, who used to live in the old town, telephoned the vet and spoke to his wife. It transpired that the vet had been at home when we called and had not heard the bell. Izzy spoke to the vet's wife and explained why I wanted to meet him. They arranged for us to call at the house two days later, after our visit to the forest.

Mrs. Z. was waiting for us by the garden door when we arrived, a smiling, well-groomed woman probably in her early sixties, wearing an elegant silk dress. She led us through the garden. In a small room overlooking the front garden, Mr. Z. stood up to greet us, a tall, gentlemanly figure with a mustache and a lock of gray hair that fell across his high forehead. His jacket, dating from earlier years, hung loosely over his frail, bony frame. To me he looked utterly English, a touch Edwardian, maybe a retired, fondly remembered schoolmaster. As we shook hands he bowed his head slightly the way Poles do.

Izzy and the vet's wife perched on the edge of a bed that occupied much of the space in the room, while the vet and I sat on chairs. I threw out some mundane opening remark, which Izzy interpreted. The vet cupped a hand to his ear. Izzy repeated the remark. The vet leaned toward him, straining to hear. His wife repeated the words, loudly, carefully articulating each syllable. The vet stared at her lips, his face taut with concentration. She shouted the words. His hearing aid began to emit a high-pitched whistle. He cupped his hands over both ears, making an even greater effort to hear.

His wife got out some books dealing with Nazi war crimes. She said they contained evidence her husband had given after the war. The vet pointed to a number of references to his name and made some comments. His voice was steady, his eyes bright, his brain sentient. He possessed all his faculties, save one. When he needed to call on it, he relapsed into a state of helplessness. I made several attempts to get through to him, but in vain.

At one point the vet produced a set of well-thumbed black-and-white photographs. I recognized their subject: the shooting of the first two hostages in Konin, the Pole Kurowski and the Jew Slodki. One of the pictures—the firing squad taking aim at the two men—was in the Memorial Book. But the vet had other pictures of the execution that I had not seen before: of the hostages being led over to the wall, a priest in a long cassock walking behind them; and a picture of them after the bullets had hit home—two dark, crumpled heaps lying on the ground, a helmeted German bending over them, the priest kneeling beside them in prayer.

I asked if the vet knew who had taken the photographs. Izzy put the question to him with no success. His wife tried, raising her voice to a shout. She started to write out my questions on a piece of paper, an idea that had crossed my mind already—Beethoven's visitors got by well enough with a slate and a piece of chalk. Halfway through writing out the sentence, she lost patience and made another futile attempt to get through to him, shouting straight into his ear. The hearing aid began whistling again. She gave up with a gesture of exasperation and frustration. It was plain how badly she was suffering on his behalf. [...]

I tried to explain why I was interested in the history of the Jews of Konin, why I wanted to speak to her husband, who had seen for himself how some of the Jews had died. Izzy did his best to help when my German broke down, but again her reply in Polish would draw a comment from him and the two of them would get carried away. "What is she saying, Izzy? What is she saying?" It was hopeless.

The vet's wife calmed down. She said we had to understand that our meeting was a difficult experience for her and her husband. He had taken special pills to enable him to cope with the stress. She had been in a labor camp during the war, and her own health was poor. His deafness was a terrible ordeal for them both. She began to cry silently. I looked across at the vet. He was bowed over, clutching his head tightly with both hands, staring down into his lap. I felt uncomfortable. Ought I to have come? Was I entitled to intrude into their lives?

The atmosphere revived the moment two attractive young women appeared from another room—their daughters, said Mrs. Z. One was an engineer, the other an actress. They did not live in Konin and were visiting their parents for the day. Their spirited personalities brightened the room. Two young grandchildren scampered after them. The sisters brought in silver and china tea things and Mrs. Z. served generous portions of cake. While we chatted, the vet sipped his tea, silent and withdrawn.

I awakened his attention by showing him the Memorial Book. He turned over the *Protokol* pages and looked at the illustrations of old Konin, recognizing each landmark with undisguised delight. He said he would love to have a copy of this book even though he could not read it. He flipped over the pages of Yiddish text until he came to the black-edged pages. I pointed out the name Ryczke, printed in Hebrew letters. He said he remembered Aron Ryczke. Izzy rolled up his sleeve and showed the vet his Auschwitz number. The vet said he had been given a number too in Mauthausen but his was on a tag around his wrist. He said he had seen people destined for the crematorium.

The sisters went in and out, preoccupied with the children playing in the next room. Mrs. Z. told us she had three daughters, all gifted in their different ways. She brought in a plaster figure about fifteen inches high which her other daughter had sculpted. It was the thin and elongated body of a man, head tilted back to an almost horizontal position, skeletal arms stretched up to the sky. Two strands of barbed wire—real barbed wire—embedded across the front of the torso gave the figure a grim power. A miniature Jesus stood at the base of the sculpture. One of the vet's experiences in Mauthausen had inspired the piece. One day, his wife related, when he was in the throes of despair, he decided to end it all by throwing himself against the electrified fence as others had done. He was about to run at the fence when his mother's voice came to him, holding him back.

While Mrs. Z. told us the story, the vet looked on, knowing what she was telling us, adding nothing to it. I wished he were more loquacious. For much of our visit it was as though he had lost his power of speech as well as his sense of hearing. Perhaps he had got too used to his wife doing the talking. Mrs. Z. asked us, almost pleadingly, if we could find him a better hearing aid in London, and we promised to try.

The visit was drawing to an end on a relaxed and cordial note. The daughters came in to say goodbye. Then, as we were about to leave the room, they did something that took us both by surprise. Reflecting on it afterward, I realized they were giving us a going-away present. Standing side by side in an open doorway, they began to sing a sweet and delicate melody, a song I had never heard before, perhaps a folk song. The engineer sang the words while her sister hummed. The two voices blended in unison, parted in melancholy harmony, came together again, separated, rising and falling with the graceful ease of birds floating on a current of air.

Their listeners had unwittingly arranged themselves as if for a painting, composed to lead the eye from one face to the next: the children gazing up, entranced; Izzy, absorbed yet instantly aware of being observed; Mrs. Z., on the edge of tears, lost in maternal pride; and the vet, bent forward, head turned away, hand cupped to ear, trying to trap the sound waves carrying his daughters' music. I listened more closely to their words and realized that the language they were singing was Hebrew.

It was Modern Hebrew. That much I could tell without understanding the words. Their pronunciation was so authentic I might have been lis-

tening to an Israeli folk duo. I closed my eyes and tried to convince myself
that I was not hallucinating, that I was indeed in a house in old Kronin,
long after all the Jews had departed, listening to two young Polish women
singing a Jewish melody. I wished the sound were loud enough to carry
to the nearby synagogue, where not a word of Hebrew, ancient or modern, had been heard for forty-eight years. I wished it were audible to
Konin's Jewish dead. And to the vet.

The afternoon was drawing to a close and we had to be on our way.
In the flurry of leaving, I failed to find out more about the song. Izzy
vaguely remembered the sisters saying they had learned it at an academy
in Poznan. (Later I discovered that the song was a modern romantic bal-
lad from Israel.) I followed Mrs. Z. out into the garden, and we stood talking for a moment near the table under the trees. She was a stalwart
woman, but she found her husband's handicap painful to observe day after
day. She said in German, "Oh, it is so sad, the way he sits here in the garden. He has no one to talk to." Her eyes filled again. He used to address
schools and talk about his experiences, but those days were over, she said.
All he did not was sit and write. She knew we had visited the forest at
Kazimierz. She could not let him go there again. The memories were too
painful. As it was, he still cried out in his sleep.

We had not talked about Kazimierz. The vet had said everything that
was to be said many years ago. But his deafness had robbed me of an
opportunity to converse with him about other things, had deprived me
of insights into the past he might have given me. Yet I felt I had gained
through being in his presence.

When we said goodby and I put my arm on his shoulder, I felt the flesh-
less bones pressing through his jacket. He bowed and said something in
Polish, which his wife translated: "He says you have great luck that he, the
last, the only one who still lives of those who saw those terrible things, is
still here. And he says you are the first to come and see him."

EPILOGUE

Second Kings, Chapter 2: A Parable

When the prophet Elijah knew that the time had come for him to ascend to heaven on a fiery chariot, his disciples respectfully drew back and averted their eyes. Only Elisha followed his master into the wilderness. "Turn back," pleaded the prophet; "my road is hard; my task is never done; the prophet's mantle hangs heavy on my shoulders; turn back." Elisha shook his head and followed his master.

The time drew near.

"What is it that you want from me?" asked Elijah.

"A double portion of your spirit!" answered the disciple.

"Hard to give, hard to receive," said Elijah. "But if you see the fiery chariot, the gift is yours."

Fire roared up into the sky, and Israel's body ascended as smoke in the air. The tree of time trembled, and a star stopped singing. Was it one chariot, or were there six million? Was there a witness? Elisha had not turned away. He saw. And his anguish screamed out into the night:

"My father, my father, the chariots of Israel and the horsemen thereof!" He tore his garments. He stumbled through the desert, falling over stones—or had it been a pile of children's shoes? He found a black cloak: it was the prophet's mantle.

And a terrible anger took hold of Elisha. He flailed the coat as though it were the staff of Moses, and the waters of the Jordan divided before him. He cried out the story. Blank unbelief: searching parties went out to seek the dust which trembled at the edges of the universe. They had not seen the chariot. They did not know. And it became the task of Elisha to tell them what had been lost and what had to be done. The salt of Elisha's tears fell into their springs of knowledge and purified the waters. Elisha replaced Elijah.

He was not a good prophet. Elijah had stood above the multitudes, had swept them along with his grandeur and power. Elisha was one of the crowd, and moved in their midst. Elijah's shadow hung over him. Elijah's cup was filled at every Seder; his chair was occupied at every manchild's birth; his place was secure in the hopes of the people. They were sure Elijah would return before the coming of the Messiah.

But Elisha had seen him leave in the fiery chariot. And whenever he acknowledged that vision and accepted it, he gained the strength to wear the mantle. He could not be a great leader. But he could be one of the people, could be a witness in their midst. He spoke of the fiery chariot, he pointed up to the sky, he lived his testimony. "My father," he wept. "My father! Oh, the fiery chariot."

There are those who say that no Messiah can come until the world stops looking for Elijah and begins to listen to the testimony of Elisha. For the Messiah's pathway—once seen by the patriarch Jacob as a golden ladder—was seared and torn by the passing of the chariots. Once the ladder was built from heaven to earth; now it must reach from earth to heaven, and must be constructed by man. And this will only happen when the quiet testimony of an Elisha among the multitudes can get them to see the passing of the chariot. They must experience the terrible grief and loss. They must cry for the past turned to fire, for the future become ashes. Etched into their vision there must be the flaming path arching up into darkness. And from their lips, with reluctance and anguish, words must rise to form the threshold of the golden ladder:

Yitgadal v'yitkadash sh'mey rabba. . . .

It is said that his payer must be repeated six million times.